CLASSICAL CHRISTIANITY AND THE POLITICAL ORDER

ERNEST FORTIN: COLLECTED ESSAYS
Edited by J. Brian Benestad

Volume 1
The Birth of Philosophic Christianity: Studies
in Early Christian and Medieval Thought

Foreword by Ernest L. Fortin

Volume 2
Classical Christianity and the Political Order:
Reflections on the Theologico-Political Problem

Foreword by Dan Mahoney

Volume 3
Human Rights, Virtue, and the Common Good:
Untimely Meditations on Religion and Politics

Foreword by J. Brian Benestad

CLASSICAL CHRISTIANITY AND THE POLITICAL ORDER

Reflections on the Theologico–Political Problem

ERNEST L. FORTIN

Edited by
J. Brian Benestad

ROWMAN & LITTLEFIELD PUBLISHERS, INC.
Lanham • Boulder • New York • London

ROWMAN & LITTLEFIELD PUBLISHERS, INC.

Published in the United States of America
by Rowman & Littlefield Publishers, Inc.
4720 Boston Way, Lanham, Maryland 20706

3 Henrietta Street
London WC2E 8LU, England

British Cataloging in Publication Information Available

Library of Congress Cataloging-in-Publication Data

Fortin, Ernest L.
Classical Christianity and the political order : reflections on the
theologico–political order / Ernest L. Fortin ; edited by J. Brian Benestad.
p.   cm. — (Ernest Fortin, collected essays ; v. 2)
Includes bibliographical references and index.
1. Christianity and politics. 2. Christianity and politics—
History. 3. Political science—Philosophy. 4. Augustine, Saint, Bishop
of Hippo—Political and social views. 5. Thomas Aquinas, Saint,
1225?–1274—Political and social views. 6. Strauss, Leo. I. Benestad,
J. Brian. II. Title. III. Series: Fortin, Ernest L. Essays ; v. 2.
BR115.P7F675   1996   261.7—dc20   96–19850   CIP

ISBN 0–8476–8276–5 (cloth : alk. paper)
ISBN 0–8476–8277–3 (pbk. : alk. paper)

Printed in the United States of America

☺™ The paper used in this publication meets the minimum requirements of
American National Standard for Information Sciences—Permanence of
Paper for Printed Library Materials, ANSI Z39.48–1984.

CONTENTS

Foreword   vii

Acknowledgments   xi

I. AUGUSTINE AND AQUINAS ON CHRISTIANITY AND POLITICS

1. The Political Thought of St. Augustine   1
2. Political Idealism and Christianity in the Thought of St. Augustine   31
3. The Political Implications of St. Augustine's Theory of Conscience   65
4. Augustine and Roman Civil Religion: Some Critical Reflections   85
5. Augustine, Spinoza, and the Hermeneutical Problem   107
6. Augustine's *City of God* and the Modern Historical Consciousness   117
7. Augustine and the Problem of Modernity   137
8. The Political Thought of St. Thomas Aquinas   151
9. Politics and Philosophy in the Middle Ages: The Aristotelian Revolution   177
10. Augustine, Thomas Aquinas, and the Problem of Natural Law   199

II. NATURAL LAW AND INDIVIDUAL RIGHTS

11. Natural Law and Social Justice   223
12. On the Presumed Medieval Origin of
    Individual Rights   243
13. The New Rights Theory and the
    Natural Law   265

III. LEO STRAUSS AND THE REVIVAL OF CLASSICAL POLITICAL PHILOSOPHY

14. Rational Theologians and Irrational Philosophers:
    A Straussian Perspective   287
15. Faith and Reason in Contemporary Perspective:
    Apropos of a Recent Book   297
16. Between the Lines: Was Leo Strauss a Secret Enemy
    of Morality?   317
17. Straussian Reflections on the Strauss-Voegelin
    Correspondence   329
18. Nietzsche and the Crisis of Nihilism   337

IV. SELECTED REVIEWS

F. D. Wilhelmsen, *Christianity and Political Philosophy*   355
R. Hittinger, *A Critique of the New Natural
    Law Theory*   360
F. Rousseau, *La Croissance solidaire des droits
    de l'homme*   362
G. Fessard, *Chrétiens marxistes et théologie de la libération*
    and *Eglise de France, prends garde de perdre la foi*   366
D. Vree, *On Synthesizing Marxism and Christianity*   369
H. A. Deane, *The Political and Social Ideas of
    St. Augustine*   371

Select Bibliography   375

Index   387

About the Author   401

About the Editor   402

FOREWORD

The remarkable pieces collected in this book reflect the immense, perhaps unequalled, learning of Ernest Fortin on the subject of the "classical Christianity" of Augustine and Aquinas, a field characterized by what the Fathers called the "noble risk" of dialectical engagement with the tradition of political philosophy. More than any other of our contemporaries, Fortin appreciates the problems associated with the Christian efforts to incorporate, tame, and transform the tradition of political philosophy, even while he recognizes the absolute indispensability of the effort. In light of the failure of all the alternatives proffered by the full range of modern secular and religious thought, Fortin affirms that there is no adequate substitute for a careful and sympathetic reconsideration of classical Christianity's confrontation with the enduring questions of nature and grace, obligations and rights, and the relationship of biblical faith to the political order.

But there are several aspects of the return to classical Christianity recommended by Ernest Fortin that are potentially disconcerting to believers and unbelievers alike, and that perhaps account for the reticence some otherwise sympathetic observers have felt about Fortin's own position on these fundamental matters. Let me state the matter boldly: Ernest Fortin does not believe, as these essays repeatedly demonstrate, that the effort to reconcile reason and revelation, Christian faith and classical political philosophy, can ever be wholly successful. A return to the "natural law" tradition in the broadest sense of the term is a prudent necessity, but it does not and never has promised any resolution of theoretical questions which by their very nature are beyond resolution. Contemporary neo-Thomists will perhaps be annoyed by Fortin's constant reminders that there can be no synthesis that ultimately resolves the tensions inherent in the effort to live and think through the conflict between Jerusalem and Athens. Some believers will be confused, perhaps disturbed, by the fact that Fortin comes to the forefront in these essays first and foremost as a partisan of that tension, rather than as a supporter of some old or new synthesis of faith and reason or as an explicit advocate of some emphatic theological parti pris. The unbeliever, on the other hand, observing Fortin's attentiveness to tensions and *aporiai* of all kinds, might be tempted to ignore or understate the distinctively theological character of his enterprise.

It seems to me that a thoughtful reader can gain some help in resolving these initial difficulties by reflecting more naively about the starting point of Fortin's reflection. Let me briefly recapitulate the problematic which inspires and animates this work.

Fortin reminds readers, in an age dominated by assorted ideological and politicized readings of Christianity and its purposes, of the essentially *transpolitical* character of the New Testament and of Christian revelation in general. Christianity, unlike Judaism and Islam, does not entail a Law which comprehensively regulates the spiritual and temporal lives of its adherents. It does not speak about the great themes of classical political philosophy, such as nature and convention, the meaning of justice, or the right ordering of a political regime. It takes its bearing from a notoriously apolitical starting point, namely, the injunction to love God with all our heart, mind, and soul and to love our neighbor as ourselves. Fortin rightfully, if a bit impishly, emphasizes the fuzzy character of these notions at least from the point of view of providing guidance for the collective lives of human beings. This indispensable transpolitical starting point of Christianity hardly prepared early Christians to deal with their confrontation with Roman authority in a decaying and decadent empire, nor provided much guidance for a prudential resolution of the immense problems opened up by the necessary coexistence of secular and ecclesiastical authority in Christian Europe. In both cases the most thoughtful and perspicacious Christian intelligences turned toward an engagement—in turns adoption, apology, co-optation, and transformation—of the political and philosophical wisdom of Greek and (to a much lesser extent) Roman antiquity. In the broadest sense, this encounter with classical philosophy allowed Christians to live within and to reflect upon the exigencies of civil society.

One of the strengths of Fortin's work is that he reveals how profound this Christian confrontation with classical thought was despite the frequent lack of adequate scholarship and information to support the Christian arguments (Augustine, for example, had limited access to Plato; Aquinas had to rely on an admirable but flawed Latin translation of Aristotle's

Politics). Fortin also does not hesitate to show us how classical Christians sometimes deliberately fudged their not-inconsiderable differences with the classical philosophers on questions of virtue, morality, and theology. They themselves knew, far better than their present-day disciples and epigones among soi-disant orthodox Christians, that there can be no final reconciliation of the worlds of faith and reason. They maintained a theological analogue of esotericism, muting their differences with their pagan predecessors in order to avoid scandal and because such a muting was necessary if classical thought was to play its salutary role.

A powerfully illuminating consequence of Fortin's work is that it clearly reveals the inadequacy of all the replacements for classical Christianity that have been trumpeted in the West since the sixteenth century. Against a wide range of influential if ultimately unconvincing authorities such as the brothers Carlyle, Jacques Maritain, Michel Villey, and Brian Tierney, Fortin insists that the origins of modern natural rights theory lie in a self-conscious break with the ancient and medieval traditions of "natural right." The modern doctrine of natural rights has provided a solution to the theologico-political problem; it has defanged religious fanaticism, but at the price of weakening the authority of civil ties and moral obligations, and, finally, at the price of severing human freedom from the natural and divine orders altogether. The natural law tradition had managed to pay due respect to the competing concerns of the body and the soul while moralizing political life and rationalizing a gospel rooted in the otherworldness of agape. Late modern and postmodern thought genuflects before the altars of science and history and, more dangerously, of idiosyncratic, ungrounded commitment. Fortin does not see the victory of these modern forms of the synthesis of faith and reason as being good for philosophy, religion, or decent common life. A world of thought and action dominated by "irrational philosophers and rational theologians," as Lessing strikingly formulated it, leads to a postmodern world of vulgar relativism and perspectivism. The invigorating tension of faith and reason, and the accompanying salutary efforts to conjugate nature and law, ultimately give way to intellectual, spiritual, and civic confusion corrupting of the very humanity of man.

In pursuing his measured, dialectical return to classical Christian thought, Fortin takes the great "Hellenic Jewish" political philosopher Leo Strauss as a guide. In doing so, Fortin is the world's only, or at least most visible and vocal, Straussian theologian. Fortin argues persuasively that the theologian must become, at least initially, a partisan of the ineliminable tension between faith and reason if he is to defend the possibility of theologizing in our time. Fortin thus is not an esoteric Averroist secretly siding with Athenian rationalism against biblical faith. Rather, as a scholarly theologian he shows that a rejection of historicism, progressivism and liberationism in all its forms is necessary if the horizon within which faith is affirmed or rejected is to become recognizable again. Leo Strauss can help us, as Werner Dannhauser has put it, to be naive again. Fortin writes movingly about Strauss's paradoxical contribution to the reinvigoration of the theological enterprise:

> By showing that modern science has not replaced God and that history has not replaced philosophy, or by showing as no one has done in four hundred years that the claims of Reason and Revelation are inherently untouched by modernity, Strauss may have performed as great a service for theology as he has for philosophy. Living as they do in an age of unbelief, that is to say, in an age in which conviction is grounded neither in reason nor in authoritative tradition, Christian theologians may yet discover that they have as much to learn from him as they do from one another or from any of their new allies about the way in which they could regain some of their lost credibility (p. 297).

But it is important to note that by turning to the noble risk which is political philosophy, Ernest Fortin, the Straussian theologian, is fulfilling what Aquinas considered one of the salutary tasks that philosophy can perform for theology. Reason must, Aquinas thought, deflect the false arguments that are posed by a specious kind of reason against the very possibility of faith.[1] Thomas knew, much better than many who invoke his name, that neither theology nor philosophy can demonstrate the truth of faith. The highest achievement of reason is to show that the arguments levelled against the faith on philosophical grounds are not compelling. In this spirit, I heartily recommend to the reader the feast of humane learning and penetrating judgment offered by Ernest Fortin.

NOTE

1. See St. Thomas Aquinas, *Exposition of Boethius's De trinitate* II.3.

Daniel J. Mahoney
Assumption College
May, 1996

ACKNOWLEDGMENTS

The author and editor wish to take this opportunity to thank all those who had a direct hand in the launching and the realization of this project, among them: Stephen F. Brown, Matthew Lamb, and Patrick J. C. Powers. Daniel J. Mahoney found the right publisher and graciously contributed the Foreword to the second volume. The idea of publishing the three volumes simultaneously and as a set belongs to Jonathan Sisk, the editor-in-chief of Rowman and Littlefield, without whose encouragement and active support the project would probably never have seen the light of day.

Invaluable assistance was provided by the editorial staff of Rowman and Littlefield and, in particular, by Julie Kirsch and Dorothy Bradley, whose expertise and endless patience won both our gratitude and our admiration. We are also grateful to Phillip Wodzinski, a doctoral student in political science at Boston College, whose research talents and proofreading skills, hitherto unknown to the world, revealed themselves to superb advantage on this occasion. Ann King, the retired secretary of the Department of Theology and Religious Studies at the University of Scranton, toiled endlessly and in a completely selfless way on virtually every page of the manuscript, at the risk of being driven out of her mind by its innumerable references to works in at least six different foreign languages, including Greek and Latin. Her dedication was paralleled by that of Shirley Gee, the omnicompetent administrative assistant of the Institute of Medieval Philosophy and Theology at Boston College. Further secretarial help was provided by Marie Gaughan, Patricia Macedon, and Barbara Quinn, of the University of Scranton. The staff of the Thomas

O'Neill Library, Boston College was always there to help whenever necessary and also deserves special mention. The author is immensely grateful for generous financial help in the form of research fellowships received from the John M. Olin Foundation, the Lynde and Harry Bradley Foundation, the National Endowment for the Humanities, and the Boston College Graduate School.

None of the articles in these three volumes could have been written without constant input from the author's colleagues and daily conversation partners in the departments of Theology, Political Science, and Philosophy at Boston College, along with friends and long-time associates in other colleges and universities here and abroad. They shall not be listed individually for fear that too many names should inadvertently be left out. If they are ever tempted to peruse these books, they will have no trouble identifying their respective contributions.

The editor is especially indebted to his colleagues at the University of Scranton, Father Richard Rousseau, S.J., and Dr. Edward Matthews, as well as to Betsy Moylan, a librarian at the University, for their expert assistance. He thanks his wife, Janet Benestad, and their daughter Katherine, for help with various aspects of the project. He also expresses his appreciation to the University of Scranton for grants to support the writing of his foreword and the typing of numerous articles, and to Dr. Thomas Hogan and Dr. Richard Passon for their support of the whole endeavor.

Chapter 1. "The Political Thought of St. Augustine" is reprinted from *History of Political Philosophy*, 3rd edition, edited by L. Strauss and J. Cropsey, © 1987 University of Chicago Press, 176-205. By permission of the University of Chicago Press.

Chapter 2. "Political Idealism and Christianity in the Thought of St. Augustine" is reprinted from a book by the same title published by Villanova Press © 1972. By permission of Villanova University Press.

Chapter 3. "The Political Implications of St. Augustine's Theory of Conscience" is reprinted from *Augustinian Studies* 1 (1970): 133-52. By permission of *Augustinian Studies*.

Chapter 4. "Augustine and Roman Civil Religion: Some Critical Reflections" is reprinted from *Revue des Etudes Augustiniennes* 26 (1980): 238-56. By permission of *Revue des Etudes Augustiniennes*.

Chapter 5. "Augustine, Spinoza, and the Hermeneutical Problem." Previously unpublished.

Chapter 6. "Augustine's *City of God* and the Modern Historical Consciousness" is reprinted from *The Review of Politics* 41 (1979): 739-46. By permission of *The Review of Politics.*

Chapter 7. "Augustine and the Problem of Modernity." Previously unpublished.

Chapter 8. "The Political Thought of Thomas Aquinas" is reprinted from *History of Political Philosophy*, 3rd edition, edited by L. Strauss and J. Cropsey, © 1987 University of Chicago Press, 248-75. By permission of the University of Chicago Press.

Chapter 9. "Politics and Philosophy in the Middle Ages: The Aristotelian Revolution" is reprinted from Aquinas's *Commentary on the Politics of Aristotle*, introduction, notes and translation by Ernest Fortin, © The Catholic University of Americal Press (forthcoming). By permission of The Catholic University of America Press.

Chapter 10. "Augustine, Thomas Aquinas, and the Problem of Natural Law" is reprinted from *Mediaevalia* 4 (1978): 179-208. By permission of *Mediaevalia.*

Chapter 11. "Natural Law and Social Justice," is reprinted from *The American Journal of Jurisprudence* 30 (1985): 1-20. By permission of *The American Journal of Jurisprudence.*

Chapter 12. "On the Presumed Medieval Origin of Individual Rights" is reprinted from *Final Causality in Nature and Human Affairs*, edited by Richard Hassing, © The Catholic University of America Press (forthcoming). By permission of The Catholic University of America Press.

Chapter 13. "The New Rights Theory and the Natural Law" is reprinted from *The Review of Politics* 44 (1982): 590-612. By permission of *The Review of Politics.*

Chapter 14. "Rational Theologians and Irrational Philosophers: A Straussian Perspective" is reprinted from *Interpretation* 12 (1984): 349-56. By permission of *Interpretation.*

Chapter 15. "Faith and Reason in Contemporary Perspective" is reprinted from *Interpretation* 14 (1986): 371-87. By permission of *Interpretation.*

Chapter 16. "Between the Lines: Was Leo Strauss a Secret Enemy of Morality?" is reprinted from *Crisis* 7, no. 11 (December, 1989): 19-26. By permission of *Crisis*.

Chapter 17. "Straussian Reflections on the Strauss-Voegelin Correspondence" is reprinted from *The Review of Politics* 56 (1994): 337-345. By permission of *The Review of Politics*.

Chapter 18. "Nietzsche and the Crisis of Nihilism" is reprinted from *Meaning, Truth and God*, edited by Leroy S. Rouner, © 1982, University of Notre Dame Press. By permission of the Notre Dame Press.

IV. SELECTED REVIEWS

F. Wilhelmsen, *Christianity and Political Philosophy* is reprinted from *The Review of Politics* 41 (1979): 578-582. By permission of *The Review of Politics*.

R. Hittinger, *A Critique of the New Natural Law Theory* is reprinted from the *Review of Metaphysics* 42 (1989): 838-41. By permission of *Review of Metaphysics*.

F. Rousseau, *La Croissance solidaire des droits de l'homme* is reprinted from the *Review of Metaphysics* 38 (1984): 693-96. By permission of *Review of Metaphysics*.

G. Fessard, *Chrétiens marxistes et théologie de la libération* and *Eglise de France, prends garde de perdre la foi* is reprinted from *Review of Metaphysics* 34 (1981): 128-31. By permission of *Review of Metaphysics*.

D. Vree, *On Synthesizing Marxism and Christianity* is reprinted from *Review of Metaphysics* 33 (1980): 807-09. By permission of *Review of Metaphysics*.

H. A. Deane, *The Political and Social Ideas of St. Augustine* is reprinted from *Cross Currents* 14, no. 4 (1964): 482-84. By permission of *Cross Currents*.

I

AUGUSTINE AND AQUINAS ON
CHRISTIANITY AND POLITICS

THE POLITICAL THOUGHT
OF ST. AUGUSTINE

St. Augustine (354-430) is the first author to deal more or less comprehensively with the subject of civil society in the light of the new situation
created by the emergence of revealed religion and its encounter with philosophy in the Greco-Roman world. As a Roman, he inherited and restated
for his own time the political philosophy inaugurated by Plato and adapted
to the Latin world by Cicero, and as a Christian he modified that philosophy to suit the requirements of the faith. He thus appears if not as the
originator at least as the foremost exponent in ancient times of a new
tradition of political thought characterized by its attempt to fuse or
reconcile elements derived from two originally independent and hitherto
unrelated sources, the Bible and classical philosophy.

Augustine writes first and foremost as a theologian and not as a
philosopher. He rarely refers to himself as a philosopher and he never
undertook a methodical treatment of political phenomena in the light of
reason and experience alone. His highest principles are drawn not from
reason but from the sacred Scriptures, whose authority he never questions
and which he regards as the final source of truth concerning man in
general and political man in particular. However, to the extent to which
the choice of his position rests on a prior consideration of the most

important alternative to that position, it presupposes an understanding of political philosophy or of political things as they appear to unaided human reason.

In the investigation of such philosophic matters, Christians had enjoyed almost from the outset a larger measure of freedom than their Jewish or, later, their Muslim counterparts; for, unlike either Judaism or Islam, the other two great religions of the Western world, Christianity did not reject philosophy as an alien or merely tolerate it but sought early to enlist its support, making room for philosophy within the walls of Christendom, where it continued to thrive with varying degrees of ecclesiastical approval and supervision. Accordingly, Augustine acknowledges in man a capacity to know which precedes faith. This knowledge, obtained without the help of Revelation, is the invention and the proper preserve of the pagan philosophers. It has since been superseded by faith as the supreme norm and guide of life, but it has not been nullified or rendered superfluous by it. Even after the final manifestation of the divine truth in New Testament times, God, the author of Revelation, not only does not forbid but positively enjoins the use of reason to acquire human knowledge. It would be foolish to think that he hates in us "that very quality by which he has raised us above the beasts."[1] The knowledge arrived at in this manner remains inadequate, but it is valid in its own right and is ultimately willed by God as an aid to the faith. Augustine compares it to the objects of gold and silver surreptitiously taken and claimed as a rightful possession by the Israelites at the time of the departure from Egypt.[2]

More specifically, philosophy serves the faith both in itself and in its relation to nonbelievers. It complements divine Revelation by supplying knowledge and guidance in areas concerning which Revelation is either silent or incomplete. Even in matters about which Revelation does speak, philosophy may be used as a tool to gain a fuller understanding of the divinely inspired truth; just as the necessarily imperfect human knowledge points toward faith as its fulfillment, so faith seeks a more perfect grasp of its own principles through the use of reason.[3] Furthermore, although the New Testament is primarily concerned with man's eternal destiny, it has much to say about the condition of rulers and subjects and, in general, about the manner in which men are called upon to live in the city; for it is by his actions in this life that man merits the blessedness of eternal life. Since the spheres of the spiritual and of the temporal constantly intersect and impinge on each other, it becomes necessary to correlate them, and any attempt to do so presupposes a knowledge not only of Revelation but of philosophy as well. Finally, dealing as it does with truths that are in principle accessible to all men, philosophy provides a common ground on which believers and nonbelievers can meet. Only by means of philosophy is the Christian able to make his position intelligible to outsiders and, if need be, to combat with their own weapons the objections that they raise against it.[4] All such objections are thereby made to serve a useful purpose in that they stimulate greater efforts on behalf of the faith and help ward off the complacency engendered by the tranquil possession of a God-given truth.

It is hardly surprising then to find that, despite their avowedly theological character, Augustine's works include numerous considerations of a strictly philosophic nature. By extracting these considerations from their native context, one might be able to reconstruct and expound methodically what could properly be regarded as Augustine's political philosophy. However, since Augustine himself, unlike Aquinas, does not look upon philosophy as a self-contained and, in its own realm, independent discipline, or since he does not in fact deal with philosophy and theology as separate sciences, it seems preferable to respect the unity of his thought and to present his views on political matters as a single, coherent whole governed by theological principles.

Augustine is, at least on the basis of extant texts, the most voluminous writer of the ancient world. His most extensive work, and his single most important political work, is the *City of God*. The *City of God*, however, does not limit itself to politics, nor does it encompass all of Augustine's most pertinent thoughts on this subject. For a thematic discussion of justice and law, one must turn above all to the treatise *On Free Choice of the Will*, and for his position on the vexed question of the use of secular power to repress heresy, to the works against the Donatists. Specific mention should also be made of *Letters* 91 and 138, addressed to the pagan Nectarius and to Marcellinus respectively, which provide a lucid defense of Augustine's views on patriotism and citizenship. There are, needless to say, numerous other works in which political considerations play a significant if subsidiary role.

The largely polemical nature of these works, dictated with rare exceptions by the circumstances of a running controversy with pagans and heretics (especially Manichees, Donatists, and Pelagians), render their interpretation difficult at times. In addition, there is evidence that Augustine shared with his predecessors, both pagan and Christian, the view that the whole truth in matters of supreme moment can be safeguarded only if its investigation is accompanied by a prudent reserve in the expression of that truth.[5] The difficulty inherent in the highest truths precludes their being made easily available to all indiscriminately. Not only error but truth itself can be harmful, inasmuch as men are not all equally well-disposed toward it or sufficiently prepared to receive it. Experience had already taught that if philosophy could be used to buttress the faith, it might under less favorable circumstances prove a positive hindrance to it.

Many of the major heresies of the first centuries could be traced back to the well-intentioned but misguided recourse to philosophic doctrines on the part of heterodox writers; and there was always the possibility that, by reasserting its claim to supremacy, philosophy would once again transform itself into an enemy and a rival of the faith. The simple presence of philosophy within the fold constituted a latent but abiding threat to Christian orthodoxy and cautioned against the premature exposure of young or foolish minds to its teachings. "He who dares to embark rashly and without order upon the study of those questions," observes Augustine, "will become not studious but curious, not learned but credulous, not prudent but unbelieving."[6]

Augustine attempts to forestall these dangers by writing in such a way as to satisfy the legitimate curiosity of the worthier and more demanding student without prejudice to the faith of the less well-informed or less perspicacious reader for whom a nonscientific presentation of dogma is all that is needed or possible.[7] His major works are for the most part addressed both to Christians who seek a deeper knowledge of the divinely revealed truth and to interested pagans who might find in them an added incentive to embrace the faith. These works may be said to constitute at once a philosophic defense of the faith, whose reasonableness they emphasize, and a theological defense of philosophy, for which they provide a justification on the basis of sacred Scripture. They explore the similarities and differences between philosophy and revealed truth for the express purpose of establishing the substantial harmony of the two, as well as the ultimate superiority of the latter over the former. They are designed to make the student who has already progressed in the knowledge of the faith more fully aware of the implications of his beliefs, and at the same time they strive to remove any obstacle that could stand in the way of an intelligent acceptance of the revealed truth on the part of the nonbeliever. In consequence, they discuss openly the points of actual or potential agreement between philosophy and Revelation, and often only hint at those points on which any such reconciliation is plainly impossible. To that extent, they make use of what Augustine himself calls "the art of concealing the truth."[8] In order to be fully understood, they require that one take into account not only the author's explicit statements on a given matter but the issues that these statements raise tacitly or implicitly. It should be added that, whereas some of the earlier Church Fathers like Clement of Alexandria and Origen defended the use of noble lies in the common interest, Augustine denounces all lies, salutary or otherwise, as intrinsically evil and, following a precedent that he alleges to have been set by Christ, admits only of indirect forms of concealment, such as omissions and brevity of speech. As he is careful to point out in his treatise *Against Lies,*

> To hide the truth is not the same thing as to utter a lie. Every liar writes to conceal the truth, but not everyone who conceals the truth is a liar; for we often conceal the truth not only by lying but by remaining silent. . . . It is therefore permissible for a speaker and an exponent or preacher of eternal truths, or even for someone who discusses or pronounces upon temporal matters pertaining to the edification of religion and piety, to conceal at an opportune moment anything that may seem advisable to conceal; but it is never permissible to lie and hence to conceal by means of lies.[9]

Augustine regarded Plato as the greatest of the pagan philosophers and as the philosopher whose thought most closely approximated that of Christianity.[10] He even goes so far as to speak of him as the philosopher who would have become a Christian if he had lived in Christian times.[11] However, his primary source of information concerning Plato's political philosophy is not Plato himself, to whose dialogues he had only limited access, but Cicero's Roman and stoicized version of that philosophy as it is found in Cicero's *Republic* and *Laws* and to a lesser extent in such other works as the treatises *On the Nature of the Gods* and *On Divination*. In the form in which it presents itself, Augustine's political thought is thus more directly Ciceronian than Platonic in content and expression. Unfortunately, both the *Republic* and the *Laws* of Cicero have come down to us in a mutilated state. Of the six books that they originally comprised, less than half survive in each case. Notwithstanding the difficulty caused by this lacuna, it is apparent that Augustine's thought differs from that of his pagan master on three important and closely related points: the notion of virtue, monotheism, and the dichotomy between religion and politics.

THE NATURE OF CIVIL SOCIETY: CHRISTIAN VERSUS PAGAN VIRTUE

The core of Augustine's political doctrine may be said to be his teaching concerning virtue, a teaching that has its roots in both the philosophic and biblical traditions. Man is by nature a social animal, who alone has been endowed with speech, by means of which he is able to communicate and enter into various relationships with other men. It is only by associating with his fellow men and forming with them a political community that man attains his perfection. Even in the state of innocence, men would have sought one another's company and would have tended together toward the final goal of human existence. The virtue that characterizes the citizen as citizen and orders all citizens to the end or common good of the city is justice. Justice is the cornerstone of civil society. Upon it depend the unity and nobility of any human society. By regulating the relations among men it preserves peace, the intrinsic common good of society and the precondition of all the other benefits that society procures. Without peace, the "tranquility of order,"[12] no society can prosper or even subsist. Quoting Cicero with approval, Augustine defines civil society or the commonwealth as "an assemblage (of men) associated by a common acknowledgement of right and by a community of interests."[13] He explains "right" by "justice" rather than by "law," and he insists that no commonwealth can be administered without justice, for where there is no justice there is no right and vice versa.

In all this, Augustine follows closely the classical tradition and stresses its substantial agreement with sacred Scripture. His chief objection to the pagan philosophers concerns not so much their doctrine of the naturalness of civil society and the need for justice within it as their inability to bring about a just society. The philosophers are the first to grant that their model of the best and most desirable city is one which has its existence in speech and private discussions only and not one which is capable of being realized in deed. They point to justice as the healthy condition of cities, but they are powerless to secure its performance.[14] There is no denying that the proposals that the philosophers make in the interest of society and for its improvement deserve the highest praise; but as practical measures these proposals fail signally, inasmuch as the obvious and inescapable wickedness of most men precludes such proposals being implemented in the political community at large. The locus par excellence of justice is the city; yet justice is seldom and perhaps never found to exist in it. By the philosophers' own admission, actual cities are characterized by injustice rather than by justice. In order to vindicate for them the title of cities in the true sense of the word, one would have to omit from Cicero's definition any reference to justice or virtue. Existing cities are assemblages of rational beings bound together not by "a common acknowledgement of right" but by "a common agreement as to the objects of their love," regardless of the quality of that love or the goodness or badness of its objects.[15] The whole argument may be accurately summed up as follows: By asserting the eminent desirability of perfect human justice and at the same time its practical impossibility, philosophy discloses its own inherent limitations; it thus proclaims at least implicitly the need to supplement human justice by a higher and more genuine form of justice. It is important to note that the case against political philosophy does not proceed from revealed premises, which nonbelievers would have been free to reject, or for that matter from premises foreign to the classical scheme. Its strength derives entirely from the fact that it appeals directly to a principle which was indigenous to the thought of Augustine's adversaries and which they were compelled to accept, even if they questioned the conclusion that he purports to draw from it.

Augustine's critique of the classical tradition resembles in many ways that of the early modern political thinkers, beginning with Machiavelli, who likewise took issue with that tradition on the grounds of its ineffectualness and impracticality. But in contradistinction to Machiavelli and his followers, Augustine does not seek to enhance the efficacy of his teaching by lowering the goals and standards of human activity. If anything, his own demands are even more stringent than the most stringent demands of the pagan philosophers. Classical political philosophy has failed, not because—by its stubborn refusal to take into account the all too deplorably human character of man's behavior—it makes unreasonable demands on human nature, but because it did not know and hence could not apply the proper remedy to man's congenital weakness.

Following a procedure that is more typical of Plato than of Aristotle, who generally prefers to deal with moral matters on their own level and without explicit reference to their metaphysical presuppositions, Augustine attempts to deduce the standards of human behavior from theoretical or premoral principles. His moral order is expressly rooted in a natural order established by speculative reason. Justice in the highest sense prescribes the right ordering of all things according to reason. This order requires the universal and complete subordination of the lower to the higher both within man and outside of him. It exists when the body is ruled by the soul, when the lower appetites are ruled by reason, and when reason itself is ruled by God. The same hierarchy is or should be observed in society as a whole and is encountered when virtuous subjects obey wise rulers, whose minds are in turn subject to the divine law.[16] Such is the harmony which would have prevailed if man had persevered in the state of original justice. In that state men would have benefitted from all the advantages of society without any of its inconveniences. They would not have been subjected against their will to other men and, instead of vying with one another for the possession of earthly goods, they would have shared all things equitably in perfect amity and freedom.

Sacred Scripture teaches that this harmony was disrupted by sin. Through sin man's lust and overweening desire to assert his dominion over his fellow men have been unleashed. The present economy is marked by the anarchy of man's lower appetites and an invincible tendency to place one's selfish interests above the common good of society. It is a state of permanent revolt, which has its source in man's initial revolt against God. The prototype of this revolt is original sin, the sin committed by Adam and transmitted in a mysterious way to all his descendants. As a result, the freedom that man once enjoyed in the pursuit of the good has yielded to oppression and coercion. Coercion is apparent in the most typical institutions of civil society, such as private property, slavery, and government itself, all of which are necessitated and explained by man's present inability to live according to the dictates of reason.[17] The very existence of these institutions is a consequence and a permanent reminder of man's fallen condition. None was part of the original plan of creation and all of them are desirable only as a means of inhibiting man's proneness to evil. The private ownership of temporal goods both gratifies and curbs man's innate and unquenchable greed. By excluding other men from the possession of the same goods, it removes the external conditions and hence the possibility of unlimited acquisition; but it does not cure the inner desire for it. The same is true of slavery and of all other forms of the domination of man by man. Even civil society as we know it is a punishment for sin. If it can be called natural at all, it is only in reference to man's fallen nature. Like private property, it too is willed by God as a further means of checking his insatiable lust to dominate. All rule is inseparable from coercion and is despotic to that degree. The whole of political society becomes punitive and remedial in nature and purpose. Its role is essentially a negative one, that of castigating wrongdoers and of restraining evil among men by the use of force.

Justice is neither the work nor the common lot of fallen man. Even the good that is proportionate to his rational nature eludes him for the most part. The remedy to this situation is not to be found among the proper resources of human nature. Man's salvation, including his political salvation, accrues to him, not from philosophy, as Plato had intimated, but from God. Divine grace rather than human justice is the bond of society and the true source of happiness.[18] But by definition this grace is given gratuitously; it can be received by man but it is not merited by him, for man's merits are themselves the effect and not the principle of the grace conferred. In the actual state of humanity, the task of securing the good life devolves specifically upon the Church as the divinely instituted and visible instrument of God's grace. The scope of civil society is drastically limited in comparison with that assigned to it by classical philosophy. At best, civil society can by its repressive action maintain relative peace among men and in this fashion insure the minimal conditions under which the Church is able to exercise its teaching and saving ministry. Of itself it is incapable of leading to virtue.

Augustine's verdict concerning the fundamentally defective character of human justice is corroborated and further clarified by his analysis of law in Book I of the treatise *On Free Choice of the Will.* Augustine begins by distinguishing clearly between the eternal law, which is the supreme norm of justice, and temporal or human law, which adapts the common principles of the eternal law to the changing needs of particular societies. The eternal law is defined very generally as the law "in virtue of which it is just that all things be perfectly ordered," and is identified with the will or wisdom of God directing all things to their proper end.[19] It constitutes the universal font of justice and righteousness, and from it flows whatever is just or good in other laws. God himself has impressed this law upon the human mind. All are capable of knowing it and owe obedience to it at all times. It is also by virtue of the eternal law that the good are rewarded and the wicked punished. Finally, the eternal law is always and everywhere the same and suffers no exceptions.

As opposed to the eternal law, which is totally immutable, the temporal law can, without injustice, vary according to circumstances of time and place.[20] As a law, it is edicted for the common good and is necessarily a just law; for a law that is not just is not a law.[21] Yet a temporal law may differ from and even be contrary to other temporal laws. If, for example, the majority of the citizens of a given city were virtuous and dedicated to the public good, democracy would be a requirement of justice and a law enjoining that the magistrates of that city be chosen by the people would be a just law. By the same token, in a corrupt city, a law stipulating that only a man who is virtuous and capable of directing others to virtue should be appointed to office would likewise be a just law. Although mutually exclusive, both laws derive their justice from the eternal law, according to which it is always proper that honors should be distributed by virtuous men rather than by wicked men; for neither compulsion, nor chance, nor any emergency will ever render unjust the equitable distribution of goods within the city.[22] This variable temporal law is precisely what distinguishes one city from another and lends to each its unity and specific character. Cities and peoples are nothing else but associations of human beings living under and bound by a single temporal law.[23]

If the temporal law is a just law, it is also in many ways an imperfect law. It exists, not primarily for the sake of the virtuous, who strive of their own accord toward eternal goods and are subject only to the eternal law, but for the sake of the imperfect, who covet temporal goods and act justly only when compelled to do so by a human law.[24] To the extent to which it takes into account, as it must, the needs and claims of morally inferior men, it represents an adjustment between what is most desirable in itself and what is possible at any given moment, permitting lesser evils for the unique purpose of averting greater and more flagrant ones.[25] Its efficacy stems directly from man's attachment to earthly goods. It is solely because men are the slaves of these earthly goods that the law has any power over them. Thus, according to strict justice, only the man who uses wealth rightly is entitled to its possession. In the interest of peace and as a concession to human weakness, however, the temporal law sanctions the private ownership of material goods, regardless of the use that is made of them by the owner. At the same time, by threatening to deprive unjust men of the goods they already possess as a punishment for their transgressions, it acts as a deterrent to further injustices and secures at least an approximation to the equitable assignment of temporal goods.[26] The most that can be said in behalf of temporal law is that it shrewdly takes advantage of man's perversity to bring about and maintain a limited measure of justice in society. For this reason alone it remains indispensable, but the justice that it embodies is no more than an image or a dilution of perfect justice.

Even within its own sphere, and despite its restricted goals, the temporal law often fails to achieve the end for which it was instituted. In the first place, it is not unreasonable to suppose that men commit many injustices which go undetected and therefore unpunished. Say that someone has entrusted a large sum of money to a friend and dies suddenly without having had a chance to claim his deposit. Assuming that no one else is aware of the transaction, what is to prevent the trustee, if he should so desire, from appropriating the money instead of returning it to the lawful heir?[27] Secondly, even when a crime is known to have been perpetrated, it is often impossible to identify the criminal. Wise and good judges are easily mistaken. Despite all their precautions to insure the proper administration of justice, they unwittingly sentence innocent men to death. In the hope of ascertaining the truth, they will occasionally resort to torture; but torture frequently does little more than involve innocent persons in suffering without leading to the discovery of the guilty party. In a dramatic way, it too, reveals to what degree human justice is shrouded in darkness.[28] Lastly and most importantly, the temporal law only prescribes and forbids external acts. It does not extend to the hidden motives of these acts, and it is even less concerned with purely internal acts, such as the desire to commit murder or adultery.[29] For that reason, if for no other, it cannot be said to instill virtue. Genuine virtue requires that one not only perform just acts but that he perform them for the right motive. It implies on the part of the doer a desire for the good commanded by the law. It therefore presupposes that one has renounced the inordinate love of worldly goods and has ordered his passions to the good of reason. Mere compliance with the temporal law is no guarantee of moral goodness, for one can abide by the law and still act for a purely egoistic or utilitarian motive. The law, for example, permits the killing of an unjust aggressor in self-defense. In so doing, it aims at the common good and is itself entirely free from passion. But the man who avails himself of the liberty thus granted to him could easily be gratifying a selfish desire for personal revenge; in which case his act, although externally just, would be morally blameworthy. It is true that by demanding just acts of everyone the temporal law predisposes men to the acquisition of virtue. But it can go no further. It therefore needs to be complemented by a "higher and more secret law,"[30] namely, the eternal law, which encompasses all of man's acts, including his internal acts, and which alone is capable of producing virtue and not merely its appearance.

Thus far Augustine's treatment of this whole question parallels closely that of Cicero's *Laws* and even bears many textual resemblances to it. The similarity ceases the moment we come to the issue of divine providence, with which in Augustine's mind the notion of an eternal law is intrinsically bound up. The distance that separates the two authors on this point is partly manifested by the difference in terminology between them. Both Cicero and Augustine distinguish the eternal or natural law from the temporal or human law; but whereas Cicero habitually speaks of the former as the "natural law," Augustine shows a marked preference for the expression, the "eternal law." This eternal law not only points to what men should do or should avoid if they wish to be happy or good, it issues commands and prohibitions. It must therefore be accompanied by appropriate sanctions, for otherwise it would be ineffectual, and all the more so as it embraces the internal acts of the will, of which other human beings are not competent judges. Since it is obvious from experience that innocent men often suffer unjustly and that the misdeeds of wicked men are not always punished here on earth, the eternal law cannot be conceived without an afterlife in which wrongs are righted and the perfect order of justice is restored. It implies the existence of a just, provident, and all-knowing God, who rewards and punishes everyone according to his just deserts. Being eternal and all-perfect, God is subject to change neither in his being nor in his actions. He cannot acquire new knowledge and must know in advance as it were all the actions to be accomplished by men in the course of time and even their most secret thoughts.

This doctrine of divine sanctions was fraught from the start with considerable theoretical difficulties. If we assume that God knows all things before they come into being, it necessarily follows that men will always act in conformity with that divine knowledge; but under these conditions it is hard to see how they could be thought to remain free. One would thus appear to be faced with a choice between two alternatives, neither of which is acceptable from the standpoint of political society. One can assert that men are free and deny that God has any knowledge of the crimes committed against the eternal law or the just deeds executed in accordance with it; but then the eternal law is left without a guarantor and is thereby deprived of any means by which it could effectively restrain potential wrongdoers and promote virtuous habits. Or else one can assert divine foreknowledge and deny free will; but in that case men can no longer be held accountable for their actions, laws lose their raison d'être, exhortation becomes futile, praise and blame are revealed to be meaningless, and there ceases to be any justice whatever in the apportionment of rewards for the good and punishments for the wicked; in short, the whole economy of human life is subverted.[31]

According to Augustine's interpretation, Cicero attempted to fight his way out of this dilemma by openly professing and privately disavowing the doctrine of divine prescience. In the very public discussion of the treatise *On the Nature of the Gods*, he sides with the pious Lucilius Balbus, who defends the gods, against the atheist Cotta, who attacks them; but in his less popular work *On Divination*, he states with approval and expounds in his own name the very theory that he feigns to reject in the former treatise. By this subterfuge, he cleverly avoided undermining the salutary belief of the multitude in divine rewards and punishments without committing himself to a teaching which the learned find incompatible with human freedom and with which in any event they can easily dispense, since they need no such inducements in order to behave justly. Thus, concludes Augustine, "wishing to make men free, he makes them sacrilegious."[32]

Against Cicero, Augustine asserts both that God knows all things before they come to pass and that men do by their free will whatever they know and sense to be done by them only because they will it. Far from destroying free choice, God's knowledge actually founds it. The answer to the question as to how these two perfections may be reconciled lies in the supreme efficacy of the divine will. God knows all things because he knows their causes; and he knows their causes because his will extends to all of them, conferring upon each the power not only to act but to act in conformity with its proper mode. Natural causes exercise a necessary causality and voluntary causes a free one. Just as there is no power in natural causes that is not already contained in God, the author of nature, and is not bestowed by him, so there is nothing in man's will that is not already found in God, the creator of that will, and cannot be known by him. Otherwise one would have to postulate the existence in creatures of certain perfections that are absent from God, the universal source of all perfection. What is true of natural and voluntary causes is also true of fortuitous causes or chance. Chance is not just a name for the absence of a cause. What men call chance is really, for Augustine, a latent cause attributable either to God or to the separate substances. A problem could still be raised in regard to evil, which cannot be traced back to God as to its cause. But the fact that God does not cause sin in no way derogates from his perfection, since a sinful act, as sinful, is an imperfection explainable only in terms of deficient causality.[33] Nor does it presuppose that God must remain ignorant of the sins that men commit. If God knows what men can and will do, he also knows what they should do and will fail to do. It is true, of course, that men's deeds are performed in time and thus belong either to the past, the present, or the future. But even this does not prevent God from knowing them immutably. Standing as he does above time and outside of it, God knows everything from all eternity by means of a knowledge that is not measured by things but is itself the measure of all things and their perfection.

Having said this much, Augustine is fully aware of the obscurity that continues to surround our knowledge of the divine essence and its operations. His explanation may leave many questions unanswered, but, on purely rational grounds, he finds it no more difficult to accept than Cicero's, and it has in his eyes the advantage of making it possible for men not only to "live well" but to "believe well." [34]

Augustine's views on human justice and law underlie and motivate his judgment concerning the societies of the past and above all his judgment concerning Rome, the last of the great empires and the epitome of the pagan world's most brilliant political achievements.[35] The groundwork for his lengthy discussion of this subject was again laid in part by Cicero. Instead of founding a perfect city in speech, as Plato had done, Cicero sought to reawaken interest in the political life by turning to the example of the old Roman republic. In accordance with this more traditional and more practical approach, he was led to magnify the past glories of his fellow countrymen. Augustine, on the other hand, sets out to unmask their vices. These vices are nowhere more conspicuous than in Rome's dealings with other nations. Because there is no internal justice in the city, there is no external justice either; for a city that is not at peace with itself cannot be at peace with its neighbors. The so-called kingdoms of this world are hardly more than gigantic larcenies. They differ from robber gangs not by the removal of covetousness but by the magnitude of their crimes and the impunity with which they commit them. From the essential viewpoint of justice, what Alexander does on a grand scale and with a huge fleet is no better than what a pirate does on a much smaller scale and with a lone vessel.[36] Even republican Rome, for which Augustine professes a much greater regard than for the Rome of imperial days, is included in the common reprobation that engulfs all earthly cities. Rome "was never a republic because true justice and law never had a place in it."[37] The corresponding section of the *City of God* presents itself as an attempt to restore, against the embellishments of the Roman philosophers and historians, what Augustine regards as a true and faithful picture of ancient Rome.

To diagnose the character of any people one has only to consult the object of its love.[38] The old Romans were not just, and their city was not a true city, because the object of their passion was not virtue. No doubt the Romans were more worthy of admiration than any of the nations they subdued. The goal for which they toiled was by no means a vile one. It extolled courage and placed self-sacrifice and devotion to one's country above the amenities of a quiet and comfortable existence.[39] But it was nonetheless a purely earthly goal. The efforts expended in its pursuit bore the mark of greatness but not of virtue. Rome, the mistress of the world, was herself dominated by the lust to conquer. Her great men were at best outstanding citizens of a bad city. Most of them did not even possess genuinely political virtues. Their determination to excel was fed not by a desire to serve their countrymen but by the thirst for personal glory. Being practiced for what was ultimately a selfish motive, their reputedly heroic virtues were in fact little more than resplendent vices.[40] To the degree to which the Romans renounced pleasure and the gratification of their lower appetites, they were entitled to some reward. God granted this reward when he allowed Rome to assert her supremacy over all other nations.[41] Thus, in extending her conquests to the limits of the civilized world, Rome was able to fulfill her deepest aspirations and attain the end implied in all earthly ambition, universal domination. But the argument stops here. In opposition to a long-standing and at the time still powerful tradition of Christian apologetics, Augustine is apparently unwilling to concede that the Roman empire was assigned a special role in the economy of salvation and that, by bringing the whole world into one fellowship of government and laws, it even remotely prepared the way for Christianity, the one true and universal religion.[42]

Augustine's polemic against Rome is all the more striking as it comes from one who is obviously impressed by the spectacle of Rome's former greatness. Livy's account of the glorious deeds of the Scaevolas and Scipios, of Regulus and Fabricius, still fired his imagination, and he takes particular delight in relating their exploits.[43] Admirable as they may be by other standards, these exploits nevertheless belong to an irretrievable past whose memory awakens a certain sadness in the mind of the beholder but which Christianity has doomed once and for all. Christ, the sun of righteousness, has eclipsed the brightest beacons of the ancient world. His advent has destroyed forever the stage on which the pagan hero could move. True heroism is Christian heroism, but it is no longer the same type of heroism. Its newness is evinced by the fact that our "heroes" are called "martyrs" or witnesses rather than "heroes."[44] Henceforth, the accomplishments of the most noble Romans serve only two purposes: they reveal, along with the depths of human greed, the ephemeral and ultimately self-annihilating character of any purely human achievement; and they remind Christians that, if the Romans were willing to undergo such hardships for the sake of earthly gain, they themselves should be prepared to make even greater sacrifices for the sake of an eternal reward.[45]

By his devastating attack on pagan virtue, Augustine is more than anyone else responsible for the disparagement of Rome which became the hallmark of any discussion of Roman politics in the Christian world. The magnitude of his accomplishment can perhaps best be conveyed by saying that, almost single-handedly, he imposed a new image of Rome which, from that moment forward, preempted in the minds of statesmen and polit-

ical writers alike the image elaborated by the Roman historians and particularly by Livy, the trumpet of Rome's eternal greatness. Not until the
Renaissance do we find a fresh attempt to recapture, beneath the massive
and relentless indictments of the *City of God,* the spirit of pagan Rome
and its distinctive way of life.

MONOTHEISM AND THE PROBLEM OF CIVIL RELIGION

According to Augustine, the real reason for which the classical scheme
is unable to make men virtuous and for which it is convicted by its own
standards is not that it is irreligious but that it is intrinsically linked to a
false conception of the divinity. This falseness is most clearly revealed in
pagan polytheism. Much of what Augustine wrote on the subject of civil
society, including the whole first part of the *City of God*, is in effect little
more than a long and detailed criticism of pagan mythology.

Following Varro, Augustine divides all of pagan theology into three
basic forms: mythical, natural or philosophic, and civil or political.[46]
Mythical theology is the theology of the poets. It appeals directly to the
multitude and its many gods and goddesses are revered for the sake of the
temporal goods or material advantages that men hope to obtain from them
in this life. Natural theology is the theology of the philosophers and is
monotheistic. It rests on a true notion of God and as such it is vastly superior to both mythical and civil theology; but it remains inaccessible to
all save a few exceptionally gifted and learned individuals and is therefore incapable of exerting a beneficial influence on society as a whole.
Civil theology, as the name indicates, is the official theology of the city.
It differs from natural theology in that it is polytheistic, and from mythical
theology in that it prescribes the worship of the pagan gods on account of
the life after death and not of this life. It is the theology that all citizens
are, especially priests, expected to know and administer. It teaches what
god or gods each man may suitably worship and what sacred rites and
sacrifices he may suitably carry out. Although civil theology imposes the
cult of false gods, it is nevertheless more tolerable than mythical theology,
for it is concerned with the good of the soul rather than that of the body
and aspires to make men better by favoring the development of the political virtues.

The most authoritative exponent of Roman civil theology is Varro, to
whom Augustine, quoting Cicero, constantly refers as a most acute and
learned man.[47] Augustine's method consists in using Varro as a witness
against himself to prove the inadequacy of civil theology. Varro defended
civil theology not because it was true but because it was useful. He
himself did not accept it and did not take its gods seriously. He insinuated
as much by the fact that he distinguished clearly between civil theology

and natural theology. The same conclusion is borne out by an analysis of his *Antiquities*, where the treatment of human things precedes that of divine things. By adopting this arrangement, Varro let it be understood that the gods of the city did not exist independently of man but were themselves the products of the human mind. This, says Augustine, is the secret of his book. In that subtle manner Varro signified his unwillingness to give priority to error over truth. If he had been dealing with the truly divine or with the divine nature in its entirety, which he regarded as superior to human nature, he would not have hesitated to reverse the order. As it is, he merely expressed a laudable preference for men over the institutions of men or, in his own words, for the painter over the painting.[48]

Varro's views in this matter were no different from those of other pagan philosophers and particularly of Seneca. Because philosophy had made him free, Seneca did not refrain from attacking civil theology in his writings; but like Varro he continued to feign respect for its sacred rites and tenets. By conforming in deed if not always in speech with the prescriptions of that theology, he showed himself to be fully aware of the fact that he was doing what the law commanded and not what was pleasing to the gods. He, too, no less than Varro, was forced into the awkward position of having to perform what he condemned or of having to worship what he decried.[49]

Varro himself was more guarded in his speech than Seneca. Out of a noble regard for the weakness of lesser minds, he did not dare censure civil theology directly and was content to reveal its censurable character by exhibiting its resemblance to mythical theology.[50] His discussion of civil theology is itself civil or political.[51] It takes into consideration, more than Seneca had done, the practical necessity of accommodating oneself to the opinions and prejudices of the multitude or, what amounts to the same thing, the practical impossibility of establishing a political order based entirely on reason or nature. Had Varro been able to found a new city, he would have written according to nature; but as he was dealing with an old one, he could only follow its customs.[52] Being the result of a compromise between nature and convention, his civil theology may be said to occupy an intermediary position between mythical theology, which demands too little of most men, and natural theology, which demands too much of them.[53] Its level is that of the citizen as citizen and it represents the only feasible means of obtaining from the majority of citizens the highest degree of virtue of which they are capable without divine grace.

If Varro felt obliged for practical or political reasons to respect outwardly Rome's civil theology, he had no such qualms about its mythical or poetic theology, with which he found fault freely and which he rejected as both unworthy of the divine nature and incompatible with human dignity. By propagating lies about the gods and depicting their conduct as unseemly and base, the poets not only commit an injustice toward them, they encourage the same immorality among men and do more than anyone else to corrupt their manners.[54] Varro himself was in full agreement with the philosophers in calling for the expulsion of poets from any well-ordered city. Unfortunately, the city with which he was concerned was far from perfect. It not only tolerated the presence of poets in its midst, it was actually dependent upon them for its survival. Poets are both the products of civil society and its creators. The morality that they profess is neither identical with the old morality nor totally different from it.[55] Insofar as their mythology overlaps that of civil theology, it must be regarded as an integral part of the city. In the final analysis, it enshrines and perpetuates the same falsehoods.

Paradoxically enough, mythical theology often proves just as helpful to the city when it departs from its traditional beliefs as when it faithfully reflects them. Poets amuse the public and excel at flattering its taste. The object of their fables is for the most part the pleasant as opposed to the useful or the noble. To that extent, their works belong to the realm of the playful rather than that of serious things. The private and vicarious enjoyment that most men derive from their performances helps to compensate for the inevitable shortcomings of the political life and provides a salutary release from the tensions that it generates. All appearances to the contrary notwithstanding, poets are not revolutionaries. Their action is at bottom a conservative one, to the point that even their innovations contribute in a roundabout way to the stability of civil society. The mere fact that the city cannot dispense with such services may be taken as further proof of its own limitations and of its radical inability to solve its problems by purely human means.

Civil theology is not only akin to mythical theology; insofar as it shares in reason, it also draws near to natural theology. Many of its teachings may be regarded as a popular or prephilosophic expression of some genuinely philosophic truth.[56] They can often be justified in terms of nature and have in fact been explained in that fashion by the pagan philosophers. For example, there is nothing to prevent one from looking upon Jupiter, the ruler of the gods, as a poetic synonym for justice, the queen of the social virtues. But there are obvious limits to these interpretations. Pagan mythology, even in its official form, can never be fully rationalized. For that reason, its hold on the minds of people is weakened by the progress of science and by the unavoidable though not always salutary diffusion of knowledge. Resting as it does on a foundation of plausible lies, it cannot maintain itself indefinitely. Seen in that light, polytheism appears as both necessary to civil society and inconsistent with its highest development. One could phrase the argument in slightly different terms by saying that the worth of any society is measured by its ability to promote the good of the intellect; but to the degree to which society is successful in achieving that goal it tends to undermine its own basis. Herein lies the fallacy of the pagan scheme. By an inner necessity and quite independently of the external influence of Christianity, the crude polytheism of the pagan city must sooner or later become purified by transforming itself into monotheism.

It should not be inferred from what has been said that Augustine accepts without any reservations the monotheistic doctrine of the natural theologians. For one thing, the pagan philosophers do not all share the same conception of the divinity. Some of them, Varro included, identified the human soul, or its rational part, with the divine nature, thereby converting man into a god instead of making of him a servant of God.[57] Such a doctrine confuses the creature with its creator and is highly questionable from a rational standpoint, inasmuch as the mutability of the human mind cannot be reconciled with the absolute perfection of the Supreme Being. Only those philosophers who distinguish clearly between God and the soul or between the creator and his creation have reached the truth about God. The most outstanding among them was Plato.[58] Just how Plato arrived at this knowledge is a question that remains open. Augustine leaves it at saying that St. Paul himself asserts the possibility of a genuine knowledge of God among the pagans.[59] Aside from the fact that philosophers sometimes err in their teachings concerning God, however, there is still one crucial element which separates them from Christianity, and that is their refusal to accept Christ as mediator and redeemer. As a seeker after independent knowledge, the philosopher is basically proud and refuses to owe his salvation to anyone but himself. His whole endeavor is motivated in the final accounting by self-praise and self-admiration.[60] On that basis, it is perhaps true to say that the philosopher is the man who comes closest to Christianity and at the same time the one who remains furthest away from it.

THE TWO CITIES AND THE DICHOTOMY
BETWEEN RELIGION AND POLITICS

Augustine's attack on pagan religion culminates in what may be regarded as his most distinctive contribution to the problem of civil society, the doctrine of the two cities. Humanity, as we know it, is divided into many cities and nations, each one of which is clearly differentiated from all the others by its laws, its manners, its rites, its language, and its general way of life. But more fundamentally, sacred Scripture distinguishes only two kinds of societies, to which all men of all times belong, the city of God and the earthly city.[61] It is only by analogy, however, that these societies are called cities. The city of God is not a separate city, existing side by side with other cities and founded on a divine law, after the manner of the Jewish theocracy or the earthly basileia of Constantine and his followers. Both the city of God and the earthly city extend beyond the borders of individual cities and neither one is to be identified with any particular city or kingdom.[62] The distinction between them corresponds to the distinction between virtue and vice, with the implication that true virtue is Christian virtue. What establishes a person as a member of one or the other of these two cities is not the race or nation that he might claim as his own but the end that he pursues and to which he ultimately subordinates all of his actions.[63] The city of God is none other than the community of the followers of Christ and the worshippers of the true God. It is made up entirely of godly men and its whole life may be described as one of pious acquiescence in the word of God. In it and in it alone is true justice to be found. Because its pattern is laid in heaven and because its perfect state is achieved only in the afterlife, the city of God is sometimes called the heavenly city; but insofar as, by adhering to Christ, men now have the possibility of leading truly virtuous lives, it already exists here on earth. For the same reason it is not to be confused with Plato's ideal city, which has no existence other than in thought and word.

In contrast to the heavenly city, the earthly city is guided by self-love and lives according to what Scripture calls the flesh.[64] The term "flesh" in the present context is not to be taken in its narrow sense, as referring only to the body and to bodily pleasures. In its biblical usage, it is synonymous with natural man and embraces all of man's actions and desires to the extent to which they are not ordered to God as to their supreme end. It applies not only to the voluptuary, who places his highest good in pleasure, but to all those who indulge in vice and even to the wise man insofar as his quest for wisdom is actuated by a false love of self rather than by love of the truth. In its widest and most comprehensive sense, the earthly city is characterized by its affectation of total independence and self-sufficiency,[65] and presents itself as the very antithesis of the life of obedience ("the mother and guardian of the virtues")[66] and of reverent submission to God. Its ancestor is the unrepentant and unredeemed Cain, and its rebellion against God renews in its own fashion the sin of disobedience that Adam committed when he first transgressed the divine command.[67]

Although Augustine occasionally equates the city of God with the Church,[68] it is clear from some of his other statements that not everyone who is officially a member of the visible Church belongs to it; and conversely, many persons who do not profess the Christian faith are, without their knowing it, members of the same holy city. Actually, anyone dedicated to the pursuit of truth and virtue may be said to be implicitly a citizen of the city of God, and anyone who abandons virtue for vice is ipso facto excluded from it. What is more, any human attempt to discriminate, except in an abstract way, between the two cities is rendered precarious by the fact that it is impossible to know with any degree of finality whether or not a man is genuinely virtuous. One can observe and narrate the actions of another person, but he cannot attain the inner core from which they proceed.[69] Even the man who performs virtuous actions has no way of determining with absolute certitude to what extent he is acting out of virtue, inasmuch as he may easily be deluded as to the nature of his motives. These motives pertain not just to the secret of the human heart, which one could reveal if he chose to do so, but to the secret intention of the heart, which remains obscure to everyone, including the agent himself. In this life, therefore, the two cities are for all practical purposes inextricably mixed, like the wheat and tares of the parable, which are allowed to grow together and must await the time of harvest before they can be separated.[70]

The fact remains that it is only as a member of the city of God and by virtue of his relationship to an order that transcends the political sphere that one has any possibility of attaining the peace and happiness to which all men, even the most wicked, aspire.[71] This does not mean that the city of God has done away with the need for civil society. Its purpose is not to replace civil society but to supplement it by providing, over and above the benefits conferred by it, the means of achieving a goal that is higher than any to which civil society can lead. Civil society itself continues to be indispensable in that it procures and administers the temporal or material goods which men need here on earth and which may be used as instruments to promote the good of the soul.[72] Hence, citizenship in the city of God does not abrogate but preserves and complements citizenship in a temporal society. What is typical of Augustine's position is very precisely the twin citizenship by which one is enrolled as a member of the city of God without ceasing to order his temporal life within the framework of civil society and according to its norms. To the extent to which this position removes from the jurisdiction of the city and reserves for a higher authority an essential part of man's life, it represents a departure from the classical tradition, but insofar as it claims to provide the solution, sought in vain by the pagan philosophers, to the problem of human living, it may be viewed as a prolongation and fulfillment of that tradition.

The sharp distinction that Augustine draws between the spheres of ecclesiastical and civil authority raises the general question of their relationship and immediately suggests the possibility of a conflict between them. In the best instance, the conflict is resolved by the coincidence of Christian wisdom and political power. This is the situation that obtains when a Christian accedes to office and exercises his authority in accordance with Christian principles and for the common good of his subjects. It is explicitly envisaged by Augustine in Book V, chapter 24 of the *City of God*, which may be read as a mirror of Christian princes.[73] Such a situation leads to a restoration of the unity of the city on the plane of Christianity and is eminently desirable from the point of view of man's spiritual and temporal welfare; but there is never any assurance that it will come about, or if it should, that it will endure for any great length of time. Nothing in Augustine's works indicates that he anticipated the permanent triumph of the city of God on earth through the definitive reconciliation of the spiritual and temporal powers.

Beyond the broad statements that set apart and define the domains of the spiritual and the temporal and their respective jurisdictions, one does not find in Augustine a detailed theory of church and state similar to the ones elaborated, allegedly on the basis of his principles, during the centuries that followed. Given the highly contingent and unpredictable circumstances of the Church's existence in the world, it is doubtful whether Augustine ever seriously considered the possibility of articulating in any but the most general way the nature of the relations between these two societies.

There is, however, one point on which he was led to take a definite stand and which deserves to be mentioned, if only because of its historical importance; namely, the appeal to the so-called secular arm to repress heretics and schismatics. The occasion was the Donatist controversy, whose roots went back to the third century and which had paralyzed the Church in North Africa throughout most of the fourth century. Augustine began by advocating persuasion as the proper means of securing the return of the dissenters to the Catholic fold and was firmly opposed to any intervention on the part of the temporal authority in a matter that could be regarded at first as purely ecclesiastical. Events soon showed that more drastic measures were needed if order was to be restored, especially since the schism had in time assumed the aspect of a nationalist movement whose rapid growth was fanned by the perennial resentment of Roman supremacy among the native African population. The peculiar intractability of Donatists, their continued agitating, and the methods of terrorism to which they frequently resorted, had made of them a persistent threat not only to the religious unity but to the social stability of the North African provinces. Reluctantly and only after having exhausted all other resources, Augustine agreed to turn the matter over to the local civil authorities. His decision to sanction the use of force appears to have been dictated in large measure by the political nature of the case rather than by theological arguments. In making this decision, Augustine asserted his conviction that no one should be constrained to accept the faith against his own will. He carefully distinguished between the Donatists who had willfully embraced the schism and those who sought the truth in good faith and were Donatists only because they were born of Donatist parents.[74] He further cautioned against excessive severity in punishing offenders and stipulated that penalties should be mitigated in favor of anyone who could be prevailed upon to abjure his errors. Unfortunately, his action established a precedent whose consequences far exceeded anything that he himself appears to have foreseen. What was, for him, a mere concession to necessity or at most an emergency measure designed to cope with a specific situation was later invoked as a general principle to justify the Church's reprisals against heretics and apostates. If such is the case, Augustine may be partly to blame for the religious persecution of the Middle Ages, which came to be looked upon as a prime example of the inhumanity fostered by the undue exaltation of moral standards and became the object of one of the principal criticisms leveled at the Church throughout the modern period.

CHRISTIANITY AND PATRIOTISM

On purely political grounds, Augustine's solution to the problem of civil society was exposed to one major objection, of which he himself was fully aware and with which he was repeatedly forced to come to grips. Christianity had staked its claim to superiority on its ability to make men better and in the eyes of nonbelievers, it could be said to stand or fall by that claim. To the impartial observer, however, it was by no means evident that Christianity had succeeded where pagan political philosophy had failed or that its diffusion had been attended by a marked improvement in human affairs. If anything, the social and political disorders that had long plagued Rome both from within and from without had seemingly increased rather than decreased, despite the fact that Christianity, once persecuted and then tolerated, had become under Theodosius the official religion of the empire. "Is it not true," asks Augustine, "that since the coming of Christ, the state of human affairs has been worse than it was before and that human affairs were once much more fortunate than they are now?"[75] An open clash between Christians and pagans had already occurred in 382 when Gratian ordered the Altar of Victory removed from the Senate, over the opposition of the pagan faction, led by Symmachus, who contended that any substantial deviation from the traditional cult and practice of Rome would sooner or later prove detrimental to the empire. The fall of Rome at the hands of Alaric and the Goths in 410 brought the whole issue to a dramatic climax. The Christians were promptly blamed for the disaster and the old charge that Christianity was inimical to the well-being of society gained widespread currency among the pagan population. It was precisely to answer this accusation that Augustine undertook to write the *City of God*.[76] Rome, so the argument ran, owed her greatness to the favor of her gods. By forsaking these gods for a new religion, she had incurred their wrath and deprived herself of their protection.

Thus crudely stated, the argument could be countered by showing that all Roman history since the beginning had been marked by endless wars and civil strife and that, since these social evils antedated Christianity, they could not reasonably be laid at its door. It is obvious, however, that this popular polemic against Christianity only partially revealed the true problem, which was political rather than religious in character. Behind the common belief in tutelary deities lay the more serious allegation that Christianity had brought about a decline in civic virtue and could with every appearance of sound reason be held at least indirectly responsible for the deteriorating political fortunes of the empire. By enlisting men in the service of a "higher and more noble country,"[77] it divided the city and weakened the unconditional claim that the city makes on the allegiance of its citizens. The dual citizenship that it imposed on its followers inevitably led to a devaluation of the whole political order and rendered more difficult, if not impossible, the full measure of dedication to the city and its regime. As Augustine himself remarks, "so far as the life of mortals is concerned, which is spent and ended in a few days, what does it matter under whose rule a man is going to die, as long as those who govern do not force him to impiety and iniquity?"[78] Worse still, many of the most characteristic teachings of the new faith seemed to conflict openly with the sacred duties and rights of citizenship. Its doctrine of the brotherhood of all men and of their equality before God, as well as its precepts enjoining the love of one's enemies and the forgiveness of offenses, all tended at first glance to undermine the military strength of the city and to rob it of its most powerful means of defense against external foes. In the minds of Augustine's contemporaries, the danger was far from illusory. Faced with the apparent and almost tragic impossibility of reconciling Christianity with loyalty to one's country, some of Augustine's own friends had for many years refused baptism even after having been instructed in the faith.[79]

One could of course point to a similar depreciation of the purely political in classical philosophy, which placed man's happiness or highest good in the theoretical or philosophic life rather than in the life of dutiful citizenship. But philosophy was addressed to a natural elite and not to all men. By its very essence it was destined to remain the preserve of a small number of wellborn and well-bred natures. Hence there was little danger of its ever becoming a political force in the same sense as Christianity or of its having the same direct and immediate impact on the life of the city.

Augustine's answer to this general objection blends in typical fashion arguments drawn both from scriptural and from philosophic sources. It consists in saying, in substance, that Christianity does not destroy patriotism but reinforces it by making of it a religious duty. The Old Testament prophets and the New Testament writers alike command obedience to civil authority and to the laws of the city. To resist these laws is to defy God's own ordinance, inasmuch as civil society is intended by God himself as a remedy for evil and is used by him as an instrument of mercy in the midst of a sinful world, as St. Paul teaches in chapter 13 of the Letter to the Romans, to which Augustine constantly refers in this connection. This being the case, one cannot justifiably allege the service of God as a reason for shunning one's civic responsibilities or refusing submission to one's temporal rulers. Indeed, Christianity is to be understood above all as a faith rather than as a divinely revealed law governing all of one's actions and opinions and called upon to replace the human laws under which men live. It is compatible with any political regime and, in temporal matters, it does not impose a way of life of its own, different from that of other citizens of the same city. Its universality is such that it can accommodate itself without difficulty to the most diverse customs and practices. The only practices to which it is opposed are the ones that reason itself denounces as vicious or immoral. By censuring these practices and by urging its adherents to abstain from them, it actually serves the best interests of the city. Its very judgment concerning the essential limitations of civil society does not, any more than that of the pagan philosophers, entail a repudiation of that society. For all its manifest imperfections, civil society is still the greatest good of its kind that men possess. Its aim is or should be earthly peace, which Christians also seek. In the pursuit of this common goal, Christians and non-Christians can be united and live together as citizens of the same city.[80]

Furthermore, any depreciation of the fatherland, if one can really speak of a depreciation, is amply compensated for by the fact that Christianity demands and very often obtains from its followers a higher degree of morality and virtue. It thus helps to counteract vice and corruption, which are the true causes of the weakness and decline of cities and nations. In Augustine's own frequently quoted words:

> Let those who say that the doctrine of Christ is incompatible with the well-being of the commonwealth give us an army of soldiers such as the doctrine of Christ requires them to be; let them give us such subjects, such husbands and wives, such parents and children, such masters and servants, such kings, such judges, in fine, even such tax-payers and tax-gatherers as the Christian religion has taught that men should be; and then let them dare to say that it is adverse to the well-being of the commonwealth. Rather, let them no longer hesitate to confess that this doctrine, if it were obeyed, would be the salvation of the commonwealth.[81]

Finally, it is unfair to assert without further qualification that Christianity breeds contempt for military valor. The New Testament does not order soldiers to surrender their arms but rather commends them for their righteousness and virtue.[82] The injunction to requite evil with good concerns not so much external actions as the inward disposition with which these actions are to be performed. It seeks to insure that war, if it must be waged, will be carried out with a benevolent design and without undue harshness. Men are compelled at all times to do what is most likely to benefit their fellow men. In some instances, peace and the correction of wrongdoers are more readily and more perfectly achieved by forgiveness than by castigation; whereas in other instances, one would only confirm the wicked in their evil ways by giving free rein to injustice and allowing crimes to go unpunished.[83] What Christianity reproves is not war but the evils of war, such as the love of violence, revengeful cruelty, fierce and implacable hatreds, wild resistance, and the lust for power. By yielding to these evils, men lose a good that is far more precious than any of the earthly goods an enemy could take from them. Instead of increasing the number of the good, they merely add themselves to the number of the wicked.[84] Just wars are therefore permissible, but they must be undertaken only out of necessity and for the sake of peace. The decision to wage such a war rests with the monarch or ruler, to whom is entrusted the welfare of the community as a whole. As for the simple soldier, his duty is to obey orders. He himself is not answerable for the crimes that may be committed in cases where it is not clear whether the orders are just or unjust.[85]

Although Augustine agrees that there would be less strife among men if everyone shared the same faith,[86] he never regarded universal peace as a goal that could be attained in this life; nor for that matter did he draw from this monotheism the conclusion that all men should be united politically so as to form a single world society. The only passage in which the question is explicitly taken up presents the happiest condition of mankind, and the one most conducive to virtue, as that wherein small cities or small kingdoms exist side by side in neighborly concord.[87] Even that condition, however, will never be fully or permanently realized. Whether men like it or not, war is inevitable. The wicked wage war on the just because they want to, and the just wage war on the wicked because they have to. In either case, independent cities and small kingdoms eventually give way to large kingdoms established through the conquest of the weaker by the stronger. The best that can be hoped for in practice is that the just cause will triumph over the unjust one; for nothing is more injurious to everyone, including evildoers themselves, than that the latter should prosper and use their prosperity to oppress the good.[88]

Augustine's remarks to that effect are directed not so much against his pagan critics as they are against his coreligionists and, in some cases, his own disciples. Many prominent Christian writers of that period—Eusebius, Ambrose, Prudentius, and Orosius among them—had interpreted in a literal or temporal sense certain Old Testament prophecies relating to the blessings of the messianic age and had predicted an era of unprecedented peace and prosperity under the auspices of Christianity and as a direct outcome of its emergence as a world religion uniting all men in the cult of the true God. Some of these writers had gone on to compare the Christian persecutions, somewhat arbitrarily set at ten, to the ten plagues of Egypt and had inferred from this parallel that the Church would no longer have to endure similar hardships until the great persecution of the end-time announced by sacred Scripture. To the Christian was promised the best of both worlds; for, according to the proposed interpretation, not only did Christianity hold out the prospect of eternal bliss in heaven, it also provided the answer to man's most urgent problem here on earth.

Augustine dismisses all such interpretations as ingenious but unfounded in Scripture and contrary to its teaching.[89] He does not deny that human art and industry have made "wonderful and stupefying advances" in the course of time, but he is quick to add that this material and intellectual progress is not necessarily accompanied by a corresponding increase in moral goodness; for if these inventions have benefitted man, they can also be used to destroy him.[90] He further rejects outright the view that evils will disappear or even diminish as time goes on. God, being all-powerful, could of course do away with evil altogether, but not without the loss of a greater good for mankind. In their own way, the evils that he permits contribute to man's spiritual advancement. They serve as a test for the just and a punishment for the wicked. They likewise insure that God will be loved for himself and not just for the material advantages accruing to men as a consequence of their good deeds; and by imposing on man the necessity of overcoming these evils both within and outside of himself, they enable him to reach an ever higher level of virtue and moral perfection.[91]

More generally, the evils of human existence are themselves part of an overall plan that God pursues among men. To that extent they may be said to be rational; but their rationality surpasses human reason. Beyond the simple fact, recorded by sacred Scripture, that history takes its course not in cycles but along a straight line,[92] that it advances through successive stages toward a preestablished goal, and that with the coming of Christ it has entered into its final phase,[93] there is little or nothing to reveal the inner meaning or purpose of human events. To the earthly observer, these events retain their fundamental obscurity even once they have occurred. Considered in its totality, the life of earthly societies appears, not as an orderly progression (*procursus*) toward a determinate end, but as a simple process (*excursus*) by which the two cities run out their earthly existence, with its characteristic mixture of successes and failures but no guarantee of salvation in this world;[94] for "only in heaven has been promised that which on earth we seek."[95]

Christianity, as Augustine understands it, does indeed provide a solution to the problem of human society, but the solution is not one that is attained or attainable in and through human society. Like that of the classical philosophers, albeit in a different way, it remains essentially transpolitical.

NOTES

1. *Epistula* (*Letter*) 120.1.3; cf. *Sermo* (*Sermon*) 43.3.4.

2. *De doctrina christiania* (*On Christian Doctrine*) II.60-61; cf. *De diversis questionibus LXXXIII* (*On Eighty-three Different Questions*), qu. 53.2; *Confessiones* (*Confessions*) VII.9.15.

3. *De libero arbitrio* (*On Free Choice of the Will*) I.2.4; I.3.6; II.2.6; *Sermo* 43.7.9.

4. Cf. *Epist.* 120.1.4; *De genesi ad litteram* (*On the Literal Meaning of Genesis*) I.41.

5. Cf. *De civitate Dei* (*City of God*) VIII.4; *Contra academicos* or *De academicis* (*Against the Academics* or *On the Academics*) II.4.10; II.10.24; III.7.14; III.17.38; III.20.43; *Epist.* 118.3.16,20; 118.4.33.

6. *De ordine* (*On Order*) II.5.17; cf. *De ordine* I.11.31.

7. Cf. *De doctr. christ.* IV.9.23; *Epist.* 137.1.3,5,18; *Epist.* 118.1.1 et passim.

8. *Epist.* 1.1.

9. *Contra mendacium* (*Against Lying*) X.23; cf. *De mendacio* (*On Lying*) X.17.

10. Cf. *De civ. Dei* VIII.4; VIII.5; VIII.9.

11. Compare *De vera religione* (*On the True Religion*) IV.6-7 and *Contra acad.* III.17.37.

12. *De civ. Dei* XIX.13.

13. *De civ. Dei* XIX.21; cf. II.21.

14. Cf. *Epist.* 91.3-4.

15. *De civ. Dei* XIX.24.

16. Cf. *De civ. Dei* XIX.21; *Contra Faustum Manichaeum* (*Against Faustus, the Manichean*) XXII.27.

17. Cf. *De civ. Dei* XIX.15.

18. *Epist.* 137.5.17.

19. *De libero arb.* I. 6,15.

20. *De libero arb.* 1.15.31; cf. *De vera relig.* XXX.58.

21. *De libero arb.* I.5.11.

22. *De libero arb.* I.6.14-15.

23. *De libero arb.* I.7.16.

24. *De libero arb.* I.5.12.
25. *De libero arb.* I.5.12.
26. *De libero arb.* I.15.32; cf. *Epist.* 153.6.26; *Sermo* 50.2.4.
27. Cf. *Enarrationes in Psalmos* (*Exposition on the Psalms*) 57.2.
28. Cf. *De civ. Dei* XIX.6.
29. *De libero arb.* I.3.8.
30. *De libero arb.* I.5.13.
31. Cf. *De civ. Dei* V.9 and 10.
32. *De civ. Dei* V.9.
33. Cf. *De civ. Dei* XII.6-8.
34. *De civ. Dei* V.10.
35. Cf. *De civ. Dei* V.12.
36. *De civ. Dei* IV.4.
37. *De civ. Dei* II.21.
38. *De civ. Dei* XIX.24; cf. II.21.
39. *De civ. Dei* V.13 and 14.
40. *De civ. Dei* V.12; cf. XIX.25.
41. *De civ. Dei* V.15.
42. *De civ. Dei* XVIII.22.
43. Cf. *De civ. Dei* II.29.
44. *De civ. Dei* X.21; cf. V.14.
45. Cf. *De civ. Dei* V.16-18; *Epist.* 138.3.17.
46. *De civ. Dei* VI.5; cf. *De civ. Dei* IV.27.
47. *De civ. Dei* IV.1; IV.31; VI.2; VI.6; VI.8; VI.9; VII.28.
48. *De civ. Dei* VI.4.
49. *De civ. Dei* VI.10.
50. *De civ. Dei* VI.7; VI.8; VI.10.
51. *De civ. Dei* III.4; VI.2; VII.17; VII.23.
52. *De civ. Dei* VI.4; cf. IV.31 and VI.2.
53. *De civ. Dei* VI.6.
54. *De civ. Dei* VI.7.
55. *De civ. Dei* VI.8.
56. *De civ. Dei* VI.8; cf. *Epist.* 91.5.
57. *De civ. Dei* IV.31; VII.5; VII.6; VIII.1; VIII.5.
58. *De civ. Dei* VIII.4; VIII.10-12.
59. *De civ. Dei* VIII.12; cf. XVIII.41 *in fine*.
60. *De civ. Dei* V.20; cf. *Epist.* 155.1.2.
61. *De civ. Dei* XIV.1; XIV.4.
62. *De civ. Dei* XVIII.2; XX.11.
63. *De civ. Dei* XIV.28; cf. *De gen. ad litt.* XI.15.
64. Cf. *De civ. Dei* XIV.2 and 4.
65. *De civ. Dei* XIV.13 and 15.
66. *De civ. Dei* XIV.12.

67. *De civ. Dei* XIV.14.

68. E.g., *De civ. Dei* VIII.24; XIII.16; XVI.2.

69. Cf. *De ordine* II.10.29.

70. *De civ. Dei* XX.9; cf. *De civ. Dei* I.35; XI.1; XVIII.49; *Post collationem contra Donatistas* (*In Reply to the Donatists after the Conference*) VIII.11; *Contra littera Petiliani* (*In Answer to a Letter of Petilian*) II.21.46.

71. Cf. *De civ. Dei* XIX.12.

72. *De civ. Dei* XIX.17.

73. See also *De civ. Dei* V.19.

74. *Contra littera Petiliani* II.83.184; *Epist.* 43.1.1.

75. *En. in Psalmos* 136.9.

76. Cf. *Retractationes* (*The Retractations*) II.43.1; *De civ. Dei* I.1.

77. *Epist.* 91.1.

78. *De civ. Dei* V.17.

79. Cf. *Epist.* 151.14 and 136.2.

80. *De civ. Dei* XIX.17; XV.4.

81. *Epist.* 138.2.15; cf. *Epist.* 137.5.20 and *Epist.* 91.3.

82. *Epist.* 189.4; *Contra Faust. Man.* XXII.75.

83. Cf. *Epist.* 138.2.13-14.

84. Cf. *Contra Faust. Man.* XXII.74; *Epist.* 138.2.12.

85. *Contra Faust. Man.* XXII.75.

86. *Epist.* 189.5.

87. *De civ. Dei* IV.15.

88. *De civ. Dei* IV.3; XIX.7.

89. *De civ. Dei* XVIII.52.

90. *De civ. Dei* XXII.24.

91. *De civ. Dei* I.29; XXII.22 and 23.

92. Cf., *De civ. Dei* XII.11-21.

93. Cf. *De catechizandis rudibus* (*On Catechizing the Uninstructed*) XXII.39; *De gen. adversus Man.* (*On Genesis, Against the Manicheans*) I.23-24; *De civ. Dei* XXII.30 *in fine*.

94. See Augustine's letter to Firmus, C. Lambot, ed., *Revue Benedictine* 51 (1939): 212. Also *De civ. Dei* XV.21; XIX.5; *Retractationes* II.43.2.

95. *En. in Psal.* 48.6.

POLITICAL IDEALISM AND CHRISTIANITY IN THE THOUGHT OF ST. AUGUSTINE

Two closely related events have altered the intellectual climate of our time and supplied the framework for its liveliest theological and political debates: the resurgence of utopianism among the prophets of radical or egalitarian democracy and the programmatic violence which in recent years has frequently accompanied the demand for a just society.

The new utopianism comes after a wave of bitter disillusionment and ubiquitous pessimism brought on by two world wars and the collapse of the liberal ideal which for centuries had been the lifeblood of the Western world and the purveyor of its most enduring hopes. It heralds the end of modern man's "journey to the end of night" and the dawn of a new Age of Aquarius, whose promises inspire the New Left in the advanced industrial societies and the liberation movements at work in the developing countries of the Third World. It issues in a call for political action and, on the Christian side, for a political theology oriented toward social reform as the primary fact with which our generation will have to come to terms. Its impact is clearly visible in the various theologies of hope abroad in the land, as well as in the realignment of forces that has made fellow travelers, and in some cases companions-at-arms, of such traditional foes as

Christians and Marxists. It culminates in the alleged discovery or rediscovery of the Gospel as a revolutionary document and in the redefinition of Christian existence as revolutionary existence.[1]

The new violence, on the other hand, finds its loudest expression in the political assassinations, the inner-city riots, and the campus disturbances of the past decade. While, on a popular level, it generally seeks to legitimize itself as the only effective form of public protest or means of self-defense against the institutionalized violence of modern society, the principles in which it is ultimately rooted go far beyond the simple repudiation of a corrupt and decaying regime. They aim at nothing less than a total critique of Western civilization and the old world of biblical and classical morality on which it was founded. To many observers, the extreme manifestations to which they occasionally give rise have become symptomatic of the deepest crisis of our time. They bear eloquent witness to the absurdity of life once the horizon of human values from which it derives its meaning has been negated—to a nihilism redeemed only by the blind act of faith that one is summoned to make in the radical newness of an indeterminate but glowing future.[2]

Neither of these two developments, needless to add, is entirely without antecedents in earlier political and social theory. Both have their common source in nineteenth-century philosophy and may be seen as typical products of the recent amalgamation of Marx's thought with that of Nietzsche and Heidegger.[3] Both likewise draw the power of persuasion that they lacked barely a generation ago from the material possibilities opened up for an increasingly affluent society by the success of modern technology and the systematic exploitation of the world's natural resources. At the same time, the ambiguity of the goal pursued, not to speak of the morally questionable nature of the methods sometimes used or advocated to promote it, has tended to provoke a reaction which in subtle ways could turn out to be as dangerous as the abuses it purports to counteract.

Be that as it may, both the desired revolution and the resistance to it have found contemporary theologians generally ill-equipped for the task suddenly thrust upon them. Assuming that there is some advantage to be gained from a clearer understanding of the older solutions to the problem of a just social order, one may feel justified in returning, after centuries of spiritual neglect, to the origins of Christian political thought and above all to St. Augustine, the most profound political thinker of the early Church and the only one to deal with the issue of political idealism in all its breadth and complexity.

Augustine's political theology presents itself first and foremost as an attempt to integrate the Christian faith and the principles of Greco-Roman philosophy. The greatest representative of the ancient political tradition, the man whom Augustine regarded as the master of those who know, was

Plato.[4] Although there is no evidence that Augustine had read Plato's major political works either in the original or in translation, he was acquainted with their spirit and much of their content through Plato's Roman disciples, Varro and especially Cicero. He himself did more than any other writer of late antiquity to restore the Platonic teaching to its native political context. Beyond the immediate circumstances that prompted its writing, the *City of God* is an answer to Plato's *Republic*, which it eventually replaced in the West as the most authoritative account of the manner in which man should live in the city. Taken as a whole, it represents the first all-out endeavor on the part of a Christian theologian to come to grips with Platonic philosophy in its integrity and on the level of its own highest principles, over against the truncated and somewhat bookish Platonism of the later or so-called Neoplatonic philosophers, whose approach remains largely metaphysical or mystical and from whose works the omnipresent and all-important political dimension of Plato's thought has virtually disappeared. In the *City of God* more than in any other ancient Christian work, the contest between Christ and Socrates, of which earlier writers had spoken, achieves its true proportions. We shall begin to glimpse the issues implied in that contest if we turn for a moment to the earliest critique of political idealism to have been written by a classical author, Aristophanes's *Assembly of Women.*

The theme of the *Assembly of Women* is democracy and, more specifically, the claim that democracy is the most just and philanthropic of all regimes, the one regime capable of insuring the largest measure of happiness for all. The story is that of a group of scheming women who disguise themselves as men and successfully conspire to take over the government of the city. Democracy aims at equality, and complete equality can neither be attained nor preserved unless all things, including women and children, become common. Hence, the basic principle of the new order instituted by the rebellious women and their heroine, Praxagora, is that henceforth "all shall participate in everything and live out of the same."[5]

To a conservative like Aristophanes such a proposal could only appear as the acme of ridicule. It brings to light the folly of the Athenians who never tire of praising democracy on the one hand and scoff at the idea that women should rule on the other. Furthermore, the scheme will not work. Not only custom but nature cries out against it. In the name of equality handsome young men end up by having to marry old hags[6] and rich citizens are required to donate their wealth to the public treasury, which they are not about to do if they can help it.[7] As might be expected, the only one to derive any profit from the revolution is its instigator, an enterprising young woman who is already married to an aged husband and who can now look forward to free dinners for her family and hitherto forbidden pleasures for herself.[8] She, at least, has managed to solve her personal problem, but in a most elegant fashion by giving it the air of a public problem. The public life has not really triumphed over the private life. In their efforts to bring about a just but impossible social order, the women of Athens have simply created a new and more ridiculous situation. Democracy, which advertises itself as the rule of all, is in fact the rule of a part which, like any other part, claims to rule in the interest of all and to be best fitted for that rule. What is most objectionable in it is that, while it pretends to benefit everyone, it discriminates against the best of those who are superior by nature. The inequalities that it produces are even more shocking than the ones it sets out to eliminate. It strives for an unattainable ideal and wreaks devastation in the pursuit of it. Since the perfect society is a delusion, one would be well-advised to settle for more moderate goals and make do with a political arrangement that promises less but in the end accomplishes more than any of its deceptively more attractive alternatives.

The challenge issued by Aristophanes was taken up in a novel way by Plato, whose *Republic* was intended as a direct reply to the *Assembly of Women.*[9] The teaching of the *Republic,* most briefly stated, is that the notion of the perfectly just society and its attendant communism, which Aristophanes had dismissed as absurd, is not ludicrous at all. Given certain very special circumstances, such a society is conceivable, but its coming into being is contingent on the one thing of which Aristophanes seems to be unaware or which in his cleverness he has forgotten, namely, philosophy. Evils will cease from the land if and when, according to that most famous of all Platonic teachings, kings become philosophers and philosophers become kings.[10]

Augustine's own *City of God* is all the more interesting from our point of view as it is directed in the first instance against the idealism of the *Republic.* The basic argument that it develops may be summarized as follows. Platonic political philosophy studies human behavior in the light of man's highest possibilities or the noblest goals to which one may aspire, that is to say, in the light of virtue; and it claims to be able to show the way to the attainment of those goals. It culminates in a discussion of the best life and, on the political level, of the best regime or the kind of rule that is conducive to the best life for everyone. By the best regime, it understands that regime which is most according to wish, a regime of the sort that wisdom and virtue would prescribe if one were in the rare and enviable position of being able to act with complete freedom in these matters.[11] The society that serves as its model is based entirely on reason and makes no concessions to prevailing customs or the lower appetites by which men are guided for the most part. In that regard it exhibits greater consistency than Roman political thought, which was forced to compromise with human weakness and officially sanctioned numerous practices that were contrary to its own principles and inimical to human dignity.[12] By resisting all such compromises, "Plato showed the Romans what their genius had left incomplete."[13]

The trouble with that approach in Augustine's view is that it compels one to speak about an ideal that has never or hardly ever been seen to exist among men and whose actualization is dependent on the unlikely confluence of an untold number of auspicious circumstances. Plato is essentially right in his estimation of what men ought to do and how they should live in society, but he was incapable of providing the means by which that ideal could be translated into practice. The just society of which he speaks is a society that exists in private discussions—*domesticis disputationibus*—rather than in the actions of the marketplace.[14] As such it is nothing but a beautiful pipe dream, setting down goals that elude most men all of the time and all men most of the time and thus destined to be deprived forever of that which it deems indispensable to the happiness of individuals and cities.[15]

The improbable, not to say hopelessly quixotic, character of the Platonic scheme is borne out for Augustine by the example of actual cities, all of which fall short of the standards established by reason and nature. Recall Cicero's definition of true or ideal cities: "assemblages of rational beings bound together by a common acknowledgement of right or justice."[16] In fact, what holds their members together, as pointed out in chapter one, is rarely anything more than their collective selfishness or, as Augustine puts it more euphemistically, a "common agreement as to the object of their love."[17] All cities suffer from the same radical defect and none has ever been known to prefer habitually righteousness to injustice. The mere fact that cities must resort to such agencies as law and law enforcement in order to secure a measure of peace among their citizens is already sufficient proof of the all too human quality of their moral life.[18] If everyone were virtuous, laws would be superfluous and men would pursue of their own accord the good that they are intended to protect.[19] As it is, few men can be trusted to seek justice for its own sake. With a view to its self-preservation, if for no higher motive, civil society must structure itself in such a way as to exploit man's perversity to its own advantage. It inhibits the potentially destructive manifestations of human egoism, not by appealing to one's reason or sense of decency, but by pitting evil passion against evil passion and using the one to countermand the other.[20] It sees to it that even scoundrels unamenable to persuasion and with no attraction for virtue will be impelled by their own self-interest to perform virtuous acts. The greedy person who seeks his own aggrandizement at the expense of others will refrain from cheating or stealing, not because he has renounced the inordinate love of material goods, but out of fear of losing those goods which he already possesses and of which the law threatens to strip him as a punishment for whatever crime he may be tempted to commit.

What is remarkable in all of this, however, is that Augustine's attack on Plato hardly does more than bring to light what was already implicit in the *Republic*, which, as closer examination reveals, must itself be read as a critique of political idealism and indeed perhaps the most devastating critique of political idealism ever written.[21] Its blueprint of the best society is one which, in the mind of its own author, can never be fully implemented in society at large. The book as a whole fulfills the function of a noble lie, calculated to incite men to as high a degree of virtue as may be reasonably expected of them, but without much hope of seeing its dream parlayed into a reality.[22] It is strictly utopian, to use a word which is not, properly speaking, Platonic but which was coined by a later disciple of Plato who had admirably captured the spirit of Plato's work. In that sense it is true to say that the *Republic* is a comedy,[23] but a comedy of the highest order, which consciously imitates and surpasses that of Plato's rival, Aristophanes. Like all great comedies, it, too, is based on an impossibility. It describes a state of affairs which could obtain only if in speaking of political matters one were able to prescind from the body and bodily passions or if one were dealing with angels instead of men.[24] It accomplishes its purpose by forcing the wise reader to reflect on the reasons for which the proposed scheme is impossible. Its comic character is evinced by the fact that its most daring and outlandish proposals—such as the perfect equality of the sexes even in regard to warfare,[25] the community of wives and children,[26] and the rule of the philosopher-king, on which the success of the enterprise is said to hinge—are not put forward as serious proposals in the usual sense of the word. Given the scarcity of truly philosophic natures,[27] the difficulty inherent in their nurture,[28] the forces that threaten their corruption,[29] and the frequent antagonism of the multitude toward them,[30] one cannot assume that the right person will always be available when needed or, if he were, that he could easily accede to power. The philosopher, whose interests lie in a direction diametrically opposed to those of the city, will never take on the burden of rulership unless compelled by some necessity to do so; and the many, who know little or nothing of wisdom, are not apt to seek or accept a wise man as their sole ruler.[31] All in all, the hoped for encounter of wisdom and political power leaves much to chance and precludes the kind of planning that could guarantee its realization at any chosen moment. Moreover, even in the unlikely event of its establishment, the new regime is faced with the necessity of maintaining and perpetuating itself; for the absolutely perfect regime, if such there be, necessarily contains within itself all that is required for its own preservation. Yet the books that follow in the *Republic* are devoted precisely to an analysis of the manner in which by a gradual process the would-be perfect regime degenerates into less perfect and eventually totally corrupt regimes;[32] which is as much as to say that the perfect regime has never existed and probably never will.

The central point of the argument is summed up in Socrates's remark, later echoed by St. Augustine, to the effect that the city whose foundation has just been described is one that has its place in speech only and is not to be found anywhere on earth.[33] Its pattern is laid up in heaven, and, in the end, it makes no difference whether it is or will be anywhere. The principles on which it is based are not susceptible of being applied directly to the concrete situation of cities and must be diluted in order to become operative. In short, the *Republic,* as Cicero had already observed, is a philosophic rather than a political book.[34] Its main purpose is to reveal the nature and hence the limitations of the political life. By so doing, it points beyond itself to another life or type of life, though not to another world, in which alone true happiness is to be encountered.

What has just been said of Plato's *Republic* applies, *mutatis mutandis,* to Cicero's *Republic,* which, despite its more traditional approach,[35] does not convey an essentially different teaching and is itself to be interpreted as a tacit admission that the problem of civil society is for all practical purposes humanly insoluble. In it Cicero explicitly takes up the question of whether justice or injustice necessarily underlies the successful management of the affairs of the state. The case for injustice is entrusted to Philus,[36] who takes the position that the faithful observance of the demands of justice runs counter to human nature and is seldom reconcilable with the demands of wisdom and self-interest. To act at all times in accordance with the rules of strict justice would be sheer folly. If Rome had done so, she would have remained a poverty-stricken village.[37] Wisdom counsels that it is the appearance rather than the substance of justice which is to be sought, for thus one may benefit from the advantages stemming from a reputation for virtue while avoiding the misfortunes that could accompany an unswerving compliance with its dictates.[38]

Philus's argument in favor of injustice is rebutted by Laelius,[39] the oldest and most conservative member of the group, who expounds the Stoic conception of natural law and is firmly convinced that the paths of justice and wisdom necessarily converge. The drift of the discussion makes it quite clear, however, that, while Laelius's uncompromising moralism is undoubtedly preferable to Philus's blatant immoralism, neither position can be regarded as adequate. All states should strive for justice but none can do more than approximate its highest standards. Even the regime which, for purposes of edification, Scipio had praised as being the most perfect was not free from injustice.[40] The harsh but inescapable conclusion at which one arrives is that for Cicero, no less than for Plato, civil society is inconceivable without injustice, however much one may deplore that situation and however eager he may be to rectify it. The perfect regime would seem to lie beyond the scope of human capacity. Whether one likes it or not, man's expectations from the political life can never equal his desires in regard to it.[41]

By denouncing the classical scheme as idealistic or utopian, Augustine was not saying anything that had not already been said or implied by Plato and Cicero. His merit is to have grasped with remarkable clarity and penetration the basic intention of the *Republic.* In this he showed himself to be an infinitely more astute critic of Plato and the Platonic tradition than his predecessor Lactantius, who remains utterly impervious to the more subtle implications of the *Republic* and sees in it nothing more than an invitation to licentiousness and promiscuity.[42] Lactantius, the Christian Cicero, was Ciceronian in style but not much else.

Augustine's indictment of the Platonic tradition is not substantially different from that of the early modern philosophers, who later broke with classical thought on the ground of its inability to produce the kind of society which it presented as essential to man's political well-being.[43] It is difficult to read Augustine's vivid account of the rapacity and ruthless depredations of nations and empires without being constantly reminded of Hobbes's famous descriptions of the state of nature as a state in which every man is at war with every other man.[44] His analysis of the mechanism of government, with its reliance on institutions rather than on education or virtue, appears at first sight to foreshadow the attempt made by the seventeenth-century theorists to establish the state on the bedrock of passion instead of reason.[45] And his endless disquisitions on the mostly evil heart of man announced from afar the approach devised by Francis Bacon, who ends up by advocating the systematic study of evil rather than of the good in the formation of the future statesman.[46]

Yet, as chapter seven will show at length, Augustine is anything but a Machiavellian or a Hobbesian before the letter. One misses completely the point of his argument if one construes it as a defense of political immoralism[47] or an anticipation of the modern contractualist theories.[48] His views on civil society are not in any way predicated on a denial of man's social nature and he never approved of anything like the divorce between ethics and politics which became prevalent in modern times.[49] His remark to the effect that Scipio's definition of the state is acceptable only with the stipulation that the word "justice" be stricken from it was not meant to be taken as an acknowledgment that states should not be concerned with justice and virtue; nor was it motivated by the desire to substitute a descriptive definition for a prescriptive one;[50] or to find a definition broad enough to fit all states regardless of the intrinsic goodness or badness of their respective ways of life.[51] It simply calls attention to the unfortunate but habitual cleavage between the "is" and the "ought" in the lives of states as well as of the individuals who make them up.

More importantly, it never occurred to Augustine to enhance the efficacy of his teaching by deliberately lowering the standards of human conduct, as was the case with the early modern political theorists. By reason of the absolute demands that they make on men, his own standards are even loftier and more stringent than the most stringent standards of classical thought. Classical thought has failed, not because it expected too much of most men, but because it was compelled to rely on purely human means to bring about the realization of the noble goals that it set for them. Thanks to the revelation of divine truth, the justice which had hitherto eluded man has at last become accessible to him, but it belongs properly to that city of which Christ is the founder and ruler.[52] As mentioned in chapter one, divine grace and not human justice is the true bond of society.[53] It alone fulfills both the ideals of pagan philosophy and the prescriptions of the Old Law, not in the sense that the Law was wanting in anything that may have been essential to it, but in the sense that it accomplishes what, despite the best of intentions, the literal command had failed in doing.[54] The *City of God* and not Plato's *Republic* is the true apology of Socrates. Just as Plato had suggested that the scheme devised by Aristophanes, absurd as it may have seemed to Aristophanes himself, might succeed if philosophers could be induced to become kings, so Plato's solution, which was never intended as a workable solution, is henceforward applicable in deed, but on one condition: that one be enrolled as a member of the city of God.

As Augustine himself was eventually forced to recognize, however, there was no tangible evidence that the new solution, even admitting its moral superiority, would yield better results. That solution, as it happens, was not without difficulties of its own, which soon became apparent as a result of the changing political situation of the time. In the eyes of Augustine's pagan contemporaries, the great objection was not that Christians did not always live up to their own high ideals—that they did not practice what they preached—but that they might some day be tempted to do so. By propagating the view that all men are equal and potentially members of a single cosmopolis ruled by God, Christianity revealed the horizon of the political life as a mere horizon, thereby destroying it and depriving the polis of the protective atmosphere within which it had thus far been able to thrive. It engendered a tendency to regard the natural differences and traditional boundaries that set men off as separate groups leading separate lives as politically irrelevant, and thus stripped the city of its status as an exclusive community, as the all-embracing whole and unique expression of that common life which stands above its individual members and binds them together as fellow citizens. Just how the universal love that it enjoined on its adherents could be reconciled with a life of dutiful citizenship was far from clear.[55] Its teaching that all men are brothers, descended from the same couple and children of the same heavenly Father, blurred the distinction between friend and foe and robbed the city of its sole reliable means of defense against external enemies.[56] Christianity proclaimed the possibility on the level of human life and action of a universalism which is restricted to the republic of spirits and is more at home in Portia's Belmont than in the cities of men. By preaching the love of all men, it, in effect, made it harder to love any. Since it prescribed what appeared to be unfulfillable duties, it proved guilty of the very defect with which Augustine had reproached classical philosophy. It was at best a tragic illusion, noble in its inspiration but blind to the necessities of the political life and irresponsible in its practical applications. As long as Christians represented only a minority of the total population, their presence was not likely to inspire any great fear on the part of the civil authorities;[57] and as long as the Empire remained secure, even large numbers of Christians within it did not constitute an imminent threat to its safety. The issue took a new turn the day the Empire was overrun and its existence menaced by hordes of invading barbarians.

It fell to Augustine to think the problem through anew and explain how Christianity, far from subverting the city or breeding contempt for it, could positively strengthen and benefit it. His whole outlook on the question finds its most striking analogy, as well as its sharpest contrast, in Plato's conception of the relation between the philosopher and the non-philosopher or between philosophy and the city, particularly as it is developed in the *Apology of Socrates.*

The *Apology* refutes the charge that philosophy was hostile to the city by showing that Socrates was neither a denier of its gods nor a corruptor of youth but a teacher of virtue. Socrates helps his fellow citizens by persuading them that they should be more concerned with improving their souls than with taking care of their bodies.[58] Unlike the Sophists, he accepts no money for his services and cannot be accused of acting for a selfish motive. His preoccupation with virtue is such that it prompts him to neglect his own affairs in order to attend to those of others.[59] Despite his poverty, he is more philanthropic than any of the wealthy citizens of Athens. Nor is there any substance to the accusation of impiety levelled against him. The proof that he does not reject the gods of the city is that his examination of his fellow citizens was undertaken at the behest of a god and carried out as a form of service to him.[60] Throughout his defense, he presents himself as a pious man who does not challenge directly the laws of the city and especially its laws concerning the gods. By assenting to these laws, he implicitly teaches that they are indispensable to the city and that it is, in part, because of their belief in the gods that most men are able to live as decent citizens within it. He does not for one moment take the city for granted and readily acknowledges that it, too, has its requirements, to which in the common interest all loyal citizens are expected to conform. His own loyalty has been amply demonstrated by his readiness to fight for his country and the courage that he subsequently displayed on the battlefield.[61] He himself is the first to recognize his debt to the city. He was not born of an oak or a stone but of human beings who were married and lived all of their lives under the protection of its laws;[62] and he was allowed to live unmolested in Athens for seventy years. Any city that can produce a Socrates and tolerate him for that long a period of time cannot be totally bad. Under the Tyranny of the Thirty, Socrates would probably have died much sooner.[63]

This does not mean that he regards all of Athens's laws as just. Some of these laws, such as the law which permits a trial of life and death to be concluded in a single day, are manifestly unjust.[64] But he is nevertheless prepared to submit to them. The only law which he cannot accept under any circumstances is the law which forbids him to philosophize;[65] for compliance with such a law would harm his soul and not merely his body.[66] The city, of course, has the power to retaliate by putting him to death, but he has nothing to fear from such a punishment. The gods of the city—those gods in whom his true judges believe—are not indifferent to the fate of good men.[67] From these gods, granting their existence, Socrates can expect a treatment that is more equitable than the one which he stands to receive at the hands of his accusers.[68] Moreover, by enforcing that law the city defeats its own purpose. It places itself in the position of not being able to meet on their own ground the philosophic attacks aimed at its most fundamental beliefs, and deprives itself of the one weapon by which it could effectively refute atheists, such as Anaxagoras, who reject even the cosmic gods and contend that the sun is no more than a stone and the moon a clump of earth.[69] It also forfeits any means by which it could redress its own unjust decrees, such as the decree in virtue of which the admirals of the Argenusai were prosecuted as a group for having abandoned their dead after the battle, even though in individual instances the action could conceivably have been dictated by prudence and may have served the best interests of the fleet.[70] A simple reflection on the inadequacy of its laws should be sufficient to convince Athens that it cannot dispense with the one thing which it is unwilling to allow. By punishing Socrates, it punishes itself. Its action is absurd and self-contradictory.

Still, the preceding remarks reflect only one side of the teaching of the dialogue and shed more light on the attitude of the city toward philosophy than on the nature of the philosophic life itself. As one penetrates beneath the surface of the argument, one soon comes to the realization that the existence which Socrates leads has little in common with that of most citizens and that its requirements differ profoundly from those of the political life.[71] His claim to piety rests on the assertion that he who believes in divine things necessarily believes in the gods;[72] but that assertion has about as much validity as the statement that the man who believes in brooms also believes in witches. When the question comes up as to what Socrates would do in the next life if he were to be put to death, the answer is that he would persist in the kind of activity in which he has always been engaged—an activity that consists essentially in interrogating others and discussing human excellence with his friends.[73] There is no longer any talk of making men better by exhorting them to virtue. It becomes apparent by this time that Socrates's understanding of nobility, justice, and piety bears little resemblance to that of the multitude. Among those whom he could anticipate meeting in the afterlife are men who have been unjustly sentenced in this life, along with their accusers.[74] The implication is that he is not satisfied with the verdict of other men or even of the gods concerning these men. He sets himself up as the judge of the justice of the gods. His entire life is devoted to a search for answers to the most basic questions, and he has no other desire than to pursue the endless or Sisyphean quest for the knowledge of truth and justice.[75]

One can only infer from these observations that Socrates is more preoccupied with wisdom than with moral virtue. His own god, as distinguished from the gods of the city, is not a god who takes an active interest in the affairs of men. He is a wise god whom one comprehends, rather than a loving god whom one accepts and obeys. The wise Socrates does what the god himself does, not what the god orders him to do. Whereas his service to the city is an activity that is imposed on him, the search for knowledge is an activity on which he embarks freely and which alone, though few men understand it, promises true fulfillment. The satisfactions that it affords are intrinsically independent of the city and are impeded rather than favored by the duties that one discharges toward one's fellow men. To the extent to which it proceeds from an awareness of the limitations of the political life, it is transmoral and transpolitical and necessitates a high degree of detachment from the city and its concerns. From the standpoint of the dedicated citizen, it is self-gratifying and heartless.[76] The philosopher lives in the cave, but as someone who is not at home in it and does not really belong to it.

The purpose of the whole discussion as it is presented to us is not so much to prove that the city needs philosophy as to offer a defense of philosophy which will render the city less hostile to it. Socrates is not interested in the city and its virtues for their own sakes but for the sake of philosophy. For, if the city needs philosophy, philosophy itself needs the city. It is not a plant that grows in any soil and it requires for its nurture certain conditions that are not encountered everywhere. There are no philosophers in the wilderness or in the land of the lotus-eaters; but neither are philosophers to be found in any city whatever.[77] Some cities are more open to philosophy and more conducive to its development than others. The city itself does not philosophize, but it can either encourage, tolerate, or persecute philosophers. For his own benefit or, better still, for the benefit of philosophy, the philosopher cannot remain completely indifferent to its life; but the efforts that he dispenses in its behalf are plainly more a matter of necessity than of choice.

Only under the best regime, such as the one sketched in the *Republic,* can the relationship of the philosopher to the city be thought to be based on nature.[78] But the perfect city of the *Republic* exists in speech only. This means that for all practical purposes the relationship in question assumes the form of a tacit contract[79] or a kind of gentleman's agreement whereby, in return for the freedom granted him, the philosopher refrains from intervening directly in the affairs of the city and agrees to exercise the greatest restraint in the public expression of his own, essentially private views. The alliance thus forged, however, is no more than a marriage of reason, entered upon for motives of calculation or mutual self-interest, rather than a marriage of love, or perhaps a kind of shotgun wedding, constantly threatened and never perfectly harmonious. That marriage was consummated by the death of Socrates. Socrates himself can hardly be thought to have been moderate in his dealings with the city, as is evident from his own behavior and that of the young men whom he influenced.[80] The *Apology* teaches that one should not imitate the young men who imitate Socrates. It thereby teaches that one should not imitate Socrates himself. By discussing philosophy only indirectly, by showing us only its political face, the *Apology* inculcates a lesson in moderation. It illustrates in dramatic fashion the tension between science and society or the ultimate irreconcilability of the demands of the philosophic life with those of the political life.

The picture changes abruptly the moment we come to the parallel issue of the relation of Christianity to the city. The distinction between the philosopher and the nonphilosopher, which Plato regarded as the most fundamental distinction among men and which underlies his treatment of the problem at hand, loses its paramount importance. By the same token, the nature of the bond that unites the Christian to his fellow men undergoes a profound transformation. Between the love of truth and the requirements of a life wholly dedicated to its pursuit on the one hand and the service of one's fellows on the other, there can no longer be any final opposition. Christian wisdom or the knowledge of the divine truth is not only reconcilable with but inseparable from the love of neighbor.[81] The responsibilities that it carries with it go far beyond anything that had previously been thought possible or desirable. They extend to all men, for one cannot love God without, at the same time, loving those whom God wants to be saved; and God wants everyone to be saved. To reject a single man is to break the covenant of love that links the Christian to all other men regardless of natural or conventional differences, inasmuch as by sinning against any member of Christ's body one sins against Christ himself.[82] The sign and locus par excellence of Christian love is the Church which is not an entity distinct from the world but the world reconciled unto itself and unto God: *mundus reconciliatus ecclesia.*[83]

Since its motive is God, the love that the Christian owes to others is in no way determined by the personal qualities that one may or may not find in them. It encompasses one's enemies as well as one's friends and fellow citizens, and it manifests itself as much by its opposition to evil as by the efforts that it displays in the pursuit of the good;[84] for the toleration of those evils which cannot be allowed to prevail without prejudice to a greater good is as much a betrayal of love as is the self-righteous and fanatical desire to extirpate forcefully all evil from among men. Its total dimension is summed up in Augustine's well-known dictum, "Love and do what you will,"[85] which expresses not only the primacy of love but its necessary concomitant, the sometimes painful duty of castigating wrong-doers. Interestingly enough, the maxim appears to have been invoked for the first time in the course of the Donatist controversy as a means of justifying reprisals against heretics.[86]

The knowledge with which the Christian has been gifted is not to be understood merely as a new theory, destined to replace a philosophic theory which, judged by its own standards, had seemingly proved inadequate, but as a new type of knowledge altogether which, once accepted, necessarily issues in deeds and is itself productive of that which it expresses.[87] By its very nature it implies a transformation of the whole person and its sole possession suffices to make him good, dealing as it does not only with things that one cannot know without knowing that one should will them, but with things that one cannot know without at the same time willing them.[88] Such a doctrine cannot be simply detrimental to the good estate of the realm and destructive of the loyalty that one owes to one's city.[89]

The specific answer to the question of how Christianity as a religion of universal love and a universal way of salvation may be reconciled with one's patriotic duties as a member of a particular society lies in the sharp distinction which Augustine introduces between the two spheres of spiritual and temporal power. That distinction finds its strongest support in Romans 13:1-7, which Augustine takes as a warning to all Christians that the freedom acquired through faith cannot be cited as a valid reason for refusing submission to one's temporal rulers.[90] To these rulers has been entrusted the administration of the material goods that all men need and use in this life. Since the Christian benefits like everyone else from the advantages of civil society, he remains subject to its authority and bound by its laws in all matters pertaining to his earthly existence. His respect for these laws is all the greater as it is inspired not by fear of punishment but by the intimate knowledge that, as he defers to them, he is fulfilling a sacred duty: "therefore whoever resists authority resists the ordinance of God" (Rom. 13:2). For this reason, his obedience, unlike that of other citizens, can never be merely feigned.[91]

The only laws in which he may not acquiesce are those which could take away what God has given in view of eternal life, over which temporal rulers have no jurisdiction. For, if it is a grave error to think that, because one is a Christian, one is not subject to civil authority, it is an even graver error to think that temporal rulers should have any say in matters relating to the faith.[92] By withholding his allegiance in such cases, the Christian exposes himself to the penalties that civil society ordinarily inflicts on those whom it regards as lawbreakers and risks being deprived of his temporal goods, among which, with noble simplicity, Augustine does not hesitate to include life itself.[93] But the harm that he suffers in his body cannot hurt his soul, inasmuch as all power, not excluding the power wielded by wicked rulers for wicked purposes, comes from God, who could never permit evil if it could not somehow be made to contribute to the spiritual welfare of innocent and unjustly punished men.[94]

Until such time, then, as one is delivered from the unrighteousness of the present life, one must accept its constraints and put up with a situation that may be better or worse according to circumstances of time and place but never as perfect as one would wish it to be. The paradoxical conclusion is that the Christian is both freer from the bonds of civil society and, by virtue of the summons received from God, more strongly obligated to it than any other man.[95] Hence, addressing a member of the municipal Senate who for years had deferred baptism because of the presumed incompatibility between Christianity and citizenship, Augustine does not hesitate to quote with approval Cicero's statement to the effect that "for good men there can be no limit, no end, to their efforts in the service of their country."[96]

One cannot claim, however, that with this answer, even if one were to accept it, the problem has been completely resolved. What constituted the strength of Augustine's position could from another point of view be regarded as its greatest weakness. That position was, in its most obvious intent, the outcome of a deliberate attempt to do justice to the legitimate demands of civil society; but one still does not see how it does equal justice to the demands of the Christian faith. If, as Augustine argues, earthly cities are necessarily imperfect, if each one is to a greater or lesser degree a "compact of wickedness,"[97] the Christian who considers it his religious duty to love his country becomes by that very fact a party to its injustice. One cannot function as a law-abiding citizen of a particular society, hold public office in it, and share its general way of life without being implicated in its inequities and actively contributing to their enshrinement. That argument, it seems, has made of injustice a requirement of love and of the Christian an instrument of its preservation. How, then, to phrase the question in more general terms, can one live as a moral man in an immoral society?

Augustine's reply to this final and decisive objection may be described as the primitive version of the natural right theory in the Christian world. That theory was expressed with greater clarity but also perhaps greater rigidity by later writers who, taking their cue from Augustine, distinguished between two forms of natural right, namely, absolute natural right, whose principles are immutable and universally applicable at all times, and conditional, relative, or secondary natural right, which presupposes the Fall and sanctions such institutions as private property, slavery, and political authority, all of which were absent from the state of original justice and are necessitated solely by man's present inability to live fully in accordance with the dictates of reason.[98]

Although Augustine himself never speaks of relative or secondary natural right,[99] he nevertheless acknowledges the impossibility of doing away once and for all with the various inequalities which human law and custom sanction but which from a higher vantage point may be looked upon as the source of the greatest injustices among men. To the extent to which men share in the unity of the faith, all such differences, whether of nation, sex, or social condition, have been transcended; but they retain their political significance and are to be accepted in conformity with present customs, lest by flouting these customs, one should bring discredit on the faith itself.[100]

The same is true of war, which is an outgrowth of the actual division of humanity into separate cities and nations and which can never be eliminated as long as that state of affairs endures. However much one may dislike and regret it, war is unavoidable, not because good men want it, but because it is not within their power to avoid it altogether, since it is imposed on them by the wicked, whose evil designs must be resisted in the interest of justice; for nothing is more injurious to mankind than that evildoers should be given free reign to prosper and use their prosperity to oppress the good.[101]

Assuming the inevitability of war in the present economy of mankind, the least one can do is to strive to humanize it within the limits of possibility. The just war theory, for which Augustine has sometimes been blamed, was obviously propounded not with the aim of extolling war and encouraging it whenever permissible, but as a means of mitigating its harshness and imposing curbs on man's innate aggressiveness. It did not recommend itself to Augustine because it settles the issue once and for all but because, everything considered, no better solution could be found.[102] Even from Augustine's viewpoint, it is doubtful whether any war can be regarded as absolutely just. The clearest instance of the so-called just war is the war waged in self-defense and for the protection of one's borders.[103] But such a view proceeds on the premise that existing boundaries are just to begin with. In the light of what Augustine says elsewhere about the origin of nations and empires and the crimes on which they were founded, it is difficult to imagine that he himself would have considered these boundaries as natural. If, in addition, one bears in mind that the state of war invariably gives rise to situations in which the ordinary rules of justice are suspended, one can only conclude that war is part of an order of things which, no matter how one looks at it, leaves much to be desired and is at best suited to the condition of an imperfect and wounded human nature.

It follows as a consequence of the views just expressed that there is, strictly speaking, for Augustine no such thing as a Christian polity. Christianity was never intended as a substitute for the political life. It transcends all regimes and is of necessity limited in its practical application by the modalities of its existence in this world. Christian wisdom and political power may occasionally coexist in a single subject, the person of the Christian ruler,[104] but even in that case, they remain distinct, cooperating with each other whenever possible but never merging one into the other.[105] Christianity liberates man neither by removing him from the cave nor by promising to dispel the shadows in which it is immersed but by supplying him with standards of judgment that are ultimately independent of the regime and the pervasive influence of its principles. It requires only that Christian citizens comply with the obligations of the political life, not that they allow their souls to be molded and determined by the taste and opinions of the regime under which they happen to live. In principle, if not always in practice, it is equally free from the intransigence of the doctrinaire and the complacency of the passive defender of the status quo.[106] Since it is neither subversive nor conformist, it cannot of itself be interpreted as a call to anarchism or as an apology for legitimism. In a spirit of moderation and charity it simply teaches that Christians should bear with equanimity the inescapable evils of life without ceasing to toil unwearyingly for the suppression of those evils which can be successfully overcome by human effort and perseverance.

One merely clouds the issue by equating the legally sanctioned injustice of a particular regime with the voluntary acts of injustice perpetrated by one individual or group of individuals against another individual or group of individuals within the same society. The Christian who, by his active presence in the city, is willy-nilly caught up in its more or less just distribution of goods and honors or its more or less just wars is not being asked to love the evils consequent on the establishment and maintenance of that society, but only the substantive justice which it embodies and which would not exist without it. One does not normally solve the problem of social justice by revolutionary action, but neither does one solve it by turning one's back on one's fellow men under the circumstances. To withdraw from society would only be to rob it of whatever contribution the Christian can still make to the betterment of its common life. Christians, who stand before others as witnesses of God's offer of salvation, must give an account not only of their actions in this world but of their separation from it.[107] It is not up to the individual Christian to decide to whom that offer should be made. The basic fallacy of Donatism, in the struggle against which Augustine's political theology reached its final form, was that it could think of no better way to preserve the integrity and holiness of the Church than by cutting itself off from the society of the nations. Its blind idealism and single-minded attachment to what it took to be the pure teaching of the Sermon on the Mount rendered service contingent on the existence of a perfect social order and thereby foreclosed the possibility of an action by which one could still work for the improvement of the existing order.[108]

This is not to deny for one moment that, in the true spirit of children of the city of God, Christians should not be moved by the sight of the evils with which they continue to be confronted in everyday life or that they can ever bear with a light heart some of the less desirable consequences of their involvement in a particular social order which never fully lives up to their hopes. These evils would be insufferable if the pain and distress they occasion were not relieved by the conviction that the ignorance and infirmity which prevent man from doing everything he would like to do, or even always seeing clearly where his duty lies, are themselves part of the secret penal arrangement and unfathomable judgement of God, with whom "there is no iniquity" (Ps. 92:16).[109] With or without its revolutions, the political life is incapable of exhausting the full range of human possibilities or satisfying completely man's longing for wholeness. When all is said and done, there is, according to Augustine, "only one life which deserves to be called blessed, the future life, in which alone the true knowledge of God is to be found."[110]

By judiciously blending the teaching of classical philosophy with that of the Bible, Augustine was able to counter the massive objections to which on political grounds Christianity was exposed, as well as the massive objections to which on Christian grounds the political life was exposed. Yet the solution at which he arrived cannot be said to have been completely harmonious or symmetrical. It reduced but did not suppress the tension between man's perfection as a citizen and his perfection as a Christian and a human being. It disposed of the problem of the political life, not by integrating the Christian fully into it, but by moving beyond it in the direction of a goal which was not only transpolitical but otherworldly. For that reason, it was called into question by later thinkers who saw fit to abandon it in favor of a radically different type of political theory which makes its appearance in the seventeenth century and which in time came to supplant traditional political thought, either in its classical or Christian form, as the dominant force in Western society.

The new theory is most clearly distinguishable from the old by its doctrinairism. It is no longer guided by a discussion of the various political regimes and, ultimately, the best political regime. Rather, it teaches that there is one and only one just or legitimate regime, and it further holds that this just regime is attainable anywhere and at any time. Its elaboration was the result of the cooperation of two basic premises: the realism or anti-utopianism which had been the soul of the modern development since its inception, and the transformation of science into a project ordered exclusively to the conquest of nature and the relief of man's estate.[111] Thanks to the benefactions of modern science and the newly posited identity of its goals with those of civil society, man could look forward, not indeed to a new heaven, but to a new earth with its glittering prospect of a "shared, abundant, and secured" but otherwise unregulated life. What had begun as a critique of utopianism had itself suddenly developed into a utopia, but this time a realizable utopia.[112] Popular enlightenment would succeed where both Christianity and classical philosophy had failed, not by effecting a change in the cave dwellers, but by inundating the cave with new light.

Since there is only one just society and since it is within man's power to achieve it, one is not only free to work for its establishment but compelled in the name of justice to do so. The Christian, along with all men of good will, is urged to convert himself into an idealist and a crusader, sharing the earthly hopes of his fellow men and assuming his portion of the burden of their struggles for a brighter future.

As the methodically planned civilization progressed, however, doubt began to arise concerning the feasibility of its goal. The new society became prosperous beyond all expectations, but there was little evidence that it had grown any less irrational in the process.[113] The alarm was sounded by Nietzsche at the end of the nineteenth century. It has since become the battle cry of the marching wing of twentieth-century thought. The change that took place in the intervening years is reflected in the transition from the Old Left to the New Left. In the hastily arranged and implausible marriage between Marx and Nietzsche, Nietzsche, not surprisingly, had emerged as the stronger of the two partners. The whole thrust of

Nietzsche's countergospel had been to restore human greatness, but on the basis of the modern critique of reason. What mattered was not the specific goal of human activity about which rational discussion was no longer assumed to be possible, but the sincerity and intensity of one's commitment to one's freely chosen goal. Concern had replaced truth as the unique and ultimate criterion of the worth of one's actions.

Nietzsche had challenged both reason and faith in the name of life. In his view, the love of God was incompatible with the love of man.[114] In the light of the events of recent history, for which Nietzsche himself must bear some responsibility, one may question whether his resolutely this-worldly solution[115] has in fact done more for the enhancement of human life than any of the solutions he so vehemently and eloquently opposed, not the least important of which was Augustine's otherworldly solution to the problem of human living.

Nietzsche regarded Augustine, along with Pascal, as the only true representative of the Christian tradition. His own philosophy may be understood, and was understood by Nietzsche himself, as a radical transformation of the whole of Western thought. One cannot fully grasp the transformation without first grasping the original form, and that alone would call for a fresh inquiry into the nature of Augustine's political thought. At the same time, one cannot help wondering whether Nietzsche's attack on the combined classical and Christian tradition was not itself prepared decisively, albeit indirectly, by Augustine's critique of classical thought in the name of faith. It would be difficult to deny that that critique has generated within the Western political tradition a tension which accounts for both its ecstasies and its agonies, but also, and perhaps more importantly, its extraordinary vitality across the centuries.

NOTES

1. See, for example, the concise but forceful remarks by R. Shaull, "Confronting the Power Structures: Cooperation or Conflict?" in *The Paradox of Religious Secularity*, edited by K. T. Hargrove (Englewood Cliffs, N.J.: Prentice Hall, 1968), 92-7. Id. "Revolutionary Change in Theological Perspective," in *Christian Social Ethics in a Changing World*, edited by J. C. Bennett (New York: Association Press, 1966), 23-43. J. M. Lochman, "Ecumenical Theology of Revolution," *Scottish Journal of Theology* (June, 1968). For a contemporary defense of utopia from a liberal point of view, cf. G. Kateb, *Utopia and Its Enemies* (New York: Free Press of Glencoe, 1963).

2. For a thematic discussion of twentieth-century nihilism and its intellectual sources, cf. Stanley Rosen, *Nihilism: A Philosophic Essay* (New Haven: Yale University Press, 1969).

3. Cf. Raymond Aron, *Maximes imaginaires: d'une sainte famille à l'autre*

(Paris: Gallimard, 1970), 123: "Marx et Nietzsche sont, à certains égards, 'extrêmes opposés'; par de multipies chemins leurs descendants se rejoignent." See also the brief but informative treatment of "Western Marxism" by J. M. Palmier, *Sur Marcuse* (Paris: Union général d'éditions, 1969), 15ff.

4. Cf. *De civitate Dei* (*City of God*) VIII.4; VIII.5; VIII.9. *De vera religione* (*On the True Religion*) IV.6-7. *Contra academicos* (*Against the Academicians*) III.17.37.

5. *Assembly of Women* V.590. For a detailed and penetrating analysis of the play as a whole, cf. L. Strauss, *Socrates and Aristophanes* (New York: Basic Books, 1965), 263-82.

6. *Assembly of Women* V.877ff.

7. *Assembly of Women* V.730ff; cf. V.777: "Surely you don't think men in their right senses will all so easily discard their goods? No, that is not our native custom." Also, V.872: "By Zeus, I must find some way of keeping my belongings while getting a share of these public dinners."

8. *Assembly of Women* V.1112ff.

9. Cf. Plato, *Republic* 451bff., and the comments by A. Bloom, *The Republic of Plato* (New York and London: Basic Books, 1968), 380-81. L. Strauss, *The City and Man* (Chicago: Rand McNally, 1964), 61-2. The numerous textual allusions to the *Assembly of Women* are listed in the footnotes of Paul Shorey's edition of the *Republic* (Loeb Classical Library, 1946).

10. Cf. *Republic* V.473c-d, where, in answer to the question relating to the possibility of the coming into being of the city that has been founded in speech, the notion of the philosopher-king is introduced as the third and biggest "wave of paradox," the other two waves being the equality of the sexes and the community of women, children, and goods, already mentioned by Aristophanes. *Assembly of Women* VI.487e.

11. Cf. *De civ. Dei* II.14.1. On the notion of the best or most desirable regime, whose actualization remains problematic though not intrinsically impossible, cf. *Republic* V.450d, V.456b-c, VI.499d, VII.540d; *Laws* IV.709d, V.742e; Aristotle, *Politics* II.1.1260b29, 11.6.1265a18, VII.4.1325b38.

12. Cf. *De civ. Dei* VI.4.2 "Thus he (Varro) confessed that, in writing the books concerning divine things, he did not write in accordance with the truth that pertains to nature but the falseness that pertains to error; this he states more clearly elsewhere, as I have mentioned in Book IV (c 31), saying that, had he been founding a new city himself, he would have written according to the order of nature; but as he had only found an old one, he could not but follow its custom." Ibid, VI.2: "What ought we to think but that a most acute and learned man (Varro), not, however, made free by the Holy Spirit, was overpowered by the custom and laws of his city, and, not being able to be silent about those things by which he was influenced, spoke of them under pretence of commending religion?" Cf. *De civ. Dei* VI.6.1.

13. *De civ. Dei* II.14.2.

14. *Epistula* (*Letter*) 91.4.

15. Cf. Plato *Republic* V.473e.

16. *De civ. Dei* II.21.2; XIX.21.1. Cf. Cicero, *De re publica* I.25.39.

17. *De civ. Dei* XIX.24; cf. *Epist.* 138.10; 155.3.9.

18. On the origin of civil society according to Augustine, cf. R. A. Markus, *Saeculum: History and Society in the Theology of St. Augustine* (Cambridge, MA: Cambridge University Press, 1970), Appendix B: "*De civitate Dei* XIX.14-15 and the Origin of Political Authority," 197-210. Markus observes, rightly, that the subject at hand is never discussed *ex professo* and in detail by Augustine. His own thesis is that whereas, for Augustine, a man's rule over his wife and children is prescribed by the order of nature, political authority would never have arisen if men had persevered in the state of innocence. As the long history of Augustinian scholarship attests, it is obviously difficult to account for every aspect of Augustine's thought on this perennially vexing question. One possible clue to a further investigation of the problem is furnished by *De libera arbitrio* (*On Free Choice of the Will*) where Augustine remarks that if all men were virtuous (as they would have been in the state of innocence), democracy would be a requirement of justice; which seems to imply that not political rule as such but coercive political rule, together with the inequalities, presupposed or engendered by it, originates in sin. There is, in addition, the fact that Augustine recognized the existence of natural inequalities and hence of a natural hierarchy among men. One might thus be led to suppose that in the purely hypothetical state of nature some form of governmental structure would have been required.

19. *De lib. arbit.* I.15.31.

20. *De lib. arbit.* I.15.32: "To explain how in all these matters the law distributes to each his due would be difficult and would take a long time, but clearly it is not necessary to our purpose. It is sufficient to see that the authority of this law in punishing does not go beyond depriving him who is punished of these things or of some of them. It employs fear as an instrument of coercion, and bends to its own ends the minds of the unhappy people to whose governance it is adapted. So long as they fear to lose these earthly goods, they observe in using them a certain moderation suited to maintain in being a city such as can be composed of such men. The sin of loving these things is not punished; what is punished is the wrong done to others when their rights are infringed." Cf. *Epist.* 153.6.26; *Sermo* (*Sermon*) 50.2.4.

21. Cf. A. Bloom, op. cit., 410.

22. "On the noble lie and its pedagogical function," cf. *Republic* II.377d, 382b; III.414b; V.459c, "and on the idea that the whole truth can be safely expressed only before an audience made up of reasonable friends," *Republic* V.45Oe; *Gorgias* 487a.

23. Cf. *Republic* 536c1. See also *Republic* III.394b-c, where Socrates restates Adeimantus's position in such a way as to include comedy along with tragedy in the definition of the dramatic form. The passage in question is an indirect description of the Platonic dialogue.

24. Cf. Plato, *Laws* V.739a: "Yet reflection and experience make it clear that a city is likely to enjoy but a second-best regime. The best regime would be possible

only if its citizens were gods or sons of gods"; *Laws* III.684c. "Now may I remind you that a legislator is commonly expected to enact only such laws as the multitude will accept of its own motion." Differently stated, legal restraints are not likely to function if they are not buttressed by habit and inner conviction. There is little real evidence to support the opinion still frequently encountered among scholars that the modified teaching of the *Laws* was the result of "bitter disillusionment" on the part of a wizened and more mature Plato. The *Republic* itself contains enough hints to the effect that the program outlined in its pages can at best be imitated and hence never fully implemented in a given society. On the notion of imitation in the present sense, cf. *Republic* V.471c. For all its "impracticability," the original ideal nevertheless serves an eminently useful purpose, for without such a model one would lack the necessary guidance in the pursuit of a just if somewhat less than perfect regime.

25. *Republic* V.451b; cf. V.471d.

26. *Republic* V.457dff.

27. *Republic* VI.491d; cf. V.476d.

28. *Republic* VI.502dff.

29. *Republic* VI.489dff.

30. *Republic* VI.487eff.

31. See the frequent references to the necessity of compelling natural rulers to assume political office, e.g., *Republic* VI.499b; VI.500d; VII.19dff., et passim. The opening scene of the *Republic* already alludes to the peculiar blend of persuasion and compulsion indispensable to the governance of the city. Socrates is enticed to remain at the Piraeus by the promise of a good meal and a pleasant spectacle and simultaneously pressured into doing so by the force of superior numbers.

32. *Republic* VIII-IX. A similar argument about the deliberately utopian and self-refuting character of the Platonic scheme could be made in relation to the injunction against incest, the city's most fundamental taboo; cf. *Republic* V.461c. Incest is strictly prohibited; yet there is no way of guarding against involuntary violations of the precept, since the community of wives and children makes it impossible to recognize with any degree of certainty one's parents and children or one's brothers and sisters. Cf. Aristotle, *Politics* II.4.1260b30ff. One should also ponder the fact that the success of the reform to which the new ruler will have to give his attention necessitates, among other things, the rustication of the entire population above the age of ten. Cf. *Republic* VII.541a. One can anticipate that such a drastic measure would meet with considerable resistance on the part of the older citizens, who can hardly be expected to abandon their homes and their city of their own accord and would therefore have to be expelled by force. But the ruler has as yet no means of compulsion at his disposal and would presumably be helpless to bring about any kind of mass exodus. It is interesting to note that, if one accepts the year 411 or 410 B.C. as the dramatic date of the dialogue, Cephalus, at whose home the discussion takes place, is already dead and Glaucon, the chief interlocutor and co-founder of the new city in speech, is less than ten years old.

33. *Republic* IX.592a-b; cf. V.472e; VI.484c. Augustine, *Epist.* 91.4.

34. Cicero, *De re publica* II.30.52: "He (Plato) established a city of the kind that is to be desired rather than hoped for—not such as to be actually possible, but in which it might be possible to perceive the nature (*ratio*) of political things."

35. *De re publica* II.1.5: "I shall, however, find my task easier if I place before you (a description of) our (Roman) commonwealth at its birth, during its growth, at its maturity, and finally in its strong and healthy state, than if I were to follow the example of Plato's Socrates and imagine a city of my own." *De re publica* II.11. 21-22: "We do see . . . also that you on your part have embarked upon a new method of argument, one that is nowhere to be found in the works of the Greeks. For that eminent Greek (Plato), whose works have never been surpassed, began with the assumption of an unoccupied tract of land on which he might build a city to his liking. His city may perhaps be an excellent one, but it is quite unsuited to men's lives and habits. Others after him have discussed the different kinds of cities and their principles without presenting any definite example or model. But you, it seems to me, mean to combine both methods; for you have approached your subject as if you preferred to attribute your own discoveries to others rather than, following the example of Plato's Socrates, to imagine a new city; and in what you say about the site of your city you provide a rational explanation for the things done by Romulus either by chance or necessity; and your discussion does not wander about but confines itself to a simple commonwealth." Cf. *Republic* II.29.51 and II.30.52: "As for me, however, employing the same principles which Plato discovered, and assuming that I am able to accomplish my purpose, I shall endeavor to seem to you to be pointing out, as with a demonstrating rod, the cause of every political good and ill, taking (as a model) not an outline of an imaginary city but a powerful commonwealth." Cf. Plato, *Republic* VI.497a-b: "But which of the current regimes do you say is suitable for it?—None at all, I said, but this is the very change I am bringing; not one city today is in a condition worthy of the philosophic nature." On Cicero's *De re publica* cf. J. E. Holton, "Marcus Tullius Cicero," in *History of Political Philosophy*, edited by L. Strauss and J. Cropsey (Chicago: Rand McNally, 1963), 130-50. L. Strauss, *Natural Right and History* (Chicago: University of Chicago Press, 1953), 155-56.

36. Cicero, *De re publica* III.5.8ff.

37. *De re publica* III.15.24.

38. *De re publica* III.17.27.

39. *De re publica* II.2.4ff.

40. *De re publica* III.21.32ff.

41. *De re publica* II.30.52. Contrary to what is sometimes affirmed, e.g., by R. Niebuhr, *Christian Realism and Political Problems* (London and New York: Scribner, 1953), 121, Augustine's views do not offer "a wholesome corrective to Cicero's . . . moralistic illusions," for the simple reason that Cicero never harbored any such illusions about civil society in the first place. Niebuhr's assertion that Augustine was, by general consent, the first great realist in Western history (ibid., 115) oversimplifies the issue and misinterprets the intention of both Plato's and Cicero's argument. See also C. Dawson, "St. Augustine and His Age," in M. C.

d'Arcy et al., *A Monument to St. Augustine* (London and New York: L. Mac Veagh, 1930), 62, who states that Augustine was led by a consideration of history "to reject the political idealism of the philosophers and dispute Cicero's thesis that the state rests essentially on justice."

42. Lactantius, *Divinae Institutiones (The Divine Institutes)* III.21-22; *Epitome* 38.

43. The basic critique is formulated with utmost clarity in Machiavelli's *The Prince*, ch. 15: "As I know that many have written of this, I fear that my writing about it may be deemed presumptuous, differing as I do, especially in this matter, from the opinions of others. But my intention being to write something of use to those who understand, it appears to me more proper to go to the real truth of the matter than to its imagination; and many have imagined republics and principalities which have never been seen or known to exist in reality; for how we live is so far removed from how we ought to live, that he who abandons what is done for what ought to be done will rather learn to bring about his own ruin than his preservation. A man who wishes to make a profession of goodness in everything must necessarily come to grief among so many who are not good. Therefore it is necessary for a prince who wishes to maintain himself to learn how not to be good, and to use this knowledge and not use it according to the necessity of the case." Francis Bacon, *The Advancement of Learning*, II.21.9: "So that we are much beholden to Machiavelli and others, that write what men do and not what they ought to do. For it is not possible to join serpentine wisdom with the columbine innocence, except men know exactly all the conditions of the serpent; his baseness and going upon his belly, his volubility and lubricity, his envy and sting, and the rest; that is, all forms and natures of evil. For without this, virtue lieth open and unfenced." Ibid., II.23.49: "As for the philosophers, they make imaginary laws for imaginary commonwealths; and their discourses are as the stars, which gives little light because they are so high." Ibid., I.20.1: "In the handling of this science, those which have written seem to me to have done as if a man that professeth to teach to write did only exhibit fair copies of alphabets and letters joined, without giving any precepts or directions for the carriage of the hand and framing of the letters. So they have made good and fair examplars and copies, carrying the draughts and portraitures of Good, Virtue, Duty, Felicity; propounding them well described as the true objects and scopes of man's will and desires; but how to attain these excellent marks, and how to frame and subdue the will of man to become true and conformable to these pursuits, they pass it over altogether, or slightly and unprofitably." Ibid., II.22.8: "But allowing his (Aristotle's) conclusion, that virtues and vices consist in habit, he ought so much the more to have taught the manner of superinducing that habit; for there be many precepts of the wise ordering the exercises of the mind, as there is of ordering the exercises of the body." Cf. Spinoza, *Political Treatise*, ch. 1, Introd.: "Philosophers conceive of the passions which harass us as vices into which men fall by their own fault, and, therefore, generally deride, bewail, or blame them, or execrate them, if they wish to seem unusually pious. And so they think they are doing something wonderful, and reaching the pinnacle of learning when they are

clever enough to bestow manifold praise on such human nature as is nowhere to be found, and to make verbal attacks on that which exists. For they conceive of men, not as they are, but as they themselves would like them to be. Whence it has come to pass that, instead of ethics, they have generally written satire and that they have never conceived a theory of politics which could be turned to use, but as might be taken for a chimera, or might have been formed in Utopia, or in that golden age of the poets when, to be sure, there was least need of it. Accordingly, as in all sciences which have a useful purpose, so especially in that of politics, theory is supposed to be at variance with practice; and no men are esteemed less fit to direct public affairs than theorists or philosophers."

44. Hobbes, *Leviathan* I.13; *De cive.* ch. 1. Cf. Herbert A. Deane, *The Political and Social Ideas of St. Augustine* (New York: Columbia University Press, 1963), 59ff., 117, 235ff., et passim.

45. Cf. Hobbes, *De homine*, Epistle Dedicatory: "To reduce this doctrine to the rules and infallibility of reason there is no way but, first, to put such principles down for a foundation as passion, not mistrusting, may not seek to displace; and afterwards to build thereon the truth of cases in the laws of nature (which hitherto have been built in the air) by degrees, till the whole have become inexpugnable." Spinoza, *Political Treatise*, ch. 1, Introd., 6: "A dominion, then, whose well-being depends on any man's good faith and whose affairs cannot be properly administered unless those who are engaged in them will act honestly will be very unstable. On the contrary, to insure its permanence, its public affairs should be so ordered that those who administer them, whether guided by reason or passion, cannot be led to act treacherously or basely. Nor does it matter to the security of a dominion in what spirit men are led to rightly administer its affairs. For liberality of spirit, or courage, is a private virtue; but the virtue of a state is its security."

46. Cf. Francis Bacon, *The Advancement of Learning* II.22.6: "But the poets and writers of histories are the best doctors of this knowledge; where we may find, painted forth with great life, how affections are kindled and incited; and how pacified and refrained; and how again contained from act and further degree; how they disclose themselves, how they work, how they vary, how they gather and fortify, how they are inwrapped one within another, and other the like particularities: amongst the which this last is of special use in moral and civil matters; how (I say) to set affection against affection, and to master one by another; even as we used to hunt beast with beast and fly bird with bird, which otherwise percase we could not so easily recover: upon which foundation is erected that excellent use of *praemium and poena,* whereby civil states consist; employing the predominant affections of *fear* and *hope,* for the suppressing and bridling the rest. For as in the government of states it is sometimes necessary to bridle one faction with another, so it is in the government within." Ibid., I.3.5, quoting Cicero, *To Atticus:* "Cato means excellently well, but he does hurt sometimes to the commonwealth; for he talks as if it were Plato's republic that we are living in, and not the dung of Romulus." On Spinoza's scientific or natural (as distinguished from moral) treatment of the passions, cf. *Ethics* Part III, Introd., and Part IV,

Prop. 7: "motion can only be controlled or destroyed by another emotion contrary thereto, and with more power for controlling emotion." Ibid., Prop. 14: "A true knowledge of good and evil cannot check any emotion by virtue of being true, but only in so far as it is considered an emotion."

47. Against John N. Figgis, *The Political Aspects of St. Augustine's City of God* (London: Longmans, Green and Co., 1921), 59ff.

48. For the ascription of "social contract" ideas to the early Christian writers, cf. E. Troeltsch, *The Social Teachings of the Christian Churches* (New York: Harper Torchbook ed., 1956, vol. I), 155.

49. See, *inter alia*, Kant's famous description of the perfectly just state composed entirely of devils, *Eternal Peace,* First Addition: "But now nature comes to the aid of this revered but practically ineffectual general will which is founded on reason. It does this by the selfish propensities themselves, so that it is only necessary to organize the state well . . . and to direct these forces against one another in such wise that one balances the other in its devastating effect, or even suspends it. Consequently the result for reason is as if both selfish forces were nonexistent. Thus man, although not a morally good man, is compelled to be a good citizen. The problem of establishing a state is solvable even for a people of devils, if only they have intelligence, though this may sound harsh."

50. Cf. S. Cotta, *La città politica di san Agostino* 24ff, 52ff.

51. Cf. C. H. McIlwain, *The Growth of Political Thought in the West* (New York: Macmillan, 1932), 157, and the critical discussion of McIlwain's thesis by H. A. Deane, *The Political and Social Ideas of St. Augustine*, 118-29. Augustine's reformulation of Cicero's definition of the state, which seems to exclude justice from the realm of politics, has given rise to a protracted debate among scholars since the beginning of the century. For a summary and a brief appraisal of the literature on the subject, see J. D. Adams, *The Populus of Augustine and Jerome* (New Haven and London: Yale University Press, 1971), 123-35. Adams's survey divides the scholars who have dealt with the question into two categories: those who see a fundamental opposition between Cicero's definition and Augustine's restatement of it (e.g., Figgis, Baynes, Cotta, Carlyle, and McIlwain) and those who deny that the two definitions are mutually exclusive (e.g., Millar, Deane, Bardy, and Adams himself, who thinks that "the two definitions are not only reconcilable, but end up by being one, in the sense that the second absorbs the first;" ibid., 131). While it may be true, as Adams suggests, that "love" is more inclusive than "justice," Augustine's emphasis is nevertheless on the absence of justice rather than on the presence of love in the life of civil societies. The love to which Augustine refers when he says that commonwealths are assemblages of human beings bound together by a common agreement as to the object of their love, rather than by a common acknowledgment of right, need not be a just or righteous love. On the distinction between the "two loves," cf. *De civ. Dei* XIV.28. This is not to deny, of course, that a measure of justice is to be found even in the worst of cities, for no city could as much as exist without it. There is no such thing as total badness. Cf. *De civ. Dei* XIX.12.2.

52. *De civ. Dei* II.21.4.

53. *Epist.* 137.5.17.

54. *Contra Faustum Manichaeum* (*Against Faustus the Manichaean* XIX.27.

55. The apparent irreconcilability of Christianity and the political life was invoked by Augustine's own friends as a reason for refusing baptism. Cf. *Epist.* 136.2 (Marcellinus to Augustine): "Another objection which he (Volusianus) stated was that Christian doctrine and preaching were in no way consistent with the duties and rights of citizens. *Epist.* 151.14: "There is, indeed, one thing in you, since you wish to hear the truth, which causes me very great distress: it is that, although qualified by age, as well as by life and character, to do otherwise, you still prefer to be a catechumen; as if it were not possible for believers, by making progress in Christian faith and well-doing, to become so much the more faithful and useful in the administration of public business. For surely the promotion of the welfare of men is the one great end of all your great cares and labors. And, indeed, if this were not to be the issue of your public services, it would be better for you even to sleep both day and night than to sacrifice your rest in order to do work which can contribute nothing to the advantage of your fellow men." For a modern statement of the same objection, cf. F. Dahn, *Die Könige der Germanen* vol. 11 (Leipzig: E. A. Fleischmann, 1908), 209, who pronounces Augustine's doctrine "logically false, morally diseased, politically corrupt, and incompatible with one's duties to the state" (Figgis, *The Political Concepts of St. Augustine's City of God*, 66).

56. Cf. *De moribus ecclesiae catholicae et de moribus Manichaeorum* (*The Catholic and Manichaen Ways of Life*) I.30.63.

57. The evidence of concern in high places becomes increasingly noticeable in the course of the third century. If Cyprian is a reliable witness, the Emperor Decius would have been less disturbed over the insurgence of a rival emperor than over the appointment of a godly bishop to the Roman See. Cf. Cyprian, *Epistula* (*Letter*) 55.9. *Handbook of Church History*, vol. I, eds., H. Jedin and J. Dolan (New York: Herder and Herder, 1965), 380.

58. *Apology of Socrates*, 30a-b.

59. *Apology* 23b, 31c, 33a, 36b.

60. *Apology* 21e, 23b, 30a, 33c, *et passim.*

61. *Apology* 28e.

62. *Apology* 34d. Cf. *Crito*, 50d.

63. *Apology* 32d.

64. *Apology* 37b.

65. *Apology* 29d.

66. *Apology* 32a.

67. Socrates reserves the title of "judges" to those who have acquitted him; cf. ibid, 18a,40a. The others are addressed simply as "Athenians" or "men," e.g., 18a, 18c, 18e, 20e, 26c.

68. *Apology* 41d.

69. *Apology* 26d. Cf. Augustine, *De civ. Dei* XVIII.41.2.

70. *Apology* 32b.

71. *Apology* 29b, 35a.

72. *Apology* 27c.

73. *Apology* 38a, 41b. Cf. *Republic* V.450b: "For intelligent men, the proper measure of listening to such discourses is a whole life."

74. *Apology* 41a-b.

75. For a fuller discussion of this passage, cf. G. Anastaplo, "Human Being and Citizen: A Beginning to the Study of Plato's *Apology of Socrates*," in *Ancients and Moderns*, edited by J. Cropsey (New York: Basic Books, 1964), 29ff.

76. On the "knowledge without heart" of the philosophers, cf. Augustine, *Confessions* VIII.8.19.

77. Cf. *Crito* 53aff.

78. Cf. *Republic* VII.520a-e.

79. *Apology of Socrates* 54c.

80. It is surely no accident that the *Apology* never mentions moderation as one of Socrates's virtues.

81. Cf. *De doctrina Christiana* (*On Christian Doctrine*) I.26.27. *De mor. eccl. Cath.* I.26.49.

82. *Sermo* (*Sermon*) 82.3.4.

83. *Sermo* 96.6-8, and the commentary by R. A. Markus, *Saeculum: History and Society in the Theology of St Augustine* (Cambridge, MA: Cambridge University Press, 1970), 105ff.

84. E.g., *Epist.* 93.2.4. Cf. Marcus, *Saeculum* 141ff.

85. In *Tractatus in Joannis evangelium* (*Tracts on the Gospel of John*) VII.8.

86. Cf. J. Gallay, "*Dilige et quod vis fac:* notes d'exégèse augustinienne," *Recherches de science religieuse* 43 (1955): 554-55.

87. Cf. *De gratia Christi et peccato originali* (*On the Grace of Christ and Original Sin*) X.11.

88. Cf. *De doctr. Christ.* I.36.40.

89. Cf. *Epist.* 138.2.5; *Epist.* 137.5.20 and 91.3. *De civ. Dei* II.19: "If the kings of the earth and all their subjects, if all princes and judges of the earth, if young men and maidens, old and young, every age and both sexes . . . were to hearken to and observe the precepts of the Christian religion regarding a just and virtuous life, then should the republic adorn the whole earth with its own felicity and attain in life everlasting the pinnacle of kingly glory."

90. Cf. *Expositio quarundam propositionum ex epistula ad Romanos* (*Exposition of Certain Propositions from the Epistle to the Romans*) 72ff; *Expositio epistulae ad Galatas* (*Exposition on the Epistle to the Galatians*) 28ff., *Contra Gaudentium Donatistarum Episcopum* (*Against Gaudentius, Bishop of the Donatists*) I.19.20. On the patristic exegesis of Romans 13, cf. K. H. Schelkle, "Staat und Kirche in der patristischen Auslegung vom Rm 13:1-7," *Zeitschrift für neuetestamentliche Wissenschaft* 44 (1952-53): 223-36; reprinted in Id., *Wort und Schrift* (Dusseldorf: Patmos Verlag, 1966), 227-38.

91. *Exposit. prop. ex epist. ad Rom.* 74.

92. *Exposit. prop. ex epist. ad Rom.* 72 and 74. On the feigned obedience of the philosophers, cf. *De civ. Dei* VI.10.3.

93. *Sermo* 62.9.14. *Tract. in Joan.* 5.12. *Ennarationes in Psalmos* (*Exposition on the Psalms*) 104.37. *Contra Faust. Manich.* 22.75.

94. *De civ. Dei* I.29; XXII.22 and 23.

95. It is remarkable that Augustine refers but rarely to Acts 5:29: "One should obey God rather than men," and even then only in an innocuous context. One gathers that the more pressing problem was to show that Christianity did not breed anarchism and was not destructive of the political life. A slightly different emphasis is found in Luther, who is more directly concerned with defining the limits of temporal power, as is suggested by the title of his treatise, *On Secular Authority: To What Extent It Should Be Obeyed.* Luther's stand is explained by his opposition to those rulers who were prescribing the "papist" faith and trying to root out the Lutheran heresy by force. Cf. H. Bornkamm, *Luther's Doctrine of the Two Kingdoms* (Philadelphia: Fortress Press, 1966), 6. This does not mean that the teaching of the Reformers was, on the whole, politically less conservative than Augustine's, with some notable exceptions, especially among the left wing of Calvinism. Cf. M. Walzer, *The Revolution of the Saints: A Study in the Origins of Radical Politics* (New York: Atheneum, 1969).

96. *Epist.* 91.1.

97. Cf. *De civ. Dei* XIX.24.

98. Ockham, *Dialogus* Part III, Treatise ii, Book III, ch. 6. R. Hooker, *Of the Laws of Ecclesiastical Polity* I.10.13: "Touching laws which are to serve men in this behalf, even as those laws of reason, which (man retaining his original integrity) had been sufficient to direct each particular person in all his affairs and duties, are not sufficient but require the access of other laws, now that man and his offspring are grown thus corrupt and sinful; again, as those laws of polity and regiment, which would have served men living in public society together with that harmless disposition which then they should have had, are not able now to serve, when men's iniquity is so hardly restrained within any tolerable bounds in like manner, the national laws of natural commerce between societies of that former and better quality might have been other than now, when nations are so prone to offer violence, injury, and wrong. Hereupon hath grown in every of these three kinds that distinction between Primary and Secondary laws; the one grounded upon sincere, the other built upon depraved nature. Primary laws of nations are such as concern embassage, such as belong to the courteous entertainment of foreigners and strangers, such as serve for commodious traffick, and the like. Secondary laws in the same kind are such as this present unquiet world is most familiarly acquainted with; I mean laws of arms, which yet are much better known than kept."

99. A theory of relative natural right is attributed to the early Christian writers by E. Troeltsch, *Social Teachings*, vol. 1, 100, 153ff., 201, et passim. Cf. Id. "Das stoisch-christliche und das moderne profane Naturrecht," *Gesammelte Schriften*, vol. IV, Tubingen, 192.

100. *De civ. Dei* XIX.17. Cf. *De civ Dei* XV.4.

101. Cf. *Epist.* 138.2.13-14. *De civ. Dei* IV.3 and XIX.7.

102. For a somewhat apolitical discussion of the problem of war in the early Church, cf. S. Gero, *"Miles Gloriosus:* The Christian and Military Service according to Tertullian," *Church History* 39 (1970): 285-98, which traces the changing attitudes toward war even prior to the Constantinian settlement. Gero's conclusion is that "the Church in North Africa could not sell her soul, so to speak, to Constantine; she had already sold it much earlier, to Septimius Severus and to Caracalla" (p. 298). The nature of the conflict between Christian ethics and the harsh realities of politics has been best expressed in our own day by Winston Churchill, *The Gathering Storm* (New York: Bantam Books, 1961), 286: "The Sermon on the Mount is the last word in Christian ethics . . . Still, it is not on these terms that Ministers assume their responsibilities of guiding states. Their duty is first so to deal with other nations as to avoid strife and war and to eschew aggression in all its forms, whether for nationalistic or ideological objects. But the safety of the State, the lives and freedom of their own fellow countrymen, to whom they owe their position, make it right and imperative in the last resort, or when a final and definite conviction has been reached, that the use of force should not be excluded. If the circumstances are such as to warrant it, force may be used. And if this be so, it should be used under the conditions that are most favorable. There is no merit in putting off a war for a year if, when it comes, it is a far worse war or one much harder to win. These are the tormenting dilemmas upon which mankind has throughout its history been so frequently impaled. Final judgment upon them can only be recorded by history in relation to the facts of the case as known to the parties at the time, and also as subsequently proved. It is baffling to reflect that what men call honour does not always correspond to Christian ethics." The same basic problem lies at the root of two opposite reactions typified in antiquity by Constantine and Julian respectively. To oversimplify for the sake of clarity, the Constantinian theologians predicted an end to all wars as the result of the emergence of Christianity as a world religion uniting all men in the cult of the true God and sought to do away with classical politics in favor of a Christian polity or a theocratic identification of the Roman Empire with the Church. Cf. T. E. Mommsen, "St. Augustine and the Christian Idea of Progress," *Journal of the History of Ideas* 12 (1959): 346-74; reprinted Id., *Medieval and Renaissance Studies* (Ithaca, New York: Cornell University Press, 1959), 265-98. "Orosius and Augustine," ibid., 325-48: "The Emperor Julian, who regarded Christians as a menace to the state and obviously thought them better at praying than at fighting for their country, determined to resolve the problem by abolishing Christianity in favor of a return to a refurbished hellenism." Cf. *Against the Galileans* 218Aff., et passim. Luther's doctrine of the two kingdoms represents a noble attempt to deal with the same issue. As a private person and a member of the kingdom on the right, the Christian is expected to live up to the ideal of the Sermon on the Mount, while as a citizen and a member of the kingdom on the left, he is compelled to abide by the laws of the state, which, despite its manifest imperfections, remains an instrument of divine

purpose. On the similarities and differences between Luther's "two kingdoms" and Augustine's "two cities," cf. H. Bornkamm, *Luther's Doctrine of the Two Kingdoms*, 19ff.

103. Cf. *Contra Faust. Manich.* 22.74-75.

104. Cf. *De civ. Dei* V.24, which is generally regarded as the prototype of a long series of mirrors of princes written during the centuries that followed. W. Berger, *Die Fürstenspiegel des hohen und späten Mittelalters,* Schriften des Reichsinstitut für ältere deutsche Geschichtskunde, no. 2 (Leipzig, 1938).

105. The essential distinction between Christian wisdom and political power comes to the fore in Augustine's portrayal of Constantine and Theodosius, the two most illustrious Christian princes of the early centuries. Cf. *De civ. Dei* V.25 and V.26.1. On Augustine's appraisal of Theodosius, which demonstrates a remarkable independence from earlier models and especially that of Rufinus, cf. J. M. Duval, "L'éloge de Théodose dans la *Cite de Dieu* (V.26,1)," *Recherches augustiniennes* 4 (1966): 135-79. Augustine's emphasis is clearly on the private rather than the public virtues of Theodosius, as well as on the eternal rather than the temporal felicity earned by the practice of those virtues. For a discussion of the apparent shift in Augustine's thought on this point and his final rejection of the Constantinian and Theodosian settlements, see, most recently, R.A. Markus, *Saeculum* 22ff., 154ff. Markus writes, *Saeculum* 149: "He (Augustine) will speak of emperors rather than empire, of kings and magistrates rather than of state or government. Thus he could continue to speak without inhibition of Christian emperors long after he had abandoned all talk about a Christian empire."

106. The strongest case for Augustine's alleged conservatism and his advocacy of an alliance between ecclesiastical authority and imperial government on the basis of the "maintenance of the social status quo" and of "romanized landowning interests" is that made by W. H. C. Frend, *The Donatist Church: A Movement of Protest in Roman North Africa* (Oxford: Clarendon Press, 1952). See also P. Brown, "St. Augustine," in *Trends in Medieval Political Thought*, edited by B. Smalley (Oxford: Blackwell, 1965), 14: "The weakness of Augustine's position is, of course, that it implies a very static view of political society. It is quite content merely to have some of the more painful tensions removed. It takes an ordered political life for granted. Such an order just happens among fallen men." For a critical assessment of Frend's thesis, cf. G. B. Ladner, *The Idea of Reform: Its Impact on Christian Thought and Action in the Age of the Fathers* (Cambridge, MA: Harvard University Press, 1959), 463-67.

107. *Contra litteras Petiliani (Against a Letter of Petilian)* II.19.43; II.31.70. *De catechezandis rudibus (On Catechizing the Uninstructed)* 21.37.

108. On Augustine's polemic against Donatism from this point of view and at the same time his indebtedness to Tyconius, the dissident Donatist theologian, cf. R. A. Markus, *Saeculum* 105ff.

109. Cf. *Contra Faust. Manich.* 27.78; *De civ. Dei* XIX.15.

110. *Retractationes (Retractations)* I.2. Cf. *Enar. in Psal.* 48.6: "For only in

heaven has been promised that which on earth we seek." *Enar. in Psalmos* 84.10. P. Brown, "St. Augustine," *Trends in Medieval Political Thought,* 18: "We are left with a dichotomy: an acute awareness of the actual condition of man in this *saeculum,* and a yearning for a city far beyond. Augustine never overcame this dichotomy."

111. Cf. F. Bacon, *The Great Instauration,* Preface. Descartes, *Discourse on Method,* Part VI.

112. On the origins of modern utopianism, cf. H. White, *Peace Among the Willows: The Political Philosophy of Francis Bacon* (The Hague: Martinus Nijhoff, 1968).

113. The paradox of advanced industrial societies, whose irrationality increases in proportion as they become more prosperous, is discussed from a different perspective in the opening sections of H. Marcuse's *One Dimensional Man.*

114. Nietzsche, *Zarathustra,* Prologue, 2.

115. Ibid., Prologue, 3: "Behold, I teach you the superman. The superman is the meaning of the earth. Let your will say: the superman *shall* be the meaning of the earth! I beseech you, my brothers, *remain faithful to the earth,* and do not believe those who speak to you of otherworldly hopes!" (Nietzsche's emphasis).

3

THE POLITICAL IMPLICATIONS OF
ST. AUGUSTINE'S THEORY
OF CONSCIENCE

"Thus conscience does make cowards of us all."
Hamlet III.1.83

The current debate on the nature of Christian ethics has raised once again the old but in more recent times often neglected question of the role of conscience in the moral life. Although by no means restricted to situations of conflict or crisis, the problem finds perhaps its most dramatic expression in the timely and sensitive issue of civil and religious disobedience. Both forms of dissent have generally been regarded as morally justifiable and publicly defensible to the extent to which they are based on an appeal to a higher law in the light of which particular laws and the acts commanded by them are deemed objectionable or unjust. Needless to say, it is frequently impossible to determine with any degree of certitude whether the dissenter is sincere or merely guided by selfish motives, especially if the law from which he seeks exemption makes harsh or unpleasant demands on him. Still, only insofar as his action is interpreted as an expression of fidelity to a principle that transcends the sphere of his private interest and personal well-being does it possess any intrinsic worth and is it capable of winning, if not the approval, at least the respect of the larger community. The higher law in question may be another positive law, such as the unwritten law that inspired Antigone's refusal to comply with Creon's decree or the divinely revealed law that prompted Luther's defiance of papal authority; but it need not be. More often than not, it will be said to have its immediate source in man himself, either alone or in society, and assumes the form of an inviolable dictate of conscience to which priority is given over all man-made laws running counter to it.

Such in barest outline is the doctrine, born of the interaction between biblical faith and philosophy, that forms part of the heritage bequeathed to us by an earlier tradition of theological thinking and subsequently incorporated in one way or another into our modern legal systems. It was injected into the constitutional discussions by Madison and is at least indirectly sanctioned by the Bill of Rights, even though the original reference to conscience was deleted in the final draft of the text.[1] It informs the reasoning underlying a number of Supreme Court or Federal District Court decisions that have aroused enormous public interest, including Judge Wyzansky's precedent-setting ruling in favor of selective conscientious objection.[2] It has come to the fore with renewed vigor and at times unprecedented acrimony in connection with the Nazi war crimes and the great political and social upheavals of the twentieth century, and it lies at the heart of some of the most widely publicized theological fracases of our day.[3] Yet the controversies that it continues to provoke suggest that its theological foundations are anything but clear. The doctrine as a whole is rejected on epistemological grounds by situationalism[4] as well as by legal positivism, which denies the very possibility of an appeal from established law to an elusive "higher law" whose existence is alleged never to have been demonstrated and on whose principles there is supposedly no general consensus among men.[5] Worse still, even its supporters are far from being in agreement as to its precise nature, as is evidenced by the numerous and divergent interpretations that the doctrine has received from assorted theologians, philosophers, social scientists, psychologists and jurists in our own time.[6] Hence, another look at its intellectual roots may not be altogether useless.

One may be tempted to search for those roots in the New Testament and particularly in St. Paul, the only New Testament author to mention conscience with any regularity; and, indeed, it is unlikely that the notion would ever have occupied so prominent a place in Christian speculation had it not been abundantly attested in Scripture. On the other hand, there does not seem to be much doubt that what Paul means by conscience is not, or is not yet, what others after him have meant by it. His own usage of the term is invariably bound up with the question of the place of the Gentiles in the Church, of their situation in regard to the Mosaic Law, and of the relation between Gentile Christians and Jewish Christians.[7] Little in the Letters suggests that he had in mind a generalized theory of conscience similar to the one elaborated, to some extent on the basis of those Letters, by the Church Fathers. It is only much later, when the specific question with which he was called upon to deal had ceased to be a live issue, that we encounter the first attempts to apply the notion of conscience to the general human condition and the timeless problem of the distinction between right and wrong.

For all practical purposes, the doctrine as traditionally understood owes its origin in largest measure to Augustine. Given the telling frequency of the references to it in his writings, it is surprising that it should have attracted but little attention thus far on the part of scholars. Aside from a brief monograph by J. Stelzenberger,[8] I know of no attempt to deal with it in a thorough and comprehensive manner. Nor is there any substantive evidence that its newness and its revolutionary character have always been fully appreciated either by Stelzenberger or by the few contemporary authors who have treated it in a more incidental fashion.[9] The cause of the failure to perceive the originality of Augustine's teaching lies in part with Augustine himself, who not infrequently conceals his own innovations and who sought to gain a wider audience for Christianity by minimizing rather than exaggerating the difference between the content of the biblical message and that of classical philosophy. The very skill with which he employed the method has often caused his commentators to be misled as to his real intentions and has given rise to the charge of hellenization leveled at him by many of his modern critics. Thanks, however, to the efforts of a small but influential group of scholars whose pioneering work has given us a new understanding of the ancient philosophers and, by implication, of their relationship to their Christian counterparts,[10] the way may have been opened to a fresh interpretation of his thought and to a more accurate grasp of the break that it represents with the pagan tradition. For if it is true that Augustine hellenized Christianity, it is no less true that he profoundly modified classical philosophy to suit the requirements of the faith. The modification is particularly evident in his uniquely Christian doctrine of conscience. The following remarks have as their purpose to call attention to the originality of that doctrine and in a more special way to its far-reaching political significance.

The word "conscience" itself, both in its Greek (*suneidēsis*) and its Latin (*conscientia*) forms, is of course broadly attested in the pre-Christian as well as the Christian periods.[11] Despite the obscurity that surrounds its appearance, its original meaning can easily be established from the writings of later authors. We know from Cicero's *Laws*[12] that the expression was commonly used to designate a shared secret or the knowledge that one possesses in common with someone else. In the simplest case it describes the state of affairs that obtains, for example, when a person is privy to some possibly incriminating information about another person and is thus in a position to testify for or against him if he should be called upon to do so. The meaning was soon extended in such a way as to include the knowledge that one shares with oneself concerning one's actions and, eventually, the witness of one's own inner self concerning the moral goodness or badness of those actions. The presence of the term in the works of historians, in the New Testament, and in a wide range of poetic or literary texts would seem to betray a popular origin.[13] However that may be, it is to the philosophic schools of antiquity that we must turn for the raw materials of what was to become the fully developed theory that we find in Augustine.

A brief survey of the philosophic literature prior to Augustine reveals that the notion of conscience initially belongs to the conventionalist rather than the natural right or natural law tradition. At the outset it has nothing to do with the practice of virtue for its own sake or with the intrinsic nobility or baseness of specific human acts. Contrary to what might be expected and to what has often been said, its first home is not Platonism, Aristotelianism, or Stoicism, but Epicureanism.[14] It is significant that the substantive *suneidēsis* is never used either by Plato or Aristotle, although one does find in Plato the verb form *autō suneidenai* ("to be conscious in oneself," "to be conscious of . . . within oneself") with some of the moral and religious overtones commonly associated with conscience. The best example of its use in that sense occurs in Book I of the *Republic*,[15] where it is linked to the fear that besets the man who is conscious of having committed injustices for which he may conceivably be punished in afterlife. But the context is clearly that of popular or ancestral religion and does not in any way reflect a teaching that could seriously be ascribed to Socrates. The speaker is the elderly and covetous Cephalus, whose piety has improved with age and for whom the preoccupation with divine sanctions assumes larger proportions as death approaches. Socrates obviously does not share Cephalus's timorous piety and indicates as much by tacitly dropping any mention of the sacrifices owed to the gods in his restatement of Cephalus's definition of justice.[16] The view of morality defended by Cephalus has its only visible support in a quotation from a poet and is subjected to a thorough criticism in the course of the ensuing discussion, at which Cephalus himself with good reason will not be present. The tone of the whole scene is unmistakably ironic, as is amply borne out by the rest of the book, where the gods of the city are replaced by the Platonic doctrine of ideas and where the belief in the nether world and personal immortality is either described as a myth or dismissed altogether.[17] Neither in this or in any other Platonic dialogue is it possible to discover even the remote antecedents of a philosophic doctrine of conscience. If anything, the whole of the *Republic* may be read as a disguised attack upon, and formal rejection of, any type of morality based on conscience or its analogues.

The same cannot be said of Epicureanism, where conscience becomes for the first time a theme of philosophy, but with a meaning that is still far removed from the one it was later to acquire especially for the Christian writers. It is the hallmark of the Epicurean doctrine that it integrates conscience into a hedonistic framework. The main features of that doctrine, as reported by Lucretius, Cicero, and Seneca, are contained in the Epicurean teaching concerning justice and civil society, a teaching that culminates in the denial of man's essentially political nature.

For all its immense power and the high regard in which it is commonly held, justice is not desirable or choiceworthy in itself; it is at best a means and not an end. Those who accept it do so only by necessity or for the sake of a lesser evil. Far from being a primary phenomenon, it arises out of the situation created by man's universal desire to procure his own advantage, if need be at the expense of others. Anyone who wishes to understand it must therefore look at it from the point of view of its beginning and not of its end. By nature men seek, not the good as such, but the pleasant in all its forms. Since the material goods to which they are mostly attracted are scarce, the stampede for them necessarily develops into a fierce contest in which the weak, despite their larger numbers, are habitually bested by the strong. Their only recourse under the circumstances is to band together and, taking full advantage of their numerical superiority, proscribe as unjust any further encroachments on their own equally selfish interests. But if that is the case, justice is no more than a subterfuge by which a large group of naturally weak men are able to turn the tables on their oppressors and obtain a measure of equality for themselves. It benefits the poor and not the rich, and is itself a form of violence, the only one of which the weak are capable. Its sole basis is the law or convention by which men engaged in a relentless struggle for the ownership of the same goods finally decide to compromise and agree to place certain limitations on their desires by calling some actions good and others bad.

Only when such an agreement has been reached can civil society come into being. Once established, however, civil society must do everything in its power to conceal its own origin. It effectually discourages any attempt to investigate its foundations and makes capital of man's persistent credulity to inculcate respect for its laws. It purposely allows the distinction between nature and convention to become obliterated and solemnly propagates the view that the principles of justice on which it rests, and without which it could not exist, are anchored in a cosmic order supported by divine authority or sanctioned by the gods themselves. It goes without saying that these gods have no existence other than in the minds of men. They both originate in and thrive on purely human passions. They are the creations of ignorant people into whose hearts the sight of lightening, eclipses, and various other natural phenomena has struck terror. By uncovering the true causes of these phenomena, science destroys superstition and removes the irrational fears in which it is grounded. It discloses a world ruled by chance and devoid of any intelligible necessity. Man himself appears as the accidental product of a long series of fortuitous events out of which the world as we see it has evolved. He is not an essential part of that world and he does not find his perfection or fulfillment in a natural order of the soul which would reflect or be reflected in the order of the universe as a whole. The only goal to which he can aspire is pleasure and above all the pure pleasure of a mind untroubled by the greatest of all fears, the fear of divine retribution in this life or in the next.

This does not mean, however, that conscience cannot effectively restrain men from evil and serve as a deterrent to crime. Although the wicked man has nothing to fear from the gods, he is still very much a prey to human justice and must contend with the punishments by which society seeks vengeance over those who flout its laws. Even the cleverest of crooks is tortured by the thought or "conscience" of his misdeeds, not because of any guilt that he might have incurred, but because he can never be sure that his crimes will not be detected or, if they are, that he will be able to escape the reprisals of his fellow men.[18] The successful tyrant, whom the multitude both hates and secretly envies, is, in fact, the most insecure and miserable of men, constantly fearing for his life and forced to take endless precautions to defend it. His mind is never at rest and, in that regard if in no other, the price that he pays for his injustices is greater than any of the advantages that he stands to gain from them.[19] For strictly utilitarian reasons, he is still better off to avoid all injustice and, following Seneca's admonition, act at all times as if he were living in a glass house.[20]

The philosophic attack on the superiority of the common good over the private good inevitably led to two opposite but equally dangerous conclusions. Like the wise man described by Lucretius, one could become indifferent to society and its problems and, disengaging oneself totally from it, enjoy from afar the endless and infinitely varied spectacle of the turmoil of human affairs;[21] or else one could decide to exploit society for one's own ends, after the manner of the vulgar conventionalist who unabashedly takes advantage of the naiveté of the law-abiding citizens who have been hoodwinked into believing that justice is preferable to injustice. In either case, the consequences were seen as disastrous both for the city and for philosophy, which depends on the city for its existence.

The result was a reaction against the Epicurean view which took the form of a return to the doctrine of the natural character of justice and found its chief exponent in Stoicism. The problem at hand is summed up by Cicero in the familiar story of the ring of Gyges, which had the mysterious property of rendering its owner invisible at will, thus allowing him to commit the most horrendous crimes with impunity.[22] The point of the fable, shorn of legendary trappings, is quite simply whether, even if one were guaranteed complete immunity, one should still side with justice against injustice. The question was answered in the affirmative by Stoicism: crime is itself its own worst penalty. No matter how well concealed, it can never go unavenged, for the sole reason that its punishment lies within itself rather than in any external source.[23] Men have ingrained in them a loathing for that which nature abhors. By indulging in injustice, they deny what is best in their own nature. The mental tortures from which they suffer stem primarily from self-contempt and exceed the most cruel exactions of human justice. Even under the most auspicious circumstances, man can never serve his own deeper interests by acting unjustly. What the wise man seeks, then, is not invisibility but moral rectitude.[24] He is the kind of person with whom one might play at odds and evens in the dark. With or without the magic ring, his behavior remains the same.

In restating the case for the naturalness of justice and civil society against Epicureanism, Stoicism radicalized it and by so doing added a new dimension to the doctrine of conscience. Not only is virtue natural to man but it is in it, and in it alone, that he finds true happiness. It is compatible with the greatest of misfortunes and requires no external goods whatever. Even whipped, racked, blinded, and abused, the virtuous man. is still happy. The knowledge of his own uprightness suffices and it matters little to him that others should regard him as the worst of criminals. Nothing can replace or surpass the joys of a good conscience. The wise man longs for no higher reward.

In spite of all the emphasis on internal disposition and the need for self-reliance, however, the role assigned to conscience in Stoic philosophy seems to have been in the last analysis entirely secondary. The word appears only on relatively rare occasions in the discussion of moral matters and, when it does, it is usually under the influence of Epicureanism and in response to it.[25] Cicero, who uses it some seventy-five times in all, avoids it altogether in the thematic treatment of Stoicism in Books III and IV of the *De finibus* and mentions it only once in passing in the *De officiis*,[26] which is expressly presented as an adaptation of the Stoic moral teaching.[27] It is perhaps no accident that the only reference to it in connection with the story of Gyges as a reason for shunning injustice occurs, not in Cicero, but in a Christian writer.[28] What is more, in none of the passages dealing with conscience is there any stress on moral obligation, except perhaps insofar as one may feel bound by himself or by nature to refrain from evil and immorality. It is likewise difficult to see how by ignoring the voice of his conscience, one could provoke God's wrath, since the Stoic God does not appear to be in any sense a personal and omniscient God who avenges the hidden sins of men.

In any event, the Stoic ideal which identifies happiness with virtue and nothing else is inseparable from philosophy and applies strictly speaking only to the wise man. It remains inaccessible to most men, whose conduct must be judged by a lower standard and for whom moral goodness is efficaciously promoted only when virtue and vice are attended by extrinsic rewards and punishments. There is no conclusive evidence that the notion of a divinely sanctioned law was, even for the Stoics, anything more than a noble lie calculated to foster as high a degree of justice as is possible among ordinary human beings. Its use is rendered necessary by the practical impossibility of demonstrating to the multitude that crime does not pay or that wickedness always leads to misery. For, although some wicked men have admitted to being wretched, there is no way of establishing from experience that all of them are.[29] The happy crook, if such there be, is not likely to brag about his success since that success depends entirely on his ability to conceal his crimes. Whatever pious terms may be used to describe it, the "law" that the criminal is said to transgress is, at least in Cicero's interpretation, really nothing else but "the highest reason inherent in the universe."[30] In the end, reason and not conscience dictates the conduct of the noble and just man,[31] and on that score the Stoic teaching remains closer to the Socratic tradition in which it originated than to the Christian tradition that it helped to mould.

It was left to Augustine, under the influence of both Stoicism and sacred Scripture, to elaborate a theory of conscience which is at most only adumbrated, if it can be said to exist at all, either in Scripture itself or in the writings of his pagan models. Although the theory is never set forth methodically or expounded for its own sake, its main lines may be reconstructed with relative ease from numerous passages of his works. The sum of these texts makes it clear that conscience constitutes an indispensable element of the apparatus of the moral life and that it is furnished for the first time with all of the key attributes that have since become familiar to us. All men are endowed with it, the wicked as well as the good. Its awakening coincides with the first manifestations of reason and there is no soul, however perverse, in which its impulses are not felt as long as reason continues to be operative in it.[32] Through it man has within himself, independently of any extrinsic source, an infallible means by which, on the most general level, he is able to discriminate between right and wrong. It is concerned with future as well as with past actions and thus functions not only as a guide but as a witness and a judge.[33] Its precepts may be transgressed and are perhaps more often transgressed than observed by most men; yet they remain normative and unconditionally binding. No one can ignore them or fail to be aware of the fact that by disregarding them he behaves in a manner contrary to what he knows to be right. The guilt that ordinarily accompanies their infractions is not an irrational feeling traceable to some psychological or cultural "complex" from the lingering and oppressive effects of which the repentant sinner has not succeeded in freeing himself; it stems from the intimate knowledge of having violated the natural order of justice, which requires that sin be avoided or, if committed, that it not go unpunished.[34]

Because conscience rules all of man's life, it represents a higher form of justice and makes demands that are both extensively and intensively more stringent than those of ordinary human justice. It applies not only to such actions as the law may prescribe or forbid but to the totality of man's external actions and encompasses even his secret thoughts and desires. For, in order to be truly virtuous, it is not enough that one perform just deeds; he must also perform them for the right motives, and over these the human law has no power. The person who pays the proper respect to the Church for the purpose of concealing a guilty conscience may fool other people and improve his reputation with them, but he is no better for it in the eyes of God. He can hide the secrets of his conscience from his fellow men; he does not thereby escape its verdict.[35] Hence the superiority of its justice over the justice of men, which is often helpless to punish even the crimes that are known to have been perpetrated. The proof is that, in an effort to obtain an admission of guilt from a suspect, honest judges are often compelled to resort to torture—an inhumane practice which illustrates in dramatic fashion the sadly inadequate character of the justice they are called upon to administer, since it measures guilt by one's sensitivity to pain or his ability to endure it and frequently accomplishes nothing more than to inflict undeserved sufferings on innocent men.[36]

Ultimately, it is before the bar of conscience rather than before that of human justice or public opinion that one's conduct is to be judged. One should of course avoid any action that might unnecessarily give scandal to his weaker fellows, even if that action is not reproved by his conscience;[37] but there are nevertheless instances when the righteous man must be content with the sole witness and consolation of a good conscience. The virgins assaulted by the barbarians at the time of the sack of Rome felt disgraced because of the suspicion of complicity that easily attaches to such matters in the minds of the many.[38] Such a feeling may be excusable in a pagan like Lucretia, who sought to vindicate her honor by committing suicide, thus demonstrating beyond all doubt that she prized virtue above everything else,[39] but it is totally out of place in the case of a Christian. It merely proves that the one who experiences it attaches greater importance to the appearance of goodness than to its reality. The genuinely virtuous person is more concerned with avoiding anything that might offend his conscience. It suffices that his own conscience be able to testify to his moral integrity.

The conclusion to be drawn from all of this is that man's moral life is invested with an objective autonomy that it did not have for any of Augustine's pagan predecessors. For conscience as Augustine understands it is not just an innate moral sense found in all or most men or a general awareness of certain broad limitations to which human conduct is subject. Nor is it a mere reflection or internalization of the ethical values and standards of a given society. Conscience cannot, for that matter, be reduced to a question of loyalty to oneself and to one's commitments, whatever those commitments might be. And conscience is even less a simple matter of sentiment divorced from reason and superior to it, as the romantic notion popularized by Rousseau would have it.[40] What Augustine's understanding of conscience basically implies is that man's life as a whole is governed by rational principles that are naturally known and universally valid even under the most extreme circumstances. Because of their fixed and unalterable character, these principles take on the form of an eternal or natural law to which all men owe obedience at all times under pain of guilt and retribution.[41] That law is conveniently summed up for Augustine in the biblical rule of thumb enjoining men to treat others as they would like to be treated by them.[42] Natural law finds its ontological basis in the natural theology and teleology which the discovery of Neo-Platonism had prepared Augustine to accept and which he was later summoned to defend against the materialistic and mechanistic cosmology propounded by Manichaeanism.[43] Its most fundamental requirements are expressed with clarity and precision in a series of precepts that explicitly denounce as contrary to nature and offensive to God such actions as murder, adultery, theft, and lying. Through natural law man accedes to a sphere that is higher in dignity than that of the most perfect human society. He becomes a member of a cosmopolis subject to the will of an omniscient and all-powerful God who rules the world with justice and by his providence orders all things to their appointed ends.

The crucial political implication is that human life acquires a universality that it did not have and could not have as long as the polis and its regime represented for most men a *total* way of life. Civil society is displaced as the locus of virtue and the object of man's deepest and most noble attachments. Its wholeness is shattered. It ceases to be, as it had been in the pagan scheme, the sole horizon lending meaning and substance to the highest activities undertaken by its citizens. The love of one's own is no longer concentrated within its borders, and by the same token citizenship itself loses its most fundamental significance. Last but not least, the gods of civil religion, which Augustine with characteristic reserve refrains from attacking directly, are deprived of their ultimate political justification and are replaced by the cult of the one true God, the author and supreme good of all things.

The practical consequences of Augustine's view are well illustrated among other ways by the stand that he was led to take on the subject of lies—a stand that is plainly at variance with the bulk of the philosophic tradition before him. Simply put, the question is whether it can ever become the duty of a good man to tell a lie.[44] The problem had received its classic solution in Plato's *Republic,* which takes the unambiguous position that rulers are not only allowed to lie but compelled to do so for the common welfare of the city. The gods on the other hand never lie. Since wisdom cannot rule without falsehood or without recourse to salutary lies, the obvious implication is that the gods do not rule.[45] Augustine readily admits that the issue is a difficult and intricate one. He is willing to grant that both the liar's intention and the matter of the lie have no small bearing on the case. The man who lies in order to save a friend's life is surely less guilty than the one who lies out of malice or for the sake of gain. Likewise, a lie in matters of religion is far more grievous than a lie pertaining to other, less vital matters. It is also the case that one may conceal the truth by refraining from speaking whenever there are good reasons to do so; for it is one thing to utter a falsehood and another to pass the truth over in silence.[46] But this does not alter the fact that all lies are intrinsically evil and sinful, no matter how praiseworthy the intention or how trivial the matter.[47] God himself, "the Father of Truth," does not deceive and does not allow others to be deceived unless they deserve it.[48] The ultimate conclusion of the argument is that the perfect man never lies even for the purpose of saving "this transitory life" for himself or for someone else; he is not free to "kill his soul" for the sake of his or another man's body.[49] No doubt, Augustine's most absolute statements are sometimes susceptible of strange qualifications;[50] but, all in all, it would be difficult to find a better example of the clear-cut difference in tone and spirit between the Christian natural law theory and the more flexible natural right theory of the pagan philosophers.

We shall grasp with greater clarity the broad political significance of Augustine's theory of conscience if we pause to examine its relationship to the notion with which at first glance it might seem to bear the closest resemblance, the famous "demon" of Socrates. The very terminology used by Augustine to describe conscience has often invited a comparison between the two doctrines;[51] but any such rapprochement merely muddies the water and obscures the novelty of the Augustinian teaching. To be sure, the question of the demon of Socrates is itself far from clear and a complete elucidation of it, assuming its possibility, would lead much beyond the scope of the present study. Even a rapid analysis of the most pertinent texts, however, should suffice to put us on our guard against any hasty identification of the two views.

The most obvious characteristic of the mysterious demon is that it restrains from action but never incites to it. It constitutes a negative rather than a positive voice and is first injected into the argument of the *Apology* to explain why Socrates habitually refuses to take part in the political life of the city.[52] Its essential function is to caution Socrates against doing anything or engaging in any activity that might endanger his life. The reference to it, interestingly enough, follows a discussion of Socrates's behavior at the battles of Potidea and Delium, two notorious Athenian defeats.[53] Socrates's courage on the battlefield is presented as a matter of public knowledge and is granted on all hands. The reader who compares the two passages is nevertheless left with the odd but inescapable impression that Socrates's reputation for bravery rests on his adeptness at beating safe retreats. Clearly, the "voice" that he hears on these and similar occasions is anything but the highest voice of moral conscience. It is, to put it bluntly, the familiar voice of self-preservation. But it is a natural voice, and therein lies precisely its relative superiority over the commonly accepted and authoritative opinions in the light of which particular cities judge the conduct of their citizens in battle or elsewhere. Its analysis leads to the discovery of the crucial distinction between nature and convention, which represents the necessary starting point of philosophic reflection. At the same time, the voice reveals the possible existence of other natural inclinations whose objects may have nothing in common with mere survival or the satisfaction of bodily needs. It points in the highest instance to the presence of an innate desire for the truth or to a philosophic eros which is perhaps not shared to the same degree by all men but which Socrates, in whom it is especially powerful, cannot be induced to forsake even at the price of death.[54]

For all his professed ignorance of the highest matters, Socrates is convinced of the injustice of the laws of Athens and does not hesitate to oppose them when the circumstances demand it.[55] But he would not be able to do so if he did not have some idea of what a good law is. The knowledge that he possesses necessarily implies more than the simple knowledge of his ignorance. It provides him with a positive standard and indeed, according to Plato, with the only standard by which one is able to rise above common opinion and rid himself of the chains that bind the ordinary citizen to the wall of the cave. There is thus revealed a new life whose demands and fulfillments differ radically from those of the political life and of which Socrates himself, who lives as a private individual in the city, stands as the perfect embodiment. We are given to understand that it is only by perfecting one's natural capacity for knowing or by developing to the fullest what is best in him that one transcends the polis and arrives at an articulation of the whole that is essentially independent of the commonly held beliefs which define its way of life. But this knowledge can in no way be equated with the knowledge of good and evil supplied by conscience. It is the preserve of a small number of exceptionally gifted and well educated individuals who have grasped the true principles of human action and, as such, it lies beyond the reach of most men, whose horizon is bounded, not by the natural whole which constitutes the object of the philosopher's quest, but by the political whole to which they belong as members of a particular society.

The true equivalent of conscience in Plato is not the demon of Socrates but the sense of shame that all men or at least all noble-minded men experience at the thought of committing evil. The kinship between the two notions is established by a passage of Plato's *Laws* in which shame is provisionally explained in terms of fear and more precisely in terms of fear of the gods, the beings before whom men tremble and to whom they owe reverence above all others.[56] The statement occurs in the context of a discussion of wine and its role in education. The paradoxical thesis upheld by the Athenian Stranger in the presence of Clinias and Megillus, two old and dignified representatives of teetotaling societies, is that, far from being harmful or conducive to vice, wine can become a powerful ally of virtue as long as its use is properly regulated. Its chief property is to restore to the soul its youthful pliability, thus rendering it more receptive to the improving influence of a wise legislator.[57] The danger, as Clinias readily agrees, is that as soon as men are allowed to drink they are likely to become insolent and lose all respect for law and authority. The objection is countered by the Athenian Stranger's remark that, even if that should happen, men could still be persuaded to curb their unruliness by the fear of divine vengeance. The remainder of the passage again makes it abundantly clear, however, that the allusion to the fear of the gods cannot be regarded as anything more than an accommodation to necessity or to popular prejudice. It has no more solid basis than the unverifiable legend according to which Bacchus was robbed of his wits by his stepmother Hera and retaliated by depriving men of their reason through the gift of wine.[58] The punitive myth, based on pious tradition and the belief in all-knowing and revengeful gods, is promptly discarded and replaced by a non-punitive account of the natural origin of wine. The upshot of the discussion is that for the well-bred man moral conduct is strictly a matter of taste and decency and not of compliance, voluntary or otherwise, with divinely promulgated and divinely enforced commands. Unlike conscience taken in its most proper sense, shame is exclusively concerned with the inherent attractiveness or repulsiveness of human actions. The person who is sensitive to it avoids evil because it is vulgar and base, not because it is forbidden by any authority, divine or human. His total pattern of behavior is not inspired by the love of the beautiful as distinguished from the love or fear of God.[59] The principles that guide him point to what should be done but do not impose it or condemn its opposite as a punishable offense against God. Their violation entails the loss of self-respect; it does not breed guilt or remorse. The difference between these principles and the principles implied in the notion of conscience is the exact measure of the distance that separates the Platonic god of reason from the Christian God of love.

Augustine's teaching on conscience and its necessary concomitant, the infrangible eternal or natural law which serves as the ultimate and infallible criterion of the justice of all human laws, is fraught with what one might be tempted to regard as the gravest of political consequences. To repeat what was said earlier, Augustine's view of conscience and natural law is founded on the assumption that there are principles of justice which are not only normally but universally valid for all men. It takes it for granted that there are assignable limits to what a political ruler is allowed to do even in cases of emergency or of extreme national crisis. From that point of view it deviates sharply from the position adopted by the classical philosophers, for whom the acceptance of natural right was reconcilable with the changeability of all rules of justice.[60] It would thus seem to provide men with a ready-made justification for civil dissent, to say nothing of revolutionary activity. The truth of the matter, however, is that the doctrine contains within itself the seeds of preservation no less than of reformation. Experience has shown repeatedly that it can be used with equal success as an instrument of political quietism and as a leaven of political change. It has been invoked to overthrow the established power, but it has also been pressed into service to legitimize and strengthen it, as the example of the "*Ordnungenstheologie*" of the thirties testifies.[61] Its fundamental ambiguity in that regard is corroborated by the fact that Augustine has been both rebuked for his conservatism and lauded for his progressivism by leading contemporary advocates of social reform.[62]

One explanation for the apparent inconsistency is that the Augustinian doctrine was joined from the outset with the well-known teaching of the Letter to the Romans which looks upon political authority as something ordained by God and urges obedience to it "for the sake of conscience."[63] On the basis of Paul's remarks and of Augustine's views on society, a distinction was made between primary natural right and secondary natural right.[64] The former obtains only in the state of innocence or of original justice and excludes private property, slavery, and all other forms of coercion associated with civil society. The latter presupposes sin and corruption and is intended by God as a remedy for them. While recognizing the essentially defective character of civil society, it proclaims its absolute necessity for fallen man, thereby sanctifying it and creating for all men a new set of inviolable duties. The unintended result was a political teaching which in many of its subsequent interpretations was less and not more revolutionary than the pure natural right teaching of the classical philosophers.

The same paradox may be accounted for by a more general reason which will come to light if we consider briefly the obvious objection to which on its own grounds Augustine's theory of conscience is exposed. The objection has to do with the fact that, although conscience is presented by Augustine as a universal human phenomenon, any true knowledge of it is predicated on the acceptance of important speculative truths which are prior to it and hence not simply known through it. It presupposes among other things that God exists, that he presides over human affairs, that the individual human soul has an eternal destiny, that there is an afterlife in which all wrongs are righted and, more generally, that it is possible for the human mind to arrive at some kind of certitude concerning such matters.[65] By Augustine's own admission, these truths are inaccessible to the multitude of uneducated men. If they are to be accepted at all by them, it can only be on the authority of a few wise and learned men. The difficulty is that wisdom is not as easily identified by most people as gold or silver. One can recognize the latter even if he does not possess them, whereas it takes wisdom to recognize wisdom and to choose rightly among the different pretenders to it.[66] At this point the argument becomes to all intents and purposes circular: conscience counsels submission to the proper authority, but it is only from the proper authority that one learns about the existence of conscience and the necessity of heeding its injunctions.

Augustine is ready to admit that on a purely human level the problem defies any completely satisfactory solution. But it is not proper to Christianity. All men are faced with it, inasmuch as wisdom is not a gift of nature but must be acquired through a long and arduous process of education. The harsh truth is that few men ever reach it and those who do are necessarily dependent on the help they receive from others. No one would ever set out in pursuit of it unless he were made aware of its existence and the possibility of attaining it by the example of those who have gone before him. Like it or not, faith precedes understanding and remains indispensable until such time as the student becomes capable of grasping the truth by himself. It is not the destruction of freedom but its universal precondition. As the inaccurate but appropriate Latin rendering of Isaiah had it, "Unless you believe you shall not understand."[67] There is always the danger that in their ignorance men will trust themselves to the wrong authority; but even so, their freedom is more seriously jeopardized by the rejection of all authority than by the manifest abuses to which the exercise of authority lends itself. Nothing would remain stable in human society if everyone suddenly determined to accept only what he is able to establish scientifically.[68] In Augustine's own words, "It is a greater misery not to be moved by authority than to be deceived by it."[69] The very evil that threatens men from the misuse of authority is an argument for it and not against it. It creates a presumption in favor of the Church, the specific authority instituted by God to lead men to the truth.[70]

Authority is finally justified, then, on the ground that it is better to obey the precepts of the wise than to follow one's own whims.[71] The case in its behalf rests squarely on the premise that the equality of all men before God does not abolish their natural differences or their fundamental inequality in regard to intellectual capacity and human perfection.[72] The issue took a radically new turn when the supremacy of wisdom was questioned by the modern natural right theorists and when, ceasing to take its bearings from man's highest excellence, political philosophy attempted to base its teachings on the low but solid footing of human passion and the desire for self-preservation.[73] If self-preservation and eventually comfortable self-preservation is the determining factor in human life, and if each individual is presumed to be the most competent judge of the means conducive to his own preservation, the intellectual and moral differences among men become politically irrelevant[74] and authority is "*eo facto*" bereft of the only true and ultimate meaning that it had for Augustine. It is hardly necessary to add that that typically modern alternative is one which Augustine apparently never considered and from which, in the spirit of his pagan teachers, he probably would have shrunk in horror.

One thing is certain: the theory of conscience that finally emerged from his reflection on Scripture and the works of the pagan philosophers is neither purely scriptural nor purely philosophic. Like the misquoted text that he borrowed from Isaiah, it stands out as a distinctively new product brought into being by the judicious mating of the New Testament with the principles of classical philosophy. The need to emphasize the difference between that theory and the strictly philosophic doctrine that it was meant to replace has again become imperative, not only because the two are still often confused but, more importantly, lest the downfall of the one should appear to entail the demise of the other.

NOTES

1. Cf. E. A. Smith, "Religion and Conscience in Constitutional Law," *Church-State Relations in Ecumenical Perspective*, edited by E. A. Smith (Pittsburgh, 1966), 245.

2. Cf. *A Conflict of Loyalties: The Case for Selective Conscientious Objection*, edited by J. Finn (New York: Pegasus, 1969).

3. As is implied, for example, by the title of Charles Davis's apologia, *A Question of Conscience* (New York: Harper and Row, 1967).

4. For an existentialist critique of the traditional "theories" of conscience, see above all M. Heidegger, *Being and Time*, trans. J. Macquarrie and E. Robinson (New York: Harper and Row, 1962), 312-348. With infinitely less subtlety J. Fletcher, *Situation Ethics* (Philadelphia: Westminster, 1966), 53, writes: "There *is* no conscience; 'conscience' is merely a word for our attempts to make decisions creatively, constructively, fittingly."

5. For a concise statement of the problem, cf. F. Oppenheim, "The Natural Law Thesis: Affirmation or Denial," *American Political Science Review* 51 (1957): 41-53.

6. A number of these interpretations are surveyed and assessed by E. Mount, Jr., *Conscience and Responsibility* (Richmond: John Knox Press, 1969).

7. Cf. K. Stendhal, "The Apostle Paul and the Introspective Conscience of the West," *Harvard Theological Review* 56 (1963): 199-215. M. Barth, "Natural Law in the Teachings of St. Paul," in *Church-State Relations in Ecumenical Perspective*, edited by E. Smith (Pittsburgh: Duquesne University Press, 1966), 130.

8. J. Stelzenberger, *Conscientia bei Augustinus: Studie zur Geschichte der Moraltheologie* (Paderborn: F. Schoningh, 1959).

9. Cf. H. A. Deane, *The Political and Social Ideas of St. Augustine* (New York: Columbia University Press, 1963), 84-88. A brief synthesis of the patristic views on conscience is to be found in P. Delhaye, *The Christian Conscience* (New York: Desclee Co., 1968), 69-99.

10. For present purposes, cf. especially L. Strauss, *Natural Right and History* (Chicago: University of Chicago Press, 1953); *The City and Man* (Chicago: University of Chicago Press, 1964); A. Bloom, *The Republic of Plato* (New York: Basic Books, 1968).

11. A useful list of Greek references is included in C. A. Pierce, *Conscience in the New Testament* (London: S.C.M. Press, 1955), 132-147.

12. Cicero, *De legibus* I.11.31. Cf. *De finibus* II.9.28.

13. Cf. Pierce, *Conscience*, 16-17.

14. The once widely held thesis of a Stoic origin has all but been abandoned by recent scholars. Cf. Pierce, *Conscience*, 13-20; Delhaye, *The Christian Conscience*, 49; J. Dupont "Syneidesis: Aux origines de la notion chrétienne de conscience," *Studia Hellen.*, 5 (1945): 125 and n. 2; W. D. Davies, "Conscience," *The Interpreter's Dictionary of the Bible* (New York: Abingdon Press, 1962) I 671-6.

15. Plato, *Republic* 331a.

16. *Republic* 331b-c.

17. Cicero, *De finibus* I.16.51. Seneca, *De clementia* I.13.3.

18. Cicero, *De finibus* I.16.53. Seneca, *Epistula* 97.13; 105-7-8.

19. Cicero, *De finibus* I.16.51; cf. *Paradoxa Stoicorum* 5.40. Seneca, *De clementia* 1.13.3.

20. Seneca, *De beneficiis* VII.1.7.

21. Lucretius, *De natura rerum* II.1-19.

22. Cicero, *De officiis* III.8.38. Cf. Plato, *Republic* 359b-360d; Herodotus I.8.

23. Seneca, *Epist.* 97.14-16.

24. Cicero, *De officiis* III.8.38.

25. Cicero, *De finibus* I.16.51; II.16.53; II.17.54; II.22.71.

26. Cicero, *De officiis* III.21.85.

27. Cicero, *De oficiis* I.2.6.

28. St. Ambrose, *De officiis* III.5.29.

29. On the same subject, see Nietzsche's remark, *Beyond Good and Evil*, 39: "But there is no doubt that for the discovery of certain portions of truth the wicked and unfortunate are more favorably situated and have a greater likelihood of success; not to speak of the wicked who are happy—a species about whom moralists are silent."

30. Compare Cicero, *De re publica* III.22.33 with *De legibus* I.6.18.

31. Cf. Dupont, "Syneidesis" 140.

32. Augustine, *Sermo* (*Sermon*) 249.2; 330.3. *De sermone Domini in monte* (*On the Lord's Sermon on the Mount*) 2.9.32. *Contra secundam Julianum responsionem* (*Unfinished Work Against Julian's Second Response*) 2.228.

33. *Tractatus in Joannis evangelium* (*Tracts on the Gospel of John*) 33.5; 41.4; *Tractatus in Epistulam Joannis ad Parthos* (*Tracts on the First Epistle of John to the Parthians*) 9.4. *De catechizandis rudibus* (*On Catechizing the Unlearned*) 16.25; *Enarrationes in psalmos* (*Exposition on the Psalms*) 30.2.8; 31.5; 57.2. *Sermo* (*Sermon*) 47.14.23; *Confessiones* (*Confessions*) 1.18.29.

34. *Contra Faustum* 26.3.

35. *Epistula* (*Letter*) 23.3.

36. *De civitate Dei* (*The City of God*) XIX.6.

37. *De bono viduitatis* (*On the Good of Widowhood*) 22.27. *De moribus Manichaeorum* 16.33-35.

38. *De civ. Dei* I.28.

39. *De civ. Dei* I.19.

40. J. J. Rousseau, *Rêveries d'un promeneur solitaire*, "quatrième promenade" in *Oeuvres complètes*, Bibliothèque de la Pléiade 1 (Paris: Gallimard, 1959) 1028: "Dans toutes les questions de morale difficiles comme celle-ci, je me suis toujours bien trouvé de les résoudre par le dictamen de ma conscience plutot que par les lumières de ma raison." Cf. *Emile*, (*Oeuvres complètes*, Bibliothèque de la Pléiade 4) 594. Rousseau's remarks on conscience should be pondered in the light of his anecdote concerning the man who was about to commit adultery and who was suddenly seized by the thought of a possible jail sentence; whereupon his "conscience" got the better of him.

41. For the most important texts on natural law cf. *De diversis questionibus LXXXIII* (*On Eighty-three Different Questions*) 53.2; De sermone Domini in monte II.9.32; *In Psal.* 57.1; 118.25.4; *Epist.* 157.15.

42. *In Psal.* 57.1; *Confessiones (Confessions)* I.18.29; *Contra Julianum (Against Julian)* IV.3.23; *In Joannis evangelium* 49.12; *De ordine (On Order)* II.8.25; *De sermone Domini in monte* II.9.32.

43. *Contra Faustum* 26.3.

44. *Enchiridion (Faith, Hope and Charity)* 18.

45. Plato, *Republic* 459c. Cf. *Republic* 380d, 382a, 450e.

46. In *Psal.* 5.7.

47. *Enchiridion* 22.

48. *De div. quaest.* 83.53.2.

49. In *Psal.* 5.7.

50. See, for example, the famous discussion of Jacob's lie, *De mendacio (On Lying)* V.5 and *Contra mendacium (Against Lying)* X.24. Also *De sermone Domini in monte* I.16, where the interesting case of the wife who commits adultery in order to save her husband's life is discussed with less rigidity than some of Augustine's other pronouncements on the same subject would lead us to expect.

51. Cf. Delhaye, *The Christian Conscience*, 86; Stelzenberger, *Conscientia bei Augustinus*, 116.

52. Plato, *Apology of Socrates* 31d.

53. *Apology* 28e; cf. *Symp.* 219e-221b.

54. *Apology* 38a.

55. *Apology* 32b-c.

56. Plato, *Laws* 671d.

57. *Laws* 71b-c.

58. *Laws* 672b.

59. Plato, *Republic* 403c.

60. Aristotle, *Nicomachean Ethics* V.7.1134b29.

61. M. Barth, "Natural Law in the Teachings of St. Paul," loc. cit. 132-133. W. H. Lazareth, "Luther's Two Kingdoms Ethic Reconsidered," in *Christian Social Ethics in a Changing World*, edited by J. C. Bennett (New York: Association Press, 1966), 120.

62. R. Shaull, "Revolutionary Change in Theological Perspective," in J. C. Bennett, ed. op. cit. 29. R. Garaudy, *From Anathema to Dialogue* (New York: Herder and Herder, 1966), 97 and 112, *Marxisme au XXe siècle* (Paris: la Palatine, 1966), 153.

63. Romans 13.5. Cf. H. W. Bartsch, "A New Theological Approach to Christian Social Ethics," in *Christian Social Ethics in a Changing World*, edited by J. C. Bennett (New York: Association Press, 1966), 74-76.

64. R. Hooker, *The Laws of Ecclesiastical Polity* I.10.13.

65. *De utilitate credendi (On the Advantage of Believing)* 13.29.

66. *De utilitate credendi* 13.28.

67. *De libero arbitrio (On Free Choice of the Will)* II.2.6; *In Joannis evangelium* 29.6; Cf. Isaiah 7.9, which the *Jerusalem Bible* translates as follows: "But if you do not stand by me, you will not stand at all."

68. *De utilitate credendi* 12.26.
69. *De utilitate credendi* 16.34.
70. *De utilitate credendi* 15.33.
71. *De utilitate credendi* 12.27.
72. *De utilitate credendi* 10.24.
73. Cf. Hobbes, *De homine*, Epistle Dedicatory.
74. Hobbes, *De cive* I.13-10; *Leviathan* I.15.

4

AUGUSTINE AND ROMAN CIVIL RELIGION: SOME CRITICAL REFLECTIONS

In the preface to the second edition of his well-known work on myth and allegory Professor Jean Pépin engages in a lengthy reply to the criticisms evoked by his interpretation of some aspects of Roman political religion.[1] The bulk of the discussion turns on the correct understanding of the *City of God* IV.27, where Augustine takes the pontiff Scaevola to task for posing as a defender of the pagan gods while at the same time slyly or tacitly denying their existence.

Augustine's information purports to be derived from Varro, from whom he quotes freely and, as far as one can tell, literally.[2] In the text under consideration, which anticipates the thematic account of civil theology in Books VI and VII, Scaevola is said to have distinguished between three kinds of gods, one introduced by the poets, another by the philosophers, and the third by statesmen. The first of these is dismissed as silly or trifling (*nugatorium*) on the ground that it ascribes to the gods things that are contrary to their nature and dignity. It often depicts their conduct as unseemly and immoral, or otherwise discredits them by telling implausible stories about them.[3] The theology of the philosophers is similarly ruled out, but for an altogether different motive. The objection this time is that its teachings are at odds with the requirements of the political life: *non congruere civitatibus*. Much of what it says about the gods is superfluous, but it also includes a number of elements the knowledge of which must be deemed prejudicial to the city at large. One need not be unduly concerned about the former since, as Augustine points out, citing Roman law, "superfluous things do no harm."[4] The real problem arises when philosophers make bold to assert that Hercules, Aesculapius, and the Gemini are not in fact gods but glorified mortals and that the statues held in veneration by cities everywhere are not genuine images of the gods, if only for the reason that a true god has neither sex, nor age, nor definite corporeal members. These are the doctrines which, according to Augustine, the pontiff was intent on concealing from the public. Then comes the crucial and somewhat startling statement: "for he did not think them false; he is therefore of the opinion that cities ought to be deceived in matters of religion": *nam falsa esse non putat; expedire igitur existimat falli in religione civitates.*

Pépin had previously observed that the words just quoted could not have been those of Scaevola as reported by Varro. They were presumably supplied by Augustine, who "perfidiously and gratuitously" took it upon himself to accuse the pontiff of "Machiavellianism and insincerity."[5] We have no evidence that Scaevola sided with the philosophers on the issue at hand or that his faith in the gods of the city was merely feigned. The more likely supposition is that he rejected their theories as objectively false and did not want the multitude to become acquainted with them lest they should be seduced by them.

This interpretation was later challenged by G. Lieberg and H. Hagendahl, both of whom contend that, while Augustine's controversial statement cannot be traced back to Scaevola, it could and probably does reflect accurately the mentality of the illustrious pontiff. Lieberg's point is that, if Scaevola had disagreed with the teachings of the philosophers, he would not have neglected to raise theoretical objections to them instead of merely declaring them politically unsound; yet we know of no such critique on his part.[6] As Pépin is quick to note, however, this argument is an argument *a silentio,* from which no firm conclusion can be drawn. It neither proves nor disproves that Scaevola refrained from attacking natural theology on its own grounds.[7] Fortunately, there are positive reasons for thinking that Scaevola was not prone to indulge in theoretical discussions of this sort, the main one being that the Romans had no interest whatever in dogma. Their religion was essentially oriented toward practice rather than doctrine. The important question was not what one believed but what one did in accordance with the laws and customs of the city. If, as one must assume, this was also Scaevola's frame of mind, one cannot reasonably expect him to have argued philosophically against the theology of the philosophers. Inasmuch as speculative preferences play no significant role in the matter, his icy *non congruere civitatibus* is actually a far more devastating critique of natural theology than would have been any direct refutation of its content.[8]

If Pépin finds Lieberg's argument inconclusive, he is even less impressed with Hagendahl's assessment of the same question. Like Lieberg, Hagendahl sees no reason to distrust Augustine's testimony as it stands. Scaevola could very well have held civil religion to be false and still not wanted his opinion to be shared by everyone else. On this point, he appears to have been in total agreement with Varro; neither one thought it expedient publicly to reveal the truth concerning the gods of the city. It matters little that Scaevola, as distinguished from Varro, was an official representative of the Roman cult, for we encounter the same attitude later on in Cotta, himself a pontiff, who does not hesitate to oppose Balbus's defense of the gods in Book III of Cicero's *De natura deorum*.[9]

None of these objections has done much to sway Pépin, who cannot bring himself to believe that Scaevola could have been anything but forthright in professing his respect for the Roman gods. Doctrines are normally and logically censured because they are noxious, and they are noxious precisely because they are false. To argue that Scaevola took exception to the theories of the philosophers because they were true is to impute to him a "complicated psychology" or a "devious turn of mind" of which he cannot in fairness be suspected, and to maintain that he deliberately allowed others to be misled in matters of religion is to cast grave doubts on his moral character. Such an allegation is not only "shocking," but runs counter to everything we know about his personality. We have it on the word of Cicero and others that Scaevola was a man of preeminent "holiness" and "justice,"[10] whom everyone admired for his personal integrity and who died a kind of martyr for the cause of the Republic, as Augustine himself recalls elsewhere in the *City of God*.[11] Nor does it help to suggest that his disregard for the truth was motivated by pragmatic reasons, for it is hard to imagine what worthwhile purpose it might possibly have served.[12] In any event, Augustine could not be privy to Scaevola's secret intentions. If he presumed to read his mind, it can only have been for the sake of disqualifying the whole of Roman religion. The charges of duplicity and "cynicism" that he implicitly levels at him are thus entirely without foundation.

As for the comparison with Cotta, it is wholly beside the point since Cotta's reply is directed, not against the gods themselves, but against Balbus's philosophic defense of them. Cotta himself is emphatic in proclaiming his allegiance to Roman religion and even goes out of his way to indicate that his faith in it rests on the authority of the ancestors—*auctoritas maiorum*—rather than on abstract reasonings, which invariably lack force and tend to breed skepticism in regard to matters that are not in themselves subject to doubt.[13] Nothing that is said about him in Cicero's dialogue warrants the slightest suspicion of insincerity.[14] True, Scaevola does not expressly declare his attachment to the civic gods, as does Cotta, but one may infer from his objections to the theology of the philosophers that he was not any less faithful to them.[15]

According to Pépin, the flaw in Hagendahl's and Lieberg's argument is that it fails to take into consideration the manifest differences between Scaevola and Varro on this issue. Following Augustine's lead, both scholars start from the premise that their views betray a similar attitude toward civil religion. Pépin denies that this is the case; for one thing, Varro objected to the cultic use of divine images, a practice to which Scaevola gives his unqualified assent. Furthermore, Varro praises natural theology and finds nothing wrong with it except for its tendency to give rise to a multiplicity of sects.[17] Scaevola, on the other hand, disapproves of it and disparages it by pronouncing it unfit for cities.[18] To be sure, Varro readily acknowledges that philosophers often raise questions which are more appropriately debated behind closed doors than in the forum: *facilius intra parietes in schola quam extra in foro ferre possunt aures.*[19] However, Pépin takes this to mean no more than that most people are indifferent to or easily impatient with abstruse philosophic disquisitions and hence that such disquisitions are best carried on within the walls of a school. He grants that Lieberg's interpretation, according to which scientific speculations about the gods require secrecy and cannot safely be conducted in the open, is theoretically possible and that it is consonant with the one proposed by Augustine, who reveals his own bias by equating *forum* with civil society.[20] If this more pregnant exegesis were to be allowed, it would dispose of a serious problem, for it greatly reduces the distance between Scaevola and Varro. But then, "why the devil would Varro have refused to the people any access to the theology of the philosophers?"[21]

That he had no intention of doing so is vouched for by the fact that his position, in contradistinction to that of Scaevola, postulates a definite relationship between the three theologies and a reciprocal dependence of each one of them on the other two. As a philosopher, Varro was understandably partial to natural theology,[22] whereas others experience a greater attraction for the theology of the poets.[23] As for civil theology, it may be said to occupy a kind of middle ground between them, drawing elements from both and adapting them to its own needs. All three theologies are in fact so closely interwoven as to justify our speaking of a single theology, which receives different specifications insofar as it originates with or is primarily addressed to philosophers, priests, or poets.

Accordingly, Augustine could not have been right in identifying Varro's *forum* with civil society, thereby implying that Varro was at one with Scaevola in excluding natural theology from the market place. What we have in Varro is the exact opposite, namely, a civil theology that is largely open to philosophic influences and a natural theology that has itself become an integral part of civil theology. Since both of these theologies are intimately bound up with each other as well as with poetic theology, it makes little sense to pretend that Varro was bent on keeping natural theology out of the hands of the people. Such is not the stand taken by Scaevola, who not only distinguishes the three theologies but maintains a sharp separation between them and denounces natural theology as both false and politically dangerous.[24] It follows that Augustine has grievously misconstrued Scaevola's thought so that it might be more easily fitted into his global reprobation of Roman religion.

Since our only source of information regarding Scaevola's position is Varro, and since Varro's testimony is known to us mainly through the few brief fragments preserved by Augustine, it is obviously difficult to arrive at a completely satisfactory solution to the problem. Still, the evidence at our disposal suggests that Augustine's assessment of the situation is perhaps not as wide of the mark as Pépin would have us believe. Regardless of whether or not Scaevola and Varro were in full accord on every point, nobody denies that they both subscribed in some fashion to the tripartite division of theology into mythical, civil, and natural. But one cannot make that distinction without implicitly raising the issue of the truth of these three theologies. To define one of them as "natural" is to insinuate that the other two are not natural or not completely natural, and hence that they belong to the lesser sphere of human institution; for what exists by nature is widely understood to be higher than what exists only by virtue of some agreement or convention among human beings. Such at any rate is the premise on which Varro and Augustine rested their case for the superiority of natural theology.[25] This does not mean, of course, that once the distinction between nature and convention is called into play, civil theology must automatically be discarded. One may wish to retain it for other reasons; but its theoretical status has become, to put it mildly, a matter of considerable uncertainty.

Pépin's opinion to the contrary notwithstanding, Scaevola's comment about the unsuitability of natural theology to the political life need not be interpreted as a denigration of that theology. It says nothing whatever about its intrinsic worth and draws attention only to the problem that it creates from the point of view of the larger or nonphilosophic context of the city. For all we know, Augustine could very well have diagnosed Scaevola's psychology correctly. The pontiff did not have any reservations about natural theology as such, which "he did not regard as false"; his sole complaint is that it was not directly applicable to the political life. Whatever else one may think of the argument, its logic is perfectly sound.

Scaevola wanted the doctrines emanating from philosophical circles to be kept from the people not because they were false but because they were true. Had they been false, it would have been easy enough to counter them with a true account of the gods. Lies of this sort may be damaging but they can be refuted, and, once exposed, they must sooner or later be abandoned. Not so with the truth, which by definition cannot be disproved by means of rational arguments and which is more likely to prevail on condition that the evidence for it be properly laid out. The wisest policy was still to maintain a judicious silence about the teachings of the philosophers and to restrict their diffusion within reasonable limits. Philosophers and their disciples could think or say what they pleased in the privacy of their chambers, as long as they showed due respect for the opinions of the city. In his capacity as *pontifex maximus,* the learned Scaevola was in no position to do otherwise. It stretches the imagination to think that an impious Scaevola would have gone about flaunting his impiety.[26]

Neither can one leave it at saying that Roman religion lacked a set of formulated dogmas, that it was not a matter of theory but of practice, that the question of the truth about the gods could not arise within the framework of Roman life, and that to raise doubts about the genuineness of Scaevola's religious convictions is to pose the problem in terms in which it did not pose itself to Scaevola and his contemporaries. Ritual actions no doubt bulk large in ancient religion, and they certainly antedate the philosophical speculations that begin to emerge, under the influence of Greek thought, during the course of the second and first centuries B.C. This hardly entitles us to ignore the impact of the new doctrines on Roman society once they had become available. Religious practices are rooted in and supported by certain opinions about the gods whose credibility is necessarily undermined by the spread of philosophic skepticism. If the works of Varro and Cicero prove anything, it is that the issue could no longer be restricted to the level of practice alone. A more thorough defense of religion was called for, of the kind that Balbus and Cotta are forced to undertake in *De natura deorum.* The basic question concerns the nature of the arguments put forward in its behalf. In that respect, there is indeed something to be learned from the example of Cotta, whose eagerness to profess his loyalty to the ancestral gods is matched only by the cogency of his case against them. Granted, Cotta's attack is supposedly made for the sake of argument rather than out of personal conviction,[27] but one cannot remain blind to the element of truth that it might contain.[28]

That Cotta was aware of the precariousness of his situation is apparent from the fact that he twice reminds his hearers that he is "a Cotta and a pontiff,"[29] that is to say, a member of a distinguished Roman family and a religious leader, as if to signify that his ready disclaimer should perhaps be understood in that light. Under the circumstances, it comes as no surprise that he should cite Scaevola as one of his authorities and praise him for his "prudence" and his "moderation,"[30] two virtues which he himself ostensibly sought to emulate. The whole question would require a much more detailed analysis of the *De natura deorum* than any that can be contemplated here, but, pending the results of such an investigation, we have no guarantee that Cotta had found a new and better way to relieve the tension between his inner "aspirations" and his responsibilities as a citizen and a pontiff.[31] As matters stand, his position remains fraught with a good deal of obscurity. Both he and Scaevola could have been sincere, but all the evidence does not point in one direction.

Even if one assumes, be it only for purposes of discussion, that Scaevola was not always completely candid in his public utterances, one wonders whether his behavior can fittingly be described as Machiavellian. Machiavelli appears to have been largely contemptuous of religion, although he had no qualms about using it for his own ends, and he abandons altogether the notion of the common good,[32] for which, to the best of our information, Scaevola exhibited a noble regard. That being the case, Scaevola's willingness to dissemble can scarcely be construed as a reflection on his moral character. The lies to which he became a party were not ordinary lies, perpetrated at the expense of others and for his own personal benefit. They were meant to serve the interests of the city and the well-being of its citizens.

In addition to stressing Scaevola's holiness and justice, Cicero tells us that he was "the best orator among lawyers and the best lawyer among orators."[33] The remark is clearly intended as a compliment, but its meaning hinges on a true appreciation of what Cicero took a good lawyer to be. Political lawyers speak on behalf of the city and are listened to insofar as they are believed to have its welfare at heart. They argue, not about the ends to which the city is dedicated, but about the means that are most conducive to those ends. Ideally, they must be well versed in all of the sciences, including the philosophic sciences;[34] but in pleading public causes they also have to be guided by considerations of prudence. By reason of their complexity, public affairs often defy rational analysis and can rarely be decided or persuasively argued on the basis of truth alone.[35] False but plausible arguments are therefore preferable to true but implausible ones, which is just a more polite way of saying that, whether he likes it or not, the orator must frequently resort to lies.[36] His conduct in such instances has nothing in common with the self-serving tactics advocated by Machiavelli. If anything, it constitutes an act of political wisdom. To impugn Scaevola's character on the ground that he willfully acquiesced in the deception of lesser minds is to obliterate the distinction between an everyday understanding of justice and the higher sense of justice that animates the true statesman. It bears mentioning that Augustine himself does not quarrel with Scaevola's intentions. He merely deplores the fact that he and so many of his fellow countrymen should have been placed in a situation that would still be hopeless were it not for the advent of Christianity and the final revelation of the one true God.

There remains the problem of the interconnection of the three theologies, which is presumed to be the point on which Varro displays the greatest originality and on which, we are told, his thought differs most conspicuously from that of Scaevola. The fact of the matter, however, is that, here as elsewhere, the texts carry no trace of a profound disagreement between the two authors. As Augustine observes on several occasions, Varro was writing, not as the founder of a new polity, but as the reformer of an ancient and well established polity.[37] He had his thoughts about what could be attempted under ideal conditions[38] and, like other philosophers, he questioned the validity of all anthropomorphic representations of the gods;[39] but he was also aware of the nature of the realities with which reformers have to contend. Had he been free to do as he pleased, he probably would have done away with the old religion altogether, but such a drastic step was sure to be resisted by those who remained attached to it or had a vested interest in it. The only practical alternative was to seek some form of accommodation with it.[40] This explains, among other things, why he was obliged to devote greater attention to poetic theology than would otherwise have been necessary. Whatever the origins of a particular religion may be, poets have an important part to play in its propagation. They function both as the unacknowledged legislators of the nation and as instruments used by actual legislators in establishing or perpetuating its religious traditions.[41] It is therefore not surprising that sizable portions of poetic theology should eventually find their way into the public cult. To that extent at least, the line of demarcation between it and civil theology is bound to remain blurred.[42] For all that, poetic theology has no official standing of its own. It lacks the authority of civil theology and is subject to whatever control the rulers, who have the final say in the matter, may wish to exercise over it.[43]

Similar considerations apply to the relation between civil theology and natural theology. Given the need for a reform of Roman religion, there was nothing to prevent Varro from trying to purge it of some of its less desirable features. We know from Augustine that his own account of the gods was selective and left out much that was no longer judged advantageous or credible.[44] This is not to say that civil theology can never coincide with natural theology, but only that, to the degree to which it draws nearer to it, it becomes less vulnerable to the attacks that reason is able to mount against it. Even in its perfected state, it still presents itself as a compromise between the theology of the philosophers, which demands too much of most people, and that of the poets, which demands too little of them.[45]

Varro did as much as he reasonably could and no more. He never doubted that the gods of the Roman pantheon were creations of the human mind and he intimated as much by the very structure of his treatise, in which the discussion of human things is made to precede that of divine things. If he had thought otherwise, he would have reversed the order and given priority to divine things, for one speaks first of the painter or the architect and only afterwards of the picture or the building.[46]

This and nothing else is the secret of his book.[47] He knew full well that, since the gods did not exist, human beings could not be descended from them, but he also realized that most people would think more highly of themselves and aspire to greater deeds if they cherished the belief in their own divine descent.[48] Therein lies the reason for which Augustine chose to classify him among those who defended the gods, not on account of this life, but on account of virtue or the life after death.[49] In short, his concerns were those of a public-spirited writer who knows that what is best for him is not necessarily what is best for everyone else and who seeks to preserve the perspective of the dutiful citizen even as he himself transcends it.[50] The reform that he projected defines accurately the possibilities as well as the limits of the political activity of the philosopher.

Except for the hypothetical reconstructions of modern scholarship, little is known of Varro's proximate sources,[51] but to all intents and purposes his program parallels closely that of the Athenian stranger in Plato's *Laws,* whose overall aim is to teach, not how one "founds" a new city in speech, as Socrates had done in the *Republic,*[52] but how one goes about improving an ancient and eminently respectable, though possibly decaying, regime. It is not without interest that the stranger's conversation is carried on with two elderly statesmen, one a Cretan and the other a Spartan, both of whom are convinced of the superiority of their allegedly god-given codes of laws and look askance at any hint that they might leave something to be desired. The problem to which the dialogue points from the beginning is that of overcoming their resistance and gradually opening them up to the possibility of change.[53] Significantly, the proposals that are about to be made are far less radical than the ones set forth in the *Republic.* They fail to include the community of wives, children and property,[54] the rule of the philosopher-king,[55] the expulsion of poets,[56] the rustication of all but the youngest members of the society,[57] and a number of other far-reaching innovations, which, we now discover, could never be implemented save among "gods or children of the gods"[58]—that is, among people to whom the attachments stemming from the body and the prospect of individual death are of no concern. The relative merit of the new proposals is that they take prevailing opinion into account and are generally content to suggest ways in which the old codes could be revised without prejudice to the authority they already enjoy.

As might have been anticipated, much of the argument centers on the role of the gods in human life and on the roots of man's religious impulse. Civil society cannot dispense with the belief in solicitous gods who lend significance to the ephemeral lives of its citizens and support the view that the just life is also the most pleasant life.[59] Most human beings find it difficult to sacrifice themselves for a cause that promises them nothing in return. They are more apt to love justice if they stand to benefit by it and to love their own country if it can claim the favor of its gods.[60] The only question has to do with the kind of gods in which they should believe. In the best instance, these ought not to be cruel or punitive gods, constantly warring against one another and hostile to human beings, but harmonious and benevolent gods, capable of providing the model of a life that more nearly approximates the life of reason.[61] On the other hand, if only that virtue which is founded on knowledge merits the name of true virtue, the city as a whole can never be expected to possess more than an "image" of it.[62] Few people live mainly for the sake of the truth, and the many who are unable or unwilling to do so have more to lose than to gain by being exposed to a philosophic education that explains all things in terms of "divine necessities" rather than of "divine will" or intention.[63] For this reason if for no other, lies will always be necessary; but the wise legislator will at least see to it that they be of a nobler and more beneficial sort.[64] Assuming the impossibility of universal or widespread enlightenment, no other decent course of action could seriously be entertained.

One gathers from Augustine's frequent remarks that this was also the rationale behind Varro's proposed reform. Whether Scaevola had a similar program in mind remains unclear for lack of more solid information. Scaevola, after all, was not a philosopher, although he does not appear to have been untouched by philosophical ideas. But there are no signs to indicate that he would have objected to the views of his younger contemporary.

The object of the first five books of the *City of God* was to refute the old but newly refurbished claim that Rome owed its enlargement to the protection of its gods and that its present weakness, dramatically attested to by the humiliation that it had lately suffered at the hands of Alaric and his Goths, was a manifest consequence of their abandonment in favor of Christianity.[65] One way to lay the argument to rest was to show that the evils for which Christians were being blamed antedated the rise of the new faith and, hence, could not have originated with it. At hardly any moment in its long history had Rome been free of war and rid of the threat that it posed to its security. The rebuttal was not foolproof, however, for it overlooked the fact that, in spite of everything, pagan Rome had not only thrived but had managed to reach the pinnacle of worldly power. Convincing as it may have sounded to the "unlearned rabble" or the "silly populace"[66] whose support was courted by both sides, it did nothing to assuage the fears engendered in certain quarters by the rapid growth of a peace-loving religion and its recent proclamation as the official cult of a nation that had formerly been "dedicated to Mars."[67] A new tack was needed, which would bring to light both the true cause of Rome's erstwhile prosperity and the absurdity of the claim that the traditional gods had anything to do with it.

To clinch his argument, Augustine had only to point out that the pagan intelligentsia itself had long since ceased to take the existence of these gods seriously, even though it continued to uphold their cult on the theory that any substantial departure from the time-hallowed customs of the city was bound to have an adverse effect on the patriotism of its citizens.[68] The manoeuvre was a clever one, based as it was on a principle whose force even his adversaries were compelled to recognize. If not only the philosophers but the pontiffs themselves could preserve or restore Roman paganism only at the expense of a blatant falsehood, how much more ready should they be to accept a religion that was both true and edifying![69] Lies cannot be maintained indefinitely. There are forces at work within society itself which, as time goes on, necessitate the abolition of polytheism and its replacement by a rationally defensible monotheistic creed.

What is striking, however, is that, even as he pokes fun at the pagan gods in general, Augustine is careful to avoid any direct assault on the last remnants of the old civil religion. It has often been remarked that his handling of this matter is hopelessly anachronistic, that it focuses on a host of picturesque but obsolete deities which it paradoxically restores to a kind of shadowy existence, that with rare exceptions his account is devoid of contemporary allusions, and that we learn next to nothing about living paganism from the pages of his book.[70] Scholars have sometimes been tempted to explain this anomaly by observing that most of Augustine's data is borrowed from Varro, whose work does not appear to have been a canon on the subject of religion.[71] But this still leaves us with the question of why Augustine should have chosen to follow Varro in the first place.

One possible answer to this intriguing question is that the approach adopted in the *City of God* was dictated in large measure by the conservative mood of the early fifth century; in which case Augustine's antiquarianism would not be his own, but that of his educated contemporaries who, in the face of the impending crisis, had themselves become "fanatical antiquarians" seeking to "invest their religion in the distant past" and preferring "any form of religion and philosophy that could boast a *litterata vetustas.*"[72] Outmoded as it may seem to us, his critique of the old gods has a sharp air of timeliness about it. Augustine was obviously not writing to please modern scholars, who tend to exhibit a livelier interest in such novel forms of religious sensibility as may have been derived from the mystery cults, Oriental religion, and Mithraism. Circumstances demanded rather that he try to "intercept" the pagans with whom he was doing battle in what had proved to be their last retreat. Admittedly, the paganism that he set out to demolish existed mainly in books, but if he looked for it there, it is because he had guessed that "the best way to reach these late pagans was through their libraries." Only by means of this otherwise baffling return to the remote past was he able to uncover the tainted origins of the ancestral cults and expose the massive "whitewash" of which they had been the object over the centuries. Viewed in this light, his attitude is not at all that of a conservative but that of "a true radical, faced with the myths of conservatism."

Even this may not tell the whole story, however. One does well to remember, first of all, that the burden of the whole first part of the *City of God* was to dismiss the view that Rome was beholden to its gods for the successes that it had achieved in former days. This alone might be thought to justify the rather one-sided emphasis on past rather than present religious practice. More importantly, we have no assurance that the quaint deities which Augustine dredges up with Varro's help and on whose names he sometimes puns shamelessly,[74] were even remembered, let alone revered, by the pagans themselves. By reverting to a book that appears to have been mostly ignored at the time,[75] Augustine was hardly meeting head-on the major concerns of his more thoughtful opponents. Besides, earlier apologists, Tertullian and Arnobius among them, had ridiculed some of the same gods in roughly the same way and for the same broad reasons.[76] One would then have to suppose that the oblivion into which these gods had lapsed was a fairly recent phenomenon, or else that the conservative trend which is said to be characteristic of the first decades of the fifth century had already set in long before that time.[77] As for the neglect of the mystery cults, historical scholarship has not yet turned up many documents to prove that they were sufficiently widespread or of sufficient public interest to rivet Augustine's attention.[78]

All of this leads to the suspicion that his seemingly odd procedure was inspired by a different and perhaps slightly more political set of motives. Augustine could simply have discerned in Varro's forgotten classic the most complete and most searching analysis of Roman religion ever produced by a Latin writer, along with a ready-made critique of that religion which could be exploited for a new and higher purpose. This much seems to be implied in the unusually lavish praise that he bestows upon its author and which would be out of place if it did not reflect a genuine admiration for his accomplishment. The actual matter of Varro's work was no longer up to date and may even have been outdated from the start,[79] but there is no reason to believe that in the interval the principles governing its treatment had shed any of their relevance.

At the same time, one wonders whether Augustine's keen sensitivity to the needs of the social life and his profound attachment to Rome, "wicked and dissolute as it was,"[80] were not such as to induce him to temper the radicalness of his own critique by couching it in terms that remain somewhat cautious. We have only a limited knowledge of the extent to which, at that relatively late date, paganism had maintained its hold on various segments of the population;[81] but that it was still a vital force in nearby circles is evidenced by the fact that some of Augustine's own friends, who had been catechumens for years, were reluctant to accept baptism for fear that its demands might conflict with the duties of citizenship.[82] To assail civil religion frontally would have been to rob the community of whatever benefit it could conceivably derive from it in an age of mounting political turmoil and instability. So long as Christianity had not yet succeeded in dislodging its antagonist from the hearts of all people, there was always the danger of adding to the confusion by creating a vacuum that no one was in a position to fill immediately.[83] Inbred habits and long custom change only with time and through a process of education that admits of no short cuts.[84] God himself had taken centuries to educate the human race. The more prudent solution, it seems, was to take issue with all archaic religion for the sake of demonstrating, if only by implication, the fundamental defect of contemporary pagan religion or, for that matter, of any form of civil religion.

It is thus fair to say that Augustine's treatment of political theology is itself political, combining as it does an unflinching commitment to the truth with a deep sympathy for the failings of ordinary human beings. As such, it bears a curious analogy to the one for which Varro had opted centuries earlier. Varro censured poetic theology openly and civil theology only indirectly by manifesting its subtle connection with poetic theology.[85] As a Christian, Augustine could not afford to be less concerned with the welfare of his fellow countrymen, including those whose religious opinions he did not share but which he was nevertheless careful not to offend any more than was necessary.[86] He obviously had no use for Varro's art of dissembling and he made it abundantly clear that lies of any kind, noble or otherwise, were not to be endorsed under any circumstances.[87] Still, he was not averse to passing some truths over in silence if there was any chance that their premature disclosure might work to the detriment of others.[88] His own strategy, whatever its merits, sheds light in retrospect on the ultimate reason for which Scaevola, Varro, Cicero, and Seneca, to list only those whom he himself mentions, were loath to condemn what they secretly repudiated and saw fit to comply with what they knew to be false.

NOTES

1. J. Pépin, *Mythe et allégorie: les origines grecques et les contestations judéo-chrétiennes*, Nouvelle édition, revue et augmentée (Paris: Etudes Augustiniennes, 1976), 12-28.

2. See the critical edition of Varro's fragments by B. Cardauns, *M. Terentius Varro, Antiquitates Rerum Diuinarum* (Mainz: Academie der Wissenschaften und der Literatur, 1976), 18 and 37, along with Cardauns's commentary, 141-142.

3. Scaevola's strictures, needless to say, are not original. They belong to an old tradition which dates back at least to Xenophanes and according to which the defects attributed to the gods in poetic literature fall under two headings: *uitia* and *miracula.* Cf. Cardauns, *M. Terentius Varro*, 142.

4. *Codex Iustinianus* VI.23.1.17.

5. Pépin, *Mythe et allégorie*, 281-282. Cf. *Mythe et allégorie*, 15, where Pépin finds independent support for his thesis in B. Cardauns, *Varros Logistoricus über die Götterverehrung (Curio de Cultu Deorum): Ausgabe und Erklärung der Fragmente* (Würzburg: K. Triltsch, 1960), 55.

6. G. Lieberg, *Die 'Theologia tripartita' in Forschung und Bezeugung*, in *Aufstieg und Niedergang der römischen Welt*, I: *Von den Anfängen Roms bis zum Ausgang der Republik*, 4, edited by H. Temporini (Berlin and New York: W. de Gruyter, 1973), 86. Lieberg's critique is aimed more directly at P. Boyancé, *Sur la théologie de Varron* in *Revue des études anciennes,* 57 (1955): 57-84 (later reprinted in his *Études sur la religion romaine* (Rome: Ecole francaise de Rome, 1972), 253-282, on which Pépin himself had drawn extensively.

7. Pépin, 15-16: "Je n'insisterai pas sur la faiblesse reconnue de l'argumentation *a silentio:* on n'a pas conservé des critiques théoriques adressées par Scaevola à la théologie des philosophes, donc il lui reconnaissait une vérité objective; cette conclusion revient exactement à la formule d'Augustin *falsa esse non putat*, dont on doit accorder au minimum qu'elle dépasse les prémisses (sans quoi elle ne pourrait être discutée); c'est un fait que l'on ne connaît l'attitude théologique de Scaevola que par le témoignage de Varron filtré par Augustin: on ne saurait garantir que toute donnée absente de ce document soit à exclure aussi de la réalité." Cf. ibid., 24.

8. Pépin, 16: " . . . dans la Rome républicaine, tous les choix religieux sont dictés par l'intérêt de l'État, que ne laisse aucune place aux préférences spéculatives; dès lors, en disant d'elle *non congruere civitatibus*, Scaevola flétrit la conception philosophique des dieux plus radicalement qu'il ne ferait en discutant le contenu."

9. H. Hagendahl, *Augustine and the Latin Classics*, II *Augustine's Attitude* (Göteborg: Universitet, 1967), 611.

10. Cicero, *Pro sexto Roscio amerino* 12.33: "Q. Scaevola vir sanctissimus atque ornatissimus nostrae civitatis . . . pro dignitate ne laudare quidem quisquam satis commode posset;" *Laelius*, I.I: "me ad pontificem Scaevolam contuli, quem unum

nostrae civitatis et ingenio et iustitia praestantissimum audeo dicere." Cf. *Val. Mas.*, VIII.15. 6 and IX.11.2.

11. *De civitate Dei* (*City of God*) III.28. As far as I know, this is the only other mention of Scaevola in Augustine's works. See also Cicero, *De natura Deorum* III.32. 80.

12. Pépin, 14: "Si les mots d'Augustin *nam falsa esse non putat* dessinent de Scaevola une psychologie alambiquée, ce qui suit attente réellement à sa moralité: *Expedire igitur existimat falli in religione civitates.* C'est une accusation de tromperie caractérisée, que n'excuse pas la considération d'on ne sait encore quelle utilité. Accusation étonnante, s'agissant d'un personnage dont les contemporains, notamment Cicéron qui fut son élève, s'entendent à célébrer la haute conscience . . . . "

13. Cf. Cicero *De nat. Deor.* III.2.6; 4.9-10.

14. Pépin, 17-18.

15. Pépin, 21: "Scaevola ne proclame pas, comme le fera le Cotta de Cicéron, son attachement aux dieux civils; mais on doit l'inférer quand on voit le pontife objecter à la théologie des philosophes; *non congruere civitatibus.*"

16. Cf. *De civ. Dei* IV.31.2; VI.7.1.

17. *De civ. Dei* VI.5.2: "Nihil in hoc gernere culpavit quod physicon vocant et ad philosophos pertinet, tantum quod eorum inter se controversias commemoravit, per quos facta est dissidentium multitudo sectarum."

18. Cf. Pépin, 21-2.

19. *De civ. Dei* VI.5.2.

20. *De civ. Dei* VI.5.2: "Removit tamen hoc genus *a foro, id est a populis;* scholis vero et parietibus clausit."

21. Pépin, 23.

22. Cf. *De civ. Dei* VI.5.3: "Quis non videat, cui palmam dederit? Utique secundae, quam supra dixit esse philosophorum." Also, *De civ. Dei* VII.5, *ca. fin.*

23. Cf. *De civ Dei* IV.32; VI.6.3.

24. Pépin, 23-28, with reference to the argument made by Augustine along these or similar lines in *De civ. Dei* VI.5 and VII.5.

25. Cf. *De civ. Dei* VI.5.3: "I see indeed why it (the civil kind) should be distinguished from the mythical, namely, because the latter is false, because it is base, because it is unworthy. But to wish to distinguish the natural from the civil, what else is that but to confess that the civil itself is erroneous (*mendosum*)? Now if one of them is natural, what fault has it that it should be excluded? And if the one that is called civil be not natural, what merit has it that it should be admitted?"

26. To bolster his point, Pépin alludes to the destruction of Porphyry's *Contra Christianos* by Constantine and his followers and observes that no one would dream of adding, "for they did not hold (Porphyry's theses) to be false," 14. The analogy does little to clarify the issue, however, especially since Constantine's motives have long been the subject of a heated and still unresolved debate among historians.

27. *De natura deorum* III.1.1 and 4: "What I have in mind is not so much to refute his (Balbus's) speech as to ask for an explanation of the points that I could not

quite understand."

28. Cotta's speech is a point by point rebuttal of Balbus, who had argued a) that the gods exist, b) that the world is rational, c) that it is ruled by the gods, and d) that these gods care for human beings. The danger implied in this habit of speaking by way of pretence is emphasized by Balbus in II.67.168: "For it is a wicked and impious habit to argue against the gods, whether it be done from conviction or only in pretence."

29. *De nat. deor.* III.2.5 and 6. Cotta had previously been reminded of the same fact by Balbus, *De nat. deor.* II.67.168: "For your part, Cotta, would you but listen to me, you would plead the same cause and reflect that you are a leading citizen and a pontiff." Assuming that Cotta had internally dissociated himself from Roman religion, it is unlikely that he would have publicly owned as much. See his remark about the risks involved in any open disavowal of the gods, ibid., III.1.3: "I think that your master Epicurus does not put up a very strong fight on the question of the immortal gods; he only does not venture to deny their existence so as to avoid any antagonism (*invidia*) or any crime (*crimen*)." The self-protection of the speaker or the writer is alluded to by Augustine, *De civ. Dei* VI.5.1 and 8.2, in connection with Varro.

30. *De nat. deor.* III.32.80.

31. Cf. Pépin, 18.

32. See, for example, *The Prince*, ch. 18: "And it must be understood that a prince, and especially a new prince, cannot observe all those things which are considered good in men, being often obliged, in order to maintain the state, to act against faith, against charity, against humanity, and against religion." Unlike its innumerable predecessors, Machiavelli's book does not once mention the common good. Its central teaching, as stated in the famous chapter 15, is that a prince must rather learn "how *not* to be good, and to use this knowledge and not use it according to the necessity of the case." On the novelty of Machiavelli's religious and moral views, see L. Strauss, *Thoughts on Machiavelli* (Glencoe: The Free Press, 1958), 174-299.

33. *De oratore* (*On Oratory*) I.39.180: "Q. Scaevola . . ., iuris peritorum eloquentissimus, eloquentium iuris peritissimus."

34. Cf. *Orator ad M. Brutus*, 14ff.; *De orat.* I.48.60; II.82.337.

35. *Orator*, 15; *De Orat.* II.44.185ff. and 49.201ff.; *Tuscalanae disputatones* (*Tuscalan Disputations*) IV.55.

36. On persuasion as the goal of rhetoric, cf. *Orator* 128; *De orat.* I.14.60; II. 53.214; *Brutus* or *De claris oratoribus* 279. Also *De orat.* II.77.310-311, where Cicero explains that the orator must hide what he is doing from his audience.

37. *De civ. Dei* IV.31.1: "What says Varro himself, whom we grieve to have found, albeit not by his own judgment, placing the scenic plays among things divine? When in many passages he exhorts, like a religious man, to the worship of the gods, does he not admit that it is not in accordance with his own judgment that he follows the things which he relates as having been instituted by Rome? Accordingly, he does

not hesitate to confess that, if he had been founding that city anew, he would have preferred to designate the gods and their names on the basis of a rule drawn from nature. But since he belonged to a nation that was already ancient, he was forced by his own admission to retain the old names and surnames as they had been handed down, his purpose being to write about them and scrutinize them in such a way that the people would be inclined to worship them rather than despise them." *De civ. Dei* VI.4.2: "Had Varro been founding a new city himself he would have written according to the rule of nature; but as he was dealing with an old one, he had no choice but to follow its traditions."

38. Cf. *De civ. Dei* VI.6.2, where Augustine accounts for some of Varro's apparent contradictions by saying that in one place Varro was speaking of what ought to be done, and in another only of what could be done: "Hic enim dixit quid fieri debeat, ibi quid fiat."

39. Cf. *De civ. Dei* IV.9; IV.31.2; VI.7.1 and 8.2; VII.5. On the Stoic opposition to these anthropomorphic representations, cf. P. Boyance, "Sur la théologie de Varron," 66.

40. Cf. *De civ. Dei* IV.29: "The more intelligent and graver Romans saw these things but were powerless against the customs of a city that was bound to observe the rites of the demons." *De civ. Dei* VI.6.1: "O Marcus Varro, you who are the most acute and without any doubt the most learned of men, but still a man . . . you are afraid to offend the most corrupt opinions and customs of the populace in their public cult, though you yourself, having considered them on all sides, perceive them to be repugnant to the nature of the gods." Also IV.9; IV.31.2; VI.2; VII.17 *et passim*.

41. See esp. *De civ. Dei* II.14, where Plato, "that demigod" (*semideus*), is commended for having been more consistent than the Romans in calling for the banishment of all poets.

42. *De civ. Dei* VI.6.3: "Civil theology is therefore not quite disjunct from that of the poets—*non ergo nulla cum poetis*." Cf. VI.8.2: "for the fabulous and the civil are both fabulous and both civil." The theatre is itself an institution of civil society; it only thrives within it and has no real existence apart from it; *De civ. Dei* VI.5.3.

43. See the allusions to the supervisory power of the Senate in such matters, *De civ. Dei* II.5 and VI.9.1.

44. *De civ. Dei* IV.31.1: "Quibus verbis homo acutissimus satis indicat non se aperire omnia, quae non sibi tantum contemptui essent, sed etiam ipsi vulgo despicienda viderentur, nisi tacerentur."

45. Ibid., VI.6.3: "Ait enim ea, quae scribunt poetae, minus esse quam ut populi sequi debeant; quae autem philosophi, plus quam ut ea vulgus scrutari expediat." Cf. *Contra Faustum Manichaeum* XIII.15 and XX.9.

46. *De civ. Dei* VI.4.2: "For he (Varro) wrote the books concerning human things, not with reference to the whole world, but to Rome; which books, he said, had been properly placed in the order of writing before the books on divine things, like the painter before the painted tablet or the mason before the building, thus most openly confessing that, as a picture or a structure, even these divine things were

instituted by men."

47. Cf. *De civ. Dei* VI.8.2.

48. *De civ Dei* III.4: "For even Varro, a very learned heathen, all but admits that these stories are false though he does not boldly and confidently say so. But he maintains it is useful for cities that brave men believe, though falsely, that they are descended from the gods, so that in this manner the human spirit, cherishing the belief in its divine origin, will both more boldly venture into great enterprises, and will carry them out more energetically, and will therefore by its very confidence secure more abundant success."

49. Cf. *De civ. Dei* VI.I.I; *Retractiones* (*Retractions*) II.43.1.

50. Varro claimed to be writing, not for himself, but for the benefit of others; *De civ. Dei* VI.I.2. His fear was that religion, which is essential to the city, was in danger of perishing from sheer neglect; *De civ Dei* VI.2.

51. On the state of the question, see Pépin, *Mythe et allégorie* 28-32 and 298-307.

52. Cf. Plato, *Republic* III.403b; IV.427c-d; V.472d-e; V.592b, and, on the greater freedom that "founders" enjoy in dealing with these matters, *Republic* II.379a: "And I said, 'Adeimantus, you and I aren't poets right now but founders of a city. It's appropriate for founders to know the models according to which the poets must tell their tales. If what the poets produce goes counter to these models, founders must not give way; however, they must not themselves make up tales,'" *The Republic of Plato*, trans. A. Bloom (New York and London: Basic Books, 1968), 56.

53. See in particular the strange discussion concerning the use of wine in *Laws*, I.637aff. and the commentary on that passage by L. Strauss, *What is Political Philosophy?* (Glencoe: Free Press, 1959), 29-34. Also, by the same author, *The Argument and the Action of Plato's Laws* (Chicago and London: University of Chicago Press, 1975), 3-21, and, for a consonant appraisal, T. L. Pangle, *The Laws of Plato*, translated with notes and an interpretive essay (New York: Basic Books, 1980), 379-96.

54. Cf. *Republic* V.457d-462e.

55. *Republic* V.473c-e.

56. *Republic* III.398a-b; X.606e-607d.

57. *Republic* VII.541a.

58. *Laws* V.739d. Plato has just made it clear that, in practice, one can never hope to obtain more than a second-best regime; cf. 739a-c. The reference to the community of wives and children in 739c appears to be the only explicit reference to the *Republic* in all of the *Laws*.

59. E.g., *Laws* II.664b-c.

60. Cf. *Laws* III.691d; 692b; 699c.

61. *Laws* V.716a-717b, and, on the question of the concordant and discordant gods, Augustine, *De civ. Dei* VI.9.2.

62. Cf. *Laws* II.668b, along with *Republic* VI.500d.

63. *Laws* VII.818a-d.

64. *Laws* II.663d-e: "*Athenian*: Even if what the argument has now established were not the case, could a lawgiver of any worth ever tell a lie more profitable than this (if, that is, he ever has the daring to lie to the young for the sake of a good cause), or more effective in making everybody do all the just things willingly and not out of compulsion?—*Kleinias*: Truth is a noble and lasting thing, but it is likely that it's not easy to persuade people of it." It should be noted that even Socrates's perfect city in speech rests on a twofold lie: its citizens must be persuaded that they are begotten of the land they inhabit and hence are all brothers, and second, that the position which they occupy within the society is determined by their natural dispositions; *Republic* III.414b, 415c. Cf. ibid., V.459c: "It is likely that our rulers will have to use a throng of lies and deceptions for the benefit of the ruled. And, of course, we said that everything of this sort is useful as a form of remedy."

65. *De civ. Dei* IV.3.

66. *De civ. Dei* IV.I; VI.I.4.

67. *De civ. Dei* IV.29.

68. Cf. *De civ. Dei* II.3; IV.I; VI, Praef. Also Cicero, *De natura deorum* I.1.4: "In all probability the disappearance of piety toward the gods will entail the disappearance of loyalty and the bond of unity among human beings as well, and of justice itself, the queen of all the virtues." Cf. *De nat. Deor.* III.2.5: "I have always thought that none of these departments of religion was to be despised, and I have held the conviction that Romulus by his auspices and Numa by his establishment of our ritual had laid the foundations of our city, which assuredly could never have been as great as it is had not the fullest measure of divine favor been obtained for it."

69. *De civ. Dei* IV.22.

70. Cf. Hagendahl, *Latin Classics*, 607-8, with further references to N. D. Madden, *The Pagan Divinities and Their Worship as Depicted in the Works of St. Augustine Exclusive of the City of God* (Washington, D.C.: The Catholic University of America Press, 1930), 6; H. Lindemann, *Die Sondergötter in der Apologetik der Civitas Dei Augustins*, Diss. (München: A. Kuspert, 1930), 20, 70ff., and E. Bickel's review of Lindemann's work in *Gnomnon* 14 (1938): 264-66. See also F. Cumont, *Les religions orientales dans le paganisme romain* (Paris: Leroux, 1929), 186: "A la vérité, si l'on se bornait a lire certains écrivains qui ont combattu l'idolâtrie à cette époque, on serait tenté de croire que rien n'était changé dans la foi nationale des Romains. Ainsi saint Augustin, dans la *Cité de Dieu,* se moque agréablement de la multitude des dieux italiques qui présidaient aux actes les plus mesquins de l'existence. Mais ces déités futiles et falotes des vieilles litanies pontificales ne vivaient plus que dans les livres des antiquaires et, de fait, la source du polémiste chrétien est ici Varron . . . L'apologétique, on l'a fréquemment fait observer, a peine à suivre les progrès des doctrines qu'elle combat, et souvent ses coups n'atteignent plus que des morts."

71. Hagendahl, *Latin Classics*, 608.

72. P. Brown, *Augustine of Hippo: a Biography* (Berkeley and Los Angeles: University of California Press, 1967), 305.

73. Brown, ibid.

74. See, for example, the almost scurrilous remarks about Pertunda in *De civ. Dei* VI.9.3.

75. For an overall assessment of the *Nachleben* of Varro's *Antiquitates*, see B. Cardauns, *M. Terentius Varro*, 125-29. Servius and Nonius appear to be the only other Latin writers of late antiquity to have had any firsthand knowledge of the work.

76. E.g., Tertullian, *Ad nationes* II.11; Arnobius, *Adversus nationes* III.23-26; IV.1-7.

77. See the remarks on this subject by P. Brown, *Religion and Society in the Age of Augustine* (New York and London: Harper and Row, 1972), 80 and 87-88, and by N. H. Baynes, *Byzantine Studies and Other Essays* (London: University of London, Athlone Press, 1955), 361-66.

78. Cf. B. Cardauns, *M. Terrentius Varro*, 129.

79. Cf. Hagendahl, *Latin Classics*, 608, who suggests that Varro's work "represented a learned reconstruction of early Roman religion rather than gave a true picture of conditions in Varro's own age."

80. *De civ. Dei* II.19. On Augustine's complex attitude toward Rome, cf. J. Straub, Augustines Sorge um die '*regeneratio imperii*': '*das imperium Romanum*' als '*civitas terrena*,' in *Historisches Jahrbuch* 73 (1954): 36-60; R. A. Markus, *Saeculum: History and Society in the Theology of St. Augustine* (Cambridge: Cambridge University Press, 1970), 45-71. Augustine's "patriotism" is denied by F. G. Maier, *Augustin und das antike Rom* (Stuttgart: W. Kohlhammer, 1955). For a survey of the literature on the subject, cf. K. Thraede's learned but somewhat obscure account, *Das antike Rom* in *Augustins De Ciuitate Dei: Recht und Grenzen eines verjährten Themas*, in *Jahrbuch für Antike und Christentum* 20 (1977): 90-145.

81. On the intellectual and religious opposition to Christianity in various parts of the Empire from the third century onward, cf. J. Geffcken's pioneering work, first published in 1920 and now translated into English, with updated notes and bibliographic references, by S. MacCormack under the title, *The Last Days of Greco-Roman Paganism* (Amsterdam and New York: North Holland Pub. Co., 1978). Geffcken's study offers a rather more balanced view of the triumph of the Christian faith than the one which G. Boissier had previously sought to accredit. "The great event of the fourth century," writes Boissier, "is the *definitive* victory of Christianity," *La fin du paganisme*, vol. 2 (Paris: Hachette, 1903), 427 (my emphasis).

82. See esp. *Epistula (Letter)* 151.14: "Since you wish to hear the truth, there is indeed one thing in you which distresses me exceedingly: it is that, although qualified by age as well as by life and character to do otherwise, you still prefer to remain a catechumen, as if it were not possible for believers to administer the affairs of the commonwealth that much better and more faithfully as they are better and more faithful Christians." *Epist.* 136.2 (Marcellinus to Augustine): "Another one of Volusianus's objections is that what Christianity enjoins and teaches is in no way consistent with the way of life of the commonwealth . . . these difficulties he thinks, may be added to his earlier question; for, though he is silent on this point, it is

manifest that the commonwealth has fallen on evil days under the rule of emperors who are dedicated for the most part to the Christian religion." Augustine's response to this objection is found in *Epist.* 138.2.9.

83. Cf. Geffcken, *The Last Days of Greco-Roman Paganism*, 226: "Seen in another way, Christianity, still a young religion, was not yet able to provide the strong support which during times of grave external danger, people needed; in their wretchedness men of all ranks, both high and low, longed for the old ways in matters of religion."

84. On the role and importance of custom in human affairs, see, for example *Confessiones* (*Confessions*) 111.8.15; *De civ. Dei* XV.16.

85. *De civ. Dei* VI.8.2.

86 He could be harsh when he wanted to, especially if he detected a note of bad faith in his correspondent; witness his reply to the pagan, Maximus of Madaura, *Epist.* 17.

87. He returned to the subject with astonishing frequency, not only in the *De mendacio* (*On Lying*) and the *Contra mendacium* (*Against Lying*) but in numerous other places as well. For the reasons underlying his uncompromising stance on lies, see E. L. Fortin, "Augustine and the Problem of Christian Rhetoric" in E. L. Fortin, *The Birth of Philosophic Christianity: Studies in Early Christian and Medieval Thought*, edited by J. Brian Benestad (Lanham, MD: Rowman and Littlefield, 1996), 79-93.

88. *Contra mend.* X.23: "To hide the truth is not the same thing as to utter a lie. Every liar writes to conceal the truth, but not everyone who conceals the truth is a liar; for we often conceal the truth not only by lying but by remaining silent . . . It is therefore permissible for a speaker and an exponent or preacher of eternal truths, or even for someone who discusses or pronounces upon temporal matters pertaining to the edification of religion and piety, to conceal at an opportune moment anything that may seem advisable to conceal; but it is never permissible to lie and hence to conceal by means of lies." Cf. *De mend.* X.17.

5

AUGUSTINE, SPINOZA, AND THE HERMENEUTICAL PROBLEM

Any serious discussion of the so-called theologico-political problem must sooner or later come to grips with the question of scriptural interpretation in which that problem is rooted. It is no accident that Spinoza, in the opinion of many the most profound theorist of modern liberalism, is famous among other things for his account of the way one ought to read the Bible. The concern with this subject was not his alone; it was shared by many seventeenth-century thinkers—Bacon, Hobbes, Locke, and Bossuet, to name only a few—who devote a considerable amount of time to it in their works.

THE THEOLOGICO-POLITICAL PROBLEM

Deriving a political program from the New Testament or justifying such a program on the basis of its teaching can be a tricky matter. This much we know from the fact that over the centuries the Christian Scriptures have been called upon to legitimate the most diverse regimes, from the sacred kingship of the Byzantine Empire, to the papal theocracy of the Middle Ages, to modern liberal democracy and such latter-day alternatives to it as Christian Marxism and liberation theology. This tendency to uncover or, if need be, invent religious warrants for any regime that one may wish to accredit is neither new nor surprising, and it is certainly not peculiar to societies dominated by revealed religion. If anything, it would appear to be as old as the political life itself.

Regimes and their laws command general respect to the extent to which they can claim a divine origin or at least divine approval, and for good reason. None of these regimes is ever perfectly just and many if not most of them fail to live up even to elementary standards of justice or decency. Although aimed in principle at procuring the common welfare, their laws tend to favor the interests of those who enact them. Equals are habitually treated as unequals and unequals as equals. This means that one segment of the population ends up by having to sacrifice itself for the other, bearing a larger share of the common burdens and reaping a smaller share of the common rewards. No wonder the beneficiaries of such arrangements are eager to defend them as mandated by God or the gods. This is true to some degree even of modern liberal democracy, purportedly the least religious and most rational of the legitimate regimes; for otherwise one fails to see why so many of its advocates would want to claim a biblical and Christian pedigree for it.

This brings us at once to what I consider to be the heart of the theologico-political problem, which is that any attempt to proclaim the sacred or divinely ordained character of the law poses a latent threat to exercise of political rule. Since divine authority is generally regarded as superior to, and more to be feared than, human authority, there is nothing to prevent subjects from appealing to it against the sovereign himself. Antigone does it in the play that bears her name, and real human beings —the early Christian martyrs, the medieval theocrats, the Protestant reformers, and countless others—have done it over and over again across the centuries. In the words of Acts 5:29, "We must obey God rather than men." All of this is to say that the means by which the unity of society and obedience to its laws are best secured can just as easily transform itself into an instrument of active or passive resistance to those laws.

There is, unfortunately, no convenient way out of the dilemma. The simplest solution, it seems, would be to roll religious and political rule into one by investing the sovereign with the power to interpret the scriptures and dictate religious practice; but while such a solution may have worked reasonably well when all religion was civil religion, it became less practicable once Christianity, an ecumenical or transnational religion presided over by an independent priesthood, had succeeded in implanting itself. This alone was enough to set the western world apart from classical paganism and force an overall reconsideration of the matter.

On all pertinent issues the Bible spoke with a firmness that far exceeded that of the religious texts of pre-Christian antiquity, and it already

had its official spokesmen, who held a virtual monopoly on its interpretation. Besides, everybody knew the Bible by heart. Tampering with
the letter of text was out of the question if only because the minutest
change would have been spotted and, if need be, denounced. It makes no
difference that modern critical editions of the Bible list no fewer than ten
thousand manuscript variants, for most of these were unknown at the time,
are minor for the most part, and rarely affect our understanding of its substance. In the *Advancement of Learning*, Bacon warns against the temp-
tation to alter old texts, especially when one is in the business of
reinterpreting them. He himself claims to have been "studious in keeping
the ancient terms" and goes so far as to rebuke Aristotle, not the most
adventuresome of writers, for taking too many liberties with these terms.
This, I take it, is Bacon's way of alerting us to the difference between the
situation created by the triumph of revealed religion and the one that had
prevailed up to that time. It is also true that the vast majority of people
instinctively resist change. Hence one should always begin by telling them
what they most want to hear, and what they most want to hear is what
they have been accustomed to hearing from their youth.[1] Spinoza is even
more emphatic. "No one," he says, "has ever been able to change the
meaning of a word in ordinary use . . . Such a procedure would be most
difficult; for whoever attempted to change the meaning of a word would
be compelled at the same time to explain all the authors who employed
it, each according to his temperament and intention, or else, with
consummate cunning, to falsify them."[2] I may be wrong, but I am not
aware of a single instance in which Spinoza, who usually quotes the Bible
in the original Hebrew or Greek, violates this rule.

THE SPINOZIST SOLUTION

For all that, the situation of the innovator was not without remedy.
Changing the words of Scripture without attracting attention was well-nigh
impossible, but, as Spinoza intimates, changing the meaning of its
sentences was definitely not impossible. Long experience had shown how
difficult it is to pin down the content of the sacred text. As Nietzsche
would later say, the trouble with the biblical God is that he cannot seem
to express himself clearly. That being the case, the same statement or set
of statements could be made to convey a fairly wide range of meanings.
Several methods were available for this purpose. By choosing one's texts
judiciously or by highlighting some while passing others over in silence,
one imparted a new twist to them. The practice was an old one, and in the
hands of a clever writer it led to interesting results. It was used to good
effect by Dante, who often reveals his intention by the manner in which
he quotes from the Scriptures. One of the literary devices employed in the

Purgatorio consists in pairing up a particular virtue with the corresponding beatitude from the Sermon on the Mount. Repentant sinners who were once guilty of, say, anger are told that the peacemakers are the ones who will be called sons of God. Those guilty of pride learn that the kingdom of heaven belongs to the humble or the poor in spirit; and so on. What the author is driving at becomes clear when one notices that two of the eight beatitudes have been tacitly omitted, the ones referring to the meek and the persecuted, whom Dante had no desire to emulate, even if that meant suppressing or distancing himself from an essential element of the New Testament message. Elsewhere in the *Comedy*, we hear only the second half of the opening verse of Psalm 32: "Blessed is he whose sins are covered." Without any fanfare, the first half of the verse, "Blessed is he whose iniquity is forgiven," has again been dropped—as if Dante, a sinner in the eyes of some people, was more eager to hide his sins than to obtain forgiveness for them.

The same kind of selectivity is at work in Spinoza, but with the intention of subverting rather than purifying the biblical tradition. Take, for example, Spinoza's often expressed interest in the miracle performed by Joshua, who is reported to have stopped the sun in its course so as to give the Israelites enough time to complete their rout of the Amorites (Jos. 10:12-14). Why the insistence on this miracle rather than on any number of others that could seemingly have done just as well? No reason is explicitly given, although one suspects that there was something about this one that made its choice particularly appropriate. In Scholastic theology, causing the sun to "stand still" and thus interfering with the course of the heavenly bodies was a miracle of the very first order, greater even than resurrection of a dead person, since it involved doing something of which nature was thought to be incapable under any circumstances; here was, so to speak, the supreme test case. If this event could be explained naturally, so could all the other supposedly miraculous events spoken of in the Bible, and Spinoza's case for the impossibility of miracles was thereby greatly strengthened.

The radicalness of Spinoza's approach comes out most forcefully in the famous chapter 7 of the *Theologico-Political Treatise*, which calls the truth of the Bible into question, albeit in ways that are calculated to spare as much as possible the sensibilities of those who still deferred to its authority. The argument in a nutshell is that the Bible as a whole, as distinguished from its individual components, is unintelligible, that there is no universally valid theoretical teaching to be extracted from it, and that one must read it, not as a divinely revealed text, but as one would read any other book, that is, in the light of such information as might be accessible to the unaided human reason. To say this is not to imply that its authors were madmen whose utterances are nothing but gibberish; it is to suggest that, contrary to popular belief, the Bible is not the work of a single divine author who uses human beings as mere instruments of the transmission of his message; that its various parts, written by different authors at different moments in history, do not cohere with one another; and, hence, that it fails to yield a consistent meaning. Its sole unity, and it is at best a dubious unity, is the one that was imposed on it by some later scribe (probably Ezra), who undertook a massive revision of the old texts during the years that followed the return of the exiles from Babylon.

Accordingly, anyone who wishes to make sense of the Bible has no choice but to look at each part separately, examine the condition of the manuscript or the printed text, verify its authenticity, restore the passage in question to what must have been its native context, determine the author's intention, and trace its subsequent evolution. This calls for an elaborate method of investigation the immediate object of which is to arrive at a better grasp of these various segments by piecing together the surviving clues to their original meaning. One needs such a method for the same reason that one needs a method to interpret nature: because the object is unexplainable in terms of a single principle or final cause and thus ultimately incomprehensible. By applying this method not only to the difficult passages of Scripture but across the board, one comes to see that contradictions of the Bible need not be imputed to the will of a mysterious or capricious God who likes to play hide and seek with his devotees; they have a natural explanation insofar as they can be shown to arise from the fact that the text is traceable to a multiplicity of authors whose conflicting views reflect the varying conditions of time and place in which they lived.

The long and the short of the story is that the Bible's only genuine or rationally defensible teaching is its moral teaching, which Spinoza reduces, first, to two virtues, justice and charity, and then to charity alone, understood in its most superficial sense as a virtue that bears no intrinsic relationship to any of the other moral virtues and has as its sole function to succor the needy and keep us from persecuting others. The lengthy argument to this effect[3] is designed to accomplish two things: (a) drive a wedge between philosophy and theology, thereby liberating the former from the tutelage of the latter, and (b) put an end to religious wars by convincing everybody that the only way to be a Christian is to subscribe to the theory and practice of universal toleration. This is a plausible if somewhat facile scriptural position. The message that finally comes across is that the truth of the biblical revelation—its *sensus plenior*, its "fuller meaning"—is modern liberal democracy, whose hallmark—freedom of thought, speech, and religion—is as much a religious obligation as it is a demand of reason. In simple terms, modern liberalism is nothing but a secularized version of biblical morality, or so Spinoza, the prototypical secularizer of the early modern period, would have us believe.

AUGUSTINE AND THE TRADITION OF
CHRISTIAN HERMENEUTICS

The true novelty of Spinoza's views comes out most clearly when one compares the *Theologico-Political Treatise* to the work against which it is implicitly directed, Augustine's treatise *On Christian Doctrine*, the only ancient work devoted in its entirety to the subject of biblical interpretation, with the possible exception of the *Rules* of Augustine's older contemporary, the dissident Donatist theologian Tyconius. The centrality of Augustine's treatise to the Christian tradition is attested to by the fact that it was the first book after the Bible to be printed from movable type when the modern press was invented in the fifteenth century.

In sharp contrast to Spinoza, Augustine starts from the premise that the Bible cannot be read like any other book. As a divinely inspired book, it must be read with the right dispositions, that is to say, piously or in a spirit of reverent submission to the word of God. The treatise begins with a synopsis of the "rule of faith" and the "rule of conduct" by which this reading is to be guided. The former includes such doctrines as those pertaining to the triune God and his attributes, Christ and his redemptive work, the Church as the body of Christ, and the last things or life after death. As for the rule of conduct, it is summed up in the dual precept of the love of God and neighbor, the alpha and the omega of the Scriptures. The whole of the Bible, we are told, is geared to the inculcation of this supreme commandment, so much so that anyone who has already grasped it can dispense with the sacred text altogether. How these dogmatic and moral truths are arrived at in the first place is a question that is not explicitly addressed. To that extent, the procedure is perfectly circular: one comes to an accurate understanding of the Bible by reading it in the light of principles that are themselves drawn from the Bible. Augustine, who occasionally hints at the problem, apparently saw no need to delve into it in a book written primarily for Christian preachers, who were presumed to be familiar with the teachings of the faith and wholly committed to them.

The second assumption, which follows logically upon the first and poses the same kind of logical problem, is that in principle, if not always in fact, the Bible is intelligible from beginning to end. For this reason, Augustine can dispense with an elaborate method of interpretation such as the one to which Spinoza will resort. To be sure, some parts of the text are obscure, but the obscurities are deliberate. God willed them as a means of arousing the curiosity of the reader and of keeping him humble. On this score, Augustine is in full agreement with Tyconius; but whereas Tyconius was confident that the application of his simple rules would dispose of all these obscurities, Augustine doubts that this will ever happen. The matter is of little practical consequence since Augustine takes it for granted that the clear teaching of the Bible cannot be contradicted by the teaching of obscure passages, whatever it may be, the reason being that a benevolent God would never deprive his faithful followers of the necessary aids to their salvation.

It should be obvious that on both counts, the divine authorship of the Bible and its fundamental intelligibility, Augustine and Spinoza are leagues apart. What needs to be added is that the distance between them is never greater than when they sound most alike. A notable case in point is the primacy accorded by both of them to charity, the premier Christian virtue. Augustine's charity bears only a distant relationship to the vague humanitarianism advocated by Spinoza. For one thing, it is inseparable from a panoply of other moral virtues, which it informs and carries to a new height of perfection. Far from being a purely natural sentiment, it is a gift of God, enjoining a way of life that befits a being created in the image of God and often prescribing activities that run counter to one's natural inclination—something that Spinoza dismisses as foolish. It is also more concerned with the proper order of the soul than with external actions. Nothing could take us further away from the notorious "soullessness" of Spinoza's philosophy.

Above all, Augustine never dreamed of invoking charity as an argument for this or that regime or political program. The Christian faith as he understood it—and he has the merit of being the first to see the problem in all its sharpness—is not only transnational but transpolitical or entirely beyond the realm of politics. As the title and the whole first book of the treatise *On Christian Doctrine* imply, Christianity is first and foremost a sacred "doctrine" or a set of beliefs. This, and not the Mosaic Law or any other law, is the fundamental Christian phenomenon and the ground of everything that pertains to the Christian life. Had Augustine been given the opportunity to read Spinoza, he would have had no choice but to reject out of hand the view that liberal democracy is either the perfection of the New Testament revelation, as Spinoza would have it, or its corruption, as many conservative religious thinkers are inclined to think. For Augustine, no direct line leads from the New Testament to any of the political arrangements by means of which human beings are wont to manage their temporal affairs. Nor, from what we know of his dealings with the heretics and schismatics of his day, would Augustine have had much patience with the view that universal toleration is a necessary derivative of Christian charity, however tolerant he himself may have been on occasion. All in all, it would be hard to find two authors whose ideological profiles have less in common.

TRADITION AND INNOVATION

There is, nevertheless, one crucial point in regard to which Spinoza remains deeply indebted to the tradition that he was determined to uproot. To repeat what was said earlier, the success of his project was contingent on his ability to develop what sounds like a traditional argument for a position that is anything but traditional. The situation was not without precedent, for there had been other moments in history when major changes had had to be justified on the ground of their continuity with what had gone before. Not the least significant of these moments is the one that witnessed the emergence of Christianity and its break with Judaism out of which it grew. Never had there been a greater need to stress not only the newness of the new but also its link with the old.

The example was set by the New Testament itself, which system-atically reinterprets the past in such a way as to give the impression that it does not teach anything the germs of which are not already present in God's revelation to the Jewish people. In accordance with the allegorical or topological method adumbrated by St. Paul, virtually all the characters and events mentioned in the Hebrew Scriptures came to be seen as prefig-urations of the realities of the new age. Everything was suddenly part of a divine pedagogy the object of which was to prepare mankind for the fullness of God's revelation. Christ, who embodies that revelation, was regularly depicted as the "antitype" of some earlier type or model. He was the new Moses, the new David, the new Solomon, the new Elijah, or the new Daniel, "fulfilling"—and thereby transforming—in his person the mission entrusted to the kings and prophets of old.

Even the expression chosen to designate the Christian dispensation and its sacred books, the "New Testament," had to come from a Hebrew source. It was inspired by Jeremiah 31:33-34, a text often alluded to in the Gospel and twice quoted in full in Hebrews 8:8-10 and 10:16-17: "This is the covenant that I will make with the house of Israel after those days, says the Lord: I will put my law within them, and I will write it upon their hearts . . . and I will remember their sin no more." It was inevitable that people who had been won over to the new faith should read into that text a Christian or pre-Christian meaning. Yet Jeremiah (or, as seems probable, the anonymous author of that section of the book attributed to him) appears to have had something quite different in mind. The law to which he refers is not the internal or spiritual law that the New Testament substitutes for the Law of Moses; it is the Mosaic Law itself, which would at long last be restored to the place of honor that belongs to it. True, the Temple had been destroyed and the people taken into captivity, but God, who does not abandon his own, would renew his covenant with them. The Temple would be rebuilt and the law would once again be placed in its "heart," that is to say, in the Holy of Holies, where the tablets had traditionally been kept. "Hearts" in the plural instead of "heart" in the singular, as the Hebrew has it, distorts the meaning of the text and gives it the inward flavor that Christians almost automatically detect in it. The law in question becomes a kind of natural law inscribed in the heart of each individual. No, Jeremiah was not looking forward to anything as startlingly new as what Christians call the New Testament. The children of the age to come, he went on to say, would be "as aforetime" (30:20). The youngest would be like the oldest. The Hebrew Bible is not a very forward-looking document. The perfection that it speaks of is located in the past and not in the future. Traditional Judaism does not know of any "New" Testament in the Christian sense of the word, for the same reason that it does not know of any "Old" Testament.

My final question is whether the New Testament writers were aware of the "violence" they were doing to their sources. The question is not an easy one, given the scantiness of the data at our disposal concerning the formation of the New Testament and the dates of its various books. Admittedly, these books do not speak with one voice on all matters and they are far from clear about the way Christianity is supposed to relate to the political order, a subject in which, truth to tell, they do not show much interest. Still, there is no evidence to suggest that in presenting the Christian message as the fulfillment of the Torah and the Prophets, their authors sought to mislead their readers.

The same cannot be said of Spinoza, whose account of liberal democracy as a typological fulfillment of the New Testament revelation deliberately manipulates the sacred text in order to make it support his political goals. But if Spinoza knew exactly what he was doing, others in his entourage must have known it as well, even though not all of them would have been persuaded by his argument. The conclusion at which we arrive is that the viability of his solution to the theologico-political problem did not require that everyone acquiesce in it. It was sufficient that it be accepted by a certain number of influential people who could vouch for its respectability and speak in favor of it when the need arose. That solution is demonstrably linked to the decay of Christendom and the divided state in which, by then, the Christian world found itself. What made it attractive is that it promised an end to the bloody wars and massacres that had been tearing Europe apart for a century or more. But this alone was not enough to make it true. It may even have cast doubts on its philosophic status since it is hard to claim universal validity for a position that is so intimately bound up with a contingent and, it could be, highly ephemeral state of affairs.

An adequate discussion of this problem would necessitate a fuller analysis of Spinoza's thought than any that I am capable of or that can be undertaken here, but this much can be said: From his own point of view, Spinoza was right in thinking that the universality of his theory was not impaired by the particularity of the circumstances that gave rise to it. Religion as he understands it is a matter of unreason or superstition rather than reason. To that extent, it is essentially unstable and varies in accordance with the passions in which it originates. No religion is likely to remain unchanged for a long period of time. The only exceptions to this rule are the Hebrew theocracy and (by implication) Christianity, whose staying power is attributable to the efficacy of certain practices not found to the same degree elsewhere; and even they achieved only limited success. The contemporary breakdown of Christendom is not an historical accident. In the long run, it was unavoidable. If Christianity manages to survive at all, it will be in the diluted, transmogrified, and barely recognizable form that Spinoza would give it. Its followers will be people who are more eager to improve their lot than to discover the true meaning of the Scriptures and who, when it comes to money, all tend to be of the same religion.

One might go a step further and ask whether Spinoza thought that the progress of science and rationality would one day cause religion to vanish altogether. Any answer to that question would have to take into account, first, his teaching concerning the absolute superiority of the theoretical life over the practical life—a teaching shared by very few other modern philosophers—and, secondly, his conviction that a permanent gulf separates the learned few from the many unwise. It was left to some of his descendants to argue that the perfectly rational society is indeed possible and that human beings never pose for themselves problems to which they do not already possess the solutions.

NOTES

1.   Cf. Francis Bacon, *The Great Instauration*, cf. "The Plan of the Work."

2.   B. Spinoza, *A Theologico-Political Treatise and a Political Treatise*, translated from the Latin with an introduction by R. H. M. Elwes (New York: Dover, 1957), ch. 7, 107.

3.   Ibid., chapter 13-14.

4.   Ibid., Preface.

5.   Ibid., chapter 17.

— 6 —

AUGUSTINE'S *CITY OF GOD* AND THE MODERN HISTORICAL CONSCIOUSNESS

Contemporary Augustinian scholarship is distinguished among other ways by its emphasis on Augustine's alleged contribution to the development of the modern notion of history. Except for a few sporadic references to a possible theology of history in the *City of God*, one finds little in the literature of the nineteenth and early twentieth centuries to indicate that the content of that work might be of particular relevance to the problem at hand.[1] The same is not true of the post-World War I period, which witnessed a sudden surge of interest in this hitherto neglected subject, to such an extent that there has scarcely been a major treatment of Augustine's thought written since that time which does not dwell on it at considerable length. Augustine, Langdon Gilkey has recently asserted, is "the father of the historical consciousness,"[2] the first author to exhibit an awareness of the fundamentally historical character of human existence, and the only early Christian writer to have brought the whole of history within the compass of a "purposive unity."[3]

It was perhaps normal that, in the midst of what was perceived as a crisis of major proportions engulfing the whole of Western civilization— witness the extraordinary success of Spengler's *Decline of the West* or

Ferrero's *Words to the Deaf*, to mention two of the most widely read books of the twenties—scholarly attention should have been drawn to the waning years of the Roman empire and the upheavals that precipitated its demise. Here was a great civilization that had not only gone under but had bequeathed to posterity a well-documented record of its own breakdown, the only corpse sufficiently well-preserved to lend itself to a dissection. Among the ancient writers to whom one might turn for information about this critical period, none was better suited than Augustine, who had himself been prompted by the dramatic events of his day to meditate on the fate of empires and the destiny of the human race. From him one could hope to learn something about what conceivably lay in store for us: whether the dislocations of our own troubled times were the necessary prelude to a larger and more powerful unity or whether they portended a return to the barbarism that had once plunged Europe into darkness for centuries; whether, as Ferrero put it, our fate was "that of the generations of Caesar and Augustus or that of the generations of Diocletian and Constantine."[4]

Yet the conflicting results to which this intensive research eventually led suggest that the quarry may be more elusive than had been anticipated. Heinrich Scholz's earlier case for the presence of an incipient philosophy of history in Augustine[5] was countered by U.A. Padovani's contention that, since Augustine's unifying principle is derived from Revelation, his views are best described as a theology rather than a philosophy of history.[6] Scholz's Hegelian account of the *City of God* was followed some years later by Wilhelm Kamlah's Heideggerian or individualistic interpretation of the same work,[7] itself soon to be challenged by Joseph Ratzinger's forceful insistence on the properly ecclesial and sacramental dimension of Augustine's thought.[8] The protracted debate, whatever else may be said about it, has had at least one notable effect. It secured accreditation for the notion of a theology of history in academic circles and enshrined it as a kind of theological *locus communis*, decked out with the aura of a tradition supposedly dating back to the early Christian centuries and the authority of no less a figure than Augustine himself.

To be sure, few people would go so far as to say that Augustine's speculations on this theme measure up to modern standards. By comparison to our own fully developed sense of history, they remain deficient and represent at best a feeble anticipation of what was to emerge with total clarity only at a much later date. What is still lacking in them, Gilkey tells us, is an appreciation of "the creativity of freedom in time and above all the sense that the course of history itself, the 'destiny' of its institutional structures, can constitute an intrinsic part of the unfolding meaning of history."[9] Accordingly, "the consciousness of history [had to] shift before this initial sense of history's meaning under God [could become] the modern consciousness of history." It is all the more remarkable that, in spite of these manifest shortcomings, Augustine should have been able to view time and the historical process as "linear, teleological, and meaningful,"[10] thereby endowing them with "an intelligibility . . . which they had not possessed before."[11] To him, more than to anyone else, belongs the honor of having laid the groundwork for a more perfect understanding of this all-important concept.

Gilkey's subtle analysis nevertheless leaves unanswered a number of basic questions that continue to perplex the assiduous reader of Augustine and of the literature of Christian antiquity. We need not concern ourselves with the issue of the superiority of the modern over the premodern conception of history, inasmuch as any decision in that regard presupposes that one has achieved an adequate grasp of both positions—a task which clearly lies beyond the modest scope of the present study and perhaps beyond the reach of all but the greatest talents. My own more limited question is whether the modern conception to which Gilkey points as the culmination of an intellectual development originated by Augustine did in fact emerge on the basis of Augustine's novel approach to history or whether it should not rather be seen as a radical departure from it.

It is worth noting, first of all, that Augustine himself employs the word *history* only sparingly (certainly much less frequently than some widely circulated translations of his works might lead us to think) and that when he does, it is without reference to an overall meaning with which the course of human events might be invested. The only thematic discussion of it to occur anywhere in his works, that of the *On Christian Doctrine*, defines history in traditional terms as the accurate and useful narration of past events: *historia facta narrat fideliter atque utiliter.*[12] As opposed to the false art of soothsaying, it does not pretend to tell us what ought to be done but only what has been done and, hence, cannot be undone. As such, it is not unlike the account that one might give of the world around us or what is sometimes called natural history.[13] To the extent to which grammarians resort to it to explicate literary texts, it bears some relationship to the liberal arts;[14] but since its function is merely to record the actions of human beings, it is not itself an art or a product of the human mind;[15] and since the objects to which it addresses itself pertain to the realm of bodily perception, it cannot be reckoned as a science either.[16] Moreover, the information that it supplies is not altogether reliable. Historians often contradict one another or deliberately seek to mislead their readers. It stands to reason that, when such contradictions occur, only the facts that accord with sacred Scripture are to be credited.[17] Yet its importance is far from negligible, for it not infrequently sheds light on the events of sacred history and furnishes us with a store of examples from which there is occasional profit to be derived.[18] At no point in the discussion do we encounter the faintest allusion to some humanly decipherable plan which a careful study of the past could help to unveil.

Granted that Augustine never uses the word history in that precise sense, one may be tempted to argue that the reality associated with it in the modern mind is not foreign to his thought. Even this, however, is open to serious question. Seen from the perspective of the Bible, human events no doubt form part of a providential order that comprises the whole of history;[19] but in the absence of any specific knowledge of the workings of divine providence, one is at a loss to say how they are related to one another or to the pre-established end to which they supposedly conduce. Anyone contemplating the sequence of these events is struck first and last not by its rationality but its patent irrationality. Civilizations flourish at one moment and then vanish just as mysteriously. While we have it on the authority of Scripture that all power wielded by human beings ultimately comes from God, the reasons for which in the course of time it passed from one people to another have not been imparted to us. What is more, there is no correlation between just or unjust rule on the one hand and earthly prosperity or misfortune on the other. Constantine, the first Christian emperor, enjoyed a long reign and the certainly no less pious Jovian a very short one.[20] God grants dominion "to whom he pleases," to Augustus one day and to Caligula or Nero the next, for motives which, though never unjust, remain impenetrable; so much so that, even after the fact, human reason is unable to determine why he does it or how precisely what he does contributes to the furtherance of the goal that he pursues among human beings.[21]

Any attempt to reduce the total succession of temporal events to the unity of an intelligible order is further thwarted by the fact that these events, to the degree to which they have their source in, or are decisively influenced by, the undetermined human will, are largely unamenable to scientific treatment. That there is such a thing as free choice is attested to by the common practice of enacting laws, engaging in exhortation, bestowing praise and blame, and administering rewards and punishments, none of which would make sense if human beings were not accountable for their actions.[22] It can likewise be shown that this freedom has its source in God himself, who confers on all creatures the power not only to act but to act in accordance with their proper mode, whether it be natural or voluntary.[23]

What is not completely clear is how, despite their radical contingency, human acts are used by God for purposes to which they are not intrinsically ordered. The least that can be said in answer to this admittedly complex question is that there is nothing contradictory in the assertion that a rational agent may be the determinate cause of events that others perceive as fortuitous. I may, for example, arrange a meeting between two strangers who have no reason to suspect that what they take to be a chance encounter was in fact premeditated by someone else. The analogy is of course imperfect, since, having no final control over the doings of others, I can never be sure that the plan will succeed. Either one of the two parties involved could turn down my invitation or suffer a heart attack before the projected meeting took place. Not so with God, the supreme ruler and architect of the universe, who weaves into the fabric of history a pattern which from a higher vantage point may yet prove to be coherent: *architectus aedificat per machinas transituras domum manentem.*[24] But to say this is to admit that the rationality of the divine plan is not in the materials used but in the mind of the user, or, less metaphorically stated, that the teleology in question remains extrinsic to the events themselves. No analysis of these events will ever lead to the discovery of an end which is at once present and operative in the process from the beginning and destined to be progressively actualized through it.

It follows that the future course of human history is totally unpredictable. History will come to an end at the appointed time, not because of anything that human beings have done or may yet do, but because God will have chosen to bring it to a close.[25] As far as anyone can tell, its completion is in no way related to emergent political structures or the general state of human affairs at any given moment. This obviously does not rule out the possibility of substantial and even "spectacular" (*stupenda*) advances in knowledge and the arts as time goes on. But if, as Augustine argues, the gains registered on this limited front are as likely to be used for destructive as for constructive purposes,[26] one fails to see how they could provide a reliable standard by which to measure the progress accomplished by the human race in the course of its long history.

As the example of some of Augustine's fellow Christians demonstrates, however, it is possible to deny that the historical process is inherently teleological and still cling to a melioristic view of the development of human society. That Augustine himself consistently refused to do so is evident from the later books of the *City of God*, whose teaching far exceeds the original intention of the work, which was to deal with the crisis provoked by the sack of Rome at the hands of Alaric's Visigoths in the year 410. Although in the opinion of some modern scholars the psychological impact produced by the incident was out of proportion to the actual damage wrought by the barbarians or their short-lived occupancy of the city,[27] its significance could not be underestimated. Not the least interesting of its corollaries was that it lent new credence to the

frequently heard charge that Christians bore a major share of the blame for
the mounting instability and teetering fortunes of the Roman Empire.
Rome had fallen because it had betrayed its tutelary deities. The latest
catastrophe was but one more sign of the displeasure of the gods, a kind
of judgment of Jove, who had retaliated by dealing in appropriate fashion
with his once loyal devotees.[28]

In its popular form, the accusation could scarcely be thought to carry
much weight with the pagan elite, most of whom had long since ceased
to take the existence of the avenging gods seriously.[29] Its real substance
on the other hand was anything but trivial; for beneath the crude polytheistic garb in which it paraded, lurked the suspicion that, as a universal
religion uniting or attempting to unite all people in the worship of the one
true God, Christianity had done a disservice to the city. By denying the
ultimate importance of the political life in favor of the belief in a heavenly
and more perfect city, it undermined public-spiritedness and made it
virtually impossible to exact from ordinary citizens the single-minded
devotion to the common good that had characterized the Roman polity at
its best.[30]

The argument could be met on its own ground by pointing out that the
evils of the present time were not without precedent in earlier Roman
history. Rome had hardly ever been without war, civil or otherwise. Since
the major portion of these evils antedated the rise of Christianity, they
could not reasonably be traced back to it.[31] Besides, other empires had
suffered a similar fate in the past, even though there was no evidence that
they had forsaken the cult of their own gods.[32] In order to substantiate the
point, however, more information was needed, and Augustine, always a
busy man, commissioned a newly recruited disciple, the Spanish priest
Orosius, to compile from all available sources a list of the disasters that
had plagued Roman political life throughout most of its notoriously
turbulent history.

The results of this inquiry are contained in Orosius's *Seven Books of
History against the Pagans*, which has the distinction of being not only
the first but perhaps the most unusual history of the world ever written.[33]
Whereas Augustine's main concern was with the city of God, Orosius
concentrated on what may fairly be called the city of the devil.[34] This
relatively short work, which enjoyed enormous popularity during the
Middle Ages,[35] is barely more than a litany of the evils known to have
been perpetrated or endured by human beings since the beginning of
recorded time. Even a superficial reading of the book reveals, however,
that in discharging his obligation Orosius went well beyond the call of
duty. The gist of his thesis, which leans heavily on Eusebius but also
prides itself on having outdone him, is that, far from boding ill for the

empire, Christianity was directly responsible for the untold blessings that had accrued to it in recent times.[36] Its auspicious birth under Augustus had coincided with an era of unprecedented peace and held out the promise of even greater benefits for the future.[37] Indeed, all of human history up to that time could be seen as a lengthy preparation for the advent and eventual triumph of the new faith. With a little coaxing, the life spans of the great empires of the past could be fitted into a neat pattern which revealed the hand of God at work in their midst. To the east, the Babylonian empire (assimilated for present purposes to the Assyrian empire) had lasted 1,400 years; to the north and south, the Macedonian and Carthaginian empires, 700 years each; to the west, Rome was already more than 1,000 years old.[38] In time, the persecutions to which the first generations of Christians were subjected had abated. The empire had not only seen fit to sanction the new religion but had become officially Christian under Theodosius. Furthermore, there was little likelihood that these accomplishments would be annulled by subsequent setbacks or the regression to a less desirable stage of human development. Just as the plagues vested on the Egyptians had stopped at ten, so the persecutions inflicted on the early Christians had ceased at the same number.[39] In the meantime, the Old Testament prophecies relating to the blessings of the messianic age were gradually being fulfilled: swords were being turned into plowshares; justice and peace were on the verge of forging a lasting alliance; under the aegis of the new emperors, the kingdom of God was about to be inaugurated, not just in heaven, as some less worldly-minded apologists for the Christian faith had predicted, but here on earth.[40]

True, innocent people were still made to suffer unjustly and the wicked occasionally enjoyed undeserved prosperity. But this meant only that the former would go to heaven a little sooner and the latter to hell a little later.[41] Orosius himself, who had managed to escape from his own troubled Spain to more peaceful shores, could afford to remain undaunted. Had he not discovered a new home in North Africa, where he joyfully found himself "a Roman among Romans, a Christian among Christians, and a man among men"—something that would never have been possible before.[42] What more was needed to prove that things were getting better and would continue to do so as time went on!

However plausible Orosius's simple-minded scheme may have appeared to some of his contemporaries and to his innumerable readers in the centuries that followed, it did not meet with the approval of Augustine, who never once mentions his collaborator in the eleven books of the *City of God* that remained to be written[43] and even seems to go out of his way to reject the position for which he had opted. Traces of his dissatisfaction with the work of his disciple may be detected in Book XVIII, where Augustine explicitly takes issue with those who would equate the triumph of Christianity with the realization of the famous messianic prophecies of Isaiah and of Psalm 72. "I do not think," he says,

> it can be rashly asserted or believed, as some have done and still do, that until the time of the Antichrist the Church will no longer have to suffer any persecutions beyond those which it has already suffered, that is to say, ten . . . Nor do I share the view that these persecutions were prophetically signified by what happened in Egypt, however nicely and ingeniously these two sets of events may have been related to each other, not by the Spirit who speaks through the prophets, but by the conjecture of the human mind, which sometimes hits the truth and sometimes misses it.[44]

Not only from the time of Christ but from that of Abel, the Church has gone forth on pilgrimage, amid both the persecutions of the world and the consolations of God; and so it will be "until the end of time."[45] As far as the prospects for the future are concerned, they remain as uncertain as always; for "in the very great mutability of human affairs, no people has even been granted such security as would free it from the dread of invasions hostile to this life."[46] Neither is it true that the rise and decline of the great world empires fall into anything like the symmetrical pattern into which Orosius had unscrupulously tried to nudge them. The Assyrian empire, for example, endured, not 1,400 years, but 1,240 years or, if one includes the reign of Belus, 1,305 years.[47] No juggling of the historical data will allow us to uncover an intimation of rational design in this random succession of worldly powers.

The same skepticism pervades Augustine's reinterpretation of the notion of a "Christian era"—*tempora Christiana*—which had recently been injected into the debate as a term of derogation by the pagan adversaries of Christianity.[48] Orosius had seized upon it not only to vindicate the Christian faith—others had done as much—but to bolster his own incremental conception of the development of Roman history: "Behold how under Christian kings and in these Christian times (*tempora Christiana*) civil wars, even when they prove unavoidable, are brought to a happy issue. The victory has been won, the city stands intact, the tyrant has been laid low."[49] Augustine is a good deal more cautious. However beneficial he may have considered the spread of Christianity to be in other respects, he certainly did not think that it carried with it any guarantee of earthly prosperity. It has been proposed, most recently by R. A. Markus, that Augustine, too, had once succumbed to a "triumphant" assessment of the emergence of Christianity and viewed the present age as the long-awaited fulfillment of the Old Testament prophecies, only to retract himself in his

later writings and subject his initial understanding of the *tempora christiana* to a "drastic devaluation" in the light of the reverses of the first
decades of the fifth century.[50] Whether or not this is the case remains
somewhat debatable.[51] There is little reason to believe that Augustine ever
sought to endow the Christian empire with quasi-messianic attributes, and
even less reason to believe that he had second thoughts about ascribing a
temporal meaning to the prophetic utterances of the Old Testament.[52] I
know of no text in which he denies that *any* of these prophecies refer to
temporal events. What he does deny, in his early as well as in his later
works, is that they contain only glad tidings. The truth of the matter, as
he sees it, is that both happy and unhappy events have been foretold by
the prophets and the gospel. Commenting again on the convulsions of his
time, he writes:

> These things should make us weep but not wonder; and we ought to cry
> unto God that, not for our merit but according to his mercy, he may deliver
> us from such great evils. For, what else was to be expected by the human
> race, seeing that these things were so long ago foretold both by the prophets
> and in the Gospel? We ought not, therefore, be so inconsistent as to believe
> these Scriptures when they are read by us, and to complain when they are
> fulfilled. It is rather those who refused to believe when they read or heard
> these things in Scripture who ought to become believers now that they
> behold the word fulfilled. Just as this great pressure of the Lord God's
> olive-press brings forth the dregs of unbelieving murmurs and blasphemies,
> so, too, it should produce a steady outpouring of pure oil in the confessions
> and prayers of believers. For, to those who never tire of hurling their
> impious complaints at the Christian faith and claim that, prior to the time
> when this doctrine was proclaimed throughout the world, the human race
> was not subjected to such great evils, an answer can readily be given from
> the Gospel. Indeed, as the Lord says, "That servant who does not know his
> master's will and does what deserves a beating shall receive a light beating,
> whereas the servant who does know his master's will and does what
> deserves a beating shall receive a severe beating" (Luke 22:47-4-8). Is it
> surprising that, in these Christian times (*christianis temporibus*), this world,
> like the servant who knows his master's will and yet does what deserves a
> beating, should be punished severely? These people notice the rapidity with
> which the Gospel is propagated, but not the perversity with which it is
> despised by many.[53]

If the new times, then, are not necessarily better or more peaceful than the
old, one cannot claim for Christianity the politically redemptive role that
Orosius and his mentor, Eusebius, had assigned to it.

The attractiveness of Eusebius's *Reichstheologie* and its Orosian analogue is that they offered what was far and away the most elegant solution
yet devised to the problem of the Christian's involvement in Roman
public life. As long as this involvement entailed the risk of complicity in
a manifestly iniquitous rule, the Christian conscience could feel justified
in adopting an attitude of uncompromising opposition to it. One is reminded in this connection of the bitter invectives of an earlier generation
of Christian extremists, represented pre-eminently by Hippolytus of Rome,
who had been taught by the Book of Revelation to identify the Roman
Empire with the harlot "seated upon the seven hills" and "drunk with the
blood of the saints and martyrs of Jesus."[54] Under such adverse conditions,
it might well be asked what indeed the Church had to do with Caesar. The
accession of a Christian, or of someone partial to Christianity, to the
imperial throne had brought about a complete reversal of the situation.
Little wonder that this unexpected turn of events should have been hailed
as the most important milestone in the history of Christianity since the
birth of Christ.[55] If public affairs were henceforth to be administered in
accordance with the rules of strict justice, if wars were destined to
disappear altogether, if the only wars remaining to be waged were demonstrably just wars, and if the newly converted empire was but an earthly
reflection of God's eternal kingdom,[56] any qualms that one might have had
about lending one's support to it could be laid to rest. The conflict
between the moral ideal of the Sermon on the Mount and the harsh necessities of the political life had happily come to an end.

One finds it somewhat easier to sympathize with Eusebius's enthu-
siastic, if seemingly uncritical, endorsement of Constantine and the
Christian empire. After all, he had witnessed the atrocities of the reign of
Diocletian (he was sixteen when the emperor acceded to the throne) and
had been forced to spend some time in jail as a young man. Given his
closeness to the new seat of power, however, it is hard to imagine that he
could have been totally blind to the darker side of his hero's policies.
There is much to be said for the suggestion that Eusebius's naivete was
more apparent than real, since by his own admission he had "related
whatever might redound to the glory, and . . . suppressed all that could
tend to the discredit, of religion."[57] Orosius's only excuse was his
ignorance or his monumental shallowness.

Unfortunately, what both of them propounded as a final answer to the
perennially vexed question of the relation of Christianity to civil society
could be seen, and was in fact seen by Augustine, as a new and more
insidious danger for at least two reasons. The first is that, by binding
Christianity to the promise of temporal rewards, it inevitably cast doubts
on the genuineness of one's sentiments in regard to it.[58] A believer may

be attracted to Christianity for a variety of human reasons, but ultimately the faith that is demanded of him cannot be accepted for any motive other than the faith itself. The fundamental ambiguity of the Eusebian or the Orosian scheme is that it rendered Christianity equally appealing to believers and nonbelievers. Without giving its claim to divine truth as much as a second thought, one might look upon the Church as a viable solution to some of the most urgent social problems of the day. Properly organized and supported, it could be pressed into service to counteract the forces that threatened the dissolution of an inordinately large and unwieldy political structure. Its spirit of moderation and law-abidingness was likely to improve the manners of society, particularly at a time when the traditional sources of morality were showing unmistakable signs of weakness. Laws are effective to the extent to which they are accompanied by habits of decency and self-restraint on the part of most citizens; left to themselves, they seldom inspire virtue and are even less capable of containing vice. Yet it was painfully obvious that neither education nor pagan religion, the two principal agencies on which governments had formerly relied for this purpose, was adequate to the task. A universal and despotic empire is not the most suitable locus of moral education, and the old religion of the city, which had been on the wane for years, was not about to be revived.

Much more could be expected from the new religion, which addressed itself to everybody regardless of language, ethnic background, or local tradition. Christians had long rejected the idea that they constituted a separate race or a *triton genos*.[59] Unlike other religious groups, they were not given to living in isolation or to withdrawing from society altogether. One found them everywhere, mingling freely with the rest of the population, sharing their customs, their dress, and, within prescribed limits, their general way of life.[60] The moral teaching to which they subscribed enjoined the practice of public as well as of private virtue. Once generally accepted, it could be counted on to curb the selfish passions and propagate sentiments of truth, justice, and harmony among a people who would regard themselves as the common children of the one true God. Thanks to its influence, the dissensions racking the empire were less apt to erupt into bloody strife. In Edward Gibbon's memorable words, "a prudent magistrate might observe with pleasure and eventually support the progress of a religion which diffused among the people a pure, benevolent, and universal system of ethics, adapted to every duty and every condition of life, recommended as the will and reason of the supreme deity, and enforced by the sanction of eternal rewards and punishments."[61]

The cost on the other side of the political ledger was, all things considered, minimal. Even the disparagement of military valor, which at other moments and under different circumstances could only be thought of as a liability, had suddenly turned into a distinct asset, favoring the ends to which in its self-interest, imperial policy had to be committed. By the same token, emperors had little to fear from a religion which derived the institution of civil government from the will of God, frowned upon sedition, and discouraged worldly ambition with as much vigor as it extolled the virtue of obedience to one's divinely sanctioned rulers. If even under the reign of Nero St. Paul had preached the duty of unconditional submission to tyrants, how much more willing would Christians be to acquiesce in the rule of a prince who was at the same time a patron and a defender! The new alliance was clearly advantageous to both parties. By a miraculous convergence, it served the best interests of both heaven and earth.

Little more was required to lay bare the essential weakness of any purely political defense of Christianity. It is significant that the *City of God* devotes barely more than two short chapters to Constantine and Theodosius, the most renowned of the Christian emperors, and that, in reviewing their reigns, Augustine stresses their private virtues to the virtual exclusion of their political virtues.[62] The conversion of the Roman Empire, which others had acclaimed as a crucial turning point in the history of the Church, is dismissed as a mere episode in an ongoing process no single moment of which is to be privileged over any other moment. Just as Augustine tacitly rejects the Byzantine theology of Eusebius, so he passes over in silence the so-called Augustus theology of Orosius, with its typical emphasis on the providential connection between the *pax romana* and the emergence of Christianity. The birth of Christ under Augustus is duly recorded, but in a single line and as a chronological coincidence from which no prognosis can be made regarding the future course of human events.[63]

There is yet another, perhaps more cogent reason for which, upon reflection, Eusebius's imperial theology in any of its forms appeared fraught with peril. If, as Eusebius and Orosius seem to have been persuaded, political institutions are bound to improve with the passing of time and if, along with this improvement, the evils to which they invariably gave rise are to vanish from the scene, one wonders what is to become of human excellence and virtue once the process reaches its completion. Later generations would be spared the trouble of overcoming the obstacles that had previously stood in the path of right action. The success of their endeavors would be assured without their having to make any of the efforts required of their less fortunate predecessors. One could look forward to the day when one need not shoulder the burden of virtue in order to reap its rewards.

Augustine's question is whether virtue can still be called virtue if success is always guaranteed. There is surely nothing wrong in following a charted course of action whose outcome is never in doubt, but there is nothing particularly glorious in it either. What gives to virtue its distinctively human character is precisely the uncertainty with which in all interesting cases one is compelled to act. People are at best responsible for the goodness or badness of their deeds, not for their results. They may deserve to be successful, but whether or not they are depends in large measure on circumstances that lie beyond their control and may not even be known to them at the time of action. A just judge who has done everything in his power to ascertain the facts of the case cannot be held to account for unwittingly condemning an innocent person, however wrong his judgment may be.[64] The paradox is that were it not for the possibility of evil, virtue itself would be in serious jeopardy. Prudence loses its raison d'être once one is relieved of the need to discern right from wrong, as does moderation, once all the impediments to the accomplishment of what has been judged right are removed.[65] The function of virtue is not to do away with evil but to conquer it.[66] Even as it does so, its victory is never secure; for "as long as the vices against which it struggles resist, the battle remains precarious, and even when defeated they do not permit a triumph of carefree ease."[67]

Nowhere is this inner struggle more apparent than when the deliberations bear on the use of force as a means of opposing injustice. For the sake of preserving the purity of one's soul, one would doubtless prefer to see an end to all wars, but even this will never be more than a pious wish. A weak justice is hardly an appropriate response to the injustices of the world. It only leads to greater injustice by allowing the wicked to prevail over the just.[68] Complete peace is not part of man's mortal condition. It belongs to that "other life" which alone is free from the corruption of sin and death and in which nothing either in ourselves or in others will be at war with any of us.[69]

Against the background of these ideas one is in a better position to measure the gulf that separates the Augustinian from the modern view of history. The philosophy of history came into being with Kant at the end of the eighteenth century and the early years of the nineteenth century in the wake of Rousseau's epoch-making attack on bourgeois morality. Its basic thrust was not only to restore genuine morality but to insure that its exercise would not be obstructed by oppressive political structures. With typical modern realism, it assumed that human good will alone could not be relied upon to overturn these evil structures and that the necessary reform would come about only through the operation of a hidden "teleology" at work in the historical process. Progress was assured neither by the simple diffusion of scientific knowledge, as others had once thought, nor by the deliberate pursuit of moral purposes on the part of human beings, but by the free interplay of the essentially immoral or self-regarding passions.[70] By their incessant preying on one another, human beings had created a situation from which they could extricate themselves only by desisting from any further attempt at aggrandizement at the expense of their fellow human beings.[71] Wars would diminish in frequency and intensity, not because their irrationality offended mankind's moral sense, but because they were proving ever more costly and suicidal.[72] An invisible hand of nature had seen to it that the antagonisms which characterize human intercourse would constrain even evildoers to accept a civic constitution recognizing the rights of all human beings and granting to each individual as much freedom as is consistent with the freedom of others.[73] The conflict between private and public morality once resolved, no one would run the risk of being punished for complying with unconditionally binding moral law.[74]

To be sure, the whole process, although morally desirable, did not of itself lead to a higher degree of morality; for the free society that it was calculated to produce could still theoretically be made up entirely of devils.[75] To that extent, Kant's solution called for a series of correctives that others after him would attempt to supply. But if the good citizen need not be a good man, at least there was nothing to prevent the good man from being at the same time a good citizen. One was henceforth spared the ignominy of having to suffer unjustly at the hands of an immoral society.

Augustine was at once more hopeful for the destiny of the individual and less hopeful for that of society at large. To repeat what was said earlier, the *City of God* was first conceived as an effort to refurbish the arguments by which Christian apologetics had traditionally sought to reconcile Christianity with the legitimate demands of the political life. It soon became apparent, however, that the incisive issue was not whether civil society could survive Christianity but whether Christianity itself could survive its integration into civil society. The problem was the more acute as the new faith was never envisaged as a purely private concern but was rather called upon to play within society a role similar to that which had once devolved upon pagan religion. Before the work was completed, the conventional defense with which it began had developed into a highly original attack on some of Augustine's fellow Christians and a far more probing analysis of the political implications of the Christian faith than any that had hitherto been undertaken.

The solution adopted by Eusebius and his followers was based on the assumption that a converted Roman empire could live up to the ethical standards of the gospel or that a perfectly just social order was possible. Augustine destroyed the ground of the argument by insisting that no society had ever conformed to the requirements of strict justice or was likely to do so. The very notion of a Christian polity, whether it be upheld seriously or for reasons of expediency, is at best a comforting and at worst a fatal illusion. Christian wisdom and political power are not only distinct but always more or less at odds with each other in accordance with the vicissitudes of history and the mostly evil inclinations of the human heart. Some regimes may be superior to others, but there is no reason to think that the regime under which one happens to live will necessarily be followed by a better one, or, more importantly, that any of them is at all capable of fulfilling man's longing for wholeness. In short, the history of which the *City of God* speaks is anything but an inside history. Its goal remains transcendent and wholly independent of any observable improvement in the political sphere.

In view of Augustine's pessimism regarding the perfectibility of human institutions and the structural foundations of society, one is entitled to ask what, if anything, the modern philosophy of history owes to him. The one point on which both views would appear to be in agreement, even though it is never explicitly discussed by Kant, concerns the linear and nonrepeatable character of the historical process. That this central premise should have been so easily taken for granted by modern philosophers of history is perhaps an indirect tribute to the persuasive power of the *City of God*. But then the notion that history takes its course along a straight line can hardly be considered an Augustinian innovation. It underlies the whole of the biblical account of human existence, for which both Kantian and Hegelian philosophy were intended as a substitute. One is still left to wonder in what specific sense Augustine might qualify as the first philosopher of history or the father of the modern historical consciousness.

NOTES

1. H.-I. Marrou, "Geschichtsphilosophie," in *Reallexicon für Antike und Christentum*, vol. 10.

2. L. Gilkey, *Reaping the Whirlwind* (New York: Seabury Press, 1956), 175. Cf. ibid., 162: "With Augustine the Western, and so the modern, sense of temporal passage comes to definitive and formative expression"; 163: "With him (Augustine) begins the tradition of philosophy of history."

3. Ibid., 164.

4. G. Ferrero, *Words to the Deaf*, B. R. Redman, trans. (New York and London: G. P. Putnam's Sons, 1926), 159.

5. H. Scholz, *Glaube and Unglaube in der Weltgeschichte* (Leipzig: J. C. Hinrichs, 1911).

6. U. A. Padovani, "La *Città di Dio* di Sant'Agostino: teologia e non filosofia della storia," *Rivista di filosofia neo-scolastica, supplemento speciale al vol. XXIII* (Milano, 1931): 220-263.

7. W. Kamlah, *Christentum und Geschichtlichkeit*, (Cologne-Stuttgart: W. Kohlhammer, 1951).

8. J. Ratzinger, *Volk und Haus Gottes in Augustins Lehre von der Kirche* (Munich: K Zink, 1954); idem, "Herkunft und Sinn der Civitas-Lehre Augustins," *Augustinus Magister*, vol. 2 (Paris: Etudes augustiniennes, 1954), 965-979.

9. L. Gilkey, *Reaping the Whirlwind*, 175. Cf. ibid., 174: "In the end, Augustine is not even interested in the kind or level of order and justice among social institutions."

10. Ibid., 163.

11. Ibid., 162.

12. *De doctrina christiana* (*On Christian Doctrine*) 2.28.44.

13. Ibid., II.29.45.

14. Cf. *De ordine* (*On Order*) II.12.37; *Epistula* (*Letter*) 101.2.

15. *De doctrina christiana* II.28.44.

16. Ibid., II.27.4-1.

17. *De civitate Dei* (*City of God*) XVIII.40. Cf. *Contra Faustum Manichaeum* (*Against Faustus, the Manichean*) 18.4; *Epist.* 101.2.

18. *De doctrina christiana* II.28.42; *De vera religione* (*On the True Religion*) 26.49.

19. Cf. *De civitate Dei* V.11.

20. *De civ. Dei* V.25. Jovian's reign lasted less than eight months, from June 363 to February 364.

21. *De civ. Dei* V.21; cf. V.19 and IV.33. On the limits of historical knowledge according to Augustine, see A. W. Ziegler, "Die Grenzen geschichtlicher Erkenntnis: Beiträge zur augustinischen Geschichtstheologie," *Augustinus Magister*, vol. 2 (Paris, 1954), 981-989.

22. *De civ. Dei* V.9.2 and V.10.2.

23. *De civ. Dei* V.9.4.

24. *Sermo* (*Sermon*) 362.7.

25. Cf. *De civ. Dei* XVIII.53.1.

26. *De civ. Dei* XII.24.3.

27. See, for example, T. E. Mommsen, "St. Augustine and the Christian Idea of Progress," reprinted in *Medieval and Renaissance Studies* (Ithaca, NY: Cornell University Press, 1959), 265-267. R. A. Markus, "The Roman Empire in Early Christian Historiography," *Downside Review* 81 (1963): 340-41.

28. *Retractationes* (*Retractations*) II.43.1; *De civ. Dei* I.1 and 3; II.3; IV.1-2; VI, Pref., etc.

29. Cf. *De civ. Dei* II.3: "There are indeed among them some who are thoroughly well educated men and have a taste for history, in which the things I speak of are open to their observation; but in order to irritate uneducated people against us, they feign ignorance of these events and do what they can to make the vulgar believe that those disasters, which in certain places and at certain times uniformly befall all mankind, are the result of Christianity, which is being everywhere diffused and is possessed of a renown and brilliancy that quite eclipse their own gods." See also Ibid., IV.1.

30. Cf. *Epistula (Letter)* 91.1; 138.2.9.

31. *De civ. Dei* I.2; I.36, et passim.

32. Cf. *De civ. Dei* IV.7.

33. For the comprehensive scope of Orosius's *Historiae adversus Paganos*, see I.1: "I intend to speak of the period from the founding of the world to the founding of the City (Rome); then up to the principate of Caesar and the birth of Christ . . . down to our own time."

34. Cf. Otto of Freising, *Chronicon sive Historia de Duabus Civitatibus*, edited by A. Hofmeister (Hanover and Leipzig, 1912), 9.

35. Cf. H.-I. Marrou, "Saint Augustin, Orose et l'augustinisme historique," *La storiografia altomedievale, Settimane di studio del Centro Italiano di studi sull'Alto medioevo*, 17 (Spoleto: Presso la sede del Centro, 1970), 64-65.

36. The point is already adumbrated in the Prologue: "I found the days of the past not only equally oppressive as these but also the more wretched the more distant they are from the solace of the true religion." Cf. v.1; VII.6; VII.43. In II.14, Orosius goes so far as to say that not only is Sicily at peace for the first time ever but even Etna "now only smokes harmlessly as if to give faith to its former activity."

37. *Historiae adversus paganos* III.8; V.1; VI.1; VI.17; VI.19-20; VI.22; VII.2, et passim. Since Erik Peterson, *Der Monotheismus als politischer Problem* (Leipzig: Hegner, 1935), 88, Orosius's political theology is often referred to as an "Augustus theology." Cf. F. Dvornik, *Early Christian and Byzantine Political Philosophy*, vol. 2 (Washington: Dumbarton Oaks Center for Byzantine Studies, Trustees for Harvard University, 1966), 725; H.-I. Marrou, "Saint Augustin, Orose et l'augustinisme historique," 81.

38. *Hist. adv. paganos* V.2.

39. *Hist. adv. paganos* VII.27.

40. Cf. *Hist. adv. paganos* V.1-2; VII-41.

41. *Hist. adv. paganos* VII.41: "For what loss is it to the Christian who is eager for eternal life to be taken away from this world at any time and by whatever means? Moreover, what gain is it to the pagan in the midst of Christians, obdurate against the faith, if he protracts his day a little longer, since he, whose conversion is despaired of, is destined to die?"

42. *Hist. adv. paganos* V.2.

43. In the Prologue, Orosius notes that Augustine was in the process of com-

pleting the eleventh book of the *City of God* when his own *Seven Books* appeared.

44. *De civ. Dei* XVIII.52.1.

45. *De civ. Dei* XVIII.51.2.

46. *De civ. Dei* XVII.13.

47. *De civ. Dei* IV.6 and XVIII.21. Cf. Marrou, "Saint Augustin, Orose et l'augustinisme historique," 75; E. Corsini, *Introduzione alle "Storie" di Orosio* (Turin: G. Giappichelli, 1968), 203-204.

48. Cf. P. Courcelle, "Propos antichrétiens rapportés par saint Augustin," *Recherches augustiniennes*, 1 (Paris, 1958): 178-183.

49. *Hist. adv. Paganos* 7.33.

50. R. A. Markus, *Saeculum: History and Society in the Theology of St. Augustine* (Cambridge, MA: Cambridge University Press, 1970), 35.

51. See the recent discussion of Markus's thesis by G. Madec, "*Tempora christiana*: Expression du triomphalisme chrétien ou récrimination païenne," in *Scientia Augustiniana: Studien über Augustinus, den Augustinismus und den Augustinerorden*, edited by P. Mayer and W. Eckermann (Wurzburg: Augustinus Verlag, 1975), 112-136.

52. For examples of Old Testament prophecies that may be thought to have been realized in New Testament times, see *De civ. Dei* XVIII.46-50.

53. *Epist.* 111.2. See also *De catechizandis rudibus* (*On Catechizing the Uninstructed*) 27.53-54; *Sermo* 81.7-9; *Sermo Denis* 24.10-13; Madec, "*Tempora christiana*," 124-125.

54. Cf. Hippolytus *In Danielem* 4.8-9. J. W. Swain, "The Theory of the Four Monarchies: Opposition History under the Roman Empire," *Classical Philology*, 35 (1940): 1-21; R. A. Markus, "The Roman Empire in Early Christian Historiography," 34-2; Markus, *Saeculum*, 48-49.

55. For a detailed account of the initial enthusiasm provoked by the Christianization of the Empire and the subsequent reaction against it, see G. Williams, "Christology and Church-State Relations in the Fourth Century," *Church History*, 20, no. 3 and 20, no. 4 (1951): 3-33 and 3-26.

56. Cf. Eusebius *Laus Constantini* 1.6; 3.5-6, *passim*, and the discussion by E. Cranz, "Kingdom and Polity in Eusebius of Caesarea," *Harvard Theological Review*, 45 (1952): 47-66.

57. Edward Gibbon, *The Decline and Fall of the Roman Empire*, chap. 16, with references to Eusebius, *Historica Ecclesiastica* 8.2, and *The Palestinian Martyrs* 12. Cf. Gibbon, chap. 18: "The courtly bishop, who had celebrated in an elaborate work the virtues and piety of his hero, observes a prudent silence on the subject of these tragic events." The year in which Constantine convoked the Council of Nicaea was also that in which he had his own son and his sister's son murdered. Orosius is candid enough to say that this was done for "unknown reasons," *Hist. adv. Paganos* 7.28.

58. Cf. *De civ. Dei* IV.33; V.25; I.8.2, with G. Bardy's remarks on this text in *Saint Augustine, La cité de Dieu, Bibliothèque augustinienne*, vol. 33 (Paris: Etudes

Augustiniennes, 1959), 767-769.

59. The designation had been applied to Christians in some early texts, e.g., *Praedicatio Petri*, frg. 5; Clement of Alex., *Stromata*, VI.5.41, and Aristides *Apology* 2.

60. Cf. *De civ. Dei* XIX.17.

61. *Decline and Fall of the Roman Empire*, chap. 20.

62. *De civ. Dei* V.25 and 26. Cf. Y.-M. Duval, "L'éloge de Théodose dans *la Cité de Dieu* (V.26.1)," *Recherches augustiniennes*, 4 (Paris, 1966): 135-179.

63. *De civ. Dei* XVIII.46; cf. *De civ. Dei* III.30.

64. Cf. *De civ. Dei* XIX.6.

65. *De civ. Dei* XIX.4.4.

66. *De civ. Dei* XIX.4.3.

67. *De civ. Dei* XIX.27.

68. *De civ. Dei* XIX.7.

69. *De civ. Dei* XIX.27; cf. *Enarrationes in Psalmos* (*Expositions on the Psalms*) 148.1-2.

70. Cf. I. Kant, *The Idea for a Universal History from a Cosmopolitan Point of View*, Fourth Thesis, in Immanuel Kant, *On History*, edited by L. W. Beck (Indianapolis: Bobbs Merrill, 1963), 15: "Thus man expects opposition on all sides because, in knowing himself, he knows that he, on his own part, is inclined to oppose others. This opposition it is which awakens all his powers, brings him to conquer his inclination to laziness and, propelled by vainglory, lust for power, and avarice, to achieve a rank among his fellows whom he cannot tolerate but from whom he cannot withdraw." Idem, *Perpetual Peace*, First Supplement, ibid., 106: "The guarantee of perpetual peace is nothing less than that great artist, nature (*natura daedala rerum*). In her mechanical course we see that her aim is to produce a harmony among men, against their will and indeed through their discord. As a necessity working according to laws we do not know, we call it destiny. But, considering its design in world history, we call it 'providence,' inasmuch as we discern in it the profound wisdom of a higher cause which predetermines the course of nature and directs it to the objective final end of the human race."

71. Kant, *Idea for a Universal History*, 16: "Man wishes concord; but Nature knows better what is good for the race; she wills discord. He wishes to live comfortably and pleasantly; Nature wills that he should be plunged from sloth and passive contentment into labor and trouble, in order that he may find means of extricating himself from them. The natural urges to this, the sources of unsociableness and mutual opposition from which so many evils arise, drive men to new exertions of their forces and thus to the manifold development of their capacities."

72. Ibid., Seventh Thesis, 18: "The friction among men, the inevitable antagonism, which is a mark of even the largest societies and political bodies, is used by Nature as a means to establish a condition of quiet and security. Through war, through the taxing and never-ending accumulation of armament, through the want which any

state, even in peacetime, must suffer internally, Nature forces them to make at first inadequate and tentative attempts; finally, after devastations, revolutions, and even complete exhaustion, she brings them to that which reason could have told them at the beginning and with far less sad experience, to wit, to step from the lawless condition of savages into a league of nations."

73. Ibid., Fifth Thesis, 16: "The highest purpose of Nature, which is the development of all the capacities which can be achieved by mankind, is attainable only in society, and more specifically in the society with the greatest freedom. Such a society is one in which there is an all-pervasive opposition among the members, together with the most exact definition of freedom and fixing of its limits so that it may be consistent with the freedom of others."

74. *Perpetual Peace*, Appendix I, 117: "Taken objectively, morality is in itself practical, being the totality of unconditionally mandatory laws according to which we ought to act. It would obviously be absurd, after granting authority to the concept of duty, to pretend that we cannot do our duty, for in that case this concept would itself drop out of morality (*ultra posse nemo obligatur*). Consequently, there can be no conflict of politics, as a practical doctrine of right, with ethics, as a theoretical doctrine of right."

75. Ibid., First Supplement, 111-112: "Now the republican constitution is the only one entirely fitting to the rights of man. But it is the most difficult to establish and even harder to preserve, so that many say a republic would have to be a nation of angels, because men with their selfish inclinations are not capable of a constitution of such sublime form. But precisely with these inclinations nature comes to the aid of the general will established on reason, which is revered even though impotent in practice. Thus it is only a question of a good organization of the state (which does lie in man's power), whereby the powers of each selfish inclination are so arranged in opposition that one moderates or destroys the ruinous effect of the other. The consequence for reason is the same as if none of them existed, and man is forced to be a good citizen even if not morally a good man. The problem of organizing a state, however hard it may seem, can be solved even for a race of devils, if only they are intelligent."

7

AUGUSTINE AND THE PROBLEM OF MODERNITY

My title assumes that modernity as a whole has become problematic and can no longer be simply taken for granted. On the other hand, it makes no effort to specify what is meant by "modernity" in this context and thus leaves open the question of Augustine's possible relationship to it, positive or negative.

THE MACHIAVELLIAN REVOLUTION AND MODERN REALISM

In the Middle Ages, the Moderns were the authors of classical and Christian antiquity who had written in Latin, as distinguished from their Greek counterparts. The distinction, a purely linguistic one, found its chronological justification in the fact that Greek literature had preceded Latin literature in time and provided the bulk of its inspiration. Conquered in battle by Rome's military might, the Greeks demonstrated their intellectual superiority to their new masters by conquering their minds. Cicero, who introduced philosophy into Rome and, by so doing, shaped the destiny of the West for centuries to come, was a self-proclaimed disciple of Plato and Aristotle. So were all, or most, of Rome's other great luminaries: Varro, Virgil, Tacitus, and Seneca, to mention only a few. Lucretius was a follower of Epicurus, another Greek. Stoicism, the most popular philosophy of the hellenistic and early Roman periods—it dominated the scene for five hundred years—was likewise a Greek export; and the list goes on. It ends only with Augustine, Boethius, and their disciples, all of whom were once classified as "moderns." No major ideological difference between the two groups, the Greeks and the Latins, was implied.

The modern use of "modern" is quite different. It goes well beyond the mere transposition of an older form of thought into a new idiom or its adaptation to a new historical setting—the Roman Empire, say, versus the small Greek polis. It rests on a radical critique of and final break with the entire tradition of ancient and medieval thought. That break, which may have been prepared or facilitated by the emergence of certain late-medieval philosophic and theological theories, nominalism in particular, was consummated by Machiavelli toward the beginning of the sixteenth century, a fact that was obscured by subsequent developments and that is still not acknowledged by everyone. A sign of the fundamental shift that takes place at this time is that Aristotle, who became the Western world's supreme authority in matters of political philosophy once the *Politics* was translated into Latin shortly after the middle of the thirteenth century, is not mentioned at all in *The Prince*, and, as far as I can see, only twice in passing throughout the rest of Machiavelli's works. This is not to deny that Aristotle is often tacitly referred to in those works, but only to suggest that his seeming absence from them tells us more about the novelty of the Machiavellian enterprise than would have any more explicit statement on Machiavelli's part.

Equally significant is the fact that Machiavelli himself is rarely mentioned in the works of the great early-modern thinkers, but this time for a different reason. Since his teaching was not on the face of it or even ultimately an edifying teaching, siding with him publicly would have been ill-advised. No one wanted to have his name associated with the man Shakespeare would soon be calling the "murderous Machiavel"[1] and whom Catholics and Protestants alike denounced as an atheist. This did not prevent his secret admirers from taking their cue from him and paraphrasing him in their works. Descartes sounds a thoroughly Machiavellian note when he says in Part I of the *Discourse on Method* that he compared the ethical writings of the ancients to "superb and magnificent palaces built only on mud and sand" and unable to provide an adequate criterion of virtue. What they called by the name of virtue, he said, was often "nothing but cruelty and apathy, parricide, pride, or despair."[2] Lest there should be any doubt about it, Descartes's high regard for Machiavelli is vouched for by the précis of *The Prince* that he included in a letter to his friend and patroness, Queen Christina of Sweden.

In a similar vein, Spinoza notes that the philosophers of the past "conceive of men, not as they are, but as they themselves would like them to be," and that, "instead of writing ethics, they have generally written satire and have never conceived a theory of politics that could be turned to use but only such as might be taken for a chimera, or might have been formed in Utopia, or in that golden age of poets when, to be sure, there was least need of it."[3] Hobbes, too, tacitly reveals his Machiavellian pedigree when, in the Epistle Dedicatory to the *De hominis natura*, he states that "as often as reason is against man, so often will a man be against reason" and goes on to dismiss the theories of his pre-Machiavellian predecessors as quixotic—as nothing but castles "built in the air."

To my knowledge, the only early modern writer to violate the unofficial code of silence observed in regard to Machiavelli is Francis Bacon, who asserts with uncommon boldness: "We are much beholden to Machiavel and others, that write what men do and not what they ought to do"[4] and then proceeds to engage in a thoroughly Machiavellian critique of premodern thought. I quote again from *The Advancement of Learning*: "As for the philosophers, they make imaginary laws for imaginary commonwealths, and their discourses are as the stars, which give little light because they are so high."[5]

All of these texts point to Machiavelli's "realism" or anti-utopianism as the heart of the modern revolution. Premodern philosophy had failed because it supposedly made impossibly high demands on people. Taking its bearings from man's "ultimate capacity," Aristotle's universal definition of virtue,[6] it set its sights on a goal so lofty as to be all but unattainable, and this despite the fact that by Aristotle's own admission, evil is what prevails for the most part among human beings. People in general are far more powerfully attracted to the good of the senses than to the good of the soul, the pursuit of which demands an effort that few of them are capable of day in and day out. For, to quote Aristotle again, the truth of the practical intellect, unlike that of the speculative intellect, is measured, not by the mind's conformity with the object, but by its conformity with the rectified appetite or desire—*omologia tê orexei orthê*,[7] something that is achieved only at the price of a painful conversion from the love of material goods to the love of spiritual goods. One becomes good by pursuing the good according to the mode of the good and not according to the mode of truth.[8] In simple terms, prudence is inseparable from the moral virtues, for it is by means of these virtues that one is ordered to the end or ends in the light of which prudential choices are to be made. As the old philosophic adage had it: as one is, so will the end appear to him. Little wonder that premodern thought should sooner or later have been decried as unrealistic. Machiavelli summed the matter up with admirable succinctness when he declared that the time had come to lay imagination aside and go to the "effectual truth of the matter"—*la verità effettuale della cosa.*[9]

It could be shown easily enough, although this is not the place to do it, that practically all the foundational doctrines of modern thought have their roots in or otherwise reflect this realism and are motivated by the same desire to enhance the effectiveness of human activity by consciously lowering its standards. I refer to such notions as individual or subjective rights and their substitution for duties as the primary moral counter; the state of nature and its concomitants, viz., social contractualism and the denial of the naturalness of civil society; the repudiation of natural teleology and its replacement by scientific mechanism; freedom as self-determination or autonomy versus heteronomy; popular sovereignty as a requirement of justice; the theory and not just the practice of religious pluralism; the idea of progress; and, more recently the extrusion of ethics from the realm of politics, value neutrality, and the radical historicity of human thought.

AUGUSTINE'S WOULD-BE MODERNITY

The amazing thing is that Augustine, who, like so many of the ancient writers was often criticized in the past for his "otherworldliness" or lack of realism, is now being credited with the paternity of these doctrines, many if not most of which are said by reputable scholars to have originated with him, either directly or else indirectly by way of a process of secularization that has emptied them of their religious content. In line with this view, Herbert A. Deane, the author of the classic treatment of Augustine's political thought in the English language, writes that for Augustine, the state

> is an external order; the peace that it maintains is external peace—the absence, or at least the diminution, of overt violence. The state is also a coercive order, maintained by the use of force and relying on the fear of pain as its major sanction for compliance to its commands. It has no weapons by which it can mold the thoughts, desires, and wills of its citizens; nor is it really concerned to exert such influence. It does not seek to make men truly good or virtuous. Rather, it is interested in their outward actions, and it attempts, with some success, to restrain its citizens from performing certain kinds of harmful and criminal acts. We have also observed that the state is a non-natural, remedial institution; like private property, slavery, and other forms of domination of man over man, it is a consequence of the Fall. It is both a punishment for sin and a remedy for

man's sinful condition; without it anarchy would reign, and self-centered, avaricious, power-hungry, lustful men would destroy one another in a fierce struggle for self-aggrandizement. This external, coercive, repressive, remedial order—and its main virtue is that it *is* an order—is clearly distinguished by Augustine from the order or hierarchy found among the angels and in the City of God; the latter is a spontaneous order of love and not an order of coercion or domination.

To this forthright if perhaps somewhat misleading statement, Deane adds pertinently,

> The reader of this brief summary of Augustine's doctrine of the state may wonder whether I am talking about Augustine, or about Hobbes or Machiavelli. Certainly, this conception of the state strikes us as essentially "modern," and we may be surprised to find it in a Christian philosopher of the fifth century.[10]

A like emphasis on Augustine's modernity or would-be modernity is present in a variety of other well-known critics and historians. In an influential book published over four decades ago and often quoted in the years that followed, Reinhold Niebuhr hailed Augustine as "the first great realist in Western history" and claimed him as the remote ancestor of the theological movement to which Niebuhr's own name was attached, "Realism," whose laudable goal was to effect a rapprochement between Christianity and liberal democracy on terms that were more or less acceptable to both sides.[11] For Hannah Arendt, Augustine, who took as his moral principle "Love and do what you will," is "the first philosopher of freedom." For Langdon Gilkey, he is "the father of the modern historical consciousness," the first author to exhibit an awareness of the fundamentally historical character of human existence, the only ancient Christian writer to have brought the whole of history within the compass of a "purposive unity."[12] For Charles Taylor, he is the bridge between Plato and Descartes, the inaugurator of the turn to the self, the man who "made the language of inwardness irresistible."[13] Others have labored valiantly to transform Augustine into a social science positivist before the letter. Much of the discussion in regard to this matter has tended to focus on Augustine's critique of Cicero's definition of a republic or commonwealth as "a group of people bound together by a common acknowledgment of right and a community of interests,"[14] a definition that Augustine rejects on the ground that actual cities rarely if ever exhibit any genuine concern for justice and right. Cicero's definition would be valid only if one were to strike from it any reference to a "common acknowledgment of right" and speak in morally neutral terms of "a common agreement as to the object of their love," which is usually nothing more than an expression of their collective selfishness.[15]

If all of this is true, Augustine, the "second founder of the ancient faith," as Possidius, his friend and biographer, calls him,[16] would have to be reckoned a prime contributor to the emergence of a project the aim of which was to subvert the very tradition that he was refounding. Since thinkers of Augustine's stature do not unwittingly contradict themselves, we are left with three possibilities: modern scholars have either misunderstood him, or misunderstood the thrust of modern thought, or misunderstood both Augustine and modern thought. The position that I shall defend is that Augustine was neither the starry-eyed idealist for which he has been taken by some, nor the hard-nosed realist for which he has been taken by others, and hence that his relationship to modernity is on the whole rather different from the one to which much of modern scholarship has accustomed us. This can be done (a) by showing how Augustine sought to reconcile the exalted moral ideal of the gospel with the painful and often sordid realities of the political life—the "dung of Romulus," as Cicero called it—and (b) by looking at what lies behind his peculiar penchant for hyperbolism, a penchant that seems to rule out the possibility of any such reconciliation. First, the attempted accommodation to the realities of the political life, the key political problem of the early Christian centuries and one that is as timely today as it was then.

AUGUSTINIAN ACCOMMODATIONISM

The problem at hand is ultimately rooted in the fact that Christianity, unlike Judaism, has no political program of its own and neither imposes nor recommends any particular form of government or social organization. The pious Jew, who had been given a divine and hence perfect law by which to live, knew that by obeying that law he was doing what was pleasing to God. The Christian, who was no longer under the Law, had no such assurance. On the one hand, he was urged to obey his temporal rulers, whoever they might be (probably Nero, when Romans 13 was written); on the other, he was told to follow Christ, a notoriously vague injunction that in itself can be taken to mean almost anything from going out into the wilderness and leading the life of an anchorite (like Antony of the desert), to preaching a crusade (like St. Bernard), conquering a new world for Christ (like the *reyes cristianos* of Spain's "golden age"), or running a soup kitchen (like Mother Teresa). To its credit, the Christian Church learned early on, in the struggle against Gnosticism, the first great internal threat to its existence, that unless it was able to demonstrate the compatibility of its teachings with life in society, it would suffer the fate of the fanatical sects of late antiquity and be suppressed.

In this process of accommodation, Christians could appeal to a noble precedent, the Book of Genesis, which, in its account of the devolution from the state of innocence to the post-lapsarian state and thence to the post-diluvian state, provided some indication as to how human beings could adapt to less than perfect conditions of humanity without losing sight of the ideal of perfection to which they are called. To cite only one example, the precepts of the Noachide convenant accorded to human beings the right to put capital offenders to death (Gen. 9:5), a loathsome practice justified only by the spread of evil in the world.

The problem, needless to say, was not unfamiliar to the classical philosophers, who had to face it like everyone else and invented their own way or ways of dealing with it. For Plato, the only form of justice worthy of the name is absolute justice, whose principles are not directly applicable to actual cities and must be diluted in order to become operative. In all but the rarest instances, obstacles stemming from their bodily nature prevent human beings from becoming perfect lovers of justice.[17] Few of them allow the love of the true and the beautiful to rule their lives and take precedence over the love of their own, a situation that rulers are obliged to tolerate, if only because any attempt to eradicate its causes would entail the use of a disproportionate amount of force and inflict even greater harm on people. Accordingly, the justice that we find in society at large, if we find it at all, is at best a shadow or a pale image of true justice. It is what Plato terms "vulgar" or "so-called" virtue.[18]

For reasons of his own, into which we cannot enter here, Aristotle opted for a different approach, defending the existence of natural right while at the same time asserting that the whole of it is variable.[19] The solution, a subtle one, consists in holding firm to the view that certain actions are intrinsically good and should be performed, while others are intrinsically evil and should be avoided. Yet, extraordinary circumstances, of the kind that tend to arise in times of war or national emergency, may occasionally render just an act that under normal circumstances would be unjust and vice versa. A classic example is the sacrifice of an innocent person for the sake of the common good when the latter cannot be preserved by any other means. In extreme cases such as these, what is chosen is not, as is often said, a lesser evil—a moral person never chooses evil, great or small—but the greater good that is secured by momentarily laying aside the ordinary rules of justice.

A third formulation was offered by Cicero, who spoke of something called the "right of nations," *ius gentium*,[20] by which he meant that part of natural right which is harmonizable with the social life and mediates between natural right in the strict sense and civil right.[21] Included in this right of nations are such matters as private property and slavery, both of which represent a departure from strict natural right: private property, because material goods do not necessarily belong by nature to their *de facto* owners, who may or may not know how to use them well or be ready to do so; and slavery, because the people who have the misfortune of being reduced to that state—usually prisoners of war—do not necessarily deserve their fate.

Cicero's solution is the one that prevailed for many centuries in the West through its incorporation into Roman law and its absorption into the Christian tradition *via* Isidore of Seville's widely disseminated encyclopedia, the *Etymologies*. It was later modified slightly and systematized under the influence of the biblical teaching by the great Scholastics of the Middle Ages. In response to Aristotle's teaching regarding the variability of natural right, Thomas Aquinas introduced a distinction between the primary and immutable precepts of the natural law and its secondary precepts, which are subject to change.[22] The distinction was not without its problems, however, for there were passages in the Bible that seemed to call into question the immutability of even the primary precepts. If these precepts are truly immutable, how could God command the killing of Isaac, the theft perpetrated by the Israelites at the time of the Exodus (Exod. 12:35-56), and Hosea's (Hosea 1:2) extramarital relations with a prostitute? Aquinas's answer is that in each of these cases the matter of the deed has undergone a change. The killing of Isaac, had it occurred, would not have been an act of murder because God, who is the author of life, is free to take it or order it to be taken whenever he sees fit. Nor was anything "stolen" from the Egyptians. God, the universal landlord and ultimate proprietor of all things, merely transferred the ownership of the goods in question from one nation to another!

Finally, in their quest for ever greater precision, some late-medieval thinkers distinguished between two forms of natural right: absolute natural right, whose principles brook no exceptions and are binding on everyone at all times, and conditional, relative, or secondary natural right, which presupposes the Fall and sanctions such institutions as private property, slavery, and coercive political rule, all of which were absent from the state of original justice and are necessitated—hence "justified"—only by man's present inability to live fully in accordance with the dictates of reason.[23]

None of these approaches corresponds exactly to the one adopted by Augustine, who, if my computer-generated information is accurate, never uses the expression *ius gentium* (with which he was undoubtedly familiar from Cicero), does not speak of primary and secondary natural law precepts, and is silent on the distinction between absolute and relative natural right. His own guiding principle is more directly biblical: the precept of the universal love of God and neighbor, in which, as he constantly reminds us, the entire message of the New Testament is summed up.[24]

A striking, though somewhat unusual, illustration of the manner in which that principle can be used to resolve concrete problems occurs in the treatise *On the Sermon on the Mount*,[25] where Augustine discusses a strange incident reported to have taken place at Antioch some fifty years earlier. The story involves a married woman whose husband was about to be executed for his failure to return a pound of gold borrowed from the public treasury; whereupon a rich fellow citizen offered to pay the debt in his stead, but only on condition that his wife, of whom he was enamored, agree to spend a night with him. Was she allowed to acquiesce in this immoral demand? Finding no precedent for such a case in the Scriptures, Augustine is at first puzzled but finally implies that the question can be answered in the affirmative[26]—that is, as long as the woman first secures her husband's permission; for St. Paul says that, although the wife has no power over her body, her husband does, and vice versa (I Cor.7:4). The deal was made, but not without further complications, for the rich neighbor was caught substituting a bag of sand for the pound of gold he had promised. For this, he was severely punished by the local prefect, who blamed himself for having created the problem in the first place by threatening to execute the husband and put up his own money to secure his freedom. Given Augustine's reputation for severity as regards sexual matters, the story is not without interest. Its language is certainly not that of an idealist who would rather let the world perish than make a single exception to his principles. Involved in the type of reasoning at work here is what I shall call Augustine's "third-party principle," according to which one can at times do for someone else's safety and well-being certain things that one is not allowed to do for one's own safety and well-being. The same principle is invoked to justify the killing of an unjust aggressor, but only as long as the unjust aggression is directed against someone else and not against oneself.[27] Engaging in heroism by proxy was happily not one of Augustine's favorite sports.

It would be a mistake, however, to think that the problem arises only in connection with isolated incidents such as the one we have just examined or the extreme situations to which Machiavelli habitually refers. In an insidious way, it affects the whole of one's life; for, by abiding by the laws and sharing the way of life of a society that is more or less unjust, as are all societies—the perfect regime exists only in speech—even the most decent citizen becomes willy-nilly a party to its systemic injustices and contributes to their perpetuation. This is the question to which Christian theology finally had to address itself.

Augustine's answer to it is that, defective as it invariably is, civil society is irreplaceable and hence a good to be defended at all cost. Human beings cannot long survive without it or attain their full moral and intellectual development outside of it. This is why Augustine, one of Rome's most severe critics, was among the first Christians to come to its defense when it became apparent that its existence was in the balance. What he loved and sought to preserve were not its injustices, against which he never ceased to inveigh, but the element of substantive justice that it embodied or made possible. As a bishop, he also realized that it is not up to the individual Christian, who stands before others as a witness of God's offer of salvation, to decide to whom that offer should be made. As a rule, one does not serve one's neighbor by abandoning him to his lot and withdrawing from society altogether, but by working for the betterment of that society.

AUGUSTINIAN RADICALISM

These sketchy remarks do not tell the whole story, however, for they fail to account for Augustine's tendency to disparage ordinary political life as that tendency reveals itself in a long series of hyperbolic statements which, taken out of context, would discourage anybody from lifting a finger in Rome's defense. To cite only a few examples from the *City of God*: Rome was never a republic;[28] all rulers are pirates in disguise and all cities "gigantic larcenies" (*magna latrocinia*) or compacts of wickedness;[29] the "virtues" of the pagans are nothing but vices;[30] disinterestedness is a mere pretense; down deep, everyone is in it for himself; what people call the *common* good is a figment of their imaginations; in a word, decent political life is an impossibility. But if so, one cannot help wondering how any man of noble character, let alone a thoughtful Christian, would want to have anything at all to do with it beyond what is absolutely necessary. Why did Augustine, who can be so eloquent when it comes to defending the role that Christians were called upon to play in Roman society, suddenly feel obliged to strike an altogether different chord?

A plausible answer to that question suggests itself when one recalls that in the *City of God* and the writings related to it, Augustine had two goals in mind. The first was to counter the charge that Christianity was to blame for the Empire's military weakness in the face of the threat posed to its existence by the massing of hordes of barbarians on its borders, a weakness dramatically illustrated by the recent sack of Rome by Alaric and the Goths in 410. This he did, as we have seen, by indicating how the gap between the pure morals of the Sermon on the Mount and the realities of Roman public life might be narrowed. The second goal was to entice the pagan elite of his time to embrace Christianity, something that a number of them were reluctant to do on the ground that it taught its followers to be more concerned with the good of their souls than with that of the fatherland and was thus incompatible with the highest duties of citizenship. The issue was brought home to Augustine in a poignant way by a friend of his, the aged Nectarius of Calama, a pagan who had imbibed from Cicero's *Republic* the loyal citizen's sentiment that there is no limit in either time or measure to the claim that his country has upon the service of right-hearted men, and who had grave reservations about a transcendent religion that was liable to dampen that sentiment.

The core of the political teaching of the *City of God* lies precisely in the tension between these two goals and the means by which they might be pursued. To attain the first goal Augustine had to reinforce the civic ardor of fellow Christians so as to attach them more firmly to the service of their earthly country; to attain the second, he had to moderate the civic ardor of his non-Christian friends so as to win them over to the Christian faith. The critique of Roman politics and religion that permeates so much of the *City of God* was specifically designed to make the pagan elite of his time aware of the problematic character of their devotion to Rome, admirable as it may have been in other respects. Hence its calculated one-sidedness, for only by downplaying the merits of Roman politics and dwelling on its shortcomings could Augustine hope to persuade these pagan "holdouts" that the time had come for them to embrace the new faith. After all, one's attachment to a given cause is in the best instance only as strong as one's conviction regarding the justice of that cause. In the present case, there was ample reason to doubt whether justice was unambiguously and in every way on the side of Rome.

The strategy that he adopted was not entirely new. It had been employed to good effect by Plato, whose criticism of Athenian politics is not any less radical than Augustine's criticism of Roman politics. In their discussion of the best regime in the *Republic,* Socrates and his young friends decide to found a city in speech because no existing city, least of all Athens, is good enough to serve as their model. Elsewhere, Socrates spends a good deal of time denigrating the most eminent statesmen of his time—Pericles, Themistocles, Miltiades, Thucydides. Warned by his *daimôn,* Socrates himself never entered politics under pretext that to do so would have been to fall in with "wild beasts" and risk his life.[31] Still, the similarity between the two approaches should not blind us to the difference that sets them apart. Whereas Augustine was writing in defense of the Faith, Plato was writing in defense of philosophy. His hero, Socrates, that compulsive body-snatcher, was luring the flower of the Athenian youth away from a life of public service into what, in the eyes of most loyal citizens, was a life of private self-indulgence. In contrast to Socrates, Augustine is more aptly described as the humble disciple who, in response to his divine master's call, becomes a "fisher of men" (Matt. 4:19; Mk. 1:17). The fact remains that both of them were engaged in behavior that was bound to arouse the suspicions of their fellow citizens. Some justification of that behavior was necessary and continued to be necessary, at least until such time as philosophy had been fully implanted in Greece and Christianity fully implanted in the West. For obvious reasons, we find it in Plato and Augustine, who were involved in a struggle to accredit either philosophy or Christianity. We do not find it to the same degree in Aristotle, who inherited a situation in which philosophy was no longer viewed as a dangerous pariah but accepted as a more or less welcome guest; and we do not find it in Thomas Aquinas, who inherited a situation in which Christianity was already well accredited.

Augustine's "radicalism," as I have labeled it, is by no means limited to his treatment of Rome. It is a standard feature of his thought and shows up in a variety of other places as well, among them his discussion of the natural law, now defined "up" as a law that imposes as a duty the possession of all the virtues, including theoretical wisdom[32]—another impossibility since, as Augustine is the first to admit, theoretical wisdom is the exclusive preserve of a handful of naturally gifted and well-trained individuals. This maximalist conception of the natural law is what accounts for Augustine's tacit refusal to endorse Cicero's notion of *ius gentium*; for by sanctioning as "just," even if only in a secondary or relative sense, certain actions that fall short of perfect justice, one accords to them a greater dignity than they deserve and would otherwise have.[33]

This brings us back to the question raised earlier: is Augustine a latent, half-baked, or premodern representative of modernity, or, if not, how exactly are we to define his position in relation to it? If we view modernity as the concerted attempt to lower the goals of human existence so as to render them more readily accessible, and to do so by lopping off the time-honored goals of wisdom and prudence for which human beings were once encouraged to strive, it is hard to see how Augustine could qualify as a modern. On the other hand, it is clear from what we have said that he was fully aware of the intractability of the moral dilemmas which human beings frequently have to face and that he could be remarkably flexible whenever necessary. His general stance and posture appears to be, if not identical to, at least consonant with the typical premodern position, which is best described as a judicious blend of high ideals and moderate expectations. As such, it stands in sharp contrast to the combination of moderate ideals and absolute expectations that characterizes modern thought at its best. What separates the two worlds is more than a question of degree, emphasis, or approach. It is a question of fundamental orientation and irreconcilable principle.

This said, one should not be gulled into thinking that the chasm which divides these two worlds is such as to render futile any further discussion between them. The charges of naive idealism, moral intransigence, or religious fanaticism once commonly leveled at Augustine are part of a caricature indulged in for the specific purpose of casting discredit on a premodernity that his critics had already rejected on extratheoretical grounds, whether it be the revulsion inspired by the Spanish Inquisition, the sixteenth-century wars of religion, or the seventeenth-century witch hunts. It is unlikely that Augustine would have renounced his convictions in favor of the new principles had he known them, and it is even less likely that he would have taken credit for originating them. However, as a scarred veteran of the intellectual wars of his day, he would undoubtedly have welcomed them as an opportunity to test the validity of his own presuppositions and, by so doing, gain a deeper insight into them.

NOTES

1. Shakespeare, *King Henry the Sixth, Part Three*, act III, scene 3, line 193.

2. René Descartes, *Discourse on Method* and *Meditations* (Indianapolis, IN: Library of Liberal Arts, 1960), *Discourse on Method*, Part I, 7.

3. *Political Treatise,* chap. 1.

4. Francis Bacon, *The Advancement of Learning*, II.21.9.

5. Francis Bacon, *The Advancement of Learning*, II.23.49.

6. *De Coelo* I.281a6-19

7. *Nicomachean Ethics* VI.1139a27-31

8. The nurse who, by mistake and through no fault of her own, administers the wrong medicine to a patient performs a morally good act even if the patient should die from it.

9. *The Prince*, chap. 15

10. H. A. Deane, *The Political and Social Ideas of St. Augustine* (Columbia University Press, 1963), 117-18.

11. R. Niebuhr, *Christian Realism and Political Problems* (New York: Scribner, 1953), 115. Niebuhr finds it "something of a mystery" that Augustine's insights into human nature and history "could have been subordinated to classical thought with so little sense of the conflict between them in the formulations of Thomas Aquinas, and how they should have become so authoritative in Roman Catholicism without more debate between Augustinian and Thomistic emphases," 127.

12. L. Gilkey, *Reaping the Whirlwind* (New York: Seabury Press, 1976), 175 and 164.

13. C. Taylor, *Sources of the Self: The Making of the Modern Identity* (Cambridge and London: Harvard University Press, 1989), 127, 131.

14. *De civitate Dei* (*The City of God*) II.21.

15. *De civ. Dei* XIX.21.

16. Possidius, *Vita Augustini* 7, (Migne *Patrologia, Series Latina* or PL 32 col. 39.

17. In *De libero arbitrio* (*On Free Choice of the Will*) III.18-22, Augustine reduces these obstacles to two kinds, "ignorance" and the "difficulty" involved in the effort to overcome one's lower self.

18. Cf. *Phaedo* 61a; *Republic* 518d.

19. *Nic. Ethic.* V.1134b18f.

20. The expression, which may have been coined by Cicero himself (cf. *De re publica* I.2; *De officiis* 3.69), is apparently modeled on Aristotle's *koinos nomos, Rhetoric* I.12, 2 and 15,4.

21. Such is the meaning attributed to the expression by Thomas Aquinas, according to whom *ius gentium* belongs in part to natural right and in part to positive right. Cf. I-II qu. 95, a.5; II-II qu. 57, a. 3. The best account that I have seen of the use of *ius gentium* in Cicero is that of M. P. Zuckert, "Bringing Philosophy Down from the Heavens: Natural Right in the Roman Law," *Review of Politics* 51 (1989): 70-85.

22. *Summa theologiae* I-II, qu. 94, a.5.

23. See, for example, Ockham, *Dialogus* Part III, Treatise ii, Book 3, chap. 6. R. Hooker, *Laws of Ecclesiastical Polity*, I.10.13. A theory of relative natural right is attributed, perhaps misleadingly, to the early Christian writers by E. Troeltsch, *Social Teachings*, vol. I, 100.153f, 201, et passim.

24. In the *De doctrina christiana*, Augustine goes so far as to say that anyone who has understood that principle can dispense with Scripture altogether.

25. *De sermone Domini in monte (On the Lord's Sermon on the Mount)* I.16.50.

26. Editor's note: The key passage in *De sermone Domini in monte* I.16.50 where Augustine discusses the woman's acquiescence in the immoral demand reads as follows: "Nihil hinc in aliquam partem disputo. Liceat cuique existimare quod velit; non enim de divinis auctoritatibus deprompta historia est." My literal translation of this passage is as follows: "From this story I offer no argument either way. Let each one form a judgment as he wishes; for the story is not drawn from divine sources." In my mind, Augustine's "third-party principle" doesn't support the consequentialist reasoning of contemporary moral theologians.

27. Cf. *De libero arbitrio* I.5.32f.

28. *De civ. Dei* XIX.21.

29. *De civ. Dei* IV.4.

30. *De civ. Dei* XIX.25.

31. Matt. 4:19; Mark 1:17.

32. Cf. *De libero arbitrio* I.752f.

33. See along the same lines and in connection with the later formulations of the problem to which we have alluded, L. Strauss, *Natural Right and History* (Chicago: University of Chicago Press, 1953), 153: "If the principles valid in civil society are diluted natural right, they are much less venerable than if they are regarded as secondary natural right, i.e., as divinely established and involving an absolute duty for fallen man. Only in the latter case is justice, as it is commonly understood, unquestionably good. Only in the latter case does natural right in the strict sense or the primary natural right cease to be dynamite for civil society."

8

THE POLITICAL THOUGHT
OF ST. THOMAS AQUINAS

Thomas Aquinas occupies a unique position in the history of political thought as the most illustrious of all Christian Aristotelians. His literary career coincides roughly with the full impact and in some instances with the initial recovery of Aristotle's works in the Western world. Both the *Politics* and the complete text of the *Ethics* in particular were first translated into Latin during his own lifetime. Through his detailed commentaries on virtually all of Aristotle's major treatises and the extensive use that he makes of Aristotelian materials in his theological works, Aquinas did more than anyone else to establish Aristotle as the leading philosophical authority in the Christian West. His own political philosophy is best understood as a modification of Aristotle's political philosophy in the light of Christian revelation or more precisely as an attempt to integrate Aristotle with an earlier tradition of Western political thought represented by the Church Fathers and their medieval followers and compounded for the most part of elements taken from the Bible, Platonic-Stoic philosophy, and Roman law.

Aquinas's endeavor to reinterpret Aristotle on the basis of the Christian faith and to reform Christian theology in terms of Aristotelian philosophy may be compared with that of the Islamic and Jewish philosophers of the Middle Ages, who also regarded Aristotle as the greatest of the pagan philosophers and who were faced with a similar problem of harmonizing Greek philosophy and revealed religion. With these Islamic and Jewish philosophers, Aquinas shared a common heritage which included the *Organon*, the *Metaphysics*, the *Physics* along with various other treatises of natural philosophy, and the *Nicomachean Ethics*. Like them, he was indebted to Aristotle for the distinction between speculative science and practical science as well as for the division of practical science into ethics, economics, and politics. But whereas Aquinas's natural philosophy, his ethics, and his political philosophy were all inspired by Aristotle, political philosophy in Islam and in the Jewish communities living in Islamic countries was based largely on the *Republic* and the *Laws* of Plato. Both of these works had been translated into Arabic at least as early as the tenth century but did not become available in the West until the fifteenth century. Alfarabi wrote commentaries on the *Republic* and the *Laws* and Averroes wrote a commentary on the *Republic*. No Arabic or Jewish commentary is known to have been written on Aristotle's *Politics* during the Middle Ages, while no fewer than seven commentaries were written on it by Christian authors from the time of the first Latin version of the text (ca. 1260) to the end of the thirteenth century.

It is possible and even likely that this first and most obvious difference between the Christian and the Judaeo-Arabic traditions was due to factors other than the mere historical accident of the availability or unavailability of the literary sources in question either in the Latin or the Arabic world. The evidence at hand suggests that the *Politics* of Aristotle had been rendered into Arabic at an early date and, in any event, its contents were known to the Islamic and Jewish philosophers through excerpts from that work as well as through the *Nicomachean Ethics* and other works of Aristotle. Likewise, the existence and part of the substance of the *Republic* and the *Laws* were familiar to the Western authors from Aristotle's *Politics* and from earlier Roman and Christian adaptations or discussions of those works by such writers as Cicero and Augustine. Yet, contrary to what was usually done in similar cases, no effort appears to have been made by either group to obtain copies or translations of the missing texts. On the strength of that and related evidence, it is not unreasonable to suppose that the use of the *Politics* by the Christian authors, and of the *Republic* and the *Laws* by the Arabic and Jewish philosophers, was at least partially the result of a deliberate choice dictated by the circumstances of the political life in these different religious communities.

We know from Alfarabi that his own works were motivated by the concern to introduce philosophy into a society from which it was absent or to restore it once it had become obscured or destroyed.[1] The specific situation to which these works address themselves called for a public defense of philosophy or its justification before the tribunal of commonly accepted opinion and religious belief. It imposed or invited an approach to the study of politics which comes to terms with or attempts to surmount the native hostility of the political and religious establishment toward any science that questions and, by so doing, threatens to undermine its foundations. It thus presented a definite kinship with the situation confronted by Plato, whose philosophy was itself developed within a predominantly political context.

Unlike Alfarabi and his successors, Aquinas was rarely forced to contend with an antiphilosophic bias on the part of the ecclesiastical authorities. As a Christian, he could simply assume philosophy without becoming publicly involved in any argument for or against it. Not only was philosophy already accredited in the West and officially sanctioned by canon law but a knowledge of it was required of all students of theology. It is typical of the Christian society of the Middle Ages, in contrast to the Islamic and Jewish communities, that its churchmen were also schoolmen. In Aquinas's works it is rather theology which is justified before the bar of reason or philosophy. The first article of his best known work, the *Summa Theologiae*, does not ask whether the study of philosophy is permissible and desirable but whether besides the philosophic disciplines another science, namely sacred doctrine, is necessary. Equally revealing from the same point of view is the fact that the reasons which Maimonides had invoked to justify the concealing of philosophic truths from the multitude could be used by Aquinas to show instead why, in addition to supernatural truths, God has seen fit to reveal certain natural truths or truths that are accessible to human reason and experience alone.[2] This unique state of affairs appears to have engendered a preference for Aristotle's *Politics*, which presupposes a larger measure of agreement between philosophy and the city and hence a greater openness to philosophy on the part of the city than Plato's *Republic*. The canonical status which philosophy enjoyed in the Christian world helps to explain at the same time why Aquinas was able to discard as unnecessary or irrelevant the esotericism common to much of the ancient philosophic tradition and purposely affected by many of the Church Fathers with whose works he was acquainted.[3]

It is impossible, however, to account fully for the decidedly Platonic character of Judaeo-Arabic political thought and the decidedly Aristotelian character of Christian political thought simply by adverting to the fact that philosophy was generally accepted in Christian society while it was often frowned upon or rejected by the Islamic and Jewish communities of the Middle Ages. One must still ask how philosophy came to be received by Christianity in the first place and why the Aristotelianism of Aquinas and his disciples eventually replaced the Platonism of the Fathers as the traditional form of Christian theology. The clue to this deeper problem is to be sought ultimately in the difference between Christianity and either Islam or Judaism as religious and political societies. The most distinctive feature of Islam and Judaism is that they both present themselves first and foremost as divinely revealed laws, or as all-inclusive social orders, regulating every segment of men's private and public lives and precluding from the outset any sphere of activity in which reason could operate independently of the divine law. Christianity, on the other hand, first comes to sight as a faith or as a sacred doctrine, demanding adherence to a set of fundamental beliefs but otherwise leaving its followers at liberty to organize their social and political lives in accordance with norms and principles that are not specifically religious. This basic difference goes hand in hand with the difference that one notes in regard to the order of the sacred sciences within each religious community. The highest science in Islam and Judaism was jurisprudence (*fiqh*), upon which devolved the all-important task of interpreting, applying, and adapting the prescriptions of the divine law and to which dialectical theology (*kalam*) was always clearly subordinated. The highest science in Christianity was theology, whose prestige far exceeded any that was ever accorded to theological speculation in the Jewish and Arabic traditions. The same essential difference led to the further consequence that Christian society, and it alone, was ruled by two distinct powers and two distinct codes of law, one ecclesiastical or canonical and the other civil; each with its own sphere of competence and each relatively free in principle from interference on the part of the other. To the first belonged the care of directing men to their supernatural end; to the second, that of directing them to their earthly or temporal end. The upshot was that one was usually able to study political phenomena in the light of reason alone without directly challenging the established religious authority or running the risk of an open confrontation with it. As a result, such specific issues as the origin of divine and human laws, the relation between the two, and the communication of divine laws through the medium of prophecy or revelation, which, as Avicenna observes,[4] are discussed as political themes by Plato but not by Aristotle, were no longer seen to be as pertinent to the Christian philosophers as they had been to their Muslim and Jewish counterparts. In short, the very structure of Christian society, with its clear-cut distinction between the spiritual and temporal spheres, bore an obvious affinity with the restricted and somewhat independent manner in which political matters are treated in Aristotle's *Politics*.

The remarks that have been made thus far concerning the general characteristics of political philosophy within the Judaeo-Arabic and the Christian traditions point to a final problem which was of paramount importance to both groups, that of the relation between philosophy and revealed religion. Aquinas's solution to this problem purports to do full justice to the claims of reason as well as those of Revelation. It differs from that of the majority of the Muslim philosophers, who, while outwardly proclaiming the supremacy of the law, regarded philosophy as the perfect science and the sole judge of the truth of Revelation; and it likewise differs from that of Augustine and his other Christian predecessors, who tend to discuss all human problems in the light of man's final end as it is known through Revelation and in whose works the mundane sciences, to the extent to which they are cultivated, form part of an integrated whole or single wisdom illumined by faith. Aquinas begins by distinguishing clearly between the domains of faith and of reason or between philosophy and theology, each of which is conceived as a complete and independent science.[5] The first proceeds under the light of naturally known and self-evident principles and represents the perfection of man's understanding of the natural order of the universe. It culminates in metaphysics or first philosophy, which remains supreme in its own realm and is not dethroned by theology as the queen of the human sciences. Even without divine grace nature is complete in itself and possesses its own intrinsic perfection in that it has within itself that by means of which it is capable of attaining its end or returning to its principle. Theology, on the other hand, offers a comprehensive account of the beginning and end of all things as they appear in the light of divine Revelation. Its premises are derived from the faith and it makes use of such philosophic doctrines as may be relevant to its purpose, not indeed as principles, but as instruments in its methodical investigation of the content of Revelation.

Far from destroying nature, divine grace presupposes it and perfects it by elevating it to an end that is higher than any to which it could aspire by its own means. Hence, between the truths of Revelation and the knowledge acquired by the sole use of reason and experience there is a distinction but there can be no fundamental disagreement. The preestablished harmony between the two orders is founded theoretically on the assumption that God, the revealer of divine truth, is also the author of nature.[6] Any discrepancy between the Bible and the teachings of the philosophers is traceable to the imperfection of the human mind which has either misinterpreted the datum of Revelation or erred in its quest for natural truth. The human soul is the weakest of the intellectual substances. All of man's knowledge originates with the senses and is obtained by abstraction from sensible things. As such it involves a multiplicity of concepts and necessarily exhibits a fragmented and discursive character. What differentiates man as a knowing being is "reason" as distinguished from "intellect" or the fact that he does not grasp the truth intuitively and all at once but arrives at it gradually through a complex rational process by means of which the mind passes in orderly fashion from the known to the unknown.[7] Because of individual differences stemming from their bodily nature, men do not all possess the same intellectual endowments and are not all equally well disposed with respect to the attainment of knowledge.[8] Neither is there any assurance that the more gifted among them will ordinarily have at their disposal the leisure or the means to devote themselves entirely to the pursuit of the truth. Moreover, although moral evil, to which man is invariably prone, does not directly impair his reasoning faculty or diminish his capacity to learn, it renders the acquisition of science extrinsically more arduous by the disorder that it provokes in his appetite.[9] Given the intrinsic limitations of the human mind and the external obstacles with which it must struggle in its search for knowledge, it is not surprising that even philosophers should lapse into error and disagree among themselves. To the extent to which they fall short of the truth, their teachings are occasionally at odds with the faith; but the fact remains that reason itself cannot demonstrate the impossibility of Revelation, any more than it can prove its real possibility. The most that can be said from Aquinas's point of view is that the arguments adduced by philosophers against divine Revelation as a whole or any part thereof never offer any evidence such that the mind is compelled to assent to them.[10]

Although Aquinas looked upon Aristotelian philosophy as the most perfect expression of natural truth and as the philosophy which was most congruent with the truth of Christianity, he was fully able to coordinate that philosophy with the Christian faith only by transforming it both in content and in spirit. For present purposes the precise nature of that transformation is perhaps best illustrated by the fact that, whereas Aristotle never speaks of natural law but only of natural right, Aquinas has generally come to be regarded as the classic exponent of the natural law theory in the Western world.

CHRISTIANITY AND POLITICS:
THE NATURE OF THE POLITICAL REGIME

The cornerstone of Aquinas's political philosophy is the Aristotelian notion of nature. More than all other animals, man is a political and social being.[11] Civil society is natural to him, not as something given by nature, but as something to which he is inclined by nature and which is necessary for the perfection of his rational nature. Man, nature's most remarkable product, is brought into the world more helpless and destitute than any other animal—unshod, unclad, and unarmed. Instead, nature has furnished him with reason, speech, and hands, with which he is eventually able to provide for himself and meet his needs as they arise.[12] It is beyond the capacity of one individual, however, to obtain all that is required for his livelihood. In order to subsist during the years that precede the development of reason and the acquisition of manual skills, as well as to live more conveniently in later years, man is necessarily reliant on the help that he receives from other men.

The first society to which he belongs and without which he could not live, let alone live well, is the family, whose specific purpose is to procure the necessities of life and thus guarantee the preservation of both the individual and the species. The various associations that it comprises—that of male and female, of parents and children, of master and slave—are all directed to the same end. The science or art that has as its object the proper management of the family is economics or household governance, which deals primarily with the acquisition and administration of such staples and commodities as are used or consumed by the members of the household.

But the family alone cannot supply all the material goods that man needs for his sustenance and his protection, nor is it capable of leading all of its members to the perfection of virtue. Paternal injunctions, which rely for their effectiveness on the natural love between father and son, normally suffice to insure that generous-minded youths will behave decently but are of limited use in the case of base souls, over whom persuasion has little or no power and who need to be coerced by fear of punishment.[13] The truly self-sufficient human association, the only one capable of securing the conditions of virtue and satisfying all of man's earthly needs and aspirations, is the city. The city is the most perfect work of practical reason. Although less natural from the point of view of its form than the family, as is evidenced by the fact that its structure exhibits a greater variety from one society to another than that of the family, it is nevertheless ordered to a higher and more comprehensive end. As a perfect society it encompasses all the other associations that human beings are capable of forming, including the family, whose end it subordinates to its own, which is the complete human good.[14] Only within the framework of civil society can man attain the fullness of life, so much so that the man who leads a solitary life away from the company of his fellow men either falls short of human perfection like a beast or has already exceeded that perfection and achieved a state of godlike self-sufficiency.[15]

Like the human body to which it is frequently compared, the city is made up of a multiplicity of heterogeneous parts, each one of which has its own special work or function. Since the individual part is often animated by passions and desires that do not coincide with those of other parts, it is essential that in a city there be a single authority whose proper task is to look after the good of the whole and to maintain order and unity among its various components. Political authority is the determining element of the city or its "form," as Aristotle had called it by analogy with the doctrine of matter and form as the constituent principles of natural beings. A city without a regime is like a body without a soul: to the extent to which one can even speak of it, it is a city in name only. Accordingly, if the city is natural, political authority, which is indispensable to it, is also natural, as opposed to slavery, which, for Aquinas and the Christian tradition before him, is rooted not in man's nature as such but in man's fallen nature.[16] Political authority differs from slavery in that it constitutes the rule of free men over free men and has as its object the good of all the citizens, who as free men exist for their own sakes. The slave, on the other hand, exists for the sake of another and hence is not ruled for his own good but for the good of the master.

It follows from what has been said that the city is more than the sum of its parts and its overall end more than the sum of the particular interests of its members. To be sure, that end is not different from the end of the single man; but since the single man depends on the city for his full development, the end of the city assumes the nature of a common good, that is to say, of a good which, while numerically one, is yet shared by every citizen of that city.[17] Just as the whole is more important than the part and prior to it as that to which the part is ordered and without which it could not exist, so the city is prior to the individual in the order of final causality and its good is higher in dignity and "more divine" than that of each man taken by himself.[18] It is paradoxical at first sight but not inconsistent to say with Aquinas that the common good of the city is itself the proper good, though obviously not the private good, of the individual citizen.[19] As a proper good, it is the object of an inclination which is stronger than that which impels a citizen to seek his private good. Thus, in the event of a conflict between the common good and the private good, the former naturally takes precedence over the latter. This explains why, in cases of extreme necessity, a man will spontaneously sacrifice himself for the city in the same way that he will sacrifice a hand for the good of the whole body.[20]

The common good and the end of political authority is in the first instance peace or the harmony of the different parts that combine to make up the city.[21] Peace exists when each part is adjusted to the whole and functions with reasonable smoothness within it. But this fundamental unity, together with the ability to counteract the forces that threaten to destroy it, represents only the minimal condition under which the city can subsist. It is the lowest and not the highest goal to which its energies may be devoted. Over and beyond mere survival, the city has as its purpose the promotion of the good life or virtue among its citizens.[22] Experience reveals that singly and collectively men are attracted to a variety of goods, such as wealth, honor, freedom or virtue, some of which are obviously more noble than others. The goal or goals which a given city actually pursues are determined in largest measure by the men who have the decisive say in that city and thereby constitute its regime. The regime in this sense is none other than the way of life of a city with particular reference to the manner in which political power is distributed within it.[23] What distinguishes one city from another and confers upon it its specific nobility or greatness is precisely the regime by which it is governed. The best regime or the question of who should rule in the city thus emerges as the central theme of political philosophy.

Since men differ from one another in many ways but most notably with respect to their capacity for knowledge and virtue,[24] and since by nature the inferior is subordinated to the superior, it stands to reason that the best man should rule over the others and that ruling offices should be distributed according to virtue. In and of itself the most desirable regime, both on the ground of unity and of the nobility of the end to which it is dedicated, is kingship or the unconditional rule of a single wise man for the sake of virtue. But if absolute monarchy is theoretically the best of the just regimes, it is also the one that is fraught with the greatest dangers. Because of the vast powers vested in him, the king, unless he happens to be an unusually virtuous man, may become corrupted and his rule may easily degenerate into tyranny, which, all other things being equal, is the worst of all rules since by its very nature it stands furthest from the common good.[25] Moreover, virtue is not as easily recognized by most people as other more obvious though less genuine qualities such as wealth or noble birth. It is a matter of common observation that politically wise and virtuous men are not always and perhaps not generally acknowledged to be such by other men, the majority of whom have little real knowledge of wisdom or virtue.[26] Nor is it permissible to assume that the unwise multitude could readily be persuaded to accept a perfectly virtuous man as its sole ruler since the interests in which he may be expected to govern would presumably run counter to its own less noble interests. The unity of the city, if nothing else, requires that the conflicting claims of the various elements within it be taken into consideration and reconciled within the limits of possibility. In all or virtually all cases, the demands of wisdom and excellence must be combined with those of consent. This means that for concrete purposes the best regime is the so-called mixed regime or the regime which blends in harmonious fashion the best features of monarchy, aristocracy, and polity. In support of this typically classical solution Aquinas could point to a sacred precedent, that of the ancient Hebrew polity, where the authority of Moses and his successors was balanced by that of a group of elders chosen from the people at large.[27]

The stability and efficacy of this regime, or for that matter of any regime, is best secured by the rule of law, which becomes most of the time a practical necessity because of the habitual scarcity of wise men and the abuses to which the rule by decree is inherently exposed. Since wise men are never very numerous, it is easier to find a few who are capable of framing good laws than to find many who are capable of judging in individual cases. Legislators also have more time to deliberate and are in a better position to take into account all the different facets of a problem than the man who is faced with the constant necessity of making decisions on the spot. Finally, their judgment is less likely to become clouded by their personal involvement in the issues upon which they are required to pronounce themselves, inasmuch as laws are proposed universally and regard future events.[28] Laws are the privileged instrument of politics and stand in relation to the works of man as universals to particulars. It is through them more than through any other agency that the ruler promotes justice and moral goodness among the citizens. Moral virtue is acquired precisely by the repetition of those acts which the law prescribes or by habitual living and education under good laws.[29] Hence, the importance of legislation, which assumes an architectonic character and constitutes the most important act of the political art.[30] It remains that laws are enacted, enforced, and, whenever necessary, amended by men. In a word, they are themselves the products of the regime in which they originate. We are thus led back to the notion of the regime as the fundamental political phenomenon and the guiding theme of political philosophy.

Up to this point Aquinas's political philosophy would appear to be in substantial harmony with that of Aristotle from which it is ostensibly derived. Closer examination nevertheless reveals that in taking over Aristotle's concept of the political nature of man and of human living, Aquinas has modified it profoundly under the influence of Christianity and Stoicism and as a consequence of the high degree of clarity and certitude that attaches to the notion of God as a lawgiver in both of these traditions. Human excellence is no longer defined or circumscribed by the conditions of the political life. Through knowledge of the natural law man accedes directly to the common order of reason, over and above the political order to which he belongs as a citizen of a particular society. By sharing in that law he finds himself, along with all other intelligent beings, a member of a universal community or cosmopolis ruled by divine providence and whose justice is vastly superior to that of any human regime. The dissociation implied in such a view between the best human regime and the perfect social order is further accentuated by the Christian and Thomistic teaching according to which the entire natural order is in turn subject to the order of grace or divine law. Hence, the simply best regime is not, as it was for Aristotle, the work of man or of practical reason guided by philosophy. It is synonymous with the kingdom of God and is actual or attainable at all times through God's saving grace. Civil society ceases to be uniquely responsible for the totality of moral virtue and is itself judged by a higher standard to which human actions must conform universally. It becomes part of a broader whole, embracing all men and all cities and is by that very fact deprived of its privileged status as the sole horizon limiting the scope of man's moral activity, setting the goals to which he may aspire, and determining the basic order of his priorities.[31]

The transpolitical character of the Thomistic doctrine is revealed, among other ways, by the manner in which Aquinas divides moral and political science. The *Commentary on the Ethics* goes out of its way to point out that the unity of the family or of the city is not an organic unity but a unity of order only and hence that the individual members of these societies retain a sphere of action that is different from that of the whole. From this observation Aquinas draws the conclusion that ethics, economics, and politics constitute not one science composed of three parts but three separate and specifically distinct sciences, thereby investing both ethics and economics with an autonomy that they do not possess in the Aristotelian arrangement.[32] This teaching finds a significant parallel in Aquinas's discussion of natural right which forms part of his treatise on particular justice and follows the tradition of Ulpian and the Roman lawyers, who treated natural right as a division of private right, rather than that of Aristotle, where the question of natural right is taken up entirely within the context of legal justice.[33] In discussing the virtuous citizen's readiness to give up his life for his country, Aquinas observes that such an act would be the object of a natural inclination if man were by nature a part of the society for which he sacrifices himself.[34] We are given to understand by this remark that man's relationship to a particular civil society, as distinct from other civil societies, is not simply natural but acquired. Although Aquinas agrees with Aristotle that the man who cuts himself off from society and the affairs of his fellow men is either more than human or less than human, his example of the superior person, whose perfection exceeds the bounds of civil society, is not that of the philosopher, which is presumably what Aristotle had in mind, but that of St. Anthony, a third-century hermit notorious among other things for his opposition to philosophy.[35] Finally, to cite only one other example, Aquinas interprets Aristotle's statement to the effect that moral virtue is relative to the regime as referring to the relative goodness of man as a citizen and not to his absolute goodness as a man. The latter is said to be inseparable from practical wisdom, whose first principles are naturally known and understood by everyone independently of the political regime.[36] Under these circumstances the notion of the best regime as the primary and indispensable condition of the happiness of individuals and cities loses its supreme importance, as does political philosophy itself, upon whose guidance the best regime is dependent for its actualization.

MORAL VIRTUE AND THE NATURAL LAW

Both the theoretical basis and the practical implications of the Thomistic position are clearly discernible in Aquinas's treatment of the moral virtues. That treatment may be described as an attempt to set forth how man should act in the light of what he is or of his rational nature. As such it appeals directly to principles which are not indigenous to moral science but rather are borrowed from natural science to which they properly belong.[37] It thus assumes on the part of the reader a determinate understanding of man's nature and of his natural end as they are apprehended by the speculative intellect. Generally speaking, it presents a more doctrinal or more strictly deductive aspect than that of Aristotle.

The difference between the two authors is already evident to some extent from Aquinas's *Commentary on the Ethics*. In Books Two to Five of the *Ethics*, Aristotle had simply listed eleven moral virtues with no precise indication as to the reason for the order in which they are presented and with little or no effort to relate these virtues to the human soul and its different parts. His discussion remains exclusively on the plane of moral virtue and confines itself to an elucidation of moral phenomena as these appear to decent or honest men as distinguished from philosophers. Its typical addressee is the "gentleman" or the man of good moral habits and opinions who takes decency for granted and does not have to be convinced of the intrinsic superiority of the moral life over the immoral life. Its avowed aim is to clarify and articulate what the wellborn and well-bred man already knows in a confused way and accepts on the basis of his own experience and upbringing but without any real awareness of its theoretical presuppositions. In accordance with this eminently practical purpose, it eschews any express reference to the speculative premises in which morality is ultimately grounded but whose knowledge is only remotely helpful to the person who is more concerned with the actual practice of virtue than with a thorough grasp of its foundations in human nature. Just as one can be a good carpenter without having studied the science of geometry, so one can be a good man without having engaged in a scientific study of human acts. Simply put, the question that the discussion as a whole raises is, What is a good man? and not, Why should one be a good man? The answer that it provides to that question draws its chief support from the evidence that morality achieves in the mind of the man for whom moral goodness has become so to speak a second nature, and not from such knowledge as may be obtained through a philosophic investigation of man as a natural being. The whole account culminates in a description of magnanimity and justice, the two general virtues which epitomize or define man's perfection as an individual and as a social being respectively.

Aquinas's interpretation of the corresponding sections of the *Ethics* goes beyond what is either explicitly stated or implicitly contained in the text by bringing to light the reasons that purportedly justify Aristotle's method of procedure. Courage and moderation have as their proper matter what Aquinas calls the primary passions, such as anger and lust. Then come the virtues connected with the secondary passions, which may relate either to external goods and evils or to external actions. To the first group belong liberality and munificence, which regulate the use of wealth; the virtues relating to honor, of which the principal is magnanimity; and mildness. To the second group belong friendliness, straightforwardness, and urbane wittiness. These in turn are followed by justice, which has as its subject matter the external actions themselves, as opposed to the internal passions with which all of the preceding virtues are concerned. The order in which these virtues are taken up by Aristotle would find its rationale in the fact that the primary passions, dealing as they do with the goods that are directly related to the preservation of life or the evils that menace its destruction, take precedence over the secondary passions, which are concerned with less vital goods, as well as in the fact that, since actions originate in the passions, the treatment of the latter understandably precedes that of the former.[38] One wonders, however, to what extent Aquinas's "scientific" explanation, regardless of its intrinsic merits, respects the tenor of Aristotle's text. The distinction that it establishes between primary and secondary passions leads for one thing to a greater valuation of courage and moderation at the expense of other more spectacular but less necessary and less common virtues, such as munificence and magnanimity, which may be taken to be one of the major focuses of Aristotle's discussion of the moral life. What is more, the proposed interpretation injects into the discussion an analytic principle that is foreign, if not to Aristotle's thought, at least to the peculiar manner in which moral matters are approached in the *Ethics*.

The same conclusion is borne out in even more striking fashion by Aquinas's treatise on moral virtue in the *Summa Theologiae*, where the Aristotelian classification is abandoned altogether in favor of a modified Platonic-Stoic framework which reduces all the moral virtues to the four so-called cardinal virtues of moderation, courage, justice, and prudence.[39] Each of these virtues is linked to one or the other of the powers of the soul which it determines and whose operations it perfects. Moderation has as its subject the appetitive or concupiscible part, into which it introduces the order of reason principally by imposing the appropriate restraints on man's desire for the pleasures associated with the senses of touch and taste. Courage is the virtue that rectifies the spirited or irascible part and enables man to overcome the fears that might otherwise deter him from the pursuit of the rational good. Justice is to be found in the will and regulates every aspect of man's dealings with other men. By all three of these virtues man is properly ordered to his natural end or the good dictated by reason. But in addition to tending toward the right end, one must also be able to deliberate about, choose, and prescribe the means that are conducive to it. Such is the role of prudence, which is an intellectual virtue insofar as it has reason as its subject, but which is also included among the moral virtues insofar as its proper exercise is contingent on the rectification of the appetite by the three preceding virtues.

All the other moral virtues are grouped under one or the other of these four general virtues either as subjective parts, potential parts, or integral parts. The subjective parts are the various species into which a given virtue may be divided according to the matter with which it deals. The prudence of the ruler, for instance, excels that of the simple subject and differs specifically from it in that it extends to the common good of the entire city or realm; yet both fulfill the definition of prudence, of which they constitute two distinct and complete forms.[40] The potential parts are those virtues which deal with some secondary act or matter of the principal virtue and hence do not contain in themselves the full essence or power of that virtue, as is the case, for example, with liberality and friendliness, whose matter, while not coextensive with that of justice, nevertheless falls within the same general purview since it has to do with the right ordering of one's relations with other men.[41] The integral parts are not complete virtues in themselves but represent the various elements that contribute to the formation of a complete virtue. Thus, memory, inventiveness, caution, circumspection, and the like are all necessary components of a single perfect act of prudence.[42] In this manner, there is gradually constituted a catalogue of moral virtues that is both exhaustive and clearly rooted in a theoretical analysis of the nature and parts of the human soul.

We shall grasp the larger significance of Aquinas's analytic procedure if we turn to a consideration of the particular difficulty raised by the Aristotelian doctrine of moral virtue as a mean between two extremes.[43] Since human actions may deviate from the norm of reason either by excess or defect, virtuous or rational behavior requires that both extremes be avoided and that the right mean be observed at all times. For the most part the mean in question is relative to the subject or the agent and can be ascertained only with reference to the individual circumstances of a given action, including the agent himself. Reason tells us, for example, that food and drink are necessary for life, but it cannot specify in any but the most general way how much this or that man should eat and drink. What is too much for one man may not be enough for another and vice versa; what is proper under certain circumstances or at a certain time may be improper and morally reprehensible at other moments and under a different set of circumstances. One can easily imagine a situation in which virtue itself might counsel that one act in a manner that is contrary to the prevailing or generally approved standards of conduct. A question immediately arises, however, as to the principle in the light of which a decision of this kind is to be made. It is characteristic of Aristotle's empirical approach that his discussion of this problem does not allude to any norm outside the sphere of morality or to any transmoral end to which one might turn in order to justify occasional departures from the common rule. The *Ethics* does state expressly that the mean of reason is the mean such as a prudent man, who is, as it were, a law unto himself, would determine it. But although this solution may be deemed adequate for purposes of action, it obviously leaves something to be desired from a theoretical point of view and actually begs the question since it does little more than suggest that the right mean is the mean as established by a prudent man, who is himself defined as a person who habitually chooses the right mean.[44]

One runs into the same difficulty if one examines Aristotle's doctrine of practical truth. Practical truth in the full sense of the expression, or as referred to action in a specific situation, is not solely a matter of knowledge. It requires that one take into account not only the nature of a given act but the various circumstances that surround it as well. But these circumstances are numberless and literally impossible to assess. If, in order to act virtuously, one were obliged to know all the relevant circumstances of his actions, one would never be able to move or to refrain from moving. It follows that a practical or prudential judgment may be objectively wrong and yet morally right. A person who, by mistake and without any negligence on his part, serves the wrong medicine to a patient performs a morally good act even though serious harm may result from it. Indeed, even if it were possible, a complete and accurate evaluation of the objective facts of a concrete situation would still not suffice to guarantee the moral character of one's action. True virtue demands that one pursue the good according to the mode of the good and not only according to the mode of thought. It implies on the part of the agent an habitual desire for the good as it appears and is known to him. The questions that solicit the attention of a moral man are not questions that can be raised in a purely objective and detached manner; they are inseparable from the questioner, and the answers to them defy analysis in terms of reason alone. Stated in slightly different words, the truth of the practical judgment is measured by the mind's conformity with the rectified appetite, as opposed to the truth of the speculative judgment, which is measured by the mind's conformity with what is or with its object. But if this is so, the whole argument, as Aquinas rightly points out, would again appear to be circular: truth or right reason in practical matters is contingent on the agreement of a particular action with the rectified appetite, which is itself determined by the fact that it agrees with right reason.[45]

Aquinas's attempt to solve this twofold problem again makes explicit what was at best only implied by Aristotle. Although adumbrated in the *Commentary on the Ethics*, it finds its most detailed and complete expression in the famous treatise on law of the *Summa Theologiae*.[46] Its originality is suggested by the fact that this treatise does not have its equivalent in Aristotle and relies for the bulk of its substance on the earlier natural law theories of Cicero and Augustine. Briefly, it consists in showing that, while it is true that the choice of the means to the end is the work of reason, the end that man pursues as a moral being is already assigned to him by nature and precontained in his innate desire for that end. Nature is to be understood precisely as the intrinsic principle of a determinate and necessary inclination or, as Aquinas defines it elsewhere, a sharing in the divine art by which even nonrational beings are made to act in a manner that conforms with reason.[47] Since man is himself a natural being, there is in him, prior to any deliberation, an inclination of his whole being toward the end or ends to which, like all other natural beings, he is uniformly ordered. Thus, as a substance, he naturally seeks his own preservation; as an animal, he shares with other animals a natural desire for the procreation and education of children; and as a rational being, he is naturally inclined toward such specifically human goods as the political life and the knowledge of the truth.[48]

Precisely because he is endowed with reason, man participates more perfectly than all other natural beings in the order of divine providence. Through the knowledge that he has of his end and of the natural inclinations that reveal its existence, he is immediately aware of the general principles that govern his conduct. As dictates of practical reason, these principles constitute a "law," promulgated by nature itself, which enables him to discriminate between right and wrong and serves as the infallible criterion of the goodness or badness of his actions.[49] Its most universal precepts form the object of a special *habitus* which Aquinas calls conscience or, more properly, synderesis, and which parallels the *habitus* of the first and self-evident premises from which all demonstrations proceed in the speculative order.[50]

The sole use of the words "conscience" (*suneidêsis*) and "synderesis," which do not occur in Aristotle but rather in the later Greek and early Christian traditions through which they were handed down to the authors of the Middle Ages, is already symptomatic of the non-Aristotelian flavor of the Thomistic teaching on this subject; there is more, however. Since they are considered to be laws in the strict and proper sense of the term, the moral principles in question take on a compulsory character that they did not have for Aristotle and the philosophic tradition generally. For the natural law not only recommends or discourages certain actions as intrinsically noble or base, it commands or forbids them under pain of retribution if not in this life at least in the next. It thus clearly presupposes both the personal immortality of the human soul and the existence of an all-knowing and all-powerful God who rules the world with wisdom and equity and in whose eyes all individual human actions are either meritorious or deserving of punishment.[51] Any violation of its precepts betrays more than a departure from reason or a simple lack of taste; it bears the mark of an offense against God, the giver and guarantor of the natural law, who, in addition to the loss of those internal goods, such as happiness and virtue, of which the sinner deprives himself, inflicts external sanctions in accordance with the gravity of the misdeed.[52] Within this context man's whole moral life acquires a distinctively new orientation; it ceases to be understood solely in terms of human completeness or fulfillment and becomes in the final instance a matter of willing and grateful compliance with a divinely authorized and unconditionally binding law.

It should be promptly added that the natural law supplies only the most general standards of human behavior or the unshakable foundation on which man's knowledge of the moral order rests. It represents the first but by no means the sufficient rule of reason among men. Only its highest principles are known to everyone without exception, and even they are usually too broad to be of immediate use in guiding one's actions. It therefore needs to be supplemented by another law which is arrived at through human effort and industry and which for that reason is called the human law. The precepts of the human law are themselves derived from the natural law either by way of specific determinations of a general rule or of conclusions from indemonstrable principles. The natural law, for example, prescribes that God should be honored and worshipped; but divine worship implies the performance of certain acts or rites which may vary according to time and place and which must be specified by human reason. Likewise, from the general principle that one should refrain from hurting others, reason infers that one should not murder, steal, or commit adultery.[53]

Needless to say, these principles do not all carry the same evidence or induce the same necessity. In most cases their universality is limited by the "deformity" or the extreme contingency of the matter with which they deal, no less than by the relative imperfection and instability of human nature. Human actions always involve particulars and their morality is likely to be affected by any one of the innumerable circumstances by which they are attended. Justice ordinarily requires that a borrowed or deposited object be returned to its owner, but this does not mean that one is morally bound to deliver a shipment of arms to a person who intends to betray his country. Moreover, not all men are capable of the same degree of virtue or moral perfection, whether it be by reason of age, natural disposition, or previously acquired habits. A moral principle that makes impossible and hence unreasonable demands on a particular subject or group of subjects must be altered to fit the situation to which it is applied.[54] The more particular the principle, the more variable and less certain it becomes. For that reason moral science, unlike natural science, offers little certitude and must be content with setting forth the truth roughly and in outline.[55]

The decisive question, then, and the real issue between Aquinas and Aristotle, is not whether moral principles are subject to change but whether there are *any* moral principles from which one is never allowed to deviate and which retain their obligatory character even in the most extreme situations. Whereas Aristotle plainly states that all of natural right is variable,[56] Aquinas distinguishes between the common or primary precepts of the natural law, with which all men must comply at all times, and its proper or secondary precepts, which are subject to variations imposed by circumstances. The former differ from the latter both by their higher degree of knowability and their greater proximity to man's natural end. Such is the case with the prescriptions against murder, adultery, and theft, which suffer no human exceptions and from which God alone, as the author of the natural law, can dispense in certain instances, as he did when he ordered Abraham to kill his son Isaac. To this category of universally valid laws belong all the precepts of the Decalogue, including the prescriptions against idolatry and the taking of the Lord's name in vain, which, unlike the ceremonial and judicial precepts of the Old Testament, have not been abrogated by the New Law.[57]

The same distinction between primary and secondary precepts is taken for granted in Aquinas's handling of the controverted issue of the justifiability or excusableness of immoral actions performed under duress. Aristotle had left the matter at saying somewhat inconclusively that there are "perhaps" some odious acts to which one should not consent even at the price of death after the most fearful sufferings and had ended his discussion with the equally ambiguous statement that "praise and blame are bestowed on those who yield to compulsion and those who do not."[58] In his commentary on that passage, Averroes explains Aristotle's assertion as relating to the fact that the man who succumbs to force may be blamed in one place but not in another, as if to suggest that, when a person is physically or morally tortured beyond the limits of ordinary human endurance, the distinction between right and wrong actions becomes by and large a matter of positive law.[59] Aquinas, on the other hand, interprets the word "perhaps" in its rhetorical rather than its literal sense. He states emphatically that certain actions are to be condemned altogether and cites, in support of this view, the example of St. Lawrence, who underwent death by fire rather than sacrifice to idols. Accordingly, he takes Aristotle's concluding remark to mean, not that the victim of compulsion may sometimes be excused or simply pitied, as Aristotle had intimated, but that he can never escape blame or censure.[60]

Since the law that prohibits such actions embodies the intention of the legislator as well as the common good of society to which that intention is primarily directed, it can never be laid aside on the ground that the legislator himself would have allowed it to be transgressed in the name of a higher law if he had been cognizant of the unforeseen circumstances that render its observance undesirable in a particular situation.[61] The most general principles of the natural law are thus directly applicable to human society and do not have to be diluted in order to become operative. The very possibility that the common good or the preservation of society should at times compel one to act in a manner contrary to these principles is eliminated once and for all. Between the requirements of justice and those of civil society there is a fundamental and necessary harmony. The perfect social order exists or is capable of existing in deed and not only in speech. Justice in the absolute sense is not only approximated by civil justice; it actually coincides with it. By the same token man's perfection as an individual turns out to be identical with his perfection as a citizen.[62]

As a consequence, both civil justice and courage, the two virtues most closely connected with the welfare of the city, acquire a new and more noble status. The issue between justice and magnanimity is decided in favor of justice, which emerges as unqualifiedly the highest of the moral virtues.[63] For the same reason Aquinas is able to remove the ambiguity inherent in Aristotle's treatment of courage and to speak unequivocally of courage as that virtue which is concerned above all with the death that one faces in defending one's country.[64] The harmonious solution that he proposes to the problem of civil society likewise does away with the need for noble lies, and all the more so as the false but salutary belief in the gods of the city is replaced by the acceptance of the one true God, which becomes itself a requirement of the natural law. Wisdom can henceforth rule without recourse to falsehood. The previously noted absence of any real esotericism in Aquinas's political teaching is explained not solely by the rehabilitation of philosophy in the Christian world but more radically by the reconciliation which the Thomistic position postulates between the demands of justice and those of civil society.

That reconciliation meets with one of its clearest illustrations in Aquinas's reinterpretation of Aristotle's doctrine of legal slavery. In accordance with Roman law and the principles of the *jus gentium*, Aquinas defends not only the necessity but the justice of that practice, which he presents as beneficial to both conqueror and conquered, since it spares the life of the latter and secures for the former the services of a subject population.[65] On this point his teaching is again at variance with that of Aristotle, who looks upon the bondage of men who are not slaves by nature as a necessary evil justified by the higher and more pressing demands of society as a whole and hence as another indication of the irremediably defective and self-contradictory character of human justice on the plane of civil society.

BIBLICAL FAITH AND PHILOSOPHY

Aquinas's natural law doctrine constitutes a prime example on the moral and political level of the Thomistic synthesis between biblical faith and Aristotelian philosophy. As a law of *nature*, the natural law shares in reason and cannot be reduced exclusively to the will of God. The actions that it commands or forbids are intrinsically good or bad; they are not good or bad simply as a result of their being commanded or forbidden by God. As a *law*, however, it also contains an explicit reference to God's will, to which it owes its moving force. It thus stands midway between the natural right doctrine of the nonreligious philosophic tradition on the one hand and the strict voluntarism of the nonphilosophic religious tradition on the other. It is distinguished from the latter in that it defines law as essentially an act of reason rather than of the will, and it differs from the former in that it conceives of God not only as the final cause of the universe or the unmoved mover who moves all things by the attraction that he exerts on them, but as a lawgiver and an efficient cause who produces the world out of nothing and by his ordinances actively directs all creatures to their appointed end. The key point in this regard, and the one on which the quarrel between philosophy and revealed religion would seem to turn, reveals itself in the last analysis as the opposition between the biblical doctrine of creation and the philosophic doctrine of the eternity of the world.

Aquinas strives to bridge the gap from one position to the other, not by ascribing to the pagan philosopher the notion of divine creation, as some of Aristotle's earlier commentators had done, but by contending that the reasons advanced by Aristotle in favor of the eternity of the world are at best only probable. His argument generally tends to follow Aristotle's *Topics*, where the eternity of the world is presented as a dialectical problem or as belonging to the class of problems that reason cannot solve, rather than the treatise *On the Heavens*, which treats the same problem from a scientific point of view and leaves little doubt concerning Aristotle's final position on the matter.[66] If the view that the world is eternal can neither be proved nor disproved by natural reason, the teaching of Revelation cannot be held to be in direct contradiction with that of philosophy. The conflict between the two teachings is further attenuated and partially blurred by Aquinas's rejection of the disjuncture between the eternity of the world and its creation by God; for, according to Aquinas, even if the world were eternal, it would still have its source in God's free will.[67] What the doctrine of creation essentially implies in the end is not the coming into being of the world (and concomitantly of time itself) at a given moment in the past, however near or remote, but the radical contingency of all beings other than God and their complete dependence upon God for their existence. It finds its metaphysical expression in the typically Thomistic doctrine of the real distinction between essence and existence in all beings outside of God.[68]

It is nonetheless true that by attributing efficient causality to God, Aquinas is compelled to preserve or restore the distinction between God's intellect and God's will. Although that distinction is to be regarded as a distinction of reason and not in any way a real distinction, it still has the effect of giving greater prominence to God's will than the Aristotelian doctrine of God as pure intellect or as the thought that thinks only itself. This conclusion is reinforced by the reasons that Aquinas puts forward to explain why, assuming the theoretical possibility of an eternal creation, God produced the world "in time" rather than from all eternity: the noneternity of the world makes it more apparent that all things owe their origin to God; it dispels any remaining doubt concerning the fact that God does not create out of necessity but through an act of his free will; and lastly, it manifests with abundant clarity God's infinite power, inasmuch as creation implies a total gift of being, of which God alone, who possesses the fullness of being, is capable.[69] The far-reaching import of such a doctrine may be glimpsed, however partially and inadequately, through the one-sided emphasis which came to be placed on will and power in modern philosophic and political thought.

Even if one were to accept Aquinas's interpretation and grant that Aristotle's teaching is not incompatible with Christian dogma, a question could still be raised as to whether, by inserting Aristotle's moral and political views into a theological framework or by complementing them with a teaching based on Revelation, Aquinas has not profoundly altered their original character. The issue of the difference between the two authors is not completely disposed of by Aquinas's occasional suggestion that Aristotle deals primarily with man's happiness in this life whereas Christianity is preoccupied above all with man's happiness in the life to come, for the simple reason that Aristotle treats the happiness of this life as the only happiness and maintains an unbroken silence on the crucial subject of the personal immortality of the soul.[70] The change in outlook effected by adding an otherworldly dimension to Aristotelian speculation is not less important for being less conspicuous. To sense that change one has only to reflect, for example, on what happens to magnanimity when it is coupled with humility—a virtue nowhere to be found in Aristotle—or on what happens to courage when life on earth is considered within the larger perspective of man's eternal destiny; for, surely, the Christian who looks forward to a heavenly reward in the event of death on the battlefield is not animated by sentiments identical to those of the heroic citizen who has no such assurance and who realizes that, by exposing his life for a noble cause, he risks the ultimate and irreparable loss of everything that men hold dear.

Formulated in broadest terms, the basic problem has to do not so much with the agreement or disagreement between the content of Revelation and the teachings of philosophy as with the contrast between faith and philosophy viewed as the grounds of total and essentially divergent ways of life. One cannot be guided at one and the same time by two different and equally authoritative norms. The acceptance of the supremacy of the life of faith or of devout response to a divinely revealed word necessarily entails the destruction of philosophy in its original sense or, what amounts to the same thing, the replacement of the natural order composed of philosophers and nonphilosophers by a supernatural order based on the more fundamental distinction between true believers and nonbelievers. When all is said and done, the gulf that separates the learned Aquinas from the learned Aristotle is infinitely wider than that which separates the learned Aquinas from the simple but pious Anthony.

The foregoing analysis suggests the true nature of the revolution initiated by Aquinas in Christian theology. Contrary to what has often been said, Aquinas did not baptize Aristotle. If anything, he declared invalid the baptism conferred upon him by his early commentators and denied him admission to full citizenship in the City of God. Instead, by casting his philosophy in the role of a handmaid, he made him a slave or servant of that city. In the light of Aquinas's own moral principles, that treatment was not unjust since, in return for his contribution to Christian theology, Aristotle received, if not the gift of grace, at least the grace to live. The proof is that, whereas he was eventually banished from Islam and Judaism, he found a permanent home in the Christian West. The place of honor that he came to occupy in the Christian tradition as the representative par excellence of the most glorious achievements of natural reason bears eloquent witness to the novelty and daring of Aquinas's enterprise.

The success of that enterprise, it should be added, was never complete or unchallenged. Because of its boldness, Aquinas ran afoul of the two most powerful (although numerically unequal) groups in the West. He aroused the antagonism of the traditional theologians, who resented the intrusion of an unregenerate pagan in the Christian fold and reproached

Aquinas with having sundered the unity of Christian wisdom; and he incurred the wrath of the newly emancipated philosophers (the so-called Latin Averroists), who objected to the enslavement of the very philosophy that they could credit with having made them free. The delicate balance that he was able to establish between the extremes of faith and reason was disrupted less than three centuries later by two revolutionary developments of which he would have disapproved but which he remotely prepared or facilitated. One is Luther's repudiation of the "Aristotelian Church" in the name of an allegedly purer and less worldly form of Christianity. The other is Machiavelli's repudiation of both Aristotle and the Church in the name of an ideal which was neither classical nor Christian but emphatically modern.

NOTES

1. Alfarabi, *The Attainment of Happiness*, 63.

2. *Summa contra gentiles* I.4; *Summa theologiae* I, qu. 1, a. 1; I-II, qu. 99, a. 2, ad 2m; *De veritate* qu. 14, a. 10. Maimonides, *Guide of the Perplexed* I.34.

3. *In librum de divinis nominibus* Proemium 2. Cf. *Expositio in librum Boethii de Trinitate*, qu. 2, a. 4; *Summa theologiae* III, qu. 42, a. 3.

4. Avicenna, *On the Divisions of the Rational Sciences*, in *Medieval Political Philosophy: a Sourcebook*, edited by R. Lerner and M. Mahdi (New York: The Free Press, 1963), 97.

5. *Summa contra gentiles* II.4; *Summa theologiae* I, qu. 1, a. 6-7.

6. *Summa contra gentiles* I.7; *De veritate* qu. 14, 1. 10, ad 7m and ad 9m.

7. *Summa theologiae* I, qu. 85, a. 3; *Summa contra gentiles* II.98; *Commentary on the Posterior Analytics* Proemium n. 4.

8. *Summa theologiae* I, qu. 76, a. 5; *Questiones disputatae de anima* a. 8; *De malo* qu. 5, a. 5; *In II Sent.* Dist. I, qu. 2, a. 5.

9. *Summa theologiae* I-II, qu. 85, a. 1-2.

10. *Summa contra gentiles* I.9.

11. *On Kingship* I.1.[4].

12. *On Kingship* I.1.[5]; *Summa theologiae* I, qu. 76, a. 5, ad 4m.

13. *Summa theologiae* I-II, qu. 95, a. 1; *Commentary on the Ethics* I, Lect. 1, n. 4; X, Lect. 14, n. 2139-42.

14. *Summa theologiae* I-II, qu. 90, a. 3, ad 3m.

15. *Commentary on the Politics* I. Lect. 1, n. 39; *Commentary on the Ethics* I Lect. 1, n. 4.

16. *Summa theologiae* I, qu. 96, a. 3-4; qu. 92, a. 1, ad 2ᵐ; *On Kingship* I. 1, [9-10].

17. *In IV Sent.* Dist. 49, qu. 1, a. 1, qu. 1, sol. 1, ad 3m.

18. *Summa contra gentiles* III.17. Cf. *Commentary on the Ethics* I, lect. 2, n. 30.

19. *Summa contra gentiles* III.24; *Summa theologiae* II-II, qu. 47, a. 10, ad 2m.

20. *Summa theologiae* I, qu. 60, a. 5; *Quodlibetum* I, qu. 4, a. 8.

21. *On Kingship* I.2.[17]; *Summa theologiae* I, qu. 103, a. 3; *Summa contra gentiles* IV.76.4; *Commentary on Ethics* III, Lect. 8, n. 474.

22. *On Kingship* II.3.[106]; II.4.[117-8]; *Commentary on the Ethics* I, Lect. 1, n. 4.

23. *Commentary on the Politics* II, Lect. 6, n. 226; Lect. 17, n. 341.

24. *Summa theologiae* I, qu. 96, a. 3.

25. *On Kingship* I.2-3; *Summa theologiae* I-II, qu. 105, a. 1, ad 2m.

26. *Commentary on the Politics* II, Lect. 5, n. 212.

27. *Summa theologiae* I-II, qu. 105, a. 1; *On Kingship* I.6.[42].

28. *Summa theologiae* I-II, qu. 95, a. 1, ad 2m.

29. *Commentary on the Ethics* X, Lect. 14; II, Lect. 1, n. 251; *Summa theologiae* I-II, qu. 92, a. 1.

30. *Commentary on the Ethics* VI, Lect 7, n. 1197; X, Lect. 17, n. 2165.

31. *Summa theologiae* I-II, qu. 72, a. 4. Cf. I-II, qu. 21, a. 4, ad 3m; qu. 91, a. 1; *On Kingship* II.1 [94]; *De perfectione vitae spiritualis* 13.

32. *Commentary on the Ethics* I, Lect. 1, n. 5-6; VI, Lect. 7, n. 1200; *Summa theologiae* II-II, qu. 47, a. 11, s. c.

33. *Summa theologiae* II-II, qu. 57.

34. *Summa theologiae* I, qu. 60, a. 5.

35. *Commentary on the Politics* I, Lect. 1, n. 35. Athanasius, *Life of Anthony*, 72ff.

36. *Commentary on the Politics* I, Lect. 3, n. 376. Cf. *Summa theologiae* I-II qu. 92, a. 1, corp. and ad 4m; I-II, qu. 58, a. 4.

37. Cf. *Summa theologiae* I, qu. 60, a. 5.

38. *Commentary on the Ethics* III, Lect. 14, n. 528.

39. Cf. *Summa theologiae* I-II, qu. 61.

40. *Summa theologiae* II-II, qu. 47, a. 11; qu. 48, a. 1; qu. 50, a. 1-2.

41. *Summa theologiae* II-II, qu. 80, a. 1.

42. *Summa theologiae* II-II, qu. 49.

43. Cf. Aristotle, *Ethics* II.6.

44. Aristotle *Ethics* II.6.1107a1.

45. *Commentary on the Ethics* VI, Lect. 2, n. 1131. Cf. *Summa theologiae* I, qu. 1, a. 6, ad 2m; qu. 14, a. 16; Aristotle, *Ethics* X.5.1176a4ff.

46. *Summa Theologiae* I-II, qu. 90-108.

47. *Commentary on the Physics* II, Lect. 1 and Lect. 14, n. 268; *Commentary on the Ethics* I, Lect. 1, n. 11. Cf. *Commentary on the Metaphysics* V, Lect. 5.

48. *Summa theologiae* I-II, qu. 94, a. 2.

49. *Summa theologiae* I-II, qu. 91, a. 2.

50. *Summa theologiae* I, qu. 79, a. 12-13; I-II, qu. 19, a. 5-6; *De veritate* qu. 16; *In II Sent.* Dist. 24, qu. 2, a. 3 The use of the word synderesis (*suntêresis*, literally, "conservation") in this context may have been due initially to a faulty transcription of *suneidêsis* ("conscience") in a widely circulated passage of St. Jerome's

Commentary on Ezechiel (I.4).

51. *Summa theologiae* I-II, qu. 18, a. 9; qu. 21, a. 4; qu. 96, a. 4; qu. 98, a. 5; qu. 99, a. 1 and 5; qu. 100, a. 2.

52. *Summa theologiae* I-II, qu. 71, a. 6, ad 5m; *Summa contra gentiles* IV.140.

53. *Summa theologiae* I-II, qu. 95, a. 1-2; qu. 91, a. 2, ad 2m.

54. *Summa theologiae* II-II, qu. 57, a. 2, ad 1m.

55. *Commentary on the Ethics* I, Lect. 3, n. 35; II, Lect. 2, n. 258-9.

56. Aristotle, *Ethics* V.7.1134b25ff.

57. *Summa theologiae* I-II, qu. 94, a. 5, ad 2m; qu. 97, a. 4, ad 3m; qu. 99, a. 3, ad 2m and a. 4; qu. 100, a. 8, ad 3m; Suppl., qu. 65, a. 1. Cf. also I-II, qu. 100, a. 1 and qu. 104, a. 1, ad 3m, where the duty to love and worship God or the injunctions against idolatry and the taking of the Lord's name in vain, while part of the natural law, are said to owe their certitude not to human reason alone but to human reason instructed by God or informed by faith.

58. Aristotle *Ethics* III.1.1110b24-33.

59. Averroes *In moralia Nicomachia expositio* (Venice, 1562), 31 I.

60. *Commentary on the Ethics* III, Lect. 2, n. 395-7.

61. *Summa theologiae* I-II, qu. 100, a. 8.

62. *Commentary on the Ethics* V, Lect. 11, n. 1003; *Summa theologiae* I-II, qu. 92, a. 1, ad 3m.

63. *Summa theologiae* I-II, qu. 66, a. 4; II-II, qu. 58, a. 12.

64. *Commentary on the Ethics* III, Lect. 14, 537.

65. *Commentary on the Politics* I, Lect. 4, n. 75 and 79.

66. *Summa theologiae* I, qu. 46, esp. a. 1; *Summa contra gentiles* II.30-38. Aristotle, *Topics* I.11.104b16; *On the Heavens* I.2-4 and 10-12; III.2.

67. *Summa theologiae* I, qu. 46, a. 2, corp. and ad 1m.

68. *Summa theologiae* I, qu. 3, a. 4; *Summa contra gentiles* I.22.

69. *Summa contra gentiles* II.38.15.

70. *Commentary on the Ethics* I, Lect. 4, n. 4; III, Lect. 18, n. 588-590; *Commentary on the Politics* II, Lect. 1, n. 170. Cf. *Summa contra gentiles* III.48.

POLITICS and PHILOSOPHY in the MIDDLE AGES: the ARISTOTELIAN REVOLUTION

Aristotle's *Politics*, the book through which the cities and nations of the Christian West were introduced to the science of politics and became fully aware of themselves as civil societies, has the distinction of being the only one of the philosopher's major treatises to have been virtually ignored for upwards of sixteen centuries. Whereas there exists a tradition of commentaries on all of his other important works that stretches back in some cases to the first century B.C., no commentary is known to have been written on the *Politics* prior to those of Thomas Aquinas and Albert the Great not long after the middle of the thirteenth century. The phenomenon is all the more striking as, in the wake of the first edition of Aristotle's complete works by Andronikos of Rhodes in 70 B.C. or thereabouts, the commentary became the privileged medium of philosophic communication within the Aristotelian school.

It was generally known from the *Nicomachean Ethics*, from the commentaries of Eustratius and other ancient authors on that work,[1] from the catalogues compiled by various historians, such as Diogenes Laertius,[2] and from remarks made by Cassiodorus,[3] Boethius,[4] and Isidore of Seville,[5] that Aristotle had devoted a treatise to the subject of politics, considered for the first time as a distinct science, but no ancient author seems to have deemed it necessary or useful to pursue its study. In a letter to Themistius, Julian the Apostate cites a brief passage from book III relative to the limitations of absolute monarchy and the necessity of the rule of law.[6] Interesting as it may be, the quotation does not betoken a profound or even a firsthand acquaintance with Aristotle's text. It appears to be taken from a collection of excerpts assembled by Julian's friend, the philosopher Priscus.[7] A hundred years later, Proclus refers to the *Politics* in his *Commentary on the Republic*, but only to reject Aristotle's critique of Plato's dialogue in Book II.[8] Beyond that, there is little to report as far as the ancient world is concerned, and the medieval harvest is scarcely more abundant. We can probably infer from a few *scholia* or notes preserved in a Berlin manuscript of the *Politics* that the eleventh-century Byzantine scholar Michael of Ephesus lectured on Aristotle's text at some time, but his seems to have been a lonely voice. Nothing more will be heard about the *Politics* until its reappearance in the Latin West two centuries later. Few outstanding philosophical works, if any, have gone practically unnoticed for so long.[9] The problem is not that the text was unavailable, for as soon as the demand for a Latin translation arose, people had no trouble finding it.

Two reasons, neither of which, as far as I know, is mentioned by any ancient writer, account for this neglect. The first is that the publication of the *Politics* coincided with the rise of the new ecumenical empires whose rulers, beginning with Alexander the Great, were presumably not eager to inform their subjects of the merits of political freedom and the ultimate superiority of the small *polis* over the vast political entities on which their hearts were set. The danger was particularly acute in view of the fact that the *Politics* offers a concrete analysis of the various regimes, democracy included, and of the means by which they might be established, strengthened, preserved, or, if need be, overturned.[10] Nothing of the kind had ever been attempted before, not even by Plato, whose *Laws*, as Aristotle notes, contains little detailed information about such matters. No doubt, one finds in Aristotle a number of powerful arguments in favor of monarchy, but by stressing certain elements of his thought at the expense of others, one could easily pass him off as a champion of popular sovereignty.[11] Under Alexander and his successors, his treatise had little chance of being received with open arms.

As for the Roman emperors, who would soon be replacing the Macedonians as the masters of the civilized world and among whom must be counted some of the most hateful tyrants known to history, it is hard to imagine that they would have had much use for it, either. Nowhere in the Roman tradition is Aristotle hailed as an authority on the subject of politics, not even by Cicero, who has the highest opinion of him but nevertheless models his political teaching on Plato's *Republic* and *Laws*. There is some doubt as to whether he had even read the *Politics*.[12]

The second reason for which no one at the time seems to have been attracted to the *Politics* has to do with the disaffection toward the political life and the accompanying surge of interest in religious, mystical, or theurgic speculation that characterize the hellenistic and Roman periods. It is significant that the later Platonic school itself—the "Neoplatonic" school, as we have been calling it since Thomas Carlyle—veered in that direction, abandoning Plato's great political dialogues, the *Republic* and the *Laws*, in favor of the *Symposium*, the *Phaedo*, and the *Parmenides*, which lend themselves more readily to nonpolitical interpretations. Whatever the reason or combination of reasons, the least that can be said is that the *Politics* was not from the beginning, and never became, a key text of imperial Rome or late antiquity.

The same neglect of the *Politics* is typical of the Islamic and Jewish philosophers of the Middle Ages, despite their unbounded admiration for Aristotle, the "master of those who know," as Dante called him, borrowing the phrase from Maimonides.[13] Whereas in all the other branches of philosophy—logic, natural science, metaphysics or first philosophy, and ethics—Aristotle was the acknowledged guide, in politics it was Plato and especially Plato's *Laws*, the book to which, according to Avicenna, one must turn for a philosophic treatment of all questions pertaining to prophecy or revealed religion.[14]

This time, the reason for shunning the *Politics* is vouchsafed to us by the Islamic and Jewish thinkers themselves. Both Islam and Judaism take the form of a God-given and, hence, perfect law. As divinely revealed, this law is not subject to criticism in the light of such criteria as may be supplied by natural reason and experience. Maimonides speaks for both of these traditions when he states that in the religious community divine revelation or the divine Law substitutes for political philosophy.[15] No one to whom the truth about the best regime has been communicated by God himself would be so bold or foolish as to spend the rest of his life searching for it. Any such quest would be either unnecessary or, if it should be motivated by doubts concerning the wisdom of the Bible, impious. One is reminded of the medieval legend about the Calif Omar, who ordered the burning of all the books contained in the famous library at Alexandria on the ground that their teaching was either identical to that of the Koran, in which case they were superfluous, or different from it, in which case they were dangerous. It is no accident that the role played by the *Politics* in medieval Islam and Judaism was always marginal at best. Elements of that work did find their way into select philosophic circles, as Shlomo Pines has shown,[16] but their sparsity is just another sign of the suspicion in which the Aristotelian approach to the study of politics was held.

The only place where the *Politics* was finally able to carve out a niche for itself is Western Christendom, where it was translated into Latin by William of Moerbeke in the 1260's.[17] The book, the last of Aristotle's major treatises to be accorded that honor, was hardly an instant success, but it would not be long before it began to attract widespread attention. In less than a century, no fewer than seven commentaries were devoted to it and the entire political literature of the West was gradually transformed by it. It is true that the oldest among these commentaries, those of Aquinas, Albert the Great, Peter of Auvergne, and Walter Burleigh,[18] are mainly preoccupied with deciphering the text and establishing its literal meaning. Only rarely do they go beyond it either to criticize it or think it through in the light of the datum of divine revelation. Most of the time, their authors are content to clarify Aristotle's method of procedure, define the terms that were likely to be unfamiliar to their readers, indicate the main divisions and subdivisions of the treatise, and illustrate its meaning by means of contemporary examples or citations from other works either by Aristotle himself or by other ancient writers.

RECOVERING ARISTOTLE'S THOUGHT

The task at hand was far more difficult than we might imagine. It is sometimes said that with the arrival of the *Politics* the Christian West came into possession of a new political philosophy. It is more accurate to say that it discovered political philosophy *tout court*. All that was previously known of that discipline consisted of an amalgam of more or less disparate fragments drawn from the Bible, Cicero, the Church Fathers (especially Augustine), Gratian's *Decretum*, and the christianized version of Roman law that most of the countries of Western Europe had adopted during the course of the twelfth century. Roger Bacon complains bitterly that the works devoted to this part of practical science, such as those of Aristotle, Avicenna, Cicero, and Seneca, either were not to be found in the libraries of his own country, were too expensive, or had not been translated into Latin. For moral philosophy, one had at one's disposal Aristotle's *Nicomachean Ethics*, and for economics or the governance of the family, Cicero's *De officiis*. When it came to politics, on the other hand, the only available resources were canon law and the civil law.[19] Dante was of the same opinion. He, too, finds that the time was ripe for a return to political science, which had been neglected for too long— *quantalibet diuturnitate neglecta*—and which alone teaches us how to live well.[20] "Among other concealed and useful truths," he says elsewhere, "knowledge of the temporal monarchy is the most useful and the most hidden; but because it is not immediately conducive to gain, it is shunned by everyone. For this reason, I propose to pull it out of its hiding-place so as to promote to the welfare of the world and reap for myself the glory in store for the winner of so great a contest."[21]

In truth, political philosophy had never been high on Christianity's list of priorities. Even St. Augustine, who knew more about it than any other Latin Father, had never undertaken a sustained treatment of it. Nor does it appear to have been of particular interest to him, save to the extent that participation in the political life confronts us with certain moral dilemmas to which no Christian who takes the Sermon on the Mount seriously can remain indifferent. Nowhere in his works does one find a *bona fide* discussion of the best regime, the highest theme of classical political theory. His thought on this subject is well summed up in the remark that "so far as this mortal life is concerned, which is lived and ended in a few days, it matters little under whose rule a man who is about to die lives, as long as those who govern do not force him to commit acts of impiety or injustice."[22] Only once in passing does he mention the different regimes according to the list that Cicero had drawn up in the *Republic*—monarchy, aristocracy, and the government of the people—but not without modifying the text, perhaps unconsciously, and thereby altering its meaning. Cicero never speaks, as does Augustine, of the "whole people," *universus populus*.[23] He says very precisely "the people itself," *ipse populus*."[24] For Cicero and the tradition that he echoes, there is no such thing as the rule of all. The city is always governed by one or the other of its parts—a king, a small group of nobles or of wealthy citizens, or "the people," that is to say, the many or the poor—each one of which claims to rule in the interest of all but invariably pursues its own interest. This is true even of a democracy, where the poor, who outnumber the rest of the population, are often in a position to impose their will upon it. The same also holds for the so-called "mixed regime," which ought to be instituted whenever possible, but which is at best a compromise designed to promote social stability by giving to every class a voice in the government of the city, whether it deserves it or not.

Not only were the Middle Ages ill-informed about the nature of political science; they did not possess anything like an adequate political vocabulary. This explains why, at every turn of the road, our commentators feel obliged to define the terms used by Aristotle. The critical edition of Aquinas's commentary lists no fewer than eighty-five definitions of this kind, considered necessary because the terms in question were neologisms.[25] The Latin world had never heard of an aristocracy or an oligarchy, two words that were not yet part of its vocabulary. It had only the vaguest idea of what Aristotle meant by a *polis*. The only political entities in existence at the time were kingdoms, principalities, duchies, seigniories, nations, or communes, none of which corresponded exactly to the small Greek city.[26] This being the case, how could the *polis* possibly be held up as a model of the "perfect" human society? As for the distinction between *politeuma*, the "body politic," and *politeia*, the "regime," it was too subtle to merit one's attention. Aquinas identifies them purely and simply.[27] He does not judge it necessary to explain that *politeuma* refers to but one aspect of the regime, the *impositio ordinis*, as distinct from the "way of life" of the city as determined by the distribution of its ruling offices.

For these and other reasons, including Aristotle's notoriously elliptical style, it was hard to obtain a decent translation of the text. In its desire to remain as literal as possible, the one provided by Moerbeke often became almost unintelligible and was not always completely accurate.[28] Every now and then, the meaning of the Greek terms seems to have eluded the translator. Thus, in Book II, 1265a12, Aristotle describes Socrates's discourses as surpassingly beautiful (*peritton*) and full of grace (*kompson*), originality (*kainotomon*), and penetration (*zêtêtikon*). Not having read Plato's dialogues, Moerbeke failed to grasp the allusion to their ironic, playful, and inventive character, and took each of these adjectives in a derogatory sense. Socrates's discourses, he says, contain much that is superfluous (*superfluum*), frivolous (*leve*), strange (*novum*), and problematic in the extreme (*quaestionibus plenum*). Given his invincible ignorance, Moerbeke can hardly be held responsible for the misinterpretation, especially since the same Greek terms have in other contexts the very meaning that he ascribes to them. *Perittos*, "out of the ordinary," can indeed be rendered in Latin by "superfluous," as it was in this case, albeit wrongly; but it can also be translated by *eximius*, a term of praise designating something rare or outstanding.[29] Similar remarks could be made apropos of the three other adjectives used by Aristotle. No doubt, the mistake left the Latin world with a less than flattering impression of the Platonic dialogues; but since most of these were inaccessible to Western readers anyway, the damage was minimal. It was nevertheless unfortunate. Medieval theologians, who are not prone to sinning by excess of humor, were scarcely in a position to appreciate it in others. Reading Moerbeke's translation would not have taught them that Socrates could be serious even when he jokes. One of the most endearing features of Greek classical thought thus remained all but completely hidden from them.

A similar problem arises in connection with *Politics*'s analysis of Plato's *Laws*. Unable to guess that Aristotle was dealing with a separate dialogue, Moerbeke assumed that the reference was to a legal code of some sort that Plato would have appended to the *Republic*. Aquinas, who shares Moerbeke's ignorance, is content to repeat slavishly Aristotle's remarks about the manifest discrepancy between the regime outlined in the *Republic* and the one adumbrated in the "laws." He had no way of knowing that the *Laws* purposely departs from the teaching of the *Republic* in order to bring to light the crucial problem with which both dialogues deal, namely, the impossibility of finding on the level of the political life a completely satisfactory solution to the problem of human justice. For Plato, as for Aristotle, no actual city, not even the best, will ever be wholly just, for this would require that all its citizens be "gods or children of gods," that is to say, perfectly rational beings, free from the constraints of the body.[30] The question is far from insignificant, for, as we shall see, it is directly related to some of the major theologico-political contestations of the Middle Ages.

Another typical mistake, this one fairly comical: unacquainted with the term *zenelasia*, Moerbeke mistook it for a proper name and came close to inventing a new founder for the Cretan regime, Zenelasias. According to his first translation, which was later abandoned, this Zenelasias is the man who would have chosen the distant island of Crete as the place on which to found a city: *Zenelasias enim longe fecit.*[31] Aristotle's thought is less original. It comes down to saying that Crete was favored in some respects by its geographical location. Having no neighbors capable of fomenting revolts among its lower classes, the Cretans lived in peace for a long time. Their very isolation had the same effect as the *zenelasia*, that is, the law prescribing the banishment of foreigners at Sparta.

Unfortunately, Crete already had a founder, and what a founder! None other than Minos, the son of Jupiter, who is mentioned twice at the beginning of the chapter. There was obviously some misunderstanding, which Moerbeke himself sought to dispel by substituting for *zenelasias* the expression *securos ab expulsione* in his second translation. Whence Aquinas's interpretation: by reason of their distance from other cities, the Cretans were in no danger of being invaded and chased out of their own territory by foreigners.[32] This was still not quite what Aristotle had in mind, but it was much better. It is amusing to note that, despite its having been retracted by Moerbeke, the notion that Crete had been founded by one Zenelasias enjoyed a long life in the political literature of the Middle Ages and continued to be cited by others as a possible explanation of the text.[33] The matter is of more than purely historical significance insofar as it draws our attention to the fact that the chapter devoted to the Cretan regime in the *Politics* is the only one in which Aristotle calls into direct question the sacred character of the ancient city, doing here openly what he does tacitly everywhere else in the *Politics*.

THE SUITABILITY OF THE *POLITICS*

Notwithstanding its imperfections, Moerbeke's translation had the merit of rendering with highly commendable literalness the substance of

Aristotle's thought,[34] to which the Latin world finally had access. The question is why the *Politics*, once all but condemned to a state of total oblivion, became in a matter of a few years one of the great philosophic texts of Western civilization. Two closely related reasons account for this momentous turn of events.

First of all, Aristotle's treatise offered a useful tool with which to deal with what had become by then the most pressing political problem of the Latin Middle Ages, that of the relationship between the spiritual and the temporal powers. By virtue of their universality, its principles could be applied to situations vastly different from the ones that Aristotle had known. Their great advantage is that they allowed for a much clearer delineation of the temporal sphere and, therewith, of the spiritual sphere. From there one could go on to discuss the manner in which the respective jurisdictions of these two spheres might be coordinated. The need for clarity in this matter was particularly acute owing to the fact that since the days of Pope Gregory VII, the Church often threatened to absorb the temporal power in accordance with a trend that the late H.-X. Arquilliére misleadingly dubbed "political Augustinianism."[35] I say "misleadingly" because it is not at all evident that the papal absolutism of Augustine's medieval disciples can be traced to Augustine himself. At the same time, the Church was thrust into the position of having to defend its own independence against the encroachments of an ever more highly centralized temporal authority. Thanks to Aristotle, philosophical arguments could now be invoked to support the claims of both the Pope and the Emperor. Dante's *Monarchia*, Giles of Rome's *De ecclesiae potestate*, and John of Paris's *Defender of the Peace*, to mention only a few contemporary, albeit vastly different works, all have in common that they are not just manifestoes, political tracts, pamphlets, legal briefs, or mirrors of princes, but veritable philosophic or theological treatises. A new genre was born to which the name of "political theology" would later be given.

Nor is this all, for the *Politics* could be mined for answers to some of the Church's internal problems as well, such as the pope's authority vis-à-vis that of bishops, the ecclesiastical possession of temporal goods, the disputes between seculars and mendicants, and the status of the laity. Important studies by Brian Tierney and James Blythe have recently cast into sharp relief the role played in these controversies by the Aristotelian notion of the mixed regime, to which Peter Olivi was already appealing toward the end of the thirteenth century and that became crucial a century later at the time of the Great Schism (1378-1417) and the Conciliar movement.[36]

The second reason for which the *Politics* seemed made-to-order is more subtle. It has to do with the very nature of Christianity, which is a nonpolitical religion, by which I mean a religion that is not of itself a "source of law" (Fustel de Coulanges)[37] and whose destiny, unlike those of Islam and Judaism, is not intrinsically linked to the existence of a particular political entity. To be sure, the New Testament presupposes the existence of civil society and alludes to it more than once, but it does not have a political program of its own, exhibits no preference for any regime, and offers no precise rules regarding the conduct of the affairs of this world. Whereas the Old Testament speaks everywhere of justice in the habitual sense of the term, the New Testament hardly ever mentions it. Its overriding concern is with justice in a spiritual sense or what Aquinas calls the "justice of the faith," *iustitia fidei*, which is the one that Christians are urged to seek in the first instance.[38] God himself will give them whatever else they need (Matt. 6:33). In all matters pertaining to the temporal order, one has only to submit to the laws of the society to which one happens to belong, so long as these laws do not command anything manifestly contrary to the teaching of the Gospel. The most openly political text of the entire New Testament simply enjoins everyone to be subject to the governing authorities (Rom. 13:1). As one reads in the anonymous but no less remarkable *Letter to Diognetus*,

> Christians are distinguished from other human beings neither by their country, nor by their language, nor by their dress. They do not dwell in cities that belong to them alone, do not speak in some strange dialect, and do not affect a manner that sets them apart from everyone else . . . . They are spread out in a variety of cities, Greek as well as barbarian, according to the lot that has befallen each one of them. They conform to local usage as regards clothing, food, and the rest of their daily needs, all the while allowing the extraordinary and truly paradoxical character of their own proper way of life (*politeia*) to be seen by everyone.[39]

The uneasiness that one is likely to experience upon hearing such words stems from the fact that the civil laws that Christians are summoned to obey are never perfect and sometimes very imperfect, as they were when, under Nero, St. Paul was writing his Letter to the Romans. It is only under the best regime that the good citizen and the morally good human being coincide.[40] But the best regime, although theoretically possible, is not to be found anywhere on earth. In Plato's words, it exists only "in speech."[41] The fact of the matter is that all actual cities are more or less unjust. If so, the Christian who shares the way of life of his city, pays his taxes, aspires to his honors, and, should the need arise, defends it in battle, necessarily becomes a party to its inequities and contributes to their propagation. How, in short, does one live as a moral human being in an immoral society? Such is the problem with which thoughtful Christians finally had to come to grips.

RECONCILING CHRISTIANITY AND THE POLITICAL LIFE

The method used by the early Church to resolve this problem is on the whole the one to which Plato resorts in the *Republic*, where all moral issues are discussed in the light of the first principles of the universe or the "ideas." For Plato, there is ultimately no such thing as moral virtue. Only such virtues as are rooted in or informed by philosophic knowledge qualify as genuine virtues. All the others are demoted to the rank of political or vulgar virtues.[42] Differently and more clearly stated, the highest moral principles are seldom if ever directly applicable to concrete situations and must be diluted in order to become operative. As we see in chapter seven, this is what caused St. Augustine to declare that what the pagans call virtues are really "vices,"[43] that all earthly kingdoms are nothing but "gigantic larcenies," *magna latrocinia,*[44] that Rome was never a "republic," and that the only city deserving of that name is the one that the Bible calls the "city of God."[45]

Aristotle's mode of procedure typically shuns these extreme utterances. It consists in looking at moral phenomena as they appear, not to the philosopher who studies all things in the light of eternity, but to decent or morally good human beings. Gone is any thought of denying to earthly societies the name of cities or to the moral qualities of their citizens the name of virtues. Aristotle, one might say, is the one who invents moral virtue by granting it a certain autonomy in regard to intellectual virtue.[46]

This more moderate approach was better suited to the realities of medieval society, whose laws and institutions bore little resemblance to those of pagan Rome. Christians were no longer being ordered to sacrifice to idols, honor the gods of the city, venerate the person of the emperor, or pay with their lives the privilege of worshipping the one true God. Plato had rendered enormous services to the apologists of the new religion at a time when Christians were only a tiny minority in the midst of a world awash in paganism. Now that Christianity had replaced imperial Rome as the energizing core of Western civilization, Aristotle could take over as its philosophical guide. All that was needed for this purpose was to touch up a few of his formulas so as to bring them into line with the biblical teaching. There was no better way of satisfying the requirements of Christian morality without imposing too heavy a burden on civil society. The typical cases of private property and slavery will show us how.

According to Aristotle, the private ownership of property is on the whole preferable to communism not because it is more just but because it is more convenient. Experience reveals that human beings take better care of goods that they can call their own, avoid disorder more easily when property is divided, and are less likely to quarrel among themselves when everyone knows in advance what belongs or does not belong to him. Is this to say that private property is in full accord with natural right? Not at all. According to the norms of absolute justice, material goods belong to those who have both the wisdom and the moral rectitude needed to use them properly. This is what in the final analysis both Plato and Aristotle teach, and it is also the position taken by a number of early Christian writers such as Augustine, who states flatly that "he who uses his wealth badly possesses it wrongly, and wrongful possession means that it is another's property."[47] However, to forestall the confusion that would result from the systematic application of such a principle, civil societies ordinarily grant to their subjects the right to keep for themselves all legally acquired goods, regardless of the use they make of them.[48]

Needless to say, the accommodation was not one with which the Christian authors could feel altogether comfortable inasmuch as it raised doubts about the truly moral character of private property. One had to be able to state unequivocally that private property was just, if not absolutely, at least in some secondary or derivative sense. This is why it was said to pertain to what Roman law calls *ius gentium* or the "right of nations," which stands midway between natural and political right and whose relative justice is vouched for by the fact that its principles are arrived at by way of deduction from the principles of absolute natural right.[49] Thus understood, the right of nations has as its proper object the highest form of justice compatible with life in society. Still, to include private property under the right of nations was to claim for it a firmer grounding in nature than Aristotle was willing to grant it.

The same type of argument was employed to sanction slavery, which, like private property, becomes more just for Aquinas than it was for Aristotle. The difficulty in the present case arises from the fact that the slave on whose services the ancient city depended for its well-being is not the natural slave of Book I of the *Politics*, a brute incapable of any kind of virtue and hence of little use to anybody. It is the political slave of Book VII, namely, the prisoner of war whose life has been spared in exchange for the work that he agrees to perform for his new masters. Such a situation, while offering certain advantages to both parties, is not necessarily just, at least to the extent that the enslaved person may have been the victim of an unjust aggression. This means that even Aristotle's best regime is vitiated by an unavoidable flaw, as he himself acknowledges when he adds that the prospect of freedom should be held out to such persons as a reward for their services.[50] As a Christian, Aquinas needed a more properly moral argument, for which he again appealed to the Roman *ius gentium*.[51] Although the compromise left something to be desired, it had the implicit sanction of the Bible, which commands slaves to obey their masters.[52]

Unfortunately, there were moments when an unbridgeable gulf appeared to separate the philosophic and the biblical traditions. Yet this did not prevent our commentators from doing their best to reduce the distance between them, either by arguing that Aristotle had spoken only by way of accommodation to pagan custom, or by proposing a benign interpretation of his views, or simply by giving him the benefit of the doubt. The thorniest text was without any doubt the one in which Aristotle authorizes abortion and the abandonment of deformed babies. According to Peter of Auvergne, his statements to this effect are not to be taken at face value. All they mean is that, just as nature bestows less care upon imperfect than upon perfect beings, so society cares less for defective than for healthy children. Fine, except that Aristotle also permits abortion and the abandonment of children born without any physical defect for no other reason than to control the size of the population. In his eagerness to defend him, Peter explains that Aristotle had no intention of justifying abortion, that he mentions it only because the societies of his time admitted it, and that in any event he had the good sense of restricting it to the early stages of the pregnancy (i.e., to the period in which the fetus has not yet received a human soul), lest by putting an innocent person to death one should become guilty of murder.[53]

An equally delicate problem presented itself in connection with the Cretan regime, whose legislator, Minos, again for the purpose of limiting the number of offspring, had encouraged homosexual relations.[54] Aristotle refuses to pronounce himself openly on the moral goodness or badness of this practice, to which he promises to return, something he never did, at least in the *Politics* as we have it. However, there is no evidence that he objected to this subordination of personal morality to public utility. On the contrary, he goes so far as to assert that on such matters Minos had shown a great deal of wisdom—that he had "philosophized," *pephilosopheken*, something that he says of no one else in the *Politics*. Aquinas, who is less preoccupied than others with moralizing Aristotle, reports his words faithfully and without further comment.[55]

Others were less restrained. Albert the Great seizes the opportunity to rail against homosexuality as a vice contrary to nature, to reason, to custom, and to both the divine and the natural law.[56] He cites as witnesses Avicenna and Alan of Lille's *Lamentations of Nature against the Sodomites*.[57] But none of this keeps him from doing his best to exonerate Aristotle by referring the reader to Book VII of the *Nicomachean Ethics*, where pederasty is characterized as a morbid state.[58] To my knowledge, no commentator thought of inquiring into the possible reasons for this discrepancy between the *Ethics*, where moral virtue is presented as something desirable for its own sake, and the *Politics*, where it is discussed in terms of its contribution to the good of society. For Aristotle, a higher degree of moral perfection may be expected on the part of the individual, or at least some individuals, than on the part of society at large. This was to postulate between private and public morality a larger gap than the one to which the Christian world was accustomed.

One final example, and a quaint one at that: toward the end of Book VII, Aristotle permits adults to attend certain celebrations in which the gods were the butt of gross or scurrilous mockeries. The text posed a curious dilemma for our commentators, for by approving this custom, as they might have been tempted to do on the ground that the pagan gods were only getting what they deserved, they ran the risk of giving to their fellow Christians the idea of poking fun at their own God. It was therefore necessary to point out, as does Peter of Auvergne, that Aristotle is merely adapting himself to a state of mind that he did not share: *loquitur secundum opinionem gentilium antiquorum*.[59] Oresme takes the further step of congratulating Aristotle for declaring this kind of spectacle off limits for young people.[60] No one asked whether in bringing up this seemingly trivial issue Aristotle did not have an ulterior motive. He could conceivably have thought that indulging in such irreverent jests had the effect of relaxing whatever hold these gods may have had on public life. To laugh at the gods is to take one's distance from them and regain one's freedom in regard to them. For a pagan in search of the truth, this freedom was the beginning of wisdom, the very condition of the philosophic quest. In that case, the point at which, in appearance, the *Politics* sinks to its lowest level could well be the one that some of the newly emancipated Aristotelians of the Middle Ages viewed as its peak.[61] Dante, whose *Comedy* often makes us laugh at things that most people hold or once held sacred, is perhaps the author who has best understood this often ignored or misunderstood side of Aristotle's thought.

By means of such emendations or glosses, and on condition that the matter not be looked at too closely, one succeeded in making of Aristotle, if not an apostle, at least a precursor of Christian morality. To be sure, he had not read the Bible, but that was not something that could be held against him. What was astonishing is that this pagan had managed to discover by himself so many truths that were corroborated by divine Revelation. There were other things as well. Aquinas and his teacher, Albert the Great, had advocated the use of Aristotelian philosophy as a means of imparting a more rigorous cast to thirteenth-century theology. Others showed themselves reticent, not without reason; for it soon became apparent that, if the *Politics* could help solve some of the nagging political problems of the hour, it also called into question the social structures and, indeed, the very foundations of medieval Christendom.[62] What it brought to the West for the first time was nothing less than a coherent and plausible analysis of the whole of human life that owed nothing to the biblical tradition and, depending on the spirit in which it was read, had all the earmarks of a viable alternative to it.

Such is the path followed by other Aristotelians, who rediscovered through the *Politics* the notion of the regime as the basic political phenomenon, as that "whole" which gives to a particular society its distinctive character, defines its way of life, determines its priorities, lends meaning to its activities, and constitutes the horizon beyond which for most people there is nothing. The only exceptions to this rule are the philosopher, who transcends that horizon, and the brute, who is incapable of rising to its level. Neither one can, strictly speaking, be considered part of the city.[63]

This rehabilitation of the political regime will allow the philosophers of that period to revalorize the notion of legal justice, the virtue of the citizen *qua* citizen, which had long given way to charity as the general virtue and which made little sense to anyone who had not read the *Nicomachean Ethics*.[64] In Aquinas, legal justice is subordinated to charity;[65] in Dante, the opposite is the case: charity becomes the handmaiden of legal justice.[66] Thanks to all of this, people will finally begin to glimpse what Aristotle's *bene vivere politice* could signify.[67] The term *politizare*, "to politicize," created by Moerbeke to render the Greek *politeuesthai*[68] and subsequently taken over by Aquinas, Dante,[69] and many others, encapsulated this conception of the citizen as someone who is authorized to take an active part in the life of the city.

Closely linked to this state of affairs was the *Politics*'s account of the role of the priesthood, which was to furnish the adversaries of the papacy with the intellectual weapons for which they were looking. What emerges clearly from Aristotle's teaching is that priests do not govern. They are old men who, while maintaining regular contacts with the magistrates, no longer discharge the functions proper to the citizen, namely, the deliberative or legislative and the judicial.[70] Aristotle's best regime is anything but a theocracy. It excludes the priests from power and considers them rather as the educators of the city. Such, not surprisingly, is the role that will be assigned to them by the fourteenth-century "imperialists" or partisans of the Empire against the Papacy, such as Dante and Marsilius of Padua, with minor modifications necessitated by the triumph of Christianity.[71]

One thinks in this connection of the preoccupations that inspired the work of Georges de Lagarde, who set out to trace through the various stages of its development the birth of what he called the "lay spirit" in the Middle Ages. For Lagarde, however, the distinction between lay and cleric applied to two groups of Christians who for some time had been drifting further and further apart within the Church itself.[72] In this he may not have gone far enough. Everything points to the fact that, not long after the middle of the thirteenth century, a growing number of philosophers went so far as to question not only the pope's temporal authority but the very

truth of divine Revelation. With assistance from Aristotle, political natur-
alism was rapidly becoming once again what it had been since the
beginning, and that for which the Church authorities had long been
suspicious of it, namely, a silent or muted critique of the reigning
religious orthodoxy at any given moment of history.

One thing is certain: the medieval theologians could no longer be satisfied with correcting Aristotle on this or that particular point. The whole
of the *Politics* had to be reconsidered in the light of Christian dogma, and
this is precisely what a good number of them undertook to do, often with
the addition of a single term. Thus, at the beginning of Book VIII,
Aristotle declares that the citizen does not belong to himself but to the
city. Fearing a trap beneath the simple words, Peter of Auvergne tries to
avoid it by inserting into his commentary the word *solum*—the citizen
does not belong to himself "alone"—without warning us of the change,
which effectively destroyed the classical notion of the regime as a total
way of life.[73]

Aquinas resorts to a similar procedure while commenting on what
Aristotle says about the supreme good of the "present life," *praesentis
vitae*, which for most people consists in pleasure, wealth, honor, or moral
virtue.[74] Aristotle is surely speaking of the "present" life, but since he does
not know of any other, he had no reason to give it that name. To use a
term that takes for granted the existence of a personal life after death is
already to christianize his thought. The implications for the conduct of
human life were not negligible. To appreciate them, it suffices to contrast
the state of mind of the pagan soldier who, by risking his life for the
defense of his country, stands to lose everything, and the state of mind of
the Christian who, by sacrificing himself for the good of others, merits
eternal salvation.

By qualifying Aristotle's text in this manner, it was thought, one was
merely rendering to Caesar what is Caesar's and to God what is God's. To
anybody who is persuaded that everything is Caesar's or that everything
is God's, this was too little. Hence other thinkers will find a way of dres-
sing up Aristotle as an "imperialist" or defender of the Empire against the
papacy—one has only to think once again of Dante or Marsilius of Padua
—or else as a patron of medieval theocracy.[75] In either case, the *Politics*
would finally enjoy its hour of glory, which lasted barely more than three
centuries. The man who put an end to its reign is Machiavelli, whose
Prince is both a *reprobatio Aristotelis*—although never mentioned by
name, Aristotle is one of the prime targets of the book—and a declaration
of all-out war against the religious tradition with which, since the thirteenth century, his name had been bound up.[76] One cannot help wondering
to what extent Machiavelli's break with the past was facilitated by the
mutilations to which Aristotle's text had consciously or unconsciously

been subjected by his Christian followers, who had otherwise done so much to bring him back to life.

NOTES

1. The Latin Middle Ages became acquainted with these commentaries through Robert of Grosseteste's translations shortly before the middle of the 13th century. Cf. H. P. Mercken, *The Greek Commentaries of the Nicomachean Ethics of Aristotle in the Latin Translation of Robert of Grosseteste, Bishop of Lincoln. Corpus Latinum Commentariorum Graecorum*, vol. VI.1 (Leiden: Brill, 1973). For the remarks on the nature of political science and its relation to the other practical sciences, see esp. 1-5.

2. Diogenes Laertius, *Lives*, V.1. On these inventories, cf. P. Moraux, *Listes anciennes des ouvrages d'Aristote* (Louvain: Editions universitaires de Louvain, 1951).

3. In keeping with the Aristotelian tradition, Cassiodorus lists politics or "civil science" as one of the three practical sciences, along with ethics and economics. Cf. *Institutiones* II.3. Migne *Patrologia, Series Latina* or *PL* 70.1168a and 1169a.

4. Boethius *Commentary on Porphyry's Isagoge* in Migne *Patrologia, series Latina* or *PL* 64. col. 11-12.

5. Isadore of Seville, *Etymologiae* II.24, 10, and 16.

6. Julian *Letter* 6 (to Themistius), 260d-261c and 263d. The passages quoted are *Politics* III.1286b, 1287a, and VII.1325b.

7. Cf. *Letter* 12 (to Priscus), where Julian alludes to these excerpts, through which he would have been introduced to Aristotelian philosophy.

8. Proclus *In Platonis rem publicam commentarii*, edited by W. Kroll (Leipzig: Teubners, 1899), II.360-67.

9. Cf. A. Dreizehnter, *Aristoteles' Politik* (München: Wilhelm Fink Verlag, 1970) XV-XXI. Aristotle, *The Politics*, translated with an Introduction, Notes, and Glosssary by C. Lord, (Chicago: University of Chicago Press, 1984), 22-24. See also, in regard to the Middle Ages, Hugh of Saint Victor, *Didaskalion* II.9, and William of Conches, *Glosae super Platonem*, edited by E. Jeauneau (Paris: J. Vrin, 1965), 60. Dominic Gundisalvi's *De divisione philosophiae*, which follows the parallel works of Farabi and Avicenna, adds to the traditional lists of the liberal arts a classification of the philosophic disciplines that includes politics. On these matters, cf. C. Martin, "Some Medieval Commentaries on Aristotle's *Politics*," *History* 36 (1951): 30. The then current notion of politics as a distinct science has been studied by Gaines Post, *Studies in Medieval Legal Thought: Public Law and the State, 1100-1322* (Princeton: Princeton University Press, 1964), esp. 494-561, and C. Nederman, "Aristotelianism and the Origins of 'Political Science' in the Twelfth Century," *Journal of the History of Ideas* vol. 52, no. 2, (1991): 179-194. Also, by the same author, "Nature and the Origins of Society: The Ciceronian Tradition in Medieval Political Thought," ibid. 49 (1988): 3-26. The upshot of these studies is that, contrary to what is often asserted, the Middle Ages acknowledged the natural character of civil society long before the

arrival of *The Politics*. It should nevertheless be added that prior to the rediscovery of Aristotle's text, the discussion of these matters often lacked precision. Cf. D. Luscombe, "City and Politics before the Coming of the *Politics*: Some Illustrations," in D. Abulafia, et al., *Church and City* (Cambridge MA: Cambridge University Press, 1992), 41-55.

10. One finds a few examples of the kind of reaction that the *Politics* could elicit even on a personal and down to earth level in the *scholia* of Michael of Ephesus, who writes, apropos of Aristotle's remark that anyone who spends money to gain office may be expected to use the office to make money (II.1273b2): "That this is most true is proved by the carrion-crows of our own time." Or apropos of Aristotle's remark that some corrupt regimes are more than ordinarily harsh (IV.1290a25): "This means despotic government, such as the kingship of our own times." Or apropos of Aristotle's remark that tyrants's are always opposed to the good (V.1334a19): "This is particularly so nowadays, my dear Aristotle, and this is why I am a beggar." Cf. Barker, ibid., 140-41.

11. See, for example, Marsilius of Padua, *Defender of the Peace*, I, ch. 12-13. On Marsilius's "populism," cf. L. Strauss, "Marsilius of Padua," in *History of Political Philosophy* edited by L. Strauss and J. Cropsey (Chicago and London: University of Chicago Press, 1987), 280f. In *Leviathan* XLVI.1.23, Hobbes writes: "He (Aristotle) calls the rule of all kings *tyranny*, and says that only in democracy is there liberty," edited by E. Curley (Indianapolis and Cambridge: Hackett Press, 1994), 476. For Aristotle's comment on Plato's *Laws* cf. *Politics* II.6.1264b29f.

12. Cf. W. Nicgorski, "Cicero on Aristotle and Aristotelians," paper presented at the 87th Annual Meeting of the American Political Science Association, Washington, D.C. 1991.

13. Dante, *Inferno* IV.131. Cf. Maimonides, *Guide of the Perplexed*, I54; II.12; II.28; and III.54. In Maimonides, the title designates Moses, although it seems to apply equally well if not better to Aristotle, who is called "the chief of the philosophers" in I.5. See S. Pines's introduction to his translation of the *Guide* (Chicago: University of Chicago Press, 1963), p. lxi, n. 8.

14. Avicenna, *On the Divisions of the Rational Sciences*, in *Medieval Political Philosophy: A Sourcebook*, edited by R. Lerner and M. Mahdi (New York: The Free Press, 1963), 97.

15. Cf. Maimonides, *Logic*, chap. 14, ibid., 190.

16. S. Pines, "Aristotle's *Politics* in Arabic Philosophy," *Israel Oriental Studies* 5 (1975): 150-160, which tries to show that the Arabic philosophers were not completely ignorant of the *Politics* and even made some use of it in their works. L. Strauss would thus have been mistaken when he denied that they had any knowledge of it. Perhaps, but if they did know Aristotle's text, one wonders why they made so little use of it. Toward the beginning of his commentary on Plato's *Republic*, Averroes notes that he had never had "Aristotle's book on government (i.e., the *Politics*) in hand." Cf. *Averroes on Plato's Republic*, translated with an introduction and notes by R. Lerner (Ithaca, NY: Cornell University Press, 1974), 4.

17. Contrary to what is often asserted, there is no evidence that the translation was undertaken at Aquinas's bidding. Cf. Thomas Aquinas, *Sententia Libri Politicorum, Opera Omnia*, vol. 48 (Rome, 1971), p. A63, n. 1. See also J. Brams, "Guillaume de Moerbeke et Aristote," *Rencontres de cultures and la philosophie médiévale: Traductions et traducteurs de l'antiquité tardive au XIVe siècle*, edited by J. Hamesse et M. Fattori (Louvain-la-Neuve Cassino, 1990), 336.

18. The common assumption that Thomas's commentary preceded that of Albert has yet to be validated. A critical edition of Albert's text, which is still lacking, could conceivably shed further light on the subject.

19. Roger Bacon, *Opera adhuc inedita*, edited by R. Steele, fasc. I (Oxford, n.d. 29 to which P. Michaud-Quantin refers in the preface to his edition of Moerbeke's first translation of the *Politics, Aristoteles Latinus*, vol. 29,1 (Bruges-Paris: Desclée de Brouwer, 1961), XVI.

20. Dante, *Epistula* V.2.6-8.

21. *Monarchia* I.1.5.

22. Augustine, *De civitate Dei* V.17.

23. *De civitate Dei* II.21.2.

24. *De re publica* 1.26.2.

25. Op. cit., p. A 215.

26. Cf. G. de Lagarde, *La naissance de l'esprit laïque au moyen âge*, vol. 3 (Louvain and Paris: Nauwelaerts, 1970), 84. Roger Bacon notes that "civil science," the equivalent of political science, draws its name from *civitas*, "city," owing to the fact in ancient times the world was divided into cities (e.g., Rome), but that it also has as its function to establish laws for kingdoms and empires, *Rogeri Baconis Moralis Philosophia*, I, Proemium, 11, 5-6 Massa.

27. *Sententia libri politicorum* III.5.23, p. A201, and 6.17, p. A204: "Dicit ergo primo quod <quia> politea nihil est aliud quam *politeuma*, quod significat ordinem dominantium in civitate, necesse est quod distinguantur politiae secundum diversitatem dominantium in civitate . . . ." It is true that Aristotle himself does not always distinguish clearly between these two terms.

28. On Moerbeke's translations, cf. G. Verbeke, "Moerbeke, traducteur et interprète: un texte et une pensée," in *Guillaume de Moerbeke: Recueil d'études à l'occasion du 700e centenaire de sa mort* (1286), edited by J. Brahms and W. Vanhamel (Leuven: Leuven University Press, 1989), 1-21.

29. Cf. *Politics* VIII.1337a39-42, where *pertta* refers to gratuitous or non-necessary things, that is to say, things that are sought for themselves rather than for their utility.

30. Cf. Plato, *Laws* V.739a. For Aristotle's analysis of Plato's *Laws* cf. *Pol.* II.1264b26f.

31. *Politica, translatio prior imperfecta*, 72b17, 54. Cf. Aristotle, *Politics* II.10.1272b15-18.

32. Loc. cit., Bk. II, *as* 1272b18, p. A175.

33. See, for example, Nicholas Oresme, *Le livre de Politiques d'Aristote*, edited

by A. D. Menut, *Transactions of the American Philosophical Society*, New Series, vol. 60, Part 6 (Philadelphia, 1960), 651, p. 108: "Et l'autre translacion dit que Zenelasius la fit loing, ce est a dire qu'il funda Crete loing des autres terres."

34. The same cannot be said of the more elegant but also much freer translation produced by Leonardo Bruni a century and a half later. For a comparison between the two translators, see J. Schmidt, "A Raven with a Halo: The Translation of Aristotle's *Politics*," *History of Political Thought* 7 (1986): 295-319.

35. H.-X. Arquillière, *L'Augustinisme politique: Essai sur la formation des théories politiques duy moyen âge*, 2d ed. (Paris, 1955), 30f, and by the same author "Réflexions sur l'essence de l'augustinisme politique," *Augustinus Magister*, vol. 2 (Paris, 1954), 991-1001.

36. B. Tierney, *Religion, Law and the Growth of Constitutional Thought, 1150-1650* (Cambridge MA and New York: Cambridge University Press, 1982), esp. 87-92. J. M. Blythe, *Ideal Government and the Mixed Constitution in the Middle Ages* (Princeton: Princeton University Press, 1992).

37. See in particular Fustel's classic work, *The Ancient City*, Book V, chapter 3, entitled "Christianity Changes the Conditions of Government" (Garden City: Doubleday Anchor, n.d.), 389-96. This book was published previously in 6 volumes between 1882 and 1892.

38. *De veritate*, qu. 12, a. 3, and 11.

39. *Epistula ad Diognetum* V.1-4.

40. Aristotle, *Politics* III.1276b30. Thomas Aquinas *Sent. Libri Politicorum*, III.4. p. A193. Dante, *Monarchia* I.12, edited by P. G. Ricci (Verona: Mondadori, 1965), 160,12.

41. Plato, *Republic* IX.592a-b. The same thought is echoed by St. Augustine, for whom the perfectly just city is to be found only in "private discussions," *domesticae disputationes* (*Epist.* 91.4.)

42. Cf. *Republic* VI.500d.

43. Cf. *De civitate Dei* XIX.25.

44. *De civitate Dei* IV.4.

45. *De civitate Dei* II.21.4.

46. The best treatment of this subject that I know of is that of L. Strauss, *The City and Man* (Chicago: The University of Chicago Press, 1964), esp. 21f.

47. Augustine *Epis.* 153.26. The rest of the text reads as follows: "Money is wrongly possessed by bad men while good men who love it least have the best right to it. In this life the wrong of evil possessors is endured and among them certain laws are established which are called civil laws, not because they bring men to make a good use of their wealth, but because those who make a bad use of it become thereby less injurious." Saint Augustine, *Letters*, vol. 3, translated by W. Parsons, *The Fathers of the Church*, vol. 20 (New York, 1943), 302.

48. In true Socratic fashion, Xenophon explains the matter with the help of a concrete case that Cyrus's preceptors once submitted to their young pupil. Let us suppose that two men one of whom owns a coat that is too big for him and the other

a coat that is too small: should they be compelled to exchange their coats? It seems eminently reasonable that they do so, but, save in the rare instances, the law does not require it and looks upon all legal possession as being just. Cf. *Education of Cyrus*, I.3.16.

49. E.g., Thomas Aquinas *Summa theologiae* I-II, qu. 95, a. 4; II-II, qu. 57, a. 2, ad 3 and qu. 57, a. 3. Cf. Cicero, *De officiis* III.17.69.

50. *Politics* VII.1339a33. Cf. Aristotle (Pseudo?) *Economics* 1344b16.

51. *Sententia libri politicorum* I.4.21, p. A91. See along the same lines *De civ. Dei* I.15, although to my knowledge Augustine never uses the expression *ius gentium*. The first Christian to introduce this notion into the debate appears to be Isidore of Seville, *Etymologiae* VI.6, entitled: *Quid sit ius gentium?*

52. See, for example, Colossians 3:22: "Slaves, obey in everything your earthly masters . . . ."; 1 Timothy 6:1: "Let all who are under the yoke of slavery regard their masters as worthy of all honor, so that the name of God and the teaching may not be defamed."

53. Thomas Aquinas, *In libros politicorum Aristotelis expositio*, no. 1241 (Turin and Rome: Marietti, 1951), 404. (Peter's commentary, which completes that of Thomas, which was left unfinished, begins with Lesson 7 of Book III.) Albert the Great notes that, by limiting abortions to the period in which the embryo was thought to be incapable of sensations, Aristotle had shown greater respect for natural piety than did most of the barbarians. Cf. *Commentarii in octo libros politicorum Aristotelis*, edited by A. Borgnet, *Opera Omnia*, vol. 8 (Paris: Vives, 1891), 739. For Aristotle's discussion of abortion and the abandonment of deformed babies cf. *Politics* VII.1335b20ff.

54. *Politics* II.1272a25.

55. *Sent. libri polit.* II.15, p. A174, 117. For Aristotle's comment on Minos cf. *Politics* II.1272a20ff.

56. Loc. cit., 182.

57. Alan of Lille, *De planctu naturae PL* 210. 430-82.

58. Cf. *Nichomachean Ethics* 1148b27 for a similar reaction, Nicholas Oresme, who cites two biblical passages where homosexuality is condemned in fairly explicit terms: Romans 1:27 (cf. 9:29, which alludes in this connection to the destruction of Sodom and Gomorrah), and 2 Maccabees, 4:12, where the high priest Jason is rebuked for building a gymnasium in Jerusalem and allowing Jews to frequent it, at the risk of indulging in the immoral practices of the Greeks. Oresme decries sodomy as a "sin against nature," (loc. cit., p. 106) and adds that Aristotle had not thought it necessary to go into the matter at greater length since the practice in question was manifestly "odious" and "bestial."

59. *In libros politicorum Aristotelis expositio*, no. 1254, 408. Cf. Aristotle, *Politics* VIII.1336b15.

60. *In libros politicorum Aristotelis expositio*, 338.

61. See on this point the pertinent remarks by R. Bartlett, *Aristotle's Best Regime*, dissertation (Boston College, 1992), 155-56.

62. See, for example, Albert the Great's invectives against the Christians who opposed Aristotelianism on those grounds and whom Albert compares to the people who put Socrates to death; loc. cit., 803-04.

63. Cf. *Politics* I.125a29.

64. The point is well made by O. Lottin, "Le concept de justice chez les théologiens du moyen âge avant l'introduction d'Aristote," *Revue Thomiste* 44 (1938): 511-21.

65. For further information concerning justice as a general virtue, cf. E. L. Fortin, "Basil the Great and the Choice of Hercules," E. L. Fortin, *The Birth of Philosophic Christianity Studies in Early Christian and Medieval Thought*, edited by J. Brian Benestad (Lanham, MD: Rowman and Littlefield, 1996), 153-168.

66. Cf. *Monarchia*, I.11.14, p. 156. Ricci: *caritas maxime iustitiam vigorabit, et potior potius.*

67. The formula is that of Aquinas *Sent. libri polit.* II.16, p. A177, 9.

68. *Politics* II.1272b24.

69. Cf. *Monarchia* I.12.10.160 Ricci: *politizantes.*

70. Cf. Aristotle *Politics* IV.1299a17; VI.1322b19f; VII.1329a27f. It goes without saying that the classical thinkers knew nothing of the typical modern theory of the separation of powers.

71. See on this point the penetrating discussion by S. Torraco, *Priests as Physicians of Souls in Marsilius of Padua's Defensor Pacis* (San Francisco: Mellon Research University Press, 1992).

72. G. de Lagarde, *La naissance de l'esprit laïque au moyen âge* vol. 1: *Bilan du XIIIe siècle*, third ed. (Paris: Nauwelaerts, 1956), VIII-IX.

73. *Aristotelis expositio*, no. 1263, p. 414. For Aristotle's discussion of the relation of the citizen to the city cf. *Politics* VII.2447a27.

74. *Sent. Libri Polit.* I.1, p. A120, 46. The same expression is used in *Sent. Libri Ethicorum, Opera Omnia* vol. 47 (Rome, 1969), I.1, p. 4, 62, and III.18, p. 178, 90 and 100. Also *Summa contra gent.* III.48.

75. As did, for example, Giles of Rome and James of Viterbo, drawing their inspiration from Aristotle's analysis of the *pambasileia* or absolute monarchy. Cf. N. Kretzman et al., *The Cambridge History of Later Medieval Philosophy* (Cambridge and New York: Cambridge University Press, 1982), 758.

76. From this point of view, Gaines Post and C. Nederman are right in emphasizing the links that unite the thirteenth century and the centuries that preceded it; cf. *supra*, note 9. The definitive break with the combined classical and medieval tradition was not effected until three centuries later with Machiavelli. For a clear statement of the nature of that break, see esp. Machiavelli's *The Prince*, chap. 15, and *Discourses* I, Introd.

10

AUGUSTINE, THOMAS AQUINAS, AND THE PROBLEM OF NATURAL LAW

Few doctrines bequeathed to the Christian West by the writers of late antiquity have had a more tumultuous career and have proved more inherently controversial than the so-called "natural law" theory. The fact that such a doctrine had been propounded by St. Augustine was enough to secure for it a prominent place in medieval ethical and legal thought. Yet the notorious debates to which it gave rise and the variety of interpretations to which it was subjected suggest that its status always remained somewhat ambiguous. The story, needless to say, does not end with the Middle Ages. It has been remarked more than once, usually by its defenders, that no single doctrine has so often risen from its ashes after having been repeatedly and solemnly pronounced dead.[1] If these cycles of decline and rebirth are a sure sign of its abiding vitality, they also testify to a no less persistent vulnerability. There is thus ample justification for dealing with it as a problem to be investigated rather than a solution to be accepted or rejected.

Part of the difficulty lies of course in the wide range of meanings that the term "natural law" has taken on over the centuries—as another name for the natural order of the universe, for the whole of divine Revelation,[2] for the fusion of biblical and classical thought that characterizes the early Christian and medieval periods, or, still more broadly, for any teaching that holds to objective standards of morality. Without questioning the legitimacy of these and other extended meanings, the present discussion will restrict itself to the common definition of the natural law as a moral law derived from nature and capable of serving as a guide to human action. The precise question to which I shall address myself is whether the existence of such a law can be defended on the basis of reason alone or whether it is ultimately dependent on revealed religion. I shall argue that, contrary to what is frequently asserted, the concept of natural law, as distinguished from natural right, plays no significant role in classical philosophy, that it is fully intelligible only within the context of divine Revelation, and, lastly, that its limitations first became apparent as a result of Thomas Aquinas's epoch-making reformulation of the Augustinian natural law doctrine. Since much of what I shall have to say hinges on a clear grasp of the distinction between natural right and natural law, some preliminary remarks about the natural right teaching of Plato, Aristotle, and Cicero would appear to be in order.

Despite the lingering tendency among scholars to speak of both Plato and Aristotle as natural law theorists, there is little to be said for the presence of a genuine natural law theory in any of their writings. The expression "natural law" does occur twice in Plato, once in the *Timaeus*, but only with reference to the cleansing of bodily fluids (hence, in the sense of a physical rather than a moral law),[3] and once in the *Gorgias,* where the position that it designates is not only different from but diametrically opposed to the one taken by Socrates.[4] The speaker in the present case is the infamous Callicles, Socrates's most outspoken adversary in the dialogue, who is anything but an advocate of the kind of morality that is normally associated with the natural law. Callicles's view, like that of Thrasymachus in the *Republic,* is the typical conventionalist view according to which right is merely the advantage of the stronger.[5] By nature human beings seek pleasure and they do so without the slightest regard for the needs of others.[6] What people call justice is nothing but a pious fraud devised by the many for the sake of defending their own selfish interests against the encroachments of other, more gifted but less numerous individuals.[7] Callicles is not unaware of the power of the social conventions to which it gives rise and he knows that, whether he likes it or not, he must defer to them; but, unlike others, he is not fooled by them. What he needs is the appearance of justice rather than its substance. His law-abidingness is strictly a matter of calculation or enlightened self-interest.

Socrates will have little difficulty in persuading, if not Callicles himself,[8] at least his other hearers that the good is not identical with but essentially different from the pleasant and hence that justice is choiceworthy for its own sake.[9] The point to be emphasized, however, is that, while he takes a firm stand on natural right, he is altogether silent on the subject of natural law; for there is no evidence that the right to whose defense he rallies forms part of a legally sanctioned order extending to the whole of human life. If, from a purely juridical point of view, the two terms are closely related and often used interchangeably in the later tradition,[10] philosophically they remain dichotomous and reflect two notably different conceptions of justice. It is one thing to claim that an action is intrinsically right, insofar as it accords with the demands of right reason, and quite another to contend that its goodness derives from its conformity to a universal law whose injunctions can never be infringed with impunity. One may be correct in assuming that a life of reason and virtue generally leads to greater happiness than a life of unreason and vice, but this is still a far cry from asserting that crime never pays and that in the end the only people who are happy are the ones who deserve to be happy. The Platonic dialogues know of no law of the cosmos certifying that justice will necessarily prevail in human affairs.[11] In the light of the later, non-Platonic natural law teaching, one could say that the choice is between a morally lawful universe in which all evils are eventually set straight and a universe in which morality, however important it may be in other respects, is left without any cosmic or suprahuman support other than that which takes the form of a myth.[12]

There is more to be said at first glance for the ascription of a natural law doctrine to Aristotle, since he at least mentions something like it in his own name, not in the *Nicomachean Ethics,* to be sure, but in the *Rhetoric.*[13] Still, it takes a good deal of imagination to see how any of the three statements borrowed from Sophocles, Empedocles, and Alcidamas which he uses to illustrate the point could possibly qualify as examples of a law that is natural in any real sense of the word.[14] One gathers from the context that the law of nature referred to in this instance is only one of a number of rhetorical *topoi* which the orator is free to employ at his discretion and which is effective to the degree to which it is accepted by his audience.[15] That the argument should be couched in legal terms is not surprising since the book as a whole is mainly devoted to a study of forensic and political rhetoric. It proves no more than that everyone "divines" (*manteuontai*) as it were, that some things are just or unjust "by nature" rather than by virtue of their legal status or any other previously reached agreement on the part of human beings.[16]

All indications thus point to the fact that the natural law doctrine is a post-Aristotelian phenomenon, which no doubt owes much to the older natural right theory of Plato and Aristotle but which nevertheless represents a significant departure from it. Yet its precise origin remains mysterious to say the least. The first fully developed and formally complete account of it that we have dates back only to Cicero, who attributes it to Zeno of Cittium, the founder of Stoicism, in whose opinion, we are told, the "natural law (*lex naturalis*) is divine and fulfills its function by commanding what is right and forbidding its opposite."[17] But Cicero himself was not a Stoic and his own treatment of the natural law raises serious questions about its alleged Stoic authenticity. With the exception of the one text from the *De natura deorum* to which reference has just been made, there is little proof that the expression *nomos phuseōs* or "natural law" was ever used by the old Stoics themselves. Zeno's thought in regard to moral matters is summed up in the famous dictum according to which the goal of the wise man is "to live conformably": *telos . . . . to omologoumenōs.*[18] If, as seems likely, Zeno derived the term *omologoumenōs* from *logos,* the formula may simply have been intended to convey the idea that one should live in accordance with the *logos* or one's essential self. It was made more specific (and perhaps less awkward) by Cleanthes's addition of the word "nature" as that to which one was urged to conform: *telos esti to omologoumenōs tē plusei zēn.*[19] In neither case is anything said about an external law by which the moral quality of human actions could be measured. Even the late Stoa still spoke only of living *logikos* or as one's inner *logos,* which is for all practical purposes identical with the universal *Logos,* would dictate.[20]

Given the absence of solid textual evidence on the one hand and of cogent historical arguments on the other,[21] one is inclined to doubt whether the natural law doctrine, at least in its moral sense, is of Stoic vintage at all, or, if it is, whether it ever gained in Stoic thought the position of prominence claimed for it by modern scholars. Professor Helmut Koester has argued persuasively that it did not and that this most famous of all Stoic contributions to the intellectual tradition of the Western world may in fact be a doctrine for which the old Stoics bear no direct responsibility.[22] It is thus not farfetched to propose that, for all anyone knows, Cicero himself may be the legitimate father of the natural law theory or at any rate the first author to furnish it with a specifically moral and political content.[23] Only in his works and nowhere else does the natural law as we have come to understand it acquire its essential characteristics not the least important of which is that it is a divinely sanctioned moral law to which are attached appropriate rewards and punishments. The question is why Cicero should have taken it upon himself to defend such a view at the risk of what appears to be a substantial deviation from the teaching of his Greek masters. The answer is perhaps to be found in the classic statement of that doctrine as it occurs in Book III of the *De re publica.*

It is certainly no accident that the spokesman for the natural law is not Cicero himself but the distinguished and eminently respectable jurist, Laelius, to whom the task of refuting the case for injustice has been entrusted by the other participants in the dialogue. Philus had previously argued for the sake of discussion that justice has nothing whatever to do with nature,[24] that "its mother is weakness,"[25] that the lip service that people pay to it serves only to mask the fact that everyone is driven by self-interest,[26] and, to make matters worse, that its demands necessarily conflict with those of practical wisdom.[27] Say that two men have been shipwrecked and find themselves vying for a plank that can only support one of them, is it likely that the stronger will sacrifice himself for the weaker especially when there is no one to observe him?[28] But if the human situation is such that the observance of justice often becomes a practical impossibility, one cannot be blamed for acting unjustly. Either justice does not exist at all or, if it does, it is "the height of folly."[29]

The argument thus far is not noticeably different from the one advanced by Callicles in the *Gorgias*. What lends new interest and greater credibility to it is that for the first time the emphasis is placed squarely on matters of foreign policy. If the Romans had been bound by considerations of justice, they would still be living in huts and Rome itself, instead of being the mistress of the world, would be no larger than the hamlet that Romulus founded.[30] Laws have "no sanction in nature."[31] They are obeyed because of the penalties that attach to them and not because they command the respect of all or most human beings. Bluntly stated, political justice is not justice but prudence, while natural justice, while it is really justice, is not prudence.[32]

Philus's blatant immoralism is obviously unacceptable to the righteous Laelius, who promptly denounces it on the ground that it runs counter to a universally binding and effective law of nature. "There is," he says, "a true law, namely, right reason, which is in accordance with nature, applies to all men, and is unchangeable and eternal; by its commands it summons men to the performance of their duties, by its prohibitions it restrains them from doing wrong." Although this law may have little effect on the wicked, it cannot be safely ignored, since it is both promulgated and sanctioned by God himself, the "common master and ruler of men." Anyone who violates it, even if he should be lucky enough to escape detection by other human beings, suffers the severest of punishments, to wit, self-contempt or the loss of his humanity.[33] The same law applies to society as a whole, which is likewise bound by its prescriptions and, to the extent that it fails to heed them, faces the prospect of imminent destruction.[34] As a patriotic citizen, Laelius is understandably loath to grant that Rome was guilty of any wrongdoing toward other peoples. The wars by which she built up her empire were "just wars," waged solely for the purpose of redressing injuries, or defending her allies, or bringing the benefits of civilization to the conquered nations. The very success of these endeavors is sufficient proof of the legitimacy of her cause.[35]

Laelius's vibrant plea for justice says more about his moral character than it does about the unimpeachable conduct of the Roman empire. It is clear from what follows that his interlocutors, who have already been treated to a detailed account of Roman history,[36] are not completely disposed to assent to it. Some of Rome's wars may have been undertaken for the sake of her allies, but this does not alter the fact that these allies never regained their independence and were often brutally repressed the moment they attempted to do so. Besides, it has never been demonstrated that a society which behaves justly toward its neighbors invariably fares well, or, inversely, that one which strays from the path of justice is punished in short order for its misdeeds. Extreme injustice may be self-defeating, but it is foolish to think that, in their relations with one another, civil societies can always be guided by standards of fairness or equity. Laelius's argument, in short, leaves much that is unsaid.

Under the circumstances, it is hardly surprising that the problem should be restated by Scipio, Cicero's mouthpiece and the leading character in the dialogue.[37] Although the mutilated condition in which the text has come down to us makes it difficult to reconstruct the argument in full detail, there does not seem to be much doubt that the more moderate solution to which our attention is finally directed is opposed both to Laelius's uncompromising moralism and Philus's ruthless Machiavellianism. The net effect, as Lactantius and Augustine correctly infer, is that the crucial objections raised by Philus are left mostly unanswered.[38] Societies never or hardly ever come into being by means that are totally just, and human affairs being what they are, it is all but inevitable that, once constituted, they should sooner or later embark upon politically expedient but morally reprehensible courses of action. This means that a measure of injustice has been permanently woven into their fabric. The practical question is not whether political power is always acquired justly—it rarely is—but what is to be done with it once it has been acquired or consolidated. There is, after all, a world of difference between the spirit of a society that thinks only of its self-preservation or its collective selfishness and one that is dedicated to the true well-being of its members. No doubt, individual human beings are capable of a higher degree of moral perfection than society at large, but their chances of attaining that perfection will be enhanced in proportion as the everyday life of the society to which they belong is informed by principles of justice and moderation. Laelius's natural law solution points in the right direction but overlooks the harsh necessities with which statesmen have to contend and it does not take sufficient account of some of the more intractable features of human nature. As it stands, it is strictly utopian. The context of Roman foreign policy within which it is developed suggests that Cicero appealed to it for political rather than theoretically valid reasons and that he looked upon it above all as a means of curbing the excesses of Roman imperialism. If

one bears in mind that Cicero himself rejected the notion of divine providence with which he explicitly connects the natural law,[39] its cognitive
status becomes even more dubious. It is virtually impossible to regard his
statements about it as more than a series of rhetorical arguments designed
to cope with what had been in the past and continued to be the most acute
problem of Roman political life.[40]

A totally different picture emerges the moment we come to Augustine,
the chief exponent of the natural law doctrine in Christian antiquity. It was
Augustine's achievement to transfer the Ciceronian teaching from a political to a religious context and to use it as a vehicle by means of which a
new synthesis between biblical morality and the insights of Greco-Roman
thought could be effected. The premises underlying Augustine's own conception of the natural law, or, as he generally prefers to call it, the eternal
law, are revealed most clearly in Book I of his early dialogue, *On Free
Choice of the Will*, which is the only place in the entire Augustinian
corpus where the topic is analyzed with any degree of thoroughness, less
for its own sake than as part of an anti-Manichaean polemic concerning
the origin of evil.

Since God, who is both good and just, cannot be even the indirect
cause of sin, human beings have only themselves to blame for the evils
that they commit and for which they are made to suffer.[41] It goes without
saying that they could not be held responsible for these evils if they
lacked the ability to distinguish between right and wrong. The knowledge
that they require is supplied in the first instance by the laws under which
they live. The problem is that mere compliance with the human law is not
by itself a sufficient warrant of moral goodness. Human laws extend only
to external actions and leave untouched the whole realm of evil desires
and intentions.[42] Even within their own restricted sphere, the standards that
they seek to enforce are far from perfect.[43] In strict justice, only the person
who uses wealth properly is entitled to its possession; yet the human law
sanctions and protects the private ownership of wealth regardless of the
use that is made of it by the owner. Society is fortunately able to utilize
this fundamentally unjust arrangement as a means of preventing greater
injustices among human beings. It does this mainly by threatening to
deprive wrongdoers of the goods they already possess in retaliation for
their crimes. If it has any power at all, it is rather because human beings
fear such punishments than because they experience a spontaneous attraction for what is just and noble. It does not even pretend to overcome the
natural love of one's own by which most people are motivated and which
is the root cause of the injustices that they commit, but merely does its
best to keep it within socially acceptable bounds.[44]

Another case in point is the law that permits the killing of an unjust
aggressor in self-defense, thereby countenancing an act from which Chris-

tians, who have been taught to requite evil with good, ought to refrain.[45] No doubt evildoers deserve to be punished; but at whatever cost to the blameless victim, the administration of justice in all such instances is best left to the legally constituted authority. Even then, Augustine finds it significant that the execution of the justly pronounced sentence is usually entrusted, not to the judge himself or to any other dignitary, but to the hangman, that is to say to some bloodthirsty individual whose inhumane cruelty might otherwise be vented on innocent people.[46]

Granted, then, that human justice is not coextensive with legal justice, one is forced to search elsewhere for a reliable criterion of moral rightness. Some "more powerful and very secret law" is needed, of which all human beings are presumed to be aware and by which they might suitably take their bearings.[47] The difficulty arises when one begins to inquire into the nature of that law. A first intimation as to what its content might be is provided by the maxim that enjoins us to avoid doing to others what we would not have them do to us. Still, it is hard to see how such a rule could serve any but the most general purposes. A man who wishes to seduce someone else's wife may be quite willing to let his own wife be seduced by a stranger, but he is not any less guilty for that reason.[48] What makes his action bad, it seems, is lust, which upon further investigation will prove to be the essence of all sin.[49] For even if it should appear that some sinful actions are prompted by fear rather than lust, it can still be shown that fear itself is rooted in lust. The slave who kills his master out of fear of being tortured does so because he wants to live free of fear. He, too, is motivated by lust. This is obviously not to suggest that all desires are blameworthy. The soldier who kills an enemy in battle also wants to live free of fear, yet no one accuses him of wrongdoing. The difference is that, whereas the slave thinks only of living as he wishes, the soldier is called upon to defend the freedom that will enable him and others to live virtuously.[50] Not any love whatever but that love alone which places ephemeral or temporal goods above those goods which depend solely on man's will and cannot be lost against his consent is to be considered evil.[51]

Such is the love that is forbidden precisely by that universal law which stipulates that "all things should be properly ordered in the highest possible degree," or, more specifically, that the higher should never be subordinated to the lower both within the individual and in society as a whole.[52] Accordingly, man is properly ordered when what is most noble in him, reason, controls the spirited part of his soul, when both reason and spiritedness combine to rule the desiring part, and when reason is itself ruled by what is superior to it, namely, God.[53] Thus understood, the natural law is none other than "the divine reason or will of God prescribing the conservation of the natural order and prohibiting any breach of it."[54] It encompasses all of man's rational activities and thus becomes synonymous with the whole of justice and virtue. As such it is inseparable from wisdom or properly cultivated reason. Nothing short of the total perfection of which human nature is deemed capable can satisfy its demands. Unlike the natural right theory of Plato, however, it not only points to this natural order as something eminently desirable but adds the crucial element of command to the findings of human reason regarding good and evil or the just and the unjust. Since its infractions are punished in accordance with a providential dispensation which sees to it that people always receive their just deserts,[55] one no longer need be disturbed by the scandal of the apparent prosperity of the wicked or the misery of the righteous.[56] Just as virtue, the mandatory and sufficient condition of happiness, is within reach of each individual, so all suffering is necessarily due to human fault.[57] The issue of the moral consistency of the universe is henceforth settled in a manner that leaves no loose ends unwrapped and satisfies man's deepest longing for rationality.

It suffices to state the problem in those terms to realize that the discussion is still far from complete. Two major objections leap to mind, of which Augustine was fully aware and which the last two books of the dialogue will attempt to resolve. The first is that, by defining justice as the proper order of the soul, the argument has tacitly prescinded from the body and the overriding obstacle that it constitutes to the implementation of the proposed ideal. Its unstated premise is that the soul rules the body despotically rather than politically and is thus able to exercise total control over it. It presupposes that human beings have it in their power to disregard whatever belongs to them as individuals in order to become perfect lovers of justice. How this could ever come about is unclear, especially since nothing has been done to forestall or alleviate the threat of conflict between the love of one's own and the requirements of justice. It is naive to think that the evils to which human beings are prone can be eradicated as long as their source is left intact. To demand that people gladly renounce the attachments springing from their bodily nature and, if need be, sacrifice all that is most dear to them for the sake of a goal that promises so little in the way of tangible returns is to ask for more than human nature can generally bear. There are obvious limits to what may be expected of most men. Since these limits have been set by nature itself, one is at pains to see how the attempt to overcome them could be called natural.

Secondly, if only the wise are happy and if wisdom itself is a condition of justice, one is similarly at pains to explain how happiness can be thought to be accessible to all human beings, including those of the meanest intellectual capacity. As Augustine readily owns, few people are capable of theoretical wisdom and fewer still possess the leisure or the inclination to dedicate themselves to its pursuit.[58] To make of it a component of moral virtue is again unrealistic and self-defeating. One does not solve the problem by saying that justice consists in giving each person his due and that this much, at least, is required of everybody;[59] for unless one is willing to settle for the most elementary form of justice, one must still be able to recognize that due. What is really owed to a person is not simply what is granted to him by law but what is good for his soul, and this can only be determined on the basis of such knowledge of human nature as is not likely to be shared by everyone. As in the case of the first objection, the whole argument would appear to be based on an abstraction or a fiction of the kind that we encounter in Plato's *Republic*.[60] It makes its point by dealing with the soul as if it were not restricted in its vision by its mysterious but intimate association with the body.[61] But then, if the desired goal is so patently unrealizable, why did Augustine bother to speak of it in the first place?

The best explanation is that such a fiction was needed in order to demonstrate *ad oculos* the futility of any purely human answer to the nagging problem of justice. It has no other purpose than to cast in sharper relief the solution that will be offered in Book III of the same work, to the effect that all men are unreservedly justified by the gift of God through the redemption wrought in Christ.[62] Without the help of divine Revelation and divine grace, human beings struggle in vain to surmount the "ignorance" (*ignorantia*) and the "difficulties" (*difficultates*) under which they labor and which keep them from being completely free.[63] They are neither wise enough to know what they should do nor strong enough to do it if they should know.[64] The impediments that stand in their way are, by all human accounts, insuperable. Lest the solution to which Augustine intends to lead the reader should sound gratuitous, however, it was incumbent on him to disclose as fully as possible the true nature of these impediments.

There is no valid reason to suppose, as some recent scholars have done, that the last two books of the *De libero arbitrio*, written sometime between 391 and 395, contain an implicit repudiation of the ideas set forth in Book I, which was completed in 388 during the months that followed his conversion.[65] If Augustine had changed his mind in the interval, it is unlikely that he would have published the work as it stands and persisted in defending it in the *Retractationes*. The fact of the matter is that the argument of Books II and III loses much of its force once it is sundered from the foundation that has been carefully laid for it in Book I. One may or may not be right in asserting that the theology of the first book is rudimentary and undeveloped,[66] but if it is, it is all the more remarkable that it should betray an understanding of the eternal or natural law that has no exact parallel in either the Ciceronian or the Neoplatonic source at Augustine's disposal.[67] The very presence of such a doctrine in the dialogue is an unmistakable sign of his ultimate dissatisfaction with a tradition of pagan philosophy to which he remained indebted but with which he had already broken decisively.

This being said, one should hasten to add that the natural law is not an item that bulks large in the Augustinian scheme. Aside from the passages previously referred to and a few more or less incidental remarks scattered throughout a variety of other works,[68] one discovers little by way of a methodical use of it in any of his writings. The fact that it figures most conspicuously in the *De libero arbitrio* and the *Contra Faustum* leads to the suspicion that he resorted to it mainly as an antidote to the Manichean disparagement of nature against which he does battle in those works. His own peculiarly Platonic understanding of nature no doubt militated against any further elaboration of the concept, such as that for which other forms of philosophic speculation unknown to him eventually pave the way. What became clear as time went on is that the thesis defended in the *De libero arbitrio* is not without fissures of its own, not the least manifest of which is that it stands or falls by one's acceptance of the scriptural premises on which it rests. To anyone viewing the problem from the vantage point of what human reason alone is able to uncover regarding the foundations of morality, it was bound to seem hypothetical. It was left to Thomas Aquinas to reinterpret the Augustinian doctrine and, by altering its fundamental thrust, to assign to it a key role in the economy of the moral life. The still unresolved problem, as we shall see, is whether Thomas himself succeeded where Augustine had failed or whether his own doctrine is immune to the philosophical objection to which that of his Christian master was open.

The non-Aristotelian character of Aquinas's teaching is vouched for by the fact that the authorities quoted in support of it are Cicero and Augustine rather than Aristotle, whose works, as we have seen, bear no trace of a bona fide natural law theory. It goes without saying that one does not find in Aristotle anything remotely comparable to the elaborate treatise on law that occurs toward the end of the *Prima Secundae*. That treatise is introduced as part of Aquinas's analysis of the extrinsic causes of the goodness or badness of human acts.[69] It expressly injects into the debate an element that is foreign to the Aristotelian view, according to which the ethical quality of human actions is ultimately determined without reference to anything other than the intrinsic standard of reason alone.

The nature of Aquinas's modification of Augustine is revealed to some extent by the manner in which law is divided by each of the two authors. Whereas Augustine speaks of two laws only, the eternal or natural and the temporal, Aquinas distinguishes four different kinds of law: the eternal, the natural, the human, and the divine.[70] At first glance one might be tempted to view the new classification as a mere refinement of the

Augustinian taxonomy; but such an interpretation, although not completely misleading, obscures the fact that nature has suddenly acquired, under the influence of Aristotle, a more determinate and pregnant meaning.

To appreciate the novelty of Aquinas's stance, one has only to think of the notorious ambiguity that shrouds Augustine's understanding of nature. No similar ambiguity stands in the way of our grasp of the Thomistic doctrine. In the process of rethinking the Christian notion of natural law on the basis of Aristotle's *Physics,* Aquinas has bestowed upon it a degree of autonomy that it never achieved in Augustine's thought. Independently of Revelation and prior to the infusion of divine grace, man has access to the most general principles of moral action and, to the extent to which his will has not been corrupted by sin, finds within himself the power to act in accordance with them. There is thus constituted a specifically natural order apart from, though obviously not in opposition to, the higher order to which human nature is elevated through grace.[71] For the single whole in the light of which man's final end had been discussed by Augustine, two complete and hierarchically structured wholes have been substituted, of which the lower or natural whole possesses its own intrinsic perfection and is capable of operations that do not of themselves require the aid of divine or properly supernatural grace. The issue was not without far-reaching practical implications. Speaking figuratively, Augustine had warned that one cannot safely appropriate the spoils of the Egyptians, that is to say, pagan learning and philosophy, without first observing the Passover.[72] Without much exaggeration, one could say that Thomas shows a greater willingness to postpone the celebration of the Passover until the Egyptians have been properly despoiled and, indeed, until such time as the whole land of Canaan has been annexed.[73]

The natural inclination toward the good postulated by the Thomistic doctrine includes, along with man's desire to preserve his own existence, to propagate himself, and to know the truth about God, an inclination toward the social life and the exercise of the moral virtues.[74] To the practice of those virtues correspond the commandments of the second table of the Decalogue, which Thomas has no qualms about equating with the immutable precepts of the natural law.[75] By severing these precepts from theoretical wisdom and limiting their scope to what all human beings can know or do from the moment reason begins to develop in them,[76] Thomas has managed to evade the problem with which the *De libero arbitrio* had had to wrestle. Augustine, for his part, is at times reluctant to identify the Ten Commandments with the natural law and simply says, rather more cautiously, that they are "copied" (*descripta*) from it, thereby hinting at a possible difference as well as a close kinship between the two.[77] The reason for the caution is obvious if one reflects on the presuppositions of some of those commandments such as the prohibition against theft, which assumes the existence of private property and hence a potentially unjust distribution of material goods among human beings. By forbidding the taking of property, the Mosaic law sanctified an institution which may not have been in every way just and which can only be defended on the ground of the law's inability to secure from most people a higher degree of conformity with the demands of absolute justice. At most, it defined the minimal rather than the maximal conditions of the moral and social life.

The basic orientation of Thomas's thought is further illustrated by his endorsement of the principle that grants to all men the right to kill in self-defense. That right is grounded in the natural inclination that impels all beings to seek their own preservation within the limits of possibility. It proves only that one is under a greater obligation to provide for oneself than to provide for others. As for Augustine's opinion to the contrary, it is rejected with the polite but not wholly convincing remark that Augustine proscribes as unjust only that act which has as its direct object, not the defense of one's own life, but the taking of the aggressor's life.[78]

The larger conclusion to be drawn from Thomas's general premises is that the demands of the natural law can somehow be met on the level of civil society and hence do not have to be diluted in order to become applicable. Since the intention of the legislator is directed simultaneously to the common good of society and to the "order of justice and virtue," the possibility of an insoluble conflict between the two is ruled out in principle.[79] The binding character of the precepts of the natural law is such that no dispensation from them can be granted, not only by human legislators, but by God himself, the giver of that law. The few instances in the Old Testament itself where God commands the performance of deeds that contravene its injunctions cannot be construed as exemptions from it. The killing of Isaac, for example, had it taken place, would not have been illegal, inasmuch as the matter of the act had been changed from outright murder to the divinely decreed surrender of a human life, which God, as the author of all life, is free to take at any time.[80] Not even in the most desperate of situations is one justified in laying aside the primary precepts of the natural law. The exceptions to the common rules of justice allowed for by the Aristotelian natural right doctrine are disposed of with the observation that they refer to lesser matters or to the "secondary precepts" of the natural law, in regard to which greater flexibility is both permitted and desirable.[81]

Augustine, needless to recall, was less sanguine about the prospects for human justice. Some of the arrangements by which human beings seek to manage their affairs are undoubtedly better than others, but none of them ever presents more than an image or a pale reflection of the justice embodied in the eternal law. Unlike his medieval disciple, Augustine stops short of referring to these legal arrangements as being just in a relative or conditional sense, lest he should appear to invest them with a greater dignity than they actually possess and convey the impression that one is sometime absolved of the obligation to aim at a higher degree of collective justice should the circumstances allow it.[82] There is no perfect human society here on earth, or, if there is, it exists only in speech or private discussion,[83] such as that in which Book I of the *De libero arbitrio* engages. Given man's fallen nature, all human endeavors to bring about the realization of a true common good among human beings are doomed to failure.[84]

Aquinas's reinterpretation of the Augustinian teaching may be viewed as part of a broad reform of Christian theology undertaken in response to the challenge of what has been called the "radical Aristotelianism" of the Islamic philosophers. The distinctive advantage of the new approach was that it deliberately sought a common ground of reason on which the age-old dispute between philosophers and theologians might fruitfully be pursued. But the advantage was bought at a price; for, by conceding the existence of a self-sufficient or self-contained realm of nature, the theologian accepted in principle the legitimacy of a philosophic critique of any doctrine advanced in the name of reason. It makes little sense from Augustine's point of view to ask whether the natural law is susceptible of a purely rational understanding, since the distinction between the orders of nature and of supernature, in the light of which the question would have to be answered, is never drawn with anything like the sharpness that is acquired as a result of the polemics of a later age. The same is not true of Aquinas, who was compelled by his own principles, if not to raise the issue, at least to face it squarely if it should arise.

One's first impression, based on the articles devoted to this topic in the *Summa theologiae*, is that Aquinas did, indeed, look upon the natural law as something that is by definition accessible to all human beings independently of divine Revelation. Other, less noticeable, features of the treatise suggest, however, that his final position may have been more guarded than these initial statements would seem to imply. As one reads the text carefully, one observes, first of all, that the thematic account of the natural law makes no specific mention of the rewards and punishments to which, like any other law, it presumably owes its coercive power.[85] This somewhat puzzling lacuna is only partially remedied by the parallel treatment of law in the *Summa contra gentiles,* which deals at great length with the question of legal sanctions but characteristically omits any reference to the natural law.[86] The omission in this instance is easily explained by the fact that the work as a whole is directed against the Arabic philosophers, in whose thought the natural law plays no role whatever. It is of course permissible to infer from a comparison of the two texts that what is said on the subject of divine sanctions in the *Summa contra gentiles* applies pre-eminently to the natural law; but one is still left to wonder why the connection between the two is never expressly established and especially why it is not established in the *Summa theologiae,* where it would most logically be expected to occur. If we recall that some of the major controversies surrounding the natural law have traditionally centered on this very issue, we may be inclined to think that Aquinas's strange silence was motivated by a deeper and more subtle reason.

A possible clue as to what that reason might be is furnished by the discussion of the relationship between the natural law and the precepts of the Decalogue in the *Summa theologiae.* The position taken at the outset is that the entire moral legislation of the old law, as distinguished from its ceremonial and judicial legislation, is summed up in the Ten Commandments and forms part and parcel of the natural law. Having conceded this much, Aquinas immediately introduces a qualification with regard to the precepts of the first table, enjoining the love and worship of God, the knowledge of which, we are told, is not simply natural but is arrived at through human reason "instructed by faith." This restructure is presumably dictated by the need to account for the prevalence of polytheism among the ancients, a practice that could not have met with universal approval if the cult of the one true God were manifestly prescribed by the natural law. As for the precepts of the second table, they are said to pertain to the natural law "absolutely speaking" and are thus held to be self-evident to all human beings.[87] One need not quarrel with this line of reasoning as long as it is taken for granted that the first and second tables of the Decalogue bear no intrinsic relation to each other. Not so, however, if it can be shown that the two are inseparable and, furthermore, that the precepts of the first table necessarily function as the ground of all the others. That this is in fact the case may be illustrated from the following consideration.

What the Thomistic theory essentially requires is not only that the content of the natural law be naturally known to all men but that it be known precisely as belonging to the natural law, that is to say, to a law which is both promulgated and enforced by God as the author of nature and hence indispensably binding on everyone. Since all laws owe their efficacy to the will of the lawgiver, such a view is clearly predicated on the assumption of a divine nature that is characterized by will no less than by intellect. It becomes intelligible only within the framework of a providential order in which the words and deeds of individual human beings are known to God and duly rewarded or punished by him. Therein lies precisely the difficulty to which on its own ground the argument is exposed; for the truth of the proposition that the God of nature is a solicitous God entitled to and demanding the love and worship of all rational creatures would appear to be secured only through the precepts of the first table, which, by Thomas's own admission, are unknowable without the aid of divine Revelation. It stands to reason that the evidence or certitude of a conclusion cannot exceed that of the premises on which it is made to rest, or, to use Thomas's own metaphor, that a river never rises above the level of its source. If the precepts of the first table are not naturally known in the strictest sense of the word, one fails to see how the precepts of the second table, which depend on them for their effectiveness, can be said to be fully natural. The whole structure of the Thomistic doctrine would thus seem to be cast in a different and rather more uncertain light. In view of the manifest circumspection with which Aquinas chose to deal with this issue, one is perhaps justified in thinking that he had his doubts about the demonstrably lawful character of the natural order and that, in his own eyes, the status of the natural law as a purely rational concept remains at best problematic.[88]

The debate took a new and dramatic turn some centuries later as the result of a series of unforeseen events whose impact on contemporary natural law speculation can scarcely be overestimated. One of the basic presuppositions of the natural law theory was that the first principles of that law were innate or naturally known to all human beings. The discovery of the new world and of primitive peoples whose patterns of behavior seemingly betrayed no awareness of a natural law called the old notions into question and forced a re-examination of the whole issue. If, as its proponents maintain, the principles of the natural law are universally accessible, how can one account for their transgression, not so much by isolated individuals (which poses no particular difficulty) but by entire nations and societies?[89] The specific form that the problem takes on at that time has to do, among other things, with the question of whether or not a war can be simultaneously just on both sides. Assuming that wars of civilization are legitimate and that the Spaniards had every right to wage war on the Native Americans, could the original inhabitants of the conquered lands reasonably be blamed for defending their territory and their way of life against a foreign invader? If not, the war would have to be regarded as just from their point of view as well. One is thus confronted with the paradox of a law that can be used to validate the mutually exclusive claims of both parties involved in the conflict. The only alternative, it seemed, was to deny that the substance of the natural law was equally available to all human beings.[90]

No less perplexing from the standpoint of a rational understanding of the natural law is the question of the rewards and penalties with which it is bound up. Can it be determined with absolute certainty that the infractions of the natural law are always punished either in this life or in the next? One had to admit that, left to itself, human reason knows little or nothing about the sufferings that may be inflicted on the guilty soul after death or, for that matter, about the continued personal existence of the individual soul in an afterlife.[91] There remains the possibility of sanctions in the present life, about which the least that can be said is that they are not all equally verifiable on the basis of experience. There is evidence enough that a life dedicated to evil is not a particularly happy life; but can one be as certain that the man who commits, let us say, a single crime by means of which he satisfies his thirst for power or riches and gets away with it will sooner or later be made to pay in proportion to the magnitude of the undetected crime? It could be the case that there is no self-evident cosmic support for justice and, hence, no compelling reason to view nature as morally lawful.

Be that as it may, the traditional natural law theory underwent a radical change when the classical notion of nature as the perfection or full development of the natural being was jettisoned in favor of an entirely different conception which takes its bearings, not from a pre-existing end to which human beings are ordered, but from a beginning that evinces no signs of directedness toward any end whatever. The new thesis was stated most forcefully by Spinoza, who argued that God's intellect is identical with God's will or, more concretely, that might makes right.[92] Nature as a term of distinction had at long last yielded to the now familiar and still powerful view that everything that is, is natural and good.

By comparison with the shift that takes place at that time, the distance separating Thomas from Augustine pales into insignificance. In retrospect, the issue between them is by and large one of approach rather than of genuine substance. Both of them succeeded to a remarkable degree in steering a difficult course between the antiphilosophic religious tradition and the antireligious philosophic tradition. Each one managed to reconcile in an ingenious way the biblical notion of law and the originally antithetical Greek concept of nature. One cannot be far wrong in stating that together they define the horizon within which the most productive debates pertaining to the nature of Christian ethics were to unfold in the centuries that followed. The basic question which their respective theories raise implicitly and to which later writers were forced to turn their explicit attention is whether the notion of natural law is fully defensible on rational grounds or whether its claim to universal acceptability is ultimately based on evidence derived from a different and presumably higher source. To that question, as far as I know, no completely satisfactory answer has yet been given.

NOTES

1. Cf. M. B. Crowe, *The Changing Profile of the Natural Law* (The Hague: Martinus Nijhoff, 1977), ix; ibid., 246: "It (the natural law) has been declared dead,

never to rise again from its ashes; but it has risen livelier than ever and buried its undertakers. It is commonplace to observe that the funeral orations for the natural law have always been premature." Also A. P. d'Entrèves, *Natural Law,* 2nd ed. (London: Hutchinson of London, 1970), 13.

2. E.g., Gratian *Decretum* I.1: "Ius naturale est quod in lege et evangelio continetur."

3. Plato *Timaeus* 83e.

4. Plato *Gorgias* 483e.

5. *Gorgias* 483d.

6. *Gorgias* 491e-492b.

7. *Gorgias* 483b.

8. Cf. *Gorgias* 513c. Callicles is not convinced by Socrates's argument, but, finding himself in the unenviable situation of having to attack justice and to defend it at the same time, he cannot refute it either. Because he cannot give an adequate account of his own doings, he is finally reduced to silence. His position is in fact self-contradictory.

9. *Gorgias* 497d-500a. The identification of the good and the pleasant on a higher level is finally achieved in Book VIII of the *Republic.* It becomes possible only in the light of a fuller understanding of philosophy, which receives short shrift in the *Gorgias.*

10. See, for example, Isidore of Seville, *Etymologiae* V.3, where law is spoken of as a species of right: "*Lex est ius scriptum.*" The distinction is likewise blurred in such expressions as *ius romanum* or *ius Francorum.*

11. For a different assessment, cf. J. Maguire, "Plato's Theory of Natural Law," *Yale Classical Studies,* 10 (1947): 151-78. Maguire's discussion ignores altogether the distinction between natural right and natural law and defines the latter in such a way as to include any independent criterion of morality. The author is thus able to assert: "It is a curious fact that, although Plato exhibits nearly all of the possible forms of the theory (of natural law) just enumerated, his importance in its history has often been denied and still more often ignored," 152.

12. Cf. *Gorgias* 523a-526d; *Republic* X.614b-621d.

13. Aristotle *Rhetoric* I.13.1373b1-17.

14. The higher law to which Antigone appeals and which is said to be of unknown origin is simply accepted on the basis of ancestral tradition and bears a closer relationship to what might be described as a divine positive law; cf. Sophocles *Antigone* 450-460. Few theorists would go so far as to include Empedocles's prohibition against the killing of animals and its implied vegetarianism among the prescriptions of the natural law. Finally, in view of what is said about natural slavery in the *Politics* I.3.1253b15sq., one fails to see how Aristotle himself could have regarded Alcidamas's rejection of it as being entirely in accordance with nature.

15. This interpretation is borne out by the remainder of the discussion, in the course of which one learns that a lawyer whose client has violated a particular statute may on occasion appeal to the general law of nature if it happens to suit his purpose;

Politics I.15.1375a26-35. What is not said, although it seems to be implied, is that, if the client is accused of some deed which the local law condones but which runs counter to one's larger sense of justice, the shrewd lawyer will stress the former rather than the latter in order to win an acquittal.

16. *Politics* I.13.1373b6-9.

17. Cicero *De natura deorum* I.14.36. The same text occurs in Lactantius, *Divinae institutiones* I.3, but since it relies on Cicero, it does not count as an independent witness.

18. In H. F. A. von Arnim, *Stoicorum veterum fragmenta,* 4 vols. (Stuttgart: Teubner, 1903-21; rpt. 1964), vol. I, 45,24.

19. *Stoicorum veterum fragmenta,* vol. I, 125,19; vol. III, 4,11; 5,16; 6,9.

20. Cf. Epictetus *Dissertationes ab Ariani digestae (Discourses)* III.1.25. On this whole issue, see the texts collected and analyzed by H. Koester, *"NOMOS PHYSEŌS:* The Concept of Natural Law in Greek Thought," in *Religions in Antiquity: Essays in Memory of E. R. Goodenough,* edited by J. Neusner (Leiden: E. J. Brill, 1968), 521-41.

21. It is by no means obvious that the emergence of the natural law theory is linked to and adequately explained by the disintegration of the Greek polis in the wake of Alexander's conquests and the subsequent establishment of a world empire seeking to unite all peoples under a common law. That view, which gained wide-spread currency in our century through R. W. and A. J. Carlyle's monumental *History of Mediaeval Political Theory in the West* (Edinburgh and London: William Blackwood and Sons, 1950), rests on the assumption that the idea of the natural equality of all men originated with the Stoics, who are to be credited with having laid the groundwork for a wholly new "theory of human nature and society of which the 'Liberty, Equality, and Fraternity' of the French Revolution is only the present-day expression" (vol. I, 8). Its sole basis is a lengthy quotation from Cicero's *De legibus* I.10.28-12.33, which, on closer analysis, does not appear to support anything like the egalitarian doctrine that Carlyle purports to extract from it. Cicero's text merely makes it plain that men are born for justice, that they are naturally social, that there is indeed a "right" (*ius*) which has its foundation in nature and not in commonly received opinion, that this right is at the root of all human fellowship, and that human beings resemble one another more closely than they do animals and other nonrational beings. In none of this do we find anything that had not been stated expressly or in equivalent terms by earlier thinkers. For a critique of the view that the notion of the homogeneity of the human race is an invention of the Hellenistic age, see, for example, H. C. Baldry, *The Unity of Mankind in Greek Thought* (Cambridge: Cambridge University Press, 1965), esp. 114-27 (with reference to Tarn's version of that idea). It might be added that Cicero himself does not seem to have been conscious of any real discrepancy between his thought and that of Plato and Aristotle, whom he professes to follow (cf. *De re publica* II.30.52; *De legibus* I.13.38; *De finibus* I.3.7). In view of his repeated insistence on the patent inequalities that characterize human beings, one is at a loss to see what, if anything, the position expounded in the *De legibus* has

in common with the egalitarianism of the theorists of the French Revolution. Carlyle, who is not blind to the objection, dismisses it with the remark that Cicero was an eclectic whose philosophy had not yet been sufficiently purged of remnants inherited from Platonic or Aristotelian thought (ibid., 12). It remains to be seen whether the inconsistency is Cicero's or that of his interpreter.

22. Koester's thesis is that, at least as far as the evidence from Greek literature is concerned, Philo was probably the creator of the theory of natural law or, in any event, the one who contributed most significantly to its elaboration; cf. Koester, 540. The earlier Latin development poses problems of its own which are not dealt with in Koester's article.

23. At best, the natural law or its equivalent seems to have been for the Stoics a theme of physics rather than of ethics. This suggestion is confirmed by Cicero and Plutarch, both of whom stress the fact that the Old Stoa was by and large apolitical and evinced no more than a speculative interest in matters of civil policy. As Cicero puts it, "Even though the Older Stoics discussed civil society, and with keen insight, their discussions were purely theoretical and not intended to be politically useful"—*non ad hunc usum popularem atque civilem de re publica disserebant* (*De legibus* III.6.14) The same view is echoed by Plutarch, who states that in writing his *Republic*, Zeno "fancied for himself, as in a dream, an image of a philosophic, well-ordered commonwealth" (*De fortuna Alexandri* 329a-b). On Zeno's *Politeia*, see Baldry, 153-63. Even the later Stoics, for all their exalted talk about world citizenship and the brotherhood of all men, never ceased to take their bearings from the traditional polis, to the extent to which they felt compelled to engage in a practical consideration of political matters, which was not always the case, as is clearly shown from the example of Epictetus. On Epictetus's return to the Stoicism of Zeno and Chrysippus, cf. Augustine *De civitate Dei* (*City of God*) IX.4.

24. *De re publica* III.8.13.

25. *De re publica* III.13.23.

26. The text, preserved by Lactantius *Instit div.* VI.9.2-4, is reproduced in Cicero, *On the Commonwealth,* translated by G. H. Sabine and S. B. Smith (Indianapolis: Bobbs-Merrill, 1929), 207.

27. *De re publica* III.9.16; 15.24.

28. Lactantius *Div.* Instit. V.16.5-13, Sabine and Smith, 215.

29. *Div. Instit.* V.16.3, Sabine and Smith, 208.

30. *Div. Instit.* V.16.4.

31. *De re publica* III.11.18.

32. Lactantius *Div. instit.* V.16.10.

33. *De re publica* III.22.33.

34. *De re publica* III.23.34; cf. III.29.41.

35. *De re publica* III.23.35.

36. *De re publica* II.2-37.

37. In the text as we have it, the conversation resumes abruptly, without the benefit of what must have been the reaction of the audience to Laelius's speech.

38. Lactantius *Div. Instit.* V.16.12, Sabine and Smith, 215: "Clearly these arguments are subtle and ensnaring; indeed, Cicero could not refute them. For though he makes Laelius answer Philus and present the case for justice, Cicero left all the objections unrefuted, as if they were traps. The result is that Laelius appears as the defender not of natural justice, which had been subjected to the charge of being mere stupidity, but rather of political justice, which Philus had admitted to be prudent, though it was not just." Cf. Augustine *De civ. Dei* XIX.21.

39. See Augustine's remarks to this effect in *De civ. Dei* V.9.

40. The "rhetorical flavor" of Cicero's discussion is noted, from a slightly different perspective, by G. Watson, "The Natural Law and Stoicism," in *Problems in Stoicism*, edited by A. A. Long (London: Athlone Press, 1971), 221.

41. *De libero arbitrio (On Free Choice of the Will)* I.1.1.

42. *De lib. arbit.* I.3.8.

43. *De lib. arbit.* I.5.13: "Videtur enim tibi lex ista, quae regendis civitatibus fertur, multa concedere et inpunita relinquere, quae per divinam tamen providentiam vindicantur, et recte."

44. *De lib. arbit.* I.15.32-33.

45. *De lib. arbit.* 1.5.11; cf. *Epist.* 47.5.

46. *De diversis questionibus LXXXIII (On Eighty-three Different Questions)* 53.2. A similar remark is made by Plotinus *Enneads* III.2.17.87, 3 vols. (Cambridge, MA: Loeb Classical Library, 1966-), 106.

47. *De lib. arbit.* I.5.13.

48. *De lib. arbit.* I.3.6.

49. *De lib. arbit.* I.3.8: "*Clarum enim iam nihil aliud quam libidinem in toto malefaciendi genere dominari.*"

50. *De lib. arbit.* I.4.9.

51. *De lib. arbit.* I.4.10.

52. *De lib. arbit.* I.6.15.

53. *De lib. arbit.* I.8.18; cf. I.13.27.

54. *Contra Faustum Manichaeum* XXII.27.

55. *De lib. arbit.* I.1.1; cf. II.19.53.

56. *De lib. arbit.* I.6.15.

57. *De lib. arbit.* I.14.30.

58. Cf. *De lib. arbit.* II.9.25.

59. *De lib. arbit.* I.13.27.

60. On the procedure adopted in the *Republic* see L. Strauss, *The City and Man* (Chicago: University of Chicago Press, 1964), 110-27.

61. On the novel doctrine of the hypostatic union of body and soul which Augustine takes over from Neoplatonism, see esp. *Epist.* 137.11 and the commentary on that text by E. L. Fortin, *Christianisme et culture philosophique au cinquième siècle* (Paris: Etudes Augustiniennes, 1959), 111-28. Fortin, "The *Definitio Fidei* of Chalcedon and its Philosophical Sources," in chapter 12 of E. L. Fortin, *The Birth of Philosophic Christianity: Studies in Early Christian and Medieval Thought*, edited by

J. Brian Benestad (Lanham, MD: Rowman and Littlefield, 1996). Also, J. Pépin, "Une nouvelle source de saint Augustin: le *Zêtêma* de Porphyre sur l'union de l'âme et du corps," *Revue des Etudes Anciennes* 66 (1964): 53-107.

62. *De lib. arbit.* III.18.51.

63. *De lib. arbit.* III.18.52.

64. *De lib. arbit.* III.18.51.

65. Cf. R. J. O'Connell, "*De libero arbitrio* I: Stoicism Revisited," *Augustinian Studies*, 1 (1970): 51: "But what is clear is this: the second book was almost certainly separated from the first by a significant time-lapse; in its bulk it covers much the same ground as the first book had, and, significantly, applies a distinct set of— Neo-Platonic—philosophic instruments. Far from being a mere prolongation of the first book, it is more of a 'retractation' of its predecessor. It must not, consequently, be invoked too easily as an illuminant on the first book: its drift may be in quite an opposite direction." Also, in the same vein, P. Séjourné, "Les Conversions de saint Augustin d'après le *De libero arbitrio*, L. I.," *Revue des Sciences Religieuses,* 25 (1951): 359, n. 2. Doubts about the validity of both O'Connell's and Séjourné's conclusions have been voiced by G. Madec in his recent edition of the *De libero arbitrio,* in *Oeuvres de s. Augustin,* Bibliothèque Augustinienne, vol. VI (Paris, 1976), 178-80.

66. Cf. Séjourné, 252 (printed by mistake as 253) and esp. 353-63.

67. Plotinus's "law of the whole" (*ho tou pantos nonos*), *Enn.* III.2.4.26, Loeb Classical Library, 57, refers only to the general orderliness of the universe and does not hold individuals infinitely responsible for the wrongs they commit. See, in particular, Plotinus's often repeated dictum, borrowed from Plato, to the effect that evils will never cease from the world, e.g, *Enn.* III.2.5.29, Loeb Classical Library, 60.

68. E.g., *De ordine* (*On Order*) II.2.7; 4.11; 8.25; 18.48. *De quantitate animae* (*On the Greatness of the Soul*) 36.80. *De vera religione* (*On True Religion*) 31.57-58. *De Div. Quaest. LXXXIII* 27 and 53.2. *Epistula* (*Letter*) 157.3.15. *Enarrationes in psalmos* (*Exposition on the Psalms*) 57.1; 118.25.4. *De sermone domini in monte* (*The Lord's Sermon on the Mont*) II.9.32. *De doctrina christiana* (*On Christian Doctrine*) I.26.27. *De civ. Dei* XIX.12.2.

69. *Summa theologiae* I-II, qu. 90, Praef.

70. *Summa theologiae* qu. 94, a. 1-4.

71. *Summa theologiae* I, qu. 1, a. 1; *Summa contra gentiles* I, chs. 5 and 7.

72. Augustine *De doctr. christ.* II.41.

73. The very first article of the *Summa theologiae* asks, in typical Thomistic fashion, "whether, besides the philosophical disciplines, any *other* science is required" by human beings.

74. *Summa theologiae* I-II, qu. 94, a. 2.

75. *Summa theologiae* I-II, qu. 100, a. 1.

76. *Summa theologiae* I-II, qu. 94, a. 4.

77. Augustine *Sermo* (*Sermon*) 81, 2.

78. *Summa theologiae* II-II, qu. 64, a. 7. From this text was later derived the

famous "double-effect" principle in moral theology. Augustine *Epist.* 47.5; *De lib. arbit.* I.5.13.

79. *Summa theologiae* I-II, qu. 100, a. 8.

80. *Summa theologiae* I-II, qu. 94, a. 5, ad 2um; cf. I-II, qu. 100, a. 8.

81. *Summa theologiae* I-II, qu. 94, a. 5.

82. See, for example, the remark about slavery in I-II, qu. 94, a. 5, ad 3um, where slavery is presented as being in some sense natural: "in hoc lex naturae non est mutata nisi per additionem." The Augustinian view is that slavery is simply due to sin; *De civ. Dei* XIX.15. Oddly enough, Thomas goes further than Aristotle in defending the institution of slavery. The slaves who form part of Aristotle's polis are not natural slaves, as is shown by the fact that they must be given some hope of regaining their freedom (*Politics* VII.10.1330a33). Their continued existence is justified only on the ground that, in an economy of scarcity, a certain amount of forced labor is necessary. What is unjust in itself becomes just by reason of a particular set of circumstances over which one has little control. Aquinas cannot rest satisfied with a solution that leaves much to be desired from the standpoint of justice. His own solution attempts to remedy the situation, not by attacking the institution itself, but by appealing to Roman law which sanctioned it as beneficial to both the conqueror and the conquered, insuring the survival of the latter in return for the services that he could render to the former; *Commentary on the Politics* I, lect. 14, nn. 75 and 79.

83. Augustine, *Epist.* 91.4.

84. See the stimulating discussion of this issue by R. A. Markus, *Saeculum: History and Society in the Theology of St. Augustine* (Cambridge: Cambridge University Press, 1970), esp. 197-210. There is some question, however, as to whether, as Markus contends, Augustine's thought underwent a radical change on this point. Markus's evolutionary thesis has been challenged by G. Madec, "*Tempora christiana:* Expression du triomphalisme chrétien ou récrimination paienne," in *Scientia Augustiniana: Studien über Augustinus, den Augustinismus und den Augustinerorden,* edited by C. P. Mayer (Würzburg: Augustinus Verlag, 1975), 112-36.

85. Cf. *Summa theologiae* I-II, qu. 90, a. 1, ad 3um.

86. *Summa contra gentiles* III.140-146.

87. *Summa theologiae* I-II, qu. 101, a. 1. See also qu. 104, a. 1, ad 3um, where the precepts of the first table are likewise said to be the object of "reason informed by faith"—*ratio fide informata.*

88. The most provocative presentation of the issue that I know of is that of H. V. Jaffa, *Thomism and Aristotelianism: A Study of the Commentary by Thomas Aquinas on the Nicomachean Ethics* (Chicago: The University of Chicago Press, 1952), which defends the view that, under the influence of the Christian faith, Thomas unconsciously modifies the teachings of his pagan master.

89. Cf. John Locke, *An Essay Concerning Human Understanding,* I.2.10.

90. For a concise but penetrating discussion of the problem, cf. T. L. Pangle,

"The Moral Basis of National Security: Four Historical Perspectives," in *Historical Dimensions of National Security Problems*, edited by K. Knorr (Lawrence, KS: University Press of Kansas, 1976), 324-32.

91. The problem is adumbrated in Aquinas's distinction between the theological understanding of sin as an offense against God and the philosophical understanding of sin as something which is merely opposed to reason, *Summa theologiae* I-II, qu. 71, a. 6, ad 5um "Ad quintum dicendum quod a theologis consideratur peccatum praecipue secundum quod est offensa contra Deum; a philosopho autem morali, secundum quod contrariatur rationi. Et ideo Augustinus convenientius definit peccatum ex hoc quod est contra legem aeternam quam ex hoc quod est contra rationem, praecipue cum per legem aeternam regulamur in multis quae excedunt rationem humanam, sicut in his quae sunt fidei." Cf. *Summa theologiae* I-II, qu. 71, a. 2, ad 4um. An intermediary solution is proposed by Suarez, *De legibus* I.15.13, who concludes that, while reason can establish the fact that the violations of the natural law deserve to be punished, it has no way of determining the mode or quantity of these punishments.

92. Spinoza, *Ethics* Part 1, Corollary 2, note and Part 1, Appendix 222.

II

NATURAL LAW AND INDIVIDUAL RIGHTS

11

NATURAL LAW AND
SOCIAL JUSTICE

To speak of the natural law today is to conjure up a doctrine that vege-tates rather than lives in the souls of our contemporaries. To be sure, efforts to revitalize it are not lacking and scarcely a year goes by without our being treated to some new book and a fair number of articles on it; yet nothing suggests that it is about to regain the position of prominence that it formerly occupied in our tradition. If these books and articles bear witness to anything, it is to the enormous difficulty that one experiences in trying to recapture the spirit that once animated that famous doctrine. One safe sign of the disfavor into which it has fallen is that few of its detractors feel the need to attack it any more, either because they no longer regard it as a force to be contended with or because they find little with which to quarrel in the bland and emasculated versions that are now being offered of it, the majority of which retain only those elements of the original synthesis that are not in open conflict with the currently most fashionable notions of justice and right. There are other signs as well, one of them being that the natural law is seldom mentioned nowadays in official church documents, where until a few years ago it was wont to figure conspicuously. Not since Friedrich Julius Stahl's monumental and unjustly forgotten *Geschichte der Rechtsphilosophie*, published toward the middle of the nineteenth century, has anyone had the urge or the patience to undertake a thorough investigation of its philosophical and historical roots. Moreover, even the few philosophers and theologians for whom it still holds some appeal as a possible antidote to the pervasive nihilism of the age cannot think of a better way to defend it than by equating it with the modern notion of human rights and its more recent offspring, social justice.

The new trend is not without precedent in our time. It goes back to the earlier years of this century and has long been enshrined in such minor classics as A. J. and R. W. Carlyle's six-volume *History of Mediaeval Political Theory in the West*, Charles H. McIlwain's *The Growth of Political Thought in the West from the Greeks to the End of the Middle Ages*, George S. Sabine's *A History of Political Theory*, and Edward S. Corwin's celebrated essay, "The 'Higher Law' Background of American Constitutional Law," first published in the 1928-29 volume of the *Harvard Law Review* and reprinted in the form of a small volume some twenty-five years later. As A. J. Carlyle writes in the opening pages of his study, "Just as it is now recognized that modern civilization has grown out of the ancient, even so we think it will be found that modern political theory has arisen by a slow process of development out of the political theory of the ancient world—that, at least from the lawyers of the second century to the theorists of the French Revolution, the history of political thought is continuous, changing in form, modified in content, but still the same in its fundamental conceptions."[1] Corwin, who is even more specific, went so far as to contend that there was not a single theme of modern political theory, whether it be popular sovereignty, the state of nature, human rights, the social contract, or the natural equality of all human beings, which had not somehow been anticipated by the writers of classical antiquity. In the Roman jurists, Corwin thought, "The natural law [was] already putting forth the stem of natural rights that [was] ultimately to dwarf and overshadow it."[2]

It is unlikely that this revolutionary thesis would ever have become as popular as it did in the academic literature of the twentieth century had the theoretical foundations for it not been laid by the philosophical giants of the late modern period. Two names deserve special mention in this connection, Hegel and Nietzsche, both of whom argued, each in his own fashion, for the fundamental continuity of the Western philosophic tradition from its origins in fifth-century Greece down to the present. In an effort to mediate the Enlightenment conflict between premodern and modern thought, Hegel tried to demonstrate that the latter had been educed from the former by means of a progressive actualization of the notion of freedom that culminated in the universal recognition of the rights of all human beings. The truth of premodern thought was the modern notion of justice, the principles of which had been secretly at work in the historical process from the beginning, even though they had come to be fully understood only in Hegel's own day. What Hegel defined as progress, Nietzsche diagnosed as a process of gradual decline or decadence, the seeds of which had likewise been sown in the remote past. The modern democratic movement, with its emphasis on rights, its noisy humanitarianism, and its levelling tendencies, was the direct heir of Christian morality, which was itself nothing more than a kind of vulgarized Platonism.[3] Its unconscious goal was the total degradation of the human species or the "last man," the man without love, longing, or aspiration of any sort.[4] No two thinkers could be less alike in their assessment of the modern world. For Hegel, the present was the highest: *die Gegenwart ist das Höchste;*[5] for Nietzsche, it was the lowest or just about. What one liked best, the other most hated. It is nevertheless significant that both were at one in thinking that what is most powerful in the present was the product of forces that predate it by centuries.

Outside of Roman Catholic circles, the only widely acknowledged challenge to this view came from Max Weber and a number of early twentieth-century religious thinkers, who sought the origins of modernity in the Protestant Reformation or, if not in the Reformation itself, in one or another of its later forms.[6] I leave it to others to pronounce on the validity of this so-called "Weber thesis," which is open to serious doubt and which has understandably enjoyed greater favor among Protestant than among Catholic scholars. What is harder to explain is why, in the past fifty years or so, Catholic philosophers and theologians, who for ever so long had been practically the only ones to offer any kind of organized resistance to the spread of modernity, should have come to the conclusion that the best case to be made for their own lost or threatened heritage is the one that proclaims its identity with a set of goals and ideals that had hitherto been regarded as basically antithetical to it. What, one wonders, has brought them to the view that the modern rights theory, which was originally intended as a substitute for, rather than a development of, the old natural law theory and which is grounded in an altogether different conception of human nature, is simply a perfected version of it? Have they mistaken the natural law for its opposite, or is it simply that the two theories have more in common than was previously thought to be the case? Do these theories merely represent distinct but complementary approaches to the problem of morality, or do they move in different directions and point to different ends? Lastly, is there anything in modern Roman Catholic thought itself that could conceivably have led to or facilitated this unexpected turn of events? Before we come to these questions, however, it may be to our advantage to look more closely at the reasons for which, over the centuries, the natural law came to play such a central role in the Christian tradition and, I might add, only in that tradition.

THE PLACE OF THE NATURAL LAW IN THE CHRISTIAN TRADITION

We hardly need to remind ourselves that the natural law is a relative latecomer among the philosophic doctrines of the ancient world. One looks in vain for any traces of it in the works of Plato and Aristotle, and even the old Stoics, to whom it is often attributed, do not appear to have been acquainted with it.[7] On the basis of the admittedly sketchy evidence at hand, the first author to speak of the natural law in an emphatically moral sense is Cicero, whose testimony remains questionable to the extent that he himself appears to have had some reservations about its theoretical status.[8] Other writers, beginning with Philo, the later Stoics, and the Church Fathers, would use the expression more freely as time went on, but without according to it anything like the place of honor that it occupies in the literature of the Middle Ages. For one thing, the Church Fathers did not make any clear-cut distinction between the natural order and the supernatural order or between the natural law properly so called and the divinely revealed law. The tendency was to look upon the realm of morality as a single whole and to treat it in the light of those truths which come to us through divine revelation. Accordingly, the natural law was usually defined as that which is contained in the Law (i.e., the Old Testament Law) and the gospel: *id quod in Lege et evangelio continetur.*[9] These older writers may also have been more keenly aware of the anomaly implied in the strange mating of the terms "nature" (*phusis*) and "law" or "convention" (*nomos*), which the Greek philosophical tradition tended to oppose rather than unite. Be that as it may, it never occurred to them to make of the natural law a kind of pivot on which all of the moral and political life could somehow be made to turn. Why it eventually attracted so much attention will become clearer if we reflect for a moment on the uniquely apolitical character of the Christian faith as it is presented to us in sacred Scripture.

The most striking feature of Christianity, as distinguished from the other great religions of the West, Judaism and Islam, is its almost complete indifference to questions of a properly political nature. Unlike the Hebrew Scriptures and the Koran, the New Testament does not call for the formation of a specific people or promulgate any law by which such a people might be governed; and, while it takes the political life for granted, it does not offer even the rudiments of a solution to the moral problems that are likely to arise when Christians attempt to live out their lives within the context of the particular society to which they happen to belong. None of its precepts qualifies as a law in the strict sense and none carries with it any indication as to how it might be adapted to the complexities of everyday life. There is no way in which such admirable maxims as "Be kind," "Be merciful," "Turn the other cheek," "Love your enemy," "Requite evil with good," and the like can be construed as a replacement for the laws by which societies seek to insure at least a minimum of compliance with the demands of the common good. This is not to say that these maxims are incapable of influencing one's behavior but only that of themselves they do not supply the effective guidance that human beings require when there are hard decisions to be made regarding their own welfare and that of their fellow citizens. Significantly, they all take the form of a personal injunction addressed to individuals who are left to judge for themselves whether or in what way it fits this or that particular situation. None is accompanied by an argument explaining its reasonableness or specifying its mode of implementation. With his usual flair for the dramatic, Paul Claudel puts his finger on the problem when he has Judas say: "After three whole years, I have yet to hear an ounce of rational discussion."[10]

It follows *a fortiori* that there is no natural law teaching to be found anywhere in the New Testament. I know of no biblical scholar who still thinks that an argument can be made for the presence of such a law in Romans 2:14, which was once thought to contain a reference to it.[11] St. Paul says only that "When Gentiles who are without the law do by nature what the law requires, they are a law to themselves, even though they do not have the law." Far from combining nature and law, the text calls attention to the distinction between them. Paul himself never uses the word "law" save in reference to the Mosaic law or, by analogy, to what he calls elsewhere the "law of Christ" (I Cor. 9:21; Gal. 6:2) or the "law of sin" (Rom. 8:2). The great novelty of the New Testament is that, while it begins by abrogating the Old Law, it does not replace it by a new one but by something that transcends all divine and human law, namely, faith in Christ. The absence of legal constraints that typifies its outlook can thus be seen as the Achilles's heel of the Christian tradition as well as the root cause of the enormous spiritual vitality that it has demonstrated across the ages. Nowhere does the New Testament give us any specific rules to live by or any inkling as to how the general rules that it does give us might apply to society at large. In all interesting cases, one is at a loss to draw any definite conclusions from the universal commandment of love, which lends itself to the most diverse interpretations and has in fact been used to justify the most diverse courses of action, from pacifism to holy wars and from passive acquiescence in the *status quo* to tyrannicide. There is perhaps no finer illustration of this point in all of Western literature than Don Quixote, that typical New Testament Christian, who in the name of

Christ is ready to slaughter any enemy, real or presumed, or to free any chain gang even if the liberated prisoners have no more pressing thing to do than to beat him up and plunder the nearest church. The Church Fathers sensed this only too well, and that is why they soon began to look elsewhere for the practical guidance that the gospel fails to supply. They tried the Old Testament for a while, since it was what they knew best, and, when it became evident that the rejudaization of Christianity was not the proper solution to the problem, they turned to the only other available source of information, political philosophy.

The snag that later theologians ran into is that until the second half of the thirteenth century political philosophy as an independent discipline was virtually nonexistent in the Latin West.[12] The little that was known of it came from Roman law, a few of Cicero's works, and such scattered fragments of it as could be gleaned from the writings of the Church Fathers. Included in this legacy was the notion of a natural law, which began to assume greater importance as the writers of the period were forced to wrestle with the nagging issue of the relationship between the spiritual and the temporal powers. The first thematic treatments of this subject date only from the twelfth century and are linked to two major contemporary events: the adoption of Roman law as the official law of the West and the systematic attempt, undertaken by Gratian, to sort out the ecclesiastical laws from the civil laws, mainly for the purpose of reem-phasizing the spiritual nature of the church, which was thought by some to have been compromised by the worldliness of the Gregorian reform.[13] Prior to that time, medieval society had been ruled by a single legal code that made no clear-cut distinction between these two types of laws. With Gratian's *Decretum*, the Church acquired its first constitution and became, so to speak, a society in its own right. Within this new framework, the natural law, which was common to both traditions and could thus serve as a bridge between them, suddenly became an object of intensive study. The result was a proliferation of tracts published under that title, all of them written by canonists and civil lawyers in defense of either the Church or the Empire. Their theological substance remains somewhat thin, however, and for the most part they shed little light on the deeper implications of that theory. Their authors simply take the natural law as one of the givens of the legal tradition without making any effort to probe its theoretical underpinnings. Nor could they have done otherwise since they lacked the philosophical understanding of nature that would have been required for such an investigation. As Etienne Gilson notes in the French edition of his *History of Christian Philosophy in the Middle Ages*, "What is still missing in the twelfth century . . . is the notion, however feeble, of a nature that has a structure in itself and an intelligibility for itself. We are at the eve of the day when this conception will be formed, and it is to Aristotelian physics that the thirteenth century will be indebted for it."[14]

AQUINAS'S NATURAL LAW DOCTRINE AND ITS MEDIEVAL CRITICS

With the rediscovery of Aristotle's *Physics* during the early decades of the thirteenth century, the natural law was finally able to come into its own. It made its formal entry into Christian theology with William of Auxerre, ca. 1220,[15] and achieved its classic expression not many years later in the works of Thomas Aquinas. The wedge was provided by the *Sentences* of Peter Lombard, the standard text on which aspirants to the title of Master in Theology were expected to write commentaries. True, Lombard himself seldom mentions the natural law, but his few references to it were enough to give birth to a plethora of disquisitions that followed one upon the other, each one longer, more complex, or more learned than its predecessor, throughout the rest of the Middle Ages.

The new or revised theory, it must be said, was admirably suited to the needs of the age. For one thing, it vouched for the integrity of the natural order and marked out a sphere within which temporal rulers were free to exercise their authority without the direct control of the Church. It also served to moralize the political life insofar as it furnished a standard by which the justice of the positive laws could be assessed. More important, it injected an element of rationality into the moral ideal of the gospel, enabled people to discover in that ideal a universality that it might otherwise be thought to lack, insured its effectiveness by spelling out some of the modalities of its application to concrete situations, and provided an added safeguard against the misuses to which it easily lends itself. The remarkable convergence of these various factors explains why medieval Christendom is the only society in which the natural law ever played anything like a determinative role. As societies governed by a sacred law that was deemed perfect and hence required no supplement, Judaism and Islam never appealed to it and never even acknowledged its existence.

One way to clarify this whole point is to compare briefly Thomas's treatment of the natural law with that of Calvin. Although Calvin accepts the natural law as part and parcel of the Christian tradition, he could not attach the same importance to it for the obvious reason that he begins by waiving the issue of natural theology, in which, for Thomas, the natural law is ultimately rooted. Yet he, too, recognized the need for a law to curb the libertarian or antinomian tendencies to which New Testament agapism continued to give rise. The only alternative in that case was to revert to the moral law of the Old Testament, which he proceeded to reinterpret in accordance with the demands of the gospel. This led him to take a much greater interest in the Decalogue than Thomas had done. Since, for Thomas, the precepts of the Decalogue belong to the natural law and can be known without the aid of divine revelation,[16] there was no reason to engage in any lengthy discussion of them. Furthermore, Thomas does not hesitate to say that the Old Law had been perfected by Christ.[17] Calvin, on the other hand, stresses the relevance of the Old Law even for Christians and criticizes those who would look for other standards by which to live. He labels the view that the Old Law was perfected by Christ "a most pernicious opinion" and thinks that it brands God's law with "undeserved abuse." Properly understood, the Old Law remains "the sole and everlasting rule of righteousness."[18] Christ did not improve upon it or add anything to it. As its true interpreter, he merely restored it to its pristine integrity.

Accordingly, Calvin is at pains to develop an exegetical method that will allow him to ferret out the intention of the divine lawgiver and derive from the Decalogue a moral code that is vastly more elaborate than that of the Old Testament itself. Part of his argument is that the sacred writers regularly make use of synecdoche, the literary device that consists in taking the part for the whole or the individual for the class. When, for example, the Bible condemns murder, it mentions only the extreme case or the most serious offense in that particular category of sins. Its purpose is not to exclude the other members of the class but to fix our minds on their extraordinary gravity. Hate, anger, and murder are all offenses against one's neighbor. By formulating the commandment as a prohibition against the most abominable among them, God makes us shudder and brings home to us the true magnitude of each one of them.[19] In like manner, the precept commanding the observance of the day of the Lord contains within it all of the other duties of piety incumbent upon us. My aim in all of this is not to take issue with Calvin's interpretation but to illustrate the point made earlier regarding the need to complement the moral teaching of the New Testament by means of a law that takes into account the realities of the political and social life.

Quite apart from the treatment that it receives at the hands of the Reformers, one has to admit that the natural law has always led a more or less precarious existence. Thomas's version of it at any rate encountered a good deal of opposition on the part of later Scholastics, who retained the expression but emptied it of much of its substance. That resistance was prompted in the main by what some theologians took to be Thomas's excessive reliance on the Aristotelian concept of nature, the implications of which seemed to pose a threat to the biblical notion of divine omnipotence. If God is the supreme master of all and if the whole of creation depends on him, not only for its coming into being but for its internal structure, it is hard to see how nature can be endowed with an intelligible necessity over which he has no control and which he is therefore bound to respect. The problem was not new by any means. It had been explicitly raised in the *Euthyphro*, where Socrates asks whether a deed is just or pious because it is pleasing to the gods or whether it is pleasing to the gods because it just or pious.[20] If the second answer was the correct one, the ideas and not God were supreme. There was even a question as to whether one might not be able to dispense with divine revelation altogether, since by knowing these ideas one already knew everything that God might demand of us.

What we witness in the period that follows is an attempt to preserve God's freedom against the encroachments of philosophical necessitarianism. Earlier writers, such as Philo, Augustine, and Thomas himself had tried to resolve the issue by placing the ideas, not above God, but in God's own mind, as if to suggest that he was not bound by anything save himself.[21] To the theologians who had since felt the full force of the Aristotelian view of nature, the solution was still fraught with too many dangers. The awareness of these dangers led Scotus to propose that the divine mind contained an indefinite number of ideas among which God was free to choose once he decided to create. In consequence, the moral principles that human beings are required to observe are grounded in an act of God's will rather than in nature. They are valid for the world that he did in fact create but not necessarily for all other possible and equally contingent worlds. The only precept that is natural in the full sense of the word is the one that requires us to love God above everything else, since he is known by human reason to be the highest good. This and this alone does not depend on the divine will, for it is not in God's power to be anything other than the supreme good and to order his creatures not to love him. All other things are good only by virtue of their having been commanded by him. Thus stated, however, the precept still did not meet the strictest requirements of the natural law, inasmuch as human beings, who are compelled to engage in a variety of other activities, cannot comply with it at every single moment of their lives. In order to be truly universal, it had to be formulated negatively: not *Deus diligendus*, "God is to be loved," but *Deus non odiendus*, "God must never be hated," becomes the one principle that is valid at all times and for all time, *semper et pro semper*, to use an expression popularized by Scotus's commentators.[22]

This noble effort to rescue Christian theology from the snares of Aristotelian philosophy was not enough to please everybody. It did not satisfy Ockham and the Nominalists, who questioned the naturalness or the eternal validity of even the love of God and carried the reaction against Thomas to its logical conclusion by denying the existence of natures altogether. Since, for Ockham, there are no universal ideas in the first place, the debate as to whether they should be located in the divine mind or above it ceases to have any meaning. God remains free at all times to do or command whatever he likes. Paradoxically, he could command us to hate him if he so desired.[23] For all that, Ockham hardly comes across as a radical innovator. His own thematic treatment of the natural law in the *Dialogue* hardly goes beyond a simple systematization of the legal theories of the Middle Ages. I mention only in passing that his thought on this controversial subject has often been misinterpreted for the accidental reason that the texts on which scholars have had to rely, the most recent of which is the Goldast edition of 1614, are garbled beyond the point of recognition. The genuine text reveals an Ockham who is religiously more conservative on this point than practically all of his medieval predecessors.[24]

FROM NATURAL LAW TO SOCIAL JUSTICE

The Nominalist attack on Thomistic theology nevertheless paved the way for two further developments that finally set the natural law theory on the course it was destined to follow down to our time. One is the return to the pre-Nominalist view, spearheaded by the great Thomistic commentators and natural law theorists of the sixteenth and seventeenth centuries, such as Cajetan, Vitoria, Vasquez, John of St. Thomas, Suarez, and Grotius. This is not the place to enter into a discussion of these authors, although it bears noting that some of them already betray the influence of the newer scientific theories of that period. The new trend is well illustrated by Grotius, who though professing a great admiration for Aristotle, claims to have gone beyond him by producing for the first time a complete and orderly treatment of what is now called international law, and, secondly, by transforming jurisprudence into an art, at the risk of removing from it the notion of prudence from which it takes its name.[25] The net result of this gigantic effort was a study of the law that is divorced from a passionate concern with justice and endowed with a formal elegance that no one had previously thought possible.

The second important development is the emergence of the modern rights theory and of the new type of natural law that is based on it; by which I mean a natural law whose principles are not self-evident or naturally known to the human mind but arrived at via a process of deduction that seeks to establish the means by which the individual's natural right of self-preservation can best be safeguarded.[26] Since one cannot give an adequate account of the end or ends of human existence by conceiving of them as posited by desires or impulses, it is not surprising that, for ever so long, the Church should have remained firmly entrenched in its opposition to the new theory. The decisive blow that Newtonian science had seemingly dealt to Aristotelian science was nonetheless sufficient to block any authentic return to premodern thought and inclined most theologians to accept the meretricious dualism of a nonteleological natural science and a teleological science of man that became prevalent in Neo-Scholastic or Neo-Thomistic circles. The tensions inherent in such a view eventually caused Catholic scholars to move away from it in the direction of a more consistent but also more thoroughly modern view, either by abandoning the natural law altogether or by redefining it in terms of human rights or what now goes under the name of "social justice," a relatively new concept which makes its first appearance in an official church document with Pius XI's *Quadragesimo Anno*.

It has become increasingly clear, however, that the notion of social justice is itself problematic for a variety of reasons, not the least troublesome of which is that no one has yet been able to define it with any degree of precision. The first author to use the term is thought to be the Roman Catholic theologian Taparelli d'Azeglio, who devotes a chapter to it in his *Theoretical Essay on Natural Right Based on Facts*, an immensely popular work that originally appeared in 1840 and that set the tone for much of what transpired in the field of moral theology during the second half of the nineteenth century. The oddity in this instance is that Taparelli himself shows no awareness of the novelty of the expression and seems to have assumed that its meaning was self-evident, something that could hardly have happened if the complex of ideas associated with it had not already been part of the intellectual landscape of the period. In fairness, it should be noted that his plight was not particularly enviable. Having been appointed to a chair of moral theology in Sicily at the age of fifty and without any previous academic experience, he had no choice but to fall back on the only manual at his disposal, that of the eighteenth-century Protestant jurist Burlamaqui, whom few people would remember today had he not had the good fortune of being attacked by Rousseau in the *Discourse on Inequality* and elsewhere. To make matters worse, the French Revolution had severely disrupted university education throughout Europe and caused a break in a badly battered Scholastic tradition that had somehow succeeded in maintaining itself up to that time.[27] As might have been expected, Burlamaqui's text proved less than adequate for Taparelli's purposes, and, instead of spending most of his time correcting it in class, he decided to write his own. The new manual turned out to be a hefty two-volume work of close to a thousand pages that inaugurated a genre which was cultivated well into the twentieth century and which is notable among other things for its typically modern preoccupation with the foundations of morality. In the middle of it there appeared, as if parachuted from heaven, something called "social justice."[28] Taparelli himself went on to become an editor of the *Civiltà Cattolica* and one of the chief promoters of the Thomistic revival that had more or less secretly been taking shape since the early years of the century, even though his involvement in that movement apparently did little to cure him of his notorious eclecticism. In the meantime, he had created for his disciples the kind of problem on which academics thrive, which was to figure out what their mentor had meant by "social justice."

The question was taken up by numerous theologians and social theorists, including the members of the Fribourg Union, whose discussions over a ten-year period in the 1880s supplied the background for Leo XIII's *Rerum Novarum*.[29] To which of the three hitherto known forms of justice—legal, distributive, and commutative—did social justice correspond, or, if it did not correspond to any of them, in what way was it different? The opinions were divided, some scholars opting for legal justice and others for distributive justice, but not without some hesitation since the use of the adjective "social" to qualify a virtue that is preeminently social to begin with evoked a different set of connotations. The hesitations were fully justified. As nearly as I can make out, social justice, in contradistinction to either legal or distributive justice, does not refer to any special disposition of the soul and hence cannot properly be regarded as a virtue. Its subject is not the individual human being but a mysterious society named "X," which is said to be unintentionally responsible for the condition of its members and in particular for the lot of the poor among them. It makes complete sense only within the context of the new political theories of the seventeenth century, the thrust of which was to shift the focus of attention from virtue or moral character to the reordering of our social structures in such a way as to insure the security and freedom of the atomic individuals who choose to enter into society or accept to remain in it for that reason and that reason alone. As such, it is of a piece with the modern rights theory, which is concerned only with the perfection of the social order as distinguished from that of the individual. Yet it goes beyond the early modern view in that it seeks to equalize social conditions as much as possible with an eye to guaranteeing the freedom of the individual by promoting the equality required for its exercise. Its immediate antecedents are to be sought in J. J. Rousseau's egalitarian scheme and the politics of compassion that goes hand in hand with it.[30] It is thus best understood as part of an all-out endeavor to ground politics in something more fundamental than the desire for self-preservation, namely, freedom or, in more recent parlance, the sacredness of the individual *qua* individual. Rousseau himself never uses the expression "social justice," but it is not unreasonable to think that he prepared the ground for it by his radical critique of civil society and his rearticulation of virtually all of the fundamental human problems in terms of the distinction between nature and history as opposed to the classical distinction between body and soul.[31]

To appreciate the overwhelming impact of Rousseau's accomplishment, one has only to observe the passionate interest evinced by later writers in such hitherto neglected classes of society as the needy, the disadvantaged, the marginalized, the criminals, and the outlaws. A classic example of this new and thoroughly Rousseauean mentality is Victor Hugo's *Les Misérables*, which places the blame for the evils that afflict human beings on society alone and whose true heroes are the convicts, the fallen women, the abandoned children, and the wayward victims of poverty or oppression, for whom it expresses unbounded pity and affection. If society and its accidental structures are the primary cause of the corruption of human beings and the evils attendant upon it, they must be changed. Social reform takes precedence over personal reform; it constitutes the first and perhaps the only moral imperative. Better institutions will give us better human beings and not vice versa. Under such circumstances, the premodern emphasis on education and moral character as the true causes of the happiness of both the individual and the community could safely be laid aside. The only true evil is social evil, just as the only sin is social sin.

THE NATURAL LAW IN CONTEMPORARY PERSPECTIVE

Assuming that there is something to be said for this all too perfunctory analysis, one is at a loss to explain why contemporary scholars should be so eager to demonstrate, not only the compatibility, but the direct continuity between the view of justice embodied in the natural law theory and its modern alternative. The trend, as was noted earlier, has been with us for quite some time. It is clearly discernible in the works of Jacques Maritain and John Courtney Murray, who labored long and valiantly to bring the two worlds closer together, and it has again surfaced in the works of John Finnis and Felicien Rousseau, to name only two authors who have recently undertaken to defend the same position by means of slightly different arguments.[32] Rousseau's oddly titled book, *The Solidary Growth of the Rights of Man*,[33] is particularly illuminating in this regard, since it offers a penetrating analysis of Thomas's natural law doctrine and then completely misconstrues that doctrine by describing it as nothing more than an earlier version of the modern "rights" theory, shorn of its individualism. Not surprisingly, all of the passages cited by Rousseau in support of this paradoxical thesis refer, not to rights, but to duties and obligations.[34] I, for one, am not aware of a single text in which Thomas speaks of universal or inalienable rights. In the Thomistic scheme, rights were contingent on the performance of prior duties. Far from being inalienable, they could be forfeited and were so forfeited by criminals, who could then be deprived of their liberty and even put to death.[35] The typical Hobbesian dilemma of the convict whom the state has the right to execute and who has the right to kill his executioner belongs exclusively to the world of modern thought. Spanning the gulf between these two views, one based on a teleological and the other on a nonteleological understanding of nature, is not as easy as one might like to think.

As for the larger implications of the premodern natural law doctrine, they appear to have been far less democratic than Rousseau makes them out to be. That doctrine was originally taken to be compatible with all legitimate regimes and did not of itself favor any one of them over the others. Rousseau's suggestion that it did much to foster the political equality of all human beings is anything but obvious, especially in view of the fact that over the centuries it was more often used to uphold the *status quo* than to change it.[36] A case in point is Thomas himself, who goes well beyond Aristotle in defending the justice of legal slavery.[37] Rousseau's anachronisms, it goes without saying, are not his alone. They come straight out of the brothers Carlyle, whose implausible argument for the homogeneity or the unbroken continuity of the Western political tradition from the time of the Stoics to the theorists of the French Revolution is one of the durable saws of the doxographical literature of the twentieth century.

To come back to our original question, then, why are Catholic thinkers and Christian ethicists generally so reluctant to accept the old natural law theory as it stands and what convinces them that in its own interest it needs to be combined with our modern theories of justice and right? A rapid glance at two of the more common objections to Thomas's position will, I hope, bring the problem into sharper focus. The first is that the natural law lacks the precision or the specificity necessary to guide our moral choices; for, by Thomas's own admission, it supplies only the common principles of human action.[38] Concrete moral decisions can only be taken in the light of "proper" principles, which function as the proximate measure of their goodness or badness. Because of its very generality, the natural law does not constitute a sufficient guide to action and must be supplemented by the human law, which is said to be "derived" from it.[39] The problem is that Thomas does not tell us how the process of derivation might be carried out. His only reply to this question is that, since prudence differs from art in that it proceeds by ways that cannot be determined in advance—*per vias determinandas*—it is impossible to lay down any fixed or detailed rules regarding such matters. Under the pretext that such a solution left too much to chance, later writers sought to replace it with a scheme the successful implementation of which is supposedly less dependent on the personal judgment of the individual moral agent.

It remains to be seen whether in the long run the new solution is not only theoretically superior to but also more workable than the old one. No one has yet been able to determine concretely what an equitable distribution of material goods might be or devise a mechanism whereby such a distribution might take place even if a consensus were to emerge in regard to it.[40] What is more, in light of recent experience, one has the right to ask whether, by reducing all the moral virtues to justice and justice itself to the conditions of peaceableness coupled with a demand for greater material well-being, one does more to elevate the tone of society than by encouraging people to subordinate their private interests to the common good of all.

The other general objection to Thomas's teaching is that it fails to distinguish clearly between human nature and animal nature and remains enmeshed in a kind of biologism from which it was never able to extricate itself. Modern scholars thus find it "extremely puzzling" that in all of his works, the earliest as well as the latest, Thomas should have unabashedly subscribed to Ulpian's definition of the natural law as "that which nature teaches to all animals"—*id quod natura omnia animalia docet*.[41] My suspicion, however, is that the argument, which does not seem to have troubled our ancestors, owes its force, not to any defect in Thomas's doctrine, but to our ingrained distrust of nature and the ensuing divorce between reason and nature to which Kantian philosophy has accustomed us. Contrary to what is often crudely assumed, Thomas had no intention of deducing human behavior from animal behavior and never suggested that human beings should take their cue from the mores of dogs or rabbits. His point is that human beings are also natural beings, endowed with certain inclinations that reveal the end or ends to which they are innately directed. The nature at work in them is not the nature that is proper to brutes; it is the nature of a rational being. But it is still a "nature," which is to say that its most basic operations are not initiated by reason and do not require its prior intervention. If someone strikes a blow at my head, I immediately raise my arm to defend myself and I do it instinctively or without pausing to deliberate. This would be impossible if human nature, like every other animate nature, were not predetermined to this type of reaction. It is precisely this *determinatio ad unum*, or directedness to a single end, which defines nature in its strictest sense. Indeed, the unity of the human being is such that even his most spiritual activities retain their dependence on those of his lower nature. On this basis, one could easily show that the precepts of the natural law are not all equally natural, and, moreover, that the most natural among them are the ones that are grounded in man's physical as distinguished from his rational nature.[42] It follows that the principles intimated to us through the inclination to preserve our own being or to procreate are more natural than the principles arising from the inclination to live in society or to seek the truth. This is not to imply that the higher is reducible to the lower, as it is for Marx, Darwin, Freud, and so many others, but only that it is rooted in it and can never completely emancipate itself from it. Such a view goes a long way toward overcoming the dichotomy between inclination and duty, or between deontology and eudaemonism, that lies at the heart of contemporary ethical theory.

To sum up, what some of the most dedicated exponents of the natural law take to be serious if not necessarily fatal flaws in Thomas's version of it could well be accounted its greatest strength. I have not forgotten a number of other, perhaps more thorny objections that might be leveled at it, particularly as regards its natural knowability,[43] but none of them should cause us to overlook its peculiar suitability to a religious and cultural tradition such as ours. In an age of unconscious but rampant nihilism, soft as it may be, it may be more important to recognize its merits than to look for its possible shortcomings, especially since there are, at the present moment, so few viable alternatives to which one might turn. Ethical theories continue to vie with one another and the competition is encouraged in the name of pluralism, Isaiah Berlin's euphemism for what bolder thinkers did not hesitate to call relativism. None has managed to win the support of a majority of our contemporaries and all of them can be seen as more or less desperate attempts to restore some meaning to human life on the basis of our modern scientific or materialistic conception of the universe. This is true of the older theories of Kant and Hegel, and it is also true of our more recent theories, most of which are barely more than revised or syncretistic versions of their predecessors.[44] No one has been able to overcome the dichotomy between the "is" and the "ought" or to maintain the "ought" in spite of the "is," and no one seriously thinks that in some crucial cases the "is" might be an "ought." The results speak for themselves, and we are daily treated to the spectacle of people who talk as if the "ought" were the only thing that matters and act as if there were nothing but the "is." Commerce prevails over culture and a more or less intelligent selfishness determines the course of their impoverished lives.[45]

The natural law theory at least had the advantage of satisfying the higher part of the soul without neglecting the lower. It saw the two as forming a unity that could not be sundered without prejudice to both of them. Because its understanding of the moral life was not guided by the abstractions of modern science, it kept alive an ideal of human wholeness that was more characteristic of former ages than it is of ours. Whether or not it can be restored today is not for me to say, but as a corrective to the extremes of fanaticism and vulgar relativism to which we have lately been treated, it may well be worth a second look.

NOTES

1. A. J. Carlyle, *History of Mediaeval Political Theory in the West*, vol. I, 2d edit. (Edinburgh and London: W. Blackwood & Sons, Ltd., 1928-1937), 2.

2. E. S. Corwin, *The 'Higher Law' Background of American Constitutional Law* (Ithaca: Great Seal Books, 1955), 16.

3. F. Nietzsche, *Beyond Good and Evil*, Preface and Part 5: "Natural History of Morals." Aph. 202 states emphatically that "The democratic movement is the heir of the Christian movement."

4. F. Nietzsche, *Thus Spoke Zarathustra*, Prologue, no. 5.

5. Hegel, *Lectures on the History of Philosophy*, end.

6. Max Weber, *The Protestant Ethic and the Spirit of Capitalism*, translated by T. Parsons (New York: Scribner, 1958). According to E. Doumergue, *Jean Calvin: les hommes et les choses de son temps*, 7 vols. (Lausanne: G. Bridel & Co., 1899-1927), Calvin is the real "founder of the modern world," vol. V, 212. See, on this subject, R. C. Hancock, *Reformation and Modernity: The Political Meaning of Calvin's Theology*, dissertation (Harvard University, 1983).

7. Cf. H. Koester, "*NOMOS PHUSEOS*: The Concept of Natural Law in Greek Thought," in *Religions in Antiquity: Essays in Memory of E. R. Goodenough*, edited by J. Neusner (Leiden: E. J. Brill, 1968), 521-41. On the problem surrounding the origins of the natural law theory, cf. R. A. Horsley, "The Law of Nature in Philo and Cicero," *Harvard Theological Review* 71 (1978): 35-59.

8. For further details, cf. E. L. Fortin, "Augustine, Thomas Aquinas, and the Problem of Natural Law," in chapter 10 of this volume.

9. Gratian, *Decretum*, I.1.

10. P. Claudel, *Figures et paraboles* (Paris: Gallimard, 1936), 24.

11. See, for example, Thomas Aquinas, *Summa theologiae*, I-II, qu. 91, a. 2, *sed contra*, which quotes the gloss on Romans 2:14: "Even though they did not have the written law, they had the natural law, by which everyone understands and knows within himself what is good and what is evil." The same view is defended by C. H. Dodd, *New Testament Studies* (Manchester: Manchester University Press, 1953), 129-42. For a critique of Dodd's argument, cf. J. L. McKenzie, "Natural Law in the New Testament," *Biblical Research* 9 (1964): 3-13.

12. See esp. W. Ullmann, *Law and Politics in the Middle Ages* (Ithaca, NY: Cornell University Press, 1975), 269.

13. For an analysis of the "theological presuppositions of Gratian's enterprise," cf. S. Chodorow, *Christian Political Theory and Church Politics in the Mid-Twelfth Century: The Ecclesiology of Gratian's Decretum* (Berkeley and Los Angeles: University of California Press, 1972).

14. E. Gilson, *La Philosophie au moyen âge*, 2d ed. (Paris: Payot, 1952), 343. Interestingly enough, this remark does not appear in the English adaptation of Gilson's work (London: Sheed and Ward, 1955), probably because in the intervening years other scholars, such as M. D. Chenu, tried to show that nature occupies a much larger

place in twelfth-century thought than had hitherto been suspected. Still, it is true to say that what was then meant by nature is a far cry from what later writers would understand by it.

15. Cf. M. B. Crowe, *The Changing Profile of the Natural Law* (The Hague: Nijhoff, 1977), 116.

16. Cf. *Summa theologiae* I-II, qu. 100, a. 1.

17. *Summa theologiae* I-II, qu. 107, a. 2; cf. qu. 98, a. 2, ad 1.

18. Calvin, *Institutes of the Christian Religion*, II.8.7.

19. Ibid., II.8.8-10. For a defense of Calvin's views on this subject, see A. Verhey, "Natural Law in Aquinas and Calvin," in *God and the Good: Essays in Honor of Henry Stob*, edited by C. Orlebeke and L. Smedes (Grand Rapids: Eerdmans, 1975), 80-92.

20. Plato, *Euthyphro* 10a-e.

21. See, for example, Augustine *De diversis questionibus LXXXIII (On Eighty-three Different Questions)*, qu. 46, "De ideis."

22. Scotus, *Questiones in III libr. sententiarum*, Dist. 37, qu. unica, *Opera omnia*, vol. 15 (Paris: Vives, 1894), 738f.

23. Ockham, *Quaestiones et decisiones in IV libros sententiarum* II, qu. 19, a. 1, ad 30; *Quodlibeta VII*, III, qu. 13, and, for a discussion of these texts. H. A. Oberman, *The Harvest of Medieval Theology*, revised edit. (Grand Rapids: Eerdmans, 1967), 92.

24. Cf. H. S. Offler, "Three Modes of Natural Law in Ockham: A Revision of the Text," 15 *Franciscan Studies* (1977): 207-18.

25. H. Grotius, *Prolegomena to the Law of War and Peace*, esp. 30 and 36. Similar departures from premodern thought are discussed by W. E. May, "The Natural Law Doctrine of Francis Suarez," 58 *The New Scholasticism* (1984): 409-23.

26. See, *inter alia*, Hobbes, *Leviathan*, I.14-15; *De cive*, I.1-3. John Locke, *An Essay Concerning Human Understanding*, II.3: *Second Treatise of Civil Government*, ch. 2-3.

27. On Taparelli, cf. L. de Sousberghe, "Propriété 'de droit naturel': thèse néo-scolastique et tradition scolastique," *Nouvelle Revue Théologique* 72 (1950): 580-607.

28. L. Taparelli d'Azeglio, *Saggio teoretico di diritto naturale appogiato sul fatto* (Livorno: Vincenzo Mansi, 1845 c 1840 in Palermo, and Rome: Civiltà Cattolica, 1855), vol. I, Bk. ii, ch. 3: "Nozioni del diritto e della giustizia sociale," Rome edition, 220-32.

29. On the work of the Fribourg Union and its concerns with matters pertaining to "social justice," see N. J. Paulhus, "The Theological and Political Ideals of the Fribourg Union" (dissertation, Boston College, 1983). (Cf. endnote 6.)

30. Cf. C. Orwin, "Compassion," *The American Scholar* 48 (1980): 309-33.

31. See, in particular, Rousseau's *Second Discourse*, which discusses "nature" in Part I and "history" in Part II.

32. For additional comments, cf. E. L. Fortin, "The New Rights Theory and the Natural Law," in chapter 13 of this volume.

33. F. Rousseau, *La croissance solidaire des droits de l'homme: un retour aux sources de l'éthique* (Montreal and Paris: Bellarmin, 1982).

34. Ibid., esp. 162-66.

35. Cf. *Summa theologiae* II-II, qu. 64, a. 2.

36. F. Rousseau, *La croissance solidaire des droits de l'homme* 15, 26, 37, 124, et passim.

37. Thomas Aquinas, *In Libros Politicorum Aristotelis*, I, Lect. 4, nos. 75 and 79.

38. E.g. , *Summa theologiae* I-II, qu. 94, a. 4.

39. Ibid., qu. 95, a. 2.

40. For a detailed discussion of the problems involved in such issues, cf. F. A. Hayek, *Law, Legislation and Liberty*, vol. 2: *The Mirage of Social Justice* (Chicago: University of Chicago Press, 1976), ch. 9: "Social or Distributive Justice," 62-100.

41. E.g., *Summa theologiae* I-II, qu. 94, a. 2.

42. Cf. F. Rousseau, *La croissance solidaire des droits de l'homme*, esp. ch. 3, 189-212.

43. See, for a brief statement of the problem, Fortin, "The New Rights Theory," in chapter 13 of this volume.

44. For some pertinent observations on this point, cf. M. Sandel, *Liberalism and the Limits of Justice* (Cambridge: Cambridge University Press, 1982), 126f.

45. Cf. A. Bloom, "Commerce and Culture," *This World* 3 (Fall, 1982): 5-20.

12

ON the PRESUMED MEDIEVAL ORIGIN
of INDIVIDUAL RIGHTS

Few issues pertaining to the history of ethical and political thought have proved more intractable over the years than that of the relationship of individual or subjective rights to the more traditional natural law approach to the study of moral phenomena. Some prominent theorists, such as C.B. MacPherson and Leo Strauss, have long argued that the two doctrines are irreducibly different and incompatible with each other,[1] whereas other scholars—Jacques Maritain, John Finnis, and James Tully, to name only three[2]—see the rights doctrine, not as a substitute for its predecessor, but either as a more polished version of it or a useful complement to it. The matter is of no small consequence for decent citizens who worry about a possible tension between the biblical component of the American Founding and the Framers' apparent commitment to an Enlightenment concept of rights that, to paraphrase Tocqueville, promotes egoism to the level of a philosophic principle. It is also a source of concern for Catholic ethicists who are uneasy with the gradual erosion of the once ubiquitous natural law and its supersession by a focus on rights in recent Church documents and Catholic theology generally. If the rights doctrine is not only compatible but essentially continuous with the natural law doctrine, any qualms that one may have about acquiescing in it may be safely laid to rest. If, alternatively, the two doctrines are demonstrably at odds with each other, the qualms may not be wholly unwarranted.

One way to tackle the problem is to inquire into the intellectual pedigree of the rights theory. Unfortunately, scholarly opinion is sharply divided on this issue as well, as can be seen from a brief survey of the recent literature on the subject. Three names stand out among others in this connection.

The first is that of Michel Villey, the distinguished French legal historian and philosopher, who in his book on the formation of modern juridical thought[3] and numerous other publications stretched out over a fifty-year period has sought to prove that the father of the rights theory as we know it is William of Ockham. For Villey, everything hinges on the distinction between objective right—"the right thing" (*ipsa res iusta*), "one's due" or one's proper share, Ulpian's *suum ius cuique tribuere*—and subjective right, by which is meant a moral power (*potestas*) or faculty (*facultas*) inhering in individual human beings. How and to what extent the two notions differ from each other becomes plain when we recall that "right" in the first sense does not necessarily work to the advantage of the individual whose right it is. In Rome, the right of a parricide was to be stuffed in a bag filled with vipers and thrown into the Tiber. Ockham, the villain of Villey's story, is the man who consummated the break with the premodern tradition by accrediting that monstrosity known as subjective rights or rights that individuals possess as opposed to rights by which so to speak they are possessed. His is the work that marks the "Copernican moment" in the history of legal science.[4] In Villey's view, a straight path leads from Ockham's nominalism, according to which only individuals exist, to the rights with which these individuals are invested; for not until the rise of philosophic nominalism in the late Middle Ages could such a novel conception of rights have seen the light of day.

The second author to be reckoned with is Richard Tuck, whose book on the origin of natural rights theories,[5] acclaimed by many as a breakthrough when it came out in 1979, is a history of the notion of subjective rights from its supposed twelfth-century origins to its full expression in the works of Locke and, before Locke, Grotius, who finally "broke the ice"[6] by casting off the shackles of Aristotelian philosophy. Tuck distinguishes between *passive* rights, by which he means rights reducible to duties incumbent on other people, and the more pertinent *active* rights or rights understood as the absolute liberty to do or to forbear.[7] Two great periods mark this history: 1350-1450, which witnessed the flowering of Nominalism, and 1590-1670, the period in which the rights doctrine finally came into its own with the publication of the great works not only of Grotius and Locke but of such other eminent theorists as Suarez, Selden, Hobbes, Cumberland, and Pufendorf. I note in passing that, with admirable intellectual integrity, Tuck has since repudiated in private conversation part of the argument of his book. I do not know whether he has yet done so in writing.

The third protagonist in this unfolding saga is Prof. Brian Tierney, who in the last ten years or so has inundated us with a spate of articles purporting to demonstrate that the now triumphant rights doctrine is indeed an early rather than a late-medieval or a specifically modern contribution to the development of political and legal theory.[8] Against Villey, Leo Strauss, and a number of Strauss's followers, among them Walter Berns (Tierney's one-time colleague at Cornell) and Arlene Saxonhouse,[9] Tierney argues that there is no significant hiatus or breach of continuity between the medieval and modern understandings of right. His thesis in a nutshell is that the subjective rights to which Villey points as the hallmark of modernity are in fact an invention of the brilliant canonists and civil lawyers of twelfth- and thirteenth-century Europe, whose writings he subjects to a far more painstaking scrutiny than either Villey or Tuck had done. In Tierney's own words,

> The doctrine of individual rights was not a late medieval aberration from an earlier tradition of objective right or of natural moral law. Still less was it a seventeenth-century invention of Suarez or Hobbes or Locke. Rather, it was a characteristic product of the great age of creative jurisprudence that, in the twelfth and thirteenth centuries, established the foundations of the Western legal tradition.[10]

Tierney's point against Villey is both well taken and ably documented. His articles have shown, convincingly in my opinion, that the definition of rights as "powers" antedates the Nominalist movement by some two centuries and that in this matter Ockham and his followers were not the radical innovators Villey makes them out to be. Further support for this conclusion is to be found in the fact that Ockham's treatment of the natural law, long a bone of contention among scholars, is anything but revolutionary,[11] as we know now that the egregious mistake contained in the printed editions of his classic statement on the subject has been corrected on the basis of a fresh reading of the manuscripts.[12] Ockham's threefold division of the natural law into principles that apply (a) to both the prelapsarian and postlapsarian stages of humanity and are therefore unchangeable (e.g., the prohibition against lies and adultery), or (b) only to the prelapsarian stage (e.g., the community of goods and the equality of all human beings), or (c) only to the postlapsarian stage (e.g., private property, slavery, and warfare) does little more than systematize what the canonical tradition routinely taught. If Ockham can be said to have innovated, it is not in regard to this issue; it is rather in regard to the theoretical foundation of the natural law, whose principles are said by him to owe their truth, not to God's intellect, but to his will alone, to such an extent that God could command us to hate him if he so desired.[13] Simply put, no human act is intrinsically good or bad; it becomes such solely by reason of its being enjoined or forbidden by God.[14]

For all its outstanding merits, however, Tierney's demonstration is not without problems of its own, one of them being, not that it uncovers traces of subjective rights in the Middle Ages, but that it constantly refers to these rights as "natural," something that few medieval authors, and none of those cited by Tierney himself, ever do, with the one exception of Nicholas of Cusa, to whom I shall return. In the vast majority of cases, the rights in question are called "rights" without qualification and appear to have been understood as civil or canonical rights. This is typically the case with Gerson, who discusses at great length the rights of popes, bishops, and local prelates, or the rights of mendicant friars to preach, hear confessions, and receive tithes, all of which manifestly belong to the realm of positive and specifically ecclesiastical rather than natural right.[15]

One does encounter the expression *iura naturalia* (natural rights) on a few scattered occasions not mentioned by Tierney, but its meaning bears little resemblance to the one that attaches to it from the seventeenth century onward. Augustine used it in the midst of the Pelagian controversy in an effort to explain how original sin, the sin committed by Adam and Eve, could have been transmitted to their descendants. The rights of which he speaks are the "natural rights of propagation"—*iura naturalia propaginis*—whereby the offspring, who are somehow precontained in the ancestor, are thought to inherit through birth the characteristic features of his fallen nature.[16] In a similar manner, St. Jerome speaks of incest as a violation of the natural rights—*iura naturae*—of a mother or a sister.[17] In other instances, the link with our modern rights theory is even more tenuous. Primasius of Hadrumetum describes the antlers that burst forth from the heads of certain animals and keep growing and growing as violating the "natural rights of places"—*naturalia locorum iura*.[18] None of this, needless to say, adds up to a *bona fide* natural rights theory imbedded in a coherent and properly articulated framework.

Nor, as I have intimated, can the concept of natural rights be said to play a significant role in medieval thought. Tierney himself acknowledges that Thomas Aquinas did not have a theory of natural rights,[19] but, to the best of my knowledge, no medieval writer either both before or after him ever tried to elaborate such a theory. If the information at our disposal suggests anything, it is that rights as the medievals understood them were subservient to an antecedent law that circumscribes and relativizes them. For Ockham, a "right" was a "lawful power," *licita potestas*.[20] For his contemporary, Johannes Monachus, it was a "virtuous power," *virtuosa potestas*, or a power "introduced by law," *a iure introducta*.[21] As the adjectives used to qualify them imply, these rights were by no means unconditional. They were contingent on the performance of prior duties and hence forfeitable. Anyone who failed to abide by the law that guarantees them could be deprived of everything to which he was previously entitled: his freedom, his property, and in extreme cases his life. Not so with the natural rights on which the modern theorists would later base their speculations and which have been variously described as absolute, inviolable, imprescriptible, unconditional, inalienable, or sacred.

In support of his thesis that rights are an invention of the Middle Ages, Tierney notes that the precept "Honor thy father and thy mother" is not only a commandment; it also means that parents have a subjective right to the respect of their children.[22] Fair enough, although these are not the terms in which the medievals were wont to pose the problem. Their question was not whether parents have a right to be respected by their children but whether it is objectively right that they be respected by them. Even if one grants the legitimacy of Tierney's inference, however, one is still left with the problem of determining which of the two, the right or the duty, comes first and of deciding what is to be done in the event of a conflict between them. Is this subjective right, assuming that it exists, inalienable, or could it sometimes be overridden by more compelling interests?

Granted, one cannot conclude from the absence of any explicit distinction between objective and subjective right in their works that the classical philosophers and their medieval disciples would have objected to the notion of subjective rights or rights as moral faculties or powers, for such they must somehow be if by reason of them human beings are authorized to do or refrain from doing certain things. Since rights are already implied in the notion of duty—anyone who has a duty to do something must have the right to do it—there appears to be no reason to dichotomize them. What they represent would be nothing more than the two sides of a single coin. If, as was generally assumed in the Middle Ages, there is such a thing as the natural law, one has every reason to speak of the rights to which it gives rise as being themselves natural.

This is in fact what appears to have been done explicitly by a small number of late-medieval writers such as Marsilius of Padua, Ockham, and Nicholas of Cusa, in whose works the expression *iura naturalia* makes an occasional appearance. Marsilius refers to certain rights (*iura*) as "natural" because in all regions "they are in some way believed to be lawful and their opposites unlawful."[23] Nothing suggests he had any intention of breaking with his predecessors, at least as regards the subordination of these rights to the natural law, about which, paradoxically, he himself seems to have had serious doubts.[24] Ockham uses the same expression at least once, but again within the context of a discussion of the natural law.[25] Nicholas of Cusa, to whom I have already alluded, does something similar when he writes:

> There is in the people a divine seed by virtue of their common equal birth and the equal *natural rights* of all human beings (*communem omnium hominum aequalem nativitatem et aequalia naturalia iura*) so that all authority, which comes from God as do all human beings . . . is recognized as divine when it arises from the common consent of the subjects."[26]

Unfortunately, Nicholas does not volunteer any further information on what he means by a "natural right" or call special attention to the expression, as well he might have if he had wanted to give it a new and more pregnant meaning. He too merely echoes the traditional medieval view according to which the early humans were free and equal insofar as they knew nothing of political authority, slavery, or private property.[27]

To repeat, nowhere in the Middle Ages does one come across a natural rights teaching comparable to the one set forth in the works of a host of early modern political writers, beginning with Hobbes. The most that can be said is that, on the basis of their own principles, the medievals could conceivably have put forward a doctrine of natural rights rooted in natural law. They never did. Why? The simplest answer is that in matters of this sort they tended to take their cue from the Bible, the Church Fathers, Roman law, the canon law tradition, and Aristotle's *Ethics* and *Politics* once they became available in Latin translation during the course of the thirteenth century. In none of these texts is there any thematic treatment of or stress on natural rights.[28] For better or for worse, natural rights in our sense of the term were largely alien not only to the medieval mind but to the literature of the entire premodern period.

One can certainly agree with Tierney that the surge of interest in legal theory from the twelfth century onward is a remarkable phenomenon, but it does not of itself signal the emergence of a new concept of right. The occasion was the recent adoption of Roman law in the West, necessitated by the pressing need to find solutions to such typical problems as the relation between the pope and the emperor, between the emperor and the lesser rulers of Christendom, between rulers and subjects, between mendicants and seculars, and so on, or else to determine such issues as the rights of property (particularly as these affected religious orders) or the rights of infidels—all of which called for an approach to moral matters that focused to an unprecedented degree on rights and duties. Ockham himself, whose supreme ambition in later life, as Tierney notes, was to have Pope John XXII declared a heretic,[29] was motivated by a similar set of concerns. In all such cases, the rights under consideration were legal rights, sanctioned either by the civil law, the divine law, or, if one wants to go beyond what the medievals explicitly taught, the natural law.

Tierney himself puts the matter in proper medieval perspective when he writes:

> In fact, one finds natural rights regarded as derivative from natural law at every stage in the history of the doctrine—in the twelfth-century renaissance of law, in the eighteenth-century Enlightenment and still in twentieth-century discourse.[30]

Part of the confusion in this instance arises from the fact that what Tierney has in mind when he refers to the eighteenth century is not the characteristic Enlightenment view of rights but Christian Wolff's assertion that "[t]he law of nature (*lex*) obliges man to perfect himself . . . *ius* is called a faculty or moral power of acting. . . *ius* provides the means for what *lex* provides as an end."[31] Similarly, when he speaks of "twentieth-century discourse," he is thinking not of Rawls and Dworkin but of Maritain and Finnis, two authors who like Wolff are committed to a basically premodern understanding of justice and morality, however much they may be influenced, as was Wolff, by modern modes of thought. None of this meets the crucial question head-on, which has to do, not with whether the premoderns had any notion of subjective rights, but with the order of rank of rights and duties.

On this score, the likeliest supposition is the one according to which there exists a specifically modern notion of rights that comes to the fore with Hobbes in the seventeenth century and distinguishes itself from all previous notions, not so much by its definition of right as a power, as by its proclamation of rights rather than duties as the primary moral counter. Nowhere is the new position formulated more clearly than in chapter 14 of *Leviathan*, which begins with a forceful assertion of the primacy of the natural right of self-preservation, that is, of the right that each individual possesses to resist anyone who poses, or is thought to pose, or could conceivably pose a threat to his existence or well-being. From this primordial *right* of nature Hobbes goes on to deduce the whole of his simplified morality and, in particular, the various *laws* of nature—nineteen of them in all—that reason devises and to which human beings bind themselves when, for the sake of their own protection, they "enter" into civil society. In Hobbes's own words,

> The RIGHT OF NATURE, which writers commonly call *ius naturale*, is the liberty each man has to use his own power, as he will himself, for the preservation of his own nature—that is to say, of his own life—and consequently of doing anything which, in his own judgment and reason, he shall conceive to be the aptest means thereunto.

This is precisely the teaching that was taken over by subsequent theorists, including Locke, who points out that "in the state of nature everyone has the executive power of the law of nature,"[32] a teaching that he himself tells us is not only strange but "very strange."[33] This teaching is clearly of a piece with the Hobbesian notion of the "state of nature," that prepolitical state in which one is not bound by any law whatsoever and is free to deal with others as one's sees fit.[34] Nothing could be further from the traditional view, which knows of no state in which human beings are not subject to some higher authority and views the meting out of punishments—Locke's "executive power of the law of nature"—as the prerogative of rulers and no one else. To refer to Thomas Aquinas once again, anyone is free to reward others for doing good but only the "minister of the law" has the authority to punish them for doing evil.[35] Gratian's *Decretum* is even more explicit, calling any private individual who takes it upon himself to put a criminal to death a "murderer": *Qui sine aliqua publica administratione maleficum interfecerit velut homicida iudicabitur, et tanto amplius quanto sibi potestatem a Deo non concessam usurpare non timuit.*[36]

The opposition between the old and the new views is equally striking when one turns to the question to which Tierney's article on Henry of Ghent is entirely devoted, namely, whether a criminal who has been justly sentenced to death is allowed to flee if the opportunity presents itself.[37] From Tierney's article we learn that a convict does have that right, but only as long as he can exercise it without injuring anyone else—*sine iniuria alterius*.[38] This position is not essentially different from the one taken by Thomas Aquinas, who also argued that a prisoner is not morally obliged to stay in jail while awaiting his execution but is nevertheless strictly forbidden to use physical force to defend himself against the executioner.[39] The only point that distinguishes the two authors, and it is a minor one, is Henry's claim that under certain circumstances fleeing may be a "necessity" or a positive duty, the reason being that refusing to flee would be tantamount to committing suicide.[40] In this matter Henry was followed by the well-known sixteenth-century canonist Jacques Alamain, who agreed that a prisoner in this situation is not only permitted to flee but obliged to do so because he is required by natural law to preserve his life and body.[41] Tierney takes this as further evidence that the key concepts of the seventeenth-century rights theorists "often had medieval origins."[42]

But did they? To stick only to the issue at hand, Tierney overlooks the crucial fact that, by the time we come to these seventeenth-century theorists, the ban against inflicting bodily harm on one's judge or executioner has been lifted. Hobbes is again the one who makes the case most pointedly when he says that no man is supposed bound by covenant not to resist violence, and consequently it cannot be intended that he gave any right to another to lay violent hands upon his person. In the making of a commonwealth, every man gives away the right of defending another, but not of defending himself . . . But I have also shown formerly that before the institution of commonwealth every man had a right to everything and to do whatever he thought necessary to his own preservation, *subduing, hurting,* or *killing* any man in order thereunto; and this is the foundation of that right of punishing which is exercised in every commonwealth. For the subjects did not give the sovereign that right, but only in laying down theirs strengthened him to use his own as he should think fit for the preservation of them all (emphasis added).[43]

The same view is affirmed, albeit with greater caution, by Locke, whose political system issues, like Hobbes's, in perfect rights rather than perfect duties. For Locke, as for Hobbes, the right of self-preservation, from which all other rights flow, is inalienable, which means that it is not in the power of human beings to surrender it even if they should wish to do so.[44] Locke's most powerful statement to this effect is the one that occurs in the *Second Treatise of Government*, where one reads:

[F]or no man or society of men having a power to deliver up their preservation, and consequently the means of it, to the absolute will and arbitrary dominion of another, whenever anyone shall go about to bring them into such a slavish condition, *they will always have a right to preserve what they have not a power to part with*, and to rid themselves of those who invade *this fundamental, sacred, and unalterable law of self-preservation for which they entered into society* (italics mine).[45]

To be sure, Locke is careful to add that, just as one is bound to preserve oneself, so one is bound, as much as one can, to preserve the rest of mankind, but—and this is the telltale qualification—only so long as one's own preservation does not "come into competition" with anyone else's.[46] I take this to be just another way of saying that in the final analysis rights take precedence over duties. On this central point, both he and Hobbes stand together against all of their premodern predecessors.

Interestingly enough, it is often when they sound most alike that moderns and premoderns are furthest apart. The fact that in dealing with this matter both groups advert to the desire for self-preservation might lead us to think that they at least have this much in common; but closer examination reveals that this is not the case. For the medievals self-preservation is first and foremost a duty: one is not allowed to commit suicide or do anything that is liable to impair one's health.[47] As Thomas Aquinas, good Aristotelian that he is, puts it, "anyone who takes his own life commits an injustice, not toward himself [by definition, justice and injustice are always *ad alios*, i.e., directed toward others][48], but toward God and toward his city, to whom he owes his services."[49] The same view is reflected in a felicitous statement by Godfrey of Fontaines that brings together both the objective and subjective dimensions of the problem:

> Because by the right of nature (*iure naturae*), everyone is bound (*tenetur*) to sustain his life, which cannot be done without exterior goods, therefore also by the right of nature each has dominion and a certain right (*quoddam ius*) in the common exterior goods of this world, which right also cannot be renounced.[50]

A very different note is sounded by Hobbes, Locke, and their followers, for whom self-preservation is not in the first instance a duty but a right that justifies not only the use of physical force against one's lawful executioner but the taking of one's own life, an act that the religious tradition always regarded as more grievously sinful than homicide and to which it attached severe penalties.[51] If self-preservation is an unconditional right and if, as Hobbes and Locke contend, such rights are to be defined in terms of freedom, that is to say, if human beings are free to exercise or not exercise them, one fails to see why it would be forbidden to commit suicide or allow oneself to be enslaved by other human beings. Needless to say, most people will prefer life to death and freedom to slavery, but these have now acquired an altogether different status. They no longer appear as moral obligations laid upon us by a higher authority but as claims that one can assert against others. To quote Locke himself, the state that "all men are naturally in . . . is a state of perfect freedom to order their actions and dispose of their possessions and persons as they think fit, within the bounds of the law of nature, without asking leave or depending upon the will of any other man."[52] It is true that Locke limits the exercise of the rights that human beings enjoy in the state of nature to what is allowed by the "law of nature," but, as we saw earlier, in the state of nature, man and not God is the "executor of the law of nature." In that state there are no restrictions other than the ones that an individual may decide to impose upon himself. This observation is only apparently contradicted by Locke's statement that "everyone is bound to preserve himself and not to quit his station wilfully," inasmuch as all human beings are "the workmanship of an omnipotent and wise Maker . . . made to last during his, not one another's pleasure."[53] Nowhere does Locke say that God has *commanded* human beings to maintain themselves in existence. What we learn instead is that human beings are directed by God to preserve themselves by means of their "senses and reason," just as the inferior animals are directed to preserve themselves by means of their "sense and instinct."[54] Both men and animals have, implanted in them by

God, a desire for survival, but only in man does this desire give rise to a right, presumably because only men have reason and are thus able to figure out what is necessary for their self-preservation as well as their comfortable self-preservation.[55] The question then is what happens to the law prohibiting suicide once the desire for self-preservation in which it is rooted is lost because of intense pain or a hopelessly weakened physical condition. Clearly, the "law of nature" of which Locke speaks is his own natural law. It is strictly a matter of calculation and has nothing to do with the self-evident principles on which the moral life is said to rest by the medieval theorists. In short, it is not at all certain that in Locke's mind there were any compelling moral arguments against suicide.[56] On this score as on so many others, he and his medieval "predecessors," as Tierney would call them, could not be further apart.

Though unable on the basis of his own principles to deny the natural right of suicide, Locke may have been loath to defend it openly, not only because doing so would have been dangerous in the extreme—his teaching was already "strange" enough—but because the whole of his political theory stands or falls by the power that the fear of death and the desire for self-preservation are capable of exerting on people's minds. Absent this bulwark, any human being could, in the name freedom, renounce the exercise of his most basic rights, whether they be the right to life, to limited government, or to freedom itself.[57] This could well be the point at which modern liberalism shows signs of recoiling upon itself. Is there or is there not at the heart of Locke's teaching a latent contradiction or, short of that, an irremediable tension?[58]

Whatever the answer to the question, the foregoing considerations permit us to glimpse the reasons that motivated the sixteenth- and seventeenth-century revolt against premodern thought and convinced so many of its promoters of the need for a fresh start. The new rights theory was perhaps not entirely consistent, and, by grounding all ethical principles in the desire for self-preservation, a self-regarding passion, it did not of itself conduce to a high level of morality. But it was public-spirited. Its aim was to procure the good of society by putting an end to the massacres and bloody wars that had hitherto marked its life.[59] To paraphrase Mandeville, the trick consisted in turning private vices to public advantage.[60] A new kind of hedonism was born that supposedly enables one to enjoy the rewards of moral virtue without acquiring virtue itself, that is, without having to undergo a painful and chancy conversion from a concern for worldly goods to a concern for the good of the soul. In the process, morality itself was drastically simplified. The only virtue needed for the success of the enterprise was the one geared to the needs of society—"social virtue," as Locke called it[61]—rather than to the proper order of the soul. Justice became not only the highest virtue but the only virtue, now reduced to the requirements of peace.[62] Tocqueville knew whereof he spoke when he said that America had managed to dignify selfishness by transforming it into a passably decent if not particularly elevated philosophy. In view of their revolutionary stand on a matter as grave as that of the origin and goals of human existence, it is not surprising that the leaders of the new movement should have been careful to express themselves in language that made them sound more conservative than they actually were. One notion well-suited to this purpose was that of the "state of nature," which began to figure prominently in their works and continued to do so for the next century and a half.

As used by Hobbes, Locke, and their many followers, the notion has highly individualistic connotations, predicated as it is on a nonteleological understanding of human nature. It derives the moral "ought" from the "is" or the "right" of self-preservation from the "desire" for self-preservation and thus denies that to be and to be good are two different things. One cannot portray human beings as atomic individuals who once existed in a so-called state of nature without implying that they are not naturally political and social or without subscribing to the view that their most basic impulse is not an attraction to the good, including the good of society, but an aversion to physical evil, along with an overpowering urge to overcome it.

By the middle of the seventeenth century, however, the "state of nature" had become a commonplace in political literature and was used indiscriminately by authors on both sides of the divide. In his short but illuminating essay, *On the Natural State of Men*, Pufendorf distinguishes at least four different meanings of the expression, which can designate not only the prepolitical state postulated by the new theorists—the Hobbesian war of every man against every man, a state only slightly more politely described by Locke as "very unsafe, very insecure," full of fears and continual dangers[63]—but the perfect state in which Adam was created, the cultural state in which human beings are presumed to have existed prior to the emergence of civil society, or any pagan or pre-Christian civil society, such as classical Greece.[64] This ambiguity is precisely what made it possible for the new theorists to pass their "strange" doctrines off as more or less standard theological fare.

Pufendorf's essay is valuable in that it gives us a better idea of how much he and his contemporaries had learned from the opposition that the "justly decried Hobbes" had aroused and how circumspect they had become in dealing with issues as explosive as these.[65] Pufendorf himself leans heavily on Hobbes, for whom he evinces an obvious preference—he was known as the "German Hobbes"—but not without injecting into the discussion a series of disclaimers that give the impression of his wanting to dissociate himself from Hobbes's most extreme positions. It is almost as if he were using the state of nature as a shield with which to protect himself. After all, no less a figure than the eminently respectable Grotius, to say nothing of others, had made use of the expression and thereby removed from it any taint of heterodoxy or impiety.

Virtually all the writers of Pufendorf's and Locke's generation, it seems, had mastered the art of concealing their "novelties" by cloaking them in more or less traditional garb. The "state of nature," with its vague theological connotations, is only one example of this procedure. Francis Bacon had already admonished radical innovators to express themselves only in familiar terms, adding that one should always begin by telling people what they most want to hear, that is, what they are accustomed to hearing.[62] This appears to be exactly what most of our seventeenth-century writers did. As a result, it became customary to pass over the crucial differences that set Grotius apart from Locke and Pufendorf and lump the three of them together as fellow travelers or members of the same ideological camp. Grotius does mention the state of nature on two occasions, but to designate pre-Christian civil society and not Hobbes's or Locke's precivil state.[67] Unlike Hobbes, Locke, and Pufendorf, in whose works Aristotle's name hardly ever appears, he holds Aristotle in highest esteem;[68] and he endorses wholeheartedly the patented Aristotelian teaching that human beings are political by nature.[69] His is still a basically classical and medieval outlook, now brought to bear on the problems of his time.

This brings us back to the question with which we started, namely, whether any ultimate reconciliation between modern and premodern ethical thought is possible. To restate that question in terms more germane to Tierney's argument: Is the seventeenth-century rights theory an offshoot of medieval theological and legal speculation or merely an accidental byproduct of its later development, if even that?

The early modern writers, with whom any discussion of the problem must begin if not necessarily end, certainly understood themselves to be breaking entirely new ground and to be doing so on the basis of a radical critique of the premodern tradition. Many of them, from Machiavelli onward, thinking that they had discovered a new continent, likened themselves to Christopher Columbus and were ready to burn their ships behind them.[70] They, at least, were convinced of the fundamental irreconcilability of the two positions and hence of the necessity to choose between them. Accordingly, they saw the war in which they were engaged, not as a civil war pitting rival factions against each other within a divided city, but as a war between two continents neither one of which could survive unless the other was destroyed. Francis Bacon stated the problem as well as anyone else when he located the opposition between the two groups on the level of "first principles and very notions, and even upon forms of demonstrations," in which case "confutations [i.e., rational arguments] cannot be employed." The only safe way to proceed, he concluded, was to insinuate one's new doctrines "quietly into the minds that are fit and capable of receiving it."[71] Hobbes is no less explicit, particularly as regards the issue of rights and duties. "Right," he says, "consists in liberty to do, or to forbear: whereas law determines and binds to one of them, so that law and right differ as much, as obligation and liberty; which in one and the same matter are inconsistent."[72] If Hobbes is to be taken at his word, the modern rights theory was no mere attempt to erect a new structure on the old foundation of classical and Christian ethics. Its ambition was to lay down an entirely new foundation, to wit, a selfish passion—the desire for self-preservation—and go on from there to devise a political scheme that would be in accord with it from the start. As usual, Hobbes is the one who stated the issue most forcefully when he wrote in the short Epistle Dedicatory to his *De natura hominis*:

> To reduce this doctrine to the rules and infallibility of reason, there is no way but, first, to put such principles down for a foundation as passion, not mistrusting, may not seek to displace, and afterwards to build thereon the truth of cases in the law of nature, which hitherto have been built in the air.[73]

Let us grant for the sake of argument that no ultimate synthesis between a consistent natural law theory and a consistent natural rights theory is possible. Does this mean that any kind of rapprochement between them is out of the question? Not necessarily. One thing is nevertheless certain: no such rapprochement can be effected on the basis of a principle that transcends the original positions, each one of which claims supreme status for itself. This leaves only one possibility: a rapprochement effected on the basis of the highest principles of one or the other of these two positions.

The need for some such mediation began to be felt in the Middle Ages when important social and demographic changes gave rise to a more complex juridical system. Tierney's studies may or may not have shown that individual rights are a product of twelfth- and thirteenth-century jurisprudence, but they do show with admirable lucidity to what extent our medieval forebears managed to find a place for rights within a human order that reflects the natural order of the universe. The modern world has been experimenting for close to four centuries with a theory that subordinates law to rights. The results have been mixed at best, and this is what lends a measure of credibility to the now frequently heard calls for a reexamination of the discarded alternative, which insisted on the subordination of rights to duties or the common good.

My immediate concern was not to argue for the superiority either of these two distinct approaches to the study of ethics and politics but to clarify the difference between them and caution against any hasty identification of one with the other. A thorough grasp of the problem would involve us in a much more methodical investigation of the implications of an ethics of virtue or character versus an ethics of rights, as well of the implications of a teleological versus a nonteleological understanding of human life. Tierney, who is more interested in the historical and legal aspects of the question than in its philosophic or theological aspects, has not seen fit to undertake this kind of investigation and I shall not undertake it, either.[74] Still, one cannot help wondering whether the argument in favor of the medieval pedigree of the modern rights doctrine does not owe much of its appeal to the fact that it combines in neat, if somewhat unexpected, fashion a deep-seated longing for a glorious Christian past with a powerful attachment to the freedoms of the modern age.[70] It would not be the first time that scholarly judgment on matters as complex as this one is influenced to a greater or less degree by considerations of an extratheoretical nature.

NOTES

1. C. B. Macpherson, *The Political Theory of Possessive Individualism* (Oxford and New York: Oxford University Press, 1962). L. Strauss, *Natural Right and History* (Chicago: University of Chicago Press, 1953), esp. 181-83. This is not to suggest that Strauss and Macpherson are in complete agreement with each other. See in this connection Strauss's review of Macpherson's book, reprinted in Leo Strauss, *Studies in Platonic Political Philosophy*, edited by T. L. Pangle, (Chicago and London: The University of Chicago Press, 1983), 229-31.

2. J. Maritain, *The Rights of Man and Natural Law* (New York: Scribners, 1943); *The Person and the Common Good* (Notre Dame: University of Notre Dame Press, 1966). J. Finnis, *Natural Law and Natural Rights* (Oxford: Clarendon Press, 1980). J. Tully, *A Discourse on Property: John Locke and His Adversaries* (Cambridge: Cambridge University Press, 1980).

3. *La formation de la pensée juridique moderne*, 4th ed. (Paris, 1975).—This paragraph and a few others that follow incorporate materials used in a previous article, "Sacred and Inviolable: *Rerum Novarum* and Natural Rights," *Theological Studies* 53 (1992): 203-33. (This article is reprinted in vol. 3, chapter 16, of Fortin's *Collected Essays* entitled *Human Rights, Virtue, and the Common Good: Untimely Meditations on Religion and Politics* (Lanham, MD: Rowman and Littlefield, 1996).

4. M. Villey, "Genèse du droit subjectif chez Guillaume d'Occam," *Archives de philosophie du droit* 9 (1964): 127.

5. *Natural Rights Theories: Their Origin and Development* (Cambridge: Cambridge University Press, 1979).

6. Tuck, 175. The expression is a quotation from Barbeyrac, *An Historical and*

Critical Account of the Science of Morality, prefaced to S. Pufendorf, *The Law of Nature and Nations*, B. Kennet trans. (London: J. J. Bonwick, 1749), 55, 63, 98.

7. *Natural Rights Theories*, 5-6.

8. These articles include "Tuck on Rights, Some Medieval Problems," *History of Political Thought* 4 (1983): 429-40. "Villey, Ockham and the Origin of Individual Rights," *The Weightier Matters of the Law: A Tribute to Harold J. Berman* (The American Academy of Religion, 1988): 1-31. "Conciliarism, Corporatism, and Individualism: the Doctrine of Individual Rights in Gerson," *Cristianesimo nella storia* 9 (1988): 81-111. "Marsilius on Rights," *Journal of the History of Ideas* 52 (1991): 3-17. "Origins of Natural Rights Language: Texts and Contexts, 1150-1250," *History of Political Thought* 10 (1989): 615-646. "Aristotle and the American Indians— Again," *Cristianesimo nella storia* 12 (1991): 295-322. "Natural Rights in the Thirteenth Century: A *Quaestio* of Henry of Ghent," *Speculum* 67 (1992): 58-68, and an as yet unpublished paper entitled "1492: Medieval Natural Rights Theories and the Discovery of America," written for the quinquennial meeting of the International Society for the Study of Medieval Thought held at Ottawa in August, 1992, which summarizes in readily assimilable form the results arrived at in the previous articles. The paper is scheduled to appear in the Proceedings of the conference.

9. Cf. Tierney, "Conciliarism, Corporatism," 88: "One school of thought holds that all modern rights theories are rooted in the atheistic philosophy of Hobbes and hence regards them as incompatible with the whole preceding Christian tradition." The reference is to an article by Walter Berns in *This World* 6 (1983): 98. "Villey, Ockham," 20, n. 74, where Berns is taken to task for having written that "natural rights and traditional natural law are, to put it simply yet altogether accurately, incompatible." In Tierney's opinion, "[s]uch views seem based on a mistaken idea that modern rights theories are derived entirely from Hobbes and on simple ignorance of the history of the concept of *ius naturale* before the seventeenth century." In "Natural Rights in the Thirteenth Century," 58, Tierney takes issue with Saxonhouse's contention that prior to the seventeenth century people did not think of individuals "as possessing inalienable rights to anything—much less life, liberty, property, or even the pursuit of happiness." Cf. *Women in the History of Political Thought* (New York: Praeger, 1985), 7.

10. "Villey, Ockham," 31.

11. On Ockham's conservatism, see Tierney's remarks in "Villey, Ockham," 19, citing John Morrall, who describes Ockham as "an interpreter and defender of the achievements of the past."

12. Ockham *Dialogus* Part III, Tr. ii, Book III,6. The most recent edition is that of M. Goldast (Frankfurt, 1614), which merely reproduces the Lyons edition of 1494, along with its mistakes. The corrected text is to be found in H. S. Offler, "Three Modes of Natural Law in Ockham: A Revision of the Text," *Franciscan Studies* 15 (1977): 207-218. The mistake in the Goldast edition concerns the second level of natural law and consists in reading the unintelligible *quod ideo est naturale quia est contra statum naturae institutae* for the *quod ideo dicitur naturale quia contrarium*

est contra statum naturae institutae of the manuscripts.

13. Cf. Ockham, *Quaestiones in librum secundum Sententiarum* II, qu. 15, ad 3 and 4, in *Opera Theologica*, vol. 5, edited by G. Gal and R. Wood (New York: St. Bonaventure, 1981), II, qu. 15, ad 3 and 4, p. 347-48.

14. See Suarez's discussion of Ockham's position in his *De legibus ac Deo legislatore*, II.7,4. English translation by G. L. Williams et al., *Selections from Three Works of Francisco Suarez, S.J.*, vol. 2 (Oxford and London: Clarendon Press and H. Milford, 1944), 190.

15. See, for example, Tierney, "Conciliarism, Corporatism," 94, who notes that *Consideratio* 12 of Gerson's *De potestate ecclesiastica*, which immediately precedes the formal definition of *ius* in *Consideratio* 13, "is devoted entirely to a discussion of *iura*—the rights of popes, kings, bishops, and lesser prelates in the conduct of church affairs."

16. Augustine, *Contra Iulianum Opus Imperfectum* (*Against Julian: An Unfinished Work*) 6.22.

17. Jerome, *In Amos*, i.1.

18. Primasius of Hadrumetum, *Commentary on the Apocalypse* 2.5.

19. "Natural Rights in the Thirteenth Century," 67. According to Busa's exhaustive *Index Thomisticus*, the word *iura* occurs a total of fifty-four times in Thomas's voluminous corpus, but never in the sense of natural rights. In all cases, the reference is to canonical or civil rights, or to the ancient as distinguished from the new codes of law, or to the laws governing warfare and the like.

20. Cf. Villey, "La genèse du droit subjectif chez Guillaume d'Occam," *Archives de philosophie du droit* 9 (1964): 117. Even without the addition of *licita, potestas* often means a "legal" power, as distinguished from *potentia*, which can designate a premoral power. It is true that the distinction between the two is not always strictly observed.

21. Johannes Monachus, *Glossa Aurea* (Paris, 1535), fol. xciv, Glossa ad Sect. 1.6.16. Tierney, "Villey, Ockham," 30.

22. "Villey, Ockham," 20.

23. *Defensor Pacis* II.12.7.

24. The gist of Marsilius's argument is that universally admitted moral principles are not fully rational and, conversely, that fully rational principles are not universally admitted. Cf. L. Strauss, "Marsilius of Padua," in *History of Political Philosophy*, 3rd editition, edited by L. Strauss and J. Cropsey (Chicago: University of Chicago Press, 1987), 292-93.

25. *Dialogus* Part III, Tr. ii, Book III,6.

26. *De concordantia catholica* (*The Catholic Concordance*), translated by P. Sigmund, slightly modified (Cambridge, England and New York: Cambridge University Press, 1991), 230. The original text is to be found in Nicholas of Cusa *Opera Omnia* III.iv,331, edited by G. Kallen, vol. XIV (Hamburg, 1963), 348. The text is cited by Tierney, who does not call attention to the rarity of the expression. Cf. "Conciliarism, Corporatism," 109.

27. Nicholas's treatise was presented to the Council of Basel in early 1434. It clearly reflects Nicholas's conciliarist leanings and was calculated to support his views on this subject. See also G. de Lagarde, "Individualisme et corporatisme au moyen âge," in *L'organisation corporative du moyen âge à la fin de l'Ancien Régime* (Louvain: Bureaux du Recueil Bibliothèque de l'université, 1937), 52.

28. The Bible certainly knows nothing of natural rights. If it is famous for anything, it is for promulgating a set of commandments or, as one might say, a Bill of Duties rather than a Bill of Rights. The term "rights" in the plural, *iura*, does not appear even once in the Vulgate, for centuries the standard version of the Bible in the West. *Ius* in the singular occurs approximately thirty times, but always to designate some legally sanctioned arrangement. Genesis 23:4 speaks in this sense of a *ius sepulchri* or right of burial apropos of Abraham, who discusses with the Hittites the possibility of acquiring a tomb for Sarah. As is clear from the context, Abraham is not claiming any kind of right and has no need to do so, for the Hittites were offering him free of charge their "choicest sepulchres" to bury his dead. The Hebrew Bible itself makes no attempt to define this or any other right. Since it has no word for "nature" and in any event does not engage in philosophic speculation, it can hardly be expected to describe such rights as "natural."

29. "Villey, Ockham," 19.

30. Ibid., 20-21.

31. C. Wolff, *Institutiones iuris naturae et gentium, Gesammelte Werke*, 26 (Halle, 1750), 23-24; quoted by Tierney, "Conciliarism, Corporatism," 102.

32. Locke, *Second Treatise of Civil Government*, nos. 6, 7, 8, and 13.

33. Ibid., no. 13. See also no. 9, where the same teaching is likewise described as "very strange."

34. Cf. Hobbes, *De cive*, I.8-9. Spinoza, *Political Treatise* II.18: "In the state of nature, wrongdoing is impossible; or, if anyone does wrong, it is to himself, not to another."

35. *Summa theologiae* II-II, qu. 64, a. 3. Also I-II, qu. 92, a. 2, ad 3, and qu. 90, a. 3, ad 2. Thomas's teaching follows roughly Aristotle, *Nicomachean Ethics* X. 15-24. Cf. Suarez *De legibus*, III.3.3; Grotius *De iure belli et pacis*, II.20.3.

36. Gratian *Decretum* I.23, qu. 8, can. 33. The text follows Augustine *De civitate Dei* (*City of God*) I.21. A literal translation of Gratian's latin is as follows: "a person without public authority who puts a criminal to death will be judged a murderer, and all the more so as he did not fear to usurp for himself a power not given by God."

37. The pertinent text by Henry of Ghent is *Quodlibet* 9, qu. 26, *Opera Omnia*, edited by Raymond Macken (Leuven: Leuven University Press, 1983), vol. 13, 307-310.

38. Ibid., 308. Cf. Tierney, "Natural Rights in the Thirteenth Century," 64.

39. *Summa theologiae* II-II, qu. 69, a. 4, ad 2: . . . . "nullus ita condemnatur quod ipse sibi inferat mortem sed quod ipse mortem patiatur. Et ideo non tenetur facere id unde mors sequatur, quod est manere in loco unde ducatur ad mortem. Tenetur tamen non resistere agenti quin patiatur quod iustum est eum pati." The

example in terms of which the problem was discussed in antiquity was that of Socrates, who could easily have fled with the help of powerful friends but chose instead to die, ostensibly in obedience to the laws of the city. As the *Crito* suggests, however, his real reasons for doing so were quite different. At the age of seventy, with at best only a few more years to live and faced with the unattractive prospect of having to spend them in some uncongenial place, Socrates had less to lose by accepting his sentence than would have been the case had he been younger.

40. Cf. Tierney, "Natural Rights in the Thirteenth Century," 64-65. Pufendorf, who deals briefly with this issue, seems to be crossing a line of sorts when he says that the magistrate is the one who should be held responsible for the convict's escape and punished for neglecting his duty. Cf. *De iure naturae et gentium*, VIII.3.4: "The delinquent is not at fault if he be not put to death. The blame lies wholly upon the magistrate." Pufendorf's statement reflects the modern tendency to compensate for the greater freedom allowed to individuals by making greater demands on the government. Laws and institutions are now considered more reliable than moral character. See on this general topic H. C. Mansfield, Jr., *Taming the Prince: The Ambivalence of Modern Executive Power* (New York: Free Press and London: Collier Macmillan, 1989).

41. Tierney, ibid., 66.

42. "Natural Rights in the Thirteenth Century," 67.

43. *Leviathan*, chap. 28. The earlier statement to which Hobbes alludes occurs in chap. 21, where it is stated that "if the sovereign command a man, though justly condemned, to kill, wound, or maim himself, or not to resist those that assault him . . . yet has that man the liberty to disobey." See in the same vein *De Cive* II.18: "No man is obliged by any contracts whatsoever not to resist him who shall offer to kill, wound, or any other way hurt his body." See on this topic Thomas S. Schrock, who writes: "Thomas Hobbes was the first political thinker to declare a right in the guilty subject to resist the lawful and lawfully punishing sovereign." Schrock adds that this teaching precipitated a "crisis" in Hobbes's political theory, for "there are reasons to doubt that the would-be Hobbesian sovereign can acquire a right to punish if the would-be Hobbesian subject has a right to resist punishment. If these two rights cannot co-exist within the same conceptual and political system, and if Hobbes will not rescind his declaration of the right to resist, his punishment dependent political theory is in trouble." "The Rights to Punish and Resist Punishment in Hobbes's *Leviathan,*" *The Western Political Quarterly* 44 (1991): 853-90.

44. The term "inalienable," which the *Declaration of Independence* popularized, does not appear to have been used by Locke himself. It shows up in the *Virginia Declaration of Rights*, but only with reference to the right of revolution.

45. *Second Treatise*, no. 149. On the derivation of all other rights from the basic right of self-preservation, see, for example, *First Treatise of Government*, nos. 86-88.

46. *Second Treatise*, no. 6.

47. Cf. Aristotle, *Nic. Ethics* V.1138a9-13. It is true that the law does not expressly forbid suicide, but "what it does not expressly permit it forbids . . . He who

through anger voluntarily stabs himself does this contrary to the right rule of life, and this the law does not allow; therefore he is acting unjustly. But toward whom? Surely toward the city, not toward himself." A similar problem arises in connection with Socrates, who was accused of a crime for which, if found guilty, he could be sentenced to death. The question is whether he had a "duty" or a "right" to defend himself. In the *Apology*, his defense is presented as being first and foremost a duty: *philosophoûntá me deîn znv* (Apol. 28e). According to the modern view, it is without any doubt a "right." Cf. Spinoza, *Theologico-Political Treatise*, chap. 20.

48. Cf. Aristotle, *Nic. Ethics* V.1134b11: "No one chooses to hurt himself, for which reason there can be no injustice toward oneself." Cf. Thomas Aquinas, II-II qu. 58, a. 2.

49. *Summa theologiae* II-II, qu. 59, a. 3, ad 2; cf. qu. 64, a. 5. See also on the prohibition against suicide Suarez, *De triplici virtute theologica: de caritate* XIII.7.18.

50. *Quodlibet* 8, qu. 11, *Philosophes Belges* 4 (1924): 105. Cf. Tierney, "Villey, Ockham," 27.

51. If the suicide attempt was successful, the dead person's property could be confiscated by the state. If it failed, other grave penalties were imposed. Until very recently, Roman Catholic canon law stipulated that anyone who committed suicide was not to be given a Christian burial.

52. *Second Treatise* no. 4. See also, for a similar argument, no. 135.

53. *Second Tr.*, no. 6.

54. *First Tr.*, no. 86.

55. *First Tr.*, no. 87.

56. For a valiant defense of the opposite view, see G. D. Glenn, "Inalienable Rights and Locke's Argument for Limited Government: Political Implications of a Right to Suicide," *The Journal of Politics* 46 (1984): 80-105. I am indebted to Prof. Walter Berns for part of my interpretation of Locke's stance and posture in regard to suicide.

57. Such a concern would be analogous to that evinced by certain present-day anti-abortionists who insist on calling all abortion murder lest, by excluding from that category abortions performed in the earliest stages of the pregnancy, they should weaken their case against it.

58. The tension reminds us in some way of the one found in Hobbes's theory, according to which the state has the right to put a criminal to death and the criminal the right to kill his executioner. Cf. *supra*, 11, n. 1. Differently and more broadly stated, Hobbes was of the opinion that a war could be just on both sides at the same time. Beccaria later tried to solve the dilemma by advocating the abolition of capital punishment. In grappling with the same problem, some twentieth-century positivists have gone further and argued that survival or self-preservation is not an antecedently fixed goal or end but a contingent fact. We are committed to it only because our concern happens to be "with social arrangements for continued existence, not with those of a suicide club." H. L. A. Hart, *The Concept of Law* (Oxford: Clarendon Press, 1961), 188. As far as I know, the first modern philosopher to rule out suicide

altogether is Kant, who argues against it not on the ground of self-preservation but because it runs counter to the categorical imperative. Cf. *Foundations of the Metaphysics of Morals*, Second Section, and, for a fuller discussion, *Lectures on Ethics*, translated by L. Infield (New York: Harper & Row, 1963), 148-54.

59. Cf. Descartes, *Discourse on Method*, First Part: "I compared the ethical writings of the ancient pagans to superb and magnificent palaces built only on mud and sand: they laud the virtues and make them appear more desirable than anything else in the world, but they give no adequate criterion of virtue; and often what they call by such a name is nothing but cruelty and apathy, parricide, pride, or despair."

60. Bernard Mandeville, *The Fable of the Bees; or Private Vices, Publick Benefits* (New York: Capricorn Books, 1962).

61. *An Essay Concerning Human Understanding*, I.2.4. The essential difference between the old and the new morality is well summed up by Locke, ibid., I.2.5: "[I]f a Christian, who has the view of happiness and misery in another life, be asked why a man must keep his word, he will give this reason: Because God, who has the power of eternal life and death, requires it of us. But if a Hobbist be asked why, he will answer: Because the public requires it and the Leviathan will punish you if you do not. And if one of the old philosophers had been asked, he would have answered: Because it was dishonest, below the dignity of man, and opposite to virtue, the highest perfection of human nature, to do otherwise."

62. Cf. Hobbes, *Leviathan*, chap. 6, where all the other moral virtues—courage, liberality, magnanimity, and the like—are demoted to the rank of passions.

63. *Second Tr.*, no. 123.

64. For a discussion of the different versions of the natural state available in the seventeenth century and in Pufendorf, see the M. Seidler's introduction to his edition and translation of Pufendorf's essay (Lewiston, N.Y.: Edwin Mellen Press, 1990), 28-31.

65. See on this subject Locke's long discussion of caution and judicious concealment in *The Reasonableness of Christianity* (Washington, D.C.: Regnery Gateway, 1965), 39-123. Cf. also, on the pains taken by Locke publicly to distance himself from Hobbes, R. Horwitz's introduction to his translation of Locke's *Questions Concerning the Law of Nature* (Ithaca, N.Y. and London: Cornell University Press, 1990), 5-10.

66. *The Plan of the Great Instauration, init.* On the use of esotericism in the premodern tradition, cf. Grotius, *De iure belli et pacis* III.1.7-20. Also, for recent assessments of the problem as it posed itself in the early modern period, P. Bagley, "On the Practice of Esotericism," *Journal of the History of Ideas* vol. 53, no. 2, (April-June, 1992): 231-247. D. Wootten, "Lucien Febvre and the Problem of Unbelief in the Early Modern Period," *Journal of Modern History* 60 (1988): 695-730.

67. *De iure belli*, II.5.15.2. See also III.7.1, where the expression *primaevus naturae status* is used in a similar sense.

68. *Prolegomena to the Law of War and Peace*, no. 42: "Among the philosophers Aristotle deservedly holds the foremost place, whether you take into account

his order of treatment, or the subtlety of his distinctions, or the weight of his reasons." Grotius nevertheless thought it possible to improve upon the teaching of his master by providing a more methodical treatment of the subject matter of his book and by illustrating his teaching by means of a larger number of historical examples. Cf. ibid., nos. 1 and 38.

69. Ibid., 6: "Among the traits characteristic of human beings is an impelling desire for society, that is, for the social life, not of any and every sort, but peaceful and organized according to the measure of their intelligence, with those of their own kind. This social inclination the Stoics called 'sociableness.' Stated as a universal truth, therefore, the assertion that every animal is impelled by nature to seek only its own good cannot be conceded."

70. Machiavelli, *Discourses*, Book I, Introduction. Cf. F. Bacon, *New Organon*, I.92: "And therefore it is fit that I publish and set forth those conjectures of mine which make hope in this matter reasonable, just as Columbus did, before that wonderful voyage across the Atlantic, when he gave the reasons for his conviction that new lands and continents might be discovered besides those which were known before; which reasons, though rejected at first, were afterwards made good by experience and were the causes and beginnings of great events."

71. *New Organon*, I.35.

72. *Leviathan*, chap. 14.

73. Hobbes, *De natura hominis*, cf. Epistle Dedicatory.

74. A more adequate discussion would obviously have to take full account of the important modification that the modern rights doctrine underwent at the hands of Kant and his followers. For all its stress on duty, however, Kant's moral doctrine is still in the end a doctrine of rights rather than of virtues.

75. On the widespread trend to rehabilitate the once discredited Middle Ages and trace to them the major achievements of the modern age, see the provocative if at times impressionistic book by N. F. Cantor, *Inventing the Middle Ages: The Lives, Works, and Ideas of the Great Medievalists of the Twentieth Century* (New York: W. Morrow, 1991).

13

THE NEW RIGHTS THEORY
AND THE NATURAL LAW

I love Carolina,
I love Angelina, too,
I can't marry both,
So what I gonna do?

Judging by the number of books and articles that have lately been devoted to it, one has the impression that the much maligned natural law doctrine is due for yet another of its periodic revivals. The new syndrome, which seems to have taken some of our contemporaries by surprise, was not totally unpredictable. As far back as 1929, even as staunch an advocate of legal positivism as the late Hans Kelsen was forced to admit that "before we had reason to expect it, a reaction (had) set in which (augured) a renaissance of metaphysics, and, thereby, of natural-law theory."[1] The reaction, he thought, was prompted by other than purely theoretical reasons. It was part of an "eternal undular movement" by which the human spirit is carried "from pessimism or optimism to the ideal of objectivity" or "from metaphysics to the critique of knowledge and back again."[2] Its immediate cause was the shaking of the social foundations brought about by World War I and the ensuing conflict among a variety of "interest groups" who naively sought to justify their claims by appealing to an illusory notion of "right."

If the shattering events of those and more recent years have taught us anything, it is indeed that human beings cannot easily dispense with objective principles of justice and right, whether they be enunciated in the form of a "transcendent law of nature and of nature's God,"[3] or for that matter in any other form. But while few thoughtful people would deny that such principles are eminently desirable, there is still considerable disagreement as to how or how well they can be established. One of the major difficulties facing the natural law theorist is that his understanding of human nature was originally bound up with a teleological view of the universe which has seemingly been destroyed by modern science. Quite apart from that, however, one does well to bear in mind that the natural law has always been in some sort of trouble, as is evident from the numerous debates it has sparked and the frequent revisions to which it has been subjected in the course of its long history.[4] In view of this situation, it is understandable that it should continue to pose a problem, not for its opponents—they have long since abandoned it as a myth-eaten anachronism—but for its own defenders.

One gathers as much from the heated discussions surrounding the abortion issue at the present moment. Although the Roman Catholic Church has not altered its official stand on this matter and gives no indication of wanting to do so, it now supports it by means of a distinctively new argument based on natural or human rights rather than on the natural law. The bottom line may be the same in both instances, but the reasoning behind it is obviously different. The old argument was mainly concerned with what abortion does to the person who performs it or allows it to be performed; the new one, with what it does to the aborted fetus. One argument emphasizes duties; the other emphasizes rights. The question, bluntly stated, is whether the two approaches are fully compatible with each other or whether at a deeper level the tension between them is not such as to caution against any hasty substitution of one for the other.

The prevailing view among Catholic scholars is that they are in fact compatible and that the modern rights doctrine is simply a perfected version of the old natural law doctrine. Such was the position taken by Jacques Maritain in a number of works, including *The Rights of Man and Natural Law* and *The Person and the Common Good*, which exerted considerable influence in the forties and fifties; and such also is the position taken, independently of Maritain and from a different perspective, by John Finnis in a recent book entitled *Natural Law and Natural Rights*,[5] which has already attracted widespread attention in Catholic as well as non-Catholic circles and which affords an excellent opportunity to explore some of the issues implied in the problem at hand.

Like Maritain, Finnis is persuaded that, properly interpreted and whatever one may think of its tainted origins,[6] the rights theory is nothing other than a more supple and differentiated way of articulating the essential demands of justice and of a just social order. His own method of procedure is largely deductive in character and resembles that of Rawls and H. L. A. Hart more than it does that of Thomas Aquinas, despite numerous references to him in the text. It consists in laying down as self-evident a number of premoral "basic values" from which by way of entailment human reason is able to fix the universal norms of private and public morality. These values represent the goals or ends to which all human activity is directed. Unlike Rawls's "primary goods," they are desired for their own sakes and not merely as a necessary means to some unspecified and freely chosen end, as would be, for example, liberty or wealth in the Rawlsian scheme.[7] Whereas Hart, on the other hand, speaks only of one such value, namely, survival or life, Finnis singles out six others for special consideration: knowledge, play, aesthetic experience, sociability or friendship, practical reasonableness, and religion. All seven values are to be regarded as "equally fundamental"[8] and none deserves to be privileged above any of the others. To pursue them in any of their various forms and combinations corresponds to what has always been understood by human fulfillment or "flourishing," Finnis's word for "happiness."

The analysis of these basic values leads in due course to the identification of the nine principles of "practical reasonableness" (originally J. Raz's term) in which for Finnis the whole of morality is summed up. Included in the list are such items as the need to form a "coherent plan of life" (shades of Rawls again), to avoid arbitrary preferences among values or persons, to refrain from actions directly opposed to any of the basic values, to behave rationally and in accordance with the requirements of practical reasonableness, to foster the common good, and to follow one's conscience at all times. The rest of the book is in large part an attempt to show how the observance of these principles conforms in all essentials to the traditional understanding of justice, both general and particular, and insures that the demands of the common good will be met. The final chapter ("Nature, Reason, and God") broadens the scope of the inquiry by placing it within the cosmic setting from which human activity draws its ultimate significance.

No brief summary will ever succeed in conveying a sense of the richness of this complex work, of the acuteness of its analyses, of its attention to detail, and of its willingness to come to grips with concrete moral and legal issues. Seldom in our time have such vast stores of historical, philosophic, and juridical information been brought to bear on the problems with which it deals, and seldom have they been deployed with such obvious mastery. Not the least of the book's many advantages is that its approach is not tied to a teleological conception of nature and is thus immune to the objections that might otherwise be leveled at it on modern scientific grounds. What we are given or promised instead is a view of justice that retains its validity even on the assumption of the nonexistence of God.[9] Another feature that deserves to be singled out is the able defense of the objectivity of moral standards against "skepticism" or scientific value relativism, which is shown to be self-defeating inasmuch as the skeptic's belief in the value of science is undermined by his denial of the scientific character of all value judgments.[10] Furthermore, the morality on behalf of which the book speaks is a noble or dignified morality, as opposed to the low-minded morality of utilitarianism (since E. Anscombe, "consequentialism"), which, as the analysis demonstrates, is impracticable anyway for the simple reason that the utilitarian has no reliable criterion by which to decide whether a particular action is or is not conducive to the greatest good of the greatest number.[11]

Finnis's theory can likewise claim the merit of ascertaining with quasi-mathematical rigor and determinateness the specific norms by which human choices are to be guided. In that respect, it overcomes one of the conspicuous deficiencies or would-be deficiencies of the Thomistic teaching, which leaves it at saying that all such norms are derived from the common principles of the natural law without stipulating any rule or method by which the process of derivation might be carried out.[12] It should be noted in passing that the discussion of Thomas's position on this as well as on other matters has a freshness that is often lacking among present-day theorists, many if not most of whom tend to read Thomas as an intruder from the past rather than as a contemporary. As a scholar trained in the best tradition of analytical jurisprudence, Finnis is noticeably unhampered by the typical historicist preoccupation with the sense of "alienness" supposedly engendered by the temporal distance that separates Thomas's century from ours. The focus of attention remains squarely on substantive moral issues, which are never allowed to disappear beneath a rubble of exegetical or methodological commentary.

The whole achievement is by any standard an impressive one, combining as it does the best of many worlds. For that reason it is sure to appeal to a broad spectrum of readers: to liberals, who generally feel at home with the language of universal human rights, but also to conservatives, for whom the best way to serve the needs of the present is to show a greater respect for the legacy of the past. Given the looseness, not to say the emptiness, of so much of the current talk about rights, one cannot imagine a more timely and challenging book.

Where there is so much to praise, one hesitates to enter even a slight demurrer. Still, in the interest of clarity, it may be worth our while to take a closer look at the other side of the picture, and all the more so as Finnis himself is the first to concede that "few problems are ever solved once for all."[13] The reader is informed early on that what he has before him is a book on "natural law"[14] and, some time later, that almost everything in it is about "natural rights."[15] Defending the synonymity or the fundamental harmony of these two originally antithetical doctrines is unfortunately not always as easy as one would like it to be. According to the original natural law theory, human beings are social and political by nature.[16] They form part of a larger whole to which they owe their primary allegiance and outside of which for the most part they are nothing. As physical beings they may be unified and self-subsisting wholes, but wholes which are nonetheless intrinsically ordered to a determinate end or ends that cannot be actualized without the collaboration of others. They do not have from the start all that they require for their well-being and attain their full development only by engaging in activities that involve them in a web of reciprocal relationships typically structured within the context of civil society—ideally, the *polis*—the comprehensive and truly self-sufficient human association and hence the only one capable of satisfying their longing for completion or wholeness. Any life other than the political life is either subhuman or superhuman.[17] Thus understood, civil society is natural, not in the sense that it is supplied by nature, but in the sense that it corresponds to the natural needs and aspirations of its members and that human nature itself inclines to it.

In contrast to the natural law theory, the natural rights theory proceeds on the assumption that these same human beings exist first of all as complete and independent wholes, endowed with prepolitical rights for the protection of which they "enter" into a society that is entirely of their own making. All rules governing their relations with one another and all principles of justice are ultimately rooted in rights and derive their efficacy from them. These principles are not indemonstrable or self-evident principles, intimated to us through the natural inclination toward the good that the individual experiences within himself,[18] but the products of a calculus of means to a desired end in which discursive reason is called upon to play the leading role. Any knowledge that one may have of them presupposes that one's intellectual capacity is sufficiently developed to engage in this kind of calculus.[19] In Hobbes's version of that theory, the one right on which everything else depends is the right of self-preservation, which alone constitutes the low but solid foundation on which the whole of the social life is made to rest.[20] The original Hobbesian view underwent a series of improvements as time went on, especially at the hands of Rousseau and Kant, but it still provided the model from which all of the most influential political thinkers of the modern period would henceforth work.

It would be surprising if, on the basis of such radically different premises, one were to come in all cases to identical or roughly similar results. By grounding the modern rights doctrine in the intrinsic dignity and worth of the human person, Finnis has unquestionably succeeded in infusing it with a properly moral content. His own view of morality would thus appear to be as far removed from contemporary utilitarianism as is Kant's moral philosophy from Hobbesian or Lockean utilitarianism. Therein lies its greatest strength. Yet the break with the utilitarian tradition is not nearly as deep or as complete as it is presumed to be. What we actually witness could more aptly be described as a simple transformation of the older rights theory, a transformation accomplished less by eliminating any element of personal advantage or expediency from the determination of the rules of morality than by prescinding altogether, as Kant had done, from the distinction between base or selfish and noble or unselfish impulses.

Accordingly, the rights whose defense the book takes up are still perceived as absolute or unconditional rights, circumscribed only by the derivative requirements of practical reasonableness and a proper respect for the rights of others.[21] This horizontal limitation guarantees that my own rights will not be infringed and for that reason I have no choice but to accept it. To do otherwise would be both immoral and foolish. On that level of generality, what is good for me is good for everyone else, but I shall not have it unless they have it too. Self-interest and public interest coalesce into a harmonious whole which does not depend for its coming into being on the conversion from a selfish concern for worldly goods to a concern for the good of the soul or the transformation of the individual into a citizen through the mediating agency of virtue. To be sure, moral virtue is not excluded, but neither is it indispensable. Courage, moderation, generosity, and the other moral virtues are not themselves basic or nonnegotiable values; they are ways or modes "deemed" by some people to fit them for the attainment of the basic values.[22] One need not acquire them in order to enjoy their benefits. Justice is always to my immediate or long-range advantage and the just life is the most pleasant life. At the extreme limit, no one has to worry about ever having to sacrifice himself for the common good.

Concrete situations are obviously not always that simple, for there are times when rights or "opportunities" come into conflict with each other, as they do, for example, when my friend's well-being "can only be secured by my ruin or destruction."[23] Self-sacrifice is too much a part of human life to be ruled out a priori. It, too, must somehow be "rational," although its "reasonableness," the defense of which is relegated to the last and most tentative chapter, is never made completely clear.[24] If virtue is not choiceworthy for its own sake, one is hard-pressed to say why anybody would want to sacrifice himself for others, save for personal or subjective reasons.

This explains why there is in fact so little talk about virtue in the book. The closest thing to it is not justice, which is not treated as a disposition of the soul,[25] but practical reasonableness, which bears a superficial resemblance to Aristotle's and Thomas's prudence and which could conceivably stand for the whole of virtue.[26] But practical reasonableness, as distinguished from prudence, does not appear to be connected in any way with the inclinations of the appetite or dependent on them for the rectitude of its judgment.[27] It functions exclusively as an intellectual capacity whose role, as was mentioned earlier, is to deduce from the postulated basic values the best, and possibly the only decent, set of rules governing human conduct. The soul, its passions, and the reordering of those passions do not enter into account. Human beings may remain as they are as long as the institutions under which they live are as they ought to be. The whole scheme, needless to say, is admirably suited to the conditions that prevail in modern liberal society which it regards as normative and to which it lends theoretical support. How such a society came into being in the first place, and whether even it could endure without some dedication to virtue on the part of its citizens, are questions that are never envisaged or fully elucidated.

The foregoing remarks are only apparently belied by the rare emphasis that is laid on the common good not only in the chapter that is expressly devoted to it[28] but throughout the book. As is his wont, Finnis has again carefully distinguished the different meanings of this tricky notion. The one for which he settles is given as an improvement on Aristotle, who allegedly lacked a "technical notion" of the common good and was, therefore, unable to supply any "distinct and enumerable" requirements of practical reasonableness.[29] It might be observed that Aristotle was not unaware of this difficulty but thought that one merely distorted moral phenomena by treating them with greater exactness than their extreme variability allowed. For him, the acme of precision (*akribeia*) was not necessarily mathematical precision but the highest degree of precision attainable in any given case.[30]

Be that as it may, Finnis's own preferred definition is more specific, though considerably weaker. It sees the common good as constituted by an ensemble of "conditions" that makes it possible for the members of a community to collaborate with one another "positively and/or negatively" in the pursuit of the basic values in terms of which human flourishing has been described.[31] Human beings are not united in a common dedication to a common goal. They are not "parts," as Thomas Aquinas still taught,[32] but atomic wholes, open to others and often in need of them, but nonetheless free to organize their lives or devise their "life-plans" as they see fit, provided they do not interfere with the freedom of others. No one has any real duties other than those entailed by the requirements of practical reasonableness or the need to protect the rights with which he was already gifted prior to his incorporation into civil society. At most, the central issue of the relation of rights to duties remains blurred and the section that deals with it thematically[33] does little to remove the ambiguity. Rights and duties are said to be correlative, as indeed they are—if I have a duty to do something, I also have the right to do it, although the converse is not always true—but this still leaves open the question as to which of the two is the fundamental moral fact. Did Socrates have a right to defend himself or was it above all his duty to do so? The query may not admit of any clear-cut answer, especially since it was never formulated in those specific terms by the ancients and since their own notion of the good as something to be pursued was free of any connotation of duty in the modern or Kantian sense. Allowing for such differences of meaning, however, the likely supposition is that they would have come out on the side of duty. They took it as a matter of course that what the law did not expressly permit, it forbade and never doubted that one's first responsibility was to the common good.[34] The same holds for the Bible, which does not promulgate a bill of rights but issues a set of commandments, duly situated within the context of a covenant of love. In both cases, duties and not rights was the principal "moral counter."[35] The individual who voluntarily harms himself or permits others to harm him commits an injustice not toward himself but toward the community by depriving it of the services that he owes to it.[36] For Socrates, to philosophize was a duty; for Spinoza, it was a right. The opposition between the two views is not reduced but merely concealed by the assertion that "human rights are not subject to the common good" if only because they are themselves an "aspect" of the common good.[37] One regrets in a way that the interesting remarks about certain African dialects in which duties are given the edge over rights were not followed up to better advantage.[38]

The usual objection to this argument is that it does not sufficiently take into account Thomas's qualification to the effect that, although the individual human being is essentially a part of the political community to which he belongs, "he is not ordered to it with regard to the whole of himself and to all that he has."[39] At first glance, this could be taken to mean that there is an important segment of human life in which the individual remains supreme and is thereby absolved from some of the obligations that the community might wish to impose on him in virtue of his participation in it. Yet Thomas also says that "each human being, in all that he is and has, belongs to the community, just as the part, in all that it is, belongs to the whole."[40] Just how these two apparently conflicting statements can be reconciled is a problem that has long divided Thomistic scholars and which would require a much fuller discussion than any that can be entered into here. According to one interpretation, the solution lies in Thomas's distinction between the human being as an "individual" and the human being as a "person."[41] By reason of their material individuality, human beings are ordered to the good of the society of which they form a part. As persons, on the other hand, they are themselves autonomous wholes, existing within society and bound to it only insofar as their own good is served by it.[42] The difficulty with this answer is that in none of the pertinent texts does Thomas invoke the distinction between individuality and personality or speak even of the "person" as superior to the common good. Rather, his point seems to be that civil society is not the sole society to which human beings are ordered. The individual person does indeed transcend civil society, but only as a member or a part of a universal community, ruled by God, whose common good is *eo facto* preferable to that of any particular society.[43] The good in which human beings find their perfection is never a "private good" but a good that is shared or capable of being shared by others and which for that reason takes precedence over any good that they could claim as theirs alone.[44] For the same reason there is no talk anywhere in Thomas of such primordial rights as would not be subordinated to the common good or contingent on the fulfillment of antecedent duties.

On this score, one is entitled to ask whether the "shift of perspective" that Finnis detects in the Thomistic commentators of the sixteenth and early-seventeenth centuries is as "drastic" as it is made out to be.[45] It is true that the characterization of *ius* or "right" as a "faculty" appears for the first time in the writers of that period, most notably in Suarez and Grotius;[46] and it is also true that prior to that time people spoke of the rightness of things rather than of the rights of persons. The significant fact, however, is that the rights to which Suarez and Grotius refer are still defined and hence limited by law. Moreover, they have to do less with u-niversal human rights than with the specific rights of rulers and subjects, parents and children, masters and slaves, property owners and workers, and the like. Contrary to what is suggested, the real "watershed" in the history of the rights doctrine is not to be located somewhere between Thomas and Suarez; it occurs with Hobbes, who set the stage for all sub-sequent discussions of this matter by denying that human beings are political by nature (something that Suarez and Grotius never did) and by proclaiming the absolute priority of rights to duties.[47]

All of the points alluded to thus far are of more than purely speculative interest. They are fraught with definite practical implications, which come to the fore when one considers, for example, Finnis's pivotal thesis concerning the fundamental equality of all basic values. His is the neutral perspective of the detached observer who surveys the world of values from an Archimedean point outside of it and is able to disregard the claims to superiority raised on behalf of these values by their adherents. Even knowledge, through which the proposed scheme is devised and which is treated extensively in a separate chapter,[48] is not objectively higher than, say, aesthetic experience, sociability, or play. It is simply *"made"* so by an individual's choice of it rather than of some other value as the one that is more important or fundamental *"for him."*[49] It follows that the life of a great scholar, statesman, or religious leader is not intrinsically superior to that of a music buff, a valetudinarian, or a ski bum. In the absence of any natural hierarchy of ends, it becomes impossible to rank people on the basis of the choice that they make of this or that particular value. Human beings are equal not only before God, or before the law, or in regard to self-preservation, but by the mere fact that they have the capacity to "realize" or, better, "participate in" any or all of the aforesaid basic values. It is entirely up to them to set their own priorities or change them if they have any reason to do so, preferring one value to another at different times and under a different set of circumstances. Thus, "if one is drowning, one is inclined to shift one's focus to the value of life as such"[50]—again a sign that the values in question cannot be ordered hierarchically.

The argument does not prove very much, however, for it suggests only that there are moments when more important things have to be set aside temporarily for the sake of more urgent ones. I may be planning to study philosophy or legal theory, but if I am suddenly stricken with appendicitis, the surgical operation will have to come first. Nor is the example of the drowning person always as unambiguous as it sounds. Suppose that *two* persons, a father and his son, are drowning and that only one of them can be saved. Would we still venture to say that the father's willingness to give up his own life is reducible to such incidental factors as "one's temperament, upbringing, capacities, and opportunities"? In all such cases, the tendency to favor the young over the old may be more than either a generally accepted convention or a matter of personal preference. It has something to do with the good of the species, which hinges on the survival of those who are most likely to propagate it. If so, does it not in point of fact direct our attention to "differences of rank of intrinsic value between the basic values"[51]? And, while we are on the subject, does not Socrates's resolve to accept death rather than stop philosophizing become trivial when viewed apart from any consideration of the hierarchy of values implied in such a choice?

Finnis's solution has neatness in its favor, but it can hardly be said to account for all the facts of experience. It is not easily reconcilable with the universal phenomenon of admiration and is bound to work to the detriment of the rarer forms of human flourishing to which that phenomenon points. Its spirit is that of democratic liberalism, whose leveling tendencies it reflects without much concern for the deprivations imposed on certain higher types of human beings, to say nothing of the community as a whole. It is doubtful whether anyone who subscribes to it will be inspired to make the almost superhuman effort required to attain the lofty goals of wisdom, prudence, or piety that an older tradition of ethical thought sought to promote. The new program serves everybody equally well, but this is as much as to say that it does not serve anybody particularly well. It can make light of the distinction between the wise few and the unwise many because, even though it can be comprehensively elaborated only by a theoretical person, it does not rely on wisdom, any more than it does on moral virtue, for its successful implementation. Trustworthy institutions, geared to the achievement of modest goals, will give us what we could never be sure of having otherwise, at the risk of making us forget that human beings once thought it possible to aspire to something higher.

Further complications arise when one ponders some of the consequences of Finnis's teaching regarding the absolute inviolability of all basic human rights, none of which, we are told, can ever be infringed, be it only for the sake of averting a catastrophe.[52] Take, for instance, the principle that prohibits the recourse to torture under any circumstances.[53] Well and good, if one thinks only of the frightening abuses to which such a practice lends itself. But how "practically reasonable" is it to refrain from torturing a known criminal if this should prove to be the only way of securing the information that will save the lives of his innocent victims? A world in which terrorism of the most brutal sort has become an almost daily fact of life may not always be able to afford the luxury of showing the same respect for assassins as for anyone else; and, besides, a morally sensitive person might have some qualms about signing away the lives of others or indulging in what, from another point of view, could just as easily be interpreted as heroism by proxy. Finnis's principle, noble as it may be, is more readily applicable to normal than to emergency situations. It owes much of its attractiveness to the fact that individuals are thereby spared the necessity of engaging in an always precarious "casuistry of duties"[54] or of wrestling with excruciatingly difficult prudential decisions of the kind over which Augustine agonizes in Book XIX, chapter 6, of the *City of God*. Whether this is enough to validate it is another matter, the laudable concern to steer clear of the pitfalls of utilitarianism notwithstanding.

Surprisingly little thought seems to have been given to the intellectual pedigree of many of these motifs. The overriding and somewhat insular preoccupation with utilitarianism and moral skepticism has resulted in a peculiar blindness to other powerful currents of thought whose language the book often speaks, as is abundantly attested to by the constant recurrence of such characteristic expressions as "personal authenticity," "commitment," "self-realization," "individual autonomy," "creativity," "values," and "lifestyles," the modern substitute for what used to be called the "good life."[55] Serious reflection on this state of affairs might have alerted the author to the enormous difficulties involved in any attempt to recapture the spirit of the natural law tradition and revealed the degree to which his own thinking remains in thrall to the dominant spiritual and political consciousness of the times. One is reminded by contrast of Tocqueville, who also thought it necessary to go along with the new trend but was much more keenly aware of the price that human beings would have to pay for acquiescing in it. Tocqueville knew from experience that the modern principles would produce a different type of human being and one which was not in every way superior to the type it was destined to replace. Because he had an alternative, dead as it may have been in his own eyes, he was able to illuminate the present situation and, in its own interest, warn of the dangers that threatened it from within. It would never have occurred to him to say that the new ideal was just like the old one, only better.

Finnis's endeavor to moralize the modern rights doctrine goes *pari passu* with a no less concerted effort to rationalize or demythologize Thomas's natural law doctrine by stripping it of any element of coercion. On his reading, the natural law, as Thomas understands it, is nothing more than an attempt (admittedly "undeveloped") to spell out what it means to live as a fully rational being. It is only "analogically law"[56] and does not impose any type of behavior under pain of sanction. It merely points to what one must do or avoid in order to fulfill oneself and hence would be just as valid even if there were no God to enforce it. The sole obligation that it carries with it is a "rational necessity of certain sorts of means to certain sorts of ends."[57] The same is also evident from an analysis of the notion of *imperium* or "command," which Thomas defines as an act of the intellect rather than of the will.[58] The very term "natural law" is a "rather unhappy" one[59] for which other expressions, such as "natural right," "intrinsic morality," or "right reason" could be substituted without any loss of meaning.[60] Its association with the notion of compulsion or obligatoriness, so prevalent today, is traceable to a misunderstanding perpetrated by Vasquez and Suarez, both of whom dismissed Thomas's concept of *imperium* as "unnecessary," "inept," or "fictitious."[61]

Finnis's interpretation is not his alone since it is already found in a number of late medieval writers from Gregory of Rimini onward,[62] and since it figures prominently in the Prolegomena to Grotius's *Law of War and Peace*; but never has it been defended so forcefully. If it were to be followed, it would go a long way toward resolving the famous dilemma of Plato's *Republic* concerning the goodness of justice in the absence of a legislating God. Yet, it was always rejected by the mainstream of the Thomistic tradition and with good reason. For all his insistence on the role of reason in matters of legislation, Thomas does not neglect to draw attention to the fact that a law or command owes its moving power to the will of the legislator.[63] The general principle that one ought to do good and avoid evil, and the more specific principles to the effect that one should not lie, steal, or commit adultery, are not or not yet moral precepts. They become precepts only when intimated in the form of an imperative: *Fac hoc*.[64] It is at this point that they cease to be simple rules of rational or sensible behavior and acquire the force of law.

That all of this applies to the natural law does not appear to be open to question. Thomas makes it plain that, insofar as it concerns human beings (as opposed to brutes), the natural law is a law in the proper sense of the word: *proprie lex vocatur*.[65] He also makes it plain that the notion of law includes two elements: first, it is a "rule of human acts," and, secondly, it has "coercive power."[66] Granted, sanctions are not explicitly mentioned in the definition of law with which the treatise opens,[67] but they are mentioned in connection with the effects of the law in Question 92.[68] The missing reference to them in the formal definition proves no more than that, following the rules of Aristotelian logic, Thomas regarded them as a "property" of the law rather than as part of its essence. There is, thus, ample reason to think that in his view the natural law is not a mere *lex indicans*, as Finnis would have it, but a *lex praecipiens*, enjoining or forbidding certain actions not only as intrinsically good or bad but as meritorious or demeritorious.[69]

If the thematic account of the *Summa theologiae* leaves little doubt about the strictly *legal* character of the natural law, it does raise some interesting questions about its *natural* character. One of the peculiarities of that account is that, while it often alludes directly or indirectly to the punishments to which acts contrary to the natural law are subject, it fails to specify the nature of those punishments. The lacuna is remedied to some extent by the parallel treatment of the *Summa contra gentiles*, which spells out in great detail the various penalties attached to the transgressions of the law, namely, in order of importance, the forfeiture of eternal bliss, the deprivation of virtue, the disorder of the natural powers of the soul, bodily pain, and the loss of external goods.[70] The oddity in this instance is that, although Thomas appears to have the natural law in view, he never refers to it by name, in all likelihood because his work was primarily intended as a Christian reply to the objections of the Arabic philosophers, in whose thought the natural law plays no role whatever. It is safe to assume that what is said here about sanctions applies preeminently to the natural law, since the acts which they cover are not specifically those described by the divinely revealed law or by the human law, but one still finds it strange that the application is not expressly made by Thomas himself and especially that it is not made in the *Summa theologiae*, where it would most normally be expected to occur.

One possible reason for the omission is hinted at in Thomas's treatment of the relationship between the natural law and the precepts of the Decalogue,[71] which we discussed in chapter 10. Briefly stated, Thomas argues that the precepts of the second table of the Decologue belong "absolutely speaking" to the natural law.[72] But Thomas argues that the precepts of the second table depends on the precepts of the first table for their effectiveness. The difficulty is Thomas's admission that not everyone has access to the precepts of the first table without the aid of divine Revelation. So the precepts of the second table cannot be regarded as simply natural.[73] Thomas's conclusion that the natural law is at best a problematic philosophical concept is borne out by what he says elsewhere about sin, which is viewed by theologians principally as a (punishable) offense against God, but by philosophers only as something that is contrary to reason.[74] Suarez, who grapples with the problem, probably comes close to Thomas's position when he argues that natural reason knows only that sins against the natural law deserve to be punished; it knows nothing about the quantity or the mode of the punishment.[75] As far as that goes, it may not even be able to tell whether in every single instance they are punished it all.[76]

Assuming that there is something to be said for this interpretation, the term "natural law" could well be a misnomer of sorts, introduced into the tradition in somewhat accidental fashion by Cicero and later enshrined in innumerable theological and legal texts to which it is indebted for the enormous prestige that it acquired over the centuries.[77] To put the matter in more concrete terms, human reason, left to itself, cannot be absolutely certain that crime never pays and that in the end the only people who are happy are the ones who deserve to be happy. There is ample evidence that a life of crime is not a pleasant one—nobody in his right mind envies Al Capone—and it is equally evident that some actions bear their punishments with them: if I eat or drink to excess, I will suffer the consequences.[78] But this still leaves the possibility that some lucky person might commit a single undetected crime by means of which he obtains the fortune or the position on which his heart is set and then, without repenting or surrendering any of his ill-gotten gains, live "honestly" and happily thereafter. Short of appealing to retribution in an afterlife, on which the unaided human reason is unable to pronounce itself, the strict natural law theorist has no option but to deny that such a person can ever be at peace with himself. As that great twentieth-century authority on the natural law, Hercule Poirot, says to the villain of *Death on the Nile*, "Mademoiselle, if you but once allow evil into your heart, it will make a home for itself there." The advice is practically sound, but this is not the same as to contend that it is demonstrably true or empirically verifiable. We sometimes hear of criminals who spontaneously turn themselves in simply because they can no longer live with themselves. There may be others who would never dream of doing as much and show no signs of being similarly afflicted by the pangs of a guilty conscience. The happy crook, if such there be, is not likely to brag about his success since it is in the nature of the case that he cannot do so without jeopardizing his situation. Nietzsche was right when he remarked that this is a species which moralists are only too eager to bury in silence.[79] The problem, as far as I can tell, remains unsolved and may not admit of any completely satisfactory solution.

All of the preceding comments were intended less as a criticism of Finnis than as a first feeble attempt to highlight but a few of the questions that his book raises or invites us to consider. In fairness, it should be promptly added that his is a philosophic work, which makes no claim to following Thomas to the letter and which will ultimately have to be judged on its merits.[80] Digesting its contents and coming to terms with its leading assumptions promises to be a long and arduous task. Suffice it to say for the time being that in scope and depth it surpasses anything that has yet been produced by a Roman Catholic scholar in our generation. In an age that has virtually given up on the possibility of establishing any kind of moral standard, let alone the highest, it fully deserves the enthusiasm with which it has been greeted, and more. The basic question is whether its dazzling amalgamation of the old and the new has eluded the danger of eclecticism and yielded the theoretically viable synthesis that we so badly need. We should have every reason to rejoice if, without further surgery, the two theories under consideration, natural law and natural rights, could be made to sit together as comfortably as we are given to understand. Even if they cannot, we may still be grateful that the groundwork has at last been laid for a fruitful comparison of their respective merits. Fortunately, the reader is not obliged to agree with everything Finnis says in order to appreciate the magnitude and quality of his effort. Critical as he may be of the central thesis, the reader will soon discover that he stands to learn more from Finnis than from most of the authors with whom he might agree.

NOTES

1. H. Kelsen, *Die Philosophischen Grundlagen der Naturrechtslehre und des Rechtspositivisimus*, translated by W. H. Kraus under the title, "Natural Law Doctrine

and Legal Positivism," in *General Theory of Law and State* (Cambridge, MA: Harvard University Press, 1949), 446.

2. Ibid., 445.

3. Cf. *Federalist*, No. 43 (Madison), *ca. fin.*

4. For a recent and reasonably complete survey of these avatars, cf. M. B. Crowe, *The Changing Profile of the Natural Law* (The Hague: Martinus Nijhoff, 1977).

5. J. Finnis, *Natural Law and Natural Rights*, Clarendon Law Series, edited by H. L. A. Hart (New York: Clarendon Press and Oxford: Oxford University Press, 1980). pp. xv + 425.

6. Finnis, 221.

7. Finnis, 82.

8. Finnis, 92-5.

9. Finnis, 49.

10. Finnis, 74-5.

11. Finnis, 111f.

12. Finnis, 34.

13. Finnis, 233.

14. Finnis, 24.

15. Finnis, 178.

16. E.g., Thomas Aquinas, *Summa theologiae* I-II, qu. 96, a. 4; I-II, qu. 72, a. 4; qu. 95, a. 4; II-II, qu. 109, a. 3, ad 1m; qu. 114, a. 2, ad 1m; qu. 129, a. 6 ad 1m; *De Regno* I.1; *In decem libros ethicorum Aristoteles ad Nicomachum* IX, lect. 10, no. 1891; *In libros politicorum Aristotelis*, I, lect. 1, etc.

17. Cf. Thomas Aquinas, *Quaestiones Disputatae* vol. 9 *de virtutibus cardinalibus*, a. 1c; *In libros politicorum Aristoteles*, I, lect, 1, no. 39.

18. Thomas Aquinas, *Summa theologiae* I-II, qu. 94, a. 2; *cf. Quodlibetum* I.4.8: "Inclinationes naturales maxime cognosci possunt in his quae naturaliter aguntur *absque rationis deliberatione*; sic enim agit unumquodque in natura sicut aptum natum est agi." Also *Summa theologiae* I, qu. 60, a. 5.

19. As Locke puts it, the natural law is "intelligible and plain" only to the "studier of that law," *Second Treatise of Civil Government*, II.12; cf. ibid., IX.124: "For though the law of nature be plain and intelligible to all rational creatures, yet men, being biased in their interest as well as ignorant *for want of studying it*, are not apt to allow of it as a law binding to them in the application of it to their particular cases" (emphasis mine). See the discussion of this early modern view by Rousseau, who points out that "it is impossible to understand the law of nature and consequently to obey it without being a great reasoner and a profound metaphysician" (*Discourse on the Origin and Foundations of Inequality Among Men*, translated by R. Masters (New York: St. Martin's Press, 1964), 94.

20. E.g., Hobbes, *De cive*, I.1.7: "Therefore the first foundation of natural right is this, that every man as much as in him lies endeavor to protect his life and members." *Leviathan*, I.13-14.

21. Finnis, 218, 225.

22. Finnis, 90-91.

23. Finnis, 372.

24. Finnis readily admits that, when it comes to that, the believer in divine revelation has an easier time of it since his faith tells him that the hoped-for convergence of the common good and the well-being of persons is insured by an all-knowing and loving God, albeit "in ways often unintelligible to us" (406). He can thus love the common good "for a new reason," namely, because God loves it. The position of the philosopher is not as enviable, but neither is it altogether hopeless. The solution to the problem, if any exists, is to be found, not in Stoic or Kantian moralism (373-78), but in Plato's concept of *logismos* (which again translates into "practical reasonableness," 408). The person who allows himself to be guided by reason need not view life as tragic. He can refuse to take success or failure too seriously and see himself as participating in a kind of cosmic game which, unlike practical reasonableness, has no point beyond itself, as Plato could have taught in Book VII of the *Laws*. The explanation has its obvious limitations, however, and Finnis himself recognizes that the "structure of practical reasonableness" remains "finally unproved." The only reason for not discarding it is that it is still "more reasonable than any logically possible alternative structures" (405). Whether it is or not is the question by which his book may be thought to stand or fall. For a slightly different and perhaps more faithful interpretation of *Laws* VII.803b-c, see T. L. Pangle, *The Laws of Plato* (New York: Basic Books, 1980), 484f.

25. Finnis, 161-97.

26. Finnis, 102.

27. Cf. Thomas Aquinas *Summa theologiae* I-II, qu. 56, a. 3; qu. 57, a. 4; qu. 57, a. 5, ad 3m; qu. 64, a. 3; II-II, qu. 47,a. 4; qu. 47, a. 13, ad 2m; *In Ethic.* VI, lect. 7, no. 1200.

28. Finnis, 134-60.

29. Finnis, 165.

30. Aristotle, *Nicomachean Ethics* I.3.1094b20f.; 7.1098a20f.; II.2.1104a1f. *Metaphysics* II.3.995a6f.

31. Finnis, 155.

32. See, among innumerable references, *Summa theologiae* I, qu. 60, a. 5; I-II, qu. 21, a. 3-4; qu. 90, a. 2; qu. 92, a. 1, ad 3m; qu. 96, a. 4; II-II, qu. 58, a. 5; qu. 61, a. 1; qu. 64, a. 5; qu. 65, a. 1.

33. Finnis, 205-10.

34. Aristotle, *Nic. Ethic.* V.11.1138a4f.

35. Finnis, 221.

36. *Nic. Ethic.* 1138a10f. Cf. Thomas Aquinas, *Summa theologiae* II-II, qu. 59, a. 3, ad 2m; qu. 64, a. 5.

37. Finnis, 218.

38. Finnis, 209-10.

39. *Summa theologiae* I-II, qu. 21, a. 4, ad 3m: "Homo non ordinatur ad com-

munitatem politicam secundum se totum et secundum omnia sua."

40. *Summa theologiae* qu. 96, a. 4: "Cum enim unus homo sit pars multitudinis, quilibet homo, hoc ipsum quod est et quod habet, est multitudinis."

41. For example *Summa theologiae* I, qu. 29, a. 4; qu. 30, a. 4; *De potentia* 9.2. Cf. J. Maritain, *The Person and the Common Good 1947* (Notre Dame: University of Notre Dame Press, 1966), 73-74.

42. Maritain, *Person and the Common Good,* 61.

43. Cf., *Summa theologiae* I-II, qu. 109, a. 3: "Manifestum est autem quod bonum partis est propter bonum totius. Unde etiam naturali appetitu vel amore unaquaeque res particularis amat bonum suum proprium propter bonum commune totius universi." Also I-II, qu. 21, a. 4-; II-II, qu. 26, a. 3; *Questiones disputatae de caritate*, 2, c.

44. Thomas's remarks on this controversial subject are obviously not meant to be interpreted in any collectivist or totalitarian sense. Civil society is not itself a person, even though it is often compared to one. Its unity is only a "unity of order" (*unitas ordinis*), as distinguished from the substantial unity of the individual person (cf. *In libros ethicorum*, I, lect. 1 , n. 5). Its function is to enable its citizens to attain their full development and it deserves its name only to the extent to which it promotes the ends to which human nature is ordered. The human beings who compose it are not destroyed by it, as they would be if they were parts of a substantial whole. The perfection that they reach through it remains intrinsic to them. Differently stated, the common good is not an alien good but the "proper good" (*bonum proprium*) of those who share in it (cf. *Summa contra gentiles* III.24). If the common good were not distributed among the members of the community, it would not be truly common; only on this condition can it be an object of desire. The good sought by any being is necessarily its own good (*bonum suum*), whether it be a particular good or the common good, for which it has an even greater natural love (*Summa theologiae* I, qu. 60, a. 5, and ad 1m). The need for justice and civic virtue is rooted in the potential conflict between these two types of good or the tendency of the part to set itself up as the whole. Were it not for this conflict, moral virtue would be expendable. Indeed, according to Aristotle, the perfect man stands in relation to others as the whole in relation to the part (*Politics* III.17.1288a27). Having no desire for goods that cannot be shared, he appears as a god among human beings (*Pol.* III.13.1284a10; see also, on the absence of moral virtue among the gods, *Nic. Ethics* X.8.1178b10f.). He is not subject to the common good because he is himself, so to speak, the common good, and hence, the source of everyone else's perfection. Only in this ideal case is the good of the individual commensurable with the common good. It matters little whether such a perfect being ever existed or can exist since the purpose of Aristotle's observation is merely to bring to light the problem inherent in any form of political rule. On Thomas's understanding of the common good, see Ch. De Koninck, *De la primauté du bien commun contre les personnalistes* (Quebec and Montreal: Editions de l'université Laval and Fides, 1943), 7-79. De Koninck's essay was widely interpreted at the time as a silent attack on Maritain and was so interpreted by Maritain himself

in his restatement of the problem, *The Person and the Common Good*, 16, n. 6. See also I. Th. Eschmann, "In Defense of Jacques Maritain," *Modern Schoolman*, 22 (1945): 183-208; Ch. De Koninck, "In Defense of Saint Thomas: A Reply to Father Eschmann's Attack on the Primacy of the Common Good," *Laval théologique et philosophique*, 1 (1945): 9-109; Y. Simon, "On the Common Good," *Review of Politics*, 6 (1944): 530-33. Simon, who professes to be in general agreement with De Koninck's views, denies that they were directed against Maritain, with whom he also agrees.

46. Suarez, *De legibus*, I.2.5. Grotius, *De iure belli et pacis*, I.1.4. The transition to the new understanding of "right" (*ius*) as a "faculty" (*facultas*) appears to have been facilitated to some extent by the frequent appearance of the word *ius* in the Vulgate. Suarez, *De legibus* refers to Genesis 23:4, where Abraham is shown negotiating with the Hittites for the purchase of a grave in which to bury Sarah. The text reads: "Give me property among you for a burying place (ᵃhuzza*t*que*b*er; Septuagint: *ktêsin taphou*) that I may bury my dead out of my sight." The Latin version, *da mihi ius sepeliendi*, could easily suggest that Abraham was demanding, not a plot of land (the first to be acquired by a member of the chosen race in Canaan), but the right to bury his dead. Suarez takes *ius sepeliendi* to mean *facultas sepeliendi*. Cf. also Genesis 31:19-21: Jacob, who has finally outwitted Laban, flees "with all that he had," which in the Latin text is rendered by "everything to which he had a right": *omnia quae iuris sui erant*. For an account of the historical evolution of the notion of right as a faculty, Cf. R. Tuck, *Natural Rights Theories; Their Origin and Development* (Cambridge and New York: Cambridge University Press, 1979).

47. E.g., *De cive* I.1.2: "The greatest part of those men who have written aught concerning commonwealths, either suppose, or require us, or beg of us to believe that man is a creature born fit for society. The Greeks call him *zôon politikon*; and on this foundation they so build up the doctrine of civil society as if for the preservation of peace and the government of mankind there were nothing else necessary than that men should agree to make certain covenants and conditions together, which themselves should then call laws. Which axiom, though received by most, is yet certainly false and an error proceeding from our too slight contemplation of human nature."

48. Finnis, 59-80.

49. Finnis, 93.

50. Finnis, 92.

51. Finnis, 94.

52. Finnis, 19-20; 224-26.

53. Finnis, 164, 213.

54. Finnis, 225.

55. Finnis, 129-30.

56. Finnis, 280.

57. Finnis, 341, n. 42, with references to *Summa theologiae* I-II, qu. 100, a. 1 and II-II, qu. 58, a. 3, ad 2m.

58. Cf. *Summa theologiae* I-II, qu. 17, a. 1.

59. Finnis, 374.
60. Finnis, 281.
61. Finnis, 339.
62. Gregory of Rimini, *In Librum Secundum Sententiarum*, dist. 34, qu. 1, art. 2; Gabriel Biel, *In Lib.Secundum Sent.*, dist. 35, qu. 1, art. 1, and the other references cited by Suarez, *De legibus*, II.6.3m.
63. *Summa theologiae* I.II, qu. 17, a. 1: "Primum autem movens in viribus animae ad exercitum actus est voluntas . . . Cum ergo secundum movens non moveat nisi in virtute primi moventis, sequitur quod hoc ipsum quod ratio moveat imperando sit ei ex virtute voluntatis." Cf. I-II, qu. 90, a. 1, ad 3m.
64. *Summa theologiae* I-II, qu. 17, a. 1.
65. *Summa theologiae* I.II, qu. 91, a. 2, ad 2m. As regards irrational creatures, the natural law is said to be a law only *per similitudinem*, i.e., by analogy or by reason of a certain resemblance with the manner in which it applies to human beings. See also I-II, qu. 93, a. 5, c. and ad 1m.
66. I-II, qu. 96, a. 5: "Lex de sui ratione duo habet: primo quidem quod est regula humanorum actuum; secundo, quod habet vim coactivam." Cf. I-II, qu. 90, a. 3, ad 2m.
67. Thomas Aquinas, *Summa theologiae* I-II, qu. 90.
68. *Summa theologiae* I-II, qu 92.
69. Cf. I-II, qu. 18, a. 5, ad 3m; qu. 92, a. 2; qu. 93, a. 6, ad 2m; qu. 100, a. 9. The principles of the natural law are generally referred to as "precepts," e.g., I-II, qu. 94, a. 1, 2, and 6. But precepts, as distinguished from simple rules or principles, are binding under pain of sanction. Cf. I-II, qu. 99, a. 5: "Quaedam moralium praecipiuntur uel prohibentur in lege, sicut Non occides, Non furtum facies. Et haec proprie dicuntur praecepta." I-II, qu. 100, a. 9: "Praeceptum legis habet vim coactivam. Illud ergo directe, cadit sub praecepto legis ad quod lex cogit. Coactio autem legis est per modum poenae." Finnis notes perceptively that for Plato "obligatum . . . is not the framework or final authoritative category of 'moral' thought" (409). But Plato was not a natural law thinker. He spoke only of natural "right," which is not quite the same thing, however frequently the two expressions may be confused, as they are, for example, in the article by J. P. Maguire, "Plato's Theory of Natural Law," *Yale Classical Studies*, 10 (1947): cited on 413.
70. *Contra Gentiles* III.1413.
71. For a more complete treatment see "Augustine, Thomas Aquinas, and the Problem of Natural Law," in chapter 10 of this volume.
72. *Summa theologiae* I-II, qu. 100, a. 1: "Quaedam enim (praecepta moralia) sunt quae statim per se ratio naturalis cuiuslibet hominis diiudicat esse facienda vel non facienda, sicut Honora patrem tuum et matrem tuam, et Non occides, Non furtum facies. Et huiusmodi sunt absolute de lege naturae."
73. *Summa theologiae* I-II, qu. 100, a. 1; qu. 104, a. 1, ad 3m: "Ad tertium dicendum quod etiam in his quae ordinant ad Deum quaedam sunt moralia quae *ratio fide informata* dictat, sicut Deum esse amandum et colendum."

74. *Summa theologiae* I-II, qu. 71, a. 6, ad 5m: "A theologis consideratur peccatum praecipue secundum quod est offensa contra Deum; a philosopho autem morali, secundum quod contrariatur rationi."

75. Suarez, *De legibus*, I.15.13: "Nam lex, imponendo necessitatem virtutis seu honestatis, consequenter facit ut transgressor legis sit dignus poena saltem apud Deum, quia suam obligationem lege impositam non observat. Quod locum habet tam in lege naturali quam in positiva, divina, vel humana, quia supposita lege actus est inordinatus, et illa dignitas poenae intrinsece sequitur ex malitia actus, etiamsi malitia fortasse fuerit ex occasione legis positivae. Est tamen diferentia in hoc inter legem naturalem et positivam, quod lex naturalis, licet faciat vel ostendat actum esse malum, tamen ut est mere naturalis non taxat modum vel quantitatem poenae. Nulla enim ratione intelligi potest hoc fieri sine decreto alicuius liberae voluntatis." Cf. *Summa theologiae* I-II, qu. 95, a. 2: "Lex naturae habet quod ille qui peccat puniatur; sed quod tali poena puniatur, hoc est quaedam determinatio legis naturae."

76. Thomas's muted reservations about the complete naturalness of the natural law come out in other ways as well. One of them is hinted at in his treatment of suicide, which is said to be contrary to the natural law and which is "always" a grievous sin. By taking his own life, the suicide commits an injustice toward the city and he commits an injustice toward God, in whose image he was created; cf. I-II, qu. 59, a. 3, ad 2m; qu. 64, a. 5. That such an act should be unjust from the point of view of the city is obvious enough, since the city is thereby robbed of the services of one of its members. That it should likewise be unjust from God's point of view is obvious only to someone who accepts the biblical teaching regarding man's creation in the image of God. The more delicate problem, however, is that the city is not necessarily hurt and might even be helped by the loss of an unproductive member, especially if it should be stricken with famine and unable to support its population. What reason sanctions in such unusual circumstances could conceivably differ from what divine revelation imposes as a universal duty. Suicide is also ruled out on religious grounds by Cebes and Simmias in the *Phaedo*, 61a-62a. Socrates does not object to the argument, although it is not completely clear whether it reflects his own thinking on the matter. Much depends on what one makes of the ensuing discussion, in which Socrates defends his resolve to die as both "wise" and "just," i.e., as something good for himself as well as for his friends.

77. The origin of the natural law doctrine is unfortunately shrouded in mystery. Scholars have generally traced it back to the Stoics, but H. Koester has shown that the expression itself does not occur in any of the surviving fragments from the early Stoa. It is attributed to Zeno of Cittium by Cicero in one and only one text whose authenticity is not corroborated by independent evidence; *De natura Deorum* I.14.36: "Zeno . . . naturalem legem divinam esse censet, eamque vim obtinere recta imperantem prohibentemque contraria." The term reappears a hundred years later in Philo, who does not seem to have been influenced by Cicero. Cf., H. Koester, "*NOMOS PHUSEÔS*: The Concept of Natural Law in Greek Thought," in *Religions in Antiquity: Essays in Honor of E. R. Goodenough*, edited by J. Neusner (Leiden: E.

J. Brill, 1968), 521-41. The close textual parallels between Philo and Cicero nevertheless point to a common source which, according to one hypothesis, could be Antiochus of Ascalon; cf., R. A. Horsley, "The Law of Nature in Philo and Cicero," *Harvard Theological Review*, 71 (1978): 35-59.

78. On the general unpleasantness of the non-virtuous life, cf., Aristotle *Politics* VII.1.1323a27-34: "No one would maintain that he is happy who has not in him a particle of courage or temperance or justice or prudence, who is afraid of every insect that flutters past him, and will commit any crime, however great, in order to gratify his lust for meat or drink, who will sacrifice his dearest friend for the sake of a farthing, and is as feeble and false in mind as a child or a madman."

79. Nietzsche, *Beyond Good and Evil*, aphorisms 39 and 197. Thomas, who was not unaware of the problem, notes that the wicked are sometimes punished by being granted the prosperity that incites them to evil; *Contra Gentiles* III.141.6.

80. Finnis, V.

III

LEO STRAUSS AND THE REVIVAL OF
CLASSICAL POLITICAL PHILOSOPHY

RATIONAL THEOLOGIANS AND IRRATIONAL PHILOSOPHERS: A STRAUSSIAN PERSPECTIVE

The coolness with which Leo Strauss's pioneering work has thus far been received in specifically Christian circles is attributable in part to the disarray that afflicts present-day theology but it also has much to do with the cultivated ambiguity of Strauss's stance and posture in regard to revealed religion. Theologians, who are not the least spirited of people, thrive on opposition but generally require a target at which they can take aim. Like politicians, they tend to be more at ease even with enemies (they have had more than their share of them over the centuries) than they are with people of whom they cannot tell for sure whether they are friends or enemies. The matter is further complicated by the absence of any thematic treatment of Christianity anywhere in Strauss's writings or of any extended commentary by Strauss on the works of an unmistakably Christian author. One must presume that Strauss's demonstrated awareness of the most compelling arguments against the truth of divine revelation encompasses Christianity as well, but the observation is hardly conclusive, since, as Strauss himself admits, the same awareness is already present in the

Christian tradition and since, in his particular case, it goes hand in hand with an explicit recognition of the inherent limitations or logical pitfalls of any systematic critique of biblical religion.

In principle, one might have expected the more conservative wing of mainline Christian theology, represented preeminently by Roman Catholicism, to be sympathetic to Strauss's attack on modernity and his attempted recovery of classical philosophy, with which for a long time its own destiny appeared to be linked. Yet this has proved not to be the case. Even the genuine, if somewhat distant, respect with which Thomas Aquinas is treated in the central section of *Natural Right and History* as well as in other places was not enough to stir more than a passing interest on the part of Catholic scholars. For one thing, that respect is accompanied by a number of strictures regarding the efforts of a few unnamed but prominent and easily identifiable Thomists about whom the least that Strauss seemed willing to say was that the right hand did not know what the left hand was doing. Secondly, the accolade, if that is the right word, came too late to be of much help to those who stood to benefit by it. It occurred at a time when, in a frantic and perhaps misguided attempt to cut their losses, Roman Catholic theologians had already begun to forsake their Thomistic legacy in favor of a variety of newer though not necessarily better approaches to the problems of ethics and politics and, indeed, of theology *tout court*. Here as elsewhere, the main thrust of the Straussian enterprise ran afoul of some of the most powerful prejudices of the age. It undermined the currently fashionable theology by bringing to light both its inner contradictions and its lack of continuity with the tradition to which its practitioners were supposedly dedicated. It is symptomatic of the prevailing climate of opinion that at the time of its appearance, John Finnis's recent book, *Natural Law and Natural Rights*,[1] should have been acclaimed by some people, and not the most hostile ones at that, as the long-awaited Catholic response to Strauss's *Natural Right and History*.[2]

Truth to tell, few Christian theologians are well-acquainted with Strauss's work and fewer still have engaged in a close study of the classics of the Western tradition of the kind that could lead to more than a superficial understanding of it. As a result of his having indirectly laid the groundwork for a fresh insight into their own heritage, Strauss could still turn out to be of considerable assistance to them. If that should ever happen, however, it is more likely to be by the roundabout way of an unpopular critique of the whole of the contemporary theological scene. My purpose is not to outline such a critique or indicate how it might proceed if it were to be undertaken, but merely to set forth a few of the reasons that seem to justify it. This may be accomplished by looking first of all at the unique position that Christianity occupies vis-à-vis the two other great religions of the western world, Islam and Judaism.

The simplest, most obvious, and hence most natural point of departure for any understanding of the specific character of Christianity appears to be the one indicated in the opening pages of *Persecution and the Art of Writing*.[3] Whereas in both Islam and Judaism, Revelation takes the form of a law or of a comprehensive social order regulating virtually every aspect of human life and thought, in Christianity it first comes to sight as a faith or a set of teachings ("dogmas," as they were later called) which do not of themselves call for or encourage the formation of any kind of political community. Anyone who takes the trouble to read the New Testament attentively from this point of view cannot help being struck by its all but total indifference to problems of a properly political nature. It will soon be discovered that it shows no awareness of the distinction between regimes, does not indicate any preference for one over the others, imposes none of its own, and makes no concrete recommendations for the reform of the social order. It was meant to be preached to all nations but was not destined to replace them or meant to compete with them on their own level. It simply takes for granted that Christians will continue to organize their temporal lives within the framework of the society to which they happen to belong and, while it strenuously opposes all forms of injustice, it leaves the administration of public affairs to the authorities whom God has ordained for this purpose. Its dominant theme is not justice but love, and love as a political principle is at best a pretty fuzzy thing. Accordingly, it does not tell us *who* should rule, but in general *how* human beings, be they rulers or subjects, ought to behave toward one another, which is a different matter altogether.

Even as regards this question, its answers are not always as specific as one might like them to be. The commandments that it issues are not universal laws of nature, possessed of an intrinsic intelligibility that would give us an inkling as to how they could be applied to particular cases; they are expressions of the will of a personal and loving God who expects, nay, demands the same kind of response from his creatures. Moreover, the situations that they envisage are typically one-on-one situations from which there are few definite conclusions to be drawn regarding the behavior that is appropriate when the welfare of the larger community is at stake. "Love your enemy" and "Turn the other cheek" may be valid maxims for the person who prefers forgiveness to revenge and would rather give up his life than take someone else's, but they are less readily applicable to multilateral situations involving the safety and well-being of a third party for whom one is responsible and whom one also has the duty to love. To put it bluntly, the God of the New Testament is not a very political animal. His own agenda is strictly transpolitical or, to use a religious term, eschatological. It follows that any attempt to derive a coherent political program from the pages of the New Testament alone is bound to end in futility or madness.

This is not to deny that Christianity was fraught from the outset with grave practical consequences. What its defenders perceived as its greatest asset was from the standpoint of a political observer its most patent liability. By calling human beings to a higher destiny and reserving the best part of their existence for the service of God, it effectively destroyed the regime as a total way of life. It cultivated a passion for an elusive kingdom of God beyond history and thus tended to turn people's minds away from the only realities that reason is capable of knowing by itself. In the process, civil society was displaced as the locus of virtue and the sole horizon lending meaning and substance to the activities of its citizens. The love of one's own was no longer confined within specific borders and citizenship itself lost its fundamental significance. Even the greatest human achievements were robbed of their former splendor.

Such are the real roots of the opposition that Christianity encountered when it first began to spread throughout the Roman Empire, and it is to this problem that its first apologists were eventually compelled to address themselves. The new religion would have gone the way of the radical sects of late antiquity had it not succeeded in demonstrating its adaptability to the needs of civil society. For the practical guidance that the gospel failed to provide, one could follow the example of some early Christians and turn to the Hebrew Scriptures; but these were hardly suited to the task since, as Augustine pointed out, they were the source of the very difficulty to which Christianity was offered as a solution. The only viable alternative, and the one that finally prevailed, was to introduce political philosophy into the Christian scheme. The feat was a remarkable one, and all the more so as the new partner in the proposed alliance had to mend her ways before the marriage could be consummated. Like the captive woman of Deuteronomy 21:10-14, to whom she was often compared, she was forced to get rid of some of her most precious adornments, in return for which she was granted a new lease on life and even allowed to prosper, albeit under more or less constant ecclesiastical surveillance. As long as she remained content with her lot and did not aspire to a higher status, her survival was insured.

For those who objected to the treatment and refused to acquiesce in it, an escape hatch was available. They could go underground, living as non-Christians in a Christian world and complying in deed, if not in thought, with what was required of everyone else. The predicament was not wholly unfamiliar to them. It had always been more or less that of the philosopher in the city and was rendered only slightly more precarious by the existence of a reasonably well-defined religious orthodoxy and of an established authority capable of enforcing it. Besides, it had its advantages; it kept alive the notion of an ideal that transcends the limits of the political life and allowed for the preservation of the books through which the nature of that ideal could be explored. If, in Strauss's eyes, even a Lessing could pass for an "orthodox Christian," the situation was not all bad. To a philosopher, the new religious society still had the appearance of a cave, but a cave that was unique in that it was characterized by the officially sanctioned presence within it of that by means of which it could be illumined for the benefit of those who were capable and desirous of such illumination. For the basic philosophic distinction between nature and convention another distinction, which only partially parallels it, was substituted, namely, the distinction between the natural and the supernatural or between what human reason at its best is capable of discovering on its own and what it could conceivably learn only from some divine source. How the two might be related is itself a thorny question a fuller discussion of which would take us much farther afield than is necessary for present purposes.

Reasonable as this novel solution may have been insofar as it did its best to respect the legitimate demands of both faith and reason, it was not good enough to satisfy the philosophers of the Enlightenment, who proceeded to mount an all-out attack on it in the name of modern science. The long-term result was not in every respect the one that had been anticipated. Instead of destroying positive religion, the attack actually paved the way for its resurgence as a spiritual force in the West during the early decades of the nineteenth century. Christianity, which throughout the preceding century had been blamed for the evils of contemporary society, was suddenly hailed as the source of all that was supposed to be good in it, science and freedom included. The modern world was indebted to it for everything—*le monde moderne lui doit tout*—as Chateaubriand proudly announced in the introduction to the first part of the *Genius of Christianity*,[4] one of the most popular books of the century and the fountainhead of so many of the ideas later to be expounded with all sorts of new twists by Tocqueville, Nietzsche, and countless others who came to the conclusion that the origins of modern political and scientific thought were to be sought in the ancient or the medieval Christian tradition. (I shall say nothing about Hegel, who restated the problem with a philosophical depth to which Chateaubriand could not and did not aspire.) Far from opposing Christianity and modernity, it became fashionable to proclaim their fundamental agreement and stress the links that bound them one to the other.

The fly in the ointment is that, quite apart from the question of its historical accuracy, the new argument was a pure and simple inversion of the old one. It pulled the bag inside out, so to speak, but did nothing to alter the terms in which the problem was posed. With rare exceptions, its leading advocates were mostly unaware of the extent to which they shared the perspective of their erstwhile adversaries. They, too, had come to look upon Christianity as a political or cultural phenomenon and could think of no better way to serve it than by defending it on those grounds. In retrospect, their account of it is barely more than a mirror image of the one they rejected. At no point does one sense that a real breakthrough had been achieved and that the issue had been raised to the level on which it could be profitably joined, if not completely resolved.

The argument had the added drawback of disqualifying in advance any attempt to probe more deeply into the problem. Part of it consisted in saying that the divinely revealed character of the Christian faith had never been questioned, let alone rejected, by the greatest thinkers of the past, as was evident from all that they had written in praise of it. The idea that they might have been "secretly incredulous" (Chateaubriand's expression) and had refrained from any frontal attack on it as a matter of necessity rather than of choice was dismissed as a contrivance of its latter-day opponents, a gigantic fraud perpetrated by the enemies of religion for the express purpose of casting further discredit upon it. It is no mere coincidence that the best case against the existence and even the possibility of an esoteric tradition extending as far back as antiquity should be the one put forward by Schleiermacher, the most famous name in early nineteenth-century Christian theology.[5]

Needless to say, the Christianity whose victory was thus secured did not emerge unscathed from the battle. It was all too often a transmogrified and secularized Christianity, seemingly bent on making its peace with the modern world on the latter's terms and acceptable to its now weary critics because what it had to offer was not noticeably different from what they had been demanding all along. Lessing, who anticipated the new trend and was one of the first to denounce it, saw more clearly than anyone else at the time what its eventual outcome was likely to be. He left little doubt as to where his own preferences lay and was as fearful of the growing irrationalism of modern philosophy as he was of the new-found rationalism of Christian theology. As he puts it in a letter to his brother:

> With orthodoxy, thank God, things were fairly well settled. A curtain had been drawn between it and philosophy, behind which each could go his own way without disturbing the other. But what is happening now? They are tearing down this curtain, and under the pretext of making us rational Christians, they are making us very irrational philosophers. I beg of you, my dear brother, inquire more carefully after this point and look less at what our new theologians discard than at what they want to put in its place. We are agreed that the old religious system is false, but I cannot share your conviction that it is a patchwork of bunglers and half philosophers. I know of nothing in the world in which human sagacity has been better displayed

and cultivated. The real patchwork of bunglers and half philosophers is the religious system which they now want to set in place of the old, and with far more influence on reason and philosophy than the old ever presumed. My neighbor's house threatens to collapse upon him. If my neighbor wants to raze it, I shall sincerely help him. However, he does not want to raze it, but rather to support and underpin it in such a way that my house will be completely ruined. He must desist from his project or I shall concern myself with his collapsing house as if it were my own.[6]

The diagnosis was amazingly perspicacious. Its accuracy is amply vouched for by all of the efforts that were subsequently made to break the old deadlock between faith and reason by relegating them to parallel but separate spheres of human existence or by collapsing them one into the other at the risk of obliterating the distinction between them altogether; so much so that, by the end of the nineteenth century, Nietzsche could dismiss all theologians as philosophic babblers and all philosophers as crypto-theologians or "Schleiermachers," that is to say, spinners of veils.

Later attempts to redress the balance, such as the one that goes under the name of Neo-orthodoxy, have only partially succeeded in rescuing Christian theology from the bondage of its new masters. Strauss's incidental remark to the effect that Neo-orthodoxy is not the same thing as Orthodoxy, for otherwise the "Neo" would be superfluous, is very much to the point. It is significant that two of the most influential theological works of our century should be entitled, one *Church Dogmatics*[7] (by Karl Barth), and the other, *Systematic Theology*[8] (by Paul Tillich). If the Cartesian and Leibnizian antecedents of the terms "dogmatic" and "systematic" suggest anything, it is that the break with the modern tradition was not nearly as clean as it claimed to be.

Although vastly different from liberal Protestantism both in its inspiration and its essential features, the Roman Catholic theology of the same period likewise failed to come up with a solution that could command universal respect. It responded to the challenge of modernity, not by settling its accounts with it, but by ignoring it in favor of a return to medieval thought in its pristine or premodern integrity. From its obscure beginnings around 1810, the movement grew to sizable proportions and gradually took the shape of a massive counteroffensive against the encroachments of modern thought. Part of the difficulty is that it inherited from its romantic past a touch of archaism of which it was never able to divest itself. Its impact, confined by and large to the Roman Catholic world, was only rarely felt by anyone outside of it. Nor did it produce any thinkers of the very first rank.

Worse still, it never fully came to grips with the single most important obstacle to any comprehensive reinstatement of premodern thought, to wit, the triumph of modern natural science. Its promoters opted instead for what Strauss describes as "a fundamental, typically modern dualism of a nonteleological natural science and a teleological science of man."[9] In this crucial respect, they were at one with their liberal Protestant counterparts, with whom, interestingly enough, they have since been drawn into ever closer partnership. Strauss's final verdict is that, their differences to the contrary notwithstanding, both groups are really "in the same boat." Their leaders and chief spokesmen "all are modern men"[10] This, more than anything else, is what lies at the root of the indifference, the skepticism, or the hostility that so often characterizes their reaction to Strauss. Their most common objection to the Straussian project is that it pays too little attention to modern science and thus fails to lay an adequate metaphysical foundation for itself. In short, Strauss's position is neither dogmatic enough nor skeptical enough to please anybody today. To anyone who has never seriously questioned the primacy of epistemology or the modern commitment to the ideal of "scientific" certitude, the objection appears to be unanswerable. One can try to answer it, as Strauss does, by pointing to its contingent source in early modern thought, but only at the risk of arousing the antagonism of one's critics. As the introduction to *Natural Right and History* reminds us with the help of a quotation from Lord Acton, "Few discoveries are more irritating than those which expose the pedigree of ideas."[11]

The deeper question, which is hardly ever addressed any more, is whether a more consistent return to the basic principles of premodern thought would be in the best interest of theology itself. What recommends the modern scientific view to a large number of theologians is that, to the extent to which it prescinds methodologically from any consideration of first principles, it leaves the domain of religion intact and, hence, poses no great threat to its supremacy. Its danger, on the other hand, is that by depriving theology of the services of its traditional handmaiden it either empties it of its intellectual content or opens it up to the influence of a host of other ideas whose compatibility with the teachings of the gospel has yet to be demonstrated.

Few people would go so far as to say that classical philosophy is the natural ally of revealed religion or deny that the decision to introduce it into the fold involved a certain risk. The Church Fathers called it a "noble risk," *kalos kindunos*, borrowing the phrase from Plato. Some of them, like Tertullian, balked at it. The shrewder ones thought it was worth taking, if for no other reason than that it could eventually lead to a better grasp of the Christian faith and of all that a wholehearted commitment to it entails. After all, it was generally admitted that philosophy could never be so sure of itself as to rule out the possibility of Revelation. As an unfinished and unfinishable quest for knowledge, it was in the position of having constantly to re-examine its own presuppositions. If no funda-mental problem can be settled once for all, it could well be that the highest achievement of human reason is to prove, not indeed that divine revelation is possible—to do that would be to disprove its strictly supernatural character by bringing it, if only to that limited extent, within the compass of reason—but that the arguments adduced against it are not sufficient to establish its impossibility. The matter finally comes down to a choice between a truth that is for the good of the intellect alone and a salutary or beatifying truth that represents the good of the whole person. Since, by definition, the issue between them cannot be decided on the level of philosophic reason alone, and since there is no higher principle on the basis of which a synthesis between the two positions might be effected, we are left with a fundamental tension at the heart of the so-called "Great Tradition," a tension which Strauss did not lament but which he thought could be fruitful as long as one knew how to live it.

By showing that modern science has not replaced God and that His-tory has not replaced philosophy, or by showing as no one has done in four hundred years that the claims of Reason and Revelation are inherently untouched by modernity, Strauss may have performed as great a service for theology as he has for philosophy. Living as they do in an age of unbelief, that is to say, in an age in which conviction is grounded neither in reason nor in authoritative tradition, Christian theologians may yet discover that they have as much to learn from him as they do from one another or from any of their new allies about the way in which they could regain some of their lost credibility.

NOTES

1. John Finnis, *Natural Law and Natural Rights* (Oxford and New York: Clarendon Press, and Oxford: Oxford University Press, 1980).

2. Leo Strauss, *Natural Right and History*, (Chicago: University of Chicago Press, 1953).

3. Leo Strauss, *Persecution and the Art of Writing* (Glencoe: The Free Press, 1952), 8-10.

4. Chateaubriand, *Genius of Christianity* (Baltimore, MD and New York: J. Murphy Company, n.d.).

5. F. Schleiermacher, *Platons Werke*, 3rd edition (Berlin: G. Reimer, 1855), vol. 1, 15.

6. Letter to Karl, Feb. 2, 1774. Lessing, *Gesammelte Werke*, IX, edited by Paul Killa (Berlin, 1956), 596-97. English translation in H. E. Allison, *Lessing and the Enlightenment* (Ann Arbor: University of Michigan Press, 1966), 84; H. Chadwick, *Lessing's Theological Writings* (Stanford: Stanford University Press, 1957), 13.

7. Karl Barth, *Church Dogmatics a Selection* (New York: Harper and Row, 1962).

8. Paul Tillich, *Systematic Theology*, 3 volumes (Chicago: University of Chicago Press, 1951-63).

9. *Natural Right and History*, 8.

10. Ibid., 7.

11. Ibid., 7.

15

FAITH AND REASON IN CONTEMPORARY PERSPECTIVE: APROPOS OF A RECENT BOOK

After centuries of heated and often futile debate, any attempt to reopen the question of faith and reason is bound to strike the modern reader as a quaint anachronism, or at best a daring challenge. For these ancient terms, once used as convenient labels to designate the two types of knowledge whose problematic relationship, it has been said, constitutes the highest theme of Western thought, our contemporaries have substituted "religion" and "experience," both of which are supposedly less controversial and more readily accessible to us. No one is likely to quarrel with the word "experience," which has a certain *prima facie* evidence that "reason" can no longer claim, and we have all learned from William James and others that there are "varieties" of religious experience, with which it is possible to become acquainted even if we have no firsthand knowledge of them ourselves.[1] Indeed, a remarkable degree of openness has come to prevail regarding these matters. Experiences can be described but require no justification. It suffices that they be "authentic." Everyone is entitled to his own without having to account for them or answer any questions about them. Since their objects are presumed to lie beyond the pale of rational discourse, all such questions are to be judged irrelevant or at the very least unanswerable.

The trouble is that it is not always easy to tell an authentic experience from one that is not. There is no mistaking the pain that I feel when I have a toothache, and, having had a number of them in the past, I know roughly what others go through when they are similarly afflicted. If, however, the content of the experience is not an object of sense perception, if it has to do with issues as subtle and elusive as those associated with religious belief, a greater measure of caution may be in order. Seemingly profound experiences often prove to be nothing more than fits of enthusiasm, passing fancies, delusions, or momentary infatuations. Others obviously have deeper roots, but even they are not wholly unambiguous insofar as they are apt to be mediated if not actually induced by the larger context of opinion to which they belong. For all practical purposes the world is what we see in it, and what we see in it is, with rare exceptions, what we have been taught to see in it. Our thoughts and feelings are rarely ours alone. They tend to be those of our time or of our society and are generally shared by other members of that society. They thus assume a public character to which they owe both their plausibility and their authority. The Hindu who is persuaded that cows are sacred is not indulging in a private fantasy or expressing a purely personal view. His "knowledge" is noticeably different from that of the party-goer who has had too much to drink and swears that the cow in his backyard has wings. Still, it is not the kind of knowledge that someone brought up in a different tradition would take for granted. This simple observation is enough to remind us that we are confronted with a multiplicity of such traditions, religious or otherwise, and that they often differ widely from one another. Hence the modern habit of speaking of "religions" in the plural rather than of "religion" in the singular, as was the custom prior to the sixteenth century. It follows that, once the normative character of these religions has been called into question, any effort to evaluate them will have to include some reference to criteria that are not indigenous to any one of them.

The great theologians of the past were not wholly unaware of the problem and that is why they preferred a more objective approach to it than the one to which we have lately become accustomed. They knew that what went under the name of "faith" was ultimately grounded in an experience of some sort, whether it be that of the prophet to whom God had spoken or of the recipient of his message, but they denied that it was a simple matter of subjective experience and insisted that the formulation of its content be submitted to the external control of reason. The assumption was that, although the divinely revealed truth exceeded the mind's natural capacity, it did not run counter to it and was not totally impervious to it. Since the God who reveals himself in the Scriptures was also the author of nature, and since he cannot contradict himself, no real antagonism between the dogmas of the faith and the independent findings of reason could be anticipated.[2] Christianity was in principle and could become in fact a universal religion.[3] It was not the preserve of any particular nation or group of people and its teachings contained nothing incongruent or demonstrably false. The assent that they commanded was a reasonable one—*rationabile obsequium*.[4] It was an assent of which all human beings were theoretically capable. There was nothing to fear from a philosophic investigation of its roots and no danger of its being damaged by it as long as the investigator was competent. If anything, the opposite was true. Philosophy could be employed, not indeed as a principle allowing one to pass judgment on the truth or falsity of Revelation, but as a tool with which to probe its meaning and counter any attack that might be leveled against it in the name of reason.

It is quite possible, however, that in its eagerness to emphasize the reasonableness of the Christian faith, medieval theology downplayed its experiential or existential component, just as, in its eagerness to react against this tendency, modern theology is prone to overlook its rational component. The singular merit of Robert Sokolowski's book, *The God of Faith and Reason: The Foundations of Christian Theology*,[5] is that it looks for a happy balance between these two approaches and that it does so, not merely by restating the problem as it posed itself in the Middle Ages, but by using the contributions of modern phenomenology to arrive at a more adequate articulation of it. As its subtitle suggests, Sokolowski's essay is an exercise in what is now called "fundamental theology." Its immediate aim is not so much to defend the compatibility of the life of faith with that of reason as to lay bare the theoretical presuppositions that enable one to make sense of the dogmas and practices of Christianity. Such a theology is said to proceed by way of clarification rather than by way of inference from premises to conclusions. It seeks above all to elaborate the horizon or "open up the logical space" within which the "meaning" of these teachings can be unfolded for the benefit of believers and interested nonbelievers alike.[6] Accordingly, it is most aptly described as a "theology of disclosure" or a "theology of manifestation," as distinguished from, though not necessarily in opposition to, a "theology of things," Sokolowski's term for the theology of the Middle Ages. Its thesis is that there is imbedded in the structures of the Christian faith a coherent pattern of thought that becomes fully manifest only when we reflect thematically on the peculiar understanding of God that underlies it and contrast it with the one that pervades the whole of pagan philosophic and religious thought. According to Sokolowski, this novel understanding is best formulated in terms of the fundamental distinction between God and the world, a distinction that has no exact equivalent outside of Christian theology. Neither in Greek philosophic thought nor in any religious tradition other than Christianity is God conceived as a being that is not in any way affected by the existence or nonexistence of the world. God is not himself a part of the world, and, even though he is responsible both for its coming into being and its continued existence, he gains nothing from its presence, just as he would lose nothing from its absence. Take God away and nothing is left of the world, but the converse does not obtain, for even if there were no world, God would still be "all that he is in undiminished goodness and greatness."[7] In him and in him alone, essence and existence coincide. When he creates, "there may be 'more' but there is no 'greater' or 'better.'"[8] This insight, as we learn from the first chapter of the book, is already implicit in Anselm's celebrated formula according to which God is the being than whom none greater can be conceived. The distinction between God and the world is unlike any of the other distinctions with which we are familiar from common experience. In all of these the two terms of the distinction imply each other and have no meaning one without the other.[9] Without a son or a daughter, there is no father or mother and vice versa. The present case is different in that the relationship of dependence between God and the world works in one direction only.[10] God is no more perfect for having created the world and would not be any less perfect for not having created it. Such a view constitutes a radical departure from all of pagan or pre-Christian thought, for which God is merely the most perfect being in the universe. "In Greek and Roman religion, and in Greek and Roman philosophies, god or the gods are appreciated as the most powerful, most independent and self-sufficient, most unchanging beings in the world, but they are accepted within the context of being." Hence "the possibility that they could be even though everything that is not divine were not, is not a possibility that occurs to anyone."[11] This is true of the Olympian gods, but it is also true of the god of Aristotelian metaphysics, for "no matter how Aristotle's god is to be described, as the prime mover or the self-thinking thought, he is part of the world, and it is obviously necessary that there be other beings besides him, whether he is aware of them or not."[12] Within this framework, the whole of nature is looked upon as a rational necessity and is treated as such. The thought that the world might never have existed simply does not arise. The same view is equally characteristic of the later Platonic tradition, despite its emphasis on the transcendence of the divine principle of all things, for even here the transsubstantial One or the Good is still "taken as 'part' of what is: it is the One by being one over, for, and in many, never by being One only alone by itself."[13]

As the rest of the book so well shows, the basic distinction to which attention has just been drawn undergirds the entire structure of Christian life and thought. It is indispensable to a proper understanding of the Trinity, the Incarnation, divine grace, and the role of the sacraments in human life, and it governs the manner in which Christians read the

Scriptures, experience the world around them, and relate to one another and to the divinity. This is not to say that once the importance of that distinction is fully appreciated, the Christian "mysteries" cease to be mysteries but only that one then begins to see more clearly wherein their mysterious character lies.[14] Such an approach has the great advantage of preserving the integrity of the faith as well as that of the natural order.[15] Contrary to what one so often finds among contemporary religious thinkers, there is no question of reducing Christian theology to a complex system of symbols designed to convey a purely human meaning. On this score, Sokolowski can also claim to be on more solid ground than either Rahner[16] or Lonergan,[17] whose "transcendental Thomism" arrives at God through an analysis of human thought and its alleged demand for complete or unrestricted knowledge. Unlike Sokolowski, Rahner and Lonergan take the createdness of the world for granted, for only on that assumption can it be regarded as transparent to God and hence "completely intelligible." As a consequence, neither of them sees the need to contrast the Christian and pagan senses of the whole. Their transcendental method thus fails to give "due recognition" to the pagan state of mind. It refuses to accept it as a real possibility and works entirely within a perspective that is biblical or Christian from the outset.[18] Without explicitly saying so, Sokolowski seems to detect in their approach a latent tendency to blur or deemphasize the distinction between the natural and the supernatural orders.[19] His own method of dealing with this issue likewise differs markedly from that of Karl Barth, who goes to the opposite extreme and repudiates metaphysics altogether but makes us pay for the "religious clarity" that this repudiation generates by leaving us in "philosophical darkness."[20]

One further point to be stressed is that the distinction between God and the world occupies a unique position within Christian theology itself. Since that distinction is not entirely beyond the scope of reason, it does not strictly speaking belong to the realm of faith, but since it has not, in fact, been discovered without the aid of divine Revelation, one hesitates to describe it as purely philosophical. Therein lies its advantage. Because it stands at the intersection of the two domains, it can serve as a bridge between them.[21] Nonbelievers will have fewer difficulties with it than they do with the dogmas of the faith, and, having accepted it or at least been made to see that it is not manifestly contrary to reason, they will be less reluctant to concede that the Christian mysteries, though not accessible to human reason alone, do not require that one turn one's back on it.[22]

Sokolowski's essay has few parallels in the theologically lean and impoverished literature of our time. As was mentioned earlier, its topic and the level on which it is taken up are more typical of former ages than of ours and the thesis that it lays before us is argued with a cogency that one admires all the more as it is so rarely found elsewhere today. One can only hope that, by raising once again the thorny issue of the rapport between faith and reason, and by raising it in a manner that is both respectful of the past and sympathetic to recent developments, the book will set a new trend in religious philosophy as well as in philosophical theology. There does not appear to be much doubt that it accomplishes what it sets out to do, namely, to show that the Christian faith can command the respect of thoughtful persons regardless of what their religious convictions may be and even if they profess no religious convictions at all. As such, it stands in the best tradition of Catholic theology, the bulk of which has prized reason and looked upon it as an ally rather than an enemy of the faith. Anyone who starts from the same premises, and they are the premises that the medieval tradition took as its point of departure, is bound to arrive at similar conclusions and will agree that the Christian faith cannot be dismissed as meaningless, that its main tenets are neither patent absurdities nor logical inconsistencies, and hence that one can subscribe to them without lapsing into obvious contradictions.

This said, one wonders whether, apart from its more modern (and sometimes more obscure) terminology, Sokolowski's "theology of disclosure" is really as new as it claims to be. In view of the extreme care that the medieval theologians brought to the distinction between the sciences and their various formalities, they can scarcely be thought to have been less concerned than we are with the manner in which things come to light, are "presenced," or manifest themselves to us. To be sure, Sokolowski has no intention of separating the two theologies, which, he says, must be kept "in tandem;"[23] but he nevertheless sees them as different. Whereas the "theology of things" takes the Christian distinction between God and the world for granted and concentrates on its two terms, the "theology of disclosure" zeroes in on the distinction itself.[24] To speak of such a distinction, however, is to imply that one has already analyzed its terms and determined as accurately as possible wherein they differ. The medievals may possibly have taken the distinction between God and the world for granted, but there is reason to think that Sokolowski, who highlights that distinction, tends to take its terms for granted.

A case in point is his insistence on the intramundane character of the Aristotelian God, which may or may not do full justice to the complexity of Aristotle's thought on this matter. Unfortunately, the texts in which the problem is taken up in the *Metaphysics* and elsewhere are relatively few in number and, as the long history of Aristotelian scholarship demonstrates, notoriously difficult to interpret. Ascertaining what exactly Aristotle may have meant by "God" is no small task, especially since the word is applied not only to the "first unmoved mover" and the other separate substances but, in accordance with earlier Greek tradition, to the outermost heaven, all of the heavenly bodies, and on occasion reason itself. The ambiguity is noted by Cicero, who observes apropos of Aristotle's lost dialogue *On Philosophy*: "At one moment he assigns divinity exclusively to the mind; at another he calls the world itself a god; elsewhere he puts some other god over the world, assigning to this god the task of regulating and sustaining the movement of the world by means of a revolution of some sort; then he calls the celestial heat (or ether) a god, not realizing that the heaven is a part of that world which he himself had previously designated by the name of god."[25] Clearly, some of Aristotle's "divine" beings belong to the whole with which the metaphysician is concerned, but it is not at all clear that the prime mover is himself a "part" of that whole. The *Metaphysics* describes him variously as "self-subsisting actuality" (*energeia ē kath autēn*),[26] an "eternal and immovable being" (*aidion ousian akinēton*)[27] "the good at which everything in the universe aims,"[28] or the principle on which the heaven and all of nature depend,"[29] even though he himself does not depend on them or receive anything from them. God is the subject of sacred theology, which appropriately begins with him and studies everything else in relation to him.[30] He is not as such the subject of metaphysics or first philosophy, which takes as its theme being qua being,[31] knows nothing of God as he is in himself, and would not speak of him at all were it not for the fact that the world as we know it becomes unintelligible without him. Significantly, God is discussed only toward the end of the *Physics* and the *Metaphysics*, where he is introduced as the extrinsic final cause of the world, as distinct from its intrinsic final cause or the order of its parts.

As for the contention that Aristotle could not conceive of a divine being whose existence was not so linked to the world as to be unthinkable without it,[32] it too may have to be re-examined in the light of other statements that bear on this subject. The problem comes up at least once in the *Metaphysics*, in connection with the discussion of the number of the separate substances. True enough, Aristotle thought it "reasonable" (*eulogon*) to suppose that this number is identical to that of the spheres, which is tentatively set at either fifty-five or forty-seven. Yet he was not prepared to rule out the possibility that there might be other separate substances whose existence is not in any way related to the realm of celestial or sublunar phenomena.[33]

Even if these remarks should prove accurate, however, they are by no means fatal to Sokolowski's general thesis; for regardless of whether one regards Aristotle's prime mover as part of the world or not, a vast difference still separates him from the God of Christian theology. That difference comes most clearly to sight in Sokolowski's discussion of the radical contingency of all beings other than God. The pages devoted to this topic bring us back to the more familiar view according to which the opposition between the religious and the philosophic traditions turns in the final analysis on the issue of creation or divine omnipotence.[34] Between a God who is defined exclusively as the thought that thinks itself, is ignorant of what goes on in this world, and has nothing to do with its coming into being or its governance on the one hand, and the all-powerful creator of the biblical tradition on the other, there is obviously no middle term. From this point of view, at least, it is certainly possible to argue for the greater transcendence of the Christian God, who not only surpasses all other beings in perfection but, as the *ipsum esse subsistens*, or uniquely self-subsistent being, already contains within himself the totality of being.

Sokolowski would appear to have reason on his side when he insists that, once the case for creation has been presented, the philosopher owes it to himself to take it seriously.[35] That it was taken with the utmost seriousness by the great thinkers of the past is amply attested to by the numerous disquisitions to which it gave rise in all three of the great religious communities of the West: Islam, Judaism, and Christianity. It does not follow necessarily that, having examined that case thoroughly, the philosopher will be more inclined to accept it. For one thing, it is hard to see how God could produce beings other than himself and still be said to be infinite or to exhaust the totality of being. As far as human reason knows, nothing can be added to infinity. To say that creation gives us something "more" but nothing "greater" or "better" provides us with a good shorthand statement of the problem but does little to elucidate it. It is equally hard to see how a God who is defined as pure and changeless actuality could create without passing from potency to act and hence without undergoing some kind of change. Finally, if God can create, he also has the power to intervene in the processes of nature and alter them as he sees fit. Anything that is not inherently contradictory becomes possible. In that case, science loses something of its necessary character and must live with the realization that its results could be overturned at any time by divine decree. Divine omnipotence may not render the world order vain, but it does inject an unknown factor or an element of unpredictability into the philosopher's quest for unchanging causes.

Much as one can admire the zeal with which the medieval theologians wrestled with these issues, it is fair to say that the problems themselves have always been clearer than the proposed solutions to them. Sokolowski seems to grant as much when he goes on to explain that the Christian distinction between God and the world is not on a par with other philosophical doctrines insofar as it "engages our affections" and demands the collaboration of both the intellect and the will. To that extent, it is inseparable from action and must be "lived" before it can even be stated.[36] While not itself a properly supernatural truth, it at least has that much in common with the truths that belong exclusively to the order of grace. It should be noted that Aristotle, for his part, did not claim to be able to prove apodictically that the world was eternal. In the *Topics* he admits that the magnitude of the problem is such as to defy any completely satisfactory solution, and he also makes it clear in the *Metaphysics* that he preferred his own alternative to the others' only because it was the one that offered the "fewest difficulties"[37] and shed the greatest amount of light on the famous issue of the one and the many or of being and becoming that had dominated the whole of pre-Socratic philosophy.[38] Since so little in the way of rational certitude awaits us on either side of this vexed question, it may be to our advantage to leave the study of nature aside for the time being and, taking our cue from Socrates,[39] turn to Sokolowski's account of human or moral things.

The discussion in this particular instance begins with an analysis of natural virtue[40] that takes its bearings from the *Nicomachean Ethics* and focuses on the nature of moral agency as well as on Aristotle's division of human types into four basic categories or formal possibilities: the virtuous, the continent, the incontinent, and the vicious. The stage for much of the argument is set by Kant, who is used as a foil to illustrate the importance attributed to moral character in classical thought. For Kant, the ethical life is conceived solely in terms of the struggle between inclination and duty or between passion and rational obligation. The virtues and habits have practically no role to play in it and the notion of human wholeness all but disappears. Kant had the right idea when he "related moral responsibility to the issue of the divine,"[41] but that is about as much as Sokolowski is willing to say on his behalf. For an adequate assessment of natural moral phenomena "we must get out from under Kant," and this is where Aristotle can be most helpful to us.[42]

The Aristotelian view of morality is subsequently contrasted with the Christian view, which modifies it to some extent and, by adding to it the infused moral virtues and the theological virtues, provides a new setting for human existence. None of these properly Christian virtues destroys the natural virtues, which continue to serve as a kind of "ballast" for Christian action.[43] This must not be taken to mean that, when the two contexts, i.e. the natural and the theological, are introduced, the individual moral agent is "split into two performers"; it means rather that "in the concrete situation, . . . what the Christian is primarily supposed to do is what the good man would be expected to do."[44] To be more specific,

> The Christian perspective does not bring in obligations that are at odds with what we ought to do according to the nature of things; the Christian illumination of what is to be done consists first of all in confirming what is good by nature, and in appreciating that what is good according to nature is not simply good in itself but also good because created and therefore willed by God. What is good by nature is not set over what is good by grace but

is integrated into it. And what is good by grace is not simply a matter of convention and arbitrary decision; rather it builds on nature and shares in the reasonableness associated with nature.[45]

While there is much to applaud in all of this, one cannot help thinking that Sokolowski's determination to absolve Christian ethics from even the faintest suspicion of irrationality has again caused him to weight the evidence in his favor. Among other things, his interpretation of the *Ethics* stresses only such elements as may be thought to be neutral in regard to the distinction that was later made between pagan and Christian virtue. Little if anything is said about the spirit that informs Aristotle's treatment of these matters, his method of procedure, the kind of reader to whom his book is typically addressed, his resolve to present moral phenomena on their own level or as they appear not so much to the philosopher as to morally good or decent human beings, and, most important, the cognitive status that attaches to moral virtue in the Aristotelian scheme. The way is thus paved for the assertion that Christian morality does not contradict pagan morality but merely redirects or refines it by privileging "certain aspects of natural moral goods."[46] Generally speaking, it exhibits a livelier concern with what human beings have in common "as created and loved and redeemed by God"; it pays greater attention to the needs and dignity of the weak, the unborn, and the poor; and it is more emphatic in its proclamation of "the natural equality of all men," later to be reasserted by Hobbes, Locke, and Rousseau.[47] None of this, not even the addition of humility to Aristotle's list of virtues, constitutes an obstacle to the pursuit of natural goodness. Humility may affect one's appraisal of one's own worth, but it does not enter into competition with noble pride or make the believer any less secure in his actions as a human being. The example of those who manage to combine in their own persons "natural pride and supernatural humility" is proof enough that the two virtues can live comfortably together.[48]

All well and good, save for the fact that we are still confronted with two vastly different types of human beings between which one is sooner or later compelled to choose. Luther may have exaggerated but he was not entirely wide of the mark when he pronounced Aristotle's *Ethics* "the worst of all books," one that "flatly opposes divine grace and all Christian virtues."[49] Even if the Christian and the pagan should happen to agree on many of the same things, the spirit that animates them and dictates their actions is not the same, and that is surely something to be considered in any analysis of moral character. Sokolowski's argument proves only that Christian belief promotes one type of morality and, depending on one's perspective, perhaps not the highest one at that. The passing remark to the effect that in Aquinas "the noble seems almost to be changed into the obligatory"[50] says a good deal about Christianity's inherent propensity to elevate justice above nobility, thereby stripping the moral life of some of its splendor.[51] Magnanimity, once it is required of everyone, inevitably ceases to be the rare achievement described in Book IV of the *Ethics*. It becomes, as Aquinas would have it, a part of courage, arguably the lowest albeit the most necessary of the moral virtues.[52] This alone does not make Christian morality any less "reasonable," but to anyone who is not inclined to measure human perfection by what is said about it in the New Testament, it could make it look somewhat less lofty. For better or for worse, there are not many "ladies" and "gentlemen" anywhere in the Bible, and the few people who tried to behave as if they were—Saul and Michal immediately come to mind—soon learned to rue their mistake.[53] Along similar lines, it is significant that the Christian tradition has often seen a parallel of sorts between Christ and Socrates (who was not a gentleman) but never, as far as I know, between Christ and Achilles, "the best of the Achaeans." Simply put, by valuing some moral "goods" so much more highly than others, Christianity risks inhibiting the development of certain parts of the soul the cultivation of which may not be any less essential to the attainment of human excellence.

The problem has larger ramifications, however, for it is far from evident that from a purely philosophical standpoint moral virtue is fully supported by nature and that its normal requirements are always consonant with the good of society as a whole. To cite only one of the examples adduced by Sokolowski, Christianity's traditional stand against abortion and infanticide can be defended on rational as well as on Christian grounds, but the reasons that purport to justify it may have to be pondered in the light of other reasons that militate against it in certain circumstances. Aristotle, Sokolowski's spokesman for natural morality, did after all propose that the number of children be limited and that deformed offspring not be allowed to live.[54] One can likewise think of numerous other cases where the strict observance of the rules of justice as ordinarily understood would be detrimental to the preservation and welfare of the city. A society that has no regard for the observance of these rules could easily jeopardize its chances of survival, but neither Aristotle nor any of his classical followers ever went so far as to maintain that an unswerving commitment to them is always and everywhere possible.

Confronted with that problem, some Christian Aristotelians of the Middle Ages questioned the universal applicability of all universally recognized principles of justice and right. As one of them expressed it in equivalent terms, what is universally admitted is not rational and what is rational is not universally admitted.[55] The question with which we ultimately come face to face is whether, in the absence of a legislating God, the moral order is internally consistent at every point and enjoys the cosmic support that most decent human beings demand for it. Sokolowski puts us on the right track when he observes that "the divine is inseparable from a sense of the good and the obligatory."[56] The moral man as such, one is tempted to say, is the natural candidate for belief in divine Revelation.

This brings us straightaway to the comparatively brief but incisive appendix that is devoted to an examination of the relationship between Christian belief and the political life.[57] Sokolowski notes perceptively that the privatization of religion necessitated or brought about by the triumph of modern liberalism has led to the neglect of religion on the part of political thinkers and of politics on the part of theologians, to the detriment of both political theory and theology. Such was not the situation in premodern times, when most philosophers and theologians were wont to take a lively interest in all questions pertaining to the place of religion in society. One notable exception to the present day rule is to be found in the works of Leo Strauss and his disciples, to whom Sokolowski gives full credit for having refocused our attention on this problem but with whom he nevertheless feels compelled to take issue on a number of crucial points. Specifically, he sees no warrant for the allegation that revealed religion renders "the political life, or at least the preservation of natural right impossible" insofar as it singles out some members of the body politic "as superior to others, not because of wealth or strength or virtue or intelligence or natural ability," but because they are the repositories of certain higher truths to which no one else is privy. His answer to that charge is that Christianity leaves the realm of nature intact and hence does not advance any political teachings that are not equally available to non-Christians or nonbelievers or establish "a group of people who are supposed to govern others by virtue of the unusual opinions they possess." None of its central doctrines, least of all the belief in creation, interferes with the normal operations of human reason or contravenes the "natural necessities" of the political order.[58]

Although Sokolowski readily acknowledges that Strauss's position on these and related matters remains somewhat elusive, he questions what appears to be Strauss's understanding of revealed religion as the "communication of commandments whose necessity is not obvious to reason" and that, as the story of Abraham and Isaac suggests, "may even appear to be irrational." Such an understanding is foreign to Christianity, which, we are again told, accentuates certain parts of natural morality more than others and expresses some of its requirements with greater clarity, but whose teachings never "work against the natural law"[59]

Equally objectionable in Sokolowski's eyes is the Straussian tendency to interpret the distinction between the natural and the supernatural as a simple variant of the distinction between nature and convention, the pivot of Strauss's political theory. On this telling, the mysteries of the faith, along with the Christian virtues and the obligations they entail, become another form of conventionalism, at the risk of losing much of their credibility. Yet Strauss himself acknowledges the threat that the weakening of the sense of the sacred poses to civil society. For the same reason, Sokolowski cannot accept the view that Athens is permanently at odds with Jerusalem or that philosophic reason and religious belief can coexist only in an uneasy and finally unresolvable tension with each other. According to Strauss, this tension is what prompted many of the philosophers of the past to conceal their innermost thoughts lest by disclosing them openly they should undermine the salutary opinions by which most people live and on which society depends for its well-being. This peculiar mode of writing may have been prevalent among philosophers in the past, but Sokolowski denies its relevance to Christianity on the ground that the Christian faith "does not enter into competition with reason" and that "its scope is other than the whole within which reason finds its home." The Christian writer can dispense with this form of concealment or deliberate dissimulation, not because he is more honest or forthright than others, but because the things he believes in "do not necessitate a conflict between what is believed and what is known."[60] Christianity is not a convention, formulating for the uneducated in a way that is persuasive to them certain thoughts about the ultimate, the sacred, the necessary, the obligatory, or the whole that philosophy then scrutinizes and reveals as mere opinion. Unlike the God of whom Strauss speaks, the Christian God is not "unfathomable will," and unlike the God of the philosophers, he is not intellect alone. As the *ipsum esse subsistens*, he is both will and intellect and neither more one than the other. Moreover, the fact that he creates and redeems does not deprive nature of its intelligibility or prevent human beings from discerning that intelligibility by the exercise of their unimpeded reason. Hence, the Christian need not prescind from the notion of creation when he speculates about the world. What he does as a philosopher is no different from what he would do if he were convinced that the world is eternal and uncreated.

Sokolowski's acute comments are all the more welcome as they reveal with unusual clarity the uneasiness that Christian theologians frequently experience when confronted with Strauss's analysis of the so-called theologico-political problem. Though critical of Strauss on the points that have just been mentioned, Sokolowski is not entirely unsympathetic to him and he fully appreciates the difficulty posed by the fact that one cannot always tell whether Strauss is speaking in his own name or merely paraphrasing the authors about whom he writes. Strauss certainly said or implied that many of these authors looked upon revealed religion as a politically useful myth, however cautious they may have been in stating that view. What is more, he never expressly disagrees with them. But neither does he profess to agree with them; for only a completed philosophy, as distinct from a philosophy that understands itself as an unfinished and unfinishable quest for wisdom, could demonstrate the falsity of revealed religion, let alone rule out its possibility. Strauss denied that he was in possession of such a philosophy. He knew that, within certain limits, the "teachings" of the classical philosophers could be harmonized with those of revealed religion, and he pointed to the achievements of Averroes, Maimonides, and Thomas Aquinas as examples of the various ways in which this harmonization could be effected. But this leaves untouched the question of whether the *bios theorētikos* or philosophy as a way of life rather than as a set of teachings or a body of doctrines is compatible with the believer's whole-hearted assent to certain truths that either exceed the capacity of human reason or cannot be nailed down by it. One may wish to quarrel with that definition of philosophy, but to be convincing to everyone, the argument against it would have to be based on premises that bear no trace of the influence of divine revelation. Sokolowski has a good point when he reproaches Rahner and Lonergan with not accepting the pagan state of mind as a real possibility, but he himself appears to be reluctant to go all the way in recognizing that possibility.

Using Strauss against himself, so to speak, Sokolowski quotes a statement to the effect that "By becoming aware of the dignity of the mind, we realize the true ground of the dignity of man and therewith of the goodness of the world, whether we understand it as created or uncreated, which is the home of man because it is the home of the human mind."[61] From that statement, he infers that by Strauss's own admission Christian belief need not be interpreted as just another convention and that the Christian thinker is not required to choose between nature on the one hand and creation and grace on the other.[62] The argument may be beside the point, however, inasmuch as Sokolowski has not proved but merely asserted that Strauss relegated religion in general and Christianity in particular to the realm of convention; but even if it is not, we should miss the full import of Strauss's statement if we were to see in it a simple acknowledgment of the fact that there is a large area of agreement between the domains of philosophy and revealed religion. The total picture comes into view only when we look at a parallel passage in the essay entitled "How to Begin to Study the *Guide of the Perplexed*," where Strauss explains that the same conclusion—in the instance under consideration, the existence, oneness, and immateriality of God—may occasionally be drawn from two different and opposed premises, to wit, the eternity of the world or its creation in time. But he is careful to add that the results in each case are not simply identical:

For instance, someone might have said prior to the Second World War that Germany would be prosperous regardless of whether she won or lost the war; if she won, her prosperity would follow immediately; if she lost, her prosperity would be assured by the United States of America who would need her as an ally against Soviet Russia; but the predictor would have abstracted from the difference between Germany as the greatest power which ruled tyrannically and was ruled tyrannically, and Germany as a second-rank power ruled democratically. The God whose being is proved on the assumption of creation is the biblical God who is characterized by Will and whose knowledge has only the name in common with our knowledge.[63]

Granted, in the vast majority of cases, the human being who takes reason alone as his ultimate guide and the one who seeks to please God above all else are likely to come to the same conclusion regarding what is to be done in a particular set of circumstances. But there is also something of importance to be learned from the few remaining cases in which their actions could conceivably differ.

As a Christian theologian, Sokolowski can hardly be blamed for taking exception to the Maimonidean and Straussian view according to which God is essentially will rather than intellect and for countering it with the Thomistic view, for which God is as much intellect as he is will. The fact is, however, that Thomas's position is a theological interpretation of the biblical datum that draws heavily on Aristotelian philosophy. If one sticks to what is said about God in the Hebrew Scriptures, which is what Strauss has in mind, a different vision emerges. As is obvious not only from the paradigmatic story of Abraham and Isaac but from innumerable other biblical passages as well, the biblical God does not give any reasons for what he does or what he demands of his followers. That outlook is only slightly modified in the New Testament, which replaces what is now called the Old Law with the new and in some fashion perhaps even more paradoxical "command" of love. It is no accident that within the Christian tradition itself the voluntaristic emphasis on the divine will again comes massively to the fore in the works of such well-known late-medieval theologians as Scotus and Ockham.

Closely related to this problem is the whole issue of esoteric writing, which figures prominently in Straussian hermeneutics but which is supposedly out of place in the Christian world. In his treatment of this matter, Sokolowski laments the fact that more is not known about the way Strauss interpreted Aquinas's works and alludes to a "Straussian oral tradition" according to which Strauss would have considered Aquinas to be "more truly a philosopher than a believer."[64] Strauss did say more than once that there is no way of knowing in advance what a truly great mind is capable of, but to my knowledge he never questioned the sincerity of Aquinas's religious beliefs. It did not surprise him that, whenever possible, Aquinas consciously and deliberately interpreted Aristotle's text in the manner that best accords with the Christian faith. Strauss was also intrigued by Aquinas's habit of muting his disagreements with some of his Christian predecessors by exposing their thought "reverently" (*reverenter*), a practice reminiscent of the reserve that marks the works of the ancient philosophers and some of their Islamic and Jewish followers. This is not to suggest, however, that he regarded Aquinas as an esoteric writer. The truth of the matter is that genuine esotericism was less frowned upon than ignored in the Christian West, where for a long time it survived mainly in the form of a pedagogical device to which the learned could resort when called upon to address the simple faithful. Aquinas, who was vaguely acquainted with it through the works of the Pseudo-Dionysius, leaves it at saying that, while it may have had its legitimate uses at other moments in history, it was now largely abandoned—*apud modernos est inconsuetus*.[65]

Be that as it may, Sokolowski traces Christianity's greater openness to philosophy to its "special understanding of God," which calls for a world in which "the mind and reason are at home" and does away with "many of the paradoxes and contradictions that Strauss so well describes between religion and philosophy."[66] The same point could be made more simply by stating that, as a charismatic religion or a religion of love rather than of the law, Christianity is not linked to any particular political community and does not lay down any particular code of laws by which such a community might be governed.[67] On that level at any rate, it was immune to the kind of philosophic criticism that could be directed against the Jewish or the Islamic Law. This is still a far cry from saying that its moral imperatives are always in full accord with the needs of the political life. As we have had occasion to observe, there are times when, in the name of reason itself, wise and decent rulers may feel compelled to embark upon courses of action that Christian morality reproves. One does not solve that problem by arguing that none of the teachings of the faith violates the "natural law"; for, the natural law properly so-called is itself a product of the Christian world and a reflection of its own understanding of natural morality.[68] What Christian theology calls "reason" is sometimes, though not always, what it has already chosen to define as reason.

It is easy, too easy perhaps, to say that "Christian Revelation leaves the natural necessities and natural truths intact, including all those that are at work in political life," and that a commitment to its beliefs does not of itself qualify one for positions of leadership in civil society.[69] Everyone knows that throughout much of its history the Church did arrogate to itself the right to exercise political authority and to impose its ethical demands on society as a whole. Sokolowski, who does not dwell on the subject, would probably reply that this is a simple historical accident based on a misunderstanding of Christian principles on the part of Church leaders. Even so, the frequency with which that misunderstanding has been perpetrated across the centuries does little to allay the fears that it continues to inspire in the minds of others. Strauss's criticisms are not proper to him and to his "school." They were first voiced by thoughtful and dedicated Christians as far back as the Middle Ages. One occasionally regrets that Sokolowski, who blames Christian theologians for their neglect of political theory, has not taken it more seriously himself. What he regards as the *primum quoad nos* or "first for us" is not the political life but the *Lebenswelt* of modern phenomenology, which is not particularly noted for its interest in politics and shows relatively little awareness of the extent to which our perception of the world around us is shaped by the realities of our political situation. This, more than anything else, is what lends to his analysis a slightly abstract quality and, despite its claim to be "closer to life,"[70] an air of remoteness from the vital concerns of everyday Christian living.

It is not necessary to add that the foregoing remarks barely touch the surface of Sokolowski's essay and are in no way meant to detract from its outstanding merits. They will have achieved their purpose if they encourage others to read the book for themselves and to read it with all the attention it deserves. Sad to say, there are few recent books of its kind that can be recommended with the same degree of confidence and enthusiasm. We live in a peculiar age, one whose leading thinkers are frequently embarrassed by the continued presence of faith and reason in our midst and, not knowing what to do with them, would just as soon ignore them altogether. *Et le combat cessa, faute de combattants* . . . Sokolowski wants them both, but he knows that their harmonious relationship is no longer as evident to us as it was to our medieval forebears. His is a courageous book, which ignores the fads and fashions of the day and refuses to be intimidated by the pomp and ceremony of the contemporary theological establishment. It is also a serene and dispassionate book, as remarkable for its defense of the faith against the latent or vestigial rationalism of our time as for its defense of reason against the irrationalism of so much of present-day religious thought. Theologians will find in it a challenging alternative to the approaches favored by Rahner and Lonergan, the two currently most influential names in Catholic theology, and it will also teach political theorists to be more moderate in their criticisms of a tradition that for the most part they have never taken the pains to investigate. A sure sign of its success is that one need not agree with everything that is said in it in order to be enlightened and perhaps even profoundly edified by it.

NOTES

1. Cf. William James, *The Varieties of Religious Experience.*
2. See, for example, Thomas Aquinas, *Summa contra gentiles* I ch. 7.
3. Cf. Augustine, *City of God* X.32.
4. Cf. Romans 12:1.
5. Robert Sokolowski, *The God of Faith and Reason: The Foundations of Christian Theology* (Notre Dame and London: University of Notre Dame Press, 1982), xiv + 172.
6. Cf. Sokolowski, xiv and 73.
7. Sokolowski, 107.
8. Sokolowski, 19.
9. Sokolowski, 32-33.
10. For a similar argument, cf. Thomas Aquinas, *Summa theologiae* I, qu. 45, a. 3, ad lum, where Aquinas explains that the relation of the creature to God is a real "relation" (*relatio realis*), whereas the relation of God to the creature is no more than a "relation of reason" (*relatio secundum rationem*).
11. Sokolowski, 12.
12. Sokolowski, 15-16.
13. Sokolowski, 18.
14. Sokolowski, 37-9.
15. Sokolowski, 21-3.
16. Cf. Karl Rahner, *Hearers of the Word* in *A Rahner Reader*, edited by Gerald A. McCool (New York: Seabury, 1975), 2-64.
17. Cf. Bernard Lonergan, *Insight: A Study of Human Understanding* (New York: Longmans, Green and Co., 1957).
18. Sokolowski, 108-9.
19. See esp., Sokolowski, 89-90 and 100-101, where the problem is taken up in much the same terms but without any mention of either Rahner or Lonergan.
20. Sokolowski, 112.
21. Sokolowski, 39.
22. Sokolowski, xii, 39 and 113.
23. Sokolowski, 93.
24. Sokolowski, 90-2.
25. Cicero, *De natura deorum* I.13.33.
26. Aristotle, *Metaphysics* 1072b27, cf. 1071b20.
27. *Metaphysics* 1071b5.
28. *Metaphysics* 1072b3.
29. *Metaphysics* 1072b14.
30. Thomas Aquinas *Summa theologiae* I, qu. I, a. 7.
31. Cf. *Metaphysics* 1003a21, 1004b15, 1025b2, etc.
32. Sokolowski, 16-18.
33. *Metaphysics* 1074a14-31.

34. Cf. *inter multa alia* Averroes, *Decisive Treatise*, in *Medieval Political Philosophy: A Sourcebook*, edited by R. Lerner and M. Mahdi (New York: The Free Press, 1963), 173-75; Maimonides, *Guide* II.13.

35. Sokolowski, 115.

36. Ibid., 123, 142.

37. *Metaphysics* 1075a27.

38. See Aristotle's summary discussion of this frequently debated topic in *Metaphysics* 1075a25-1076a5.

39. Cf. Xenophon *Memorabilia* I.1.10-15.

40. Sokolowski, 53-68.

41. Ibid., 56.

42. Ibid., 55.

43. Ibid., 83.

44. Ibid., 82.

45. Ibid., 83.

46. Sokolowski's remarks concerning the difference between natural and Christian morality are set within the context of a comparison between the Augustinian and Thomistic views of natural virtue (cf. 78-79 and 88). In simple terms, for Augustine natural virtue without faith is "false" virtue; for Aquinas, it is "true" virtue, albeit only relative virtue. This apparent discrepancy is rightly said to find its explanation in the fact that Aquinas distinguishes more sharply between the order of nature and the order of grace. It is not unimportant to note, however, that Augustine, who generally works within a Platonic framework, tends to study all things in the light of their highest principles. Just as Plato denies that virtue without true knowledge is genuine virtue, so Augustine denies that virtue without faith is true virtue.

47. Sokolowski, 83, 96.

48. Ibid., 85.

49. Luther, *An Open Letter to the German Nobility*, in *Three Treatises* (Philadelphia: Muhlenburg Press, 1947), 93-94.

50. Sokolowski, 81.

51. On p. 77, Sokolowski notes by way of comparison that, whereas "natural temperance, for example, moderates our use of food and drink in view of health and the exercise of reason . . . infused virtue will urge us toward asceticism." No one denies, of course, that Christian virtue is more ascetical than purely natural virtue, but the interesting point in Sokolowski's statement is that it reflects a purely instrumental conception of natural virtue, which is regarded as a means to a further end whether it be bodily health or the healthy condition of the mind. No mention is made of the Aristotelian notion of moderation and moral virtue generally as something "noble" (*kalon*) or desirable for its own sake; cf. *Nicomachean Ethics* 1115b13 and 24; 1116a12 and b20; 1117a17; 1119a18 and b17; 1120a23, et passim.

52. Thomas Aquinas, *Summa theologiae* II-II, qu. 129, a. 5.

53. Cf. I Samuel 15:l-9; II Samuel 6:16-23.

54. Aristotle, *Politics* 1135b20-26.

55. Cf. Marsilius of Padua, *The Defender of the Peace* II.12.7-8.

56. Sokolowski, 55.

57. Ibid., 157-64.

58. Ibid., 158.

59. Ibid., 159.

60. Ibid., 162.

61. L. Strauss, "What Is Liberal Education?" in *Liberalism, Ancient and Modern* (New York: Basic Books, 1968), 8.

62. Sokolowski, 161.

63. L. Strauss, ibid., 180.

64. Sokolowski, 161.

65. Thomas Aquinas, *In librum B. Dionysii de divinis nominibus*, edited by C. Pera (Turin: Marietti, 1950), Prooemium II.1.

66. Sokolowski, 163.

67. On that basis, Sokolowski argues for the greater transcendence of the New Testament conception of God over against that of the Old Testament (cf. 124-29). The God of the Old Testament, we are told, is an "interventionist" God who does not allow things to be according to their own natures. His creative power and dominion over the world no doubt set him apart from everything else, but for all that, when the Jewish writers speak of him, "they speak of 'the same thing' that the gentiles speak of with their god and gods, except that the Jews consider themselves to be speaking truly while the others are in error" (p. 25). As Sokolowski himself eventually recognizes, however, this supereminently transcendent character of the Christian God is often obscured in ordinary Christian piety. The whole argument, which is as subtle as it is profound, would require a much more detailed examination than any that can be accorded to it here. One regrets only that more is not said about the Old Testament's highly original notion of the "holiness" (in modern parlance, the "transcendence") of God, which could cast the problem in a slightly different light.

68. As recent studies have shown, the origin of the natural law theory presents a riddle that no one has yet been able to crack. Cicero, the author of the oldest known works in which the expression is used in a clearly moral sense, identifies the natural law with right reason, thereby depriving it of its strictly legal status (cf. *De re publica* III.22). The Church Fathers refer to it only sparingly and more as a commonplace than as a fully developed doctrine. The first theological treatises devoted expressly to it date only from the thirteenth century and are proper to the Christian West, where the natural law proved especially helpful as a means of bridging the gulf between the ecclesiastical and the temporal powers. Since the end of the nineteenth century, the claim has frequently been made that the Church itself is the authentic interpreter of the natural law, a fact that may seem somewhat strange if, as is likewise asserted, the natural law is accessible to the unassisted human reason. On this point, see the puzzling remarks by T. E. Wassmer, "Natural Law: Contemporary Theology and Philosophy," *New Catholic Encyclopedia*, vol 10: 262.

69. Sokolowski, 158.

70. Ibid., 97.

16

BETWEEN THE LINES: WAS LEO STRAUSS A SECRET ENEMY OF MORALITY?

History's final verdict on Leo Strauss is not yet in and is not likely to be in for quite some time. Meanwhile, one cannot help noticing that since his death in 1973, Strauss's reputation has been growing by leaps and bounds. Barely known beyond a small circle of colleagues, students, and friends when I first encountered him in the 1950s, he is now a name to be reckoned with, one of the gurus of our age, the focal point of a swirling and oftentimes bitter controversy. A sure sign of this posthumous success is that everybody in academic circles has to pretend to know him. People have made a career of attacking or defending him. A good number of them have been promoted or denied promotion on the basis of their affiliation with him.

For better or for worse, Straussianism has become a school, a "movement," an establishment of sorts, a minor but expanding and apparently exportable industry. Although concentrated on the North American continent, Straussians have begun to crop up elsewhere, in various European countries as well as in such far away places as India and Japan. They have not only infiltrated the academy but occupy key positions in government, the media, and on the boards of large foundations. I do not wish to give the impression that the country is about to be taken over by them, as some of their critics fear, for nothing could be further from the truth. We are still talking about a relatively small and to some extent persecuted minority, but a minority that, like the early Christians, has managed to attract more attention than would have been thought possible when it began to form a short generation ago.

Strauss had a knack for turning students into disciples, and disciples, as we know, are both a blessing and a curse. The gospel, which does not have too many good things to say about them, reminds us that they are forever (a) vying among themselves for first place and (b) distorting the master's teachings. And, in fact, the once-monolithic Straussian core has evolved into a surprisingly diversified group, encompassing within its ranks: right-wing and left-wing Straussians; fundamentalist or reactionary and revisionist or avant-garde Straussians; paleo- and neo-Straussians; philosophical, political, and literary Straussians; naive and thoughtful Straussians; firsthand, secondhand, and thirdhand Straussians; fanatical, mainstream, and lukewarm or borderline Straussians; moralizing and non-moralizing Straussians; Socratic, Machiavellian, and Nietzschean Straussians; front-door, back-door, side-door, and revolving-door Straussians; renegade and born-again Straussians; avowed and closet Straussians; hard-core and soft-core Straussians; pious and irreverent Straussians; East coast and West coast Straussians; urban, agrarian, and prairie Straussians; genial and grumpy Straussians; professional and amateur Straussians; Sunday and week-day Straussians; full-time, part-time, and intermittent Straussians; and with that the enumeration has hardly begun.

The development, an utterly amazing one, is not a mere fad, for it has already lasted longer than most fads. Not its least interesting feature is that it has given us the rare opportunity to observe at first hand a phenomenon previously known to our generation only from history books, namely, what happens to the thought of a *bona fide* master once he is no longer around to restrain the enthusiasts and keep a lid on things.

Given this state of affairs, it was inevitable, first of all, that a book should sooner or later be written on Strauss, and secondly, since old-time Straussians are generally reluctant to speak publicly about the master, that the author should be someone who never knew Strauss. For this we can be grateful. Closeness is not a guarantee of objectivity and has been known to constitute a serious obstacle to it. Kierkegaard tells us that the apostles, who shared Christ's life for three years, did not necessarily understand him better than we can since they lacked the perspective that comes only with temporal distance. It is also true that a person whose critical faculties have not been dulled by a partiality bred of long acquaintance frequently achieves insights that are denied to others. I hasten to add that none of this automatically makes of Shadia B. Drury a more reliable guide to Strauss's thought than anyone else, for closeness to the subject and enlightened partiality, whatever their dangers, have their own advantages.

Be that as it may, the aim in the present case appears to be an eminently laudable one. Professor Drury comes neither to praise Strauss nor to bury him. Her goal, she tells us candidly in *The Political Ideas of Leo Strauss*,[1] is to interpret and understand him, and this she has tried to do in the only way possible—by disentangling his thought from the numerous commentaries on older authors in which for the most part it is imbedded. Her book is not a piece of research in the usual sense of the word. She has not taken the pains to figure out why, for instance, in reprinting some of his articles, Strauss occasionally left out passages that seem most intriguing to us. She has likewise refrained from engaging in a number of favorite Straussian pastimes, such as counting paragraphs, tallying numbers, locating the center of this or that enumeration, or uncovering the mysteries supposedly buried in footnotes that are hard to track down. (In one of its versions, Strauss's essay "What is Political Philosophy?" has a total of 66 paragraphs. It also happens to be introduced by a quotation from chapter 66 of Isaiah. Wow!)

Nor, as far as I can see, did she avail herself of the hitherto unused materials contained in the Strauss archives at the University of Chicago. Her study is based exclusively on Strauss's published works. Even here, no attention is paid to the distinction between the pieces published by Strauss himself and the *Nachlass* edited by others (as is the case with the important essay on "The Mutual Influence of Theology and Philosophy," of which much is made in the book). Interestingly, Professor Drury wonders why Strauss is silent about Freud, whom she considers relevant to his project and whom, unlike Strauss, she seems to hold in high esteem as a thinker. In that connection, she goes so far as to invent a little dialogue between them. Reading Strauss's unpublished essay on Freud might have been both prudent and helpful.

What we have before us, then, is something that presents itself as a straightforward, no-nonsense account of Strauss's thought or, as she prefers to say, using a term that Strauss himself would probably have avoided, his "ideas." Any newcomer who reads the book will have the good fortune of being introduced to some of the great themes with which Strauss's name is associated, even if they are not always highlighted in the same way by Professor Drury.

I refer to such matters as the following: First, the quarrel between the ancients and the moderns, which had been all but forgotten and which Strauss had the merit of reopening in all its breadth and scope. Second, the nature of "modernity," as we now routinely call it. Third, the role of Machiavelli as the founder of the modern tradition in this emphatic sense, a role which, up to that time, was virtually unrecognized by modern scholars, mainly for the reason that few of Machiavelli's early modern followers wished to be known as disciples of the man described by the greatest of all English bards as the "murdrous Machiavel." Fourth, the recovery of political philosophy and the re-emergence of classical political philosophy as a live alternative to modern thought. The matter is of some consequence since for well over a century the only debates worth mentioning in the field of ethics and politics had been between utilitarians or teleologists on the one hand and deontologists or Kantians on the other. Who would have predicted fifty years ago that the ancients and not the moderns would be at the heart of our most heated debates? Finally, so as not to prolong the list, the notion that the development of Western tradition exhibits a unity that can be traced from its Socratic beginnings down to our time; that its evolution, without being predetermined, follows something like a logical order; and that its foremost representatives were all engaged as partners in a dialogue that spans the centuries.

It is significant that by and large Professor Drury's book follows the order of Strauss's *Natural Right and History*[2] working its way up (or down, as the case may be) from the classics, through the likes of Machiavelli, Hobbes, Locke, and Rousseau, to Nietzsche and his twentieth-century epigones. The framework of the book is clearly taken over from Strauss, as was practically inevitable in a work of this sort, and the discussion itself is carried out in terms that are mostly those of Strauss. Professor Drury is modest enough to admit that she has learned a great deal from Strauss. Indeed, she avows on more than one occasion that she would not have bothered to write a book on him had she not held him in high regard.

How much did she learn from Strauss? The question poses itself in acute form when we come to the last chapter, in which, abandoning any pretense at objectivity, Professor Drury launches into a blistering attack on him. The language suddenly becomes sharper and the accusations almost fiery. Strauss's ideas, we are informed, are never frivolous, but they may be "perverse." He himself is a dangerous man, who equips his students with a "philosophical kit" that will see them through any situation and "always save the day." His commentaries force the text and compel the reader to surrender to the Straussian logic. Worse still, Strauss "corrupts," and this, more than the power of his intellect, is the source of his fiendish attraction. His elitism is "among the most radical that has ever been encountered in the history of Western thought." Accordingly, his students are for the most part a bunch of snobs who think they belong to "a privileged class of individuals that transcend ordinary humanity."

Drury finds Strauss's manner all the more insidious as it encourages students to "discover" for themselves the very things he wants to teach.

It is almost as if in dealing with him, one were conducting an experiment with the devil, for Strauss has a low opinion of morality and denies that it has any place in politics. Equally alarming is the "vulgar nature of his vision of the philosopher-superman," whose nobility is altogether "spurious." The real Strauss, we had previously been told, is "surprising, shocking, outrageous." Now we know why. He is nothing but a "heroic 'Epicurean'" (Harry V. Jaffa's term) whose "idea of philosophy as *eros* is a splendid excuse for being one of the Hugh Hefners of the philosophic set." So much for the direct quotations, which should suffice to give us an idea of the tone of the book and the flavor of the argument. Professor Drury's prose rises to new heights on two sets of occasions: when she paraphrases Strauss, as she often does, and when she attacks him.

My own image of Strauss is more positive. Perhaps I am just one of those dupes who need to be made aware of their naiveté, but the Strauss whom I knew was not nearly so offensive and downright immoral as Drury pictures him. In any event, my first contact with him took place under more favorable auspices. This was not the pre-packaged Strauss with or against whom it is now fashionable to line up. I was a young student struggling to complete a dissertation on St. Augustine's doctrine of the soul and running into all sorts of difficulties with which my mentors, world-famous scholars all of them, were unable to help me. Strauss's major works were just beginning to come out and, lo and behold, there were the answers I was seeking, or if not the answers themselves, some valuable clues as to how one might go about looking for them. This man knew something that the others did not know and was thus able to shed light on problems that most people did not even recognize as problems. At last, I was in business. This, of course, proved to be only the beginning of a much longer story the details of which are not of sufficient general interest to detain us here.

The trouble with Professor Drury's diatribe is that it appears to be motivated by a non-theoretical animus that casts doubts in retrospect on the validity of her findings. It slowly comes across to us that she is more interested in warning people, and especially young students, against Strauss than in discovering what, if anything, Strauss might have to teach them. One could formulate this question in slightly different terms by asking for whom her book was primarily written. Some answer to that question is provided toward the end of chapter one, where, foreseeing that she may be denounced by Strauss's devotees, Professor Drury writes:

> Those who understand fully the truth of my interpretation of the hidden meaning of Strauss's thought will repudiate the book only to remain true to Strauss's desire for secrecy. The rest of his students who are veritably ignorant of his real meaning will be genuinely horrified and appalled by

what they will consider to be violent distortions of their master's sacred views.

If I understand correctly, there are two groups of people who, more than anyone else, stand to benefit from Professor Drury's book: the naive Straussians, who need to be made aware of the poisonous character of Strauss's teaching, and potential Straussians, who run the risk of succumbing to the same deadly attraction.

The author of this timely book is clearly a person who is sure that she has understood Strauss, is convinced that he is wrong on the most fundamental issues, and has taken upon herself to alert the unwary to the dangers to which they are exposing themselves by dabbling in him. This may not be the most auspicious beginning for anyone who wants to get to the bottom of Strauss's thought. No decent person, not even a dyed-in-the-wool Straussian, would have any objection to protecting the innocent. The problem is that by shielding gifted students in this manner one deprives them of a unique opportunity to reflect on certain basic problems which, unless they are properly dealt with at that time, may come back to haunt them later on in life. Three points in particular seem to stick in Drury's craw: Strauss's vaunted defense of esotericism, his ambiguous stance in regard to the status of morality, and his idiosyncratic account of the rapport between faith and reason. My hunch is that on all three counts Strauss is closer to both the pre-Christian and the Christian traditions than Professor Drury herself.

First, the question of esotericism, about which the least that can be said is that it was taken for granted by virtually everyone until roughly the end of the eighteenth century. Professor Drury is of the opinion that the truth is not nearly so terrible as Strauss thinks it is and hence that there is no reason to withhold it from the multitude. All truths are salutary. This obviously runs counter to the teaching of Plato's *Republic*, which defends noble lies, but it also runs counter to a teaching found everywhere in Greek patristic literature.

Origen, who did so much to shape the early Christian tradition, states flatly that it is always dangerous to talk about God. His predecessor, Clement of Alexandria, had already coined the expression *engraphos agrapha* to explain how a truth that is unfit for general consumption but useful to the learned may be silently inscribed in a written text. Oscar Wilde, not the least perceptive of writers when it comes to such matters, knew whereof he spoke when he alluded to the "aura of mendacity that adorns the pale brow of antiquity."

Not all intellects are capable of the highest truths. Scripture itself tells us that the number of the unwise is infinite—*stultorum infinitus est numerus*,[3] as the Latin translation of the Bible used by Augustine had it.

It likewise warns that the person who digs a pit and leaves it uncovered is responsible for anyone who might fall into it. The Church Fathers took that to mean that certain thorny questions were not to be discussed in the presence of the simple faithful, lest they should prove unsettling to them. Only the shallowest of persons, who has nothing of importance to say anyway, would state publicly everything he thinks exactly as he thinks it.

This is not the place to enter into a full discussion of this matter, whose fascinating history has been told many times, most notably by Grotius in the seventeenth century and by Cardinal Newman in the nineteenth century, much to the dismay of Newman's former co-religionists. The question is not whether esotericism was condoned and practiced by our forebears—it obviously was—but why we have so much trouble accepting it today. Two factors appear to have precipitated its demise: first, the Enlightenment notion that knowledge is power and, hence, that the end of science and that of civil society coincide; and second, the idea of progress, with its serendipitous faith in the irreversibility of an historical process that leads to ever-higher stages of human development.

Secondly, Professor Drury objects even more strenuously, if that is possible, to Strauss's supposed immoralism. All I can say is that the Strauss I knew was anything but the scoundrel the book makes him out to be. Far from denigrating morality, he was fond of quoting the famous text from the beginning of Book VII of the *Politics,* in which Aristotle says pointedly: "No one would maintain that he is happy who has not in him a particle of courage or moderation or justice or prudence, who is afraid of every insect that flutters past him, and will commit any crime, however great, in order to gratify his lust for meat or drink, who will sacrifice his dearest friend for the sake of an obol, and is as feeble and false in mind as a child or a madman."[4]

Professor Drury's eagerness to paint Strauss as an immoralist reveals itself among other ways in the tendency to put the worst possible face on some rather innocuous statements. A case in point is her understanding of Strauss's remark to the effect that "not everything just is noble," which she takes to mean that "a certain ignobility may be just if it is deemed necessary under the circumstances." Maybe so, but the statement also has a simpler meaning. It reminds us that the Greeks had no word for what we today call "morality." They spoke instead of the "just" and the "noble," thereby calling our attention to the fact that some human activities are rarer and more resplendent than others. The distinction is not unimportant. A streetsweeper who does his work well and pays his debts is without any doubt a just man. Yet no one who wishes to do justice to the full range of moral phenomena would dream of calling him noble for that reason alone.

The deeper issue concerns the ultimate status of morality, and on this score, Drury cannot come up with a better way of characterizing Strauss and his followers than by calling them highbrow consequentialists or thoroughgoing hedonists. They deny, she says, that moral virtue has any support in nature and have no qualms about bypassing it altogether when this can be done without any social inconvenience to themselves. That may or may not be the case, but given the importance that Professor Drury attaches to this issue, one wonders why she refuses to engage in any thematic discussion of it. Is there or is there not any cosmic support for justice? Is the universe structured in such a way as to insure that justice will not only predominate but always prevail within it? In simplest terms, is the world completely fair? We know that certain types of behavior are harmful to the individual who indulges in them and can thus be said to carry their own punishments with them. Eat or drink too much and you suffer the consequences. We also know that a life dedicated entirely to the pursuit of crime is liable not to be a happy one. But this still does not prove that all crimes will eventually be punished and that the only rewards that people reap in life are the ones to which in justice they are entitled.

This is what might be referred to as the problem of the happy crook, and it is a problem that is not easily resolved if one limits oneself to what natural reason is able to discover on its own. One would like to think that justice always redounds to the good of the one who practices it, but (to borrow a phrase from Shakespeare) that may be more than we know. Nature could very well be indifferent to the plight of the just. If this is the kind of secret that Strauss and his disciples are bent on keeping to themselves, they are not hiding very much. There is nothing here that has not been said or hinted at over and over again by the most unimpeachable authorities. After all, Plato and Aristotle are not the only ones to raise questions about the goodness of justice in the absence of a legislating and avenging God. The cat that Professor Drury boldly lets out of the bag is a pretty small animal.

The third and perhaps most delicate of Drury's three charges concerns Strauss's understanding of the relationship between faith and reason, the highest theme of the Western tradition as it has developed over the centuries. As is well known, Strauss stresses the tension between these two poles and denies that they can ever be fully reconciled. Perfected reason or philosophy cannot disprove the claims of divine revelation and divine revelation cannot establish its own claims except by means of arguments that are fully convincing only to those who have already acquiesced in its authority. Indeed, if faith in divine revelation is to mean anything, it cannot ultimately be accepted on any ground other than the faith itself. What we end up with is a kind of standoff in which neither side is able to defeat the other. Strauss is nevertheless quick to add that such a tension need not be deplored as long as one is willing and able to live it. To it, he thought, could be attributed the abiding vitality of the Western tradition.

Professor Drury, I gather, is unhappy with this formulation of the problem. Unlike Strauss, she apparently believes in a preestablished and demonstrable harmony between the two domains. She rejects Strauss's contention that the biblical God is a God of justice rather than of theoretical wisdom and cites in support of her view the New Testament saying, "The truth will make you free." She objects to Strauss's characterization of philosophy as the embodiment of what Genesis calls the knowledge of good and evil, and she is less than comfortable with the view that emphasizes the total suprarationality of the assent of faith.

Each of these crucial points would require a much lengthier discussion than any that can be accorded to them here. The least that can be said by way of a cursory reply is that on all three of them Strauss's views are close to, if not actually identical with, those of any number of orthodox theologians, beginning with Thomas Aquinas, who insists that unaided human reason is powerless to establish the possibility, let alone the truth, of divine revelation. Thomas will go no further than to say that the highest achievement of natural reason is to prove, not that divine revelation is possible—to administer such a proof would be to deny implicitly the supernatural character of revelation—but that the arguments leveled against it on rational grounds are never such as to compel our assent.

The precise issue, Strauss insisted, is not whether some rapprochement between divine revelation and philosophy as bodies of doctrines is feasible. The whole of medieval philosophy shows that it is, and Strauss himself is the first to admit it. It has to do rather with the choice between faith and reason as the respective grounds of two ways of life that are mutually exclusive in so far as each one claims absolute superiority over the other. Nor, in speaking of God, is it unbiblical to stress his justice rather than his wisdom. Contrary to what Professor Drury suggests, the freedom that Christ promises when he tells us that the truth will make us free is not primarily freedom from error, which is what the philosopher seeks, but freedom from sin. St. Augustine, who in the *Confessions* attributes his passion for speculative truth to Cicero and not to the Bible, knew that only too well. As for the equation of philosophy with the knowledge that Adam and Eve were forbidden to seek, it was taught by no less of an authority than St. Bonaventure, who declares in the plainest of terms that "philosophy is the tree of the knowledge of good and evil."

Professor Drury can hardly be blamed for wishing to protect morality and religion from the insidious assault supposedly mounted against them on philosophic grounds by Strauss and his school. I did not know what to make of her book when I first read it, and I am not sure what to make of it now. Here is an ostensibly orthodox thinker writing on behalf of moral and religious orthodoxy and putting people on their guard against those who would subtly undermine it. All well and good, except that most, if not all, of the positions impugned as both unorthodox and dangerous are identical or nearly identical to the ones taken by staunch upholders of the orthodox tradition. What in heaven's name is going on? I was perplexed. Then the truth dawned on me: perhaps Drury's book is a masterpiece of esoteric writing!

Every teacher knows without having to be told by Allan Bloom how hard it is to get young students to take serious writers seriously these days. Practically the only way to do it is to pick one such writer and attack him while pretending to give a scrupulously fair and impartial analysis of his thought. No reader runs the risk of missing the outwardly anti-Straussian thrust of Drury's argument, which is the only one that needs to be put across to most of them. This leaves open the possibility that a tiny minority of more perceptive readers will be mesmerized by the eloquent passages in which Strauss's views are laid out—often in Strauss's own words—and will catch a glimpse of an unknown world whose beauty surpasses anything he has ever imagined. What happens after that is anybody's guess, but, as Strauss once remarked, passages such as these, encountered in the midst of an otherwise dull book, could conceivably signal the beginning of a new life for them.

Drury's coup was all the more brilliant as it scored a double hit. It enabled her to rehabilitate Strauss and at the same time put the nasty Straussians in their places. She made it clear from the start that she had no intention of doing what she says Straussians usually do: build a shell around Strauss in order to preserve his secret. Her task was rather to tear down that protective shell. The strategy—let us call it the *Purloined Letter* strategy—could not be more clever. Drury makes us see the real Strauss, but without letting on that this is what she is doing. Fooled or distracted by her exoteric attack, the casual reader will conclude that what Strauss and the Straussians discover in philosophic texts is always the same old thing—no creator God, no divine providence or divine foreknowledge, no personal immortality, and the like—and he will not look for anything beyond that in Strauss's books.

None of this information will come as a great surprise anyway, since it does not take a genius to realize that the God of Aristotelian metaphysics, the "thought that thinks itself," has little in common with the loving and solicitous God of Abraham, Isaac, Jacob, and Jesus. Nor, if he is a believer, will the casual reader be unduly disturbed by it, for by their own admission philosophers have little to say with absolute certitude about any of the things about which they speak. The casual reader knows

for having been told by Drury that their approach is mainly "zetetic"
—rarely arriving at conclusions that are more than hypothetical. As a
result, our casual reader is a sure bet to miss what is most exciting in
Strauss. Never having personally experienced the siren call of a truly philosophic life, he will not be tempted by it and will dismiss it as nothing
but hedonism in disguise. Hence, the chances of his responding to Strauss
as the body snatcher and Pied Piper of souls that he is are virtually nil.

All of this is to say that Professor Drury has done what no one has
succeeded in doing for forty years: she has taught Straussians a lesson in
Straussianism. Anyone with a modicum of curiosity can read her book
and, sinking back into his complacency, come away with the impression
that he knows all there is to be known about Strauss, an impression no
Straussian has ever had.

The only thing wrong with this interpretation of Drury's work is that
it takes far too much for granted. It assumes that Drury herself has understood Strauss and is therefore free to disclose or conceal his "secrets" as
she sees fit and to whom she sees fit. This is to assume a great deal,
especially since there is not a shred of evidence that she has reflected
deeply on any of the authors whom Strauss claimed as his greatest
teachers and to whom he constantly directs our attention. In consequence,
nothing assures us that the student who has only her book to go by will
come within striking distance of its elusive quarry, save perhaps by some
unusually rare and happy accident.

NOTES

1. Shadia B. Drury, *The Political Ideas of Leo Strauss* (New York: St. Martin's
Press, 1988).

2. Leo Strauss, *Natural Right and History*, (Chicago: University of Chicago
Press, 1953).

3. Ecclesiastes 1:15.

4. Aristotle, *Politics* VII.1.1323a27-34.

17

STRAUSSIAN REFLECTIONS ON THE STRAUSS-VOEGELIN CORRESPONDENCE

In the final analysis, Leo Strauss is supposed to have said, there are two interesting things in life, God and politics, and furthermore, today we have neither. Apocryphal or not, the statement would no doubt have met with Voegelin's approval. The two men obviously had a lot in common, so much in fact that at one point Voegelin thinks he can refer to Strauss as a "kindred soul."[1] Together they did more than anyone else in our century to restore (a) political philosophy to the position of prominence that it once occupied among the human disciplines and (b) the theologico-political problem to its central position within political philosophy. It is, therefore, not surprising that most Voegelinians should have a general interest in Strauss (though not necessarily a good knowledge of him) and most Straussians a general interest in Voegelin (though not necessarily a good knowledge of him, either).

It would be futile in the limited space at my disposal to try to list all of the intellectual concerns that they shared. Both come across as critics and diagnosticians of modernity in its emphatic and not merely its chronological sense. Both are advocates of a dialectical return to premodern modes of thought, by which I mean a return informed by an awareness of the modern critique of classical thought, although not on the basis of that critique. Both are convinced that a "bracketing of modern thinking" is needed in order to effect such a return, that "radical doubt about the dogmas of the last three centuries is the beginning of wisdom," and that the common "objective of combating the presently reigning idiocy is more important than their differences," whatever these may turn out to be.[2] To read the fifty-odd letters that they exchanged, especially between 1942 and 1954, is to become acquainted with most of the great themes of the Western tradition: reason and Revelation, belief versus unbelief (according to Goethe, "*the* single most profound theme of world and human history"), the foundations of the philosophical enterprise, the intellectual roots of modernity, the quarrel between the ancients and the moderns, the problem of secularization, *logos* and myth, symbolism versus the "doctrinization" of Christianity, philosophy and law, theory and practice, philosophy and sophistry, positivism and historicism as the archetypal pathologies of twentieth-century thought, hermeneutics and the art of reading—the list could be extended almost at will.

Nor should we pass over in silence the priceless comments made by the two interlocutors about some of the intellectual gurus of our age. Several fascinating subplots unfold beneath the surface of these letters, one of them having to do with Strauss's initially less than candid attempt to involve Voegelin in a move to block Karl Popper's appointment to the faculty of the New School for Social Research by obtaining from him a written opinion about the candidate. The ploy not only worked; it elicited from the outspoken Voegelin a few of the correspondence's raciest remarks. I refer to his characterization of Popper as a "primitive ideological brawler"—"rascally," "impertinent," and "loutish"—and to Popper's work as "coffeehouse scum," "ideological rubbish," "impudent, dilettantish crap," and "a scandal without extenuating circumstances."[3] The informality and presumed confidentiality of the epistolary genre clearly has the advantage of allowing one to say things that would be ruled out of order in a text written for publication.

These little sideshows should not blind us to the fact that we are dealing here, not with run-of-the-mill academics, but with synoptic thinkers whose grasp of the Western tradition, ancient as well as modern, has rarely been matched in our time. If philosophy is an erotic quest for the truth about the whole and not simply about the parts independently of the whole, then they exemplify it to an uncommonly high degree. Both men are actuated by that rarest of passions, the passion for knowledge understood as something to be sought for its own sake and not, as in the case of the Sophists, for the prestige, power, or monetary rewards it might bring. The hankering for this knowledge is, as Strauss says (borrowing the expression from Plato), the philosopher's "highest mania."[4] Its object is not any truth whatever but a truth that engages the totality of one's being and thus constitutes the *unum necessarium*, or one thing, with which anybody caught up in its pursuit can never dispense.

This or something like it, I gather, is what first attracted the two interlocutors to each other. Part of the suspense generated by the letters stems from the fact that, the first contacts having been initiated, neither one knows exactly where the other stands on the issues at hand.[5] Finding the answer to that question is a knotty affair, in part because of the numerous semantic problems to be overcome. The same terms often mask serious differences of opinion, and different terms large areas of agreement. For a while it almost looked as if the loftiest kind of friendship, one that is based on a common understanding of the most vital matters, might blossom between them, even though by the time their paths crossed they were both well into middle age and hence beyond the point at which such friendships are likely to develop. It never did. When the smoke of polite battle finally lifted, at least three insurmountable barriers stood between them.

The first of these concerns the classic issue of the relationship between faith and philosophy. Strauss intimates as much when he says that his own premises are "very simple: *philosophari necesse est* ['it is necessary to philosophize'] and philosophy is radically independent of faith," to which he adds: "the root of our disagreement lies presumably in the second thesis."[6] The same thought is expressed in different ways on a variety of occasions in the letters that follow. Strauss is adamant in his denial that faith and philosophy can be synthesized. *Fides,* represented by the Middle Ages, is one thing; *epistêmê* or scientific knowledge, represented by classical antiquity, is something else. *Noêsis,* however understood, is not *pistis*; the two are irreducibly different.[7] This is not to rule out the possibility of any rapprochement whatever between them but only to say that such a rapprochement can never give rise to a *tertium quid* compounded of the two and superior to either one taken separately.

Voegelin is of a different mind. He fails to see how Strauss can "get around the historical fact of the beginning of philosophy in the attitude of faith of Xenophanes, Heraclitus, and Parmenides."[8] He attributes the same attitude to Plato, whose philosophy would likewise be rooted in myth, and he does not hesitate to call Aristotle, that paradigmatic rationalist, a "mystic," albeit an "intellectual" or "unmythical" mystic, in whose works the mythical image has been conceptualized.[9] Having read Strauss's *Philosophy and Law,* Voegelin has the impression that Strauss has "retreated from an understanding of the prophetic (religious) foundation of philosophizing . . . to a theory of *epistêmê*" and that he refuses "to see the problem of *epistêmê* in connection with experience, out of which it emerges."[10] I, for one, cannot imagine what gave Voegelin the idea that Strauss once thought philosophy had a prophetic origin, and Voegelin himself does not bother to tell us.

Strauss defends himself by pointing out that the distinction between revelation and human knowledge to which Voegelin objects is in harmony with "the Catholic teaching."[11] Judging from the context, what he has in mind is the Catholic teaching as distinguished from the typical Protestant teaching, i.e., the philosophically informed Catholic teaching of, say, Thomas Aquinas, who holds that nature is not destroyed but perfected by grace, so that even with the gift of grace it retains a discernible integrity. This is indeed standard Catholic fare, although not one that suits every-body's theological palate equally well. Thomas's doctrine, at least as commonly interpreted, was often called into question in the past and has again been vehemently attacked in our own day by a number of well-known Catholic theologians, such as the late Henri de Lubac, for whom Voegelin professed a profound admiration. Lubac's objection to it is that it looks upon grace as something added to nature from without and is thus guilty of an "extrinsicism" that he considers fatal to a proper under-standing of the relationship between them.

Thus formulated, the problem appears to be insoluble. Lubac's thesis, which, as far as I can tell, Voegelin accepts, is that there is no such thing as "an order of pure nature"[12] for the simple reason that the only nature of which we have any experience is a nature that has already been elevated to the supernatural order. Implied in this statement is a distinction between "graced" and "nongraced" nature or between nature in its "natural" state, so to speak, and nature in its "supernatural" or "trans-natural" state. How the two might differ from each other we have no way of knowing save by comparing them, and this we shall never be able to do since we have no access to nature in its original state. What we are finally left with is grace and only grace. The trouble is that, if all is grace, nothing is grace. Without its correlate, nature, grace simply ceases to be a term of distinction.[13] Using that term merely adds a spurious dignity to a discussion that can just as easily be carried on without it. The only way out of the impasse is to appeal, as Voegelin does, to the kind of intuitive and affective knowledge that is commonly associated with the mystical life. Strauss, who is more apt to question the claims of mystics than to take them at face value, is quick to distance himself from that particular approach to the question. As he observes, we are dealing here with an intra-Christian problem rather than a "universal-human" problem, one that arises on the basis of "a *specific* faith" and thus transcends the only level on which he can claim a measure of competence, namely, that of philosophy *qua* philosophy.

This brings us to a second key difference between our protagonists, namely, their stance and posture in regard to History with a capital "H" or "historicism," as they both call it. Voegelin's position on this all-important issue was for a long time unclear to Strauss. At one moment, he suspects Voegelin of being an historicist, later revises his opinion, and finally concludes that he is one after all, however qualifiedly. But a qualified historicist is still an historicist, and that is more than Strauss can take. He is willing to grant that "history" is a "condition" of truth, the search for which requires leisure, something not found in all societies, but not that it is the "source" of truth.[14] As a philosopher, he is not inclined to accept Voegelin's argument that the whole of human thought could be grounded in experiences that are not in principle accessible to all human beings at all times. Nor can he accept that the "Platonic-Aristotelian philosophy was put to rest by Christianity"[15] or that "philosophy in the Platonic sense . . . was made obsolete by revelation."[16] Nowhere in the correspondence does the gap between the two thinkers appear to be greater. Voegelin finds the classical perspective provincial, myopic, and time-bound. Reinstating it, he declares, is neither feasible nor desirable. Too much has happened since then. One must take into account the advances made not only by the Church Fathers and the Scholastics but by such contemporary authors as Bergson, Gilson, Jaspers, de Lubac, and von Balthasar,[17] all of them people about whom Strauss is either silent or whom he did not hold in highest esteem, with the possible exception of Bergson. The implication is that Plato and Aristotle are still in the cave, whereas he, Voegelin, who knows so much more than they did, is out of it and not about to go back into it.

A third major point on which our correspondents failed to reach agreement is the vexed question of the ideological roots of modernity. Voegelin, who does not think that atheism is possible, is convinced that modern philosophy, like all philosophy before it, is grounded in religious experience. It emerged by way of a "radical immanentization" or secularization of premodern Christian thought. Modernity has no independent principle of its own. It is essentially parasitic, a Christian heresy as it were, and, hence, a secondary or derivative phenomenon. One already finds "half-baked" versions of it in a variety of medieval authors, among them the Calabrian monk Joachim of Flora, in whose writings the notion of history as an ontological category, which would achieve its full development in Hegel six centuries later, first comes to the fore.[18]

What is wrong with this account in Strauss's view is that it does not pay sufficient attention to the turn that occurred "within philosophy" itself, which Strauss considers far more significant than any role, instrumental or otherwise, that Christianity might have played in the genesis and eventual triumph of modernity.[19] What is there in modern thought that cannot be accounted for without reference to Christianity? When all is said and done, very little, however hard Hegel, Nietzsche, Whitehead, and others like them may have tried to prove that modernity is a linear descendant of the Christian faith. In the pregnant sense in which Strauss speaks of it, modernity defines itself precisely in terms of its unflinching opposition to *both* Christianity and classical philosophy. As far as its own self-understanding is concerned, it is anything but a transmogrified Christianity, even though for political purposes it may occasionally have sought to pass itself off as just that.

Partial as he may have been to the ancients, Strauss never ceased to be fascinated by the moderns and to admire them for the originality, grace and subtlety of their writings. A telltale sign of this is his passing remark about Machiavelli, on whom he was writing a "small" book (some 350 pages long, as it turned out) and of whom he says with refreshing candor, "I can't help loving him—in spite of his errors."[20] This remarkably sympathetic disposition stands in sharp contrast to that of Voegelin, who hates the moderns and has trouble finding a single redeeming feature in them. Typical in this regard is his assessment of Locke, his *bête noire*, for whom he reserves some of his harshest judgments. Locke is not only mistaken, he is a "dirty," morally corrupt impostor consciously engaged in a gigantic "swindle" and ultimate "destruction" of *ratio*, a "nihilistic destroyer" who camouflages his real thought in order to "cover his work of destruction from the attentiveness of the qualified."[21] The danger is that, having written Locke off as a scoundrel and a rogue, Voegelin was hardly in a position to appreciate him at his true worth, great or small as it may be, and penetrate to the bottom of his thought. Ironically, this left him more vulnerable than might otherwise have been the case to the subtle influence of modern philosophy, so well represented by Locke. Although he is too polite to say so, Strauss seems to have concluded that Voegelin's break with modern thought was not radical enough and his return to premodern thought not complete enough. Part of the reason for this is that Voegelin's serious turn to the classics did not occur until he had all but finished his graduate studies under some famous positivists, as he himself mentions in his splendid *Autobiographical Reflections*.[22] The apparent harshness of Strauss's verdict is somewhat tempered by his observation that at the time the "preliminary studies" needed for a genuine recovery of the classical tradition were lacking.[23] To a large extent, they still are.

It is significant that the debate pursued in these letters came to an abrupt end in 1954, although, since the two correspondents were still at the peak of their intellectual powers, it could have gone on for another twenty years. Instead, it died a kind of natural death. Neither party seems to have been eager to prolong it. Why? The most plausible explanation is that they both sensed they had gone as far as they could along the road to mutual understanding and that there was no point in keeping the dialogue alive by artificial respiration. The discussion had not been in vain by any means, for it had helped them to clarify their thinking and at the same time made them more keenly aware of the fact that total agreement on fundamental issues is something that is rarely achieved even among great minds. As in the old Homeric tales, the moment had come for the two sides to disengage themselves from the battle, even though neither one was yet ready publicly to declare victory and hang up his trophies. This leaves the reader in the unenviable position of having to decide who won. When it comes to such difficult matters, an old teacher of mine, a famous Neoscholastic who was himself a scarred veteran of the theological wars of the early part of this century, used to say, "We shall know in purgatory." Strauss displays the same kind of modesty when he says at one point, "God knows who is right."[24]

For us more or less innocent bystanders, two questions remain to which, here again, there are no ready-made answers. First, which of the two, Strauss or Voegelin, is more sympathetic to religion? Most people would opt for Voegelin, and that is why, I suppose, scholars with a strong theological bent tend to be more attracted to him than to Strauss, who often passes for a skeptic and a nihilist among those who know little about him. Yet there may be at least as much to be said for Strauss's position, which Strauss himself calls with more than a semblance of good reason the "Catholic" position and which has the merit of being in some way less ambiguous than Voegelin's. After all, the contention that faith and reason, understood not merely as sets of doctrines but as total ways of life, are irreconcilable in the sense that one must ultimately choose one or the other as one's supreme guide redounds to the glory of the faith as much as it does to the glory of philosophy; for the former would lose its transcendent character and cease to be what it is if its truth could be established by means of philosophical arguments. Secondly, which is more compatible with revealed religion, classical philosophy, with which Christianity has been uneasily allied since the age of the Fathers, or modern philosophy, which, to the extent that it shuns any discussion of first principles, presents less of a threat to the primacy of religious knowledge? It is a tribute to the quality of this unique correspondence that it prompts us to raise these questions for ourselves and exemplifies in truly admirable fashion the spirit in which the elusive answers to them might be sought.

NOTES

1. Cf. *Faith and Political Philosophy: The Correspondence Between Leo Strauss and Eric Voegelin, 1934-1964.* Edited by P. Emberly and B. Cooper, (University Park, PA: Pennsylvania State University Press, 1993).

2. *Correspondence*, 59.

3. Ibid., 67-9.

4. Ibid., 63.

5. See, for example, p. 66: ". . . we are in more fundamental agreement than I believed." p. 72: ". . . I fully agree." p. 76: "We will not be in 'agreement'. . . " p. 98: "Externally, our efforts are to a surprising degree extensively in accord."

6. *Correspondence*, 72

7. Ibid., 76, 78.

8. Ibid., 74.

9. Ibid., 8-9.

10. Ibid., 77.

11. Ibid., 89.

12. On the "inconceivability and practical impossibility of an order of pure nature" and the passionate debate to which de Lubac's defense of this view gave rise in the forties and fifties, see, most recently de Lubac's own *Mémoire sur l'occasion de mes écrits* (Namur: Culture et verité, 1989), 262f.

13. I note in passing that a similar objection to de Lubac's position was raised by the distinguished French philosopher Maurice Blondel in a letter to de Lubac, which de Lubac himself subsequently published in his *Mémoire*, 189-90.

14. *Correspondence*, 65.

15. Ibid., 6.

16. Ibid., 91.

17. Ibid., 99, n 97.

18. Ibid., 73.

19. Ibid., 75.

20. Ibid., 98.

21. Ibid., 94-6.

22. Eric Voegelin, *Autobiographical Reflections*, edited by Ellis Sandoz (Baton Rouge and London: Louisiana State University Press, 1989), 30, 39, et passim.

23. Correspondence, 59.

24. Ibid., 91.

NIETZSCHE AND THE CRISIS OF NIHILISM

Given his low opinion of professional philosophers and his almost patho-logical fear of being misunderstood, Nietzsche would hardly have been pleased with the current surge of interest in his writings. On the theory that the more novel one's teaching is, the less likely it is to be well received by one's contemporaries, he once suggested that *Beyond Good and Evil* should not be read until about the year 2000.[1] He could have said the same thing of *Thus Spoke Zarathustra*, which is typically subtitled, *A Book for Everyone and No One*. The problem is further complicated by his often oracular style, the self-acknowledged intellectual evolution that he underwent over a productive period of less than twenty years,[2] and above all the unfinished character of his thought. Paradoxically, Nietzsche, who shares with Marx the dubious honor of being the most outspoken of philosophers, is at the same time the most secretive writer of his gener-ation. It is therefore not surprising that the interpretation of his works should continue to give rise to profound disagreements on the part of competent scholars.

Was Nietzsche the radical innovator that he claimed to be,[3] the herald of a new gospel,[4] the first philosopher in whom the entire tradition of Western metaphysics finds its fulfillment and therewith its ultimate trans-formation?[5] To these and similar questions, Walter Kaufmann responds with a resounding "No!"[6] For all his iconoclastic bombast and his manifest opposition to the ruling consciousness of his day, Nietzsche is anything but the irrationalist and the immoralist that his Marxist adversaries have made him out to be. Neither is he simply a reactionary bourgeois who found an artificial solution to the creeping decadence of the modern world. According to Kaufmann, his blunt defense of reason in *The Gay Science* proves sufficiently that he had no desire to turn his back upon it.[7] His dislike for Christianity, as distinguished from Christ, is unmistakable, but even then he only attacked it on the ground that it denigrated reason. The same holds for his criticism of all philosophical systems, to which he objected not because they were too rational but because, by refusing to question their own assumptions, they were not rational enough.

As regards Nietzsche's call for a sweeping "revaluation of all values," Kaufmann is of the opinion that it cannot in any way be construed as an all-out assault on morality itself, since its sole purpose was to rid contemporary morality of the ingredients of hypocrisy, comfortableness, and laxity with which it had long been infested. Like Kierkegaard, Nietzsche was attracted to both Christ and Socrates, but whereas Kierkegaard preferred Christ, Nietzsche opted for Socrates, whom he sought to emulate by vivisectionally applying the knife to the counterfeit values of his time. Accordingly, his moral program is not a new legislation. Its aim is rather to restore the old values, which had suffered a drastic revaluation at the hands of Christianity. By revaluating the revaluation or negating the negation, Nietzsche has in fact performed a positive and much-needed task.[8] To reproach him with having hastened the advent of nihilism, as many have done, is to overlook the fact that he merely helped topple what was already falling and pave the way for the recovery of the genuine virtues that centuries of Christian living had successfully repressed.

While one should be grateful to Kaufmann for having denazified Nietzsche and rescued him from the crude prejudices to which his reputation had fallen victim between the two world wars, one wonders whether his stunning rehabilitation does full justice to the complexity of the subject at hand.[9] A closer look at Nietzsche's concept of nihilism, which receives short shrift in Kaufmann's treatment, will, I hope, bring to light a number of elements that coexist only in an uneasy tension with, and perhaps even flatly contradict, the Socratic ideal to which Kaufmann points as the core of the Nietzschean enterprise.

THE CONCEPT OF NIHILISM

In his last and most controversial book, Nietzsche predicted that his name would one day be associated with a crisis the like of which had never been seen on earth.[10] The nature of that crisis is best expressed by the word *nihilism,* which occurs with increasing frequency in his works from the year 1886 onward and which designates what he gradually came to perceive as the fundamental fact of European history. Although the term itself is older than Nietzsche, having been applied by Turgenev and others to a growing number of young radicals who challenged the traditional values of Western society in the name of scientific progress, it is fair to say that it acquires in his later works a depth of meaning that goes far beyond anything that attaches to it in the literature of the nineteenth century.[11] The reality to which it refers is not a specific world-view, comparable to other contemporary or older world-views, but a pervasive phenomenon engulfing the whole of modern life and thought—the spiritual style, so to speak, of the Western world. In its most advanced pre-Nietzschean form, it is coextensive with historicism or historical relativism and manifests itself most clearly in the final repudiation of all absolute or eternally valid norms of conduct. As such, it constitutes the root cause rather than the consequence of the corruption and moral decay of modern society. Its motto is "Nothing is true; everything is permitted,"[12] which represents the only consistent and legitimate response to the emptiness of life without a compelling horizon of values.

The distinctive features of the new movement will come into sharper focus if we glance briefly at the two older philosophical positions to which it seems to bear the closest resemblance, skepticism and classical conventionalism. Skepticism, in contrast to nihilism, is essentially ahistorical. It is not bound to a particular historical configuration and presents itself as accessible to human reason at all times. It merely regards all notions of right and wrong as based on the arbitrary decisions of the community and makes no effort to correlate them with the conditions that prevail in actual societies at any given moment.

Classical conventionalism, represented philosophically by Epicureanism and, on a more popular level, by the Sophists of antiquity, is likewise ahistorical. It, too, rejects the commonly accepted principles of justice and morality on the ground that they have their source in human convention rather than in nature. It shares with its foremost competitor, the natural right theory of Plato and Aristotle, the fundamental distinction between nature and convention, as well as the notion of the superiority of the former over the latter. Like the natural right theory, it views philosophy as an ascent from public opinion to private knowledge or as an attempt to grasp the eternal order whose existence is presupposed by, though only imperfectly reflected in, the officially sanctioned dogmas by which societies are governed. Yet it refuses to consider justice as something desirable or choiceworthy for its own sake. By nature, human beings seek their own pleasure or their own aggrandizement, if need be at the expense of others. The rules of morality on which society depends for its well-being are just a series of expedients invented by the weaker members of that society to defend themselves against the encroachments of their betters. They are not inherently binding and serve only to obscure the normative character of nature, to which the wise person must turn for a true understanding of the goals of human existence.[13]

Nihilism, on the other hand, does away with the dichotomy between nature and convention altogether. One might say in a provisional way that it looks upon all right, legal or otherwise, as conventional. As opposed to both skepticism and conventionalism, it does not pretend to be coeval with human reason but is said to be related to an unprecedented situation in which all notions of right and wrong, and indeed the very distinction between right and wrong, have become questionable. Its emergence is linked to the catastrophic context of the present crash of all horizons or the total dissolution of all viable syntheses of meaning and value.[14] It culminates in the view that no value or set of values, whether it be those of civilization or those of cannibalism, is demonstrably superior to any other value or set of values. Its essence is summed up in the formula "God is dead,"[15] which, as its paradoxical wording indicates, is to be taken not as a simple profession of faith in atheism and hence as a theoretical statement belonging to the same order of truth as its opposite, theism, but as an emphatically historical statement calculated to bring home to us the uniqueness of the predicament within which it comes to light. It should be added that the God whose demise it proclaims stands not only for the Christian God but for all other gods as well.[16] In the highest instance, *God* is synonymous with the transcendent realm of metaphysical ideas and ideals from which, since Plato or at least the Hellenistic and Christian interpretations of Plato, the sensory world of human experience has been thought to derive its significance. Since, as we are told elsewhere, the gods themselves now "philosophize,"[17] or, to express the same view in less metaphorical terms, since there is no truth to be found in this or any other world, human beings are left without anything by which they might take their bearings. Like the madman to whom the announcement of the death of God is entrusted in *The Gay Science,* they suddenly find themselves "straying as through an infinite nothing."[18] The crisis that they face is a *total* crisis, provoked by the structural disintegration, not of this or that particular ideal, but of the whole world of classical and biblical thought which had hitherto made possible and supported all forms of civilized life as we have known them or could imagine them. All moral precepts having been revealed to be matters of blind preference, it would be sheer foolishness or hypocrisy to allow oneself to be determined by them in one's actions. At the extreme limit, anything that anyone will dare to do becomes permissible.

Thus understood, nihilism is only the last stage in a process that has already lasted for a century and whose roots stretch back to the origins of the philosophic tradition. Its remote ancestor is none other than Socrates, the "prototype of the theoretical man,"[19] who destroyed the primal unity of Greek culture by establishing reason as the master of the instinctual life. It is to Socrates that the West owes the "sublime metaphysical illusion that thought can penetrate the deepest abysses of being."[20] Via Christianity, what was nonetheless only a "tendency" in Socrates has since come to inform and dominate all subsequent modes of thought up to and including historicism, to the degree to which it still adheres to the notion of scientific objectivity.

The point to notice, however, is that the present crisis was not generated from without but is the end product of an internal and thoroughly moralistic development. Had Western civilization merely succumbed to a more powerful external enemy, it could have gone down with honor, proud of itself and convinced of the superiority of its own cause. As it is, it bore within itself and from the outset the seeds of its ultimate destruction. The theoretical impulse at work within it made it inevitable that sooner or later its supreme values should not only be devalued but should "devalue themselves."[21] Indeed, once the belief in a suprasensory world of eternal ideas is seen to be without foundation, any attempt to cling to it becomes a mere pretense. At this point, truthfulness turns against itself and puts an end to all forms of self-deceit.[22] In the name of intellectual probity or honesty, the last of our remaining virtues,[23] one is compelled to face that most terrible of all truths, the truth that there is no truth. It may be observed that in the process truthfulness itself, whose role as a moral virtue was strictly provisional, is called upon to disappear, leaving room for the single virtue that characterizes Nietzsche's philosopher of the future, the new historical sense.[24]

THE BASIS OF NIHILISM

The Nietzschean view regarding the illusory character of all objective norms and standards is sometimes said to be rooted in the experience of history, which confronts us with an apparently endless array of conflicting goals and ideals and thus seems to call into question the intrinsic validity of all human goals and ideals. There is considerable doubt, however, as to whether the evidence supplied by history warrants the conclusion that nothing whatever is right by nature. History reveals that the ideals pursued at different times by different individuals or groups of individuals often contradict one another; it does not prove that they refute one another, and it says even less about their relative merits or the possible superiority of one over the other. Natural right would be free of controversy only if its principles could be shown to be immediately available to everyone. If, on the other hand, the discovery of these principles is contingent on the use of properly cultivated reason, as most natural right theorists argued, one would normally expect people to disagree about them, but one would also be inclined to ascribe these disagreements to human error rather than to any defect in the theory itself. In short, what the experience of history taken by itself suggests is that the knowledge of what is right by nature is difficult, not that it is impossible. Furthermore, the awareness of the indefinite variety of human ideals was never absent from the philosophic tradition and was even regarded by older thinkers, not as an argument against natural right, but as the necessary condition for the emergence of natural right. For without such an awareness, it would not dawn on anyone to look for an understanding of justice that is grounded in something other and presumably higher than human agreement or consent.[25]

In light of these remarks, one is led to conclude that the view espoused and philosophically elaborated by Nietzsche is predicated not on the experience of history as such, but on a particular interpretation of that experience, prompted by and growing out of the prior conviction that theoretical knowledge of any kind is not only difficult but impossible. It goes without saying that a complete analysis of Nietzsche's position on this score would require a much lengthier discussion than space and time permit. At the risk of considerable oversimplification, I shall limit myself to a bare summary of the argument as it occurs in the first chapter of *Beyond Good and Evil,* which offers as clear and concise a statement of the issue as is to be found anywhere in his works. As already noted, philosophy was originally conceived as an attempt to understand all things in the best possible manner by the sole use of one's reason. Its aim was to replace the opinions about the whole that most people share, but never question, with a genuine knowledge of the whole. To be sure, it never contended that a perfect knowledge of the whole had been reached or was even attainable. To the extent to which the whole remains elusive, it defies any perfectly lucid and rational account that one might be tempted to give of it. Yet philosophy does not stand or fall by its ability to answer all questions or even by its ability to provide a final answer to any of them. It requires for its justification only that human reason have access to the fundamental problems, as well as to the limited number of alternative solutions to those problems. It is thus more properly defined not as wisdom but as the love of wisdom or an unending quest for wisdom. However much philosophers may have disagreed among themselves in the past, they were nevertheless united in a common search for a common truth.

This desire to know or, as Nietzsche calls it, this "will to truth,"[26] is what eventually proves to be most problematic. Philosophers, who are notorious for questioning everything, have never seriously questioned their own impulse to raise questions. All of them gratuitously posited the

existence of a preestablished order, which each one claimed to have discovered and articulated more perfectly than any predecessor or rival. Like
Oedipus, they took it for granted that the riddle to be solved existed
outside of themselves and did not think of asking what "in them" had
caused them to seek an answer to it in the first place.[27] At no time did it
occur to them that the mystery could conceivably lie with the inquirer
rather than with the object of inquiry. Even their disagreements were at
bottom mere lovers' quarrels, serving only to confirm them in their love
for an object whose existence was never doubted. Their systems are all
based on a dogmatically asserted premise which, upon examination, turns
out to be a delusion. In Nietzsche's phrase, they are "beautiful and strong
asses,"[28] some more impressive than others perhaps, but all of them
equally stupid. Contrary to popular belief, one finds nothing in them that
is impersonal or detached. Philosophers are "lawyers" who defend their
own causes by means of arguments invented after the fact.[29] Their thought
is best described as a species of unconscious autobiography, which invariably tells us more about the authors themselves than the reality they purport to investigate.[30]

It follows that there is no permanent order of being to be uncovered
anywhere, just as there are no permanent problems of being to which a
solution of some kind, however tentative, might be sought. All human
thought rests finally on premises which, far from being self-evident, are
imposed upon us by history or by fate. Thought necessarily belongs to a
particular perspective, which it can enlarge but which it can never transcend and beyond which it has no meaning. One can of course analyze its
conditions, but since by definition the analysis is itself historically
conditioned, it remains subject to the same basic criticism. The ultimate
at which one arrives in analyzing any thought is a free act of the will in
the light of which everything else is understood but which is not itself in
the light. The same goes for Nietzsche's own philosophy, which must
likewise be seen as an interpretation.[31] The only feature that distinguishes
it from other interpretations is that it is conscious of the fact that it is an
interpretation. Its sole claim to superiority is that, as the first perspective
to be aware of the law of perspectivity, it ranks as the highest possible
perspective. What we end up with is not just a new philosophy but a new
type of philosophy which parts company with the whole tradition of
philosophic thought by denying the very possibility of philosophy as it
had always been understood.[32]

THE SELF-OVERCOMING OF NIHILISM

We scarcely need to remind ourselves that the notion of historical perspectivism did not originate with Nietzsche, since it was already present

and operative in much of earlier nineteenth-century thought. If Nietzsche is to be credited with anything, it is rather with having been the first to perceive the nihilistic consequences of that insight. As he saw it, the immediate danger to which it gives rise is not that, once persuaded that nothing is true, human beings will feel free to embark upon ruthless and destructive courses of action, but that they will lack the incentive to do anything at all. Human greatness hinges on one's willingness to devote oneself heart and soul to the pursuit of a noble cause. It presupposes that one is convinced of the righteousness of that cause and prepared to make whatever sacrifices it may require. Yet it is doubtful that one who has glimpsed the ephemeral character and hence the ultimate vanity of all such causes will ever be motivated to sacrifice oneself for any of them. Human life can only thrive within a limited horizon.[33] It requires for its well-being a protective atmosphere that restricts one's vision and blinds one to the injustice implied in the choice of any goal. By disclosing all specific horizons as mere horizons, perspectivism necessarily destroys those horizons and poisons the wellsprings of human activity. It teaches not only that all ideals are perishable but, inasmuch as life is inseparable from injustice, that they deserve to perish.[34] Its truth is in fact a "deadly truth,"[35] breeding inertia or apathy and leading in the end to the blessed narcosis of a life dedicated only to the pursuit of comfortable self-preservation or the satisfaction of one's bodily needs.

The long-range but inevitable result of this state of affairs is the complete degradation of the human race or the universal domination of the lowest human beings, who are not even aware of the extent to which they have degenerated, who no longer have any desire to rule or to be ruled, and whose sole ideal, if it can be called an ideal, is that of the single fold without a shepherd.[36] The depths to which the modern herd animal has already sunk is nowhere more clearly visible than in the barbarism that afflicts the bulk of present-day art. By opening themselves up to all sorts of foreign influences indiscriminately, contemporary artists have forfeited any chance of developing a style of their own. The tasteless amalgamation of heterogeneous elements with which their works present us is symptomatic of the plight of the modern world in its totality, which knows everything but is incapable of loving anything and is itself nothing.[37]

This is not to suggest that there are no legitimate uses to which the practice of history may be put to remedy the situation. Insofar as it furnishes us with examples of former greatness, it could still stimulate activity and provide a necessary antidote to the evils of the present. It is thus more proper to say that what we suffer from is not history itself but an excess of history or an overdose of the antidote.[38] Interestingly enough, the modern historical movement, which bears most of the blame for these evils, was originally in the service of life and probably would not have survived had it not been nurtured in its infancy by an ardent love of the fatherland. Its first promoters were dedicated patriots whose attachment to their national past was intensified by the crushing defeat that they had recently been dealt by the Napoleonic armies. The misfortune is that the learned habit acquired in the process soon took on a life of its own, which persisted long after the springs of piety had dried up, transforming itself into an insatiable curiosity for anything old and greedily devouring "every scrap that falls from the bibliographical table." What had begun as national history became universal history, carrying in its wake a "restless cosmopolitanism" which preserves the corpse but is utterly incapable of instilling new life into it.[39]

It is nevertheless true that the situation just described represents only the most acute form of nihilism yet reached by Western thought. For the most part, the nihilism typical of nineteenth-century society is, in Nietzsche's view, only an "imperfect" or "incomplete" nihilism,[40] which shows itself under two different guises, one optimistic and the other pessimistic. The first of these is the cheerful or serene nihilism of the free spirits who rejoice in the death of God ("God is dead, thank God!") but cling that much more firmly to the faith in Christian morality and the dignity of the human being. Its fashionable representative is the liberal theologian David Strauss, who proclaims with "admirable frankness" that he has ceased to be a Christian and hails Darwin as a great benefactor of humanity, but whose boldness is limited to words and who thinks he can continue to live as if nothing had changed. The fallacy in Strauss's argument is that it assumes that one can get rid of the architect and keep the building or do away with the lawgiver and still claim the protection of the law. A more consistent Strauss would have realized that his premises lead straight to a "new Hobbesian war of every man against every other man."[41] Christian belief and Christian morality go together, to such a degree that the latter cannot long survive the death of the former. As Nietzsche puts it in a later reference to the essay on Strauss, "When one gives up the Christian faith, one pulls the right to Christian morality right out from under one's feet."[42] More generally stated, if traditional speculative thought is jettisoned, then traditional morality, which is rooted in it, will also have to be forsaken and replaced by a totally new morality that has nothing but the name in common with the older moral doctrines. Without knowing it, Strauss is living on borrowed time. His naive optimism, inherited from Hegel and illogically maintained after the abandonment of the Hegelian notion of the end of history, is more aptly described as philistinism, or, if one prefers, cultured philistinism.[43]

The inconsistency is not Strauss's alone. It is characteristic of the entire modern democratic movement and its unruly tail, socialism, with its cherished belief in progress, its inherent low-mindedness, its utter dedication to mediocrity, and its slavish resentment of all forms of superiority. All of these people are unconscious heirs of the Christian tradition,[44] who have merely replaced the authority of God with that of reason and exchanged the otherworldly goal of everlasting bliss for the earthly happiness of the greatest number. Severed from their Christian moorings, they must suffer the same fate. The same applies to anarchists, who would gladly overthrow bourgeois society for the sake of a better world but cannot imagine anything radically different from the values they set out to destroy.[45]

Side by side with this optimistic nihilism one finds the morbid nihilism of the pessimist, who, far from taking pride in the accomplishments of his contemporaries, has become thoroughly disenchanted with the flatness of modern life and seeks to escape from it by every possible means. The new mood is discernible in the romantic longing for a heroic but irretrievable past, or, for those who find the past too remote, in such other forms of evasion as the cult of art for art's sake or Schopenhauer's futile attempt to annihilate the will through an act of the will.[46] All of these attitudes are reflective of the generalized paralysis with which the age is stricken, and in none of them do we encounter anything like a genuine revaluation of values.

To these more or less developed forms of nihilism Nietzsche opposes his own brand of nihilism, which he labels "active nihilism," and which is identical with the epoch-making shift from historical consciousness to hermeneutical consciousness, or, to state the matter in terms that more closely approximate Nietzsche's own, from theoretical historicism to radical historicism.[47] Assuming that the belief in objective truth is indispensable to all higher forms of life, one might at first be tempted to substitute a new myth or a "mighty lie" for the deadly truth of historicism.[48] But it does not take much effort to see that this solution, which is the one that Plato had adopted, will no longer work. For one thing, a fabricated myth is not a genuine myth and will always lack the effective power of a genuine myth. For another, the demands imposed upon us by our newly acquired intellectual probity are such as to preclude any recourse to lies, however beneficial or well-intentioned.

Nietzsche's solution consists not in rejecting but in accepting and radicalizing the historicist premise regarding the relativity of all truths by applying it to scientific history itself. That solution comes to sight when one begins to perceive the essential limitations of scientific history as well as of all other forms of objective knowledge. The trouble with nineteenth-century historicism is that it did not take history seriously enough. It presumed to be able to arrive at a genuine knowledge of the past and failed to take into account the fundamental disproportion between life, which presupposes a commitment to substantive principles of thought and action, and modern historical science, which renders any such commitment impossible. As a mere onlooker, the scientific historian is in no position to recover the substance of the past, for it takes a committed person to understand another person's commitment. What is resurrected is not the past itself, which can only be grasped by what is most powerful in the present, but an impoverished version of it.[49]

There is an entirely different conclusion to be drawn from the nihilistic devaluation of all values, which is that human beings can now do consciously what their predecessors could only do unconsciously and under the false assumption that they were complying with God-given or otherwise demonstrably valid norms of behavior. They are at last free to create their own values in a manner that no longer suffers from the limitations under which people had previously labored. The name given to this radically new project is the "will to power," as opposed to the old will to truth on the one hand and the will to mere life on the other.[50] Its most perfect embodiment is the "superman," who has yet to come into being and whose emergence is by no means assured, but in whom Nietzsche's redeemed humanity finds its ultimate meaning. It needs to be stressed that the new project is itself the product of an unpredictable creative act, which as such is not deducible from the experience of nihilism, although it assumes it and remains in complete agreement with it.[51]

THE DILEMMAS OF NIETZSCHEAN NIHILISM

The Nietzschean attempt to overcome nihilism from within and on the basis of its own premise is open to a number of serious objections to which Nietzsche was forced to devote greater attention as time went on. Not the least obvious of these objections is the seeming contradiction implied in the thesis that there are no timeless truths, which at first hearing has all the earmarks of a timeless or trans-historical truth. If all philosophy is interpretation, it is not easy to see how Nietzsche can exempt himself from his own verdict and claim for his philosophy a finality that he denies to every other philosophy. The truth of relativism cannot be asserted absolutely. One has to assume that, as a mere interpretation, Nietzsche's philosophy is itself provisional and subject to revision. The objection need not be decisive, however. On purely logical grounds, it may be countered by saying that the radical dependence of thought on fate is not a truth that is accessible to human beings as human beings. It is the preserve of one and only one moment, namely, that privileged moment in which human thought is given an intuition into its own nature and becomes, as it were, transparent to itself. It thus remains uniquely historical, differing from other historical insights only by reason of a peculiar self-awareness that it, and it alone, happens to possess.

The more pertinent objection concerns the hierarchy of values postulated by the antithesis between the "superman" and the "last man," which, as an expression of the will to power, can with equal reason be thought to lack any objective status. The objection is only partially resolved by the observation that, since the superman distances himself from the last man by creating his own nature, his superiority is not to be judged in terms of any eternal or pre-existing standard but is itself its own standard or measure. For even if this should prove to be the case, one could still ask whether, in the absence of any assignable limits to what it can do, the will to power is not capable of overcoming itself by decreeing the abolition of the superman, along with the entire hierarchical structure of being to which his appearance gives rise. Nietzsche apparently thought that the clue to this thorniest of all questions lay in the notoriously difficult doctrine of the eternal recurrence of the identical, on which the whole of his philosophy was finally made to turn. By guaranteeing the return of all things exactly as they have always been, and hence of the last man as well as the superman, the eternal recurrence rules out forever the possibility of an eventual total degradation of humanity. It views the past with all its fragments, its scattered parts, and its horrible accidents, not as something to be conquered, as Hegel and Marx had taught, but as something to be affirmed and willed as the necessary condition of the redemption of the human race.[52]

To my knowledge, no one today subscribes to any of the three closely related doctrines that lie at the heart of Nietzsche's philosophy: the will to power, the superman, and the eternal return. This is not to say, however, that the problems which Nietzsche attempted to solve by means of these doctrines can be safely disregarded by anyone who remains committed to a historical understanding of human existence. I shall mention only three such problems with which subsequent thinkers have had to contend and to which, as far as I can see, no completely clear solution has yet been offered.

The first has to do with the guidance that the new kind of thinking initiated by Nietzsche is able to provide in human affairs. Nietzsche's highly unsystematic philosophy may with some justification be seen as an extreme reaction against Hegel's completely systematic philosophy, which was wholly oriented toward the past and which did away with the need for ethics altogether. From that point of view at least, Nietzsche shares one of the major concerns of pre-Hegelian philosophy, which was to direct human action. The question is whether that concern can be adequately met by the substitution of historical standards for the now discarded universal standards. There are, admittedly, no concrete norms of behavior to be derived from past history, which is essentially nonrepeatable. Moreover, unless one is convinced beforehand that the victorious cause is necessarily the best cause, one would hesitate to say that the acceptance of an emerging trend or consensus is always preferable to the rejection of that trend or consensus. Given the lack of any identified or identifiable moral norm, all that remains, it seems, is a unique kind of formal ethics which takes the form of an appeal either to Nietzschean creativity or to its more recent analogue, Heideggerian authenticity. Both appeals are fraught with difficulties, a full discussion of which mercifully lies beyond the scope of a brief essay.

The second problem is related to the manner in which, on the basis of the Nietzschean premise regarding the historicity of human thought, one is able to understand any of the older or nonhistorical philosophies for which the new philosophy was intended as a replacement. Unlike modern scientists, who can rest content with their theory as long as it produces the desired results, philosophers are never dispensed from the obligation to retrace their steps and reexamine their point of departure. The choice of their own way necessitates the consideration of alternative or competing ways, which cannot be dismissed until such time as they have been thoroughly scrutinized and found wanting. This amounts to an admission that continued efforts at self-understanding are inseparable from an effort to understand others as well. According to Nietzsche and his followers, however, such an effort can never be expected to yield more than limited results. One cannot possibly hope to understand the authors of the past as they understood themselves; one can, at best, understand them differently.[53] Yet the rejection of any or all of these authors necessarily entails a criticism of their respective positions and hence the implicit claim to have understood them better than they understood themselves. Furthermore, one fails to see how the impossibility of an objective or detached understanding of an older author can be established from history itself. There is no denying that the authors of the past have been understood differently by different people over long periods of time. But one cannot infer from that observation that none of the interpretations that have been given or could still be given of them is the correct one. In order to be absolutely certain that it is not, one would have to know both the author's thought and that of the interpreter. Since a completely objective knowledge of the first and perhaps even of the second is supposedly impossible, one is left without any real basis for judgment.[54]

The final unresolved problem concerns the notion of a privileged or absolute moment with which Nietzsche's philosophy and any strictly historical philosophy is inescapably bound up, an absolute moment similar to the one presupposed by Hegelian philosophy, although obviously not identical with it since it is no longer dependent on the assumption of the completeness of the historical process. The existence of this absolute moment is vouched for by the fact that the discovery of the fundamentally historical nature of human thought coincides with the rise of nihilism or the collapse of all horizons, which alone makes that discovery possible. More simply put, the discovery of the historical nature of human thought is itself historical or historically conditioned. It belongs properly to our time. For that reason, it was not shared and could not have been shared by earlier ages, all of which were firmly convinced of the objective validity of their own norms and values. For the same reason, one must suppose that the situation within which it arises will sooner or later give way to a different situation calling for a different type of hermeneutics. Yet neither in Nietzsche nor in any of his successors, do we find the suggestion that a major change in philosophical orientation is to be expected. If anything, the insight into the historicity of human thought is regarded as definitive. It is here to stay and is not likely to be affected by future developments. One wonders in that case whether the new hermeneutics does not again claim for itself a universality or an infinity that is implicitly ruled out by its own admission of the finite character of all human experience.[55]

The movement of Nietzsche's thought may be described as a movement from history to nature which bypasses the primacy of reason and sees nature itself as a creation of the universal will to power.[56] That movement has been correctly diagnosed by Heidegger as a relapse into traditional metaphysics. Whether Heidegger succeeded in purging Nietzschean philosophy of the metaphysical remnants with which it remains infected is a question that may conveniently be left to others to decide. The relapse does, however, reveal a greater closeness of Nietzsche to Socrates than the thrust of the preceding argument may have led us to think. Nietzsche's fascination with Socrates is undeniable. There also appears to be little doubt that he looked upon Socrates as his most formidable adversary. It is significant that he is himself the first philosopher to have taken issue with Socrates, who, as the originator of philosophy, had previously been immune to all attack even on the part of those who rejected the whole of classical philosophy. That Nietzsche's first book, the *Birth of Tragedy,* should have dealt in the main with Socrates, and that an important segment of one of his last books, the *Twilight of Idols,* should be entitled "The Problem of Socrates," is ample evidence that Socrates was from the beginning and remained to the end the crucial problem. It likewise suggests that the victory which he claimed to have won over him may not be as final as he himself would sometimes have us believe. Nietzsche's entanglement in the thicket of the idea of values was due in large part to the influence of Socrates. According to Heidegger, that entanglement is the reason for his failure to attain "the true center of philosophy." But, as Heidegger is also quick to point out, "Even if a future philosopher should reach this center—we of the present day can only work toward it—he will not escape entanglement, but it will be a different entanglement. No one can jump over his shadow."[57]

Nietzsche's valiant endeavor to resurrect a mummified Socrates, if only for the purpose of refuting him, raises two questions, which may never be fully answered but which can no longer be avoided. The first is whether Nietzsche's new perspective is indeed broader than, and therefore superior to, that of his antagonist. The second is whether, beyond the indefinite variety of particular perspectives with which history acquaints us, there is not *the* perspective or *the* horizon which lends meaning to all of them and renders the disagreements among philosophers intelligible, even though it may never suffice to resolve them.

NOTES

1. Friedrich Nietzsche, *Selected Letters of Friedrich Nietzsche,* edited and translated by Christopher Middleton (Chicago and London: University of Chicago Press, 1969), 256, letter of September 14, 1886, to Malwida von Meysenbug.

2. Ibid., 285-86, letter of February 19, 1888, to Georg Brandes. See also Friedrich Nietzsche, *The Gay Science,* translated by Walter Kaufmann (New York: Vintage Books, 1974), no. 370.

3. Cf. Nietzsche, *The Gay Science,* no. 124.

4. Nietzsche, *Selected Letters,* 311, letter of September 14, 1888, to Paul Deussen.

5. Martin Heidegger, "The Word of Nietzsche: 'God Is Dead'," in *The Question Concerning Technology and Other Essays,* translated by William Lovitt (New York: Harper and Row, 1977), 112.

6. Walter Kaufmann, *Nietzsche: Philosopher, Psychologist, Antichrist* (Princeton, N.J.: Princeton University Press, 1974), 110

7. Ibid., 230, with references to *Gay Science* nos. 2 and 359.

8. Ibid,. 111-12.

9. For a critique of Kaufmann's book on this score, see W. Dannhauser, *Nietzsche's View of Socrates* (Ithaca, NY: Cornell University Press, 1974), 26-41.

10. Friedrich Nietzsche, *Ecce Homo* and *On the Genealogy of Morals,* translated by Walter Kaufmann (New York: Vintage Books, 1967), "Why I Am a Destiny," no. 1 in *Ecce Homo.*

11. See in particular Turgenev's famous portrait of the "nihilist" Bazarov in *Fathers and Sons* (1862). The word *nihilism* appears to have been coined by Jacobi in his letter to Fichte, March 21, 1799, where idealism is described as a form of nihilism; cf. F. H. Jacobi, *Werke,* vol 3 (Leipzig, 1816), 44. A modern edition is Jacobi's *Werke,* edited by F. Roth and J. Koefpen (Darmstadt: Wissenschaftliche Buchgesellschaft, 1980).

12. Friedrich Nietzsche, *Thus Spoke Zarathustra,* translated by Walter Kaufmann (New York: Viking Press, 1954), pt. 4, "The Shadow." Also *Genealogy of Morals,*

III, 24.

13. On the difference between skepticism and conventionalism on the one hand and nihilism on the other, cf. L. Strauss, *Natural Right and History* (Chicago: University of Chicago Press, 1953), 10-12, 20. The distinction between skepticism and nihilism remains somewhat blurred in S. Rosen's otherwise penetrating study, *Nihilism: A Philosophical Essay* (New Haven, Conn. and London: Yale University Press, 1969).

14. Friedrich Nietzsche, *Will to Power*, translated by Walter Kaufmann and R. J. Hollingdale (New York: Vintage Books, 1968), no. 11. On Nietzsche's concept of nihilism in general, see Heidegger, "Word of Nietzsche," 60-70, and Martin Heidegger, *Nietzsche*, vol 1, *The Will to Power as Art*, translated by David Farrell Krell (New York: Harper and Row, 1979), 151-61.

15. Nietzsche, *The Gay Science*, nos 125, 343; also Nietzsche, *Zarathustra*, Prologue, 2.

16. Cf. Nietzsche, *Zarathustra*, pt. 1: "On the Gift-Giving Virtue," no. 3.

17. Friedrich Nietzsche, *Beyond Good and Evil*, translated by Walter Kaufmann (New York: Vintage Books, 1966), nos. 294-95.

18. Nietzsche, *The Gay Science*, no. 125.

19. Friedrich Nietzsche, *Birth of Tragedy*, translated by Walter Kaufmann (New York: Vintage Books, 1967), secs. 13 and 15. On Socrates as the "first decadent," see *Ecce Homo*, "The Birth of Tragedy," 1.

20. Nietzsche, *Birth of Tragedy*, sec. 15.

21. Nietzsche, *Will to Power*, no. 2.

22. Ibid., nos. 3-5; *Genealogy of Morals*, III, 27.

23. Nietzsche, *Beyond Good and Evil*, no. 227.

24. Ibid., no. 224.

25. See, on this point, Strauss, *Natural Right and History*, (Chicago: The University of Chicago Press, 1953), 9-10, and for a concise analysis of the so-called experience of history as it was finally understood after Nietzsche, 20-22.

26. Nietzsche, *Beyond Good and Evil*, nos. 1-2.

27. Ibid., no. 1.

28. Ibid., no. 8.

29. Ibid., no. 5.

30. Ibid., no. 6.

31. Ibid., no. 22.

32. Ibid., no. 2.

33. Friedrich Nietzsche, *Use and Abuse of History*, translated by Adrian Collins (Indianapolis: Bobbs-Merrill Educational Publishing, 1957), secs. 1 and 7.

34. Ibid., sec. 3.

35. Ibid., sec. 9.

36. Cf. Nietzsche, *Zarathustra*, Prologue, 5.

37. Nietzsche, *Use and Abuse of History*, sec. 4.

38. Ibid., sec. 10.

39. Ibid., sec. 3.

40. Cf. Nietzsche, *Will to Power*, nos. 18, 22, 28, *et passim*.

41. Friedrich Nietzsche, *David Strauss, the Confessor and Writer*, translated by Anthony M. Ludovici, in *Thoughts out of Season*, pt. 1 (New York: Macmillan, 1911), sec. 7.

42. Friedrich Nietzsche, *Twilight of the Idols* and *The Antichrist*, translated by R. J. Hollingdale (Harmonsworth, England: Penguin Books, 1979), "Expeditions of an Untimely Man," 5; cf. Nietzsche, *Will to Power*, nos. 19-20.

43. Nietzsche, *David Strauss*, sec. 8.

44. Cf. Nietzsche, *Beyond Good and Evil*, no. 202.

45. See, for example, Nietzsche, *Will to Power*, nos. 753, 784.

46. Nietzsche, *Genealogy of Morals*, III, 5-6; *Twilight of the Idols*, "Expeditions of an Untimely Man," 24; *Will to Power*, nos. 82-85, 843-49, 1021.

47. Cf. Nietzsche, *Will to Power*, no. 3 ("radical nihilism") and no. 22 ("active nihilism").

48. Nietzsche, *Use and Abuse of History*, sec. 10.

49. Ibid., sec. 6.

50. Cf. Nietzsche, *Beyond Good and Evil*, nos. 1, 13.

51. Nietzsche, *Will to Power*, Preface, 4.

52. Cf. *Zarathustra*, pt. 2: "On Redemption," and, for a further elaboration of the doctrine, pt. 3: "On the Vision and the Riddle" and "The Convalescent."

53. Cf. Heidegger, "Word of Nietzsche," 58. On the antecedent history of that particular formulation of the problem, see O. Bollnow *Das Verstehen: Drei Aufsätze zur Theorie der Geisteswissenschaften* (Mainz: Kirchheim, 1949).

54. See, for a similar assessment, D. C. Hoy, "History, Historicity and Historiography," in *Heidegger and Modern Philosophy*, edited by M. Murray (New Haven, Conn. and London: Yale University Press, 1978), 329-53.

55. On this subject see the remarks by L. Strauss, Correspondence Concerning *Wahrheit und Methode, The Independent Journal of Philosophy* 2 (1978): 5-7. The connection between the approaching "world night" and the new hermeneutics is likewise emphasized by Martin Heidegger, *An Introduction to Metaphysics*, translated by Ralph Mannheim (Garden City, NY: Doubleday, 1961), 37-38, 41.

56. Cf. L. Strauss, "Relativism," in *Relativism and the Study of Man*, edited by H. Schoeck and J. Wiggins (Princeton, NJ: Princeton University Press, 1959), 153-54. For Nietzsche's use of the word *nature*, see *inter alia: Beyond Good and Evil*, no. 188, and *The Antichrist*, no. 57

57. Heidegger, *Introduction to Metaphysics*, 167.

IV

SELECTED BOOK REVIEWS

Fredrick D. Wilhelmsen. *Christianity and Political Philosophy*. Athens: University of Georgia Press, 1978, 243 pp.

Fredrick Wilhelmsen's essay is a vibrant plea for the restoration of political theory to its long-lost Christian dimension. The wide range of topics that it covers—Cicero, early Christian and medieval political thought, the American political tradition, nineteenth-century European conservatism (Donoso Cortès), contemporary political theory (Voegelin, L. Strauss)—makes it all but impossible to summarize its rich content, let alone do it full justice. The reviewer can only try to highlight some of the principles that govern the inquiry and lend a measure of unity to it.

Unlike most writers on these subjects, Wilhelmsen is motivated by a keen awareness of the spiritual crisis afflicting the whole of Western civilization. His work is modestly described as diagnostic rather than therapeutic. Philosophers have no recipes to offer and none is expected of them. Their function is to determine the causes of the crisis while leaving it to others, on the basis of their analysis, to come up with the appropriate response. If the West is no longer "sailing" but "drifting," it is above all because it has lost all sense of transcendence. This much is apparent from an examination of the currently most fashionable modes of thought, whether it be positivism, historicism, existentialism, or Marxism, all of which culminate in the extrusion of metaphysics from the realm of human thought. Any chance that we may have of regaining our collective bearings hinges on our willingness to be guided by a sound metaphysical conception of human existence of the kind that is found in Greek philosophy. Yet classical political philosophy alone will not suffice. Plato and Aristotle had the right idea but were unable to provide for its realization. Neither one succeeded in exorcising the demon of chance or unreason from human affairs. Although there is still much to be learned from them, any thought of going back to them is strictly out of the question (cf. pp. 9, 22). What the modern world needs is not just any metaphysics but a metaphysics that is open to Revelation and thus capable of producing a public orthodoxy in harmony with the laws of being. Such is the metaphysics embodied in the "Christian existentialism" of Thomas Aquinas, Fortescue's medieval constitutionalism, or Donoso's ideal of a decentralized monarchy informed by Christian principles.

The proposed solution is contrasted with those of Eric Voegelin and Leo Strauss, to whom Wilhelmsen professes his indebtedness but with whom he finds himself in profound disagreement. Voegelin is guilty of reducing Christianity to a form of "mythic or mystic experience whose only authority is itself" (p. 8). This is particularly true of *The Ecumenic Age*, which, in Wilhelmsen's opinion, constitutes a substantial departure from the somewhat more orthodox views reflected in his earlier works. Nothing is said about Voegelin's own reply to this frequently voiced objection (see, for example, *Journal of the American Academy of Religion*, 43 [1975]: 765-772). Strauss and the Straussians, on the other hand, refuse to take Christianity seriously or tend to ignore it altogether. Thus, by Wilhelmsen's accounting, only five of the thirty-four theories discussed in the well-known *History of Political Philosophy*, edited by Strauss and Cropsey, can be "specifically described as Christian" (p. 238 n. 2). We are not told how that number is arrived at or what other leading Christian theories ought to have been added to the list, which by the editors' own admission is subject to criticism. Wilhelmsen is quick to note that Straussians have "a fascination and a peculiar reverence for the figure of Averroes" (p. 209). One wonders in that case why Averroes himself was not included in the *History*, where he is barely mentioned three times in passing (twice in connection with Thomas Aquinas). Perhaps Straussians are given to discriminating against their own as well as against Christians.

The more serious allegation is that, by divorcing reason and Revelation, Strauss and his "school" (a term for which Strauss had little use) have violated their Aristotelian principles and perpetrated a fallacy that casts grave doubts on the validity of their enterprise. According to Aristotle, all philosophical knowledge is rooted in experience. Since Christianity has been an essential ingredient of the Western tradition for close to two thousand years, it necessarily forms part of the horizon of experience from which any attempt to philosophize must henceforth proceed. By denying its relevance, H. V. Jaffa, on whose statement of the Straussian position the discussion concentrates, has mainly tried to develop a presuppositionless philosophy. His view is not only logically inconsistent but primed by the historicist prejudice that because philosophy began in classical Greece, it must remain there (p. 224). As far as I know, neither

Strauss nor Jaffa ever subscribed to the Cartesian notion of a presup-positionless science. The basic issue concerns the nature of the experience at hand. The *empeiria* of which Aristotle speaks has little or nothing to do with religious experience in any of its forms; it is simply the experience generated by the memory of a series of sense perceptions from which universal knowledge is ultimately derived (cf. Prior Analytics II.19.100a6 ff.; *Metaphysics* I(A).1.980a28ff.). Unless one is prepared to reduce the Christian faith to an object of sense perception one fails to see how it could serve as the basis of a properly philosophic understanding of reality. There is reason to fear that by seeking to ground philosophy in the experience of a particular tradition, Wilhelmsen has left himself open to the charge of historicism which along with Melvin Bradford he gratui-tously levels at his opponent.

Wilhelmsen nevertheless agrees with Jaffa that the reconciliation between philosophy and Revelation can only be effected by means of a synthesizing principle which as such is not part of the final synthesis. As a Thomist, he readily concedes that philosophy and divine revelation are distinct modes of knowing but rejects the idea that the polarity which characterizes them implies an opposition between reason and revelation. To the extent that the Christian faith is a "reasonable faith" it allows for such a synthesizing principle which is none other than "reason itself as an act" (p. 220). The flaw in Jaffa's argument is that it mistakenly equates reason with philosophic reason. There are other uses to which reason may be put either prior to the acceptance of the faith and as a preparation for it or within the context of the faith once it has been accepted. The unanswered question is whether the evidence of the conclusions at which reason operating in this capacity arrives is always such as to compel the assent of everyone including nonbelievers. Wilhelmsen "knows" that it is. What he regards as certain, however, may appear considerably less so to one who faces the issue without the benefit of the guidance accruing to us from some divine source. One cannot leave it at saying that any educated person living in the West today, whether he be Christian or not, *is* acquainted with and hence compelled to take into account the "philo-sophical truths" belonging to what Christian apologetics calls the *praeambula fidei*, to wit, that God exists, that he is one, good and just, and the like (cf. pp. 219, 223). What is at stake is not the meaning of these truths but their cognitive status. Few thoughtful people, Jaffa least of all, would argue that they are absurd or meaningless. Wilhelmsen surely has every right to dismiss Tertullian's familiar *credo quia absurdum* as unrepresentative of the Christian tradition as a whole. Still, it is one thing to admit that a given statement is not absurd, that is, that it contains nothing manifestly contrary to reason and another thing altogether to contend that its truth has been demonstrated beyond all reasonable doubt. To say nothing of other more complex matters, it makes perfect sense to speak of the creating and provident God of Revelation and Thomistic philosophy as being good and just; but this does not entitle us to forget the reasons that caused so many great medieval thinkers to suspend their judgment regarding the notions of creation and divine providence. The situation is not helped by Wilhelmsen's personal observation that since the government of the universe can conveniently be left to God, any given and supposedly legitimate regime has the duty to pursue "the particular good of its own society" even if the achievement of this good "demands the destruction of civilization" (p. 104). Philosophers, Maimonides once remarked, are prone to emphasize God's wisdom; the Jewish tradition, his justice. Wilhelmsen wants both and thinks he has them. Maybe he does. The wonder is that he seems surprised to find that not everyone agrees.

Even this formulation of the problem does not get to the heart of the matter, however, for it merely takes philosophy and Revelation as two parallel teachings that can be compared and eventually harmonized within specified limits. The perspective changes radically the moment philosophy is viewed, not as a body of doctrines, but as an autonomous and essentially open-ended quest for the truth, that is to say, as a way of life which by its nature is the very antithesis of the life lived on the basis of a God-given and presumably final truth. No one can serve two masters each one of whom makes an absolute claim on the allegiance of his followers—unless, of course, it is proved beforehand that they both require the same thing of him or at the least do not impose conflicting demands upon him. Since philosophy as we have just defined it is non-dogmatic even in regard to its own possibility, it is difficult to imagine how that proof could be administered. Ironically, Wilhelmsen detects a note of arrogance in Jaffa's insistence that the only knowledge to which the philosopher lays claim is the knowledge of his ignorance (p. 225). The point would be well taken if the noetic claims of revealed religion were themselves totally unambiguous. But by definition divine revelation transcends natural reason, which means that it is never without an element of mystery. Like it or not, we continue to be confronted with a choice between two irreducibly different alternatives, neither one of which is able to establish its superiority over the other. Philosophy in its original sense will not go away simply because Wilhelmsen prefers to ignore it. Granted the believer is under no compulsion to engage the philosopher on his native turf, but if he does, he must be ready to accept the consequences; bearding the lion in his den involves a certain risk. The Church Fathers referred to it as a "noble risk," *kalos kindunos,* borrowing the expression from Plato. Some of them, like Tertullian, balked at it. The better ones decided it was worth taking if only because it could lead to a full grasp of all that a wholehearted commitment to the Christian faith entails.

Wilhelmsen's last appeal is to the Gilsonian notion of a "Christian philosophy," a tricky notion at best which is bound to strike some of his readers as a futile endeavor to square the circle (cf. Heidegger *Introduction to Metaphysics*, translated by Mannheim, p. 6). Voegelin, whatever else may be said about him, is more consistent. He avoids the pitfall by denying that the essence of the Christian faith is to be found in a set of propositional truths. Wilhelmsen would locate the core of both revelation and philosophy in a set of propositional truths (cf. p. 219). He, too, wants to get rid of the uncomfortable but nonetheless creative tension between faith and philosophic reason—in a different way, to be sure, but for the same motive.

In Wilhelmsen's eyes, the fact that Strauss and Jaffa do not pretend to speak as Christians makes them safer than Voegelin in that people are less liable to misread their intentions. It might be added that, by resurrecting classical political theory, Strauss has paved the way for a genuine recovery of the Christian classics as well. One regrets that with few exceptions Christian scholars have yet to avail themselves of his groundbreaking work in order to gain a fresh insight into their own heritage. There is much to be said for the return to a sane natural law teaching, especially at a time when, bereft of any but the crudest of moral standards, Western society gropes aimlessly for a solution to its most pressing problems. The case for that view would have been strengthened if, instead of falling back on a traditional interpretation of the traditional natural law doctrine, Wilhelmsen had faced squarely the objections to which on its own terms that doctrine is exposed as regards its knowability, its immutability, and its coercive power. As it stands, his account has little chance of convincing anyone who is not already won over to his position. The same applies to his analysis of Cicero's political theory, of Augustine's celebrated critique of that theory, and of Fortescue's praise of the English regime, a praise that may be more guarded than Wilhelmsen would have us believe.

These strictures notwithstanding, the book has the outstanding merit of alerting us to the plight of political theory in the Christian world. It comes as a timely reminder both of the task to be accomplished and of the distance that separates us from its accomplishment. Christian scholars and theologians owe it to themselves to regain a foothold in an area which through contempt or neglect they have long since forfeited to others. Our hope is that the "new flowering of Christian political wisdom" for which the author calls will indeed come to pass. Wilhelmsen may not have led us all the way but he has pointed us in the right direction. For this we can all be grateful.

Russell Hittinger. *A Critique of the New Natural Law Theory*. Notre Dame: University of Notre Dame Press, 1987, vi + 232 pp.

This relatively short but dense volume, which has been hailed as a "veritable God-send" by no less of an authority than Henry B. Veatch (*The New Scholasticism* 62 [1988]: 353), has the merit of being the first book-length study of the controversial version of the natural law theory propounded in recent years by Germain Grisez and the Oxford legal theorist, John Finnis. The task, an arduous one in view of the abundance and the frequent opacity of the materials at hand, was further complicated by the fact that Grisez and Finnis do not see eye to eye on all particulars, as well as by the fact that their theory has undergone a number of tacit revisions of which the reader is simply presumed to be aware. Sad to say, the author could not count on much help from Grisez and Finnis themselves, who do not take kindly to criticism and rarely respond to it, save perhaps by way of another tacit reformulation of their positions (as, for example, in their article, "Practical Principles, Moral Truth, and Ultimate Ends," *American Journal of Jurisprudence* 32 [1987]: 99-151). Such features lend to their voluminous and still growing corpus an oracular quality that automatically places it beyond the ken of any mortal who has not reached the top of the sacred mountain. Conflicting interpretations of that corpus are bound to proliferate as time goes on. If successful, the new theory could spawn a scholasticism, the like of which has not been seen since the late Middle Ages.

One thing is certain: while Grisez and Finnis frequently borrow their terminology from the natural law tradition, theirs is anything but the traditional or "conventional" natural law theory, combining as it does elements native to an assortment of distinct and competing moral systems. The emphasis on premoral goods smacks of Hobbes and the utilitarian tradition that grows out of him; the role assigned to practical reason, understood apart from any natural end or ends to which human beings might be ordered, recalls Kant and his present-day descendants; the place reserved for human "flourishing" reminds us in a roundabout way of classical eudaemonism; and the generous sprinkling of such terms as "lifestyles," "creativity," "values," "authenticity," and "commitment" bears witness to the pervasive if unacknowledged influence of modern existential thought. The basic question is whether the final product is a genuine synthesis effected on the basis of a principle that transcends the plane of the original positions, or an eclectic compromise ultimately weaker than any of its individual components (cf. p. 163). Hittinger's reservations about key elements of the system suggest that he leans strongly in the second direction.

One of these reservations has to do with the so-called first principle of practical reason (*Fppr*), "Good is to be pursued and evil avoided," which in the Grisez-Finnis scheme functions as a premoral rather than as a properly moral principle. But if the *Fppr* is only a premoral principle, one is faced with the old problem of bridging the gulf between the "is" and the "ought," i.e., of deducing genuine morality from something that is not itself moral at the risk of stripping it of its status as a primary phenomenon. Grisez and Finnis, it seems, would equate morality with moral obligation. One can surely grant that the *Fppr*, not being stated in the form of an imperative, is not a moral *precept;* but that alone is not enough to remove it from the pale of morality. If it were, the whole of Aristotle's *Ethics,* which knows nothing of moral obligation, would have to be relegated to the premoral realm.

A second series of difficulties concerns the parity that the Grisez-Finnis system postulates among the basic goods in the attainment of which human beings find their fulfillment (life, science, friendship, play, and the like). In practice, this means that it is morally permissible to pursue any basic good or set of basic goods as long as this is not done "exclusivistically," that is, as long as one does not deny the validity of the other basic goods or question anyone's right to pursue them (cf. p. 75). Prior to choice, none of these goods can be said to be superior to any other. Human types cannot be ordered hierarchically, and nonexclusivism becomes the touchstone of morality. Thus, there is no objective reason to think that the individual who dedicates himself heart and soul to the pursuit of knowledge or holiness ranks higher than, say, the one who would rather spend his life playing the kazoo.

Similar problems arise in connection with Grisez's and Finnis's treatment of religion, which, as a basic good, must be kept on a par with all the other basic goods. Hittinger's questions this time are formulated for the most part in terms of James Collins's methodical distinction between two views of religion, one that sees it as belonging to the foundations of practical reason and one wherein it is brought in by implication, so to speak, and only once the foundations have been laid, as is the case in Kantian philosophy (cf. pp. 155ff.). If I understand the argument correctly, the least that can be said is that, in the Grisez-Finnis arrangement, religion receives far less than what would formerly have been considered its due.

There are other complaints as well, not the least of which is that, as the theory unfolds, one never catches a glimpse of the "inside" of the human subject (p.186). All inwardness has vanished and morality is transformed into a kind of intellectual game, the object of which is to avoid any move that would jeopardize the integrity of the basic goods with which play begins. The overall framework is still the one that has dominated the intellectual scene for a century or more, namely, the debate between Kantians or deontologists on the one hand and utilitarians, consequentialists, or proportionalists on the other.

Grisez and Finnis are understandably dissatisfied with both of these approaches, but, having ruled out natural teleology as a reliable guide to action, they have no viable alternative to offer. Neither of them has been profoundly touched by the rediscovery of premodern thought, by far the most significant development of the past fifty years in the field of ethics (cf. pp. 1ff.). Their system does not take its bearings from the highest human possibilities; it merely tells us that anyone who complies with it is sure to avoid all wrongdoing. As such, it shares with the rest of modern ethical thought a tendency to lower the goals of human activity for the sake of enhancing its effectiveness.

Moreover, since it has been decided that nature has nothing to contribute to ethical behavior, one looks in vain for some other powerful force capable of motivating human beings to act in accordance with the demands of the abstract morality generated by the new system. Unbeknownst to them, the authenticity for which Grisez and Finnis occasionally call, is at root nothing but the Heideggerian antidote to the latent nihilism of the age. But even this is not taken seriously. A simpler and more familiar premise undergirds their efforts: the liberal democratic dogma of the equality of all ends and "values," casually or uncritically accepted. The game, it turns out, has been rigged. The only results with which we come up are the ones it was set up to yield (cf. p. 48).

The foregoing remarks will have achieved their purpose if they give the reader at least a rough idea of Hittinger's toughminded dissection of what is nonetheless the most ambitious enterprise launched by Catholic ethicists in our generation. My only regret is that the author did not go for the jugular instead of taking us through a maze of intricate detail from which we eventually emerge with the odd feeling of having lost our way on more than one occasion. The natural law may, indeed, be "the stone which the builders rejected" (Veatch, quoted p. 190), but more work is apparently needed before it can be retrieved and pressed into service.

F. Rousseau. *La croissance solidaire des droits de l'homme: un retour aux sources de l'éthique.* Montreal, Bellarmin, and Tournai: Desclée et Cie, 1982, 315 pp.

There are two sides to this oddly titled book, one good and one bad. The good side is its penetrating analysis of Thomas Aquinas's natural law theory, to which fortunately the major portion of the essay is devoted. Much of its inspiration comes from the late Jasmin Boulay, a charismatic teacher who published little in the span of his relatively brief academic career but had a profound influence on the few students who were privileged to study with him. One can be grateful that, through the diligence of a close associate, Boulay's insights have now been developed and made available to a broader public.

It is hardly necessary to remind ourselves that the natural law doctrine, once considered the cornerstone of Christian ethics, has long been toppled from the position of prominence that it formerly occupied in our tradition. Periodical efforts to revive it in the face of the ethical relativism or nihilism that threaten us have been halfhearted at best and generally retain only those elements of the Thomistic synthesis that do not conflict openly with the currently most fashionable notions of justice and right. The great merit of the present work is that it treats Thomas's teaching as a coherent whole and refuses to be intimidated by the attacks that continue to be leveled at it on modern scientific or historical grounds. The first chapter rightly insists on the importance of Thomas's definition of law as a work of reason rather than of the will. It dwells at length on the connection between speculative and practical reason and proceeds to investigate the "sources," i.e., the premoral foundations of the natural law in the order of nature itself. From a close examination of Thomas's notion of nature, the author is then able to show that the precepts of the natural law are not all equally "natural" and, moreover, that the most natural among them are the ones grounded in man's physical as distinguished from his rational nature. It follows that, for Thomas, the moral principles intimated to us through the inclination to preserve our own being or to procreate are more natural than the principles arising from the inclination to live in society or to seek the truth. This is not to say that the higher is reducible to the lower but only that it is rooted in it and is never totally independent of it. On the basis of these and similar observations, we are made to see more clearly how Thomas could endorse Ulpian's definition of the natural law as that which is common "to all animals" without lapsing into the "biologism" of which he is so frequently accused. The final chapter applies some of these notions to such timely issues as the legitimacy of private property, the right use of material goods, and sexual morality. Among other things, it suggests ways in which, by following Thomas's lead, Catholic theologians could conceivably arrive at a more nuanced position on the problem of birth control.

The net result of all of this is an interpretation of the natural law that is at once more faithful to the spirit of Thomas's text and less rigid than the one that has been handed down to us from the Scholastic commentators of the late medieval and early modern periods. Through it, one can better appreciate the remarkable subtlety of the Thomistic doctrine, about which the least that can be said is that it does its utmost to preserve the integrity of human life and carefully avoids the dichotomy between reason and nature on which so much of modern ethical thought has been foundering for close to two centuries.

The bad side of the book is its valiant but stillborn attempt to demonstrate that Thomas's doctrine is nothing but an earlier version of the modern "rights" theory, shorn of its individualism. Significantly, all of the texts adduced in support of this paradoxical thesis speak, not of rights, but of duties and obligations (see especially pp. 162-66). The parallel suggestion that the Decalogue constitutes the "oldest charter of the rights of man" (p. 173) is equally baffling and makes us wonder why the content of that famous document is always referred to as the "ten commandments" rather than the "ten rights." The truth of the matter is that there is no such thing as a biblical or medieval inalienable rights theory.

Rousseau, who is not totally unaware of the problem, tries to get around it by arguing that duties and rights are correlative and, hence, inseparable from one another. If I am morally bound to give others their due, they must have the right to receive it. Still, this does not explain how such a right can be described as "inalienable" (pp. 12, 16, 20, 165 *et passim*). Rights, to the extent that they were thought to exist, were contingent on the performance of prior duties. Far from being inalienable, they could be forfeited and were so forfeited by criminals, who could then be deprived of their liberty and even put to death (cf. Thomas Aquinas, *Summa Theologiae* II-II, qu. 64, a. 2). The typical Hobbesian dilemma of the convict whom the state has the right to execute and who has the right to kill his executioner belongs exclusively to the world of modern thought. The further contention that the two theories in question find their common denominator in the principle of self-preservation is likewise misleading, insofar as the conclusions drawn from that principle are vastly different in each case. For the medievals, the inclination to preserve one's existence meant that one had no right to take one's life or do anything that would impair one's health, e.g., by mutilating oneself or refusing to eat. For the moderns, it is a powerful and essentially self-regarding passion, which grounds the claims that one can make on others or the rights for the protection of which governments are established. Bridging the gulf between these two views, one of them based on a teleological and the other on a nonteleological understanding of nature, is not an easy task.

As for the larger implications of the premodern natural law doctrine, they appear to have been far less democratic than Rousseau makes them out to be. That doctrine was originally taken to be compatible with all legitimate regimes and did not of itself favor any one of them over the others. The idea that it did much to promote the political equality of all human beings (pp. 15, 37, 124, 26) is anything but obvious, especially in view of the fact that over the centuries it was more often used to uphold the *status quo* than to change it. A case in point is Thomas himself, who goes well beyond Aristotle in defending the justice of legal slavery (see his *Commentary on the Politics of Aristotle*, I. Lect. 4, nos. 75 and 79). In fairness, it should be added the Rousseau's anachronisms are not his alone. They can be traced back to A. J. and R. W. Carlyle, whose implausible argument for the unbroken continuity of the Western political tradition from "at least the lawyers of the second century to the theorists of the doxographical literature of the twentieth century" (cf. *A History of Mediaeval Political Theory in the West*, vol. 1, p. 2, and Rousseau, p. 124).

Rousseau's attempted "reconciliation" of the medieval natural law and the modern natural rights doctrines goes hand in hand with a strong emphasis on the distance that separates Thomas from Aristotle on many of the points under consideration. The former's teaching, we are told, is less elitist than that of his pagan mentor (pp. 104, 126) and pays greater attention to the "essential" as distinct from the more "excellent" features of human life (pp. 266, 271, 275). It also allows more room for the exercise of prudence on the part of ordinary citizens (e.g., p. 110). Above all, it specifies more clearly the ends of human existence and thus avoids the apparent circularity of Aristotle's treatment of this subject, which defines the right end as the one pursued by the good man and the good man as the one who pursues the right end (cf. pp. 121-22). So be it. The crucial question is whether Thomas's position is fully defensible on rational grounds or whether it makes complete sense only against the background of divine revelation. Interestingly enough, Thomas himself seems at times to lean toward the second alternative, or so one gathers from his admission that the precepts of the first table of the Decalogue are known to human reason only as "instructed" or "informed" by faith (cf. *Summa Theologiae* I-II, qu. 100, a. 1; qu. 104, a. 1, ad 3m). It may be that natural reason alone is unable to prove with absolute certitude that the universe is ruled by a just and loving God who requites everyone according to his deeds. This would account for the fact that the notion of natural law has always been more readily acceptable to believers than to nonbelievers. One regrets that Rousseau has not seen fit to address himself to this troublesome and still much debated issue.

To end with a small but not insignificant point: It is by no means obvious that Thomas's definition of law in *Summa Theologiae* I-II, qu. 90, a. 4 applies only to the positive law. If anything, the answer to the first objection in that article suggests the opposite. The word "positive" in the citation from Thomas (p. 22) does not appear in the original text and was presumably added by Rousseau.

G. Fessard. *Chrétiens marxistes et théologie de la libération: Itinéraire du Père G. Girardi.* Paris: Lethielleux, 1978, 424 pp.

G. Fessard. *Eglise de France, prends garde de perdre la foi.* Paris: Julliard, 1979, 317 pp.

The author of these two complementary essays, neither of which he lived to see in final published form, was one of the most distinguished Jesuit scholars of his generation. Alexander Kojève, whose seminar on Hegel Fessard attended from 1934 to 1939, once remarked that he could have been "easily and by far" France's best Marxist theorist if he had so desired (see his review of Fessard in *Critique* 3-4, Aug.-Sept. 1946, pp. 308-12). Partly because of the topical nature of his works, but perhaps even more because of his philosophic depth, he was never read as widely outside of France as are his illustrious confrères, Henri de Lubac and Jean Daniélou. Of the one-hundred and twenty-odd items listed in his bibliography (not counting a considerably larger number of book reviews) only three articles have thus far been translated into English. Yet this impressive literary production could well become one of the landmarks of contemporary French Catholicism.

In the two books under consideration, Fessard returns to a theme that had haunted him throughout most of his professional life, namely, the gradual infiltration and "subversion" of Catholic thought by Marxist principles since the end of World War II. The first is a piece by piece commentary on the works of Giulio Girardi, the unacknowledged founder of liberation theology and the original purveyor of the ideas that have since gained a world-wide audience through the writings of Gustavo Gutierrez. The opening pages advert to the deep kinship between Christian Marxism (esp. Moltmann and Metz) and liberation theology, two movements which, though not identical—one is more theoretical, the other emphasizes practice—nevertheless have their common source in Marxist ideology. They also call attention to the European origins of liberation theology, however eager its more recent proponents may be to pass it off as a native Latin-American product. The second work, which is modestly described as a "brochure" (p. 15), but to which the author seems to have attached particular importance, likewise takes the form of a commentary, this time on a series of documents issued by the French hierarchy and its semi-official organs on the subject of Catholic involvement in the socialist movement since 1972. Its title is clearly meant to suggest a parallel with two of Fessard's earlier pamphlets: *France, Beware Lest You Should Lose Your Soul*, published clandestinely in 1941, and *France, Beware Lest You*

Should Lose Your Freedom, published in the midst of the euphoria generated by the liberation of his country four years later.

The story that these two books tell is not a happy one. Fessard is persuaded that in Marxism the Church faces a deadly and insidious rival, given to the use of "seduction" as a means of securing the "compromises" that will eventually "corrupt" and "destroy" its enemies. His basic thesis is that Marxism forms a unitary system whose premises and the practice they inspire are fundamentally at odds with the Christian faith. Much as some churchmen would like to separate them, historical materialism is indissolubly wedded to the philosophic materialism in which it finds its roots. By acquiescing in a typically Marxist critique of capitalist society while rejecting Marx's atheism, the bishops, their theologians, and their spokesmen unwittingly commit themselves to a view of human life that, as Christians, they are bound to repudiate.

Fessard does not doubt that their recent statements stem from the impulses of a generous heart. What troubles him is that the authors and promulgators of these statements are blind to their larger implications and hence guilty of inconsistency. Where Paul VI had spoken of the "dynamism of the Faith," the bishops speak of the "dynamism of the labor movement." They now subscribe as a matter of course to the Marxist notions of "class conflict" (often extended so as to include the Church itself) and of the "collective memory of the working class." Even the idea of a valid "socialist option with Marxist reference" barely gives them pause to reflect. True, they still prefer the word "socialisms" in the plural to "socialism" in the singular, as if to signify their desire to stand above party politics; but since one and only one brand of socialism is intended, the precaution is illusory and ineffectual. The few among them who try to buck the trend meet with little success. They are mercilessly set upon, sometimes by their own colleagues, and pursued with an inquisitorial animus that has no parallel in history. Therein lies the tragedy. Unable to articulate or agree upon a coherent position of its own, the hierarchy has no other course but to "react" passively to pressures from without. This, more than anything else, is what is responsible for the chaotic state of the Church in France.

Words such as these strike hard at times (the French reader is almost tempted to pun on the author's name), but they are authorized by no less a figure than Thomas Aquinas, who is quoted as saying that, when the faith is in imminent danger, as Fessard believes it now is, even a subject has the duty publicly to take issue with his prelates, provided he do so with inner respect and the proper external deference (cf. *Eglise de France,* p. 8, with reference to Thomas Aquinas, *Summa Theologiae,* II-II.33.4, ad 2um). None of Fessard's readers will accuse him of failing to live up to these criteria. It was his habit to reread every page he wrote with a view to removing from it any remark that might give personal offense to others. Both of his books stand at a lofty distance from the vulgar and noisy polemics to which we have lately become accustomed. Their sole purpose is to elaborate the theoretical framework from which the routinely accepted slogans of popular Marxism take their significance. Fessard is too much of a philosopher to think that "conviction" can ever substitute for "reflection" (cf. *Eglise de France*, p. 84) or that there is any clarity to be achieved by subjecting truth to the passionate and distorting climate of political activism. If he can be reproached with anything, it is with being too meticulous. In his endeavor to be completely fair to his opponents, he is apt to multiply subtle distinctions to the point of obscuring the main thrust of the argument.

Needless to say, Fessard is not the only contemporary writer to denounce the phony alliance between Marxism and Christianity. What sets him apart from others, however, is that he brings to this complex issue a competence that grows out of a lifelong meditation on the works of Marx and his philosophic source, Hegel. It is to his credit that he was the first French critic to make use of Marx's 1844 manuscripts and that he did so long before they became available to the general public. As Kojève observes in the review mentioned earlier, his unique strength is that he knows Marxism better than his Marxist adversaries, most of whom have only a superficial acquaintance with Marx and no acquaintance to speak of with Hegel.

Chrétiens marxistes proves sufficiently that he is willing to engage in dialogue with those whose views he opposes, but it also shows that he has reflected more deeply than they have on the conditions that make such dialogue possible. The Christian who adopts a defensive posture in regard to Marxism has already conceded too much to his interlocutor and weakened the position that he sets out to defend. Contrary to what Girardi may think, genuine dialogue is not a simple matter of "will," "sincerity," or "good faith" (cf. p. 25). It presupposes a measure of agreement on the nature of the problem to be debated as well as on the terms in which it should be posed, and it can only take place under conditions, not indeed of neutrality, but of "impartiality." Girardi is shrewd enough to realize that there are at least as many obstacles to dialogue on the Marxist side as there are on the Christian side; but whereas he dwells at length on the latter, he is virtually silent about the former. By insisting that the problem be defined in Marxist categories, he has in fact prejudiced the outcome of the debate and foreclosed the possibility of a fruitful encounter between the two parties. The circularity of his argument is attested to by the very manner in which it is conducted.

The paradox is that, for all their awareness of a deepening crisis within the Church, Fessard's books sound a strangely positive note, dedicated as they are to the defense of reason against the rampant irrationalism of the age. There is no trace in them of the somberness that came to characterize the works of his disenchanted and more pessimistic collaborators. Fessard is too lucid to ignore the possible tension between the demands of rationality and the commitment to a particular creed. Still, in the best tradition of the Society of Jesus, he is convinced that faith can and should be an incentive rather than a hindrance to learning. One regrets that his knowledge of modern philosophy is not matched by an equally profound knowledge of premodern philosophy. Only this broader perspective could have given him the means of disclosing the full range of human possibilities and enabled him finally to overcome the essential limitations of our own time. The impression that comes across is that his ascent from the cave of modern thought is guided in large part by his appreciation for the *Spiritual Exercises* of Ignatius of Loyola, on which he has written two sizable volumes and which he has done much to reaccredit in religious circles (see, for example, *Eglise de France,* pp. 136-44). Excellent as this point of reference may be, there is some question as to whether it suffices by itself to guarantee the universality of his teaching and win for it the broad audience that it deserves.

Pronouncing a final verdict on the lasting worth of these two unfashionable studies will take some time. Certain it is that anyone who undertakes to write a history of contemporary French theology will find in them a wealth of information and perspicacious judgment that cannot safely be ignored.

D. Vree. *On Synthesizing Marxism and Christianity.* New York and London: John Wiley and Sons, 1976, xxii + 206 pp..

Vree's essay is a penetrating assessment of the now famous dialogue in which Christian and Marxist thinkers here and abroad have been engaged since the late fifties and early sixties. Its claim to novelty is that, unlike most other books of its kind, it purports to be written from a strictly "neutral" or nonpartisan frame of reference (p. viii). What this means in effect is that the author has little sympathy for either of the two dialoguing parties, well-intentioned as they appear to be.

The trouble with the so-called "Christian-Marxist dialogue," simply put, is that it is neither Christian nor Marxist. The participants on the Christian side, represented for present purposes by Harvey Cox and Jürgen Moltmann, fail to measure up to the standards of normative Christianity, minimally defined by the teachings of the first seven Ecumenical

Councils, to which the whole Church subscribed throughout seventy-five percent of its history and which continue to be accepted by seventy-five percent of all Christians today. They ignore original sin, view the kingdom of God as something to be brought about by human effort, and promote a kind of eschatological politics that leaves no room for genuine transcendence. Their thought thus smacks of the archetypal heresies of Gnosticism, Pelagianism, and Montanism. The protagonists on the other side are revisionists whose "studied ambiguity" matches that of their Christian counterparts (p. 87, 155, *et passim*) and who, like them, embroil themselves in contradictions of which they hardly seem to be aware. They generally prefer the early or humanistic Marx to the mature or "scientific" Marx of *Capital,* or else tend to blur the difference between them, possibly for political reasons. Sobered by recent experience, both sides have retreated slightly from the extreme positions with which they became identified in the 1960s, but only at the price of greater inconsistency.

There is even some doubt as to whether their discussions can truly qualify as a dialogue. Over the years, the two groups have converged to such a degree that they now speak with virtually one voice and are less apt to be at odds with each other than with their own traditions. Their great hero is Joachim of Flora, the twelfth-century monk whose chiliastic speculations were supposed to usher in the age of the Spirit. Shorn of its accidental trappings, their program reduces to a single common denominator, namely, democratic socialism, which they unabashedly proclaim as the truth of their respective gospels. Neither group, it might be added, has given much thought to the type of human being that this new bourgeoisification of society is likely to produce.

Vree's conclusion is that genuine Christianity and genuine Marxism are disjunctive systems which cannot be synthesized without compromising their integrity. For all his early vacillations and the philosophic thinness of his doctrines, Marx never wavered on the issue of atheism. His contempt for religion was such that he would not even have deigned to attack it had he not discovered it to be more tenacious than he originally anticipated. As for the Christian God, he is not a "politician God" (p. 24) but a transcendent God who promises not only something more but something other than political redemption. Nothing is left of the radical newness of the Christian message once its transpolitical core has been evacuated.

Unbiased students of Marx and of the Christian tradition will find little with which to quarrel in all of this. They will also learn much from Vree's subtle analyses, to which no brief summary can do adequate justice. Greater pains could, nevertheless, have been taken to trace Cox's and Moltmann's theories to their proximate source in modern thought. Vree leaves no doubt that both of them are derivative thinkers, but the comparison with Gnosticism, Pelagianism, and Montanism does little to disclose the specific nature of the phenomenon at hand. Nor is the analogy with Joachim of Flora particularly instructive, however much the old (and often maligned) Calabrian seer may have done to stir things up in his day. The works of Cox and Moltmann would not have struck a responsive chord in the hearts of so many people if our own world had not already been pounded for over three centuries by the twin dogmas of formless freedom and the relief of man's estate, into which their democratic socialism ultimately resolves.

The case against a Christian-Marxist synthesis would likewise have been strengthened if a more positive note had occasionally been sounded. Vree is right in thinking that he may have unwittingly cast himself in the role of a "mischievous rogue" (p. 179), but his last-minute attempt to redress the balance falls somewhat short of the mark. The real danger is that his book will sound more cranky than impish to some liberally-minded Christians who might otherwise have been attracted to it. True, Christianity is not essentially political, but it is not apolitical either. One could perhaps best describe it as transpolitical. Inasmuch as it presupposes the existence and the legitimacy of the political order (not necessarily this or that political order), it invites careful reflection on the nature of the Christian's involvement in it. This being the case, one would have appreciated at least a thumbnail sketch of what a viable alternative to the politicized Christianity of Cox and Moltmann might be. The low level of current political discourse within the theological community may be as much to blame for this lacuna as the author himself. Christian theology still has a long way to go before it is able to retrieve the whole of its legacy. In the meantime, theologians of a more traditional stripe must not be surprised to find their place usurped by newcomers who are forced to look elsewhere for the guidance they have failed to provide.

It is a tribute to its quality that the essay has not aged in the four years that have elapsed since its publication, except to the extent to which recent developments have further served to expose the shallowness of much of what Vree's "dialogical Christians" or practitioners of theological *détente* like to pass off as a requirement of the Gospel. One hopes that a second book will follow which would undertake the difficult but urgent task to which the present volume implicitly points.

Herbert A. Deane. *The Political and Social Ideas of St. Augustine.* New York and London: Columbia University Press, 1963, 356 pp.

Augustine was the greatest political thinker of Christian antiquity and one of the most influential writers of the entire Western tradition. Despite his intrinsic importance and the contemporary relevance of much of what he wrote, there existed, surprisingly enough, no book-length study of his political thought in the English language. Herbert A. Deane's work, *The Political and Social Ideas of St. Augustine*, fills this lacuna in a manner that is both thorough and objective. The stated purpose of the book is to present, in a single volume, the most significant passages from Augustine's work on the subject of civil society; to organize this material in the light of the general principles that underlie Augustine's thought; and finally to situate Augustine's ideas on political man within the general framework of his thought, assess their coherence, and point out their strengths and weaknesses. Anyone who is the least bit acquainted with the subject matter will readily appreciate the difficulty of such an enterprise. Augustine was, with Cicero, the most voluminous writer of the ancient world. His most important views on man and society, however, unlike those of Cicero, are not condensed in one or two books but scattered throughout many works, most of which are of a polemical and controversial nature. Moreover, under the pressure of circumstances, he was compelled to change his position on a number of important points, as he himself has admitted.

The author has dealt with the matter at hand under the following general headings: theology and psychology of fallen man; morality and justice; the state and its functions; war and the relations among cities; and, finally, Church, state, and heresy. Among the book's many assets is its lucid account of the Donatist controversy and of the different stands that Augustine was forced to take, in the course of that controversy, on the use of secular power to coerce heretics. The only serious omission of the book has to do with Augustine's polemic against pagan religion. No doubt many of the details of that polemic are of only peripheral interest to the modern reader; yet, given the role that religion plays in classical political theory, it is difficult to see how one can appreciate fully the revolutionary character of Augustine's thought without taking into account his discussion of mythical, civil, and natural theology in the first half of the *City of God*.

Deane's sympathetic attitude toward Augustine is inspired by the apparently broad-minded view that no single thinker can be credited with having expressed the whole truth about man and society, since each great writer is so completely taken up with his original insight into one dimension of human reality that he becomes blind to other aspects of the same reality. According to this view, the greatest thinkers are necessarily one-eyed giants who owe their abiding importance to their penetrating analysis of certain new facets of human existence to the exclusion of others. The greatness of their accomplishment is thus directly related to the partiality of their vision. Hence, one can arrive at a complete picture of reality only by combining the specific contributions of all the great writers of the past.

Deane's central thesis is that Augustine was a realist in political matters and that his pessimistic view of fallen man led him to conceive of the state, not as an association whose function is to guide man to the perfection of virtue, but as an agency essentially designed to restrain evil among men by the use of force. This pessimism and this realism would explain in part the fascination that Augustine has exerted on theologians and secular thinkers in our own day. Deane himself does not feel that grim realism is the only solution to the problems that beset us, nor is he convinced that Augustine's brand of realism is the one that comes closest to the truth; but he is willing to concede that in an age of bankrupt ideals and widespread disillusionment, there is room for Augustine's somber and powerful view of the human condition. Beyond these general remarks, he prefers to abandon to the reader the task of determining to what extent Augustine's ideas are applicable to our own situation. He justifies his reticence in this matter on the ground that one demonstrates an "unwarranted smugness of contemporaneity" by congratulating or rebuking a great thinker of the past for having expressed views that agree with or differ from currently fashionable ideas. If by this humble statement he implies that one cannot speak of an author's relevance without using the commonly accepted ideas of a given age as one's criterion of judgment, he may be accused by some of his readers of having jumped from the frying pan of Hegelianism into the fire of historicism.

A closer comparison of Augustine's principles with those of Cicero might have revealed a closer kinship between these two authors than Deane is prepared to admit; for Cicero too, no less than Augustine perhaps, was aware of the intrinsic limitations of the political life, to such an extent that he made of these limitations the theme of his major political work, the *De re publica*. The principal difference between Augustine and his Roman predecessor would thus seem to lie not so much in the realization that actual cities are for the most part unjust as in the former's attempt to shift the center of gravity of justice from this world to the next. In so doing, Augustine introduced for the first time into political thought a dichotomy from which, for better or for worse, it has never completely recovered.

Whatever one's final verdict concerning these writers, Deane's book is the one to which scholars and students will turn henceforth for a useful account of Augustine's thought on a subject to which neither Christian nor secular thinkers can remain indifferent today.

SELECT BIBLIOGRAPHY

1. **Editions of Early Christian Writings in the the Original Languages**. (A standard abbreviation follows each entry.)

Bibliotheque Augustinienne (Oeuvres de Saint Augustin). Paris: Etudes Augustiniennes, 1947ff. This edition has a French translation on the facing page. BA

Corpus Christianorum, Series Latina. Turnhout, Belgium: Brepols, 1953ff. CCL

Corpus Scriptorum Christianorum Orientalium. Louvain, 1903ff. CSCO

Corpus Scriptorum Ecclesiasticorum Latinorum. Vienna, 1866ff. CSEL

Loeb Classical Library. London and Cambridge, MA: Harvard University Press, 1912ff. This edition has an English translation on the facing page. It only contains a few texts of early Christian writers. LCL

Patrologiae Cursus Completus Series Latina. 222 volumes in-quarto. Edited by J.-P. Migne Paris, 1844-1855. PL

Patrologiae Cursus Completus Series Graeca. 168 volumes in-quarto Edited by J.-P. Migne. Paris, 1857-1868. This edition has a Latin translation. PG

Patrologiae Latinae Supplementum 5 volumes in-quarto. Edited by A. Hamman. Paris, 1958-1974. PLS

Sources chrétiennes. Paris, 1942ff. This edition has a French translation on the facing page. SC

2. **English Editions of Early Christian Writings in Series** (A standard abbreviation follows each entry.)

Ancient Christian Writers. New York, NY and Mahwah, NJ: Paulist Press, 1946ff. ACW

The Ante-Nicene Fathers. Buffalo, NY, 1885-1896. Reprinted by William B. Eerdmanns Publishing Co. of Grand Rapids, MI, 1951-1956. ANF

The Catholic University of America Patristic Studies. Washington, DC: The Catholic University of America Press, 1922ff. CUA or PSt

The Fathers of the Church. Washington, DC: The Catholic University of America Press, 1947ff. FC

The Library of Christian Classics. Philadelphia: Westminster, 1953ff. LCC

A Library of the Fathers of the Holy Catholic Church. Oxford, 1838-1858. LF

A Select Library of Nicene and Post-Nicene Fathers of the Christian Church. First Series. Edited by Philip Schaff. Buffalo, NY, 1886ff. Reprinted by William B. Eerdmans Publishing Co. in 1956. NPN

A Select Library of Nicene and Post-Nicene Fathers of the Christian Church. Second Series. Edited by Philip Schaff and Henry Wace. New York, 1890ff. Reprinted by William B. Eerdmans Publishing Co. in 1956. NPN, 2nd Ser.

The Works of Saint Augustine, A Translation for the 21st Century. Edited by John E. Rotelle. Hyde Park, NY: New City Press, 1990ff. This new series will eventually publish the complete works of Augustine in English. WSA

3. **Editions of St. Augustine's Writings in Series**

The following list is a complete record of St. Augustine's writings that are published as part of a series in the original Latin or in English translation. A few works are still not available in English. Augustine's works are listed alphabetically according to the Latin title. The English title in parentheses immediately follows the publication information on the Latin text. Standard abbreviations, as noted in sections 1 and 2, are used to identify the publisher of each work. *Patrology*, volume IV, edited by Angelo Berardino with an introduction by Johannes Quasten, is an invaluable source for publication details and other information on each of St. Augustine's works. With a few exceptions, the dates listed are those indicated in the Berardino volume. For more information on the dates of Augustine's works cf. S. Zarb, *Chronologia operum sancti Augustini* Rome, 1934; and A. M. Bonnardière, *Recherches de chronologie Augustinienne*, Paris: Etudes augustiniennes, 1965.

392 *Acta contra Fortunatum Manichaeum* BA 17; CSEL 25, 1; PL 42
  (*Proceedings against Fortunatus, the Manichean*) NPN 4
399 *Ad catechumenos de symbolo* CCL 46; PL 40
  (*To the Catechumens, on the Creed*) FC 27; NPN 3
415 *Ad Hieronymum presbyterum* or *Epistulae* 166-167 CSEL 44; PL 33
  (*To the Priest Jerome* or *Letters 166-167)* FC 30
c. 400 *Ad inquisitionem Januarii* or *Epistulae* 54-55 CSEL 34; PL 33
  (*In Answer to the Inquiries of Januarius* or *Letters 54-55*) FC 12
399 *Adnotationes in Iob* CSEL 28,3; PL 34
  (*Notes on Job*)
415 *Ad Orosium contra Priscillanistas et Origenistas* CCL 49; PL 42
  (*To Orosius, against the Priscillianists and the Origenists*)
c. 411 *Breviculus collationis cum Donatistis* CCL 149; CSEL 153; PL 4
  (*An abridgement of the Conference with the Donatists*)
c. 427 *Collatio cum Maximino Arianorum* PL 42
  (*A conference with Maximinus, Bishop of the Arians*)
397-400 *Confessiones* BA 13-14; CCL 27; CSEL 33; LCL (2 volumes);
  PL 32
  (*The Confessions*) FC 21; LCC 7; LCL (2 volumes); NPN 1
386-387 *Contra Academicos* or *De Academicis* BA 4; CCL 29; CSEL 63;
  PL 32
  (*Against the Academics* or *Answer to Sceptics* or *On the Academics*)
  ACW 12; FC 5
392 *Contra Adimantum manichaei discipulum* BA 17; CSEL 25,1;
  PL 42
  (*Against Adimantus, a Disciple of Manicheus* or *Mani*)
c. 420 *Contra adversarium legis et prophetarum* CCL 49; PL 42
  (*Against an Adversary of the Law and the Prophets*)
c. 405-406 *Contra Cresconium grammaticum partis Donati* CSEL 52;
  PL 43
  (*Against Cresconius, a grammarian of the Donatist party*)
c. 420 *Contra duas epistulas Pelagianorum* BA 23; CSEL 60; PL 44
  (*Against Two Letters of the Pelagians*) NPN 5
400 *Contra epistulam Parmeniani* CSEL 51; PL 43
  (*Against a Letter of Parmenian*)
c. 396 *Contra epistulam Manichaei quam vocant fundamenti* CSEL 25,1;
  PL 42
  (*Against the letter of Mani which is called "the foundation"*) NPN 4
397-398 *Contra Faustum Manichaeum* BA 17; CSEL 25,1; PL 42
  (*Against Faustus, the Manichean*) NPN 4
397-98 *Contra Felicem Manichaeum* BA 17; CSEL 25,1; PL 42
  (*Against Felix, the Manichean*) NPN 4
? *Contra Gaudentium donatistarum episcopum* BA 32; CSEL 53;

PL 43

(*Against Gaudentius, Bishop of the Donatists*)

c. 421 *Contra Iulianum* PL 44

(*Against Julian*) FC 35

398-401 *Contra litteras Petiliani* BA 30; CSEL 52; PL 43

(*Against a Letter of Petilian*) NPN 4

428 *Contra Maximinum Arianum* PL 42

(*Against Maximinus the Arian*)

420-21 *Contra mendacium* BA 2; CSEL 41; PL 40

(*Against Lying*) FC 16; NPN 3

428-430 *Contra secundam Iuliani responsionem opus imperfectum*
CSEL 85; PL 45

(*Unfinished Work Against Julian's Second Response*)

399 *Contra Secundinum Manichaeum* BA 17; CSEL 25,2; PL 42

(*Against Secundinus, the Manichean*)

418 *Contra sermonem Arianorum* PL 42

(*Against a Sermon of the Arians*)

404 *De actis cum Felice Manichaeo* BA 17; CSEL 25; PL 42

(*Concerning Proceedings with Felix the Manichaen*)

c. 396 *De agone christiano* BA1; CSEL 41; PL 40

(*On Christian Combat*) FC 2

? *De anima et eius origine* CSEL 60; PL 44

(*On the Soul and Its Origins*) NPN 5

c. 400 *De baptismo, contra Donatistas* BA 29; CSEL 51; PL 43

(*On Baptism, against the Donatists*) NPN 4

386-87 *De beata vita* BA 4 AND 4/1; CCL 29; CSEL 63; PL 32

(*On the Happy Life*) FC 5; PSt 72

c. 401 *De bono conjugali* BA 2; CSEL 41; PL 40

(*On the Good of Marriage*) FC 27; NPN 3

414 *De bono viduitatis* BA 3; CSEL 41; PL 40

(*The Good* or *Excellence of Widowhood*) FC 16; NPN 3

399 *De catechizandis rudibus* BA 11; CCL 46; PL 40

(*The First Catechetical Instruction* or *On Catechizing the Unlearned*
or *Uninstructed*) ACW 2; NPN 3; PSt 8

413-426 *De civitate Dei* BA 33-37; CCL 47-48; CSEL 40; LCC (7 volumes; PL 41

(*The City of God*) FC 8,14,24; LCC (7 volumes); NPN 2

c. 420 *De coniugiis adulterinis* BA 2; CSEL 41; PL 40

(*Adulterous Marriages*) FC 27

c. 400 *De consensu evangelistarum* CSEL 43; PL 42

(*On the Harmony of the Evangelists*) NPN 6

After 412 *De continentia* BA 3; CSEL 41; PL 40

(*Continence*) FC 16; NPN 3

417 *De correptione donatistarum* or *Epistula* 185 CSEL 57,2; PL 33
   (*On the Coercion of the Donatists* or *Letter 185*) FC 30; NPN 4
c. 426 *De correptione et gratia* BA 24; PL 44
   (*Admonition and Grace* or *On Rebuke and Grace*) FC 2; NPN 5
424-25 *De cura pro mortuis gerenda* BA 2; CSEL 41; PL 40
   (*On the Care to Be Taken for the Dead*) FC 27; NPN 3
After 4 April 397 *De diversis quaestionibus ad Simplicianum* BA 10;
   CCL 44; PL 40
   (*To Simplicianus on Various Questions*) LCC 6
388-396 *De diversis quaestionibus LXXXIII* BA 10; CCL 44A; PL 40
   (*On Eighty-three Different Questions*) FC 70
406-408 *De divinatione daemonum* BA 10; CSEL 41; PL 40
   (*On the Divination of the Demons*) FC 27
397, 426-27 *De doctrina christiana* CCL 32
   (*Christian Instruction* or *Christian Doctrine*) FC 2; NPN 2
? *De dono perseverantiae* BA 24; PL 45
   (*On the Gift of Perseverance*) FC 86; NPN 5; PSt 91
392 *De duabus animabus* BA 17; CSEL 25,1; PL 42
   (*On the Two Souls*) NPN 4
413 *De fide et operibus* BA 8; CSEL 41; PL 40
   (*On Faith and Works*) ACW 48; FC 27
393 *De fide et symbolo* BA 9; CSEL 41; PL 40
   (*On Faith and the Creed*) FC 27; LCC 6; NPN 3
After 399 *De fide rerum quae non videntur* BA 8; CCL 46; PL 40
   (*On faith in Things Unseen*) FC 4; NPN 3; PSt 84
401-415 *De Genesi ad litteram* BA 48-49; CSEL 28, 1; PL 34
   (*On the Literal Meaning of Genesis*) ACW 41,42
393 *De Genesi ad litteram liber imperfectus* CSEL 28,1; PL 34
   (*An Unfinished Book on the Literal Meaning of Genesis*) FC 84
c. 389 *De Genesi adversus Manichaeos* PL 34
   (*On Genesis, against the Manicheans*) FC 84
417 *De gestis Pelagii* BA 21; CSEL 42; PL 44
   (*On the Proceedings of Pelagius*) FC 86; NPN 5
418 *De gratia Christi et peccato originali* BA 22; CSEL 42; PL 44
   (*On the Grace of Christ and Original Sin*) NPN 5
c. 425 *De gratia et libero arbitrio* BA 24; PL 44
   (*Grace and Free Will*) FC 59; NPN 5
c. 412 *De gratia novi testamenti ad Honoratum* CSEL 44; PL 33
   (*To Honoratus on the Grace of the New Testament*) FC 20
428-429 *De haeresibus* CCL 46; PL 42
   (*On Heresies*) PSt 90
387 *De immortalitate animae* BA 5; PL 32
   (*On the Immortality of the Soul*) FC 4; PSt 90

388, 391-395 *De libero arbitrio* BA 6; CCL 29; CSEL 74; PL 32
(*On Free Choice of the Will*) ACW 22; FC 59
388-391 *De magistro* BA 6; CCL 29; PL 32
(*On the Teacher*) ACW 9; FC 59; LCC 6
395 *De mendacio* BA 2; CSEL 41; PL 40
(*On Lying*) FC 16
388-89 *De moribus ecclesiae catholicae, et de moribus Manichaeorum*
BA1; PL 32
(*The Catholic and Manichean Ways of Life* or *On the Way of Life of
the Catholic Church and the Way of Life of the Manicheans*) FC 56;
NPN 4
388-89 *De musica* BA 7; PL 32
(*On Music*) FC 4
399 *De natura boni* BA 1; CSEL 25, 2; PL 42
(*On the Nature of the Good*) LCC 6; NPN 4; PSt 88
415 *De natura et gratia* BA 21; CSEL 60; PL 44
(*On Nature and Grace*) FC 86; NPN 5
Between 419-420 *De nuptiis et concupiscentia* BA 23; CSEL 42; PL 44
(*On Marriage and Concupiscence*) NPN 5
c. 415 *De natura et gratia* BA 21; CSEL 60; PL 44
(*On Nature and Grace*) FC 86; NPN 5
c. 426 *De octo Dulcitii quaestionibus* BA 10; CCL 44A; PL 40
(*On the Eight Questions of Dulcitius*) FC 16
? *De octo questionibus ex vetere testamento* CCL 33; Pl 35
(*Eight Questions out of the Old Testament*)
401 *De opere monachorum* BA 3; CSEL 41; PL 40
(*On the the Work of Monks*) FC 16; NPN 3
386-387 *De ordine* BA 4; CCL 29; CSEL 63; PL 32
(*On Order*) FC 5
415 *De patientia* BA 2; CSEL 41; PL 40
(*Patience)* FC 16; NPN 3
412 *De peccatorum meritis et remissione* CSEL 60; PL 44
(*On the Consequences and Forgiveness of Sins*) NPN 5
c. 415 *De perfectione iustitiae hominis* BA 21; CSEL 42; PL 44
(*On the Perfection of Human Righteousness*) NPN 5
429 *De praedestinatione sanctorum* BA 24; PL 44
(*On the Predestination of the Saints*) FC 86; NPN 5
417 *De praesentia Dei* or *Epistula* 187 CSEL 57; PL 33
(*On the Presence of God* or *Letter* 187) FC 30
387 or 388 *De quantitate animae* BA 5; PL 32
(*On the Magnitude* or *Greatness* or *Quality of the Soul*) ACW 9;
FC 4
c. 401 *De sancta virginitate*

(*On Holy Virginity*) FC 27; NPN 3

415 *De sententia Iacobi* or *Epistula* 167 PL 33
  (*Concerning Jacob* or *Letter 167*) FC 30

391-394 *De sermone Domini in monte* CCL; 35; PL 34
  (*On the Lord's Sermon on the Mount*) ACW 5; FC 11; NPN 6

c. 412 *De spiritu et littera ad Marcellinum* CSEL 60; PL 44
  (*On the Spirit and the Letter to Marcellinus*) LCC 8; NPN 5

399-420 *De trinitate* BA 15-16; CCL 50, 50A; PL 42
  (*On the Trinity*) FC 45; LCC 8, WSA; NPN 3

c. 411 *De unico baptismo contra Petilianum* BA 31; CSEL 53; PL 43
  (*On One Baptism, against Petilian*)

Between 398-401 *De unitate ecclesiae* or *Epistula ad catholicos de secta
  donatistarum* BA 28; CSEL 52; PL 43
  (*Concerning the Unity of the Church*)

391 *De utilitate credendi* BA 2; CSEL 25,1; PL 42
  (*On the Advantage* or *Usefulness of Believing*) FC 4; LCC 6; NPN 3

408-412 *De utilitate ieiunii* BA 2; CCL 46; PL 40
  (*The Usefulness of Fasting)* FC 16; PSt 85

390 *De vera religione* BA 8; CCL 32; CSEL 77; PL 34
  (*On the True Religion*) CC 6

413 *De videndo Deo* (*Epistula* 147) CSEL 57; PL 33
  (*On the Vision of God* or *Letter 147*) FC 20

392-420 *Enarrationes in psalmos* CCL 38-40; PL 36-37
  (*Expositions on the Psalms*) ACW 29,30; NPN 8

421 *Enchiridium ad Laurentium* or *De fide spe et caritate* BA 9; CCL 46;
  PL 40
  (*Enchiridion* or *Faith, Hope and Charity*) LCC7; FC 2; ACW 3;
  NPN 3

386-430 *Epistulae* BA 46B; CSEL 34, 44, 57, 58; LCC (selected letters);
  PL 33
  (*Letters*) 1-82 FC 12; NPN 1
  (*Letters*) 83-130 FC 18; NPN 1
  (*Letters*) 131-164 FC 20; NPN 1
  (*Letters*) 165-203 FC 30; NPN 1
  (*Letters*) 204-270 FC 32; NPN 1
  (*Letters*) LCC
  Select Letters LCC

? *Epistulae ad Romanos inchoata expositio* CSEL 84; PL 35
  (*An Unfinished Exposition of the Epistle to the Romans*)

? *Expositio 84 propositionum ex epistola ad Romanos* CSEL 84;
  PL 35
  (*Exposition of 84 Propositions Concerning the Epistle to the Romans*)

? *Expositio epistulae ad Galatas* CSEL 84; PL 35

(*An Explanation of the Epistle to the Galatians*)

418 *Gesta cum Emerito Donatista* BA 32; CSEL 53; PL 43
These are minutes of meeting that took place between the Donatist Emeritus, and Augustine on September 20, 418.

? *Locutionum in Heptateuchum* CCL 33; CSEL 28,2; PL 34
(*Of Expressions in the First Seven Books of the Bible*)

c. 411 *Post collationem contra Donatistas* CSEL 53; PL43
(*Against the Donatists after the Conference of 411*)

? *Psalmus contra partem Donati* BA 28; CSEL 51; PL 43
(*A Psalm against the Donatist Party*)

? *Quaestiones Evangeliorum* CCL 44B; PL35
(*Questions on the Gospels*)

Between 406-412 *Quaestiones expositae contra paganos* VI (*Epistula* 102) CSEL 34,2; PL 33
(*An Explanation of Six Questions against the Pagans*) FC 18

419 *Quaestionum in heptateuchum* CCL 33; CSEL 28,3; PL 34
(*Questions on the Heptateuch*)

? *Quaestionum septemdecim in Evangelium Matthaeum* CCL 44b; PL 34
(*Seventeen Questions in the Gospel of Matthew*)

? *Regula ad servos Dei* PL 32
(*The Rule of Saint Augustine*)

426-427 *Retractationes* BA 12; CCL 57; CSEL 36; PL 32
(*The Retractations*) FC 60

c. 418 *Sermo ad Caesariensis ecclesiae plebem* CSEL 53; PL 43
(*Sermon to the people of the Caesarean Church*)

? *Sermo ad catechumenos de symbolo* CCL 46; PL 40
(*Sermon to Catechumens on the Creed*) FC 27; NPN 3

398 *Sermo de disciplina christiana* CCL 46; PL 40
(*Sermon on the Christian Life*) FC 16

c. 410 *Sermo de urbis excidio* CCL 46; PL 40
(*Sermon on the Destruction of the City*) PSt 89

? *Sermo de utilitate ieiunii* BA 2; CCL 46; PL 40
(*Sermon on the Usefulness of Fasting*) FC 16; PSt 85

390-430 *Sermones* PL 38-39; CCL 41
(*Sermons*) FC 38; ACW 15; NPN 6; WSA (*Sermons* 1-400 in 10 volumes)
Sermons for Christmas and Epiphany ACW 15

c. 386-387 *Soliloquiorum* BA5; PL 32
(*The Soliloquies*) LCC 6; FC 5; NPN 7

c. 427 *Speculum de Scriptura sacra* CSEL 12; PL 34
(This work is a collection of moral precepts from the Bible)

? *Tractatus adversus Iudaeos* PL 42

(*In Answer to the Jews*) FC 27
Between 413-418 *Tractatus in epistulam Joannis ad Parthos* PL 35
  (*Tracts on the First Epistle of John*) NPN 7; LCC 8
? *Tractatus in Joannis evangelium* CCL 36, 38, 39, 40; PL 35;
  BA 71, 72, 73A, 73B
  (*Tractates* or *Tracts on the Gospel of John*, 1-10) FC 78; NPN 7
  (*Tractates* or *Tracts on the Gospel of John*, 11-27) FC 79; NPN 7
  (*Tractates* or *Tracts on the Gospel of John*, 28-54) FC 88; NPN 7
  (*Tractates* or *Tracts on the Gospel of John*, 55-111) FC 90; NPN 7
  (*Tractates* or *Tracts on the Gospel of John*, 112-124) FC 92; NPN 7

4. Separate Editions of St. Augustine's Writings in Translation.
The following list is a partial record of works published separately.

Against the Academicians (*Contra Academicos*) & *The Teacher* (*De magistro*). Indianapolis, IN: Hackett Publishing Co., 1995

Augustine of Hippo Selected Writings. Translated with an introduction by Mary T. Clark. New York and Mahwah, NJ: Paulist Press, 1984.

Basic Writings of Saint Augustine. Volumes 1 and 2. Introduction and notes by Whitney J. Oates. New York and Toronto: Random House, 1948.

The City of God (*De civitate Dei*). Translated by M. Dodds. New York: Modern Library, 1950.

Confessions (*Confessiones*). Translated by Frank J. Sheed. Introduction by Peter Brown. Indianapolis, IN: Hackett Publishing Co., 1993.

Confessions (*Confessiones*). Translated with an Introduction and notes by Henry Chadwick. Oxford and New York: Oxford University Press, 1991.

Confessions (*Confessiones*). Volume I, Introduction and Text; Volume II, Commentary on Books 1-7; Volume III, Commentary on Books 8-13. Commentary by James J. O'Donnell. Oxford and New York: Clarendon Press, 1992.

The Confessions of St. Augustine (*Confessiones*). Translated with an introduction and notes by John K. Ryan. New York and London: Doubleday, 1960.

On Christian Doctrine (*De doctrina christiana*). Translated with an introduction by D. W. Robertson, Jr. Indianapolis and New York: The Bobbs-Merrill Company, Inc.,1958.

On Free Choice of the Will (*De libero arbitrio*). Translated by Anna S. Benjamin and L. H. Hackstaff. Introduction by L. H. Hackstaff. Indianapolis and New York: The Bobbs-Merrill Company, Inc., 1964.

On Free Choice of the Will (*De libero arbitrio*). Translated by Thomas Williams. Indianapolis, IN: Hackett Publishing Co., 1993.

Political Writings. Edited by Ernest L. Fortin and Douglas Kries. Indianapolis, IN: Hackett Publishing Co., 1994. This is the most accurate readable translation of well chosen selections from *De civitate Dei* (*The City of God*). It also contains selections from other writings on politics.

5. Bibliographical Tools

Bavel, T. Van. *Répertoire Bibliographique de saint Augustin,* 1950-1960. New York: Oxford University Press, 1963.

Di Berardino, Angelo, ed. *Patrology*, Vol IV, *The Golden Age of Latin Patristic Literature From the Council of Nicea to the Council of Chalcedon.* Translated by Placid Solari, Westminster, MD: Christian Classics, Inc., 1988.

Donnelly, Dorothy F., and Mark A. Sherman. *Augustine's De civitate Dei: An Annotated Bibliography of Modern Criticism, 1960-1990.* New York: Peter Lang, 1991.

The *Revue des Etudes Augustiniennes* carries a critical bibliography of all the books and articles published each year on St. Augustine.

St. Thomas Aquinas

Aquinas never wrote a treatise dealing exclusively and comprehensively with the subject of politics. His teaching on these and directly related matters is to be found above all in the sections on law and on moral virtue of the *Summa theologiae* and in parallel passages of the *Summa contra gentiles* and other theological works. They are expounded methodically, albeit from a restricted point of view, in the short treatise *On Kingship*, written at the request of the King of Cyprus. Finally, they may be gleaned in somewhat more incidental fashion from his commentaries on the *Ethics* and on the first two and a half books of the *Politics* of Aristotle. (It should be noted that the rest of the commentary on the *Politics* in the manuscript tradition and the printed editions of that work was written, not by Aquinas himself, but by his disciple, Peter of Auvergne.)

The *Summa theologiae*, or *Summa theologica*, as it is sometimes called, is not a treatise in the ordinary sense of the word, after the manner of Aristotle's treatises, let us say. Because its method of procedure is generally unfamiliar to the modern reader, a few words of explanation in regard to it may be in order. The work as a whole is divided into three parts. The First Part has as its overall theme God and creation. Part Two contains an exposé of Aquinas's moral theology and is itself divided into two parts: the first is devoted to a treatment of man's final end and of the principles of human actions in general, whether intrinsic (the virtues and vices) or extrinsic (law, grace); the second treats mainly of the virtues and vices in particular. Part Three deals on the whole with Christ and the sacraments or with the way through which, in the actual economy of salvation, man returns to God. Each of these three parts is divided into a series of questions and each question into a series of articles which adhere uniformly to the pattern of the so-called "disputed question." The individual articles are given a title in the form of a question, which is immediately followed by an enumeration of the most important or most relevant objections to the thesis defended in the article. Aquinas then states his own position with the support of an acknowledged authority, such as a quotation from Scripture, the Church Fathers, Aristotle, or Cicero, and proceeds to establish that position by means of theological or philosophical arguments in the body of the article. The article ends with a point by point answer to the objections raised at the outset.

Aquinas's commentaries on Aristotle belong to a literary form known in the Middle Ages as the *commentarium ad litteram* or literal commentary, as distinguished from the simple paraphrases of glosses commonly employed by his Latin predecessors. They are characterized by the extreme care as well as the sympathy with which the text of Aristotle is scrutinized. The subject matter of each work and the mode of procedure to be adopted in dealing with it are indicated either in a preface or at the beginning of the commentary itself. Aquinas then divides and subdivides the text of Aristotle for the purpose of revealing its overall structure along with the relation of each part to its immediate context and to the whole. The commentary follows the order of the books into which Aristotle's treatises are traditionally divided and breaks them down into smaller segments of varying length, each one of which forms the object of a single *lectio* or lesson. Finally, each unit of thought or ultimate subdivision within these segments is explicated briefly or in greater detail, as the circumstances of the case demand.

The general aim of the commentary is to interpret Aristotle's text accurately and objectively, not to add to it or develop from it an original philosophic teaching. Whenever needed, the commentary clarifies the meaning of the most important words and gives their Latin equivalents. It indicates in relation to each specific point the precise nature of the argument used by Aristotle. In some instances, it supplies the reasons which tacitly underlie his statements or makes explicit what was only implicit in the original text. On rare occasions, it calls attention to the difference between Aristotle's teaching and that of the Bible. Any difficulties, ambiguities, or apparent contradictions in the text are elucidated by means of plausible hypotheses based on principles which are those of Aristotle himself and which are preferably taken from the same work. To what extent Aquinas's interpretations remain faithful at all times not only to the letter but to the spirit of Aristotle is, not unexpectedly, a question that has given rise to considerable debate among scholars. Whatever the answer to that question, it cannot be denied that, both individually and collectively, his commentaries reveal an extraordinary grasp and mastery of the entire corpus of Aristotle's works.

A complete bibliography of the writings of St. Thomas may be found in the *Dictionnaire de Théologie Catholique* under the heading Thomas D'Aquin *Ecrits*. The French theological dictionary lists St. Thomas's writings under headings: (1) commentaries on sacred Scripture; (2) commentaries on Aristotle and the *Book of Causes*; (3) systematic works such as a) commentaries on Peter Lombard's 4 books of Sentences, b) the *Summa contra gentiles*, c) the *Summa theologiae*, d) *Disputed Questions*, e) *Questiones Quodlibetales*, f) 47 *Opuscula* (the authenticity of some *Opuscula* is disputed), g) Sermons and h) *Principia*.

Another valuable source is Vernon Bourke's *Thomistic Bibliography* 1920-1940, St. Louis, MI: The Modern Schoolman, 1945. Bourke classified St. Thomas's writings under five headings: 1) major theological works (*Commentaries on the Sentences of Peter Lombard*, the *Summa contra gentiles* and the *Summa theologiae*); 2) theological questions (*Questiones quodlibetales* and *Questiones disputatae*); 3) scriptural commentaries on the Old and New Testaments; 4) commentaries on Aristotle, Boethius, and the *Liber de Causis*, and the Opuscula c. 30 miscellaneous works.

Bourke gives a chronological list of all of Thomas's writings (79 separate works) with references to the Latin editions in which they can be found. In addition, he provides a list in chronological order of the chief editions of Thomas's *Opera omnia* between 1570 and 1880. Furthermore Bourke provides references to editions of separate works as well as a list of some translations of Thomas's works in English, German, French, Spanish and Italian.

Leo Strauss

A bibliography of Leo Strauss (1899-1973) is readily accessible in two works: Leo Strauss, *An Introduction to Political Philosophy: Ten Essays*, edited with an Introduction by Hilail Gildin, Detroit, MI: Wayne State University Press, 1989. Pages 347-355, and Leo Strauss, *Studies in Platonic Political Philosophy*, with an Introduction by Thomas Pangle, Chicago and London: The University of Chicago Press, 1983. Pages 249-258.

INDEX

Abel 124
abortion 188, 196n53, 262n57, 266, 307
Abraham 168, 260n28, 283n46, 308, 311, 326
Abulafia, D. 192n9
Achilles 227, 307
Acton, Lord 294
Adam 7, 19, 246, 254, 325
Adams, J. D. 57n51
Adeimantus 52n23, 102n52
Agapism 229
Alamain, Jacques 250
Alan of Lille 188, 196n57
Alaric 22, 94, 121, 146
Albert the Great 177, 180, 188-89, 193n18, 196n53, 196n62
Alcidamas 201, 217n12
Alexander the Great 13, 178, 217n21
Alexandria 179
Alfarabi 152-53, 173n1, 192n9
Allison, H. E. 295n6
Ambrose, St. 26, 82n28
American Founding 243
Anastaplo, G. 59n75

Anaxagoras 41
Andronikos of Rhodes 177
Anscombe, E. 268
Anselm, St. 300
anti-utopianism 139
Antigone 66, 216n14
Antiochus of Ascalon 286n77
Antony of the desert, St. 142, 161, 172
antiquarianism 95
Aquinas, Thomas St. 3, 144, 148, 149n11, 150n21, 151-53, 155-56, 158-63, 165-66, 168-73, 177, 180-83, 185, 187-91, 193n17, 195n40, 195n49, 196n53, 196n67, 200, 209-10, 212-15, 221n82, 222n91, 229-31, 235-37, 239n11, 241n37, 246, 250-51, 260, 262n48, 267-68, 271-73, 276-79, 280nn16-18, 281n27, 281n36, 282n44, 284n67, 286n79, 288, 306-7, 310-12, 314n2, 314n10, 314n30, 315n52, 316n65, 325, 332, 356, 362-65, 367

Arendt, Hannah 141
Aristophanes 33-34, 36, 39,
    51n10
Aristotelian philosophy 231,
    311
Aristotelianism 68, 153,
    196n62, 212
Aristotle 7, 51n11, 53n31, 68,
    83n60, 109, 137-39, 143-44,
    150n20, 151-54, 156, 158,
    160-63, 165-73, 174n43,
    174n45, 175n56, 175n58,
    175n66, 177-84, 186-91,
    192n9, 194n31, 195n40,
    195n50, 196n59, 197n70,
    197n73, 200-201, 209-10,
    216n14, 221n82, 226, 229,
    232, 236, 248, 255, 260n35,
    261n47, 262n48, 271,
    281n30, 281n34, 286n78,
    300, 302-7, 312, 314n26,
    315n38, 315n54, 323-24,
    327n4, 331, 333, 339,
    355-57, 361, 365
Arnobius 96, 104n76
Aron, Raymond 50n3
Arquilliére, H.-X. 184, 194n35
Athanasius 174n35
atheism 340, 367, 370
Augustine 1-4, 6-8, 11-16, 18-
    27, 29n94, 32-36, 37-40,
    44-48, 50, 57n51, 58n69,
    59n76, 62n105, 67-68, 72,
    74-75, 78-80, 82n32, 85-89,
    91-97, 99n11, 100n29,
    104n80, 104n82, 112-13,
    117-26, 128, 130-31, 134n58,
    137, 140-42, 144-49, 152,
    155, 166, 180-81, 184, 186-
    87, 194n22, 195n41, 195n47,
    199, 204-6, 208-12, 215,
    219n39, 220n72, 221n77,
    221n83, 231, 240n21,

    259n16, 260n36, 275, 290,
    314n3, 315n46, 321, 323,
    325, 372-73
Augustinianism 184
Augustus 118, 120, 123, 128
Averroes 152, 168, 175n59,
    193n16, 310, 315n34, 356
Avicenna 154, 173n4, 179-80,
    188, 192n9, 193n14

Bacon, Francis 38, 55n42,
    56n46, 63n111, 107, 109,
    116n1, 139, 149nn4-5, 255,
    264n70
Bacon, Roger 180, 193n19,
    194n26
Bagley, P. 263n66
Balbus 87, 90, 99n27,
    100nn28-29
Baldry, H. C. 217n21, 218n23
Balthasar, Hans Urs von   333
Barbeyrac, Jean 257n6
Bardy, G. 57n51, 134n58
Barth, Karl 293, 295n7, 301
Barth, M. 81n7, 83n61
Bartlett, Robert 196n61
Bartsch, H. W. 83n63
Baynes, N. H. 57n51, 104n77
Beccaria, Cesare 262n58
Beck, L. W. 135n70
Benestad, J. Brian 105n87,
    196n65, 220n61
Bennett, J. C. 50n1, 83n61
Berger, W. 62n104
Bergson, Henri 333
Berlin, Isaiah 238
Bernard, St. 142
Berns, Walter 245, 258n9,
    262n56
Bickel, E. 103n70
Biel, Gabriel 284n62
Blondel, Maurice 336n13
Bloom, Allan 51n9, 52n21,

81n10, 102n52, 241n45, 326
Blythe, James M. 184, 195n36
Boethius 177, 192n4
Boissier, G. 104n81
Bollnow, O. 353n53
Bonaventure, St. 325
Borgnet, A. 196n53
Bornkamm, H. 60n95, 62n102
Bossuet, Jacques 107
Boulay, Jasmin 363
Boyancé, P. 98n6, 101n39
Bradford, Melvin 357
Brahms, J. 193n17, 194n28
Brandes, Georg 351n2
Brown, P. 62n106, 62n110,
    103nn72-73, 104n77
Bruni, Leonardo 194n34
Burlamaqui, J. J. 233
Burleigh, Walter 180

Caesar 118, 126, 133n33, 191
Cajetan 232
Caligula 120
Callicles 200, 203, 216n8
Calvin, John 229-30, 239n6,
    240nn18-19
Calvinism 60n95
cannibalism 340
Canonical tradition 245
Cantor, N. F. 264n75
Caracalla 61n102
Cardauns, B. 98nn2-3, 98n5,
    104n75, 104n78
Carlyle, A. J. 239n1
Carlyle, A. J. and R. W.
    57n51, 217n21, 224, 236,
    365
Carlyle, Thomas 179
Cassiodorus 177, 192n3
Cephalus 53n32, 68
Chadwick, H. 295n6
Chateaubriand, François-René
    291-92, 295n4

Chenu, M. D. 239n14
Chodorow, S. 239n13
Christian Marxism 107
Christian tradition 50, 112,
    144, 154, 158, 166, 172,
    226-27, 229, 258n9, 287,
    307, 322, 370
Christian virtues 306
Chrysippus 218n23
Churchill, Winston 61n102
Cicero, Marcus Tullius 1, 5-6,
    11-13, 15, 33, 35, 37- 38, 45,
    52n16, 54n34, 54n36, 54n41,
    56n46, 57n51, 67, 69, 71-72,
    81n12, 81n17, 81n19, 82n22,
    82n24-25, 82n27, 82n30, 87-
    88, 90-91, 97, 98n10, 99n13,
    100n36, 137, 141-44, 147-48,
    150nn20-21, 152, 166, 178,
    180-81, 195n49, 200-202,
    204-5, 209, 217n17, 217n21,
    219n40, 226, 228, 278,
    285n77, 286n77, 303,
    314n25, 316n68, 325, 355,
    359, 372-73
classical paganism 108
Claudel, Paul 227, 239n10
Cleanthes 202
Clement of Alexandria 4,
    135n59, 322
Collins, Adrian 352n33
Collins, James 361
Columbus, Christopher 255,
    264n70
common good 100n32, 227,
    237, 256, 257n2, 267,
    270-73, 281n24, 283n45
communism 186
Constantine 19, 61n102,
    62n104, 99n26, 126, 128
Cooper, B. 335n1
Cortès, Donoso 355-56
Corwin, Edward S. 224, 239n2

Cotta 12, 57nn50-51, 87-88,
    90-91, 100nn28-29
Courcelle, P. 134n48
Cox, Harvey 369-71
Cranz, E. 134n56
Creon 66
Cretan regime 188
Cretans 183
Crete 183
Cropsey, J. 54n35, 59n75,
    193n11, 259n24, 356
Crowe, M. B. 215n1, 240n15,
    280n4
Cumberland, Richard 244
Cumont, F. 103n70
Curley, E. 193n11
Cyprian 58n57

Dahn, F. 58n55
daimon of Socrates 75-76, 147
Daniel 114
Daniélou, Jean 366
Dannhauser, W. 351n9
Dante 109-10, 179-80, 184,
    189-91, 193n13, 194n20,
    195n40
d'Arcy, M. C. 54n41
Darwin, Charles 238, 345
Davies, W. D. 81n14
Davis, Charles 81n3
Dawson, C. 54n41
Deane, Herbert A. 56n44,
    57n51, 81n9, 140-41,
    149n10, 372-73
Decius, Emperor 58n57
De Koninck, Ch. 282n44,
    283n45
de Lagarde, Georges 190,
    194n26, 197n72, 260n27
Delhaye, P. 81n9, 81n14,
    83n51
de Lubac, Henri 332-33,
    336nn12-13, 366

democracy 33-34, 178, 181
d'Entrèves, A. P. 216n1
deontology 238
Descartes, René 63n111, 138,
    141, 149n2, 263n59
de Sousberghe, L. 240n27
Deussen, Paul 351n4
Diocletian 118, 126
Diogenes Laertius 177, 192n2
doctrinairism 49
Dodd, C. H. 239n11
Dolan, J. 58n57
Don Quixote 227
Donatists/Donatism 3, 21-22,
    29, 48, 59, 62
Doumergue, E. 239n6
Dreizehnter, A. 192n9
Drury, Shadia B. 318-27,
    327n1
Duns Scotus, John 231,
    240n22, 311
Dupont, J. 81n49, 82n31
duty/duties 140, 146, 148,
    150n33, 175, 247-49, 251-52,
    256, 260n28, 262n47, 266,
    272-73, 289, 305, 364
Duval, Y.-M. 62n105, 135n62
Dvornik, F. 133n37
Dworkin, Ronald 249

ecclesiastical laws 228
Eckermann, W. 134n51
Elijah 114
Emberly, P. 335n1
Empedocles 201, 216n14
Enlightenment, the 224, 243,
    249, 291, 323
Epictetus 217n20, 218n23
Epicurus/Epicureanism 68-69,
    71, 100n29, 138
Eschmann, I. Th. 283n45
esotericism 153, 322, 323
Eudaemonism 238, 360

Eusebius 26, 122, 125-28, 130, 134nn56-57
Eustratius 177
Eve 246, 325
existentialism 355

Fabricius 14
fanaticism 148, 238
Fattori, M. 193n17
Ferrero, G. 118, 131n4
Fessard, Gaston 366-69
Fichte, Johann Gottlieb 351n11
Figgus, John N. 57n47, 57n51, 57n55
Finn, J. 81n2
Finnis, John 235, 243, 249, 257n2, 266-68, 270-71, 273-77, 279, 280nn5-15, 281nn21-26, 281nn28-29, 281n31, 281n35, 281n37-38, 281nn59-61, 283nn48-57, 284n59-61, 286n80, 288, 295n1, 360-62
Fletcher, J. 81n4
Fortescue 356, 359
Fortin, E. L. 105n87, 196n65, 239n8, 220n61, 240n32, 241n43, 257n3
French Revolution 224, 233, 236, 365
Frend, W. H. C. 62n106
Freud, Sigmund 238
Fribourg Union 234, 240n29
Fustel de Coulanges 184, 195n37

Gal, G. 259n13
Gallay, J. 59n86
Geffcken, J. 104n81, 105n83
Gemini 86
Gero, S. 61n102
Gerson 246, 258n8, 259n15
Gibbon, Edward 127, 134n57

Giles of Rome 184, 197n75
Gilkey, Langdon 117-19, 131nn2-3, 132n9, 141, 149n12
Gilson, Etienne 228, 239n14, 333
Girardi, Giulio 366-68
Glenn, Greg D. 262n56
Gnosticism 142, 370, 371
Godfrey of Fontaines 252
Goethe 330
Goldast, M. 258n12
Gratian 22, 180, 216n2, 228, 239n9, 250, 260n36
Great Schism 184
Greek tradition 302
Gregory VII, Pope 184
Gregory of Rimini 276, 284n62
Grisez, Germain 360-62
Grotius, H. 232, 240n25, 244, 255, 260n35, 263n66, 273, 276, 283n46, 323
Gundisalvi, Dominic 192n9
Gutierrez, Gustavo 366
Gyges 71

Hagendahl, H. 86-88, 98n9, 103nn70-71, 104n79
Hamesse, J. 193n17
Hancock, R. C. 239n6
Hargrove, K. T. 50n1
Hart, H. L. A. 262n58, 267, 280n5
Hayek, F. A. 241n40
hedonism 253, 327
Hefner, Hugh 321
Hegel 131, 224-25, 238, 239n5, 291, 333, 345, 348, 366, 368
Hegelianism 373
Heidegger, Martin 32, 81n4, 350-51, 351n5, 352n14, 353n53, 353n57, 359

Hellenism 61n102
Henry of Ghent 250, 260n37
Heraclitus 331
Herodotus, 82n22
Hippolytus of Rome 134n54
historicism 346, 355, 373
Hittinger, Russell 360-362
Hobbes, Thomas 38, 56nn44-45, 84nn73-74, 107, 141, 193n11, 240n26, 244-45, 248-52, 254, 256, 258n8, 260n34, 263n62, 264n73, 269, 273, 280n20, 306, 320, 360
Hofmeister, A. 133n34
Hollingdale, R. J. 352n14, 353n42
Holton, J. E. 54n35
homosexuality 188
Hooker, R. 60n98, 150n23
Horsley, R. A. 239n7, 286n77
Horwitz, R. 263n65
Hosea 144
Hoy, D. C. 353n54
Hugh of Saint Victor 192n9
Hugo, Victor 235
humanitarianism 113, 225
hyperbolism 142

idealism 148
Ignatius of Loyola 369
Infield, L. 263n38
Isaac 144, 211, 308, 311, 326
Isaiah 79, 124
Isidore of Seville 144, 177, 192n5, 195n51, 216n10
Islam 2, 152, 154, 172, 179, 184, 226, 229, 288-89, 304

Jacob 326
Jacobi, F. H. 351n11
Jaffa, Harry V. 221n88, 321, 356-59

James, William 297, 314n1
James of Viterbo 197n75
Jaspers, Karl 333
Jeauneau, E. 192n9
Jedin, H. 58n57
Jeremiah 114, 115
Jerome, St. 174n50, 246, 259n17
Jewish tradition 358
Joachim of Flora 333, 370-71
Johannes Monachus 246, 259n21
John XXII, Pope 248
John of Paris 184
John of St. Thomas 232
Joshua 110
Jovian 132n20
Judaism 2, 114-15, 142, 154, 172, 179, 184, 226, 229, 288-89, 304
Judas 227
Julian the Apostate 61n102, 178, 192n6
jurisprudence 245, 256, 268

Kallen, G. 259n26
Kamlah, Wilhelm 118, 132n7
Kant, Immanuel 57n49, 129-31, 135nn70-71, 238, 264n74, 269-70, 305, 360
Kateb, G. 50n1
Kaufmann, Walter 337-38, 351n2, 351n6, 351n10, 351n12, 352n14, 352n17, 352n19
Kelsen, Hans 265, 279nn1-2
Kierkegaard, Soren 318, 338
Knorr, K. 222n90
Koester, Helmut 202, 217n20, 218n22, 239n7, 285n77
Kojève, Alexander 366, 368
Koran, the 179
Kraus, W. H. 279n1

Kretzmann, N. 197n75
Kroll, W. 192n8

Lactantius 38, 55n42, 204,
    217n17, 218n26, 218n28-29,
    218n32, 218n38
Ladner, G. B. 62n106
Laelius 37, 202-4, 219nn37-38
Lambot, C. 29n94
Latin Averroists 173
law
  Canon 153, 248
  Canon law tradition 248
  civil law(s) 180, 185,
      195n47, 228, 248
  constitutional 80
  Divine 248, 154, 160
  eternal 8-11
  law of nature 249-50, 252-
      53, 256, 258n6, 263n65,
      266
  natural 11, 37, 68, 74-75,
      78, 144, 148, 156, 160,
      166-70, 175n57, 188,
      199-202, 204-6, 208-15,
      216n1, 216n11, 216n14,
      223-26, 228-29, 231-32,
      236-38, 243, 245, 247-
      50, 253, 257n2, 266,
      276-79, 280nn4-5,
      284n69, 312, 316n68,
      359, 362-63
  natural law doctrine
      200-202, 205, 235-36,
      265-66, 279n1, 359, 363
  natural law theory 200,
      239n7, 256, 269, 360,
      362
  natural law tradition 276,
      360
  new 168
  Roman 86, 144, 150n21,
      151, 169, 180, 187, 228,
    248
  Sacred 229
  unwritten 66
Lawrence, St. 169
Lazareth, W. H. 83n61
legal theory 248
legal justice 234
Leo XIII, Pope 234
Lerner, R. 173n4, 193n14,
    193n16, 314n34, 315n34
Lessing, G. E. 292, 295n6
liberalism 107, 111, 253, 275,
    308
Lieberg, G. 86-88, 98n6
Lindemann, H. 103n70
Livy 14, 15
Lochman, J. M. 50n1
Locke, John 107, 222n89,
    240n26, 244-45, 250-55,
    260nn32-33, 263n65,
    280n19, 306, 320, 334
Lombard, Peter 229
Lonergan, Bernard 301, 310,
    313, 314n17
Long, A. A. 219n40
Lord, C. 192n9
Lottin, O. 196n64
Lucilius Balbus 12
Lucretia 73
Lucretius 69-70, 82n21, 138
Ludovici, Anthony M. 353n41
Luscombe, D. 192n9
Luther, Martin 60n95, 61n102 ,
    66, 173, 306, 315n49

MacCormack, S. 104n81
Machiavelli 7, 55n43, 91,
    100n32, 138-41, 145, 173,
    191, 197n76, 255, 264n70,
    319-20, 334
Machiavellianism 86
Macken, R. 260n37
Macpherson, C. B. 243, 257n1

Macquarrie, J. 81n4
Madden, N. D. 103n70
Madec, G. 134nn51, 134n53, 220n65, 221n84
Madison, James 66, 280n4
Maguire, J. P. 216n11, 284n69
Mahdi, M. 173n4, 193n14, 314n34
Maier, F. G. 104n80
Maimonides 173n2, 179, 193n13, 193n15, 310, 315n34, 358
Mandeville, Bernard 253, 263n60
Manichaeanism 74
Mannheim, Ralph 353n55, 359
Mansfield, H. C., Jr. 261n40
Marcellinus 3, 58n55, 104n82
Marcuse, H. 63n113
Maritain, Jacques 235, 243, 249, 257n2, 266-67, 282nn41-42
Markus, R. A. 52n18, 59n83, 62n105, 62n108, 104n80, 124, 132n27, 134n50, 134n54, 221n84
Marrou, H.-I. 131n1, 133n33, 133n37, 134n47
Marsilius of Padua 190-91, 193n11, 247, 259n24, 316n55
Martin, C. 192n9
Marx, Karl 32, 49, 238, 337, 348, 368, 370
Marxism 355, 366-68, 370
Marxists 32
Masters, R. 280n19
Maximus of Madaura 105n86
May, W. E. 240n25
Mayer, C. P. 134n51, 221n84
McCool, Gerald A. 314n16
McIlwain, Charles H. 57n51, 224

McKenzie, J. L. 239n11
Menut, A. D. 194n33
Mercken, H. P. 192n1
Metz, J. B. 366
Michal 307
Michaud-Quantin, P. 193n19
Middleton, Christopher 351n1
Millar 57n51
Miltiades 147
Minos 183, 188, 196n55
Mithraism 96
Moerbeke 182-83, 190, 193n19, 194n28
Moltmann, Jürgen 366, 369-71
Mommsen, T. E. 61n102, 132n27
Monachus, Johannes 259n21
monotheism 5, 18, 25
monotheistic 95
Montanism 370, 371
Moraux, P. 192n2
Morrall, John 258n11
Moses 114, 159, 193n13
Mount, E. Jr. 81n6
Murray, M. 353n54
Murray, John Courtney 235

natural order 226, 229
Nectarius of Calama 3, 147
Nederman, C. 192n9, 197n76
Neoplatonism 74, 219n61
Nero 120, 128, 142, 185
Neusner, J. 217n20, 239n7, 285n77
New Left 31
Newman, Cardinal 323
Nicgorski, W. 193n12
Nicholas of Cusa 246-48, 259n26, 260n27
Niebuhr, Reinhold 54n41, 141, 149n11
Nietzsche, Friedrich 32, 49-50, 63n114, 82n29, 109, 224-

25, 239nn3-4, 279, 286n79,
291, 293, 320, 333, 337-39,
341-51, 351n1, 351n4,
351n10, 351n12, 352n14,
352n24, 352n26, 352n37-38,
353n51
nihilism 32, 224, 238, 338-40,
345-47, 350, 351n11,
352n13, 362-63
nominalism 138, 244
Numa 103n68

Oberman, H. A. 240n23
Ockham, William of 60n98,
150n23, 231-32, 240n23,
244-48, 258nn11-12, 259n13,
262n50, 311
O'Connell, R. J. 220n66
Oedipus 343
Offler, H. S. 240n24, 258n12
Olivi, Peter 184
Oppenheim, F. 81n5
Oresme, Nicholas 189,
194n33, 196n58
Origen 4, 322
original sin 246
Orlebeke, C. 240n19
Orosius 26, 61n102, 122-25,
128, 133n33, 133n37,
133n43, 134n57
Orwin, C. 240n30
Otto of Freising 133n34

pacifism 227
Padovani, U. A. 118, 132n6
pagan tradition 67
paganism 95-97, 104n81,
105n83, 186
Palmier, J. M. 51n3
Pangle, T. L. 102n53, 222n90,
257n1, 281n24
Parmenides 331
Parsons, T. 239n6

Pascal 50
Paul VI, Pope 367
Paul, St. 18, 24, 66, 78, 114,
128, 145, 185, 227
Paulhus, N. J. 240n29
Pelagian controversy 246
Pelagianism 370-71
Pépin, Jean 85-89, 98n1, 98n5,
98nn7-8, 99n12, 99nn14-15,
99n18, 99n21, 99n24, 99n26,
100n31, 102n51, 220n61
Pera, C. 316n65
Pericles 147
Pertunda 104n74
Peter of Auvergne 180, 188-
89, 191
Peterson, Erik 133n37
Philistinism 345
Philo 226, 231, 285n77,
286n77
philosophic nominalism 244
philosophic tradition 342
Philus 37, 202-4, 219n38
Pierce, C. A. 81n11, 81nn13-
14
Pines, Shlomo 179, 193n13,
193n15
Pius XI, Pope 233
Plato 5, 7, 8, 13, 18-19, 33-40,
51n9, 52n15, 52n24, 54n35,
68, 75-77, 81n15, 83n45,
83n52, 83n56, 83n59, 93,
101n41, 102n52, 137, 141,
143, 147, 152-54, 178-79,
182, 185-87, 193n16,
194n30, 195n41, 200-201,
207-8, 216nn3-4, 226,
240n20, 277, 281n24, 294,
315n46, 322, 324, 330-31,
333, 339-40, 346, 355, 358
Platonic tradition 300
Platonism 33, 68, 154, 225
Plotinus 220n67

pluralism 140, 238
Plutarch 218n23
Poirot, Hercule 279
political idealism 32, 33, 36, 55n41
political theory 224, 253, 313, 359
political thought 224
political tradition 32, 50, 355, 365
polytheism 15, 17-18, 95, 213
Popper, Karl 330
Porphyry 99n26
Portia 40
Possidius 142, 149n16
Post, Gaines 192n9, 197n76
Praxagora 33
Primasius of Hadrumetum 246, 259n18
Proclus, Julius 178, 192n8
Protestant Reformation 225
Protestantism 293
Prudentius 26
Pufendorf, S. 244, 254-55, 258n6, 261n40, 263n64

radicalism 148
Rahner, Karl 301, 310, 313, 314n16
Ratzinger, Joseph 118, 132n8
Rawls 249, 267
Raz, J. 267
realism 139-41
Regulus 14
relativism 238, 363
religious tradition 252
right/rights
    Canonical 246
    human 224
    modern rights theory 225, 246, 256, 258n9, 364
    modern rights doctrine 257, 264n74, 266, 270, 276

natural right(s) 68, 78-80, 143-44, 150n23, 156, 161, 168, 170, 186-87, 200, 224, 244, 246-49, 253, 257, 259n19, 260n28, 260n38, 261n40, 261n42, 276, 279, 280n5, 280n20, 308, 341-42
natural rights doctrine 365
natural right(s) theory 75, 201, 269, 246, 256
new rights theory 253
Robert Grosseteste 192n1
Robinson, E. 81n4
Roman tradition 178
Roman paganism 95
Rome 13-16, 22, 37, 94, 96-97, 100n37, 101n46, 104n80, 137, 145-48, 244
Romulus 54n35, 56n46, 103n68, 142, 203
Rosen, Stanley 50n2, 352n13
Rousseau, Felicien 235, 240n33, 241n33, 241n36, 241n42, 364-65
Rousseau, J. J. 74, 82n40, 129, 233, 235-36, 240n31, 269, 280n19, 306, 320
Rufinus 62n105

Sabine, George 218n26, 219n38, 224
Sandel, M. 241n44
Sandoz, Ellis 336n22
Sarah 260n28, 283n46
Saul 307
Saxonhouse, Arlene 245, 258n9
Scaevola 14, 85-91, 94, 97, 98n3, 99n11, 99n15
Schaull, R. 50n1, 83n62
Schelkle, K. H. 59n90

Schleiermacher, F. 292-93, 295n5
Schmidt, J. 194n34
Schoeck, H. 353n56
Scholz, Heinrich 118, 132n5
Schopenhauer, A. 346
Schrock, Thomas S. 261n43
Scipio 37-38, 204
Seidler, M. 263n64
Séjourné, P. 220nn65-66
Selden 244
self-preservation 35, 76, 80, 249, 251-54, 256, 262n58, 269, 274, 344, 364
Seneca 16, 69, 81n17, 81n19, 81n20, 81n23, 97, 138, 180
Septimius Severus 61n102
Shakespeare, W. 138, 149n1, 324
Shorey, Paul 51n9
Sigmund, P. 259n26
Simon, Y. 283n45
Smalley, B. 62n106
Smedes, L. 240n19
Smith, E. A. 80n1, 81n7
Smith, S. B. 218n26, 219n38
social justice 224, 233, 234
Socrates 33, 37, 39-41, 43, 51n5, 52n23, 54n35, 58n67, 68, 75-76, 93, 103n64, 147, 182, 196n62, 200, 216n8, 231, 261n39, 262n47, 272, 274, 285n76, 305, 307, 338, 341, 350-51, 351n19, 352n19
Sokolowski, Robert 299, 301-13, 314n5, 314n9, 314n11, 314n15, 314n18, 314n24, 314n32, 315n35, 315n40, 315n48, 315nn50-51, 315nn56-60, 316n62, 316n64, 316nn66-67
Solomon 114
Sophocles 201, 216n14

Sparta 183
Spengler, Oswald 117
Spinoza 55n43, 56n45, 107, 109-16, 116n2, 116n5, 139, 215, 222n92, 262n47, 272
Stahl, Friedrich Julius 223
Steele, R. 193n19
Stelzenberger, J. 67, 81n8
Stendhal, K. 81n7
Stoa 202, 285n
Stoicism 68, 71-72, 138, 160, 201, 218n23, 220n65
Straub, J. 104n80
Strauss, David 345
Strauss, Leo 51n5, 54n35, 81n10, 100n32, 102n53, 150n33, 193n11, 193n16, 195n46, 219n60, 243, 245, 257n1, 259n24, 287-88, 293-95, 295nn2-3, 308-13, 316n61, 316n63, 317-27, 327n2, 329-35, 335n1, 345, 352n13, 352n25, 353nn55-56, 355-57, 359
Suarez 222n91, 232, 244-45, 259n14, 260n35, 262n50, 273, 276, 278, 283n46, 285n75
Swain, J. W. 134n54
Symmachus 22

Tacitus 138
Taparelli d'Azeglio 233, 240nn27-28
Taylor, Charles 141, 149n13
Temporini, H. 98n6
Teresa, Mother 142
Tertullian 61n102, 96, 104n76, 294, 357-58
theism 340
Themistius 178, 192n6
Themistocles 147
Theodosius 22, 62n105, 123,

128
theology
  Catholic 243, 302
  Christian 145, 151, 154,
    172, 229, 231, 288, 301,
    303
  civil 15-17, 88-89, 92, 97
  fundamental 299
  liberation 107, 366
  moral 233
  natural 15-17, 86-89, 92,
    229
  political 31, 32
  Sacred 303
  scholastic 110
  Thomistic 232
Thraede, K. 104n80
Thrasymachus 200
Thucydides 147
Tierney, Brian 184, 194n36,
  245-50, 253, 255-57, 258n9,
  259n15, 259nn21-22,
  260n38, 261nn40-41, 262n50
Tillich, Paul 293, 295n8
Tocqueville, Alex de 243, 254,
  291
Torraco, S. 197n71
Troeltsch, E. 57n48, 60n98,
  150n23
Tuck, Richard 244, 257n6,
  258n8, 283n46
Tully, James 243, 257n2
Turgenev, Ivan 339, 351n11
Tyconius 62n108, 112

Ullmann, W. 239n12
Ulpian 237, 244, 363
utilitarianism 268, 270, 275
utopianism 31, 63n112, 139

Vanhamel, W. 194n28
Varro 15-18, 33, 51n12, 85-90,
  92-97, 98n2, 100n29,
  100n37, 101nn37-38,
  102n48, 102n50, 104n79,
  138
Vasquez 232, 276
Veatch, Henry B. 360, 362
Verbeke, G. 194n28
Verhey, A. 240n19
Villey, Michel 244-45,
  258nn9-10, 257n4, 259n20,
  262n50
Virgil 138
Vitoria 232
Voegelin, Eric 329-35,
  336n22, 355-56, 359
Volusianus 58n55, 104n82
von Arnim, H. F. A. 217n18
von Meysenbug, Malwida
  351n1
Vree, D. 369-71

Walzer, M. 60n95
Wassmer, T. E. 316n68
Watson, G. 219n40
Weber, Max 225, 239n6
West, the 33, 81n7, 226, 228,
  248, 260n28, 291, 304, 341
Western tradition 324-25, 330,
  356, 372
White, H. 63n112
Whitehead, Alfred N. 333
Wiggins, J. 353n56
Wilde, Oscar 322
Wilhelmsen, Fredrick D. 355-
  59
William of Auxerre 229
William of Conches 192n9
William of Moerbeke 179
Williams, G. 134n55, 259n14
Wolff, Christian 249, 260n31
Wood, R. 259n13
Wootten, D. 263n66
World War I 266
World War II 366

Wyzansky, Judge 66

Xenophanes 98n3, 331
Xenophon 195n48, 315n39

"Zenelasias" 183

Zeno of Cittium 201-2,
    218n23, 285n77
Ziegler, A. W. 132n21
Zuckert, M. P. 150n21

ABOUT THE AUTHOR

A native of Rhode Island, Ernest L. Fortin, A.A., received his B.A. degree from Assumption College (Worcester, MA) in 1946, his Licentiate in Theology from the Angelicum (Rome) in 1950, and his Doctorate in Letters from the Sorbonne in 1955. He has also done post-doctoral work at the Ecole Pratique des Hautes Etudes (Paris) and the University of Chicago. He taught at Assumption College from 1955 to 1970, and as a part-time visiting professor of philosophy at Laval University from 1965 to 1972. Since 1971 he has been teaching theology and political theory at Boston College, where he also co-directs (with C. Bruell) the Institute for the Study of Politics and Religion. He has lectured widely to scholarly audiences both in America and in Europe. His publications include *Christianisme et culture philosophique au cinquième siècle: la querelle de l' âme humaine en Occident* (Paris, 1959); *Medieval Political Philosophy: a Sourcebook,* edited with M. Mahdi and R. Lerner (New York, 1963); *Dissidence et philosophie au moyen âge: Dante et ses antécédents* (Paris and Montreal, 1981); *Dantes Göttliche Komödie als Utopie* (Munich, 1991), and *Augustine: Political Writings*, edited with D. Kries (Indianapolis, 1994). His articles, review articles, and book reviews have appeared in a wide variety of professional journals and symposia. An English translation, with an introduction and notes, of Thomas Aquinas's *Commentary on the Politics of Aristotle* is scheduled to appear in 1997.

ABOUT THE EDITOR

J. Brian Benestad is professor of theology at the University of Scranton, a Jesuit University in Northeastern Pennsylvania. He has been teaching at Scranton since the fall of 1976. A native of New York City, he received his B.A. from Assumption College in 1963, a Licentiate in Theology from the Gregorian University (Rome) in 1968, and a Ph.D. in political science from Boston College in 1979. In 1981 he co-edited a collection of the U.S. bishop's policy statements issued between 1966 and 1980, and authored *The Pursuit of a Just Social Order* (1982). Most recently he completed an article entitled "Ordinary Virtue as Heroism," published in *Seedbeds of Virtue*, edited by Mary Ann Glendon and David Blankenhorn.